AGRICULTURAL PRACTICES AND WATER QUALITY

AGRICULTURAL PRACTICES
AND WATER QUALITY

EDITED BY TED L. WILLRICH AND GEORGE E. SMITH

THE IOWA STATE UNIVERSITY PRESS / AMES, IOWA

The chapters of this book are a result of a conference, The Role of Agriculture in Clean Water, held
at Iowa State University, Ames, Iowa, November
18–20, 1969.

Composed and printed by
The Iowa State University Press

First edition, 1970

International Standard Book Number: 0–8138–1745–5

Library of Congress Catalog Card Number: 70–114798

LIST OF AUTHORS

MINORU AMEMIYA, Associate Professor and Extension Agronomist, Department of Agronomy, Iowa State University, Ames, Iowa.

D. E. ARMSTRONG, Assistant Professor of Water Chemistry, University of Wisconsin, Madison, Wisconsin.

E. R. BAUMANN, Professor, Department of Civil Engineering, Iowa State University, Ames, Iowa.

HAROLD BERNARD, Chief, Agricultural and Marine Pollution Control, Office of Research and Development, FWPCA, Washington, D.C.

C. A. BLACK, Professor, Department of Agronomy, Iowa State University, Ames, Iowa.

C. S. BRITT, Assistant to Director, Soil and Water Conservation Research Division, ARS, USDA, Beltsville, Maryland.

G. M. BROWNING, Regional Director, North Central Agricultural Experiment Station Directors, Iowa State University, Ames, Iowa.

R. S. CAMPBELL, Professor of Zoology, University of Missouri, Columbia, Missouri.

P. A. DAHM, Professor, Department of Zoology and Entomology, Iowa State University, Ames, Iowa.

R. J. DEMINT, Research Chemist, Crops Research Division, ARS, USDA, Denver, Colorado.

S. L. DIESCH, Associate Professor, Department of Veterinary Microbiology and Public Health, University of Minnesota, St. Paul, Minnesota.

R. H. DOWDY, Research Soil Scientist, SWCRD, ARS, USDA, Morris, Minnesota.

W. E. FENSTER, Assistant Professor and Extension Specialist in Soils, Department of Soil Science, University of Minnesota, St. Paul, Minnesota.

P. A. FRANK, Plant Physiologist, Crops Research Division, ARS, USDA, Denver, Colorado.

L. R. FREDERICK, Professor, Department of Agronomy, Iowa State University, Ames, Iowa.

M. C. GOLDBERG, Research Hydrologist, U.S. Geological Survey, USDI, Denver, Colorado.

L. D. HANSON, Associate Professor and Extension Specialist in Soils, Department of Soil Science, University of Minnesota, St. Paul, Minnesota.

T. E. HAZEN, Professor, Department of Agricultural Engineering, Iowa State University, Ames, Iowa.

H. G. HEINEMANN, Director, North Central Watershed Research Center, SWCRD, ARS, USDA, Columbia, Missouri.

N. W. HINES, Professor of Law, College of Law, University of Iowa, Iowa City, Iowa.

R. F. HOLT, Director, North Central Soil Conservation Research Center, SWCRD, ARS, USDA, Morris, Minnesota.

H. P. JOHNSON, Professor, Department of Agricultural Engineering, Iowa State University, Ames, Iowa.

SHELDON KELMEN, Assistant Professor, Department of Civil Engineering, Iowa State University, Ames, Iowa.

H. E. LE GRAND, Research Hydrologist, Water Resources Division, U.S. Geological Survey, USDI, Raleigh, North Carolina.

R. I. LIPPER, Professor, Department of Agricultural Engineering, Kansas State University, Manhattan, Kansas.

T. M. MC CALLA, Microbiologist, USDA, Lincoln, Nebraska.

R. E. MC KINNEY, Professor, Department of Civil Engineering, University of Kansas, Lawrence, Kansas.

W. P. MARTIN, Professor and Head, Department of Soil Science, University of Minnesota, St. Paul, Minnesota.

J. R. MINER, Assistant Professor, Department of Agricultural Engineering, Iowa State University, Ames, Iowa.

W. C. MOLDENHAUER, Research Soil Scientist, SWCRD, ARS, USDA, Ames, Iowa.

J. A. MOORE, Instructor, Department of Agricultural Engineering, University of Minnesota, St. Paul, Minnesota.

H. P. NICHOLSON, Chief, Agricultural and Industrial Waste Control Programs, Southeast Water Laboratory, FWPCA, USDI, Athens, Georgia.

R. A. OLSON, Professor, Department of Agronomy, University of Nebraska, Lincoln, Nebraska.

G. L. PALMER, Instructor, Department of Agronomy, Iowa State University, Ames, Iowa.

J. T. PESEK, Professor and Head, Department of Agronomy, Iowa State University, Ames, Iowa.

D. C. PETERS, Professor, Department of Zoology and Entomology, Iowa State University, Ames, Iowa.

H. B. PETTY, Professor and Extension Entomologist, University of Illinois, Urbana, Illinois.

J. M. RADEMACHER, Regional Director, Missouri Basin Region, FWPCA, USDI, Kansas City, Missouri.

G. A. ROLICH, Director, Water Resources Center, and Professor, Sanitary Engineering, University of Wisconsin, Madison, Wisconsin.

F. J. STEVENSON, Professor, Soil Chemistry, Department of Agronomy, University of Illinois, Urbana, Illinois.

D. R. TIMMONS, Research Soil Scientist, SWCRD, ARS, USDA, Morris, Minnesota.

F. L. TIMMONS, Research Agronomist, Crops Research Division, ARS, USDA, Laramie, Wyoming.

J. F. TIMMONS, Professor, Department of Economics, Iowa State University, Ames, Iowa.

JACOB VERDUIN, Professor, Department of Botany, Southern Illinois University, Carbondale, Illinois.

C. H. WADLEIGH, Director, Soil and Water Conservation Research Division, ARS, USDA, Beltsville, Maryland.

G. H. WAGNER, Associate Professor, Department of Agronomy, University of Missouri, Columbia, Missouri.

J. R. WHITLEY, Supervisor, Water Quality Investigations, Missouri Department of Conservation, Columbia, Missouri.

T. L. WILLRICH, Professor, Department of Agricultural Engineering, and Extension Agricultural Engineer, Iowa State University, Ames, Iowa.

TABLE OF CONTENTS

ix

FOREWORD

THE Water Resources Research Act of 1964 (Public Law 88–379, as amended by 89–404) provided for the investigations of water problems through organizations at the land-grant universities. In the midcontinent area, which produces the major portion of the nation's grain and meat, a substantial portion of the research conducted by these organizations has been concerned with pollutants that could originate from farmland.

At a regional meeting of the organization directors and research workers from state universities in April 1968, "Pollution of Water by Agriculture" was the subject for discussion. It proved to be a topic of intense and widespread interest. It was apparent that the subject was so broad and complex that well-trained specialists in specific research fields were not communicating with their research associates in other departments.

This group agreed that there would be an increasing interest in water quality in the Midwest, particularly in those areas where agricultural production is a major portion of the economy, and where crop and livestock enterprises might prove to be important and growing sources of pollution. It was decided that there was need for an exchange of ideas and an understanding of basic chemical and biological processes by those most knowledgeable in specific fields relating to agriculture as a source of water pollutants. It was further agreed that only fundamentals and established research facts (not opinions) should be considered and presented at a level that could be understood by representatives from other disciplines.

A committee consisting of Professors Don Kirkham, Robert L. Smith, and George E. Smith was appointed to arrange a regional conference on "Agriculture and Clean Water." Subsequently a conference was held on the Iowa State University campus November 18–20, 1969. Dr. T. L. Willrich of Iowa State University and Dr. George E. Smith of the University of Missouri served as cochairmen of the conference. Professor R. L. Smith (University of Kansas), Doctors Don Kirkham, Lee Kolmer, E. R. Duncan, H. P. Johnson, E. R. Baumann, J. R. Miner, and D. C. Peters (all of Iowa State University) assisted with the initial planning. In addition to sponsorship by Mid-Continent State Research Organizations and Iowa State University, the Federal Water Pollution Control Administration also cooperated. The conference was also funded in part by Iowa Community Services under Title I of the Higher Education Act of 1965.

The participants in the conference were some of the most outstanding research workers in their respective fields. The conference was attended by about 250 individuals from 32 states. Many disciplines, including engineers; agricultural, biological and social scientists; geologists; hydrologists; and specialists (including legislative representatives) from other fields, attended.

The planning committee was pleased with the interest, the scientific soundness of the presentations, and the participation. The conference accomplished the original objectives of the water resources research directors. The information published in this proceedings is probably the most factual material in one volume on the chemical and biological reactions in soils and on crop and livestock production as they may be potential contributors to the degradation of water quality. This proceedings provides valuable information to those persons genuinely interested in the relation of modern agricultural technology to the water environment.

DON KIRKHAM, Director
  Water Resources Research Institute
  Iowa State University
  Ames, Iowa

G. E. SMITH, Director
  Water Resources Research Center
  University of Missouri
  Columbia, Missouri

R. L. SMITH, Chairman
  Department of Civil Engineering
  University of Kansas
  Lawrence, Kansas

PREFACE

Environmental pollution is a major concern to many people. When sources of water pollution are enumerated, agriculture is, with increasing frequency, listed as a major contributor.

Except for chemical pesticides, many materials now designated as water pollutants, such as sediments, nitrates, phosphates, and organic materials, have entered streams and lakes since the first sod was plowed, and even prior to that time. However, the concentration of these pollutants in water has generally increased with time. A portion is from agricultural lands. The remainder is from nonagricultural operations.

Movement of pollutants into water is controllable if it results from man's activities. However, water quality degradation by natural causes also occurs, and this may not be controllable.

As the nation makes an effort to correct abuses to its water resources, there is a need to determine the causes of water quality degradation and to quantify pollution contributions from the many sources.

Until such time as adequate facts are made available through research to delineate causes and sources, conflicting opinions will continue to flourish and programs to control and abate pollution will be less effective and efficient in the use of limited resources.

Existing knowledge indicates that agricultural operations can contribute to water quality deterioration through the release of several materials into water: sediments, pesticides, animal manures, fertilizers, and other sources of inorganic and organic matter.

Sediment from land erosion can be a pollutional material in surface water. Although soil loss from cultivated land is the major source of sediment in streams and reservoirs in most areas, highway construction, rural roads, stream bank erosion, gully erosion, housing developments, strip mines, and logging operations are also important contributing sources to production of sediments. Sediment reduces the storage capacity of reservoirs and lowers their value for recreational uses. Sediment, depending on origin, contains different inorganic minerals and organic compounds. Both supply plant nutrients. These nutrients can stimulate the growth of undesirable aquatic plants that on decomposition can cause eutrophication and increase costs when surface water is treated for domestic use or for industry. Decomposition of the organic material can utilize dissolved oxygen in water. Residues of slowly degradable pesticides used in agricultural production are adsorbed on sediments. These may serve as a reservoir to be taken up by aquatic plants and eventually enter the food chain.

Production economics and a shortage of farm labor have caused some livestock and poultry operations to develop as an agribusiness with large numbers of animals concentrated on small land tracts. Concentrated animal wastes have created problems of waste disposal and water pollution through runoff and leaching. Animal manures for soil fertility maintenance are no longer considered as valuable as they once were. Nutrients required in crop production can frequently be applied in chemical fertilizers at a lower cost than the cost of hauling and spreading animal wastes. However, land application of animal manures continues to be the least-cost disposal alternative in most situations and the preferred method to reuse the plant nutrients they contain. Lot runoff has less nutritive value than concentrated manure, but the plant nutrients and organic matter that it contains can pollute a receiving body of water. Consequently, many states have or are in the process of regulating feedlot runoff discharges to prevent water quality degradation.

The use of chemical fertilizers, with other practices, has provided ample crops for domestic consumption and export to meet the needs of an exploding world population. At least one-third of this nation's food production can be attributed to the use of chemical fertilizers. Therefore, fertilizer use is essential to prevent mass starvation. However, a portion of the applied fertilizer may be removed from the soil by leaching or runoff and thus enter a groundwater or surface-water body along with plant nutrients from other sources. Inadequate data are available to separate nutrient contributions from the many sources: chemical fertilizers; weathering of soil minerals; mineralization of nature's storehouse of humus; crop residues; animal manures; atmospheric contributions of nitrogen through rainfall, soil adsorption, and legume fixation; and many domestic, municipal, and industrial wastes.

The problem of pesticides as pollutants is complex. The use of these compounds, combined with other management practices, has permitted the production of an abundance of a wide variety of foods. However, some of the more effective pesticides degrade only slowly. Some may dissolve in water or be sorbed on sediments. The more resistant materials may accumulate and enter the food chain. Given a choice, few consumers would buy foods which contain insects, are affected by disease, or are contaminated by rodents—no matter how low the price. It is doubtful if sufficient food could be grown, stored, and processed that would meet the requirements of the Food and Drug Administration without the use of pesticides. There is, however, a need to develop effective new compounds that do not persist in soil, water, or plant or animal tissue.

Laws, public interest, and political motivation point to clean water as a major national issue in coming years. Streams, lakes, and groundwater that are polluted must be cleansed. Future pollution must be prevented. However, prevention cannot be attained without adequate knowledge concerning the causes and sources of pollution.

The opinions of the uninformed that misinform the public can only retard effective progress to assure an adequate supply of clean water.

The materials contained in this volume should be both informative and useful. It was assembled by knowledgeable scientists, representing many disciplines, to identify the role of agriculture in clean water; more specifically, to present and evaluate the existing body of facts as they identify agriculture's contributions to polluted water and reveal alternative solutions to provide clean water.

TED L. WILLRICH
   Extension Agricultural Engineer
   Iowa State University
   Ames, Iowa

GEORGE E. SMITH, Director
   Water Resources Research Center
   University of Missouri
   Columbia, Missouri

ISSUES IN FOOD PRODUCTION AND CLEAN WATER

CECIL H. WADLEIGH and CLARENCE S. BRITT

W E AMERICANS are carnivorous.

The average person's dinner plate accounts for 238 pounds of flesh per year. Three-fourths of this consumption is of red meat, and nearly half of the total is beef. Poultry now provide one-fifth of our total meat consumed, while lamb and fish account for a rather small percentage of the total.

We are eating just twice as much beef per capita today as we were 30 years ago. In fact, if a visitor from outer space were to enter one of our wonderful restaurants, he would gain the impression that the favorite indoor sport of Americans is that of attacking a juicy steak.

I am delighted to be an American!

Our inventory of beef cattle has been increasing at about twice the rate of our population. Since our numbers of dairy cattle have been decreasing rather markedly during the past 20 years, total cattle population appears to be leveling off at about 110 million.

A big Holstein cow will produce 75 pounds of fecal wastes a day, along with 20 to 30 pounds of liquid wastes. A little effort with a slide rule will tell you that a 100-head dairy produces 1,800 tons of wastes a year, exclusive of bedding. Obviously, every dairyman has no small problem in working out a system of materials handling.

Beef steers out on the range may produce only 30 pounds of fecal wastes a day, and 15 to 20 pounds of liquids. Cattle being fattened in feedlots daily produce between 35 and 60 pounds of fecal wastes and between 18 and 25 pounds of liquids.

The poultry industry also faces major problems in waste disposal. Per capita consumption of fryers has increased 26-fold in the last 30 years. Furthermore, in terms of 1968 dollars, the farm price per pound of broilers is only one-fourth of what it was 30 years ago. How could one have a more vivid picture of what improved agricultural technology means to the food consumer?

CECIL H. WADLEIGH is Director of the Soil and Water Conservation Research Division, ARS, USDA. CLARENCE S. BRITT is Assistant to Director of the Soil and Water Conservation Research Division, ARS, USDA.

Now let us consider a few of the problems that have developed because of increased production of animal wastes and the demands of a burgeoning population in suburbia that voices loud concern about the quality of its environment, with special emphasis on air and water.

Many of these suburbanites have emigrated into the rural fringe in order to live in the pastoral delights of a rural atmosphere—and then have vigorously complained about some of the rural atmosphere they have received. Many of them have problems in water supply and waste disposal.

We can now recognize that our current animal waste disposal problems were markedly affected by two developments that took place in 1912. We can assume beyond all reasonable doubt that the distinguished German chemist, Fritz Haber, had no idea that he was sowing the seeds of a massive manure disposal problem in the United States when in 1912 he succeeded in synthesizing ammonia by passing H_2 and N_2 over hot iron filings at high temperature and pressure. The seeds were not long in sprouting. Haber's process, with the developmental work of Karl Bosch, was a tremendous contribution to Germany's armed might during World War I by making Germany independent of Chilean nitrate (Taylor, 1953).

This synthesis of ammonia was first performed in the United States in 1920 at the Fixed Nitrogen Laboratory set up by the War Department in 1919. By the late 1920s, synthetic ammonia for fertilizer use was in commercial production. Figure A shows that during the past 50 years, use of fertilizer nitrogen has doubled about every 10 years until in 1969 we used nearly 7 million tons. This increase in usage has been abetted by the relatively low cost of nitrogen. For example, during this past year many a ton of nitrogen was applied to fields at a cost of less than 5 cents a pound.

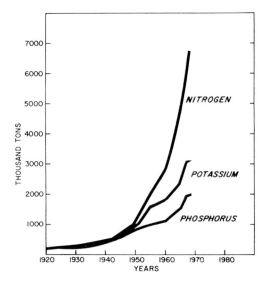

FIG. A. Use of plant nutrients, 1920 to 1968.

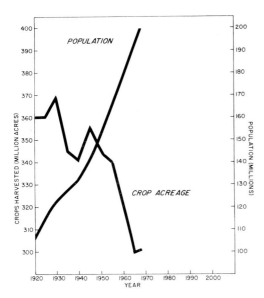

FIG. B. Acreage of 59 principal crops harvested, plus acreages in fruits, tree nuts, and farm gardens. Total United States population, including persons in our military forces in this country and abroad.

This rapid increase in the use of chemical nitrogen, along with other purchased inputs, is closely associated with the fact that although the United States has had a sharp increase in population, there was a marked decline in acreage of cropland harvested as shown in Figure B. The rapid increases in use of weed killers and farm machinery are other inputs that have contributed to this tremendous increase in efficiency of land use to meet our population growth. Our corn crop, which is a primary source of feed in animal production, provides an example of the effect of enhanced farm technology on land requirements in producing an abundance of animal feed at low cost.

During the past 20-odd years, the corn acreage harvested has decreased markedly, so it is only about two-thirds of what it was in 1945. Nevertheless, our corn production over this period has increased very significantly, to double the total bushels produced in 1940. These trends took place because of the rapid increase of average corn yield per acre since 1940 due to the increased use of fertilizer and other purchased inputs upon corn land. As a consequence the price of corn to the farmer in 1968 dollars has shown a very significant general decline since 1940, which, in turn, has its implications on the price of the tremendous amount of meat we eat. The corn crop has received a high degree of sophisticated mechanization, including eight-row planters that sow seed, distribute fertilizer, and apply pesticides all in one fell swoop.

This rapid increase in field mechanization reminds us of another very significant event that took place prior to World War I that now has a very marked bearing on our animal waste disposal problems. During 1912–14, Henry Ford started mass production methods, including continuously moving assembly lines. This immediately made possible the assembling of a Model-T in 93 minutes. This innovation in materials handling sparked the American industrial revolution. The value of man's labor was greatly increased. With the adoption of electronic controls to assembly-line methods, industry made further advances in efficiency of production. With the advent of World War II, farm labor became in short supply. Innovative poultrymen and cattle feeders began installing labor-saving devices involving automated silos, conveyor belts, mixers, and all manner of schemes to expedite the handling of feed. Thus one man became able to feed thousands of cattle and tens of thousands of birds. In due course, feedlots came into being that carried 50,000 head, and poultry enterprises developed that involved over 100,000 birds. Waste production was concurrently concentrated in large masses. Unfortunately, efficient methods of handling waste materials by no manner kept pace with improved efficiency in feeding operations. In many instances the stuff accumulated as miniature mountains. A number of economic studies indicated that the value of the manure to the land was so low that it was cheaper for the farmer to get his plant nutrients from the fertilizer bag than to haul manure from feedlots to the field.

There is indeed a vast materials handling problem when you consider that total cattle wastes alone amount to 1.4 billion tons a year. Wastes from all of our domestic livestock come to 1.6 billion tons; and when bedding, dead carcasses, and the offal from slaughtering are added, the total is close to 2 billion tons a year. Obviously, large feedlots carrying 100,000 head of cattle produce tremendous masses of material.

To consider the magnitude of the problem, we have to recognize that a fattening steer will give off in the neighborhood of 110 pounds of nitrogen, 125 pounds of potassium, and 365 pounds of biochemical oxygen demand (BOD) in its excrement each year. This means that a feedlot with a stocking rate of 200 head per acre will deposit a really tremendous amount of plant nutrients and readily oxidizable organic matter on each acre.

The Monfort Feedlot near Greeley, Colorado, carries 90,000 head on 320 acres. The feeding and waste handling procedures are really something to see.

We know that most of the nitrogen deposited on a feedlot goes into the atmosphere as a result of denitrification processes, but we also know from soil cores taken from feedlots in Colorado that there can be deep percolation of nitrate-nitrogen in comparatively high amounts. We also know some of these nutrients and organic materials can enter into runoff water.

As a matter of fact, it has been common practice to locate feedlots on a hillside above a waterway in order to provide good drainage and a disposal area for the runoff. Some feedlots traverse a stream course with the assumption that the stream will carry away the wastes.

On a smaller scale, we find that even some of the best dairy farmsteads in the Northeast are built along stream courses so that the barnyard will drain into the brook. Farmers running dairy farms or feeder operations in the North prefer to apply manure to the land during the wintertime when labor demands for other tasks are at a minimum. This means that much of this manure may be spread right on top of an accumulation of snow. It also means that if there is rapid snowmelt in the spring, with a comparable rate of runoff, there will be appreciable amounts of the wastes with plant nutrients and BOD moving off the fields and into streams. Studies on Lake Mendota near Madison, Wisconsin, indicate that much of the pollution coming into that lake during the spring months has its source in runoff from barnyards or fields on which manure was applied during the winter.

We must recognize that runoff carrying manure can be a cause of major fish kills. In fact, the Federal Water Pollution Control Administration reports that of 8 major fish kills in 1967, 3 of them were due to manure drainage (U.S. Department of the Interior, 1968). It is also of interest that the one really serious fish kill was caused by food products, which frequently have an effluent exceedingly high in BOD. It is also of interest that not one of these listed was caused by pesticides.

Studies in Kansas (Smith and Miner, 1964) show what may happen in a stream receiving drainage from a feedlot. Their studies on the Fox River were made at a point about a mile below a feedlot during November. Figure C shows that in 20 hours after a 1-inch storm the water in the stream 1 mile below the feedlot contained 90 ppm of BOD and just about zero ppm of oxygen. Fish cannot survive if oxygen content of water falls below 4 ppm. At the point of sampling, the BOD dissipated rapidly and the oxygen content of the water recovered.

It is also important to note that in this study Smith and Miner found the pollution from fecal coliform bacteria rose to a tremendous level 20 hours after the storm and then dissipated rather rapidly. By contrast, the count for fecal streptococcus bacteria rose to an enormous count and continued at that high level of infestation for the duration of the sampling period (Table A).

As with cattle, the tremendous growth of the broiler industry in concentrated chicken factories has resulted in the production of large quantities of manure in local areas.

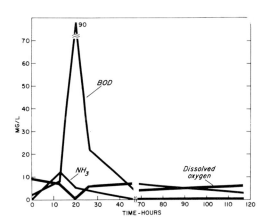

FIG. C. Water quality parameters. (From Smith and Miner, 1954.)

TABLE A. Fox creek bacterial pollution (average counts per 100 ml sample, Nov. 1962).

Condition	Fecal Coliform	Fecal Streptococcus
Mean dry weather	1,148	13,800
After rainfall (11–27)	542,000	1,600,000
After rainfall (11–28)	17,200	1,410,000
After rainfall (11–29)	23,000	1,600,000
After rainfall (11–30)	7,900	1,600,000

Source: Adapted from Smith and Miner (1964).

In the Southeast alone, 9 million tons of chicken litter are produced annually. When this chicken litter is spread on fescue grass in September at the rate of 16 tons per acre, it supplies 640 pounds of nitrogen and 250 pounds of potassium per acre. If it is applied at higher levels, it may even kill the fescue grass and allow useless weeds to take over. Even a modest application of chicken manure to fescue pastures will produce fescue hay in November that contains 0.6% nitrate-nitrogen. This grass may not only induce nitrate poisoning in the cattle but may also be "grass tetany prone"—that is, too high in potassium and too low in magnesium.

High applications of chicken litter to oats in late winter will encourage a lush growth that is very susceptible to lodging and dangerously high in nitrate-nitrogen.

It is not unusual to see cattle that have been eating a high nitrate forage gather in farm ponds to keep cool. They often pant continuously. They do this because the nitrate in the grass becomes nitrite in the rumen, and this causes some of the hemoglobin in their blood to be changed to methemoglobin, which does not carry oxygen. In other words, the cattle pant and try to keep cool because of an oxygen deficiency in their systems.

We hear much about agricultural endeavor causing the eutrophication of our surface waters. Eutrophication is nutrient enrichment enabling the growth of plant life in water. It is nature's way of providing fish food. As already documented, feedlots can be a good source of plant nutrients. We can see tremendous eutrophication in drainage ditches in western Minnesota or streams in eastern Maryland. Lakes in Minnesota that are completely removed from any agriculture may accrue an excess of water plants.

We ought to look at this movement of nutrients into water and recognize that it is more complex than just the supplying of nitrogen and phosphorus that causes an excess of plant growth. There are any number of publications on fish production in farm ponds, or fish farming, that indicate the need for the addition of 800 to 1,200 pounds of 8-8-4 fertilizer per acre of pond surface per year in order to assure good fish production. This fertilizer is essential to enable good growth of water plants that provide food for the fish.

Studies on agricultural and wooded watersheds at the U.S. Hydrologic Field Station, Coshocton, Ohio, show the phosphorus delivery per acre per year is only 0.03 to 0.06 pounds. Nitrogen yield from the watersheds is appreciably higher but still low in terms of nitrogen needs of plants for fish food.

If there is an excess of organic matter high in BOD going into the water along with the nutrients, the depletion of oxygen will kill the fish—as one can sometimes see along the banks of the Potomac River. In fact, there are places in the Potomac estuary, below the Blue Plains sewage disposal facility that dumps into the river, where nothing seems to grow but ugly water plants. The oxygen content of this water is so low that the fish which would normally eat some of the plankton and other plants are eliminated by oxygen deficiency.

Fish can also be eliminated by pesticides. The heavy fish kills in the Mississippi River in 1964 were alleged to have been caused by endrin. The source of the suspected endrin was not land runoff. There have been no end of fish kills attributed to pesticides moving into water. Here again, if these pesticides kill the fish, ecological balance is upset; that is, there is no curb on the growth of water plants. When an overproduction of water plants takes place, some will die and rot, contributing to further oxygen depletion, nutrient release, and initiation of a vicious cycle of an abundant plant growth incurring water environment inimical to the growth and survival of fish and other faunal life. The process becomes one of forming a muck bog out of the lake. Yet, we are inclined to the view that plant nutrients in water should not be considered as pollutants. Rather, we ought to look upon such nitrogen and phosphorus as potential protein.

Possibly we should even paraphrase the words of George Clemenceau when he stated that "war was just too important a matter to be left in the hands of generals" (Seldes, 1966), and say that water contamination is just too important a matter to be left in the hands of sanitary engineers.

Consider a few data.

A good fish pond will produce over 1,000 pounds of fish per acre per year. One thousand pounds of fish contain 200 pounds of dry matter, of which 150 pounds are protein that contains 24 pounds of nitrogen. The conversion factor from plant protein to flesh protein by foraging fish ranges from 5 to more than 20 to 1. Thus, at least 120 pounds of plant protein nitrogen are needed to produce these 1,000 pounds of fish. However, fish biologists often find P deficiency in surface waters as the main limiting factor in fish production.

We ought to ask fish and wildlife experts to prescribe optimal aquatic ecologies for the production of adequate food for abundant fish not only for man's food and recreation but also for the benefit of fish-eating wildlife. This will certainly require minimal delivery to our surface waters of such fish killers as putrescible matter, acids, sediment, insecticides, and other chemicals. It may also require use of herbicides with high biochemical specificity on unwanted water plants. It may mean manipulation of fish population to attain proper balance between foragers and carnivores.

What are we doing in agriculture to solve water pollution problems?

First of all, we in agriculture feel strongly that every measure feasible must be taken to minimize or eliminate possible adverse effects from the use of pesticides. We are now using about a billion pounds of these chemicals a year. Some of them are very persistent in the environment; some of them volatilize and become widely dispersed; some of them can be very toxic to insects, plants, or wildlife which we want to protect. And yet we also recognize that it is mandatory that the ominous threat of insect pests, diseases, and weeds to our production of food and fiber must not be ignored. We must ever seek chemicals carrying a minimum of danger and adverse side effects. We must seek improved technology in handling and application of these chemicals, and wherever feasible, seek methods of biological control or nonchemical control.

Toward minimizing the damages that may occur from pesticides and all other pollutants that may occur in runoff from the land, we must recognize the long-proved advantages of conservation practices that will curb runoff and soil delivery. Water moving across the land is completely indiscriminate. It will pick up and move that which is movable, whether it be soil particles, manure, plant residues, pesticides, fertilizers, or other chemicals. Use of grass waterways has proved very effective in minimizing the transport of any undesirable burdens in the runoff water.

We need to develop water diversion structures around our farmsteads and feedlots so that none of it runs directly into a watercourse, but rather into a storage lagoon where oxidation of degradable materials may take place.

Under some conditions there probably ought to be secondary or even tertiary lagoons to make certain that runoff finally entering into the watercourse is fairly well reclaimed (less than 20 ppm BOD). Lagoons have been used with good success around poultry operations in the South if they were designed to be of adequate capacity and were operated without intermittent loading.

Some hog operations use lagoons satisfactorily, yet many in the northern states are failures. They do not control the emanation of foul odors. There is a large hog operation near Pendleton, Oregon, that is of interest. The hogwash is collected in lagoons and then distributed through a large sprinkler irrigation system that covers 140 acres of cropland in one rotation. In this particular operation the hogwash aids in producing 10 tons of alfalfa hay per acre. The hay is ground and used as hog feed. The operation is a good example of recycling of wastes—an objective that should be followed whenever feasible.

Cattlemen and dairymen in the northern states, where restrictions have been imposed on spreading manure on frozen ground, are using slatted floors with the collection of the excrement in enormous vats. The liquified manure is spread upon the land by use of either movable sprinkler systems or large mobile tanks. Many dairymen have constructed concrete receiving basins for manure that eliminate runoff to stream channels while enabling the easy operation of loading equipment to get the manure on the land expeditiously.

Let us go back to the Monfort Feedlot in Greeley, Colorado.

The hundreds of thousands of tons of manure produced on this feedlot are picked up by high-efficiency loading equipment and trucked to over 10,000 acres of land growing corn for cattle feed. Chopped corn so produced is ensiled in the amount of about 200,000 tons. The ensilage is then mixed with cooked grain by automated equipment and fed to the cattle by specially designed trucks.

This operation is a very excellent example of the recycling of wastes.

Finally, we must stress again that a key contribution in making beneficial use of agricultural wastes, and minimizing any loss of these wastes from the farm, can take place through sound conservation farming. It also contributes to beauty of the countryside.

We must make sure that every watershed above our water impoundments is effectively protected so the quality of the water in the reservoir may be used without concern for fishing, recreation, supplemental irrigation, and even for municipal water supply. Obviously, we who are involved in agricultural technology still have a big job to do.

REFERENCES

Seldes, G. 1966. *The great quotations,* p. 162. New York: Lyle Stuart.

Smith, S. M., and Miner, J. R. 1964. Stream pollution from feedlot runoff. *Trans. 14th Ann. Conf. Sanit. Eng.* Bull. Engineering and Architecture 52. Lawrence, Kans.: Univ. of Kans. Publ.

Taylor, G. V. 1953. Nitrogen production facilities in relation to present and future demand. In *Fertilizer technology and resources in the United States*, ed. K. D. Jacob, pp. 15–61. New York: Academic Press.

U.S. Department of the Interior. 1968. *Pollution caused fish kills, 1967.* CWA-7.

PART ONE

SEDIMENT AS A WATER POLLUTANT

CHAPTER ONE

POLLUTION BY SEDIMENT: SOURCES AND THE DETACHMENT AND TRANSPORT PROCESSES

H. P. JOHNSON and W. C. MOLDENHAUER

W HILE erosion has been active over geologic time, man has often altered the process to the detriment of his environment. Considered by many people more innocuous than sewage, suspended solid loads delivered to streams and lakes as sediment in surface runoff are equivalent by weight to more than 700 times the load from sewage (U.S. Department of Agriculture, 1968). Sediment reduces water quality and often degrades deposition areas. Sediment pollutes when it occupies space in reservoirs, lakes, and ponds; restricts streams and drainageways; reduces crop yields in a given year; alters aquatic life in streams; reduces the recreational and consumptive use value of water through turbidity; and increases water treatment costs. Sediment also carries other water pollutants such as plant nutrients, chemicals, radioactive materials, and pathogens.

Because the sediment pollution problem is so broad, we do not attempt to describe the entire problem but do (1) identify problem areas, (2) define present understanding of the erosion and transport process, and (3) indicate research needs. We discuss continuum from field erosion to streams, but our primary emphasis is given to agricultural aspects of erosion and sedimentation in the humid central region of the United States. Only mechanical processes are considered; chemical and biological processes are omitted. Detailed coverage of the erosion-sedimentation process is available from several sources (Colby, 1963; Einstein, 1964; Gottschalk, 1964; Wischmeier and Smith, 1965; Raudkivi, 1967).

To express relatively the status of understanding of the various

H. P. JOHNSON is Professor of Agricultural Engineering, Iowa State University. W. C. MOLDENHAUER is Research Soil Scientist, ARS-SWC, USDA, and Professor, Iowa State University.

Contribution from Agricultural Engineering Department, Iowa State University, Ames, and Corn Belt Branch, Soil and Water Conservation Research Division, ARS, USDA, Ames. Journal paper No. J-6393 of the Iowa Agriculture and Home Economics Experiment Station, Ames. Project Nos. 1266 and 1776.

TABLE 1.1. Analysis approaches.

	System Inputs	System Operation	Limitations
Frequency diagrams of system output	Given little consideration	None defined; (plot output)	Neglects change in system with time; need representative data over long period
Multiple correlation	Selected then screened by statistical analysis	Defined by correlation equations	Need representative data; accuracy of results
Physical models	Specifically selected; defined dimensionally	Model integrates inputs	Range of data; design require- ments of model
Mathematical models (deterministic)	Equations, data describing processes	Defined by flow diagrams; equations solved	Accuracy of equations describ- ing processes; input data
Laws of mechanics	Selected data; appropriate equations	Solve equations	Often difficult to relate to entire system; often a component of mathematical models

processes involved in erosion and sediment transport, we comment on approaches to problems. As understanding of a problem improves, we proceed from empiricism to physical "laws." This should not condemn empirical approaches; in many instances these are the only approaches available to planners and designers.

As we proceed from empiricism to laws, however, we are better able to define the factors involved in a process (inputs) and can better explain the interaction of the factors (system operation). Table 1.1 presents an attempt to describe analysis approaches. Although all approaches are used in erosion and sedimentation studies, the application of mathematical models to unsteady state problems is only beginning. Most design approaches are based on field observations, and it is ironical in this time that most design is based on observation and not on Newtonian physics.

GROSS EROSION FROM LAND

The ability to predict on-site sheet and gully erosion and the transport of eroded material to a point of concern is extremely important in planning, design, and economic analysis. The total on-site sheet and rill erosion (gross erosion) is not delivered to streams. The amount of sediment that completes the route of travel from the point of erosion to a point of concern in a watershed is termed sediment yield. The amount of sediment that travels this route involves factors related to sheet and gully erosion.

Sheet Erosion

EMPIRICAL—THE EROSION EQUATION

In the early 1930s the U.S. Department of Agriculture established ten soil erosion research stations. Using some of the data collected at these and at state stations, Smith (1941), Browning et al. (1947), and Musgrave (1947) attempted to systematize the calculation of erosion losses by using the pertinent causative factors.

In 1954 a Runoff and Soil Loss Data Center was established at Purdue University by the Agricultural Research Service of the U.S. Department of Agriculture. All available data from soil and water loss experiments throughout the United States were assembled for summarization and analysis. A major result of this summarization was the so-called Universal Soil Loss Equation (see Wischmeier and Smith, 1965, for development and use). This equation is $A=RKLSCP$, in which A is the computed soil loss in tons per acre, R is the rainfall factor and is the number of erosion index units in a normal year's rain. K is the soil erodibility factor and is the erosion rate per unit of R for a specific soil in cultivated, continuous fallow on a 9% slope, 72.6 feet long. L is the effect of slope length and S is the effect of slope gradient. C is the crop management factor and is the ratio of soil loss from a field with specified cropping and management to that from the fallow condition on which the factor K is evaluated. P is the erosion control practice factor and is the ratio of soil loss with contouring, strip-cropping, or terracing to that with straight-row farming up and down slope. All factors are dimensionless except A and K, which are in tons per acre, and R which is the number of EI units.

R, the rainfall factor, is the rainfall erosion index developed by Wischmeier (1959) and Wischmeier and Smith (1958). It is the annual summation of $EI/100$, where E is the kinetic energy of a rainstorm and I is its maximum 30-minute intensity. The E and I values can be obtained from recording rain-gage charts. Expected locational values were published in 1962 in the form of an iso-erodent map (Wischmeier, 1962). The proved high correlation of EI with soil erosion has made this equation usable anywhere in the world where the R and K values can be characterized.

Values of K have been determined for 23 major soils on which erosion plot studies were carried out (Wischmeier and Smith, 1965). Values for many other soils have been approximated by interpolation and extrapolation at joint ARS-SCS workshops. Recently, Wischmeier and Mannering (1969) developed an equation by using multiple regression analyses which estimates K on the basis of soil properties and their interactions. This equation will allow more accurate determination of K than can be done by interpolation and extrapolation.

The slope length and gradient factors $(L$ and $S)$ are ratios to field slope losses from a 72.6-foot length and 9% slope, respectively. L may be expressed as $(\lambda/72.6)^m$, where λ is field slope length in feet and m is an exponent determined from field data. $S = (0.43 + 0.30s + 0.43s^2)/6.613$ where s is the slope gradient expressed in percent. Together they may be expressed as $LS = \sqrt{\lambda}(0.0076 + 0.0053s + 0.00076s^2)$.

The cropping management factor C is the ratio of the soil loss from a field with specified cropping and management to that from the fallow condition on which the factor K is evaluated. Five crop-stage periods are used that reflect the changes in plant cover and surface residues through the year. Productivity level, crop residue management, crop sequence, plow date, and length of meadow periods are all considered (Wischmeier, 1960). The erosion control practice factor P is concerned with only contouring, strip-cropping, or terracing. Improved tillage practices, sod-based rotations, fertility treatments, and greater quantities of crop residue left on the field are included in the C factor.

The Universal Soil Loss Equation was developed from many years of plot data assembled from many locations. In the past 12 years rainfall simulators have been used to update the information from earlier plot studies and to field test new concepts and practices (Meyer et al., 1965). Most of the plots used were 72.6 feet long and 0.01 to 0.025 acre in area. The plot sites represented major soil types over a large part of the United States. All the plots were on uniform slopes. Consequently, the more uniform the slope in the field, the more accurate were the predictions. In developing this equation for field use, researchers recognized that data were most lacking for predicting K values and for dealing with more complex field topography. Onstad et al. (1967), Young and Mutchler (1969), and others have found that erosion from a concave slope is less than that from a uniform slope because sediment tends to deposit at the bottom. Erosion from a convex slope is greater than that from a uniform slope. Incorporating this type of information into the Universal Soil Loss Equation can improve predictions. Wischmeier and Smith (1965) recommend use of the complete slope length with the gradient of the lower one-third to determine the value of LS for concave or convex slopes.

The Universal Soil Loss Equation was designed to predict field losses on an average annual basis. When it is used to predict sediment content of streams and losses from watersheds, factors must be added to account for deposition in terraced and bottomland areas adjoining streams and for contributions from streambanks and gullies. It is difficult to check the equation's accuracy on a field basis. The geometry of most fields does not allow measurement of field soil loss because of interception above the gaging point. Hadley and Lusby (1967), however, found very close agreement between measured and predicted erosion (13 vs. 15 tons per acre). In 1965 at the Treynor Experimental Watersheds in Iowa, Piest and Spomer (1968) found measured values in May and early June were greater than predicted. After early June, predicted values were higher. It is expected that predicted values would always be higher because sediment deposition on alluvial and colluvial areas of the watershed would remove some sediment actually lost from the hillslopes. Higher measured early losses may be due to development of rills in the plow-through drains as noted by Piest and Spomer. Once the rills reach the depth of the plowed layer, the rill growth seems to slow considerably or stop altogether where the slope gradient is low. Because of significant interactions of the management and practice factors (C and P) with storm size and antecedent soil moisture, single-storm or short-term predictions tend to be less accurate than longer-term predictions. Spraberry and Bowie (1969) correlated total measured sediment from 12 watersheds ranging from 243 to 32,000 acres with computed gross erosion. They found a coefficient of correlation of 0.97 between total measured sediment and the sum of erosion computed from active gullies and sheet errosion computed by the Universal Soil Loss Equation. The coefficient of correlation was 0.95 when the Musgrave (1947) equation was used. They also found that computed gross erosion from cultivated land 2% slope and above, and from active gullies, correlated better with total measured sediment yield than the erosion computed from the entire contributing area.

GEOLOGIC MEASUREMENTS

Some studies in geomorphology are of interest from an agricultural point of view. For example, Leopold et al. (1966) estimated slope erosion by using a system of pins and washers. They also studied deposition in an attempt to determine a sediment budget. They obtained an average value of surface erosion of 0.015 feet per year on sparse range vegetation in a semiarid area in New Mexico. This amounts to an erosion rate of 30 tons per acre per year from 10% slope. They estimated from their data that sheet erosion is by far the largest source of sediment. Channel deposition is only about half of the total sediment trapped, and this is only about one-quarter of the total sediment produced. They point out that sediment spread thinly over colluvial areas does not show up in their measurement data. Their sediment accumulation data compare very favorably to those of Hadley and Schumm (1961). Both groups conclude that sediment accumulation per unit area of basin decreases rapidly with increasing drainage area. Data of Hadley and Schumm were also collected in a semiarid area.

Hillslope erosion resulting from runoff from a high-intensity thunderstorm near Matt, Colorado, was measured by Hadley and Lusby (1967). They also used pins previously driven in the ground for measurement of erosion losses. From a 12-acre watershed, they found an erosion of 18 tons per acre during a 0.90-inch storm with a 0.51-inch runoff. The maximum intensity of rainfall for a 10-minute period was 1.98 inches per hour. Here, again, the climate was arid to semiarid, the average annual precipitation being 8.3 inches. Although this would not be considered an unusual storm in the Corn Belt, runoff and erosion of this magnitude from this type of storm would be highly unusual in the Corn Belt unless antecedent moisture was very high.

Ruhe and Daniels (1965) measured deposition that had occurred over a period of several thousand years and for the period from when the area was first settled until the present. Older deposition rates were determined by carbon dating, and deposition rates during the postsettlement period were measured from tree-ring data. These data are very interesting, but because of the long periods involved, it is impossible to relate the deposition to a postsettlement event or series of events. Postsettlement (125 years) deposition, however, corresponded to soil losses of 10 tons per acre per year on an Adair County, Iowa, site compared with 1.0 ton per year in the preceding 6,800 years.

Some general comments can be made about the applicability of geological data to the pollution problem. Most of the detailed studies of erosion seem to be in the arid and semiarid areas. Measurements are made on the range or pasture land or in badlands areas where there is little vegetation. Many studies are made on spectacular examples where land features stand out rather than on more subdued arable fields. Most estimates are on the basis of deposition and for long periods—hundreds of years. Shorter-term estimates are seldom on an individual storm basis. Schumm (1964) emphasizes that the need for data on erosion processes is pressing, not only as a guide for better land management, but also as a basis for explaining land forms as functions of current erosion processes and erosion rates. He is particularly interested in semiarid regions of the western United States where erosion proceeds at above average rates.

Schumm (1969) shows the relationship of erosion and deposition to landform characteristics. Studies such as these are very helpful in understanding the role of geomorphic processes in field erosion.

RESEARCH APPROACHES—MECHANICS OF EROSION

A concentrated effort is being made by the Soil and Water Conservation Research Division of the Agricultural Research Service, U.S. Department of Agriculture, to develop an erosion model. The basic model, as now conceived, considers (1) soil detachment by rainfall, (2) transport by rainfall, (3) detachment by runoff, and (4) transport by runoff. These are considered as separate but interrelated phases of soil erosion by water (Meyer and Wischmeier, 1968). An example of erosion model results is given in Figure 1.1 for a complex slope averaging 8%. Rainfall intensity was 2 inches per hour, and infiltration rate was 1 inch per hour. Comparable results can be obtained from a number of slope shapes and rainfall intensity-infiltration relationships. The general model can be expanded to a more detailed one by introducing other components.

The advantage of this model over the empirical model is that the dynamics of each phase will be described by fundamental hydraulic and hydrologic relationships and by parameters describing the soil properties that influence erosion. Each phase is now being studied as a segment or submodel by workers at various locations. Analytical studies of raindrop splash are being carried out, and this effect is related to soil properties as well as to raindrop size, shape, and velocity.

Studies of soil particle detachment by raindrops from soil beds consisting of a number of soil types, conditions of soil management, and size distribution of clods are being made at Ames, Iowa. Non-

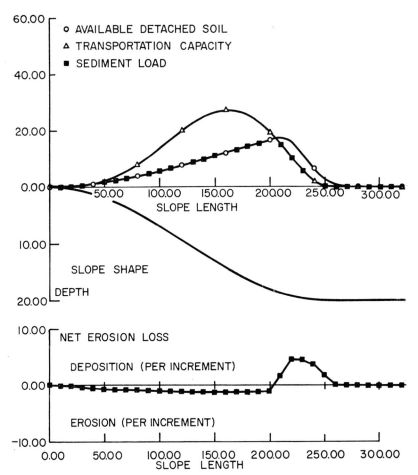

FIG. 1.1. Erosion model results plotted for a complex slope averaging 8% steepness. Rainfall intensity was 2.0 in/hr, and infiltration rate was 1.0 in/hr. Graph ordinates are relative, but the slope units have been assumed to be in feet and the erosion units may be considered as pounds per foot of slope width. The upper graph shows the available detached soil, the transportation capacity, and the resulting sediment load plotted against slope length. The middle graph shows the slope shape studied with an expanded vertical scale. The lower graph shows the net erosion loss for each increment. (Meyer and Wischmeier, 1968.)

cohesive soils (sands) have shown the highest detachment by raindrops. When large clods (one-fourth to one inch) were concentrated on the surface, peak rates of detachment were delayed (Moldenhauer and Koswara, 1968). Clod stability to raindrop impact was inversely related to clay content. The higher the content of montmorillonite clay, the weaker were the clods. Concentrating the large aggregates in the surface kept the infiltration rate high longer than if they were mixed with fine material (Moldenhauer and Kemper, 1969). The effect of surface sealing on detachment has been studied (Molden-hauer and Koswara, 1968).

Work is being done to determine the effect of the suction (tension) gradients on stability, and consequently their effect on detachment and erosion. Plans are being made to develop a computer model for infiltration, runoff, clod breakdown, and soil detachment from the beginning of the first rain after tillage throughout each succeeding rain.

When pore size at the soil surface has been reduced to the point that rainfall intensity exceeds intake rate, runoff begins. As runoff water becomes concentrated in the lower areas of the surface microrelief, small rills begin to form because of detachment and transport of soil by flowing water. This process is being studied at Lafayette, Indiana.

Gully Erosion

In most areas of the humid region, gully erosion is a relatively small percentage of gross erosion. A study of 113 watersheds (Glymph, 1956), ranging from 23 acres to 437 square miles and located in the humid area of the United States, showed that sheet and rill erosion accounted for 90% or more of the sediment yield in half the watersheds. In about 20% of the cases studied, however, 50% or more of the sediment was derived from gullies. In most instances of relatively large sediment production from gullies, watersheds of less than 1 square mile were involved. In three instances, stream channel erosion contributed more than 40% of the sediment yield. In a region of loess-covered sands in Mississippi, gully erosion contributed about 20% of the sediment yield for watersheds ranging from about 8 to 120 square miles (Miller et al., 1963).

The prediction of gully growth rates has received little attention, although such information is often needed for design and cost-benefit analysis for the Public Law 566 program. A study of 61 gullies in the deep-loess area of southwest Iowa (Beer and Johnson, 1963) related change in gully area to such factors as watershed area, precipitation, channel geometry, and terraced area. The R^2 statistic used to measure the relative fit (R^2 measures the percentage of total deviation attributed to regression) varied between 0.70 and 0.89 for 5 linear regression models with 6 or 7 "independent" variables. The R^2s for logarithmic models were lower, but fewer problems with correlation between "independent" variables were encountered. Using the ratio of the predicted growth rate (equation derived from same field measurements) to the growth rate measured in the field as a standard, Beer was able to predict growth rate within 50% in half the cases. A study (Thompson, 1964) of 210 gully heads located in 6 states related gully advancement to area, a soil factor, rainfall, gully depth, and channel slope. R^2 value for the equation of best fit was 0.77. An Israeli study (Seginer, 1966) related gully advance to area. Both Thompson's and Seginer's studies showed the gully head growth rate to be proportional to the square root of the contributing watershed area. The scarcity of reported literature and the approaches taken to date indicate that the mechanics of gully growth are poorly understood. Predictions of gully growth are usually made by projecting observed rates obtained from the recent past through use of aerial photograph measurements and by interview.

SEDIMENT YIELDS

Sediment yields are ordinarily reported in tons per acre per year in agricultural literature and in tons, or acre-feet, per square mile per year in engineering and geological literature. The ratio of sediment yield to gross erosion is termed sediment delivery ratio, a ratio commonly used in design of small reservoirs. The sediment delivery ratio is used to express the fact that the sediment production per unit area decreases as the watershed area increases. There is strong evidence to support this as shown in Table 1.2 (Gottschalk, 1964). Even though qualitative reasoning would indicate this is true, no cause and effect relationships are available to represent the decrease in the sediment delivery ratio with area. The percentage of area of lesser slopes increases with drainage area. Groundwater in contrast to surface water ordinarily contributes a larger percentage of flow to a stream, and local storms initiate erosion in only a portion of a watershed. From this it would seem that sediment production per unit area should decrease with size of watershed if all other factors remain constant.

The primary sources of sediment-yield information are reservoir sedimentation surveys and suspended load samplings. Reservoir surveys have the advantages of providing long-term information in some instances and of including bed-load sediments (sediment moving but not in suspension). Disadvantages of the surveys are loss of sediment through spillage, unavailable individual storm runoff events, and difficulty in measuring sediment density. A summary of reservoir sediment deposition surveys is published periodically (U.S. Department of Agriculture, 1969). Suspended load samplings have the advantage of providing data for specific storm events; time required to obtain long-term records, difficulty in obtaining accurate data, and cost are disadvantages. Federal agencies are the primary source of the limited sediment-yield data. Most of the suspended sediment-yield data are published by the U.S. Geological Survey.

TABLE 1.2. Sediment production rates for drainage areas in the United States.

Watershed Size	Number of Measurements	Average Annual Rate
(square miles)		(acre-feet/square mile)
Under 10	650	3.80
10–100	205	1.60
100–1,000	123	1.01
Over 1,000	118	0.50

Source: Gottschalk (1964).

Sediment Yields from Watersheds

Because of the complexity of the sedimentation process, only statistical attempts have been used to relate yield to selected observed measurable system inputs. Several regression equations have been developed, primarily for watersheds less than 50 square miles. Some estimate of the gross erosion (on-site sheet plus gully erosion) is required for most of these equations. Other factors related to drainage density and channel geometry are added.

Glymph (1954) discusses several of the equations. Equations were developed for South Dakota stock ponds, California forested watersheds, and western Iowa and Texas watersheds. The equations typically present sediment yield as some function of climate, area, watershed geometry, watershed management (if variable), and relative capacity of the reservoir if predictions are based on reservoir sedimentation surveys. An example of such an equation (Glymph et al., 1951) was developed for 36 western Iowa and eastern Nebraska watersheds ranging in area from 0.036 to 2,800 square miles.

$$\text{Log } S = 1.0078 \text{ Log } E + 0.6460 \text{ Log } 10 \ N - 0.1354 \text{ Log } 100 \ W - 1.4130$$

where
  $S = $ Sediment yield, tons per square mile per year
  $E = $ Gross erosion, tons per square mile per year
  $N = $ Number of rainfall events (average annual number equal to or exceeding one inch per day during the growing season)
  $W = $ Net drainage area, square miles.

About 90% of the sediment-yield data points calculated by the above equation were within $\pm$ 50% of the points determined by field measurement.

A more severe test for such prediction equations is to use data from the same or a similar area (Beer et al., 1966) but independent of the equation development. Four methods, three based on equations and one based on gross erosion, delivery ratio, and trap efficiency, were tested by plotting the ratio of predicted yield to measured yield for 24 reservoirs. Figure 1.2 shows the discrepancy among equations for the various reservoirs. About 40% of the plotted points lie in a band in which the actual deposition was predicted within $\pm$ 50%.

The sediment delivery ratio approach is used in Soil Conservation Service watershed designs (Adair and Renfro, 1969). A plot of delivery ratio against watershed area is defined for a given land resource area and is limited to that land resource area. Recent studies for river basin planning (U.S. Corps of Engineers, 1968) indicate a similar approach was used in developing logarithmic plots of annual sediment yield as a function of area for a given land resource area. Lines for all land resource areas are drawn parallel and indicate an exponent (slope) of about $- 0.11$. The annual sediment yields representing field data range from about 30% to about 300% of the yields indicated by plotted lines. A similar earlier logarithmic plot

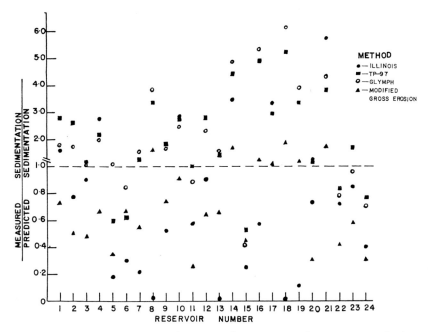

FIG. 1.2. Comparison of measured reservoir sedimentation with that predicted by four methods.

(Glymph, 1951) of data from 51 suspended load measurement stations and reservoirs from different parts of the country showed a slope of the data envelope lines of about − 0.12. The sediment-yield plots from the upper Mississippi basin study ranged over three logarithmic cycles for the entire basin drainage area; Glymph's data ranged over somewhat less than two cycles.

Thus, measurements indicate that extreme variations in sediment yield may occur in a region made up of different land resource areas defined by land use, topography, climate, and soil types. Iowa provides a good example of the effects of topography and soil types in a region in which agricultural land use is heavy and rainfall characteristics are similar. The relatively flat and recently glaciated area of north-central Iowa, which is characterized by surface depressions, has sediment yields of about 50 tons per square mile per year for a 100-square-mile watershed. The rolling loess hills of western Iowa produce sediment at a rate of about 6,000 tons per square mile per year for a 100-square-mile watershed (U.S. Corps of Engineers, 1968).

Reservoir Sedimentation

Three aspects of reservoir sedimentation related to delivered sediment are trap efficiency, specific weight of deposited material, and distribution of sediment. The trap efficiency of a reservoir is a measure of the efficiency of the structure to retain the incoming sediment, expressed in percent. The trap efficiency depends primarily on the particle fall velocity and rate of flow of water through the reservoir. Trap efficiencies of reservoirs usually decrease with time as sediment accumulates. Trap efficiency studies (Brune, 1953) indicate most large reservoirs have trap efficiencies greater than 80%. Brune presented envelope curves of trap efficiency as a function of the ratio of reservoir capacity (acre-feet) to annual inflow (acre-feet). Few good data are available on trap efficiency, especially for small reservoirs.

The specific weight of sediment is needed to obtain a meaningful measure of deposited sediment. The specific weight is expressed in terms of dry weight per unit volume in place. Recent studies provide a measure of in-place specific weight (Heinemann and Dvorak, 1963; Lara and Pemberton, 1963). The range of specific weights for dominant grain sizes is as follows:

Dominant Grain Size	Permanently Submerged	Aerated
	(pounds per cubic foot)	
Clay	40–60	60–80
Silt	55–75	75–85
Sand	85–100	85–100

Specific weights within reservoirs can be estimated if the sand, silt, and clay percentages and reservoir drawdown characteristics are known. Lara and Pemberton's data indicate standard errors of prediction of 11 to 14 pounds per cubic foot for 1,316 samples obtained from many reservoirs under different types of operation. Some river bed sediments were included. The standard error indicates that 68% of the measured specific weights were within 11 to 14 pounds per cubic foot of the independently predicted specific weight. The correlation coefficients (R) ranged from 0.57 to 0.84.

The distribution of deposited sediment is affected by particle size and velocity of flow through the reservoir. The sediment may be deposited in the form of a delta at the head of a reservoir or deposited as a blanket over the bottom of the reservoir. The delta deposits contain primarily the coarser material in transport; the bottom deposits are primarily clay. Graphs derived for different reservoir shapes have been developed that indicate the proportion of the sediment located below indicated percentages of reservoir depth (Borland and Miller, 1960). In a study of 23 small reservoirs (Heinemann, 1961), a regression equation was developed that expressed the percentage of original reservoir depth filled with sediment in terms of percentage of original storage depleted, reservoir geometry, storage capacity, and the capacity-watershed ratio. The coefficient of determination, R^2, for the equation was 0.91. Graphs of sediment distribution were also presented.

SEDIMENT IN TRANSPORT

Sediment transported by a stream may be divided between bed load and suspended load, depending on mode of transport. Bed load moves on or very close to the bed, but suspended load is maintained in the flow by turbulence. Another term sometimes used is "wash" load or that portion in transport made up of fine particles not found in quantity in the bed. The term bed-material load describes that portion in transport of which the bed is largely composed. The bed-material load may be in suspended transport. Although it is arbitrary and depends on velocity, water temperature, and sediment size available, a division in size may be made at 62μ.

Suspended Transport

The suspended load in transport through a unit width of stream cross section is determined by the product of concentration times velocity integrated over the depth of flow. Several measurements of vertical distribution of sediment are usually taken at a cross section, except in very small streams. Most samples are taken with a depth-integrating sampler which intercepts a representative sample in the profile while the sampler is lowered and raised. The point-integrating sampler intercepts a water-sediment sample at a point in the profile and enables construction of sediment concentration curves.

In most streams of the humid area of mid-America, most sediment in transport is suspended. Measurements in the Mississippi River at St. Louis over 10 years indicated that 95% of the total sediment discharge was as suspended load; 85% of the suspended load was silt and clay (Jordan, 1965). In Iowa probably more than 85% of transported sediment is in suspension; 90% or more of the suspended particles are in the silt and clay range, as indicated from average particle size distributions of 7 rivers (Hershey, 1955). Although there are exceptions, most reservoir deposits contain less than 10% sand (Gottachalk, 1964). For 303 samples collected from 32 reservoirs in Illinois the sand content was usually 2 to 5% of the sample (Stall, 1966).

The capacity of a stream to transport fine particles is restricted by the available supply; the supply is usually much less than the stream can convey. In instances where the bed load is appreciable the supply of particles is usually greater than the stream can transport. Thus the amount transported as bed load depends on flow characteristics.

The amount of sediment in suspension is extremely variable and depends on local hydrologic conditions. In general, the suspended load increases faster than the discharge and can be expressed by $L = aQ^b$, where L = sediment load in tons per day, Q is stream discharge in *cfs*, and a and b are constants. The constant b typically lies between 2 and 3 (Leopold and Maddock, 1953). Although the equation roughly expresses the relationship, a scatter over two logarithmic cycles is not uncommon. The concentration of suspended sediment is related to climate and physiographic area. For example, the maximum concentrations of sediment in the portion of the Des Moines River that drains the most recently glaciated area is seldom over 5,000 ppm, but records for the Soldier River located in western Iowa deep loess show several concentrations over

200,000 ppm (U.S. Corps of Engineers, 1951). An instantaneous concentration of 276,000 ppm was sampled in Waubousie Creek of that region (Hershey, 1955). As indicated previously, the concentration of suspended sediment in a downstream direction generally decreases.

The wash load of a stream travels at about the velocity of the water. Thus the travel time of clay and silt to a critical downstream point would be about the same as that of dissolved solids. Bed-load material would move more slowly because of the nature of transport. The peak concentrations associated with surface runoff occur near, and in most cases before, the peak discharge in very small watersheds (Dragoun and Miller, 1966). The changes in concentration with time occur rapidly. In larger watersheds the peak concentrations tend to coincide with the peak flows, although local inflow from small watersheds may significantly alter concentrations.

The distribution of sediment in a stream varies laterally across the stream and through the vertical flow profile. Examples indicate that a variation from the average stream concentration of ± 20% is common (Task Committee on Sedimentation, 1969). Very large variations may occur at stream sections below a tributary stream with different sediment transport characteristics. Sediment particles in the coarse silt through clay range tend to be uniformly distributed in the vertical. But the sand concentration gradient decreases from the stream bed upward. A mathematical expression (based on theory of turbulence) is available that defines the concentration gradient for a given particle size, if the concentration of the given size at a given elevation is known (Rouse, 1938).

Bed Load

Considerable effort has been expended in developing bed-load formulas, but there is not agreement in the literature regarding which approach is best (Shulits and Hill, 1968).

Several comparisons have been made (Vanoni et al., 1961; Jordon, 1965). Variation between predicted (by formula) and measured bed loads may be greater than 100%. The most commonly used formulas are the Einstein, Schoklitsch, and Meyer-Peter and Muller formulas (Shulits and Hill, 1968). Some of the formulas are used routinely in planning and operations (Adair and Renfro, 1969).

If the fall velocity (particle size), average stream velocity, and nature of the channel are known, an estimate of the bed load may be made. Curves relating bed-material discharge per foot of width and mean velocity have been developed for sand-bed streams (Colby, 1961). The bed-load discharge may also be estimated in terms of percentage of suspended load, where data on suspended load are available (Lane and Borland, 1951). Suspended load concentration, type of material forming the channel, and texture of suspended material are needed for the estimate. In some cases where the concentration is over 1,000 ppm, channel material is sand or consolidated clay, and the suspended material is less than 25% sand, predicted bed load varies from 2 to 15%.

CONCLUSION

Although considerable progress has been made in the last 30 years, the science of erosion and sediment transport needs to advance considerably if it is to be sufficiently flexible for use in detailed planning. Most of the approaches to design and planning are empirically based and are subject to the restraints of the observations from which they are developed. Considerable study of on-site erosion and river transport, especially of sand-bed streams in the West, is evident. The relationship between on-site erosion and the subsequent response in streams is poorly defined quantitatively.

A few points stand out in relation to pollution. Most material in transport is in suspension, and is in the silt and clay size range. Most of the fines in transport in streams are evidently derived from surface erosion. In regions of erosive soils and well-defined drainage systems, 10 to 30 tons per acre per year are delivered to streams if vegetation cover is poor. Concentrations of suspended sediment of 25,000 to 150,000 ppm are encountered for short times. On the other hand, in flat country with poor drainage development, the sediment loads and concentrations are relatively low even though the land is cropped intensively. While bed loads are low, the effect of man on bed transport may be small.

The works of man are primarily related to change of cover and alteration of the hydraulic system through which is transported the water and sediment. The options of altering cover and channels remain open.

According to Vanoni (1963):

> The theoretical treatment of the sedimentation problem is very difficult, and will develop slowly. It will be based on the understanding gained from experiments rather than by some break-through by a stroke of theoretical genius. However, in order for the experiments to contribute understanding, they must be designed carefully to answer certain questions or to prove or disprove hypotheses based on reasoning and results of other investigations. Considering the primitive state of knowledge of sedimentation, contributions can be made in many ways.

REFERENCES

Adair, J. W., and Renfro, G. W. 1969. Sedimentation considerations in watershed design. Paper No. 69–209 presented at the meeting of the Am. Soc. Agr. Engrs., June 1969, Lafayette, Ind.

Beer, C. E., and Johnson, H. P. 1963. Factors in gully growth in the deep loess area of western Iowa. *Trans. Am. Soc. Agr. Engrs.* 6:237–40.

Beer, C. E., Farnham, C. W., and Heinemann, H. G. 1966. Evaluating sedimentation prediction techniques in western Iowa. *Trans. Am. Soc. Agr. Engrs.* 9:828–33.

Borland, W. M., and Miller, C. R. 1960. Distribution of sediment in large reservoirs. *Trans. Am. Soc. Civil Engrs.* 125 (1): 166–80.

Browning, G. M., Parish, C. L., and Glass, J. A. 1947. A method for determining the use and limitation of rotation and conservation practices in control of soil erosion in Iowa. *Am. Soc. Agron. J.* 39:65–73.

Brune, G. M. 1953. Trap efficiency of reservoirs. *Trans. Am. Geophys. Union* 34:407–18.

Colby, B. R. 1961. *Effect of depth of flow on discharge of bed material.* U.S. Geol. Survey Water Supply Paper 1498-D.

———. 1963. *Fluvial sediments—a summary of source, transportation, deposition, and measurement of sediment discharge.* U.S. Geol. Survey Bull. 1181-A.

Dragoun, F. J., and Miller, C. R. 1966. Sediment characteristics of two small agricultural watersheds. *Trans. Am. Soc. Agr. Engrs.* 9:66–70.

Einstein, H. A. 1964. River sedimentation. In *Handbook of applied hydrology,* ed. V. T. Chow, pp. 17–35 to 17–67. New York: McGraw-Hill.

Glymph, L. M. 1951. *Relation of sedimentation to accelerated erosion in the Missouri River Basin.* USDA, Soil Conserv. Serv., SCS-TP-102.

———. 1954. Studies of sediment yields from watersheds. *Intern. Union Geodesy Geophysics,* Intern. Assoc. Sci. Hydrol. Publ. 36, pp. 178–91.

———. 1956. Importance of sheet erosion as a source of sediment. *Trans. Am. Geophys. Union* 38:903–7.

Glymph, L. M., Heinemann, H. G., and Kohler, V. O. 1951. Unpublished study from files of U.S. Soil Conserv. Serv., Lincoln, Nebr.

Gottschalk, L. C. 1964. Reservoir sedimentation. In *Handbook of applied hydrology,* ed. V. T. Chow, pp. 17–1 to 17–34. New York: McGraw-Hill.

Hadley, R. F., and Lusby, G. C. 1967. Runoff and hillslope erosion resulting from a high-intensity thunderstorm near Mack, western Colorado. *Water Resources Res.* 3:139–43.

Hadley, R. F., and Schumm, S. A. 1961. *Hydrology of the upper Cheyenne River basin.* U.S. Geol. Survey Water Supply Paper 1531-B.:137–98.

Heinemann, H. G. 1961. *Sediment distribution in small floodwater retarding reservoirs in the Missouri basin loess hills.* USDA, ARS 41–44.

Heinemann, H. G., and Dvorak, V. I. 1963. Improved volumetric survey for small reservoirs. In *Proc. Federal Inter-Agency Sedimentation Conf.* USDA Misc. Publ. 970.

Hershey, H. G. 1955. *Quality of surface waters in Iowa.* Iowa Geol. Survey Water Supply Paper 5.

Jordon, P. R. 1965 *Fluvial sediment of the Mississippi River at St. Louis, Missouri.* U.S. Geol. Survey Water Supply Paper 1802.

Lane, E. W., and Borland, W. M. 1951. Estimating bed load. *Trans. Am. Geophys. Union* 32:121–23.

Lara, J. M., and Pemberton, E. L. 1963. Initial unit weight of deposited sediments. In *Proc. Federal Inter-Agency Sedimentation Conf.* USDA Misc. Publ. 970.

Leopold, L. B., and Maddock, T. 1953. *The hydraulic geometry of stream channels and some physiographic implications.* U.S. Geol. Survey Prof. Paper 252.

Leopold, B., Emmett, W. W., and Myrick, R. W. 1966. *Channel and hillslope processes in a semiarid area, New Mexico.* U.S. Geol. Survey Prof. Paper 352G, pp. 193–253.

Meyer, L. D., and Wischmeier, W. H. 1968. Mathematical simulation of the process of soil erosion by water. Paper 68–732 presented at the 1968 winter meeting of the Am. Soc. Agr. Engrs., Dec. 10–13, 1968, Chicago.

Meyer, L. D., Mech, S. J., Mutchler, C. K., Hermsmeier, L. F., Palmer, R. S., Swanson, N. P., Brubenzer, G. D., and Moldenhauer, W. C. 1965. Symp. on simulation of rainfall for soil erosion research. *Trans. Am. Soc. Agr. Engrs.* 8:63–75.

Miller, C. R., Woodburn, R., and Turner, H. R. 1963. Upland gully sediment production. *Intern. Assoc. Scientific Hydrol.,* Commission of Land Erosion Publ. 59, pp. 83–104.

Moldenhauer, W. C., and Kemper, W. D. 1969. Interdependence of water drop energy and clod size on infiltration and clod stability. *Soil Sci. Soc. Am. Proc.* 33:297–301.

Moldenhauer, W. C., and Koswara, J. 1968. Effect of initial clod size on characteristics of splash and wash erosion. *Soil Sci. Soc. Am. Proc.* 32:875–79.

Moore, C. M., Wood, W. J., and Renfro, G. W. 1960. Trap efficiency of reservoirs, debris basins, and debris dams. *Am. Soc. Civil Engrs. Proc. J. Hydraulics Div.* 86, HY2:69–87.

Musgrave, G. W. 1947. The quantitative evaluation of factors in water erosion, a first approximation. *J. Soil Water Conserv.* 2:133–38.

Onstad, C. A., Larson, C. L., Hermsmeier, L. F., Young, R. A. 1967. A method of computing soil movement throughout a field. *Trans. Am. Soc. Agr. Engrs.* 10:742–45.

Piest, R. F., and Spomer, R. G. 1968. Sheet and gully erosion in the Missouri Valley loessial region. *Trans. Am. Soc. Agr. Engrs.* 11:850–53.

Raudkivi, A. J. 1967. *Loose boundary hydraulics.* 1st ed. New York: Pergamon Press.

Rouse, H. 1938. *Fluid mechanics for hydraulic engineers.* New York: McGraw-Hill.

Ruhe, R. V., and Daniels, R. B. 1965. Landscape erosion—geologic and historic. *J. Soil Water Conserv.* 20:52–57.

Schumm, S. A. 1964. Seasonal variations of erosion rates and processes on hillslopes in western Colorado. *Ann. Geomorphol.* Supplement 5:215–38.

———. 1969. A geomorphic approach to erosion control in semiarid regions. *Trans. Am. Soc. Agr. Engrs.* 12:60–68.

Seginer, I. 1966. *Gully development and sediment yield.* Israel Ministry of Agr. Soil Conserv. Div. Res. Rept. 13.

Shulits, S., and Hill, R. D. 1968. *Bedload formulas.* University Park, Pa.: Dept. Civil Eng. Hydraulics Lab. Bull.

Smith, D. D. 1941. Interpretation of soil conservation data for field use. *Agr. Eng.* 22:173–75.

Spraberry, J. A., and Bowie, A. J. 1969. Predicting sediment yields from complex watersheds. *Trans. Am. Soc. Agr. Engrs.* 12:199–201.

Stall, J. B. 1966. *Man's role in affecting the sedimentation of streams and reservoirs.* Ill. State Water Survey Reprint Series 68.

Task Committee on Sedimentation. 1969. Sediment measurement:

fluvial sediment. *Proc. Am. Soc. Civil Engrs.* 95 (HY5): 1477–1514.

Thompson, J. R. 1964. Quantitative effect of watershed variables on rate of gully-head advancement. *Trans. Am. Soc. Agr. Engrs.* 7:54–55.

U.S. Corps of Engineers. About 1951. *Suspended sediment in the Missouri River, daily record for water years 1937–1948.* Corps of Engrs., Missouri River Div., Omaha.

———. 1968. Fluvial sediment. In *Upper Mississippi River comprehensive basin study,* Draft 3, appendix G. North Central Div., Chicago.

U.S. Department of Agriculture. 1968. *A national program of research for environmental quality.* Joint Task Force Rept. of the USDA and the state universities and land-grant colleges.

———. 1969. *Summary of reservoir sediment deposition surveys made in the United States through 1965.* Misc. Publ. 1143.

Vanoni, V. A. 1963. Review of research activities in sedimentation. In *Proc. Federal Inter-Agency Sedimentation Conf.* USDA Misc. Publ. 970.

Vanoni, V. A., Brooks, N. H., and Kennedy, J. F. 1961. *Lecture notes on sediment transportation and channel stability.* Pasadena, Calif.: W. H. Keck Lab. of Hydraulics and Water Resources, Calif. Inst. of Technol. Rept. KH-R-1.

Wischmeier, W. H. 1959. A rainfall erosion index for a universal soil-loss equation. *Soil Sci. Soc. Am. Proc.* 23:246–49.

———. 1960. Cropping-management factor evaluations for a universal soil-loss equation. *Soil Sci. Soc. Am. Proc.* 24:322–26.

———. 1962. Rainfall erosion potential. *Agr. Eng.* 43:212–15.

Wischmeier, W. H., and Mannering, J. V. 1969. Relation of soil properties to its erodibility. *Soil Sci. Soc. Am. Proc.* 33:131–37.

Wischmeier, W. H., and Smith, D. D. 1958. Rainfall energy and its relationship to soil loss. *Trans. Am. Geophys. Union* 39:285–91.

———. 1965. *Predicting rainfall-erosion losses from the cropland east of the Rocky Mountains.* USDA Handbook 282.

Young, R. A., and Mutchler, C. K. 1969. Effect of slope shape on erosion and runoff. *Trans. Am. Soc. Agr. Engrs.* 12:231–33, 239.

CHAPTER TWO

CHEMISTRY OF SEDIMENT IN WATER

R. F. HOLT, R. H. DOWDY, and D. R. TIMMONS

T HE sediment that is carried off sloping lands and transported into surface water supplies has been called the greatest single pollutant of our natural waters. In a certain sense its physical effects are much more obvious than its chemical effects. The clogging of navigation channels and the silting of lakes and reservoirs are expressions of the physical existence of the sediment. It is also a costly existence, for millions of dollars are spent annually for dredging operations to remove this material from its place of deposition. Relatively little is known about the chemical effects of sediment on the water supply in which it resides or its influence on the chemical status of flowing water during transport.

There has been growing concern for the quality of surface waters, particularly in terms of the nutrient levels that permit nuisance growth of aquatic plant life. The two elements most closely associated with these noxious growths are nitrogen and phosphorus. These elements are also closely associated with agriculture, for they occur in all plant life. Since these are the chemicals most apt to be in insufficient supply for crop growth, they are the nutrients most frequently supplied as fertilizers. Fertilizers are applied to the surface of soils and thus are quite vulnerable to removal by erosion. It is this eroded topsoil which makes up the bulk of the sediment being fed into surface water supplies, and it is this material that we are concerned with in this discussion.

CHARACTER OF THE SEDIMENT

The mineralogical composition of sediment, both suspended and bottom material, is as complex as that of the soil from which it was

R. F. HOLT is Soil Scientist, USDA, and Professor, University of Minnesota. R. H. DOWDY is Soil Scientist, USDA, and Assistant Professor, University of Minnesota. D. R. TIMMONS is Soil Scientist, USDA. Contribution from the Corn Belt Branch, Soil and Water Conservation Research Division, ARS, USDA, Morris, Minn., in cooperation with the Minnesota Agricultural Experiment Station.

derived. Little is known about the mineralogical composition of natural water sediments. However, from soil erosion literature it has been established that erosion is selective (Massey and Jackson, 1952; Massey et al., 1953). While a discussion of soil erosion is beyond the intent of this chapter, some observations are appropriate. Mannering and Wischmeier[1] observed that the sediment from five soils containing 60 to 75% silt was higher in silt than the original soil. It was also observed that clay was preferentially removed from two soils of high sand content.

Working with a Connecticut watershed, Frink (1969) reported a large decrease in sand content of the lake sediment compared to that of the watershed soils, 18 and 60 to 65%, respectively. On the other hand, the clay content of the sediment was fivefold greater than that of the upland watershed soils. Similarly, the silt content increased from 20 to 25% for the watershed soils to 34% for the lake sediment. Stall (1964) reported the following representative comparison between Illinois lake sediments and the watershed soils from which they were derived: (1) the sand content of the two remained the same at approximately 5% and (2) the clay content of the sediment was 39% compared to a 15% clay content for the watershed soils. These types of observations strongly support the hypothesis of the selective, size-sorting nature of erosion. It is the product of this erosion that becomes the colloidal stream load and sediments of natural waters.

The clay mineralogy of sediment reflects the mineralogy of the soils from which it was derived. Frink (1969) identified vermiculite (40%), "illite" (hydromica, 35%), and kaolinite (25%) in the lake sediment he studied. Vermiculite concentration decreased in the sediment compared to that of the watershed soils, while illite and kaolinite concentrations increased. In the southeastern United States where kaolinite is the predominant clay mineral in soils, it is likewise observable in the sediments of that region (Pomeroy et al., 1965). Sediments derived from western Minnesota soils high in montmorillonite contain montmorillonite as the major clay mineral (Burwell et al.[2]). Working with a Tennessee lake bed sediment, Lomenick and Tamura (1965) observed that "illite" (hydromica) was the predominant clay mineral present in the sediment as well as in the shale formations of the surrounding area. Information as to the presence of X-ray amorphous clay material (i.e., crystalline relics, amorphous Fe, and Al hydrous oxides) is indeed limited, but this material must exist in young sediments and suspended water load if these clay size particles were present in the source materials. Work by Frink (1969) showed the presence of free Fe oxides in a neutral, freshwater lake. The free Fe oxide content was highly correlated with the clay content of the sediment which suggested that this material also obeys size sorting.

The chemistry of sediments is in reality the surface chemistry and properties of the colloidal (inorganic and organic) fraction of those sediments. To understand the behavior of the colloids, one must

---

1. Personal communication.
2. Unpublished data.

first look at the structure and characteristics of the colloidal material. For a complete discussion of clay minerals, the book by Grim (1968) is recommended.

Clay minerals are defined as two-dimensional arrays of Si/O tetrahedra and Al/ or Mg/O/OH octahedra. In soil science we often use the term "clay" to include all inorganic particles 2μ in equivalent spherical diameter. Hence, clay could include 2μ quartz as well as hydrous Fe and Al oxides. The structure of clay minerals is the superimposition of tetrahedral and octahedral sheets in many different arrays. When one tetrahedral and one octahedral sheet are superimposed to form a layer, the resultant is referred to as 1:1 type clay mineral or the kaolin group. The 2:1 type clay minerals are characterized by two tetrahedral sheets sharing a central octahedral sheet. For both the 2:1 and 1:1 type clays, the crystals are formed by the stacking of unit layers with a constant periodicity. The third type of clay minerals is the 2:1:1 minerals or the chlorite group. It is formed by interlayering 2:1 type minerals with a brucite sheet (either iron, aluminum, or magnesium hydroxide or any combination); hence, 2:1:1 type minerals.

From a physicochemical perspective, the two most important properties of clay colloids are electrical charge and surface area. To discuss these characteristics in any detail is beyond the scope of this chapter; however, the magnitudes of these properties for some clay materials are shown in Table 2.1. As a general rule, clays carry a net negative charge. This negative charge arises from two sources: (1) isomorphous substitution in the crystal structure, and (2) broken bonds on crystal edges. Isomorphous substitution refers to the replacement of tetravalent Si by trivalent Al in the tetrahedral sheet of a clay crystal and/or replacement of trivalent Al by divalent cations such as Mg in the octahedral sheet. This type of substitution gives rise to a permanent negative charge on the clay crystal which is balanced by a surface layer of cations too large to penetrate to the crystal structure which can be replaced by another cation—hence the term exchangeable cation. The site and magnitude of this substitution are used to differentiate clay minerals. Vermiculite is substituted in the tetrahedral sheet, while montmorillonite is substituted octahedrally. For this reason and the fact that vermiculite possesses

TABLE 2.1. Cation exchange capacity and surface area of several clay minerals.

Clay	Cation Exchange Capacity	Surface Area
	$(me/100\ g)$	(M^2/g)
Vermiculite	100–150	600–800
Montmorillonite	80–120	600–800
Hydromica	10–40	65–100
Chlorite	10–40	25–40
Kaolinite	3–15	7–30
Hydrous oxides	2–6	100–800

a higher surface charge, montmorillonite will expand more readily and to a greater extent in aqueous solutions than does vermiculite. In contrast to these expanding 2:1 type clay minerals, hydromica has a much higher surface charge which is satisfied with K ions. The electrostatic interactions in hydromica are so great that expansion upon hydration is not observed generally. Hence, the K ions are nonexchangeable, with the result that hydromica has a lower exchange capacity than vermiculite or montmorillonite.

Kaolinite has very little isomorphous substitution (permament charge). Its ion exchange capacity is derived from a second source of charge, which is broken bonds at the edges of crystals. The charge arising from broken bonds is a function of particle size and pH. As particle size decreases, so does the ion exchange capacity. It may be either positive or negative, depending upon the pH of the system. However, for pH values in the neutral and alkaline range, the edge charge will be neutral or negative (Schofield and Sampson, 1954). Other clay minerals have similar pH-dependent charge, but such charge becomes of less importance as the permanent negative charge increases in magnitude. Amorphous, clay size, hydrous oxides of Fe and Al possess positive charges due to the protonation of a formerly shared OH group—for example $[(- OH_2)^{+\frac{1}{2}}]$ (Rich, 1968).

Organic colloids are a significant constituent of natural sediments. Losses of organic matter in eroded soil can be as high as 1,100 pounds per acre (Barrows and Kilmer, 1963). Since organic matter is concentrated in the soil surface and has a low density, it is among the first components to be removed. Thus, the eroded soil contains more organic matter than the surface soil from which it came, and enrichment ratios of about 1 to 5 have been reported. Unfortunately, little definitive information is known about the physicochemical character of this material, perhaps due to the lack of understanding of the chemical character of soil organic matter from which it is derived. The organic colloids may be cationic and/or anionic in nature or exist as neutral entities with functional groups such as hydroxyl, carboxyl, and amino, which may ionize in the same manner as other organic compounds. If organic colloids of sediments bear any relationship to those in the soils from which they were derived, a cation exchange capacity from 250 to 400 me/100 g soil can be expected. What role selected erosion may play in the qualitative nature of the organic sediment is unknown. Likewise, the physicochemical character of organic colloids produced in natural waters is unknown.

Chemical reactions of sediments with the properties discussed above can be divided into two groups: (1) interactions with charged ions, and (2) interactions with neutral compounds. Adsorption of charged ions by colloids is referred to as ion exchange and is the straightforward process of maintenance of electrical neutrality by the interaction of oppositely charged species. Both inorganic and organic cations are adsorbed on negatively charged clay colloid surfaces. The ease or difficulty with which an inorganic cation can replace an adsorbed cation is dependent upon numerous factors which include (1) cation concentration, (2) complementary adsorbed cation, (3) solution anion, (4) nature of the clay mineral, (5) temperature of suspension, and (6) nature of replacing the cation. These factors are discussed by Grim (1968). As a general rule, the higher the valence, the greater the replacing power of an ion. Also, the replacing power for ions of the same valence tends to increase with increasing atomic radius and decreasing hydration.

Cation exchange can play a very important role in the chemistry of natural waters. In some instances, cesium-137 is a major radionuclide contaminant of natural waters (Lomenick and Tamura, 1965). Sawhney (1964) and Colman et al. (1963) have shown that vermiculite and hydromica fix Cs against Ca extraction. Lomenick and Tamura (1965) observed that hydromica in lake sediments fixed large quantities of Cs-137 from contaminated waters. Hence, sediments can serve as chemical scavengers of contaminated natural waters. Diagenesis of illite from vermiculite by the exchange and fixation of K from lake waters as suggested by Frink (1969) is another important exchange reaction in nature.

Adsorption of anions such as phosphates is of great interest to those concerned with the fate of nutrients in natural waters. Rich (1968) stated that amorphous Al and Fe hydrous oxides and hydroxides are the most reactive soil colloids with respect to anion adsorption. This type of reaction is an electrostatic interaction. Anions may also enter into exchange with hydroxyl groups exposed at the broken edges of crystals or on the surfaces of amorphous hydrous oxides. By studying the adsorption of sulfate in soil suspensions, Chao et al. (1965) concluded that sulfate ions were exchanging for "structural" hydroxyl groups. It is suggested that reactions of the same type can occur in natural colloidal suspensions.

The second type of adsorption on sediments is the interaction of colloids with neutral polar molecules. In natural waters it must be remembered that water is the solvent and that one is studying an aqueous system. Hence, in any equilibrium adsorption reaction, the adsorbate is competing with an extensively hydrated adsorbent. This is why Hoffmann and Brindley (1960) observed that adsorption of alcohols from aqueous suspensions of montmorillonite did not occur until the compound contained five or six carbon atoms. This same phenomenon occurs in the adsorption of sugars onto clays. Clapp et al. (1968) reported the adsorption of polysaccharides on montmorillonite from aqueous suspension, while it is not possible to show an adsorption of mono- and disaccharide under the same conditions (Dowdy[3]). While an exact division between adsorption and no adsorption of sugars on a size basis cannot be made, it is possible that molecular weights in the tens of thousands are required before adsorption occurs from aqueous suspension. However, once adsorption of uncharged polymers occurs, it is very difficult to remove them from the clay surface (Greenland, 1963). This very strong interaction can be explained by the development of many weak polymer-surface bonds (van der Waals, H-bonding) and the statistical improbability

---

3. Unpublished data.

of simultaneous rupture of all bonds at a given time (Greenland, 1965). In light of the above discussion, the published information about adsorption of neutral polar molecules must be studied very critically, if extrapolations are to be made to sediments in natural waters.

Lotse et al. (1968) determined that adsorption of lindane on lake sediments from aqueous suspensions was correlated significantly with both clay and organic matter content of the sediment. In some cases the interactions of clay with organic compounds can enhance adsorption reactions. Lee and Hoadley (1967) showed that the sorption of organic materials from natural water onto clays activated new adsorption sites. They noted increased adsorption of parathion on the clay-organic complex versus adsorption on clay alone. Hence, in some natural situations it may be possible to observe "chemical scavenging" of uncharged pollutants in natural waters.

Another physicochemical phenomenon worthy of note in natural waters is the production of sediments by precipitation. Theabold et al. (1963) observed the precipitation of hydrous oxides of Fe, Al, and Mn when waters containing these elements came into contact with a body of water of sufficiently high pH. Once formed, these hydrous oxides enter into other chemical reactions such as the adsorption of phosphates. In aquatic environments supporting photosynthesis, it is possible to have sufficient CO_2 evolved to increase the pH of the water to exceed the solubility product of $CaCO_3$—hence, precipitation of $CaCO_3$. Upon cessation of photosynthesis, Lee and Hoadley (1967) suggest that the pH will return to its original equilibrium level, followed by solution of the precipitated $CaCO_3$. However, Chave (1965) observed that in some situations $CaCO_3$ did not redissolve and postulated that it had been coated with resistant organic material. Lee and Hoadley (1967) also stated that Sr^{2+}, Pb^{2+}, and Zn^{2+} can be co-precipitated with $CaCO_3$ if present in the given system.

OXIDIZED AND REDUCED ZONES IN SEDIMENTS

A waterlogged soil becomes differentiated into a surface-oxidized layer and an underlying reduced layer. The thickness of this oxidized zone has been reported to vary from 1 or 2 millimeters to several centimeters with an average of about 20 mm (Mortimer, 1942; Gorham, 1958; Holden, 1961; Patrick and Mahapatra, 1968). There is general agreement among researchers that these zones exist, but different mechanisms have been proposed as to how the two layers are formed and maintained.

Mortimer (1942) described the existence of an oxidized zone and believed this oxidized layer was maintained by the diffusion of oxygen from water into the sediment. He suggested the distance of this diffusion into the sediment during winter depended mainly upon the reducing power of the sediment. In waterlogged soils, Patrick and Mahapatra (1968) stated the thickness of the oxidized layer is determined by the net effect of the oxygen consumption rate in the soil and the oxygen supply rate through the overlying water. A soil with an abundant source of organic matter (energy) will utilize oxygen faster than it can be supplied through the water, and this high consumption rate results in a thin oxidized zone. When the oxygen consumption rate is low, the oxidized layer becomes thicker.

Gorham (1958) suggested the thickness of the oxidized zone of lake sediment may depend on two factors: (1) the turbulent displacement of the uppermost sediments into the overlying aerated water, and (2) the reducing power of the sediments. When sedimented plankton decomposes, the winter oxidized zone may disappear from the surface downward because of the greater oxygen consumption. Gorham placed more emphasis on the turbulent mixing of the sediments with aerated water than on the reducing power of the sediment. Regardless of the exact mechanism involved in forming the oxidized and reduced zones, these two layers are extremely important in conversions and equilibrium phenomena involving chemical nutrients.

When soils are submerged, the oxidation-reduction (redox) potential decreases. Patrick and Mahapatra (1968) reported a range of -300 to $+700$ millivolts redox potential in waterlogged soils. Since aerated soil measures about 400 to 700 millivolts potential, it appears the oxidized layer of sediment would be within this same range, and the reduced layer redox potential should range from -300 to $+400$ millivolts.

The reduction of oxidized inorganic components is generally a sequence of the various redox systems (Fig. 2.1). Oxygen was found to disappear at $+320$ to $+340$ millivolts (Turner and Patrick, 1968), nitrate became unstable at $+225$ millivolts (Patrick, 1960), ferric iron was reduced at $+120$ millivolts (Patrick, 1964), and sulfate reduction started at -150 millivolts (Connell and Patrick, 1968). Usually the reduction of one component is not completed before reduction of the next most easily reduced component begins.

REACTION OF NITROGEN FORMS WITH SEDIMENT

The chemistry that is important in the influence of sediments on the quality of water involves the nitrogen and phosphorus relations between the sediment and the water. Nitrogen relationships are difficult to study because many conversions to different forms occur for different biological and chemical conditions.

When sediment is transported to surface waters, it contains

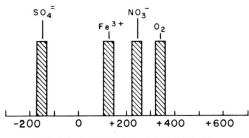

FIG. 2.1. The approximate oxidization-reduction potentials at which oxidized forms of several inorganic redox systems become unstable. (After Patrick and Mahapatra, 1968.)

REDOX POTENTIAL—MILLIVOLTS
(CORRECTED TO pH 7)

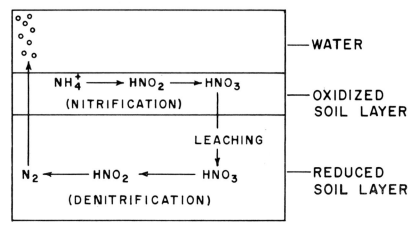

FIG. 2.2. A schematic diagram of the processes by which ammonium fertilizer can be lost from a waterlogged soil. (After Mitsui, 1954.)

nitrogen in the forms of organic-, NH_4-, NO_2-, and NO_3-N. Before being deposited the sediment will probably lose soluble organic-, NO_2-, and NO_3-N, whereas the insoluble organic N and NH_4-N will essentially remain with the sediment. Flooded soils would react similarly except losses of the soluble components would probably be slower because more diffusion and less turbulence would be involved.

The scheme for nitrogen reactions in submerged soils has been depicted by Mitsui (1954) and is shown in Figure 2.2. Under anaerobic conditions, nitrogen mineralization cannot proceed past the NH_4-N stage because insufficient oxygen is available to convert NH_4-N to NO_3-N. Since the organisms involved in anaerobic organic matter decomposition are less efficient than their aerobic counterpart, the conversion of organic matter to NH_4-N is slower in waterlogged soils (Tenny and Waksman, 1930). Although the conversion rate was slower in waterlogged soils, Waring and Bremner (1964a, 1964b) found that more nitrogen was mineralized for several soils under waterlogged conditions than under aerobic conditions.

According to Patrick and Mahapatra (1968), denitrification is one of the major mechanisms by which nitrogen is lost from a flooded soil. In the oxidized zone, NH_4-N from organic matter decomposition or already present on the sediment base exchange is converted to NO_3-N. This NO_3-N either diffuses or is leached into the reduced zone where it is converted by certain facultative anaerobic organisms to N_2 or N_2O and lost to the atmosphere. Broadbent and Stojanovic (1952) found that only 0 to 6% of the NO_3-N denitrified in a waterlogged soil was reduced to NH_4-N. Only in specialized cases is NH_4-N volatilization an important mechanism of nitrogen loss from a waterlogged soil.

The rate of NO_3-N reduction after submergence of a soil can be quite rapid. With no additional energy source, Patrick (1960) reported a NO_3-N reduction rate of 15 ppm per day in reduced soil, whereas Bremner and Shaw (1958a, 1958b) recorded a loss of 1,000 ppm NO_3-N in 4 days from a submerged soil which had an energy source added.

Sediments are apparently poor conservers of nitrogen supplies. Attempts to overcome poor utilization of fertilizer nitrogen by rice under flooded conditions have resulted in the development of a system in which denitrification of added nitrogen is minimized. This involves deep placement of ammonia nitrogen in the reduced soil layer where it is protected from nitrification and subsequent denitrification.

The increase of fresh organic material to the surface sediments in lakes and reservoirs by the periodic deposition of aquatic vegetation should create conditions favorable for the rapid loss of NO_3-N, with perhaps slight increases in NH_4-N.

REACTION OF PHOSPHORUS WITH SEDIMENT

When phosphorus is added to an aerated soil, it is converted rapidly to water-insoluble forms and becomes extremely immobile. If the soil is submerged continuously or becomes sediment in a lake or stream, there may be a marked increase in the availability of native and applied phosphorus compared to well-aerated conditions. The mechanism of this phosphate release, as given by Patrick and Mahapatra (1968), consists of (1) reduction of insoluble ferric phosphate to the more soluble ferrous phosphate, (2) release of occluded phosphate by reduction of the hydrated ferric oxide coating, (3) displacement of phosphate from ferric and aluminum phosphates by organic ions, (4) hydrolysis of ferric and aluminum phosphates, and (5) phosphate exchange between clay and organic anions. However, the phosphate that becomes soluble from reduction of ferric phosphate can be refixed if sufficient alumnium is available, and can also be refixed as ferric phosphate if Fe^{2+} is oxidized to Fe^{3+} in the oxidized zone. Thus, submergence of soil does not necessarily increase phosphate solubility and availability.

Under waterlogged conditions, organic matter affects the mechanisms of reduction and chelation. Shapiro (1958) reported both processes increase soil phosphate solubility and availability, so the addition of organic matter to the surface of sediments should create conditions favoring increased availability of phosphorus. However, others (Bartholomew, 1931; Paul and DeLong, 1949) have reported that a transformation of inorganic phosphorus to the organic form in flooded soils reduced the availability of the phosphorus. It is a complex system and contradictory findings are not unusual.

The equilibrium reactions involving phosphorus in sediments, water, and aquatic plants are influenced by many biological, chemical, and physical factors, making this dynamic system very difficult to study in situ. Studies using radiophosphorus placed either in the bottom sediments or in the surface water have provided needed data about the behavior of phosphorus.

Rigler (1956) found that only 3% of the radiophosphorus added to the surface of a small, acid-bog lake was lost to the sediments.

He concluded there was a turnover of "mobile" phosphorus of the epilimnion with phosphorus of the littoral organisms in 3.5 days. The turnover time (in summer) for soluble inorganic phosphorus was about 5 minutes. Hayes et al. (1952) reported that lake sediment increased in radiophosphorus for 10 days after deposition in the lake surface, but suggest that in addition to the sediments, aquatic organisms are very active in the exchange process.

Using sediment core samples in the laboratory, Holden (1961) concluded that bottom sediment can slowly take up large amounts of phosphate and that about 85% of the phosphate removed by the sediment occurred in the aerobic zone which extends to about 20 mm. In unfertilized lakes, the phosphorus content of the sediment surface was very high relative to the equilibrium concentration in the overlying water.

Harter (1968) also found that lake sediment can absorb a large amount of phosphorus from the water. When more than 0.1 mg phosphorus was added it was adsorbed in a loosely bonded form, and he suggests that large influxes of phosphorus into a lake may be held temporarily and subsequently released to aquatic plants.

Phosphorus equilibria between lake bottom sediments and calcium phosphate solutions were studied on samples collected from two eutrophic lakes in western Minnesota (Latterell et al.[4]). When solutions containing up to 42 ppm phosphate were equilibrated with sediment, the resulting solutions contained about 0.03 ppm phosphate, so the sediment adsorbed large amounts of orthophosphate.

The release of phosphorus from lake sediments to lake water was investigated for several lakes at Madison, Wisconsin, by Sawyer et al. (1944). They reported that continuous leaching of 1-liter sediment samples for 220 days released 12 and 5 mg of phosphorus from Lake Monona and Lake Waubesa sediments, respectively, as compared to 180 and 90 mg from undigested sewage sludge and storm sewer sludge for these two lakes, respectively. The amount of phosphorus removed by this continuous leaching, however, does not indicate the equilibrium concentration.

Diffusion of phosphorus from sediment into the overlying water is negligible in undisturbed systems. Hasler (1957) found that the percentage as well as the amount of phosphorus released to the superimposed water was very small when it was placed at depths greater than 1 cm.

In a similar study, Zicher et al. (1956) reported that phosphorus placed at ½ inch below the sediment surface showed only a very slight tendency to diffuse into the above water and did not diffuse into the water at all when placed at 1-inch depth. Water samples taken near the sediment surface contained a higher percentage of soluble phosphorus than water samples taken at greater distances from the sediment surface.

The establishment of an upper oxidized layer and lower reduced layer may be expected in sediments left undisturbed for appreciable periods of time, but sediments covered by shallow waters and sub-

---

4. Unpublished data.

jected to wave action may not exhibit the same characteristics. Stephenson (1949) found that agitation of sea water with bottom mud may either increase or decrease the concentration of phosphate in solution. The changes in phosphate levels are ascribed to (1) destruction of organisms with release of protoplasm, (2) breakdown of this protoplasm by bacteria with release of phosphate, and (3) absorption of phosphate by bacteria.

Certain benthic ciliates are capable of splitting inorganic phosphorus from dilute solutions of organic phosphates that occur in lake sediments (Hooper and Elliott, 1953). This process may provide a source of energy supplementary to that obtained from ingestion of particulate organic matter and bacteria, but its importance in nutrition is unclear.

Sediment plays an important role in the assimilation of phosphate during transport in waters. Keup (1968) has quoted Gessner (1960) on studies of the turbid Amazon River that indicate when soluble phosphorus concentrations exceed 0.01 ppm, it is sorbed on finely divided inorganic suspended material.

Obviously, bottom sediments can remove relatively large amounts of dissolved phosphate from waters but the partition of this removal is not well understood. It is probable that these sediments act as a control, removing phosphate from the water when the concentration is above the equilibrium value and releasing phosphate to the water when the concentration falls below the equilibrium point. The contribution that these sediments make to support algal growth is not known, but without thermal or mechanical mixing it is doubtful that sufficient phosphate could diffuse at a rate fast enough to support algae more than a few inches from the sediment.

SUMMARY

Sediment can be considered a major pollutant of surface waters. However, its contribution to the dissolved chemicals in lakes and streams is largely unknown. The composition of sediment closely resembles the soil from which it is derived but is generally higher in silt, clay, and organic matter.

Chemical reactions involving sediment are essentially the surface chemistry of their colloidal fractions which is a function of their surface area and electrical charge. As a result, reactions with sediment can be divided into interactions with charged ions and with neutral compounds. Cation exchange, an example of the former, can play an important role in the uptake and release of elements from sediments. Adsorption of anions such as phosphates is also of great interest with respect to the fate of nutrients in natural waters. Similarly, the adsorption of neutral polar molecules influences the chemical composition of the surface water supplies and may have distinctly beneficial effects.

The chemistry of sediments in situ can be surmised from studies of submerged soils. An oxidized zone exists at the soil-water interface and a reduced zone is established beneath the oxidized zone. Nitrogen transformations that occur in these two zones may be postulated to explain the inefficiency of nitrogen utilization in submerged culture. Also, an effective mechanism for controlling the percolation of nitrates into groundwater supplies becomes operative when these zones are established. The existence of anaerobic conditions in the sediment may increase the availability of phosphorus above that anticipated under aerobic conditions.

Sediments carry relatively large amounts of total nitrogen and phosphorus into surface waters, but in both cases only a small proportion of this total is readily available to the biosystem. Sediments apparently have a high capacity to remove phosphate from solution, but without turbulence the release of phosphate from bottom sediments will not support algal growth at appreciable distances from the sediment. However, if the concentration of phosphorus in the surrounding solution drops low enough, the sediments will release phosphorus. Nitrogen may be added to or removed from the biosystem by nitrification or denitrification in the bottom sediments. Thus, it appears that sediments have a leveling influence on nitrogen and phosphorus concentrations in surface waters.

Available inorganic nutrients, particularly phosphorus, are rapidly taken up by the biosystem in natural waters. They eventually become a part of the organic fraction of the sediment and their release back to the waters is not well resolved.

REFERENCES

Barrows, H. L., and Kilmer, V. J. 1963. Plant nutrient losses from soils by water erosion. *Advan. Agron.* 15:303–16.

Bartholomew, R. P. 1931. Changes in the availability of phosphorus in irrigated rice soils. *Soil Sci.* 31:209–18.

Bremner, J. M., and Shaw, K. 1958a. Denitrification in soil. I. Methods of investigation. *J. Agr. Sci.* 51:22–39.

———. 1958b. Denitrification in soil. II. Factors affecting denitrification. *J. Agr. Sci.* 51:40–52.

Broadbent, F. E., and Stojanovic, B. F. 1952. The effect of partial pressure of oxygen on some soil nitrogen transformations. *Soil Sci. Soc. Am. Proc.* 16:359–63.

Chao, T. T., Harward, M. E., and Fang, S. C. 1965. Exchange reactions between hydroxyl and sulfate ions in soil. *Soil Sci.* 99:104–8.

Chave, K. E. 1965. Carbonates: association with organic matter in surface seawater. *Science* 148:1723–24.

Clapp, C. E., Olness, A. E., and Hoffmann, D. J. 1968. Adsorption studies of a dextran on montmorillonite. *Trans. 9th Intern. Congr. Soil Sci.* 1:627–34.

Coleman, N. T., Craig, D., and Lewis, R. J. 1963. Ion-exchange reactions of cesium. *Soil Sci. Soc. Am. Proc.* 27:287–89.

Connell, W. E., and Patrick, W. H., Jr. 1968. Sulfate reduction in soil: effects of redox potential and pH. *Science* 159:86–87.

Frink, C. R. 1969. Chemical and mineralogical characteristics of eutrophic lake sediments. *Soil Sci. Soc. Am. Proc.* 33:369–72.

Gessner, F. 1960. Investigations of the phosphate economy of the Amazon. *Intern. Rev. Hydrobiol.* 45:339–45.

Gorham, E. 1958. Observations on the formation and breakdown of the oxidized microzone at the mud surface in lakes. *Limnol. Oceanog.* 3:291–98.

Greenland, D. J. 1963. Adsorption of polyvinyl alcohols by montmorillonite. *J. Colloid Sci.* 18:647–64.

———. 1965. Interaction between clays and organic compounds in soils. I. Mechanisms of interaction between clays and defined organic compounds. *Soils Fertilizers* 28:415–25.

Grim, R. E. 1968. *Clay mineralogy.* New York: McGraw-Hill.

Harter, R. D. 1968. Adsorption of phosphorus by lake sediments. *Soil Sci. Soc. Am. Proc.* 32:514–18.

Hasler, A. D. 1957. Natural and artificially (air-plowing) induced movement of radioactive phosphorus from the muds of lakes. *Intern. Conf. Radioisotopes in Scientific Res., UNESCO/NS/RIC/188 (Paris)* 4:1–16.

Hayes, F. R., McCarter, J. A., Cameron, M. L., and Livingstone, D. A. 1952. On the kinetics of phosphorus exchange in lakes. *J. Ecol.* 40:202–16.

Hoffmann, R. W., and Brindley, G. W. 1960. Adsorption of non-ionic aliphatic molecules from aqueous solutions on montmorillonite. *Geochim. Cosmochim. Acta* 20:15–29.

Holden, A. V. 1961. The removal of dissolved phosphate from lake waters by bottom deposits. *Verhandl. Intern. Ver. Limnol.* 35:247–51.

Hooper, F. F., and Elliott, A. M. 1953. Release of inorganic phosphorus from extracts of lake mud by protozoa. *Trans. Am. Microscop. Soc.* 72:276–81.

Keup, L. E. 1968. Phosphorus in flowing waters. *Water Res.* (Great Britain) 2:373–86.

Lee, G. F., and Hoadley, A. W. 1967. Biological activity in relation to the chemical equilibrium composition of natural waters. *Advan. Chem. Ser.* 67:319–39.

Lomenick, T. F., and Tamura, T. 1965. Naturally occurring fixation of cesium-137 on sediments of locus trine origin. *Soil Sci. Soc. Am. Proc.* 29:383–87.

Lotse, E. G., Graetz, D. A., Chesters, G., Lee, G. B., and Newland, L. W. 1968. Lindane adsorption by lake sediments. *Environ. Sci. Technol.* 2:353–57.

Massey, H. F., and Jackson, M. L. 1952. Selective erosion of soil fertility constituents. *Soil Sci. Soc. Am. Proc.* 16:353–56.

Massey, H. F., Jackson, M. L., and Hays, O. E. 1953. Fertility erosion on two Wisconsin soils. *Agron. J.* 45:543–47.

Mitsui, S. 1954. *Inorganic nutrition, fertilization, and soil amelioration for lowland rice.* Tokoyo: Yokendo.

Mortimer, C. H. 1942. The exchange of dissolved substances between mud and water in lakes. *J. Ecol.* 30:147–201.

Patrick, W. H., Jr. 1960. Nitrate reduction rates in a submerged soil as affected by redox potential. *Trans. 7th Intern. Congr. Soil Sci.* 2:494–500.

———. 1964. Extractable iron and phosphorus in a submerged soil at controlled redox potentials. *Proc. 8th Intern. Congr. Soil Sci. Bucharest, Roumania* 4:605–10.

Patrick, W. H., Jr., and Mahapatra, I. C. 1968. Nitrogen and phosphorus in waterlogged soils. *Advan. Agron.* 20:323–59.

Paul, H., and DeLong, W. H. 1949. Phosphorus studies. I. Effects of flooding on soil phosphorus. *Sci. Agr.* 29:137–47.

Pomroy, L. R., Smith, E. E., and Grant, Carol M. 1965. The exchange of phosphate between estuarine water and sediments. *Limnol. Oceanog.* 10:167–72.

Rich, C. I. 1968. Applications of soil mineralogy in soil chemistry and fertility investigations in mineralogy in soil science and engineering. *Soil Sci. Soc. Am. Spec. Publ.* 3, pp. 61–90

Rigler, F. H. 1956. A tracer study of the phosphorus cycle in lake water. *Ecology* 37:550–62.

Sawhney, B. C. 1964. Sorption and fixation of micro-quantities of cesium by clay minerals: effect of saturating cations. *Soil Sci. Soc. Am. Proc.* 28:183–86.

Sawyer, C. N., Lackey, J. B., and Lenz, A. T. 1944. Investigation of the odor nuisance occurring in the Madison lakes, particularly Lakes Monona, Waubesa, and Kegonsa from July 1943 to July 1944. Report to the Governor's Committee, State of Wisconsin.

Schofield, R. K., and Sampson, H. R. 1954. Flocculation of kaolinite due to the attraction of oppositely charged crystal faces. *Discussions Faraday Soc.* 18:135.

Shapiro, R. E. 1958. Effect of organic matter and flooding on availability of soil and synthetic phosphates. *Soil Sci.* 85:267–72.

Stall, J. B. 1964. Sediment movement and deposition patterns in Illinois impounding reservoirs. *J. Am. Water Works Assoc.* 56:755–66.

Stephenson, W. 1949. Certain effects of agitation upon the release of phosphate from mud. *J. Marine Biol. Assoc.* 28:371–80.

Tenny, F. G., and Waksman, S. A. 1930. Composition of natural organic materials and their decomposition in the soil. V. Decomposition of various chemical constituents in plant materials, under anaerobic conditions. *Soil Sci.* 30:143–60.

Theabold, P. K., Jr., Lakin, H. W., and Hawkins, D. B. 1963. The precipitation of aluminum, iron and manganese at the junction of Deer Creek with the Snake River in Summit County, Colorado. *Geochim. Cosmochim. Acta* 27:121–32.

Turner, F. T., and Patrick, W. H., Jr. 1968. Chemical changes in waterlogged soils as a result of oxygen depletion. *Proc. 9th Intern. Congr. Soil Sci. Australia* 4:53–65.

Waring, S. A., and Bremner, J. M. 1964a. Ammonium production in soil under waterlogged conditions as an index of nitrogen availability. *Nature* 201:951–52.

———. 1964b. Effect of soil mesh-size on the estimation of mineralizable nitrogen in soils. *Nature* 202:1141.

Zicher, E. L., Berger, K. C., and Hasler, A. D. 1956. Phosphorus release from bog lake muds. *Limnol. Oceanog.* 1:296–303.

CHAPTER THREE

LAND AND WATER MANAGEMENT FOR MINIMIZING SEDIMENT

MINORU AMEMIYA

SEDIMENTS are primarily soil particles washed into streams by water. They are products of land erosion and are largely derived from sheet and rill erosion from upland areas, and by cyclic erosion activity in gullies and drainageways. It is estimated (Wadleigh, 1968) that at least half of the 4 billion tons of sediment washed annually into tributary streams in the United States is coming from agricultural lands.

Erosion can be natural or can be accelerated by man's activities. Natural or geologic erosion pertains to that occurring under natural environmental conditions. Man-made or accelerated erosion is that induced by man through reduction of natural vegetative cover and improper land use, and occurs at a rate greater than normal for the site under natural cover.

Although sediment yield and soil erosion are not synonymous, they are closely related—and occasionally used interchangeably. Sediment yield can be defined as the quantity of soil material transported into a stream. Soil erosion refers to detachment and movement of soil particles on site, but does not imply movement into stream channels. Thus, soil erosion is a primary requisite for sediment production. The most logical and direct approach to solving our agriculturally related sediment problem is the stabilization of the sediment source by controlling soil erosion through the use of proper land and water management practices or structures. In short, to minimize sediment yield, soil erosion must be minimized.

Soil erosion occurs in two basic steps (Smith and Wischmeier, 1962): (1) detachment of soil particles from adjacent particles by raindrop impact and splash, and (2) transport of detached particles by flowing water. Only when conditions for these steps exist does soil erosion become a serious problem as a direct source of sediment. Soil erosion by water is a physical process requiring energy, and its control involves the dissipation of energy—that of falling raindrop impact and splash, and that due to elevation differences which affect the flow velocity of water.

MINORU AMEMIYA is Associate Professor and Extension Agronomist, Department of Agronomy, Iowa State University.

The present state of knowledge concerning the mechanics and hydrology of soil detachment and transport have already been adequately reviewed (see Chapter 1). The properties of sediments from agricultural lands have been described and interpreted (see Chapter 2). It is the purpose of this chapter to briefly review management practices for controlling soil erosion to minimize consequent sediment production from agricultural lands. Emphasis will be on sediments derived from sheet-rill or microchannel erosion. This does not imply that sediments resulting from gully or macrochannel erosion are not serious contributors to total sediment yield. However, it has been shown that the best method of controlling gully erosion is to minimize runoff and sheet erosion above a gully or potential gully site (Jacobson, 1965).

FACTORS AFFECTING SOIL EROSION BY WATER

The Universal Soil Loss Equation (Smith and Wischmeier, 1962) provides a framework for discussing erosion control measures. In this equation, soil erosion is described as a function of rainfall, soil properties, slope length and steepness, cropping sequence, and supporting practices.

At present, little can be done to readily change the amount, distribution, and intensity of rainfall per se, but measures can be adopted to modify its erosiveness—that is, to decrease raindrop impact and splash energy or to decrease the amount and velocity of overland flow, or both—to minimize sediment production.

Soil properties affect both detachment and transport processes. Detachment is related to soil stability, size, shape, composition, and strength of soil aggregates and clods. Transport is influenced by permeability of soil to water which determines infiltration capabilities and drainage characteristics, aggregate stability which influences crusting tendencies, porosity which affects storage and movement of water, and soil macro-structure or surface roughness which creates a potential for temporary detention of water.

The slope factor determines the transport portion of the erosion process since flow velocity is a function of hydraulic gradient which is influenced by slope length and steepness. The remaining two factors, cropping sequence and supporting practices, serve to modify either the soil factor or the slope factor or both, as they affect the erosion sequence.

Water runoff and accompanying soil erosion resulting from rainstorms are inversely related to the water infiltration capacity of soil, plus any surface storage capacity. Hence, one way to prevent erosion would be to maintain high water intake rates and surface ponding capacities at levels sufficient to prevent runoff from all rainstorms (Meyer and Mannering, 1968). This is seldom possible, but any increase in infiltration capacity and surface and subsurface storage capacity can greatly reduce erosion as well as benefit crop water supply. In most cases water intake and storage capacities are not sufficient to prevent runoff. Soil erosion then becomes a func-

TABLE 3.1. Effect of rates of applied wheat straw mulch on runoff, infiltration, and soil loss from Wea silt loam with 5% slope.

Mulch Rate	Surface Cover	Water Applied*	Runoff	Infiltration	Soil Loss
(tons/a)	(%)	(inches)	(inches)	(inches)	(tons/a)
0	0	6.25	2.83	3.42	12.42
¼	40	6.25	2.50	3.75	3.23
½	60	6.25	1.58	4.67	1.42
1	87	6.25	0.30	5.95	0.30
2	98	6.25	0.09	6.16	0.00
4	100	6.25	0.00	6.25	0.00

Source: Adapted from Mannering and Meyer (1963).
* Water applied at constant intensity of 2.5 inches per hour.

tion of runoff velocity and the resistance of the soil to the forces of flowing water.

Laboratory studies have shown that the amount of energy required to initiate runoff was a function of clod size (Moldenhauer and Kemper, 1969). Rough, cloddy surfaces enhanced water intake and contributed to surface detention of water, even after water intake was reduced by pore sealing. It was apparent that large clods created many steep micro-slopes. Dispersed particles from soil peaks eroded into depressions, leaving exposed areas still receptive to water.

A vegetative cover or surface mulch is one of the most effective means of controlling runoff and erosion (Duley and Miller, 1923; Borst and Woodburn, 1942; Baver, 1956; McCalla and Army, 1961; Smith and Wischmeier, 1962). Wheat straw mulch applied on freshly plowed land at a rate exceeding one ton per acre almost completely eliminated runoff from, and controlled erosion on, a 5% slope, as shown in Table 3.1 (Mannering and Meyer, 1963). Mulch on the surface protected it from raindrop impact energy, reducing detachment of soil particles and surface sealing. In so doing, high water intake rates were maintained. The effectiveness of mulch in maintaining high intake rates was correlated with the proportion of the surface covered. In addition, the mulch created barriers and obstructions that apparently reduced flow velocity and carrying capacity of runoff. This was evident especially at the ¼- and ½-ton mulch applications where total runoff was 87 and 56%, respectively, of the zero mulch treatment. In contrast, soil loss was 27 and 11%, respectively, of the zero rate.

In another study (Meyer and Mannering, 1968), runoff velocity was measured as a function of mulch rate. Five inches of simulated rain were applied at a constant intensity of 2.5 inches per hour to soil treated with straw mulch at various rates. Data shown in Table 3.2 indicate that small amounts of surface mulch caused considerable reduction in flow velocity. Moreover, large reductions in erosion rates were associated with relatively small reductions in flow velocity. This was not unexpected because the quantity of material moved is considered proportional to about the fourth power of velocity.

In a laboratory study, Kramer and Meyer (1968) studied the effects

TABLE 3.2. Effect of applied wheat straw mulch on run-off velocity, and soil loss from Wea silt loam with 5% slope.

Mulch Rate	Runoff	Runoff Velocity*	Soil Loss
(tons/a)	(inches)	(ft/min)	(tons/a)
0	3.3	26	14.5
1/4	2.8	14	5.8
1/2	2.4	12	3.7
1	2.0	7	1.7

Source: Adapted from Meyer and Mannering (1968).
* After application of about 5 inches of rainfall when runoff rates were essentially constant.

of mulch rate, slope steepness, and slope length on soil loss and run-off velocity. Using a glass bead bed to simulate a soil slope, they showed that less than a ton of mulch on the surface reduced erosion on slopes greater than 70 feet long at 4% slope. Mulch rates of less than 1 ton reduced erosion from moderate to steep slopes (4 to 6%). However, on slopes of 8 and 10%, 1/8- and 1/4-ton mulch rates did not greatly decrease erosion compared to no mulch. Erosion more than doubled as slopes increased from 8 to 10%. Again, mulch rates 1/4 ton or greater reduced runoff velocity considerably. It was noted that for some conditions low mulch rates increased erosion as compared to no mulch. This was attributed to increased flow velocity and turbulence around mulch pieces, causing particle movement.

In some area soil wettability is considered a factor in soil erodibility. Water repellency, often developed as a result of fires on some soils, can cause much sediment production by curtailing infiltration and encouraging runoff. Reduction in erosion is effected by modifying the wetting characteristics of hydrophobic soil. By mechanical or chemical means, soil wettability can be increased so that infiltration rate is increased (Osborn and Pelishek, 1964; De Bano, 1969).

Another means of preventing runoff and increasing total infiltration is through surface storage. Rough soil surfaces can retain several more inches of rainfall than smooth surfaces, due to water being trapped in the depressions of the rough topography (Larson, 1964). Available subsurface storage capacity has also been recognized (Holtan, 1965) to be important in the infiltration process. Thus, for soils to have high infiltration capabilities, they must have a high inherent permeability to water, show resistance to crusting, and have a high surface and subsurface storage capacity.

PRACTICES FOR EROSION CONTROL

Practices or structures for erosion control are designed to do one or more of the following: (1) dissipate raindrop impact forces, (2) reduce quantity of runoff, (3) reduce runoff velocity, and (4) manipulate soils to enhance the resistance to erosion (Meyer and Mannering, 1968).

TILLAGE METHODS AND EROSION CONTROL

The relationship between tillage methods and soil erosion has been reported by many investigators. Principles involved have been well documented (Larson, 1964; Mannering and Burwell, 1968). Some tillage methods deter soil erosion by creating rough surfaces which provide surface storage, reduce runoff, and delay or prevent surface crusting. Other tillage methods provide increased subsurface storage, and still others provide both. There are tillage methods that leave all or part of the residue from previous crops on or near the soil surface, protecting the surface from raindrop forces and enhancing water infiltration. Excessive tillage can be a factor in soil erosion, however, because tillage is a source of energy for breaking soil into erodible sizes just as are rainfall and runoff. Tillage-induced soil conditions play a significant role in soil erosion through effects on the infiltration capabilities of soil (Burwell et al., 1966; Burwell et al., 1968).

On a silt loam soil, 6.7 inches of simulated rainfall, applied at a constant intensity of 5 inches per hour, infiltrated a surface created by moldboard plowing before runoff began. When the soil was plowed, disked, and harrowed, only 2.1 inches of water infiltrated before initiation of runoff. Comparable values for untilled and rotary tilled soil were 0.4 and 0.9 inch, respectively. Cumulative water intake was fifteen times greater on rough, plowed soil and three times greater on plowed, disked, and harrowed soil than on untilled soil. These differences were related to plow layer porosity and to surface roughness (Burwell et al., 1966).

Another study conducted on the same soil compared infiltration of simulated rainfall of mulch-tilled and clean-tilled surfaces (Burwell et al., 1968). The soil was previously cropped to oats. Mulch tillage consisted of a pass with a chisel-type cultivator to a depth of 6 inches. This tillage operation incorporated about half of the oat stubble residue, leaving about 0.6 ton per acre on the surface. Clean tillage consisted of moldboard plowing in the fall, with and without secondary disking and harrowing the following spring, and spring plowing alone. Table 3.3 is a summary of this study. Fall mulch-tilled surfaces provided nearly eight times greater infiltration capacity

TABLE 3.3   **Influence of tillage treatment on water infiltration.**

Tillage		Infiltration	
Fall	Spring	To initial runoff	During 2″ runoff
		(inches)	(inches)
Chisel	None	6.7	3.8
Plow	None	1.2	1.6
Plow	Disk, harrow	0.9	0.8
None	Plow	2.1	1.5

Source: Adapted from Burwell, Stoneker, and Nelson (1968).

before runoff started and four times greater infiltration capacity during runoff than did fall-plowed surfaces, disked and harrowed in the spring. Infiltration for fall mulch-tilled surfaces was more than three times greater than for spring-plowed surfaces. Fall-plowed surfaces were altered by fall to spring weathering, resulting in little, if any, infiltration advantage over fall-plowed, spring-disked, and harrowed surfaces. Rainfall action, wetting-drying, and freezing-thawing cycles between fall plowing and spring planting act to disperse soil material which seals the surfaces by filling in depressions and open channels created by plowing.

These representative data indicate that the amount of water entering soil can be controlled significantly by soil physical conditions created by tillage operations. Conventional tillage (plow, disk, harrow) usually creates conditions that restrict water movement. Mulch and other so-called minimum tillage systems can produce soil conditions conducive to water intake. Plowing, followed by disking and harrowing, usually leaves the soil clean or void of crop residue. Rain falling on these bare or only partially covered surfaces washes fine soil into depressions and open channels, resulting in progressive soil sealing. Rate of sealing depends on how cloddy or how rough the surface is after tillage. Where clean tillage is practiced, it should create rough, cloddy surfaces that resist dispersion and subsequent surface sealing so as to delay the first runoff event during the spring.

In a recent summary (Burwell and Larson, 1969) it was shown that prior to initial runoff, tillage-induced roughness accounted for most of the variation in infiltration, whereas differences in pore space caused only minor variations. In contrast, during a 2-inch runoff period, water intake was little affected by roughness or porosity—indicating that surface seals were already formed when runoff started, and overshadowed roughness or porosity changes induced by tillage.

Mulch tillage—a tillage system that loosens the soil without soil inversion—leaves all or most crop residue on the soil surface. This creates a condition highly resistant to raindrop and runoff forces. A comparison of runoff and soil loss from conventional and mulch tillage is typified in Table 3.4. In each instance the benefits of this type of tillage are apparent.

Deep tillage or subsoiling of some soils can reduce soil losses by increasing volume of subsurface storage available for infiltrated water. If deep tillage shatters or fractures a soil pan, this increased storage may be much greater than indicated by the increased depth of tillage. However, subsoiling generally has not been effective unless channels were kept open to the soil surface. If subsequent tillage obliterates subsoiler slots in the surface few inches, little difference in soil loss or infiltration can be expected (Meyer and Mannering, 1968).

Postplanting tillage is used with most tillage systems. If a surface seal has developed, cultivation to break it may materially increase water intake. In a 5-year tillage study (Mannering et al., 1966), cultivation of minimum tilled treatments reduced average runoff from 3.5 to 2.1 inches and soil loss from 16.3 to 9.5 tons per acre as compared to the same treatments uncultivated. Under some condi-

TABLE 3.4. Effect of mulch tillage on runoff and soil losses in the Corn Belt.

Location, Soil, and Slope	Field Practice	Tillage	Runoff	Soil Loss
			(inches)	*(tons/a)*
Wisconsin				
Miami sl, 6%	Noncontoured	Conventional	3.1	22.3
		Mulch	2.5	6.7
Miami sl, 9%	Contoured	Conventional	0.8	1.4
		Mulch	0.06	0.01
Fayette sl, 16%	Contoured	Conventional	0.6	2.0
		Mulch	0.05	0.03
Ohio				
Muskingum sl, 9–15%	Contoured	Conventional	1.14	7.8
		Mulch	0.05	0.03
Indiana				
Russell sl, 5%	Noncontoured	Minimum	3.12	10.7
		Mulch	2.24	0.5

Source: Adapted from Mannering and Burwell (1968).

tions, cultivation of rough, cloddy surfaces may increase erodibility by decreasing soil aggregate size, decreasing surface roughness, and reducing existing crop residue surface cover.

SLOPE MODIFICATION FOR EROSION CONTROL

Contour planting and tillage function to control runoff and soil loss from storms that are moderate in extent, or until capacity of soil to hold or to conduct runoff is exceeded. In field practice, rows are oriented on the contour, generally with a slight grade toward a waterway. On slopes of moderate steepness and length, average annual soil loss can be reduced by about 50% (Smith and Wischmeier, 1962). Runoff is ponded and flows slowly around the slope rather than downslope. However, when smooth tillage is used, or when infiltration rates are low, runoff from high intensity rains may overtop rows, reducing runoff and erosion effectiveness. In addition, because contouring generally results in point rows and irregular field shapes, its use as an erosion control practice is declining. Large farming equipment and narrow rows are not compatible with point row farming.

Contour strip-cropping is the practice of alternating strips of a close-growing meadow or grass crop with strips of grain or row crops across a hillside. The erosion control aspect of strip-cropping is the reduction in length of slope of land in row crop. In addition, flow velocity of runoff water is reduced as it moves through the close-growing grass strip, causing sediments to drop out. The sod literally acts as a filter strip. The reduction in soil erosion from a strip-cropped slope is proportional to the fraction of the slope that is in grass strips (Wischmeier and Smith, 1965).

Terracing is one of the oldest practices used to control erosion. Terraces are combinations of ridges and channels laid out across the slope to trap water running downslope, and to conduct the water to suitable surface or subsurface outlets at a nonerosive velocity. The primary benefit of terracing is the reduction in slope length. Since erosion is approximately proportional to the square root of slope length (Smith and Wischmeier, 1962), reducing slope length in half can reduce erosion by more than 20%. Bench-type terraces also provide for a reduction in slope steepness. Terracing with contour farming is generally considered more effective as an erosion control practice than strip-cropping, but it is also more expensive. With both practices soil loss is confined within field boundaries. In strip-cropping the saved soil from one storm event is deposited in the sod strip and can be transported further downslope during subsequent storms. With terracing, the deposition is in the terrace channel which offers positive sediment retention, unless overtopping occurs.

Although effective for erosion control, conventional broad-based terrace systems are not compatible with efficient tillage operations or modern farm equipment. In addition, herbicides are making it increasingly difficult to maintain grassed waterways. To overcome these problems, a system of bench terraces with permanently vegetated backslopes is gaining popularity (Jacobson, 1966). In this system, all runoff is collected in low spots in the terrace channel and if necessary removed through underground tile outlets, thus grassed waterways. Parallel terraces materially straighten field alignment and eliminate objectionable point rows. In time sediment deposited in the channel reduces the slope in the terrace intervals.

Studies on instrumented watersheds in western Iowa on deep loess soil indicate that although terracing did not affect total water yield from a watershed, the surface flow component of water yield was significantly reduced. Only 14% of water yield from terraced watersheds was surface flow, while on unterraced but contour-farmed watersheds, surface flow accounted for 64% of water yield (Saxton and Spomer, 1968). These differences in surface flow were associated to sediment yield from these watersheds as shown in Table 3.5 (Piest and Spomer, 1968).

OUTLOOK

Slope modification measures combined with soil-conserving tillage practices can be effective in reducing soil erosion from cropped land. However, to become widely accepted, such practices must fit efficient farming operations and must be economically feasible. If presently available practices do not meet these requirements, new practices or systems that will control erosion and sediment production without loss of net income to the operator must be developed.

For example, consider a system where sheet erosion is controlled through till-plant tillage, and runoff is controlled by storage fills constructed across waterways (Jacobson, 1969). The fills, like bench terraces, would have favorable uphill slopes with a seeded backslope. Water would be removed from fills by tile outlets. It is anticipated

TABLE 3.5. Effect of land treatment on sediment yield of watersheds in western Iowa.

Watershed	Size	Crop	Land Treatment	Sediment Yield		
				1964	1965	1966
	(acres)				*(tons/a)*	
1	75	Cont. corn	Field contoured	30	60	8
2	83	Cont. corn	Field contoured	30	45	10
3	107	Grass	None	2	2	1
4	150	Cont. corn	Level terraced	2	2	1

Source: Adapted from Piest and Spomer (1968).

that such a system would almost eliminate soil loss from cropped fields on slopes up to 6%. Soil-moved sheet erosion is stored in the fills and eventually helps reduce slopes. Again, troublesome hillside waterways are eliminated. Straight row farming is possible, adding to farm adaptability. And the cost of such a system should be relatively low. Tillage costs will be lower, and building the system of storage fills often would be less costly than building waterways. On lands with slopes steeper than 6%, farming becomes progressively difficult. Unless the slope can be reduced to permit more efficient machinery operation, economics will force the retirement of much of these lands from row-cropping (Jacobson, 1969). Erosion control on such land will require bench terraces with tile outlets.

To reiterate, nearly all sediment is the result of man's removal or disturbance of natural soil cover of trees and grass. Since all land cannot be returned to its original cover, wise land use planning and careful use and treatment of land can reduce soil erosion, the source of sediment. Although the mechanics of the erosion process are not completely understood, guidelines have been developed, satisfactorily tested, and translated into erosion control practices, measures, and structures. Existing erosion control technology has not been universally accepted and used, primarily because of direct or indirect economic considerations (Swanson and MacCallum, 1969). The challenge to agriculturists, conservationists, engineers, and economists is to continue their efforts to develop an improved erosion control technology that will be compatible with modern requirements and economically feasible. Only when this challenge is met will there be a significant reduction in sediments redrived from agricultural lands.

REFERENCES

Baver, L. D. 1956. *Soil physics.* 3rd ed. New York: John Wiley.

Borst, H. L., and Woodburn, R. 1942. *Effect of mulches and surface conditions on the water relations and erosion of Mulkingum soil.* USDA Tech. Bull. 825.

Burwell, R. E., and Larson, W. E. 1969. Infiltration as influenced by tillage-induced random roughness and pore space. *Soil Sci. Soc. Am. Proc.* 33:449–52.

Burwell, R. E., Allmaras, R. R., and Sloneker, L. L. 1966. Structural alteration of soil surfaces by tillage and rainfall. *J. Soil Water Conserv.* 21:61–63.

Burwell, R. E., Sloneker, L. L., and Nelson, W. W. 1968. Tillage influences water intake. *J. Soil Water Conserv.* 23:185–88.

De Bano, L. F. 1969. Water repellent soils. *Agr. Sci. Rev.* 7 (2): 11–18.

Duley, F. L. 1939. Surface factors affecting rate of intake of water by soils. *Soil Sci. Soc. Am. Proc.* 4:60–64.

Duley, F. L., and Miller, M. F. 1923. *Erosion and surface runoff under different soil conditions.* Mo. Agr. Exp. Res. Sta. Bull. 63.

Ellison, W. D. 1947. Erosion studies, Parts I, II, and III. *Agr. Eng.* 28:145–46, 197–201, 245–48.

Holtan, H. N. 1965. A model for computing watershed retention from soil parameters. *J. Soil Water Conserv.* 20:91–94.

Jacobson, P. 1965. Gully control in Iowa. In *Proc. Fed. Inter-agency Sedimentation Conf. 1963,* pp 111–14. USDA Misc. Publ. 970.

———. 1966. New developments in land terrace systems. *Am. Soc. Agr. Engrs. Trans.* 9:576–77.

———. 1969. Soil erosion control practices in perspective. *J. Soil Water Conserv.* 24:123–26.

Kramer, L. A., and Meyer, L. D. 1968. Small amounts of surface mulch reduce erosion and runoff velocity. Paper 68–206 presented at meeting of Am. Soc. Agr. Engrs., 18–21 June 1968, Logan, Utah.

Larson, W. E. 1964. Soil parameters for evaluating tillage needs and operations. *Soil Sci. Soc. Am.Proc.* 28:119–22.

McCalla, T. M., and Army, T. J. 1961. Stubble mulch farming. *Advan. Agron.* 13:125–97.

Mannering, J. V., and Burwell, R. E. 1968. *Tillage methods to reduce runoff and erosion in the Corn Belt.* USDA Information Bull. 330.

Mannering, J. V., and Meyer, L. D. 1963. Effects of various rates of surface mulch on infiltration and erosion. *Soil Sci. Soc. Am. Proc.* 27:84–86.

Mannering, J. V., Meyer, L. D., and Johnson, C. B. 1966. Infiltration and erosion as affected by minimum tillage for corn (*Zea mays* L.). *Soil Sci. Soc. Am. Proc.* 30:101–4.

Meyer, L. D., and Mannering, J. V. 1968. Tillage and land modification for water erosion control. In *Tillage for greater crop production,* pp. 58–62. St. Joseph, Mich.: Am. Soc. Agr. Engrs. PROC-168.

Moldenhauer, W. C., and Kemper, W. D. 1969. Interdependence of water drop energy and clod size on infiltration and clod stability. *Soil Sci. Soc. Am. Proc.* 33:297–301.

Osborn, J. F.. and Pelishek, R. E. 1964. Soil wettability as a factor in erodibility. *Soil Sci. Soc. Am. Proc.* 28:294–95.

Piest, R. F., and Spomer, R. G. 1968. Sheet and gully erosion in the Missouri Valley loessial legion. *Trans. Am. Soc. Agr. Engrs.* 11:850–53.

Saxton, K. E., and Spomer, R. G. 1968. Effects of conservation on the hydrology of loessial watersheds. *Trans. Am. Soc. Agr. Engrs.* 11:848, 849, 853.

Smith, D. D., and Wischmeier, W. H. 1962. Rainfall erosion. *Advan. Agron.* 14:109–48.

Swanson, E. R., and MacCallum, D. E. 1969. Income effects of rainfall erosion. *J. Soil Water Conserv.* 24:56–59.

Wadleigh, C. H. 1968. *Wastes in relation to agriculture and forestry.* USDA Misc. Publ. 1065.

Wischmeier, W. H., and Smith, D. D. 1965. *Predicting rainfall erosion losses from cropland east of the Rocky Mountains.* USDA Agricultural Handbook 282.

CHAPTER FOUR

WORKSHOP SESSION

G. M. BROWNING, Leader
H. G. HEINEMANN, Reporter

Browning: There are four or five things that we want to do. We should consider what is known about soil as a pollutant. A good bit of that evidence was discussed at the session yesterday morning. We should also consider where we are now and what we know—and what additional knowledge we need to get to where we want to be in the next 5 to 10 years. A workshop such as this is an excellent way to identify and get a consensus of what the important problems are and to learn how we might do something about them.

Verduin: I think the whole picture is really long term—very encouraging, from what I have heard since I got here. Amemiya's paper shows that if you have farmland so good that you want to farm it but it has too much slope, you can terrace it, and you won't lose much from it—any more than you did from grassland, which we consider pretty good soil-holding land. The whole thing, of course, is tied to our problem of feeding the people who need food, but we have been doing that with less and less acreage. It seems to me that in the 20-year future, we may well have all farmland that does not erode. We have a chance to get our erosion under control in this country and set a model for the whole world.

Browning: Does anyone want to respond to that?

Laflen: We have had erosion control practices since sometime in the late eighteenth or nineteenth century. Our terracing program started out fairly strongly with the USDA in the thirties, and today we still have between 5 and 8 million acres of cropland that needs terracing. With the independent farmer, I don't see how we are going to get the terracing done in the near future.

Browning: I am concerned because I doubt that we are keep-

G. M. BROWNING is Regional Director, North Central Agricultural Experiment Station Directors, Iowa State University. H. G. HEINEMANN is Director, North Central Watershed Research Center, SWCRD, ARS, USDA, Columbia, Missouri.

ing up with this. On a lot of the land that is in tilled crops, with 8, 10, and even 12% slope, you can terrace and control this sediment. But modern-day 6- to 8-row equipment doesn't fit on irregularly shaped slopes very well. So, if we are going to any more than keep up on those areas, we need to devise new and acceptable methods and procedures that will help control erosion. We are not in the ball game economically with 2- or 4-row equipment when compared with the 6- and 8-row equipment of farmers on flatter ground. So we have some really tough going, admitting that we know what needs to be done and could do it. We have made a lot of progress in the past 20 or 30 years, but we still have a whale of a long way to go.

Herpich: I am wondering if the voracious appetites Americans have for meat and the limited acreage on which we can put cattle to produce it will force us to retire a lot of this poor land to the production of crops that we could use to produce livestock. It would probably help to solve the problem.

Browning: We all know, of course, that grass is a wonderful conservation practice and there is a lot of land in crops that should be growing grass if we are going to control erosion from a practical standpoint.

Verduin: What you said is being said in a number of situations. The pollution people are saying it. We have the technology but it is going to be expensive. You look at the actual capacity of our society and at the fact that the farmer, over the past 20 years, has practically been held steady with a little bit of subsidy—and then we say we can't subsidize him any more. Why can't we? We are subsidizing everyone else more.

Herpich: We live on an economy of waste. You have only to travel in some of the European countries to understand what I mean. We have great big, wide turn rows and waste land on waterways. If we are really concerned with producing food, we can put pipelines down the waterways and plant something on them.

Kerr: It bothers me that we deal so much in the ideologies of what we are trying to do and spend so little time in how to do it. We are talking about the sediment deposition and the ramifications that it is going to have over a period of time—and we know that this is very serious. But what are we going to do about it? If we take a good look at history, we learn that the Soil Conservation Service has accomplished some water conservation and some pollution abatement as an incidental thing to what it is really trying to accomplish. Its prime objective when it was formed was to save the soil. This needed to be done, but since then we have evolved through a couple of steps with the Soil Conservation Service in its small watershed program. I think most people agree that a small watershed program is the best tool for keeping soil and water where it is supposed to be. I can't see how we are going to accomplish sediment control for pollution purposes any more effectively than we could with the principles of the small watershed project. So I think that the SCS should be permitted to accept benefits accruable from pollution abatement. It cannot do that at this time.

Cochran: I like to hear that, because in Iowa we do have the tools. If we could get the Iowa Legislature to pass a bill, we could do the job that everyone has been talking about. Back in 1965 I had what turned out to be the grand opportunity of being a member and becoming the chairman of a committee in Iowa to revise the drainage codes, which were 50 years out of date. We began to realize that drainage was related to flood control, soil conservation, water pollution, recreation, and all the things that go hand in hand with controlling soil erosion and water pollution. And so we launched a program and developed the Conservacy District Bill, which is an enlargement of the watershed program. We presented this to the Legislature in 1969. We divided Iowa into six conservacy districts; so, for example, we are now in the Des Moines River Conservacy District and any water that falls on Iowa soil that eventually gets to the Des Moines River is in that conservacy district. According to our Conservacy District Bill, we start in the upper reaches of our various tributaries and begin to solve the erosion problem on the individual pieces of land, then work downward on the tributaries to our major streams. The farmer is responsible for setting up soil conservation practices found in any conservation handbook. The Conservacy District is responsible for internal improvements, flood control, dams, and other structures. We have set goals to be met by voluntary action. If it is not voluntary, we will set up rules and regulations which will have to be abided by. We can control pollution with this method. In Iowa, we have the bill, and now we have to convince the Legislature.

Jones: My question is: What do we need to know? We would like to know what is a tolerable level for sediment as it moves off the land. We have the universal soil loss equation. The Soils people tell us that we can lose so many tons per acre per year from our soils and still maintain production. Yet, if we look at some sedimentation surveys of some lakes where we have public water supply and work this information back, we will find that the lakes are accumulating something like a quarter of a ton per acre per year from these watersheds, and the people are up in arms at the rate at which they are losing their water supply from sedimentation. This quarter of a ton per year is a far cry from the 3 to 4 tons per acre per year that our Soils people say is a satisfactory level for controlling soil loss. So I think we need to reevaluate what is a reasonable level of soil loss from our fields.

Morris: I would like to address the Representative from the Legislature about the problem of air pollution. I think it may be wise to include an air study which is being emphasized right now by large societies.

Cochran: In 1967 we *did* pass an air pollution bill set up by a State Air Pollution Commission; however, our later bill concerns soil erosion and water pollution from the standpoint of water and wind erosion.

Culbertson: I was happy to hear Mr. Jones say what he did. Very shortly we are going to have to set standards for suspended sediment in streams. This will be extremely difficult. These rivers have adjusted to a certain base—depending on slopes, widths, depths, etc., and if we cut off the sediment, we will have tremendous bank scours, bed scours, etc. Now, our problem will be to determine from past records what the sediment supply should be in a river. We don't want the situation that occurs below dams. So I think you have to start in the erosion phase on the land and see what you can allow to go into your streams and then those of us who work in the rivers (the transport phase) will have to take it from there. Now you may have the erosion problem solved, but we certainly do not have the transport problem solved. And this relates to what Mr. Kerr said. If we had some standards for sediment concentration, if it were exceeded, this could be considered pollution or damage. Maybe this is the first step, before including it in the damage benefit ratio.

Verduin: You mean, for example, that the clearing up of the water in the Missouri is causing injury to all those dams because there is not enough silt in the water?

Culbertson: Definitely. Certain types of river beds will readjust the entire regime of the system downstream to a delicate balance between sediment load, water discharge and velocity, and stream width and depth.

Verduin: Yes, but before the dams the Missouri changed its course every year. The Missouri has been doing that since the glacier pushed down. I still think that the best silt load is as near zero as you can get.

Culbertson: This is unnatural.

Verduin: I am not sure of that. When a country is well vegetated, there is not much silt in the water. The streams are clean. I would say that the base of most of the rivers in this country is pretty low in silt.

Herpich: From what vantage point are we defining this word "pollution"? It seems that we must establish this before we can say this is or is not pollutant.

Browning: What about this? Does this mean that we have more than one goal? When the erosion factor was developed, we had in mind what you might lose from the soil so that you could maintain production. It seems to me that you probably have different levels for different things you are trying to do.

Kerr: I wonder if we are using what we already know. I think we have acquired a lot of knowledge. What bothers me is that we don't get more action. Why don't we get the tools that we need, as Iowa is trying to with legislation?

Herpich: I can't help but feel that the action program is a little behind the research. I think we need something positive to start to catch up.

Morris: Some active research has already been done in which streams have had viscosity reduction, and when that happens, there has been a higher velocity flow, and therefore a change in stream beds. We at the University of Nevada are making a hydrologic study of the Trucky River system from Tahoe to Clearming Lake. I think that things like that are necessary to make the stream behave naturally over a large number of years.

Browning: I have a letter from Roland E. Pine, Program Coordinator, Water Quality and Environmental Programs, Washington State Water Pollution Control Commission. I will just read sections of the letter.

> Irrigation of agricultural lands is the largest, single consumptive use of water, and the resulting runoff from this activity is one of the nation's major sources of water pollution. The Yakima and Columbia River Basins in south-central Washington are devoted almost entirely to agriculture and comprise one of the most extensively irrigated regions in the nation. Nearly the entire summer flow in the lower 80 to 90 miles of the Yakima River is composed of irrigation return water.

> The sediment load, and adsorbed nutrients and pesticides, is a significant contributor to water pollution problems associated with irrigation return flows. The control of irrigation return flows and their associated contaminates must be through proper land and water management practices which can and will reduce the quantity of such contaminates carried into the receiving water.

> It must be shown that such practices are highly economic practices, beneficial to the farmer and to his neighbors with respect to crop yield, quality of the crop and cost of production.

Laflen: The points that Pine made pertain to the failure of our terrace practices to be accepted. It is very difficult to show to the farm owner that conservation practices do put dollars in his pocket within a reasonable length of time. What we need are conservation practices that will compete for his dollar as fertilizers do.

Gattis: Economic reason has brought about more conservation in our state than terraces have in the past 20 years. The simple reason is that when the land was in row crops it had to be terraced. It got to the point where you couldn't make a living on those terraced lands, so those fields are now in pasture or in woodland. With that, we have done more to reduce the sediment stream than we have in the previous 20 years.

Shrader: On this matter of the permissible rate of erosion, I think it is becoming increasingly clear that that is one of the basic things. We have many fields with a loss of 20 tons per acre, because it is in the farmer's economic interest to let that land erode. He discounts the future very heavily. His idea of what is permissible soil loss is just another magnitude different from the person that is looking at the reservoir problem. We obviously need some way to use the land that will maximize the return for the whole population for the whole watershed.

McGill: Mr. Culbertson has raised an entirely new thought to me. Assuming that he is correct and assuming that desirable standards could be achieved or set, what could you do about increasing the suspension?

Culbertson: It will increase by itself. If sediment is taken from the river and there is an unlimited supply in the stream bed and banks, the flowing water will pick up enough sediment to bring itself back into balance and equilibrium. We cannot stop it. The only way you can stop this entirely is to use a TVA-type network, where the backwater from one dam goes right up to the foot of the upstream dam.

McGill: Seventy percent of the terrain in my part of the state lends itself well to the growing of forage crops and pasture land. We have done wonders and we have hardly scratched the surface in improving our pastures. We can carry 2 to 3 head of cattle where we have had only 1 before. In southern Iowa we would do well to get the tax off our breeding cattle—or reduce it—and get this land back into production of red meat. That would take care of the erosion problem.

Amemiya: It has been mentioned about the detrimental effects of decreasing the silt load in the streams, insofar as the stream channel is concerned. And it has been alluded to that there is an equilibrium established in these stream channels. But the equilibrium is changing, and as we alter our land use patterns upstream on the watersheds, we are going to reduce the amount of water getting into our streams, and the stream flow is going to be less and more uniform; so we will have to look for a new equilibrium. I can't see how we can assume that the stream flow pattern will remain the same when we put these upland treatments into effect.

Morris: It might be possible to establish some kind of workable equilibrium for each of the rivers that are so investigated.

Cochran: Does siltation in water reduce its energy? Is this why, if we take silt out of the water, we have more energy to cut the stream banks and stream bottoms?

Culbertson: You can't destroy the energy. Sediment uses some of the energy and it reduces the turbulence that does the cutting. The problem in erosion and deposition, as I see it, is not after it enters the large tributary or stream. Sediment damages, as the farmer sees it, are those that are carried on within his land and in the immediate vicinity of the small channel. When we get to the large streams, I personally wonder what the effect of additional erosion control would do to the stream system.

Kirkham: In the past few years we have thought of sediment as a pollutant because it carries nitrogen and phosphate and other fertilizers and pesticides into the river. It is these materials that the sanitary engineers are concerned about, because they see this tremendously excessive stuff over and above that that they find from their waste disposal plants.

Duncan: I would like to ask Dr. Shrader to comment on the recent geological development of, particularly, northern Iowa. Erosion really isn't anything new. We have had 600 or so inches deposited on the west side of the state fairly recently. It took quite a little wind to deposit that from somewhere and there weren't very many people farming then.

Shrader: I think Duncan has answered his question fairly well. I will try to put some of this in perspective, as I see it. Yes, we've had about 100 feet of deposition in the western part of the state, of loess piled up there, blown out of the Missouri bottom over a period of several thousand years, stopping a few thousand years ago. But, to keep our perspective, I think we have to accept the fact that we have grossly accelerated the rate of erosion here in Iowa since the time of settlement. We are eroding our landscape in tens of years, at a rate that would ordinarily take hundreds or even thousands of years in certain parts of our landscape. Any way you look at it, some of our lands are eroding at an astounding rate and the end is not yet in sight.

Holt: I think Dr. Kirkham has a point in that people are now associating pollution and siltation with nutrient enrichment. However, I am not convinced that we have greater nutrient enrichment now than we had before man came here. We have more sediment going into our streams, and this sediment is carrying nutrients. There is no question about this. But the source of these nutrients is an unknown.

Browning: Do you have some evidence to prove this?

Holt: We have some evidence that grasslands are contributing more nitrogen and phosphorus, generally, than cultivated land, in terms of solubles and nutrients in the water supply. We do have evidence that the total amounts of nitrogen and phosphorus coming off in the sediment are greater. We can't evaluate their availability, but so far evidence is that they are not generally very available. The best evidence we have is that before man came, the prairies were supplying as many nutrients or more than are presently being supplied.

Verduin: Where does the phosphorus come from for that prairie soil?

Holt: There is an abundant supply of native phosphorus in our soils, as Dr. Black pointed out.

Browning: We have talked about a good many problem areas; the problems are undoubtedly different in different states. It has been emphasized also that we have a lot more knowledge than we are using. Little has been said about very pressing problems on which we need more research, but we have emphasized that we do need action.

Cochran: I have listened to a lot of experts the past few years— Dr. Morris from the University of Iowa, for example. He didn't take us back to before the time of civilization, but he did give us some results of the monitoring program on various streams and major rivers of Iowa, and he pointed out that the nitrogen content in the water is rising each year—and rising rather rapidly—not too far from Des Moines. Dr. Morris correlates it with the ever-increasing use of fertilizer, and as that rate goes up, more and more nitrogen is getting into our streams as we use more cultivation and less conservation.

Duncan: This was an excellent study, as I recall it; it was a study of fertilizer applied on a grass slope. Measurement of the runoff showed a very high concentration—in fact, a relatively high percentage—of the nutrients that had been applied ran off. What the study did not indicate was the probability of receiving precipitation in this amount. It was a 2½-inch rain in about an hour and a half, but this was not reported. Certain kinds of monitoring will produce the same data, particularly out of small streams.

Cochran: Dr. Kirkham raised an interesting question the first day of the conference when he asked, "Why doesn't the government just decide to allow crops to be planted on land where erosion isn't a very serious problem and just not plant crops and not fertilize heavily on the slopes where erosion takes place?" I thing that is a perfectly fair question. Maybe the government should reconsider its policy on this, if erosion and pollution are serious problems.

Browning: This gets back, I think, to your real basic question. A lot of this would be solved if we would use the land the way it should be used. We don't really have a countrywide land use policy. Your policy might say that any land having an excess of some predetermined slope isn't suitable for crops because it will wash away and fill streams, and if you fertilize, it is going to carry fertilizer with it and contaminate water, etc., so that land can't be used for row crops. We are a long way from that kind of regulation, but I think that when we realize our problems and what causes them, we will be able to move people, and when they decide they want something done we will get action. I think we are making real progress, but progress is slow.

Morris: Maybe it would be better if we had state legislation, because the subdivision developers in the small watersheds of Sierra and the hills that you have out there are another erosion problem.

Browning: I think the national, state, and local governments should look at this thing and try to develop procedures that would be as practical as possible.

Kerr: I don't think any one of us wants the federal government to dictate land use policy. But the thing that the United States does have and can use is an incentive based on the power of the purse. The United States could use pollution as an incentive to assist in the control of siltation, because the whole idea of pollution control is very, very popular nationwide at this time. It seems that this is a very opportune time to get some of these things under a legislative umbrella.

McGill: We take the position that we own the land; we hold title to it and we do about what we want to with it. I think, however, that if I am doing something that affects my neighbors, maybe it is logical that I have some compulsion about the way I use the resource.

There has been a bill in the State Senate the past two sessions that I have been interested in. It would require anyone who shares in cost-sharing benefits under conservation practices to file an application for a farm plan at the local SCS office. Farm plans have been very beneficial and farmers have followed them voluntarily, in most instances.

Jones: The man from Nevada mentioned that we should have state legislation for land use plans. I don't know about other states, but the basic law establishing Soil Conservation Districts in Illinois says that Soil and Water Conservation Districts shall establish land use plans. Perhaps the emphasis from the urban population will put some pressure on these districts to move in this direction.

Culbertson: Last October a national meeting of county officials was held in Washington on the subject of sediment control. County officials were urged to go back and try to set up these types of controls within their counties. The counties in the Washington area have actually had laws passed that require a builder who tears up the land to erect a building (anything with a specified number of square feet or acres) to install sediment control measures to insure that the sediment that comes from that freshly dug ground would not go onto someone else's property. This system appears to be working very well. The state highway departments are entering into this in new construction. One or two counties started this and it moved from county to county.

Herpich: Was the real emphasis for this sociological, esthetic, or economic in nature?

Culbertson: I think it must be a combination of all factors. Economically, it is all tied together; it's like water and sediment— you can't separate them.

Duncan: A year ago last spring, quite a bit of dust blew around Iowa and in Illinois and Minnesota. We have increased our soybean acreage from about 2½ million acres to about 5½ million the past 4 or 5 years and it will probably go up another million. Land following soybeans is easy to work on, but we need to find out why land following soybeans tends to blow so much. This is an easy place to start. I don't know why we don't work on some of the easy problems instead of trying to work on the difficult research.

Browning: I am surprised that no one has talked about tillage, though some folks have been working on it. It relates partly to what Duncan said, because if you leave that soybean straw on the surface, it doesn't blow a heck of a lot; but we have to rake it in the fall or plow it under. Some work shows that you can raise almost as many beans on land that you disk or minimum till as when you plow. I would like for someone to respond to what Duncan has said.

Duncan: Iowa has an absolute economic advantage producing soybeans in the western part of the state. Farmers are finding this out; and as a result soybeans are moving in on this deeper soil.

Holt: Ten years ago when I first went to western Minnesota to visit with the farmers out there, they mentioned two big problems. One was that they were going out of growing soybeans because it leaves the land too loose and it is too difficult to control weeds. The other problem was controlling erosion on complex slopes. We have been working on tillage practices as an approach to this. Generally speaking, some form of multitillage is effective on these complex slopes, where other practices are not. Back to soybeans—I suspect that there may be something in the microorganisms that loosens this soil. We have been checking roots lately, and when a soybean plant matures and the leaves drop off, the root system is completely gone— so I suspect there is some tie-in between the microorganisms which exist under a soybean crop and this looseness and tendency to blow.

Browning: I figured this out 27 years ago and wrote a paper about it. In the first place, soybeans have roots that grow a lot in about 6 weeks; they use a lot of water and then dry out, and the wetting and drying and freezing and thawing have a granulating effect. The second answer is: they have a lot of nodules in the roots, and that is quite a stimulant for microbiological activity—it is about 40 times as active in this area. We carried on studies with corn and soybeans under identical conditions; if we left that residue on, it was loose and there was little runoff or erosion from the soybeans.

Amemiya: We can, through tillage, affect the infiltration of rainwater into the soil, and in so doing, cut down the runoff and soil loss problems. Some of the work of my colleague Bill Moldenhauer indicates that corn following soybeans erodes much more than corn following corn.

Moldenhauer: We had about 40% more water erosion from corn following soybeans than we did from corn following corn. We haven't measured wind erosion.

Jones: I think one of our primary needs in research right now is good economics of soil conservation. In Illinois we haven't had a good study since 1954.

McGill: Is it a reasonable assumption that the younger farmers are more susceptible to these conservation practices and new ideas and will voluntarily be more concerned with soil? Or will they look at the almighty dollar and go at it like our grandfathers did and plow the hills straight up and down, etc.?

Jones: I think they are more computer based and look at the net return. And I think they are even less prone than were their fathers or their grandfathers to use the moral side as impetus for soil conservation.

Holt: There was a study in recent months in Illinois by Swanson (*Journal of Soils*) on the economics of conservation work. Swanson said that it doesn't pay, even up to 50 years' projection.

Amemiya: I think this study was based on strip-cropping, crop rotation, and contouring. It didn't include some of the major slope modification practices that we talked about.

Verduin: We're getting hung up again as to whether or not it pays. We should pay a man for terracing if we are convinced that that's what should be done to hold that soil over the next 10 generations.

Laflen: There is a lot of competition for the tax dollar, and it is going to have to be spread around a lot. Where is the money to come from? It is going to cost 800 million dollars or more to terrace Iowa.

Verduin: That is the biggest problem, and I don't know whether any research has been done on it. How can we get the thing going to do the things that almost anyone will admit need to be done?

Wiersma: It's a matter of priorities again, is it not? I think that if people who are going to pay for this are informed of the problem in the right manner, we will get the priority and I think we've got to talk in terms of "we" rather than "they."

Browning: How do you establish priorities on things? In our process, we get people agitated and then we get things done. So I think it behooves people in these areas to dig out the facts and present as well as they can alternative solutions and what they're going to cost with and without our program. Then the people can and will decide. I think we are going to be forced to do more of this, and the better job we do of identifying the priorities and showing how the benefits will accrue against the cost, the better our chance will be of sharing in the short dollars that are available.

Wiersma: How did they get the money to put this man on the moon? They didn't do that on economics, did they? Haven't we a lot more concrete evidence in agriculture than they have?

Browning: Agriculture has far more specific things to show and put values on than practically any other area—and we have probably done less of it than anyone. We must do this.

Herpich: Our Congress has already established some priorities. They said "pollution."

Browning: We must begin to establish some of these guidelines. We'll have some evidence but we won't have nearly enough. But we'd better get ourselves in that position or we won't get the support needed to do the job that's in the best interest of the public.

Kerr: Right now, our gimmick is pollution. We're in a better position than we have ever been, if we can just proceed correctly.

Morris: Why not use air pollution also to get at the urban population, increasing the number of people who might be interested in pollution. If we enlist the urban development as well as the rural development, we might be able to make the package better than we could with the single increment, pollution.

Browning: This is the key to obtaining support in these areas. Looking at legislation history, money comes in fairly large chunks—usually a good many years after somebody has been talking about it.

You have to have a genuine problem that the public will recognize. The Congress will find the money, priority wise. If we've done our jobs right, we'll get the kind of support we need.

Kirkham: One of these days, the American public will get so sick of that war in Vietnam that it will be stopped. Then there should be some extra money, and it's up to us to be ready for it.

Gattis: For many years we've known what slopes should be to control erosion under given cropping systems. Maybe we should work toward putting the slope on ground that will conserve the soil and keep it in place. This is being done in some areas at a cost per acre that is less than the cost of terracing the land. Your steep land here would cost more, but slope alterations would be something of a more permanent nature.

Evans: Sediment is a pollutant if man thinks it is. It is a resource out of place. Sediment can be useful, and it can be harmful. Economics is at the core of this. We must find economical means of recovering our sediment and utilizing it. We need to take an environmental approach to pollution. We must enlist the help of ecologists. This area has been neglected. We need to develop some type of land use plan that involves not only agriculture but also the urban areas, and it's got to take in transportation, manufacturing, agriculture—the whole business. We must think in terms of the future and try, as educators and scientists, to get as many people as possible thinking in this direction and trying to promote legislation.

Amemiya: Sediments are a problem, whether they're pollutants or not. They are pollutants, not only because of their physical significance but because of their chemical significance. Sediment costs taxpayers money in maintaining irrigation ditches, canals and estuaries, ponds, lakes, and reservoirs. I think that proper land use, especially on the upland areas, will go a long way toward minimizing the sediment that enters our streams.

Pine: If sediment interferes with another beneficial use of water, it is a pollutant. When sediment gets into lakes, reservoirs, and other areas, it is a pollutant.

Culbertson: Many of you realize there is a problem, but we need figures to work with. The only way to get them is to collect water and sediment data and evaluate the problem. The Geological Survey is one federal agency that will put up half of the money and cooperate with any state agency or city, on a fifty-fifty basis, to make these investigations. So I would suggest that if you want definite values to attack a problem, propose this to my organization and we can make these evaluations.

Verduin: If a river flowing into a lake contains so much silt that it reduces the light penetration to a point where 1% of surface light doesn't reach the middle of the water, then silt is a real pollutant.

Manges: I think that within 5 years, society is going to tell us sediment is a pollutant and we will be forced to do something about it. We must be prepared to suggest a program.

Browning: Thank you very much for your participation here this evening. This is the end of the session.

PART TWO

PLANT NUTRIENTS AS WATER POLLUTANTS

CHAPTER FIVE

SIGNIFICANCE OF PHOSPHORUS IN WATER SUPPLIES

JACOB VERDUIN

T HE pollution of surface waters by domestic sewage and by industrial waste has long been recognized as a serious evil in our society. Unfortunately, action to ameliorate these long-recognized sources of water deterioration has lagged far behind the recognition of the problem. But only in recent years has a more subtle problem come to light. It is the problem of superabundant plant nutrients in our surface waters. These are invisible; they do not show up in the classic BOD test used by sewage treatment plant operators to measure the efficiency of their treatment process. And the presence of these nutrients is usually recognized only after we see the nuisance levels of aquatic plant growth which they support (Sawyer, 1947; Verduin, 1964, 1967, 1968, 1969).

At first glance one would consider the addition of plant nutrients to rivers and lakes as beneficial. This is especially true when the low level of plant nutrients in natural waters is considered. For example, forest streams and lakes which receive no urban or agricultural runoff have phosphorus concentrations of less than 7 μg/liter (parts per billion) and the waters of our great Lake Superior are mostly still in such condition. Nitrogen also is scarce in such natural waters, and one would imagine that a bit of enrichment would be appreciated.

However, to appreciate the damage done by even relatively small quantities of fertilizer we must examine the *modus vivendi* of the aquatic community. It has evolved, of course, under the low level of nutrients described above. It consists of three major components: (1) the microscopic autotrophic plants in the water, (2) the heterotrophic organisms in the water, and (3) the organisms that live on the bottom. These form a delicately balanced web of life which can survive only so long as the delicate balance is preserved. There are of course many complex interactions in this community, but as an example let us consider the problem of oxygen supply. Oxygen has a low solubility in water (about 8 mg/liter at summer

JACOB VERDUIN is Professor, Department of Botany, Southern Illinois University.

temperatures), and it must be transported to the bottom by vertical mixing in the water column. If we add fertilizer to the lake, its plant population will increase, and the quantity of organic matter settling on the bottom will increase proportionately. As it decays there, it consumes oxygen, but we have not increased the vertical mixing rate, consequently the bottom organisms will be subjected to lower oxygen than ever before in their history—with catastrophic consequences. Such a sequence of events has been documented in Lake Erie. Dr. N. Wilson Britt (1955) has described the catastrophic extermination of the mayfly *(Hexagenia)* population in western Lake Erie in 1953. This population was never reestablished, but a population of bloodworm larvae *(Chironomus)*, more tolerant of low oxygen, has displaced it. Several other changes have been documented in Lake Erie. Large numbers of dead clams have risen to the surface during calm weather (the periods of lowest mixing rates) and the dominant fish species has changed from walleye *(Stizostedion)* to yellow perch *(Perca)*. There is little doubt that all these changes are attributable primarily to enhanced supplies of plant nutrients.

To focus more specifically on the levels of plant nutrients, examine Table 5.1. It shows what to an agriculturist must seem to be fantastically low levels of plant nutrients. Hydroponic solutions, for example, are made up in mg/liter instead of the μg/liter used in Table 5.1. But once the shock of this feature has been overcome, there are two highly significant features to notice: (1) While nitrogen supplies increased by about 30% during the 20-odd years covered by the table, phosphorous supplies increased by 480%, and in doing so (2) the N/P ratio changed from a value of 35 to 9.2. Even an elementary plant physiologist will recognize that a N/P ratio of 35 represents a medium in which phosphorus is severely limiting, but a ratio of 9 is a well-balanced medium because the ratio of N/P in protoplasm is about 8. Consequently the 20-year period covered in Table 5.1 was one of greatly increased plant growth in Lake Erie as a response to nutrient enrichment, with phosphorus enrichment playing a spectacular role.

PRESENT LEVELS OF PHOSPHORUS IN OUR SURFACE WATERS

To appreciate the extent of the plant nutrient problem in our surface waters an examination of the present phosphorus levels is most revealing. Figure 5.1 presents such information for the years 1965–66. The data were provided by the Federal Water Pollution Control Administration. Each figure on the map is the average of 2 or more stations in the vicinity of the number, with the exception of the Sioux Falls, South Dakota, station (1,618 μg/liter) which is in a class by itself! The data represent samples drawn primarily from drinking water intakes. But it is well known that for many cities the drinking water intake draws samples of the diluted sewage effluent from the city upstream. So it would not be unrealistic to regard these numbers as representative of the diluted sewage effluents of our cities, plus the contributions from agricultural drainage.

TABLE 5.1. Comparison of nitrogen and phosphorus data in western Lake Erie for 1942 with data for 1965–66.

Year	Available Nitrogen NH_3-N plus NO_3-N	Soluble Phosphorus	N/P Ratio
	($\mu g/liter$)	($\mu g/liter$)	
1942*	261	7.5	35.0
1965–66†	330	36.0	9.2

* Average of 28 samples, April through December. Data of Chandler and Weeks (1945).

† Average of 20 samples, June, July, August 1965, and March, April, May 1966. Data of J. Kishler (private communication). Samples analyzed by the Great Lakes Ill. River Basin Project Lab., Chicago.

The degree of enrichment that our waters have experienced can be appreciated when we compare the phosphorus levels in Figure 5.1 with those observable even today in streams of forested areas. Sylvester (1961, as reported by Mackenthun, 1965) reported soluble phosphorus levels of 7 µg/liter for such streams. It seems likely that our prairie streams had similar plant nutrient levels before the prairies were converted to farmland. Therefore the aquatic communities that originally occupied our lakes and streams were adapted to such low nutrient levels. The data in Figure 5.1 reveal that such low nutrient levels are found today only in the open areas of the Great Lakes. All of the major streams of the United States exhibit phosphorus levels five to thirty times higher than this "natural" plant nutrient level.

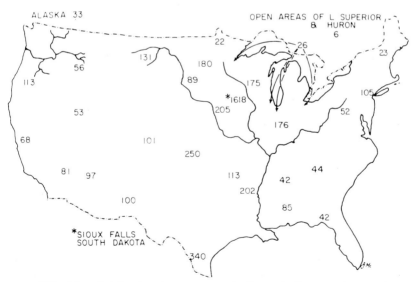

FIG. 5.1. Total phosphorus concentrations (ortho-, meta-, and organic) in water supplies of the United States. Data provided by FWPCA, 1965–66, averages of 18 months' collections.

TABLE 5.2. Correlation between metabolism of Cladophora communities and phosphorus concentrations in Lake Erie.

Location	Phosphorus Concentration	*Cladophora* Community	
		Photosynthesis	Respiration
	(μg/liter)	(μm CO_2 absorbed /g/hr)	(μm CO_2 evolved /g/hr)
Western Lake Erie	35	142	12
Eastern Lake Erie	10*	39†	6†

* Average of 21 samples. Unpublished data of B. A. Thumm, E. E. Klum, and D. Lentz, Dept. of Chemistry, SUNY College at Fredonia.

† Unpublished data, K. G. Wood, Dept. of Biology, SUNY College at Fredonia.

The influence of such enrichment was recognized many years ago. More than 20 years ago a study of lake fertilization by tributary streams (Sawyer, 1947) revealed that nuisance blooms of algae arose when phosphorus concentrations exceeded 20 μg/liter. More recently the nuisance level of filamentous algal growth (*Cladophora glomerata*) in the littoral zones of the lower Great Lakes has occasioned some investigation. Table 5.2 presents data (Verduin, 1968) showing a correlation between the phosphorus supply and the metabolic rate of the *Cladophora* community in Lake Erie. The western Lake Erie community, which is bathed in water having about 35 μg of phosphorus per liter, exhibits a photosynthetic rate about 3.7 times that of the eastern Lake Erie community (Dunkirk, New York), which is bathed in waters having about 10 μg of phosphorus per liter. The respiration rate of the western Lake Erie *Cladophora* community is also distinctly higher than that of the eastern Lake Erie community. These data suggest that the metabolism of the *Cladophora* community increases almost in linear proportion to increases in phosphorus supplies, within the range of values presently encountered in the Great Lakes.

The influence of enhanced plant nutrient levels is widespread today. They are responsible for foul tastes and odors in our drinking water, clogging of water intake filters, and windrows of decaying algae on our beaches. They also result in oxygen depletion in deeper parts of our lakes, with catastrophic destruction of fish and of bottom-dwelling organisms, and they support the weed-choked condition of shallow areas. It is significant that the 1966 annual report of the Division of Health and Safety of the Tennessee Valley Authority devotes three pages to the problem of counteracting nuisance growths of aquatic plants in the large TVA reservoirs. The following quotation from that report is pertinent: "In Cherokee Reservoir, in June, the last of three surveys showed oxygen nearly depleted below the thermocline. Analysis of survey results over the past few years revealed earlier oxygen depletion each ensuing year. The Holston River below Kingsport was found to be highly eutrophic . . . supporting dense masses of aquatic weeds." The report postulates that organic contributions by the aquatic weeds may have influenced the oxygen depletion in the hypolimnion. No monitoring of phytoplankton crops in the epilimnion is mentioned. It seems likely that enrichment of the Holston River, which flows into Cherokee Reservoir, has supported greater phytoplankton growth there, with a resultant increase in the organic load settling into the hypolimnion. The TVA report describes countermeasures taken to reduce nuisance growths of aquatic plants. These include scouting of dense plant concentrations by aerial surveillance, and the helicopterized application of 2, 4-D pellets. Thus we counteract the pollution due to plant nutrients by adding another chemical pollutant, a plant toxin!

THE RELATIVE CONTRIBUTIONS OF URBAN SEWAGE, PHOSPHATE DETERGENTS, AND AGRICULTURAL DRAINAGE TO THE PHOSPHORUS LEVELS IN SURFACE WATERS

Up to this point we have been concerned primarily with establishing the significance of plant nutrients as water pollutants, and with an inspection of the level of a key plant nutrient, namely phosphorus. Because this symposium is concerned about the role of agriculture in clean water, we can best advance that concern by trying to evaluate agriculture's contribution to the phosphorus levels now prevailing in our surface waters. Such evaluation can be made by examining the concentrations in streams whose watershed represents agricultural land and does not include urban runoff. Table 5.3 presents data of this kind compiled from several sources. These

TABLE 5.3. Soluble phosphorus concentrations reported for waters from agricultural watersheds.

Author	Watershed	Phosphorus
		($\mu g/liter$)
Engelbrecht and Morgan, 1960*	Kaskaskia River (Ill.)	60
Sawyer, 1947*	Watershed, farmlands agricultural drainage around Lake Mendota	48
Putnam and Olson, 1960*	St. Louis and Black rivers, tributaries of western Lake Superior	40
Harlow, 1966†	Raisin River (Mich.)	60
Owen, 1965†	Ontario agricultural watershed	33
Hardy, 1966†	Big Muddy (Ill.) river system, upstream portions	110
	Average	58

* As reported by Mackenthun (1965).
† Private communication, plus papers presented at the 9th Conf. on Great Lakes Res., Chicago, 1966.

TABLE 5.4.   Comparison of upstream station phosphorus values (assumed to represent agricultural runoff and drainage) with values at the mouth of the Big Muddy River (representing the combined contribution from agricultural and urban effluents).

Four upstream stations, average of 4 samples at each station	110 μg/liter
River mouth station, average of 4 samples	350 μg/liter
Percentage of total attributed to agriculture	31%

Source: Private communication. Hardy supervised collection of samples. Chemical analyses were performed by the Great Lakes Ill. River Basin Project Lab. in Chicago. Statistical analyses were made by Richard Rowe of the Southern Ill. Univ. School of Technology.

data show that runoff from rural watersheds represents a significant fraction of the phosphorus appearing in our surface waters. The data in Table 5.3 represent rural watersheds from the upper Mississippi and Great Lakes region, the same region for which phosphorus levels of 175 μg/liter are shown in Figure 5.1. The average value of 58 μg/liter in Table 5.3 suggests that approximately one-third of the phosphorus contribution may come from agricultural watersheds. Some data collected by George Hardy, a sanitary engineer with the Illinois Department of Health during the summer of 1966, permit a similar evaluation for a single river system, the Big Muddy in southern Illinois. Table 5.4 presents these data. This analysis also indicates that about one-third of the phosphorus concentration found at the mouth of the Big Muddy may be attributed to agricultural sources. Upon consulting with fertilizer dealers in the Big Muddy watershed, it was learned that farmers apply fertilizers in such quantity that the PO_4 added amounts to about 100 lb/acre. If 1% of this addition is dissolved in the annual runoff and drainage it would create a phosphorus concentration of about 50 μg/liter, which is similar to the average value in Table 5.3. Obviously the farmer is not going to be impressed by the fact that 1% of his phosphate application is lost in runoff and drainage; neither do any practical measures for reducing this contribution come to mind.

A somewhat encouraging aspect of the above analysis, at least for the agriculturist, is that agriculture appears to be responsible for less than half of the phosphorus supplies in our waters. The supply from urban sources seems to represent the major fraction. In urban sewage effluents, detergents seem to contribute about three times more phosphate than is contributed by the organic matter in sewage, according to Engelbrecht and Morgan (Mackenthun, 1965). Consequently, detergents would appear to be the most significant single source of phosphates enriching our waters today. Unfortunately their use is still increasing. I am told that some weed and orchard sprays contain these detergents to prevent clogging of spray nozzles. And our northern cities are now adding these detergents to salt applications on icy streets. The detergents presumably act as rust inhibitors.

THE SIGNIFICANCE OF PRESENT PRACTICES OF ANIMAL MANURE DISPOSAL

There is a fairly recent development in agricultural practice that is most distressing. For hundreds of years the successful farmer has been spreading animal manures and decayed vegetable composts on his land. But in recent years feedlot operators have been installing lagoons to decompose the animal manures. These ancient, tried and true soil improvers are now being digested in lagoons, and the plant nutrients that remain in solution after the digestion is completed are discharged to our surface waters in the lagoon overflow! Prepare yourselves for a dogmatic statement: Manure belongs on the land. To be sure, the agricultural economist may be able to demonstrate that it is cheaper to buy chemical fertilizers than to spread manure. But it certainly cannot be a great deal cheaper, and if our Agricultural Stabilization Service can pay the farmers for not raising feed grains or cotton, then it should certainly consider paying the feedlot operator for not lagooning animal manure, because manure belongs on the land. Manure contains many trace elements, vitamins, soil conditioners, etc., which chemical fertilizers do not provide, and organic manures represent the only economically feasible source of CO_2 fertilization. With our modern crop densities the CO_2 content of air among the leaves drops spectacularly, especially in quiet weather (Verduin and Loomis, 1944). A healthy layer of decaying organic matter will serve to augment the atmospheric CO_2 supply significantly. The method we use in solving a problem is profoundly influenced by the initial conception of the problem. If we regard a concentration of animal manure as a disposal problem, we are likely to adopt the least expensive means of disposal available, and the lagoon may well fit the bill. But if we regard a concentration of animal manure as a valuable source of fertilizer and soil conditioner, the problem is one of transportation and application—it is not a disposal problem at all, and a lagoon will never be considered a solution to the problem.

METHODS OF ALLEVIATING THE PROBLEM OF WATER POLLUTION BY PLANT NUTRIENTS

Phosphorus is a key element in the problem of pollution by plant nutrients because it is present in such low concentrations in natural waters and because it has undergone much more spectacular increases than any other plant nutrient. The agricultural practices which would tend to reduce the agricultural phosphorus contribution are simply sound soil conservation practices: (1) methods of cultivation which minimize runoff, (2) insuring intimate mixture of fertilizer with soil, (3) improving soil texture by addition of animal manures and ploughing in legume stands, and (4) particularly, abandoning the practice of lagooning animal manures. But the fact that the major phosphorus contributions come from nonagricultural sources shifts the burden of problem solution elsewhere. However, the solution is of interest to the agriculturist as well as to any other citizen, and more so because agriculture can make distinct contributions to the solution of this problem.

The contribution of agriculture to the solution of the problem has two facets: (1) The same condemnation made above of the decomposition of animal manures in a lagoon applies to the decomposition of organic matter in urban sewage treatment plants. This organic matter, considerably enhanced today by the use of garbage disposal units in our kitchens, is as good for the land as animal manure, and it should be so utilized. Again, if we stop thinking of the problem as a waste disposal problem and look at it as a problem in processing, transporting, and applying a valuable soil conditioner, our attack on it will be drastically altered. Because the organic matter includes human excrement we have a pasteurization problem, but the fact that the organic matter is suspended in water introduces a drying problem. If the drying is done at sufficiently high temperature, pasteurization will be automatic. Moreover, we may well be able to utilize the "waste" heat from thermal electric power plants—heat which is now being widely decried as thermal pollution! Once the organic matter is pasteurized and dried we should call in the chemical fertilizer industry to add as much of their product as is needed to provide a maximally advantageous fertilizer. Then we should pelletize this product so the farmer can dispense it from attachments on his plough, disc, drill, and planter, thus avoiding extra trips over the landscape.

(2) Even after all settleable solids are removed from the sewage, a high level of dissolved organic matter and plant nutrients, especially detergent phosphorus, will remain in the urban effluents. The most promising method of treating such effluents is again an agriculture-related treatment. It is the "living filter" described by Kardos in the AAAS symposium on Agriculture and the Quality of our Environment (Kardos, 1967). If such sewage effluents are allowed to percolate through the root zone of crop plants or trees, the dissolved materials are removed effectively and diverted to promote valuable plant growth. The water emerging from tiles beneath these root zones can be released to our surface waters without fear of serious pollution.

It is obvious that agriculture has a primary role to play in the solution of the pollution problem. Where it is contributing plant nutrients directly, it should attempt to minimize such contributions, but wherever plant nutrients are entering our surface waters from nonagricultural sources, we should recognize the agricultural potential of such plant nutrient sources and attack the problem of restoring them to the land. In the problem of removing concentrated nutrients from water, agricultural technology can make a major contribution in the application of the living root zone filter to the process of plant nutrient removal.

REFERENCES

Britt, N. W. 1955. Stratification in western Lake Erie in summer 1953: effects on the *Hexagenia* (Ephemeroptera) population. *Ecology* 36:239–44.

Chandler, D. C., and Weeks, O. B. 1945. Limnological studies of western Lake Erie. V. Relation of limnological and meteorological conditions to the production of phytoplankton in 1942. *Ecol. Monographs* 15:435–56.

Engelbrecht, R. S., and Morgan, J. J. 1959. Studies on the occurrence and degradation of condensed phosphate in surface waters. *Sewage Ind. Wastes* 31:458–78.

Kardos, Louis T. 1967. Waste water renovation by the land—a living filter. In *Agriculture and the quality of our environment,* ed. Nyle C. Brady, pp. 241–50. Norwood, Mass.: Plimpton Press.

Mackenthun, K. M. 1965. *Nitrogen and phosphorus in water.* U.S. Health, Education and Welfare Publ.

Sawyer, C. N. 1947. Fertilization of lakes by agricultural drainage. *J. New Engl. Water Works Assoc.* 61:109–27.

Tennessee Valley Authority. 1966. *Annual report of Division of Health and Safety.*

Verduin, J. 1964. Changes in western Lake Erie during the period 1948–1962. *Verhandl. Intern. Ver. Limnol.* 15:639–44.

———. 1967. Eutrophication and agriculture in the United States. In *Agriculture and the quality of our environment,* ed. Nyle C. Brady, pp. 163–72. Norwood, Mass.: Plimpton Press.

———. 1968. Reservoir management problems created by increased phosphorus levels of surface waters. *Am. Fish. Soc. Symp.,* pp. 200–206. Athens: Ga.: Univ. of Georgia Press.

———. 1969. Man's influence on Lake Erie. *Ohio J. Sci.* 69:65–70.

Verduin, J., and Loomis, W. E. 1944. Absorption of carbon dioxide by maize. *Plant Physiol.* 19:278–93.

CHAPTER SIX

BEHAVIOR OF SOIL AND FERTILIZER PHOSPHORUS IN RELATION TO WATER POLLUTION

C. A. BLACK

THE principal objective of this chapter is to present an account of selected aspects of the behavior of soil and fertilizer phosphorus as a basis for understanding how phosphorus from these sources may contribute to the phosphorus content of waters in the soil and leaving the soil. An attempt is made to place these matters in perspective in the broad picture without undue encroachment on the aspects of the subject covered by other contributors to the symposium.

Although the basis for the subjects discussed is mostly chemical, an exhaustive review of current knowledge of the chemistry of phosphorus in soils and fertilizers will not be attempted because such a review would lose sight of the objective. Chemically oriented reviews have been published by Dean (1949), Wild (1950), Hemwall (1957), Larsen (1967), Mattingly and Talibudeen (1967), and Huffman (1968). Taylor (1967) published a review on phosphorus and water pollution with emphasis similar to that in this chapter.

PHOSPHORUS CYCLE IN SOIL

Vertical cycle

Plant roots continually absorb small amounts of phosphorus from soil, generally less than 15 kg per hectare annually. The major portion of the phosphorus is transported to the above-ground organs. The phosphorus not contained in harvested parts is returned to the surface of the soil in the plant residues.

The phosphorus added to soil in plant residues is constrained against downward movement by a mechanical sieving action of the soil, which is effective on the solid residues, and by a chemical siev-

C. A. BLACK is Professor, Department of Agronomy, Iowa State University.

Journal Paper No. J–6373 of the Iowa Agriculture and Home Economics Experiment Station, Ames. Project No. 1183.

ing action, which is effective on the phosphorus that has been released from the residues to the water in the soil. The existence of a chemical sieving action is suggested by data by Ponomareva et al. (1968) showing that the concentrations of phosphorus in micrograms per milliliter in drainage water from successively deeper layers in a soil from the USSR were 0.005, 0.001, 0, 0, and 0. Similarly, Barber et al. (1962) measured an average concentration of 0.18 μg of inorganic phosphorus as orthophosphate per milliliter of the saturation extract of the 0- to 15-cm layer of soils of midwestern United States and 0.08 μg per ml of the saturation extract of the 46- to 61-cm layer of the same soils.

The combination of upward transport of phosphorus in the soil profile by plants and the retention of phosphorus by the soil against downward transport by water may significantly alter the vertical distribution of phosphorus in the soil. In soils that have been subjected to moderate weathering and leaching, a minimum in the concentration of total phosphorus in the soil may be found a small distance below the surface (Fig. 6.1).

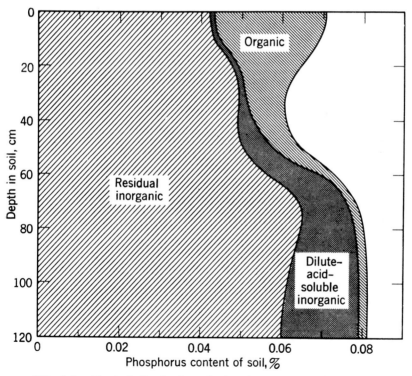

FIG. 6.1. Vertical distribution of phosphorus in a soil developed on loess under grass vegetation in Iowa. (Pearson and Simonson, 1939; Pearson et al., 1940. Reproduced by permission of John Wiley & Sons, Inc., New York.)

Chemical cycle

The phosphorus plants absorb from soil is presumably inorganic orthophosphate. In plants, perhaps half of the phosphorus occurs as inorganic orthophosphate and almost all the remainder as various organic forms. Plant residues therefore return to the soil some inorganic phosphorus and some organic phosphorus.

Inorganic phosphorus, present in relatively high concentration in the plant sap, diffuses readily from the dead plant material into the soil. In the soil it reacts with the soil minerals, and the concentration in solution is much reduced, as may be inferred from the experiment by Ponomareva et al. (1968) discussed previously.

A small proportion of the organic phosphorus probably diffuses out of the plant residues into the soil, but most of it is not readily soluble in water and presumably must be acted upon by microorganisms before it is released. Despite rapid decomposition in the first few months, however, complete disappearance of added organic matter requires a long time. A consequence is that during soil development organic phosphorus is produced at the expense of inorganic phosphorus. The accumulation of organic phosphorus parallels the accumulation of organic carbon, nitrogen, and sulfur (Jackman, 1964), and the content of organic phosphorus is usually greatest at the surface and decreases with depth, as is true also of other organic constituents (Pearson and Simonson, 1939). Figure 6.1 shows the vertical distribution of organic phosphorus in one soil profile. In time, presumably, a steady state is reached in which organic phosphorus changes to the inorganic form as rapidly as it is produced.

When soils are cultivated, the previously existing balance between formation and decomposition of organic phosphorus is upset. Generally the content of organic phosphorus decreases (Haas et al., 1961; Cunningham, 1963).

One other aspect of the chemical cycle worthy of particular mention is that inorganic orthophosphate ions in the soil solution exchange continuously with inorganic orthophosphate ions held by the soil solids (but not with organic orthophosphate). The classic paper on this subject was published by McAuliffe et al. (1948). In each soil, some of the solid-phase phosphorus exchanges readily with added radioactive phosphorus, some exchanges more slowly, and usually most exchanges extremely slowly, if at all. Phosphorus is supplied to the solution from the readily exchanging fraction in response to removal of phosphorus from the solution and is transferred from the solution to the readily exchanging fraction in response to addition of phosphorus to the solution from external sources. The readily exchangeable fraction, in turn, gains phosphorus from other sources in the soil when its level is decreased, and it loses phosphorus to other forms when its level is increased by phosphorus additions. Larsen (1967) gave an exceptionally clear picture of these transformations.

GEOLOGIC PHOSPHORUS CYCLE

Soil contributes to the geologic phosphorus cycle by supplying phosphorus in solution to groundwater and surface water and by supplying phosphorus in suspended solids to surface water and air. Emphasis here will be on the parts involving water.

Loss of phosphorus from soil by drainage into the groundwater is a normal part of the geologic phosphorus cycle. Indirect evidence of various kinds (Clarke, 1924; Weir, 1936; Wild, 1961; Ludecke, 1962) indicates that during the time required for soil to develop from parent material, a substantial part of the original phosphorus may have disappeared, presumably as a result of downward movement of water through the soil. The annual losses are so small in relation to the amount present, however, as to be undetectable by analyses made of the soil over a span of a few years or perhaps even a lifetime.

Loss of phosphorus due to downward movement of water through the soil on a short-time basis is commonly determined by analyzing the drainage water from a lysimeter, in which the depth of soil is usually no more than a meter, or by analyzing water from tile drains. The concentrations are usually less than 0.1 μg of phosphorus per milliliter (Voelcker, 1874; Kohnke et al., 1940; Morgan and Jacobson, 1942; Sylvester and Seabloom, 1963). Analyses for phosphorus are often omitted because the concentrations are so consistently low.

Two difficulties in interpretation of values obtained as just described are that (1) part of the water in tile drains has passed through strata beneath the tiles and (2) the phosphorus filtering process that goes on in soil proper takes place even more effectively in unconsolidated material underlying the soil. Occurrence of a zone of relatively high phosphorus content in the unconsolidated material below the soil (Huddleston, 1969) is evidence that some of the phosphorus leached from the soil is retained by the material beneath and that the estimate of loss of phosphorus to the groundwater by leaching may depend on the depth at which the water is collected.

Because of the effectiveness of soil and underlying material in retaining phosphorus, the phosphorus content of groundwaters is normally low. A value of 0.011 μg of phosphorus per milliliter is obtained by averaging 63 of the 65 analyses reported by White et al. (1963) in a survey of data. Two high values not included in the average were 0.15 and 0.36 μg of phosphorus per milliliter. Juday and Birge (1931) reported an average of 0.016 μg of phosphorus per milliliter in water from 17 wells near lakes in northeastern Wisconsin (2 additional wells had phosphorus contents of 0.086 and 0.197 μg per milliliter) and an average of 0.023 μg of phosphorus per milliliter of lake water. Groundwaters may thus be expected to be low in phosphorus in most instances.

Surface waters present a different sort of problem because they contain phosphorus in both dissolved and particulate form. The solids are derived primarily from surface soils (Gottschalk, 1962),

FIG. 6.2. Concentration of phosphorus in solution after equilibration of soils of France with superphosphate versus calculated concentration in solution due to phosphorus added. Two parts of water were equilibrated with one part of soil. Each line represents a different soil. (Demolon and Boischot, 1951.)

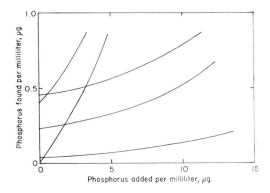

most of which have, in the soil solution, concentrations of phosphorus exceeding the value of 0.015 μg per milliliter, quoted by Mackenthun (1965) as a concentration of phosphorus sufficient to produce a subsequent nuisance growth of algae in water. Data on phosphorus in soil solutions were published by Pierre and Parker (1927) and Barber et al. (1962). Another source of phosphorus in surface waters is dead plant residues on the surface of the soil. These residues release phosphorus readily, and the initial phosphorus concentrations are much above those generally found in soil solutions.

The suspended solids impart to the stream a phosphorus-buffering quality, illustrated in principle in Figure 6.2. That is, when the solids are initially suspended in rainwater or when the stream is later diluted by low-phosphorus water, release of phosphorus from the solids will make the concentration of phosphorus in the final mixture closer to that in the original soil solution than would be predicted from a simple dilution effect. Conversely, if a stream receives high-phosphorus water from another source, such as sewage, the soil-derived solids will take up phosphorus from the water and will reduce the concentration of phosphorus in solution.

Whether the entrance of groundwater into streams increases or decreases the concentration of phosphorus in the stream water depends on the relative concentrations of phosphorus in the two. If the stream is one that carries substantial amounts of suspended solids from surface soils and receives sewage effluent at intervals, it seems unlikely that entrance of the groundwater will raise the concentration of phosphorus. But, even if the groundwater originally has a lower concentration of phosphorus than the stream water, the groundwater may not much lower the concentration in the stream because of the buffering effect of the solids. Groundwater enters streams mainly through the sides and bottom of the channel, and it must pass through the previously deposited sediments in the stream bed and must be substantially at equilibrium with them by the time it enters the stream proper.

Concentrations of inorganic orthophosphate in the water of streams and lakes are extremely low by conventional standards. Plants are extremely efficient in absorbing phosphorus, however, and if other conditions are favorable, will reduce the external concentration of phosphorus essentially to zero. Absorption of dissolved phosphorus by aquatic plants starts a biological cycle in which animals feed on the plants and the residues of both decompose, with release of inorganic orthophosphate that starts around the biological cycle again.

This biological cycle continues after the water has reached the oceans. But the depth and circulation of oceans introduce some changes. Photosynthesis occurs only near the surface because of the requirement for light. The residues of both plants and animals sink and decompose at great depths or on the bottom, where there is little synthesis. Consequently the inorganic phosphorus content of surface water is low, and that of deeper water is higher. Circulation of the oceans brings up water from the depths and renews the supply of phosphorus for the biological cycle.

Despite the annual addition of an estimated 2 million metric tons of dissolved phosphorus to the oceans (McKelvey et al., 1953), the phosphorus concentration in ocean water remains low because of continuous loss of phosphorus from the biological cycle, the principal loss being due to formation of the mineral apatite. According to Kazakov's theory (McKelvey et al., 1953), the cold ocean water from great depths, which contains a relatively high concentration of carbon dioxide and inorganic orthophosphate, becomes supersaturated with respect to apatite as it flows upward, warms, loses carbon dioxide, and increases in pH. Solid-phase apatite is then slowly formed. Apatite is forming now off the coast of California under these conditions, according to Dietz et al. (1942). If the apatite is formed in a place that receives little extraneous sediment, a substantial and high-grade bed of "phosphorite" or "phosphate rock" may be developed over geologic time. If, later, the bed of phosphorite is uplifted and occurs above sea level, the geologic phosphorus cycle begins again with loss of phosphorus by leaching. Phosphorus in phosphorite reenters the geologic cycle in another way in that beds of this substance located now on land supply almost all the phosphorus used for fertilizers and other purposes.

REACTION OF FERTILIZER PHOSPHORUS WITH SOILS

Nature of fertilizer phosphorus

The phosphorus in phosphorite is present as orthophosphate (PO_4^{---}), and it remains as orthophosphate when phosphorite is processed to form the more soluble phosphate compounds that contain the bulk of the fertilizer phosphorus. In some modern fertilizers, however, a part or most of the phosphorus is now appearing as condensed phosphates, in which two or more orthophosphate groups are joined through an oxygen atom. The solubility of condensed phosphates decreases with an increase in size of the molecules.

The chemistry of condensed phosphates is somewhat different from that of orthophosphates (Huffman, 1968). For present pur-

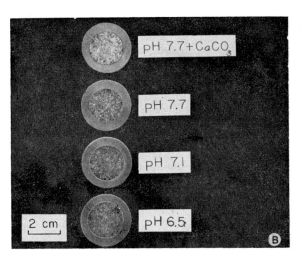

FIG. 6.3. Crystalline phosphates formed from the interaction of phosphate fertilizers with soils. **A.** Crystals of calcium ammonium phosphate [$Ca(NH_4)_2(HPO_4)_2.H_2O$ (dimorph B)] formed on calcium carbonate in a calcareous soil to which dibasic ammonium phosphate was added as fertilizer. The fertilizer was added in a thin layer and moved upward into the soil. The surface of the calcium carbonate shown in the picture was oriented perpendicular to the layer of fertilizer and parallel to the direction of movement. (Bell, 1968.) **B.** Variation in content of calcium ammonium phosphate [$Ca(NH_4)_2(HPO_4)_2.H_2O$ (dimorph B)] with original pH of a soil when dibasic ammonium phosphate was allowed to move upward into a column of soil from a thin layer at the bottom. The soil is dark colored, and the intensity of the sprinkling of white indicates the relative amount of calcium ammonium phosphate formed. The sample in each case was taken from a 2-mm layer of soil adjacent to the fertilizer and had been pressed into a brass ring pre-

paratory to examination by X-ray diffraction. (Photograph courtesy of L. C. Bell.) **C.** Crystals of magnesium ammonium phosphate hexahydrate ($MgNH_4PO_4.6H_2O$) developed in a soil high in exchangeable magnesium when monobasic ammonium phosphate moved upward into a column of the soil from a thin layer of the salt at the bottom. Values for cation-exchange capacity, exchangeable calcium, and exchangeable magnesium in the soil were 54, 38, and 12 m.e. per 100 g, respectively. (Photograph courtesy of L. C. Bell.) **D.** Cross section of an originally neutral, high-calcium soil, adjacent to a granule of concentrated superphosphate, showing development of crystals of dibasic calcium phosphate dihydrate ($CaHPO_4.2H_2O$). Although the soil contains a large amount of the newly formed crystalline phosphate, most of the crystals are too small to be identified at this magnification. Only a few relatively large crystals may be seen.

poses, however, it is perhaps sufficient to say that (1) condensed phosphates spontaneously decompose in soil, gradually forming orthophosphates, and (2) in the meantime they are present in forms that are probably no more readily lost from the soil than are orthophosphates.[1]

Reactions at high phosphorus concentrations

The quantities of phosphate fertilizers added to soil are rarely great enough to produce a high phosphorus concentration in the soil solution if the fertilizer phosphorus were uniformly distributed, but uniform distribution is never accomplished in practice. Initially the solution is usually saturated with the fertilizer salt at the immediate site of application, and the concentration of phosphorus is of the order of 1 million times greater than the concentration of phosphorus in soil solutions and streams.

Soils invariably contain cations that form phosphates of low solubility (calcium, magnesium, aluminum, and iron are of principal importance), and such phosphates form rapidly in soil in the presence of the high concentrations of phosphorus found near the site of the fertilizer. Some of the phosphates are crystalline, and the crystals may be seen under a microscope and occasionally even with the unaided eye. Figure 6.3 shows some examples. The kinds and amounts formed depend on the nature of the soil and fertilizer and on other factors as well (Bell, 1968; Huffman, 1968). Formation of these compounds greatly decreases the tendency of the phosphorus to move in the soil water by either mass movement or diffusion.

The crystalline phosphates that form quickly in soil when soluble phosphate fertilizers are added disappear with time when the concentration of phosphorus decreases. They may simply dissolve (Larsen et al., 1964), or they may leave a less soluble phosphate as a residue (Bell, 1968). In either case the phosphate released does not stay in solution but is retained in some way by the soil solids. There is some evidence for eventual formation of crystalline phosphates of extremely low solubility (Nagelschmidt and Nixon, 1944; Australia, 1956; Bell, 1968). On the other hand, if the phosphorus concentration is maintained, the quickly forming phosphates may be stable indefinitely. This situation will be discussed in the section on reaction capacities.

---

1. Scott (1958) investigated the reaction of orthophosphate and condensed phosphates (from calcium metaphosphate fertilizer, vitreous calcium metaphosphate, sodium metaphosphate, and ammonium metaphosphate) with soils and found that the soils tested sorbed the condensed phosphate more strongly than the orthophosphate. Sample (1965) was quoted by Huffman (1968) as having found that pyrophosphate was taken up by soil more rapidly than orthophosphate but was retained less strongly. Gunary (1966) found that most soils he tested had a higher "adsorption maximum" for pyrophosphate than for orthophosphate. The adsorption concept is discussed in a subsequent section.

Reactions at low phosphorus concentrations

Reactions at low phosphorus concentrations are important at the perimeter of the zone of soil containing fertilizer phosphorus and also in stream waters, where suspended and sedimented solids interact with waters having low concentrations of phosphorus. Figure 6.2 shows that as phosphorus was added to suspensions of soil in water the concentration of phosphorus in solution increased, slowly at first and then more rapidly, but the concentrations of phosphorus in solution with no addition and the rates of increase with phosphorus additions differed among soils. These observations signify that soils react most strongly with the first increment of added phosphorus and less strongly with succeeding increments and that the reaction has both an intensity aspect and a quantity aspect.

The Freundlich and Langmuir equations used in colloid chemistry to describe adsorptions have both been used to express the reactions of soil with low concentrations of inorganic orthophosphate. Recently attention has been focused on the Langmuir equation. Olsen and Watanabe (1957) used the equation in the form

$$\frac{C}{x/m} = \frac{1}{kb} + \frac{C}{b}$$

in which C is the equilibrium phosphorus concentration, x/m is the quantity of phosphorus adsorbed per unit weight of soil, b is the maximum quantity of phosphorus that can be held by adsorption per unit weight of soil, and k is a parameter related to the bonding energy of the soil for phosphorus. If experimental data fit the equation, a plot of $C/x/m$ against C should yield a straight line with slope $1/b$ and intercept $1/kb$, from which b and k may be evaluated. The quantity of phosphorus found in the soil by isotopic dilution of radioactive orthophosphate was used as an estimate of the phosphorus already present in adsorbed form.

Figure 6.4 shows Olsen and Watanabe's data for two soils. From the equations, it may be seen that Pierre clay had a higher adsorption capacity ($b = 25.9$ mg P/100 g soil) than Owyhee silt loam ($b = 13.3$ mg P/100 g soil) and that Pierre clay bonded phosphorus more strongly ($k = 1.32 \times 10^4$ liters/mole) than did Owyhee silt loam ($k = 0.94 \times 10^4$ liters/mole).

The constants in the Langmuir equation provide a convenient way to represent the phosphorus-adsorbing properties of soils in the presence of low concentrations of phosphorus in solution and provide reasonable bases for comparing different soils if the procedures are standardized. Moreover, the Langmuir equation may be used to describe phosphorus release or desorption from soil as shown by Fried and Shapiro (1956).

The experience obtained in use of the Langmuir equation with soils suggests that it may be useful also for describing phosphorus adsorption and release by solids suspended in streams. Nevertheless, the results should not be taken too seriously because the equation is empirical as applied to interaction of phosphorus with soil, and the

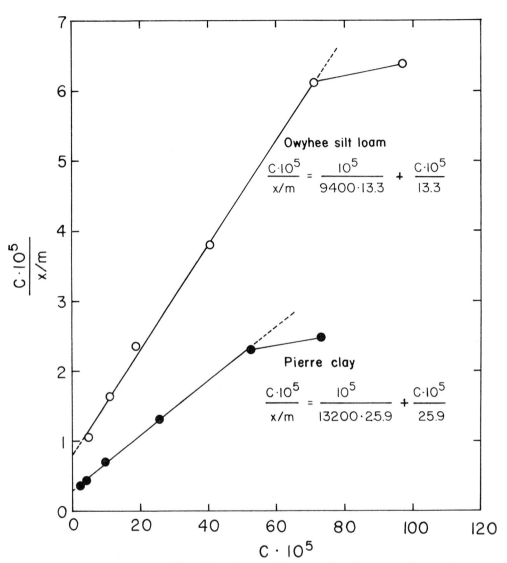

FIG. 6.4. Plot of phosphorus adsorption data for two soils according to the Langmuir equation. In each case the first five points fall close to a straight line, indicating conformance to the equation, and the sixth point deviates from the line. (Olsen and Watanabe, 1957.)

equation does not fit data from all soils (Fried and Shapiro, 1956; Olsen and Watanabe, 1957; Thompson et al., 1960). Deviation of the data from a linear plot at high concentrations, illustrated in Figure 6.4, is a common problem; this means that the adsorption capacity must be calculated and not determined directly. Olsen and Watanabe (1957) quoted other work suggesting that the deviation might be due to formation of crystalline phosphates.

Reaction capacities

Of great importance in the behavior of phosphorus in soil in relation to water pollution is the capacity of soil to react with phosphate. There is much confusion on this matter because soils are so complex, conditions are so many, and measurement capabilities are so limited.

For present purposes, it seems reasonable to describe, conceptually, three kinds of capacities. Each is significant under different circumstances.

First is the capacity of the soil to react with phosphorus at low concentrations. This is the so-called adsorption capacity discussed in the preceding section. It is of significance in both soils and streams.

Second is the capacity of soil to react rapidly with phosphorus added at high concentrations, as when water-soluble phosphate fertilizers are added as solids. This capacity is significant in determining the capability of soil to capture fertilizer phosphorus in new solid phosphate species and to retain the phosphorus near the site of its introduction into the soil. This capacity could be defined operationally in many different ways, yielding many different values. Under conditions such as those of practical concern in the field, this capacity or these capacities far exceed the adsorption capacity discussed in the preceding paragraph.

Third is the ultimate capacity of soil to react with phosphorus. The ultimate capacity is equal to the phosphorus retained by the total amount of cations in the soil capable of forming phosphates of low solubility. This capacity is far greater than the capacity of soil to react rapidly with phosphorus added at high concentrations.

The ultimate capacity is evoked when soil has been in contact with a solution of high phosphate concentration for a long time. The original carbonate, hydrous oxide, and silicate minerals are then decomposed, with release of soluble silica from the silicates, and the product is a bed of phosphates.

There is no known instance in which soil has been thus altered by addition of phosphate fertilizer, but there is no doubt of the validity of the concept. In a classic paper, Gautier (1894) traced a layer of clay that had entered a cave in France through a fissure in the rock and found that the clay had been altered to an aluminum phosphate where it had been contacted by water derived from bat guano. Many instances are known of alteration of rocks to phosphates under the influence of leachings from guano in caves and on ocean islands. Teall's (1898) photomicrographs of thin sections of trachyte slightly

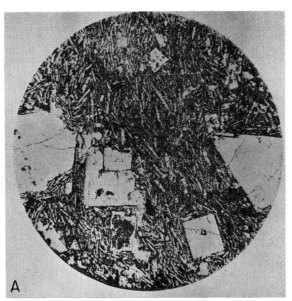

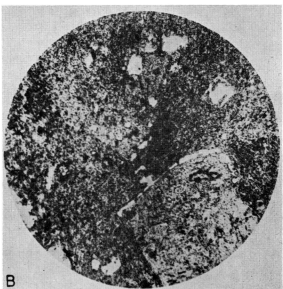

FIG. 6.5. Photomicrographs of thin sections of trachyte altered by phosphate from overlying guano on Clipperton Atoll. **A.** Altered trachyte, showing phenocrysts of sanidine set in a groundmass of microlitic feldspars and brown interstitial matter. In the central lower portion of the photomicrograph is a crystal of the feldspar crowded with brown inclusions. The phosphorus is present in the brown substance. **B.** Highly altered trachyte, showing the replacement of feldspar by phosphate with concretionary structure. The groundmass is replaced by a similar material, but without concretionary structure. The outline of one of the feldspar crystals is clearly seen in the lower right portion of the photomicrograph, but the original substance has been replaced by the phosphate. (Teall, 1898.)

TABLE 6.1. Chemical composition of trachyte at different degrees of alteration under guano on Clipperton Atoll.

Constituent	Least Altered Sample	Considerably Altered Sample	Highly Altered Sample
	(%)	(%)	(%)
SiO_2	54.0	43.7	2.8
P_2O_5	8.4	17.0	38.5
Al_2O_3	17.9	...	25.9
Fe_2O_3	4.4	...	7.4
CaO	1.4	...	...
K_2O	4.5	...	...
Na_2O	5.0	...	...
Loss on ignition	3.8	12.3	23.0
Matter insoluble in HCl	...	...	2.2
Total	99.4	...	99.8

Source: Teall (1898).

altered and strongly altered by bird guano are reproduced in Figure
6.5, and his data showing the change in chemical composition of the
rock with degree of alteration are given in Table 6.1. The inverse
relationship between phosphorus content and silicon content is particularly noteworthy.

Laboratory work has verified that soils, clay, and minerals may
indeed be altered to phosphates. Gautier (1894) demonstrated the alteration of gelatinous alumina, clay, siderite, and chalk to phosphates.
Tamini et al. (1964) reported recent work on gibbsite and soils and
reviewed some of the previous work. Clarke (1924) reviewed early
work. Modern researchers have better tools than their predecessors
and now can determine more easily the nature of the phosphates
formed. Figure 6.6 shows, for example, a cross section of a crystal
of calcite, the surface of which had been altered by a sodium phosphate solution to a calcium phosphate identified by X-ray diffraction
as apatite.

The second and third kinds of capacities are usually great
enough to enable soil to retain a tremendous amount of phosphorus
near the site of application of soluble phosphate fertilizer. At the
same time, the combined effect of all three kinds of capacities keeps
the concentration of phosphorus in the soil solution at a low value in
soil only a few centimeters away.

Addition of phosphate fertilizers in agriculture is never continued to the stage at which the ultimate capacity of soil to react
with phosphate is satisfied because such additions would be accompanied by unfavorable effects on plants. The maximum favorable
effects are achieved with comparatively small additions.

In terms of the concentration of phosphorus in solution, the consequence of adding so much phosphate fertilizer that the soil is converted to a phosphate bed would depend on the circumstances. One
solid figure—the value of 0.15 μg of phosphorus per milliliter of
groundwater from the Phosphoria phosphorite formation of Garrison,

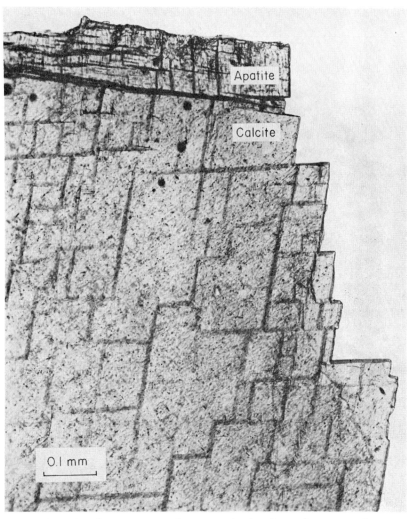

FIG. 6.6. Cross section of a crystal of calcite showing a layer of apatite developed on the surface when the calcite was immersed for 2 weeks in a 0.1-molar solution of tribasic sodium phosphate. (Ames, 1961.)

Montana—was recorded by White et al. (1963). This value is to be regarded as a minimum that might be reached some years after application of soluble phosphate had been discontinued. Higher concentrations would be expected as long as more soluble phosphates of the type illustrated in Figure 6.3 remained.

DISTRIBUTION OF FERTILIZER PHOSPHORUS IN SOIL

Inorganic phosphorus

Most phosphate fertilizer is added to soil as a solid. The highly soluble phosphates attract water from the surrounding soil and form a saturated solution of the fertilizer, first in the fertilizer itself and then in the surrounding soil as the solution is drawn into the soil by capillarity. If the bulk soil is relatively dry, the soil around the fertilizer is visibly wetted by the water that has accumulated (see Fig. 6.7). This process was described by Lehr et al. (1959) and Lindsay and Stephenson (1959).

During outward movement of the solution the concentration of phosphorus decreases because of reaction with the soil, exhaustion of the soluble salts in the fertilizer, and dilution of the solution with water in the soil. Eventually the concentration of the solution becomes low enough so that water is no longer drawn to any appreciable extent from the surrounding soil. Within a few weeks the concen-

FIG. 6.7. Wetted zone of soil around a granule of concentrated superphosphate. The granule of fertilizer was imbedded in the smooth surface of a dry soil, and the soil was exposed to an atmosphere saturated with water vapor. The fertilizer took up the water vapor, forming a solution, and the solution moved into the soil by capillarity.

1 mm

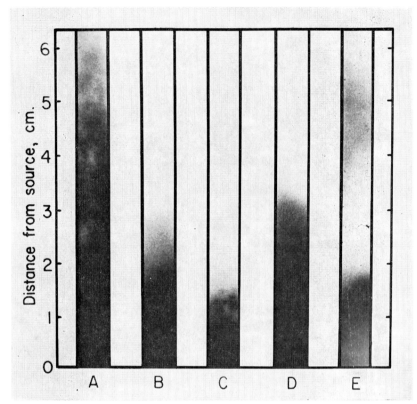

FIG. 6.8. Autoradiographs, showing distribution of radioactive phosphorus along water-saturated columns of soil 2 weeks after placement of phosphate fertilizer at the lower end of the columns. The darker areas represent higher concentrations of radioactive phosphorus. $A =$ Cecil sandy loam, $KH_2P^{32}O_4$ source; $B =$ Elliott silt loam, $Ca(H_2P^{32}O_4)_2$ source; $C =$ Fargo silty clay loam, $KH_2P^{32}O_4$ source; $D =$ Miami silt loam, $KH_2P^{32}O_4$ source; $E =$ Miami silt loam, $Ca(H_2P^{32}O_4)_2$ source. (Bouldin and Black, 1954.)

tration of phosphate in solution is so low that little further movement occurs over a much longer time by either diffusion or mass movement in moving water.

Generally, the concentration of total phosphorus in soil a few weeks after addition of a soluble fertilizer is greatest at the site of, or immediately adjacent to, the fertilizer and gradually decreases with distance from the site of the fertilizer. The distribution pattern, however, is not always like this. Figure 6.8, for example, shows an instance (autoradiograph E) in which there were two maxima in the distribution of phosphorus with distance from the source. Bell (1968) observed occurrences of bands of crystals of dibasic calcium phosphate dihydrate in glass-fiber filter paper imbedded in soil in which phosphorus was slowly moving from a layer of soluble phosphate fertilizer. The phenomenon of periodic precipitates or Liesegang rings

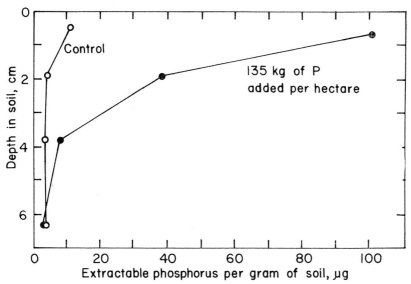

FIG. 6.9. Extractable phosphorus at different depths in unfertilized and phosphate-fertilized silt loam soil in Wisconsin. The soil received a surface application of superphosphate equivalent to 135 kg of phosphorus per hectare on April 25 and was sampled on October 15 of the same year for analysis by Truog's (1930) method. (Midgley, 1931.)

thus seems to have application in soil as well as in more homogeneous media usually studied by chemists.

Results of three field experiments on movement of fertilizer phosphorus in soil will be cited. Figure 6.9 shows an instance in which the increase in extractable phosphorus in the soil in the autumn following an early spring topdressing of superphosphate was confined to the surface 6 cm. Results such as this are characteristic of soils with moderate capacities to react rapidly with phosphate added at high concentrations.

In the second experiment (Ozanne, 1962), the equivalent of 225 kg of P^{32}-labeled superphosphate per hectare was broadcasted on a fallow siliceous sand in the winter season in Western Australia. After 38 days, during which a total of 23 cm of rain was received, more than 50% of the labeled phosphorus had penetrated more than 1 meter below the surface of the soil. These results are characteristic of soils that have little capacity of any kind for reaction with phosphate.

The third experiment (Fig. 6.10) shows the measurable accumulation of phosphorus that occurred with time when repeated additions of superphosphate were made to a soil with moderate capacity to react quickly with fertilizer phosphorus. The downward penetration was such that after 31 years the plots receiving 60 kg of phosphorus per hectare at presumably annual intervals could be clearly distinguished from the control plots by analyses of samples of soil from the 40- to 60-cm depth. Plots receiving 180 kg could be clearly

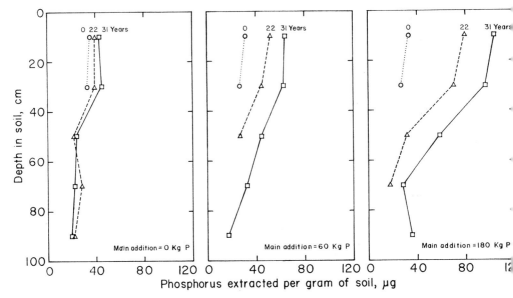

FIG. 6.10. Extractable phosphorus at different depths in soil fertilized repeatedly with superphosphate and sampled at different times during a 31-year field experiment in the Soviet Union. All plots received 20 kg of phosphorus per hectare in a row application each time sugar beets were grown in the crop rotation, plus main applications of 0, 60, or 180 kg of phosphorus per hectare at presumably annual intervals. Extractable phosphorus was determined by the Truog (1930) method. (Alekseeva, 1968.)

distinguished from the control plots by analyses of samples of soil from the 80- to 100-cm depth.

Organic phosphorus

Some, but not all, organic-phosphorus-bearing substances react with soil to form combinations of extremely low solubility, like inorganic orthophosphate. Hannapel et al. (1964a) found that when plant materials or sucrose (with ammonium nitrate) were incubated with the upper portion of a column of soil, most of the phosphorus obtained subsequently in drainage water was organic when excess water was added at intervals to the top of the column of soil. The greatest increase in organic phosphorus in the leachates resulted from addition of sucrose, which contained no phosphorus. Most of the organic phosphorus removed by leaching after incubation of soil with sucrose and ammonium nitrate was present in microbial cells and cellular debris retained by a filter with 0.45μ pores (Hannapel et al., 1964b).

The findings just described provide an explanation for previous observations by Dyer (1902) and Stephenson and Chapman (1931), indicating deeper penetration of phosphorus derived from manure than of phosphorus derived from inorganic fertilizers. The findings have further relevance to attempts to use soil to remove phosphorus from sewage or livestock wastes. The efficiency of soil for this purpose may not be as great as it is for removing inorganic phosphorus. Koelliker and Miner (1969) reported that water from drain tiles at a depth of 122 cm contained 0.5 μg of phosphorus per ml during a season in which the soil was irrigated with livestock wastewater containing 552 kg of phosphorus per hectare. The chemical oxygen demand of the tile water was 37 μg/ml, which suggests that much of the relatively high concentration of phosphorus was organic.

REFERENCES

Alekseeva, E. N. 1968. Migration of phosphorus down the soil profile during long-term use of fertilizers. (Translated title.) *Agrokhimiya*, 1968, No. 8, pp. 78–82.

Ames, L. L., Jr. 1961. Anion metasomatic replacement reactions. *Econ. Geol.* 56:521–32.

Australia. 1956. Commonwealth Scientific and Industrial Research Organization, Ann. Rept. 8:18–19.

Barber, S. A., Walker, J. M., and Vasey, E. H. 1962. Principles of ion movement through the soil to the plant root. *Trans. Joint Meeting Com. IV & V, Intern. Soc. Soil Sci. (New Zealand, 1962)*, pp. 121–24.

Bell, L. C. 1968. Nature and transformation of crystalline phosphates produced by interaction of phosphate fertilizers with slightly acid and alkaline soils. Ph.D. Thesis, Iowa State Univ., Ames.

Bouldin, D. R., and Black, C. A. 1954. Phosphorus diffusion in soils. *Soil Sci. Soc. Am. Proc.* 18:255–59.

Clarke, F. W. 1924. *The data of geochemistry*. U.S. Geol. Survey Bull. 770.

Cunningham, R. K. 1963. The effect of clearing a tropical forest soil. *J. Soil Sci.* 14:334–45.

Dean, L. A. 1949. Fixation of soil phosphorus. *Advan. Agron.* 1:391–411.

Demolon, A., and Boischot, P. 1951. Réaction des sols à l'apport de phosphates solubles. Doses isodynames. *Compt. Rend. Acad. Sci.* 233:509–12.

Dietz, R. S., Emery, K. O., and Shepard, F. P. 1942. Phosphorite deposits on the sea floor off southern California. *Bull. Geol. Soc. Am.* 53:815–47.

Dyer, B. 1902. *Results of investigations on the Rothamsted soils*. USDA, Office of Exp. Sta. Bull. 106.

Fried, M., and Shapiro, R. E. 1956. Phosphate supply pattern of various soils. *Soil Sci. Soc. Am. Proc.* 20:471–75.

Gautier, A. 1894. Sur un gisement de phosphates de chaux et d'alumine contenant des espèces rares ou nouvelles et sur la genèse des phosphates et nitres naturels. *Ann. Mines* (Ser. 9) 5:1–53.

Gottschalk, L. C. 1962. Effects of watershed protection measures on reduction of erosion and sediment damages in the United States. *Intern. Assoc. Sci. Hydrol. Publ.* 59, pp. 426–47.

Gunary, D. 1966. Pyrophosphate in soil; some physico-chemical aspects. *Nature* 210:1297–98.

Haas, H. J., Grunes, D. L., and Reichman, G. A. 1961. Phosphorus changes in Great Plains soils as influenced by cropping and manure applications. *Soil Sci. Soc. Am. Proc.* 25:214–18.

Hannapel, R. J., Fuller, W. H., Bosma, S., and Bullock, J. S. 1964a. Phosphorus movement in a calcareous soil: I. Predominance of organic forms of phosphorus in phosphorus movement. *Soil Sci.* 97:350–57.

Hannapel, R. J., Fuller, W. H., and Fox, R. H. 1964b. Phosphorus movement in a calcareous soil: II. Soil microbial activity and organic phosphorus movement. *Soil Sci.* 97:421–27.

Hemwall, J. B. 1957. The fixation of phosphorus by soils. *Advan. Agron.* 9:95–112.

Huddleston, J. H. 1969. Local soil-landscape relationships in eastern Pottawattamie County, Iowa. Ph.D. Thesis, Iowa State Univ., Ames.

Huffman, E. O. 1968. The reactions of fertilizer phosphate with soils. *Outlook Agr.* 5:202–7.

Jackman, R. H. 1964. Accumulation of organic matter in some New Zealand soils under permanent pasture. I. Patterns of change of organic carbon, nitrogen, sulphur, and phosphorus. *New Zealand J. Agr. Res.* 7:445–71.

Juday, C., and Birge, E. A. 1931. A second report on the phosphorus content of Wisconsin lake waters. *Trans. Wis. Acad. Sci. Arts Letters* 26:353–82.

Koelliker, J. K., and Miner, J. R. 1969. Use of soil to treat anaerobic lagoon effluent: renovation as a function of depth and application rate. Paper presented at meeting of Am. Soc. Agr. Engrs., June 1969, Purdue Univ., West Lafayette, Ind.

Kohnke, H., Dreibelbis, F. R., and Davidson, J. M. 1940. *A survey and discussion of lysimeters and a bibliography on their construction and performance.* USDA Misc. Publ. 372.

Larsen, S. 1967. Soil phosphorus. *Advan. Agron.* 19:151–210.

Larsen, S., Gunary, D., and Devine, J. R. 1964. Stability of granular dicalcium phosphate dihydrate in soil. *Nature* 204:1114.

Lehr, J. R., Brown, W. E., and Brown, E. H. 1959. Chemical behavior of monocalcium phosphate monohydrate in soils. *Soil Sci. Soc. Am. Proc.* 23:3–7.

Lindsay, W. L., and Stephenson, H. F. 1959. Nature of the reactions of monocalcium phosphate monohydrate in soils: I. The solution that reacts with the soil. *Soil Sci. Soc. Am. Proc.* 23:12–18.

Ludecke, T. E. 1962. Formulation of a rational fertiliser programme in tussock country. *Proc. New Zealand Grassland Assoc.* 24:29–41.

McAuliffe, C. D., Hall, N. S., Dean, L. A., and Hendricks, S. B. 1948. Exchange reactions between phosphates and soils: hydroxylic surfaces of soil minerals. *Soil Sci. Soc. Am. Proc.* 12:119–23.

McKelvey, V. E., Swanson, R. W., and Sheldon, R. P. 1953. The Permian phosphorite deposits of western United States. *Congr. Geol. Intern. Compt. Rend. 19th Sess.* 11:45–64.

Mackenthun, K. M. 1965. *Nitrogen and phosphorus in water.* U.S. Dept. Health, Education, and Welfare, Public Health Serv., Div. Water Supply and Pollution Control.

Mattingly, G. E. G., and Talibudeen, O. 1967. Progress in the chemistry of fertilizer and soil phosphorus. *Topics Phosphorus Chem.* 4:157–290.

Midgley, A. R. 1931. The movement and fixation of phosphates in relation to permanent pasture fertilization. *J. Am. Soc. Agron.* 23:788–99.

Morgan, M. F., and Jacobson, H. G. M. 1942. *Soil and crop interrelations of various nitrogeneous fertilizers. Windsor lysimeter series B.* Conn. (New Haven) Agr. Exp. Sta. Bull. 458.

Nagelschmidt, G., and Nixon, H. L. 1944. Formation of apatite from superphosphate in the soil. *Nature* 154:428–29.

Olsen, S. R., and Watanabe, F. S. 1957. A method to determine a phosphorus adsorption maximum of soils as measured by the Langmuir isotherm. *Soil Sci. Soc. Am. Proc.* 21:144–49.

Ozanne, P. G. 1962. Some nutritional problems characteristic of sandy soils. *Trans. Joint Meeting Com. IV & V, Intern. Soc. Soil Sci. (New Zealand, 1962)*, pp. 139–43.

Pearson, R. W., and Simonson, R. W. 1939. Organic phosphorus in seven Iowa soil profiles: distribution and amounts as compared to organic carbon and nitrogen. *Soil Sci. Soc. Am. Proc.* 4: 162–67.

Pearson, R. W., Spry, R., and Pierre, W. H. 1940. The vertical distribution of total and dilute acid-soluble phosphorus in twelve Iowa soil profiles. *J. Am. Soc. Agron.* 32:683–96.

Pierre, W. H., and Parker, F. W. 1927. Soil phosphorus studies: II. The concentration of organic and inorganic phosphorus in the soil solution and soil extracts and the availability of the organic phosphorus to plants. *Soil Sci.* 24:119–28.

Ponomareva, V. V., Rozhnova, T. A., and Sotnikova, N. S. 1968. Lysimetric observations on the leaching of elements in podzolic soils. *Trans. 9th Intern. Congr. Soil Sci. (Australia)* 1:155–64.

Scott, C. O. 1958. Sorption of orthophosphate and nonorthophosphate phosphorus by soils. Ph.D. Thesis, Iowa State Univ., Ames.

Stephenson, R. E., and Chapman, H. D. 1931. Phosphate penetration in field soils. *J. Am. Soc. Agron.* 23:759–70.

Sylvester, R. O., and Seabloom, R. W. 1963. Quality and significance of irrigation return flow. *J. Irrig. Drain. Div., Proc. Am. Soc. Civil Eng.* 89, No. IR3, pp. 1–27.

Tamini, Y. F., Kanehiro, Y., and Sherman, G. D. 1964. Reactions of ammonium phosphate with gibbsite and with montmorillonitic and kaolinitic soils. *Soil Sci.* 98:249–55.

Taylor, A. W. 1967. Phosphorus and water pollution. *J. Soil Water Conserv.* 22:228–31.

Teall, J. J. H. 1898. A phosphatized trachyte from Clipperton Atoll (northern Pacific). *Quart. J. Geol. Soc. London* 54:230–32.

Thompson, E. J., Oliveira, A. L. F., Moser, U. S., and Black, C. A. 1960. Evaluation of laboratory indexes of absorption of soil phosphorus by plants: II. *Plant Soil* 13:28–38.

Truog, E. 1930. The determination of readily available phosphorus of soils. *J. Am. Soc. Agron.* 22:874–82.

Voelcker, A. 1874. On the composition of waters of land-drainage. *J. Roy. Agr. Soc. Engl.*, 2nd Ser. 10:132–65.

Weir, W. W. 1936. *Soil science.* Chicago: J. B. Lippincott.

White, D. E., Hem, J. D., and Waring, G A. 1963. *Data of geochemistry, sixth edition. Chapter F. Chemical composition of subsurface waters.* U.S. Geol. Survey Prof. Paper 440-F.

Wild, A. 1950. The retention of phosphate by soil. A review. *J. Soil Sci.* 1:221–38.

———. 1961. A pedological study of phosphorus in 12 soils derived from granite. *Australian J. Agr. Res.* 12:286–99.

CHAPTER SEVEN

SOURCES OF NITROGEN
IN WATER SUPPLIES

MARVIN C. GOLDBERG

NITROGEN, like silicon, carbon, and phosphorus, has the unique ability to act as a Lewis acid or base. It has three p electrons, presumably unpaired, each capable of entering into chemical reaction. Also, with all three valence electrons tied up, the inner 2s shell electrons act as an electron pair donor and gave nitrogen its electronegative character in secondary amines and other such compounds. Nitrogen is a gas at standard temperature and pressure; its density is 0.81 g/ml. When combined in compounds, nitrogen exhibits oxidation states from -3 to $+5$. The elemental state is extremely electronegative with a value of 3 on the Pauling scale. Only a few of the nonmetals, for example, O, F, and Cl, have electronegativity of equal or greater value.

Nitrogen concentration in the dry atmosphere of the earth is 757.4 g/cm^2 of earth's surface, according to Hutchinson (1954). The total atmospheric mass is 38.65 geograms. (A geogram is 10^{20} grams.) The mass of water in the hydrosphere is 14,000 geograms. The amount of dissolved nitrogen is 0.26 geograms, or equivalent to 5.2 g/cm^2 of the earth's surface. The average nitrogen concentration in igneous rocks is about 0.005% by weight. It occurs in the form of ammonium substituted for potassium in mineral lattices.

CHEMISTRY OF NITROGEN IN WATER

Ammonia and other reduced forms such as nitrous oxide, nitrites, etc., are oxidized by nitrifying bacteria to nitrates in water. Organic nitrogen is primarily formed and degraded by biological action. Common species of organic nitrogen are proteins, protein derivatives, purines, pyrimidines, and urea. Some of these materials are readily degradable and some are not. Pyrimidines and purines are important components of nucleotides and eventually may end up as genetic components such as DNA and RNA. Urea, on the other hand,

MARVIN C. GOLDBERG is Research Hydrologist, U.S. Geological Survey, Denver Federal Center, Denver.
Publication authorized by the Director, U.S. Geological Survey.

is a decomposition product of proteins or amino acids and is readily hydrolyzed enzymatically in natural waters into ammonia and carbon dioxide. Urea is a highly available form of nitrogen for biological synthesis.

Another species of bound nitrogen in water is the solute from geochemical organic deposits. Most of this type of material, which remains undissolved, does not enter the nitrogen cycle. Usually the nonreactive character of geo-organic nitrogen is due to adsorption onto clay minerals or formation in complex forms which are polymeric and exist in water as polyelectrolytes. Only about 5 to 10% of this material is in the form of nucleic acids, 30 to 40% is in the form of proteins, and 10 to 15% is amino sugars. The remainder has been uncharacterized. The majority of soluble organic nitrogen in lakes is present in the form of amino groups.

For each 15 atoms of available nitrogen in water, there are 510 atoms of dissolved molecular nitrogen and a relatively unlimited supply of elemental nitrogen both in the atmosphere and the sediments. Hence, nitrogen becomes a limiting nutrient in water bodies only because of the slow rate at which atmospheric nitrogen is fixed or the slow rate at which organic nitrogen deposits are degraded.

OBJECT

Water supplies can be categorized as surface waters or groundwaters. This discussion will examine representative studies of nitrate entrance to both types of water supplies, with summaries of some of the many laboratory and field studies described in the current literature. As the literature is voluminous, only some exemplary studies are mentioned.

ENTRANCE OF NITROGEN INTO WATER

Mechanisms for the introduction of various fixed forms of nitrogen into water are categorized as nitrogen fixation from the air, ammonia entrance from "rainout," entrance of organic nitrogen from decomposing plants and animals, and land drainage. Water solutions usually contain nitrogen in either organic or ionic form. Ammonium, nitrite, and nitrate are the most common ionic forms of nitrogen found in water. In water itself, as the nitrogen cycle illustrates, proteinaceous material is decomposed by bacterial action. The inorganic ions which result from this decomposition are in turn used as nutrients to form new cell material. The forms of the new cell material are controlled by the environmental conditions imposed upon the biological systems involved. Grill and Richards (1964) examined nutrient regeneration from phytoplankton and observed that at the end of an experiment dealing with phytoplankton decomposition, 33% of the total nitrogen was ammonia, 39% was in particulate matter, and 28% was in dissolved organic compounds.

NITROGEN SOURCES IN WATER SUPPLIES

A catalogue of some sources of nitrogen in water supplies would include:

Agriculture
  Irrigation
  Rural runoff
  Tile drainage
Animals
Atmospheric
  Air pollutants from industrial sources
  Pollen
  Precipitation
Feedlots
Fertilizer
Geologic
  Caves
  Minerals
Industrial wastes
Lake sediments
Pond water
Rural waste
  Barnyards
  Feeds
  Privies
Storm water
Topsoil
Urban waste
  Leaking sewers
  Sanitary landfills
  Septic tanks
  Sewage
  Sludge lagoons
  Waste stabilization ponds
  Water treatment plants

ATMOSPHERIC PRECIPITATION AS A SOURCE OF NITROGEN

Precipitation might be the most important single source of nitrogen in surface waters (Feth, 1966), and thus it would also be an important source of nitrogen in groundwater.

Most of the nitrogen in the atmosphere is in the molecular form of N_2; however, there are small amounts of ammonia as well as various oxides of nitrogen and their hydration products, such as nitric acid. Much atmospheric ammonia is attributed to industrial air pollution. Additional sources are released from soil decomposition products and photochemical reactions occurring in the stratosphere. The most abundant oxide of nitrogen is probably N_2O_4 produced by internal combustion engines. Ion molecule reactions which occur in the stratosphere and upper ionosphere account for formation of nitrogen molecules other than N_2.

Stable aerosols composed of ammonium sulfate and ammonium persulfate occur at altitudes between 15 and 25 kilometers above the earth. Particles are in a constant condition of fallout from the stratosphere to lower layers of the atmosphere where they are incorporated into falling rain or snow. In a study by Junge (1968), it was reported that nitrate and ammonium concentrations in rainwater were low near coastlines. During April 1958 to March 1959 about 59% of total inorganic nitrogen in rainwater at Yangambi, Belgian Congo, was ammoniacal nitrogen (Meyer and Pampfer, 1959). Nitrous nitrogen did not exceed 3% of the nitric nitrogen. Of special interest is the fact that examination of individual downpours showed that the smaller the downpour, the higher the concentration of nitrogen, especially ammoniacal nitrogen. Matheson (1951) reports 6.5 kg nitrogen per hectare per year as accumulate nitrogen fall contained in precipitation and atmospheric sediments collected at Hamilton, Ontario, with 61% of the total nitrogen collected on 25% of the days when precipitation occurred. The balance is due solely to sedimentation of dust. Fifty-six percent of the total was ammonia nitrogen. In a New Zealand experiment (Miller, 1961) it was observed that total nitrogen collected at the Taita Experimental Station from rainwater was double the concentration of inorganic and aluminoid nitrogen. Contributions from rainwater to nitrogen in soil would probably be not less than 3.36 kg/ha/yr.

Feth (1967) lists tables of data indicating bulk precipitation of nitrate in the Mojave Desert Region, California, between March 1965 and March 1966. Values for nitrate nitrogen ranged from a trace to as high as 16 mg/l of rain, depending upon time of year and location.

Wind-borne sources of nitrogen also exist. For example, McGauhey et al. (1963) have shown the amount of nitrogen contributed by pollen may be as high as 2 to 5 kg/ha/yr in a forested area.

GEOLOGICAL SOURCES OF NITROGEN

Examples of geological sources of nitrate are the estimated 227 teragrams of nitrate of soda on the plateau of Tarapaca in Chili and the significant amounts of nitrate in the Amargosa Valley, Inyo County, California. Nitrate deposits have been found in soils or geologic formations in all of the 11 western states. Most of the states in the Ozark and Appalachian plateaus have natural nitrate accumulations in caves. Other geological sources of nitrate are igneous rocks, coal, peat beds and muck soils, cave deposits, caliche deposits, and playa deposits. In addition, all the world's organic matter, both living and dead, plus that in sedimentary rocks, are potential sources of nitrogen.

According to notes on the Conference on Nitrogen Chemistry held by the U.S. Geological Survey in Menlo Park, California (1965), fixed nitrogen in rocks may amount to a total 50 times as great as the amount of fixed nitrogen in the atmosphere. Rocks, however, are not a ready source of nitrogen because of access problems, attributed to small exposed surfaces. Only limited zones near the surface are in position to yield their nitrogen freely to circulating air and water. They can be considered, however, as groundwater nitrate sources under certain circumstances (Smith, 1967)—for example, in those localities where conditions have altered the geologic strata in such manner that there is collapse of cavern roofs or burial of ancient playa deposits which become geographically placed in the zone of saturation.

Organic-rich shales can also be a source of nitrogen. It has been reported that in sedimentary rocks, concentrations as high as 600 mg/kg dry weight of nitrogen may be present. Miocene shale from the Los Angeles Basin, California, can contain up to 8,600 mg/kg nitrogen.

The largest geologic concentrations of nitrogen seem to be present in the younger rocks; they are highest in clay, slate, and argillite, and generally low in metamorphic rocks. Water released during metamorphism tends to be high in ammonia. Igneous and sedimentary rocks may contain nitrogen in amounts ranging from 40 to 500 mg/kg, but organic shales contain nitrogen in much higher concentrations.

NITROGEN IN LAKES

Nitrogen from Lake Sediments

In 14 samples from the upper 10 cm of Lake Tahoe sediments analyzed by the Kjeldahl method, nitrogen concentrations ranged from 0.06 to 16.6 mg/g dry weight and carbon nitrogen ratios from 3.7 to 28.4 (McGauhey et al., 1963).

Decomposition Processes in a Lake as a Source of Nitrogen

Koyama and Tomino (1967) studied the mineralization of nitrogen-containing materials in a lake. Their results are typical of many such studies and show primarily (1) that during the early stages of the stagnation period, nitrogen fixation is generally more active than denitrification. Denitrification gradually exceeds nitrogen fixation with progressive stagnation and (2) at the end of the stagnation period, the amount of denitrified nitrogen is large when compared with other mineralized nitrogen compounds. Denitrification is the dominant process determining nitrogen metabolism in the lake water. The ratio of mineralized carbon to nitrogen at the end of the stagnation period is 3.5, considerably smaller than the value for plankton of 5.7. Mineralization rates of carbon and nitrogen in the organic detritus of the lake studied were 51% per year and 76% per year, respectively.

Nitrate Metabolism in Lakes

The following regime has developed in Sanctuary Lake, Pennsylvania (Dugdale and Dugdale, 1965): (1) a spring bloom when ammonia nitrogen, nitrate nitrogen, and molecular nitrogen are assimilated strongly, in that order of importance; (2) a midsummer period when weak assimilation of ammonia nitrogen and molecular nitrogen, but not nitrate nitrogen, occurs; and (3) a fall bloom with intense nitrogen fixation and some ammonia nitrogen uptake, but characterized by a low nitrate nitrogen activity. Nitrogen fixation and ammonia nitrogen uptake appear to proceed at the same time, although ammonia uptake dominates in the spring and nitrogen fixation dominates in the fall.

Biogenic interactions affect nitrogen sources in waste—for example, fixed nitrogen entering a reservoir is synthesized into the biomass as protein and liberated upon death of the biological entity. As much as 40% is released to the aqueous environment, some diffuses to the surface and escapes as a volatile gas, some is denitrified (going from the +5 oxidation state to −3) and some is permanently incorporated into the bed sediments.

Examination of a nitrogen cycle (Ehrlich and Slack, 1969) revealed that nitrogen assimilation in a laboratory study, where the sole nitrogen source was a stream of calcium nitrate, followed the characteristic pattern. The nitrogen was assimilated by plant life, in this case algae, with slight denitrification occurring at high nitrate concentrations. The organic nitrogen was converted to ammonia by proteolytic bacteria, with the possible escape of some ammonia. The ammonia from the organic compounds was partly assimilated by algae and partly nitrified by bacteria. The nitrate, of bacterial origin, was assimilated by algae. Nitrification apparently was not of major importance in converting organic nitrogen to algal biomass.

Analysis of surface and subsurface samples from western Lake Superior (Putnam and Olsen, 1959) showed that ammonia nitrogen was present in trace amounts only, usually less than 0.1 mg/l. It was found that the range of organic nitrogen during the year was from 0.08 mg/l in the hypolimnion to 0.28 mg/l at the surface. The bulk of nitrogen in the lake existed in the form of nitrate and ranged from 0.93 mg/l at the surface to 1.15 mg/l in the hypolimnion. Nitrite was practically indetectable. Waters that entered Lake Superior from its tributary streams contained very little free ammonia. Nitrate concentrations in the rivers were lower than that observed in the lake and varied from 0.16 mg/l to 0.47 mg/l. Nitrite was either absent or present only in trace amounts. In a second publication (Putnam and Olsen, 1960) it was stated that nitrate-nitrogen concentrations were directly related to the depth of the sample and in no case was the concentration lower in the deeper water layers than near the surface. As expected, nitrate nitrogen in all tributary streams except one was considerably lower than that observed in the lake. In August the nitrate nitrogen range was 0.01 to 0.44 mg/l.

AGRICULTURAL SOURCES OF NITROGEN IN WATER

Agricultural sources of nitrogen result primarily from organic and inorganic materials added to soils for crop nutrition. Movement

TABLE 7.1. Estimate of nutrient contributions from various sources.

Source	Nitrogen		Phosphorus	
	Pounds per year	Usual concentration in discharge	Pounds per year	Usual concentration in discharge
	(millions)	*(mg/l)*	*(millions)*	*(mg/l)*
Domestic waste	1,100–1,600	18–20	200–500	3.5–9.0
Industrial waste	>1,000	0–10,000	†	†
Rural runoff:				
Agricultural land .	1,500–15,000	1–70	120–1,200	0.05–1.1
Nonagricultural land	400–1,900	0.1–0.5	150–750	0.04–0.2
Farm animal waste .	>1,000	†	†	†
Urban runoff	110–1,100	1–10	11–170	0.1–1.5
Rainfall*	30–590	0.1–2.0	3–9	0.01–0.03

Source: Task Group 2610-P Report (1967). Reprinted from the March 1967 issue of *J. Am. Water Works Assoc.* Copyright 1967 by the Am. Water Works Assoc., Inc.

* Considers rainfall contributed directly to water surface.

† Insufficient data available to make estimate.

of these materials has been traced from their soil origin to entrance into surface and groundwater supplies. Several of the following studies indicate the fate of agricultural nitrogen-containing materials after entrance into the environment.

A review paper (Smith, 1967) describes the use of fertilizer salts to supplement nitrogen in soils. This nitrate source feeds vegetation, is lost to the atmosphere by denitrification, and is removed from the soil by erosion and leaching. Organic-matter nitrogen lost from soils is usually attributed to mineralization.

Estimate of Nutrient Contributions from Various Sources

Table 7.1 characterizes nitrate sources in water. The relative magnitude of runoff from agricultural land is noticeably large.

Rural Runoff as a Nitrogen Source

Approximately 742 million hectares of rural land in the United States produce runoff. Major factors in rural runoff are amount of water applied and land use. For example (McGuinness et al., 1960), runoff is greatest for a corn crop, somewhat less for wheat, and least when the land is in meadow. The mean concentration given in milligrams per liter of total nitrogen constituents per storm event with land planted to wheat varies between 6 and 9 (Weidner et al., 1969). These data are losses from a watershed varying in agricultural use.

Agricultural drainage waters contain nitrogen concentrations ranging from 1 to 60 mg/l, mostly in the form of nitrate. Sediment suspended in flowing water may carry relatively high amounts of ammonium nitrogen as well as particulate organic nitrogen. Distribution of nitrogen in river waters in the United States ranges roughly from 0.1 mg/l to 3.0 mg/l.

Annual average nitrogen loss from a watershed drainage of an apple orchard in Ripley, Ohio, was 1.0 kg total nitrogen per hectare. The mean-runoff nitrogen concentration per storm for the apple orchard was 4.9 mg/l total nitrogen. The results of this work indicate that rural runoff is a factor in stream pollution and must be considered as a source of nitrogen in water supplies.

Timmons et al. (1968) have conducted a definitive study on the loss of crop nutrients through runoff. As can be seen from Table 7.2, a study of the Barnes-Aastad Soil, Water, and Conservation Research Association farm near Morris, Minnesota, showed 29.1 kg/ha nitrogen loss in the year 1966, with a high of 9.65 cm of runoff, and 100.7 kg/ha nitrogen loss in 1967, with a high of 11.76 annual centimeters of runoff. Nitrate accounted for the majority of the nitrogen loss and in 1966 was 0.89 and in 1967, 2.9 kg/ha.

UREA MATERIALS

Several materials used as agricultural fertilizers are salts of nitrogen. One of the materials used commercially in large quantities is ureaform. When evaluated as a nitrogen-loading material in soils,

TABLE 7.2. Annual nutrient loss for two seasons for the natural-rainfall erosion plots.

Cropping Treatments	Avg Annual Kilograms Per Hectare Soil Loss	Avg Annual Centimeters Runoff	Avg Kg per Hectare Nutrient Loss				
			Total N*	NH_4-N	NO_3-N	P	K
			1966				
Fallow	8,518.0	9.65	29.1	0.33	0.90	0.04	2.0
Corn-continuous ..	807.0	2.31	4.48	0.11	0.11	0.11	0.56
Corn-rotation	426.0	5.20	2.24	<0.11	0.33	0.11	0.67
Oats-rotation	22.4	0.51	0.11	0.0	<0.11	0.0	<0.11
Hay-rotation	0.0	8.66	0.34	0.0	0.11	0.11	0.90
			1967				
Fallow	23,044.0	11.76	100.8	0.22	0.54	2.9	5.1
Corn-continuous ..	7,039.0	7.56	21.5	0.34	0.90	0.04	1.3
Corn-rotation	1,389.0	5.96	7.5	0.11	0.08	0.11	0.67
Oats-rotation	2,286.0	5.30	10.5	0.11	0.18	0.11	0.67
Hay-rotation	0.0	9.72	6.4	0.0	0.04	0.33	5.8

Source: Timmons et al. (1968). Reprinted with permission.

* Excludes NH_4- and NO_3-N.

it was found to be relatively long lived (about 1 year) and stable (Brown and Volk, 1966). Losses did occur once the nitrogen entered the soil biological cycle. If water-soluble nonurea portions of urea-form were incubated anaerobically with soil, appreciable quantities of hydrogen were produced. Simultaneously NH_4NO_3 was evaluated and in studies where the initial rate of application was 168 kg of nitrogen per hectare it was found that 2 to 5% of the ammonium nitrate was in the soil to a depth of 0 to 15 cm. Ureaform was found in amounts of 18 to 24% in soil from 0 to 15 cm in depth. Of the 168 kg nitrogen per hectare application it was noted that the percent excess was 9.091 of ammonium nitrogen and 8.973 of nitrate nitrogen, whereas the ureaform excess produced was 9.907 ureaform nitrogen.

The loss of urea nitrogen on leaching as traced by lysimeter studies was examined (Overrein, 1968) during a 12-week experimental period, and it was shown that at urea application rates of less than 250 kg of nitrogen per hectare, loss was slight. At application rates of 1,000 kg of urea nitrogen per hectare, treatment was followed by a leaching loss equivalent to 5% of the added fertilizer nitrogen. The volatile ammonia gas loss was also characterized. The highest total of accumulated loss of ammonia was equal to 3.5% of the added urea nitrogen. No gaseous nitrogen oxides were produced. Trace amounts of tagged molecular nitrogen were recovered in the atmosphere above lysimeters receiving the urea nitrogen during tests in which the higher application rate was used.

NITRATE AND AMMONIUM MATERIALS

Ammonium nitrate and urea differ considerably in the extent to which they are adsorbed by the soil. It is reasonable to expect that they vary in their susceptibility to loss from the soil by leaching into surface runoff water. Urea, however, is hydrolyzed to ammonium ion and ammonium ion is nitrified to nitrate in soils. A time interval, therefore, must be allowed between fertilizer application and occurrence of rainfall before computing nitrate runoff into surface waters. Such a study was conducted (Moe et al., 1968) and the ammonium nitrogen losses from urea-treated plots were approximately equal to those from the ammonium-nitrate-treated plots during artificial rainfall applications. In a second set of artificial rainfall applications, losses of ammonium nitrogen averaged 40% less. It was concluded that the ammonium nitrogen is less susceptible to runoff loss in the urea-treated plots than in the ammonium-nitrate-treated plots. An explanation is that ammonium nitrate, because of its high ionization, would be adsorbed and held near the surface of the soil. A non-ionized urea would be carried farther down into the soil with the first increment of rainfall and would be less subject to surface runoff loss.

It was found that urea is rapidly hydrolyzed to ammonia in the soil; the only measurable amounts of urea occurred in the runoff from sod plots and resulted from the direct washing of urea from the surface vegetation. Total nitrogen losses from all plots ranged between 2.4 and 12.7%. These results are very similar to those of Moe et al.

(1968). As a general conclusion, the amount of nitrogen in the run-off water from soils treated in this manner would not contribute appreciably to nitrate pollution of surface-water resources.

White et al. (1967) studied movement of NH_4NO_3 applied on a soil surface at the concentration of 224 kg/ha. Six and three-tenths centimeters of artificial rainfall were applied in a 2-hour period, during which the runoff from fallow soil was 4.9 mg/l and from sod 2.1 mg/l. After a few moments, most of the soluble nitrogen moved into the soil and was inaccessible to erosion processes.

On the southern high plains (Lotspeich et al., 1969) estimates are that 0.2% of the fertilizer nitrogen applied is found in surface-water runoff. In nearly all the playas of the southern high plains, the nitrate content is less than 1.0 mg/l, revealing the fact that nitrogen fertilizer applied to the farmland adds little nitrate to the surface water.

A clue to nitrogen runoff from soil, resulting in enrichment of nitrogen in water, may be discovered in the data of Pratt et al. (1967). It was found that the ratio of nitrogen removal to total crop yield was higher with $Ca(NO_3)_2$ treatment than with ammonium sources. The largest amount of nitrogen removed by drainage water as well as the highest nitrogen depletion occurred in a soil relatively high in organic content. Lack of organic matter may explain low nitrate runoff on the southern high plains.

A study of 82,029 irrigated hectares (Carter et al., 1969) illustrated that subsurface drainage water contains more nitrate nitrogen than does the irrigation water, but concentration rarely exceeds 5.0 mg/l of nitrogen. Concentrations of nitrogen in surface drainage waters are only slightly higher than concentrations in the irrigation water.

A study in Britain demonstrated that the amount of nitrogenous fertilizers applied to agricultural land has doubled in the last 10 years. Land drainage has been shown to contribute much inorganic nitrogen to rivers. In the Great Ouse River (Owens and Wood, 1968) sewage effluents contributed a small proportion of the total concentration of nitrogen, silicon, chloride, and sulfate; however, the bulk of the phosphorus could be attributed to the effluent sources. Table 7.3

TABLE 7.3. Ranges of some selected nutrients in sewage effluents and land drainage entering the Great Ouse: Concentrations in the river water are also included.

Nutrient	Sewage Effluent	Land Drainage	River Water
	(mg/l)	(mg/l)	(mg/l)
Carbon (soluble)	6.7–24.0	2.8–8.0	3.5–12.4
Ammonium-N	0.0–48.0	0.0–0.5	0.0–9.8
Nitrate-N	0.0–35.0	5.5–29.4	3.0–14.2
Nitrite-N	0.0–14.5	0.01–0.1	0.01–0.4
Organic-N	0.0–13.6	0.3–0.9	0.0–2.9
Potassium	16.0–32.0	6.0–16.5	6.8–9.0
Total soluble phosphorus ...	3.0–14.0	0.02–0.3	0.17–0.73
Silicon	1.9–11.0	0.7–5.0	0.07–5.0

Source: Owens and Wood (1968). Reprinted with permission from M. Owens. Copyright 1968, Pergamon Publ. Co.

(Owens and Wood, 1968) lists the nutrients entering the Great Ouse River yearly and their sources.

Figure 7.1 shows the estimated total quantity of nutrients supplied by sewage effluents in comparison with the total load of nutrients in the river. Only about 10% of the nitrogen in the river could be accounted for by the amounts discharged in sewage effluents. It was assumed that increase in river flow between the influent streams and the downstream limit of the reach, other than that from the sewage effluent, was derived from land drainage and that this land drainage would have the same average concentration of nutrients as the land drain sampled. Estimated nutrient loads are between 1.0 and 2.3 times greater than those actually determined. Hence, the assumption that the increase in load results from land drainage may be in error.

About 3.15×10^6 kg of nitrogen were carried by the Great Ouse River in 1966. If all of the material flowing down the river were derived from land drainage, the flows of nitrogen per unit of catchment area would be 18.5. The amount of nitrogen applied per unit

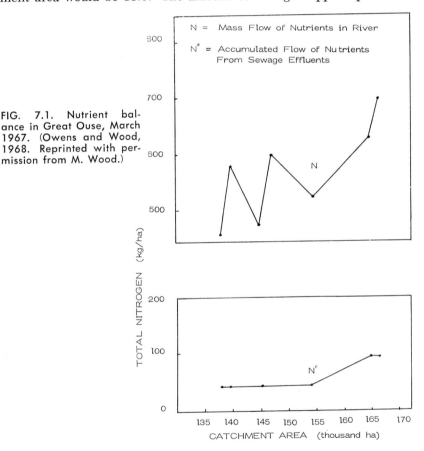

FIG. 7.1. Nutrient balance in Great Ouse, March 1967. (Owens and Wood, 1968. Reprinted with permission from M. Wood.)

N = Mass Flow of Nutrients in River

N^e = Accumulated Flow of Nutrients From Sewage Effluents

TOTAL NITROGEN (kg/ha)

CATCHMENT AREA (thousand ha)

area in the Ouse basin, according to statistics supplied by the Ministry of Agriculture, Fisheries and Food, was 65 kg/ha.

TIME VARIATION

One study (Olsen et al., 1969) related that more leaching of nitrate nitrogen occurred between fall and spring than during the growing season and more under fallow than cropped conditions.

TILE DRAINAGE EFFLUENT

Effluents from a tile drainage system in irrigated areas in the San Joaquin Valley of California showed that initial tile effluent from a previously unirrigated, noncropped area had a nitrogen concentration of 1.0 mg/l. Another system that had been planted to alfalfa had a low discharge over a year's period and yielded a range of nitrogen between 2.0 and 14.3 mg/l. In systems where high rates of nitrogen fertilizer were applied, the concentrations ranged up to 62.4 mg/l. Concentrations of nitrate in all systems ranged from 1.8 to 62.4 mg/l, with a weighted average of 25.1 (Johnston et al., 1969).

Nitrogen can be carried directly into surface drains with tailwater from fields where fertilizer is being applied in the irrigation water. In addition, nitrogen can also come from nonirrigated agricultural land. A further source of nitrogen is soil from erosion, with resulting increase in sediment load, plant nutrients, and pesticides. Soil nitrogen is sporadically released to water, such release being produced and greatly influenced by intensity of precipitation.

It was shown that in sand columns (Preul and Schroepfer, 1968) the breakthrough curve for ammonium nitrogen occurs between 0.5 and 1.0 in units of throughput volume per column weight measured in liters per kilogram of soil. Flow rates varied from 200 to 1,170 ml/day, pH ranged from 7.1 to 7.6, and nitrogen absorption ranged from 24.7 to 126.0 μg/g of ammonium nitrogen, at equilibrium. Discharge velocities were approximately 4.93 cm/day at flow rates of 1,000 ml/day. The conclusions of this study are that movement of nitrogen in soils is controlled by adsorption and biological action, and that where nitrogen is in a nitrate form at the pH of usual wastewaters there is no impairment to nitrogen movement. Biological interference is minimized under flow conditions with limited oxygen tension. These results indicate a minimal vertical flow. In the study indicated, the major part of nitrification was restricted to within 0.61 meter of the surface. The possibility of lateral flow, however, would tend to move nitrogen into surface waters. Leachates of nitrogen (NH_4NO_3)-treated soil (Krause and Batsch, 1968) contained 4 to 7 mg/l ammonium nitrogen; the soil lost 88% of its treated nitrogen between September and December. Untreated soils slowly lost nitrate nitrogen.

IRRIGATION RETURN FLOW

A study of irrigation return flow in the Yakima River Basin, Washington (Sylvester and Seabloom, 1963), was made for an irrigated area of 151,870 hectares during an irrigation season extending from April through September. Average water diversion was 20,000 m³ per hectare per year of which approximately 5,240 m³ was applied to land; the remainder was lost in canal seepage and canal evaporation wastage.

It was established that the evapotranspiration loss in the irrigation water return would result in a salt concentration of 1.7. The nitrate content of the return due to evapotranspiration, leaching, and ion exchange was 10 times greater than in the applied water. Removal of 37 kg/ha of nitrate resulted from irrigation leaching.

Salts and sediments are of great concern to water users (Peterson et al., 1969). Salt and silt create the most difficult problems to irrigation, agriculture, and subsequent users of return flow. Under certain conditions, however, animal waste, plant nutrient, and toxic elements become equally important.

Nitrogen Movement in Soils

In a leaching experiment (Sinha and Prasad, 1967), urea was found to be distributed mainly within the top 10 centimeters of the soil column and very little of it leached down below this depth. Retention of urea in soils appears to be due to its conversion to ammoniacal form.

In a typical situation in the San Joaquin Valley from 1962 to 1966, it was found that the subsurface drainage water of fields irrigated with water containing 1.7 mg/l of nitrate nitrogen had nitrate levels averaging 44.5 mg/l. Fertilization consisted of adding 187 kg nitrate nitrogen per hectare per year (Doneen, 1968).

It was also found that nitrate concentrations of drainage waters from different areas generally paralleled the amount of fertilizer nitrogen.

LATERAL MOVEMENT OF NITRATES

Smith (1967) cites data to illustrate the diminishing concentration of nitrates 61 to 91 meters from the source origin. A second conclusion was that at the site under observation, leaching of fertilizer nitrogen was relatively insignificant in comparison to other sources.

FATE OF NITRATE NITROGEN IN TROPICAL SOILS

Macrae et al. (1968) in a study of submergence of tropical soils determined that considerable proportions of applied nitrate nitrogen had been immobilized into the soil organic fraction. Six Philippine soils were used in the study to trace the fate of added nitrate nitrogen after submergence.

Occurrence of Nitrates in Well Water

Shallow wells frequently contain greater nitrate concentrations than deep wells. As has been shown by many workers, this may be a result of improper well construction. Shallow wells and deep wells can be polluted by nitrates, either leached from the aquifer or transmitted to the aquifer by percolating waters. Sources of nitrogen in deep wells are strata through old wells which have been abandoned, pumped wells with rusted or perforated casings, improper sewage and waste disposal, natural sinkholes, and river valleys recharge. Nitrate levels fluctuate in wells on an annual basis.

A survey of nitrates in private water supplies in Morgan County, Missouri, made by the Missouri Division of Health (Inglish, 1967) showed that in 157 well waters tested, 40 contained no nitrate, 27 contained less than 1 mg/l, 44 contained between 1 and 20 mg/l, 20 contained between 20 and 45 mg/l, and 23 contained over 45 mg/l, with the highest value being 200 mg/l. Of these wells only 13 were cased to a depth of 30.5 meters or more and only 4 were free of nitrate.

Nitrates in Groundwater Supplies

Appearance of excessively high amounts of nitrates in groundwaters has been considered an indication of wastewater infiltration into the supply. The wastewater may originate from septic tank effluents, waste stabilization ponds, waste treatment plant effluents, sludge lagoons, sanitary landfills, privies, barnyards, leaking sewers, irrigation systems, and similar sources. Of course, these sources carry public health implications. Comly (1945), Metzler (1950), and Whitehead and Moxon (1952) have reported on the hazard of nitrogen in water supplies. One manifestation of nitrates is the disease infant methemoglobinemia. Livestock, chiefly hogs and cattle, are affected adversely and exhibit poor growth characteristics. Nitrates can cause gastroenteritis and diarrhea. In some instances, high nitrogen levels in water can be lethal.

LIMITS OF NITROGEN IN WATER SUPPLIES

Forty-five mg/l nitrate is the upper limit set by the U.S. Public Health Service for city potable water supplies.

Some of the most immediate sources of nitrate and nitrite in groundwaters are domestic sewage effluents, fertilizers, and wastes from corrals. Mean concentrations of nitrate nitrogen from wells in nonirrigated and irrigated regions of southern Oahu were 1 ± 0.22 mg/l and 8.2 ± 2.4 mg/l, respectively (Mink, 1962). Mink attributed

TABLE 7.4.   Characterization of waters in the San Luis Valley, Colorado.

Water Characteristics Rio Grande River		Aquifer Characteristics
Total dissolved solids	41–120 mg/l	Unconfined to depth of 100 feet
Character	Ca(HCO₃)₂	Wells are 35–100 feet in depth
pH	6.7–7.4	Total dissolved solids 100–400 mg/l
		pH 7.0–7.8

Source: R. K. Glanzman and J. M. Klein. (Data to be published.) Private communication.

this difference to percolation of nitrate materials previously added to the system in the form of fertilizer.

A study made by the U.S. Geological Survey in the San Luis Valley, Colorado, conducted by Glanzman and Klein[1] of the Colorado District found relatively high nitrate concentrations in wells at depths of 11 to 30 meters.

The San Luis Valley has an arid high-altitude climate with 15 to 18 cm of rainfall annually. The Rio Grande is the major surface-water source; its nitrate concentration ranges from 0.0 to 2.3 mg/l. Table 7.4 gives the other characteristics. Soil characteristics are given in Table 7.5.

Nitrogen application on the surface soils of San Luis Valley was 112 kg of nitrogen per hectare per year in the form of ammonium sulfate. The nitrogen was applied by disking, banding, or sideband-ing. These treatments were followed by copious applications of water. Considering that the water table was within 30 cm of the surface, it is likely that the high nitrogen content in wells was due to percola-tion from surface applications and especially from irrigation ditches, which are used to disperse the fertilizer in liquid form to soil sur-faces.

Figure 7.2 is a contour map showing concentrations of nitrate in the San Luis Valley. The irrigation ditches correspond to the lines of high nitrate concentration. It is reasonable to conclude that some of the nitrate infiltration is coincident with the surface route of the main irrigation ditches.

The fertilization practices followed in this valley incorporate large amounts of ammonium sulfate, applied as dissolved solute, in irrigation water. Considering the high water table and the general lack of other nitrogen sources such as feedlots, septic tanks, and sewage-processing tanks, it appears that in this case the nitrogen source is inorganic fertilizer.

ANIMAL VARIATION

Nitrates tend to accumulate at the top of a groundwater column. As leaching through a soil is a function of physical parameters, such

---

1. Glanzman, R. K., and Klein, J. M. (Data to be published.) Private communication.

TABLE 7.5. **Characterization of the principle on the fan, San Luis Valley, Colorado.**

Gunbarrel loamy sand	0–48 inches course loamy sand 48–60 inches sand to sand and gravel

	Percent Passing Sieve Size			pH	Per- meability	Water- holding Capacity
	No. 4	No. 10	No. 200		(in./hr)	(in./in.)
0–48"	90–100	90–100	15–30	7.9–9.0	2.5–5.0	0.05
48–60"	75–90	65–80	5–15	7.9–9.0	>5.	0.05

	Depth to sand and gravel	24–60 inches
	Water table range	1–5 feet

Sand	83–92%	pH	
Silt	4–11%	Salinity millimhos/cm	1.3–1.8
Clay	4–7 %	Organic matter	0.4 or less
		CaCO₃ equivalent percent	0.7–2.3

Moisture at saturation 19–20
Cation exchange capacity 5.0–8.3

Source: R. K. Glanzman and J. M. Klein. (Data to be published.) Private communication.

as soil permeability, soil porosity, temperature, rainfall, snow melt, or volumes of irrigation water, it is obvious that nitrate concentration in a water supply will vary according to the season of the year and the amount of water flow at any given time.

ANIMAL SOURCES OF NITROGEN

Numbers of livestock vary throughout the United States as follows: 74% of the hogs, 42% of the cattle, and 39% of the poultry are contained in the north-central region (Loehr, 1969); the south-central and western regions contain 41% of the cattle; and the poultry population is evenly divided throughout the country. Dramatic increases in numbers of cattle have been noted in the United States. For example, an increase of 36 million head has occurred during the past 25 years, and 17 million of this increase occurred during the last 8 years. The poultry industry today is a $3.4 billion industry. Cattle feedlots have expanded rapidly also in the last few years. Livestock on American farms produce about 1,814 teragrams of manure each year. In units of population equivalents, the nitrogen contribution of domestic wastes is estimated to be 3.6 to 5.4 kg per year, or 0.015 kg per capita per day. For chickens, the nitrogen contribution per animal per day is 0.001; for swine, 0.02; for dairy cattle, 0.18; and for beef cattle, 0.14. Swine, dairy cattle, and beef cattle on a population-equivalent basis produce more nitrogen per capita per day than that derived from domestic sewage wastes. The production of animal wastes in the United States exceeds the waste produced by the human population by about 5 to 1 on a BOD (biological oxygen demand) basis, 10 to 1 on a total-dry-solids basis, or 7 to 1 on a total-nitrogen basis (Table 7.6).

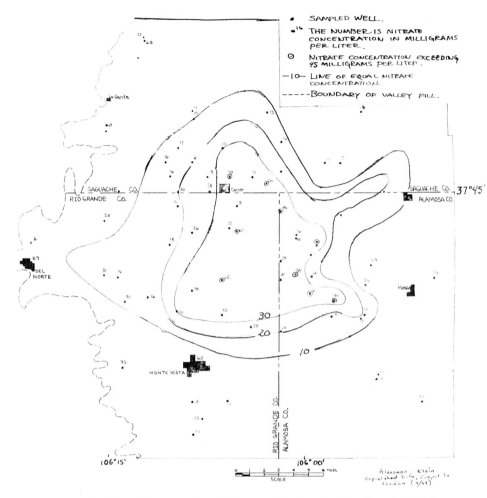

FIG. 7.2. Concentration of nitrate, Rio Grande Fan, San Luis Valley, Colorado.

Nitrates in Wells

Analysis of 6,000 rural water supplies (Keller and Smith, 1967; Smith, 1967) indicated that the sources of nitrogen were animal wastes, improperly constructed shallow wells, and septic-tank drainage. There was some evidence of nitrogen infiltration from heavy annual applications of nitrogen fertilizer. The soil was an alluvial sand. Clay soils generally do not transmit nitrogen. In this study, livestock were considered a more important source of contamination than nitrogen fertilizer. None of the reservoirs sampled showed increases in nitrate due to fertilization. It was thought that nitrate infiltration is relatively slow. The infiltration mechanism involves

TABLE 7.6. Average animal waste characteristics.

| Specie (1) | Kilograms per Animal per Day | | | Per Capita Equivalent*† | | |
	BOD₅ (2)	Total dry solids (3)	Total‡ nitrogen (4)	BOD₅ (5)	Total dry solids (6)	Total nitrogen (7)
Chickens	0.0068	0.027	0.001	0.11	0.09	0.11
Swine	0.136	0.41	0.023	1.7	1.7	1.5
Dairy Cattle ..	0.45	4.54	0.18	8.0	18.0	12.0
Beef Cattle	0.45	4.54	0.14	6.0	18.0	9.0

Source: Loehr (1969). Reprinted with permission from R. C. Loehr.

* Based on average characteristics in municipal sewage: 0.077 kg BOD₅ per capita per day; 0.25 kg total solids per capita per day; and 0.015 kg total nitrogen per capita per day.

† Number of people equivalent to one animal.

‡ Total Kjeldahl nitrogen.

trapping soil fissures during drought and further infiltration washed during times of heavy rains. Indeed, without microorganism populations to reduce nitrates to ammonia, the nitrates persist.

Nitrogen from sinkholes and cave leaching is a source of nitrate in wells. It was estimated that as many as 1,450 known caves in Missouri contain bat guano. In Cooper County, Missouri, nearly 50% of drilled wells, over 85% of dug wells, and 80% of springs contained more than 5 mg/l nitrogen. Keller and Smith (1967) attribute this to the following sources: fertilizers, feedlots, bat guano, and biological waste materials.

Waterfowl as a Source of Nitrogen

Duck wastes are quoted as being as high as 0.95 kg of fixed nitrogen per duck per year. Estimating 100 million waterfowl in the United States, they would produce 91 to 227 million kilograms of nitrogen per year. Wild duck nutrient contributions to 1,416-hectare Lake Chautauqua in Illinois were 14.3 kg of total nitrogen per hectare of water (Paloumpis and Starrett, 1960).

Feedlots as a Source of Nitrogen

Many workers have shown that feedlot runoff pollutes streams; such runoff has high ammonia concentrations and reduces the oxygen content. At 4.41 cm of rain per hour, nitrogen concentrations in the form of ammonia can run as high as 400 mg/l within an hour after the rain starts. Water which has moved through feedlots commonly contains nitrates and ammonium compounds, and has an offensive odor. The animal wastes in feedlots and in other areas of containment can, under the proper conditions, act as sources of nitrogen in both surface waters and groundwaters. Typical examples are given below.

It has been confirmed that groundwater under feedlots is usually contaminated by nitrate (Stewart et al., 1967, 1968). It has also been shown, however, that nitrate levels in the range of 10 to 30 mg/l are found in groundwater beneath irrigated fields.

Atmospheric ammonia measured near feedlots (Hutchinson and Viets, 1969) was as much as 20 times greater than near control sites. The conclusion was that surface waters in the immediate vicinity of a feedlot can become enriched in nitrogen by absorption of atmospheric ammonia volatilized from the feedlot. These data seem to indicate that not only are runoff and percolation sources of nitrogen from feedlots, but atmospheric pollution is a serious consideration as well.

Data from the above study show that at a sampling station 0.4 km west of a 90,000 unit feedlot, 2.8 kg/ha of ammonia were absorbed each week, which would be 146 kg/ha on an annual basis. In other sites where no feedlots were located, the weekly ammonia nitrogen absorption was 0.15 kg/ha.

Hanway et al. (1963) found evidence for the fact that nitrates are more concentrated below or near the area of a waste accumulation or disposal, such as manure piles, feedlots, septic tanks, disposal fields, cesspools, and privies, than in other areas of a fertilized field. Nitrate also may be marshalled in water under low areas and waterways that convey runoff from higher ground. Water which percolates through feedlots, decomposing peat soils, heavily mineralized soils, or other nitrogen sources moves nitrates to the groundwater.

Stewart et al. (1968) found that nitrate concentrations in soil under feedlots ranged from none to more than 5,604 kg/ha in a 6.1-meter profile. They found that even though the ratio of irrigated lands to feedlots was 200:1, calculations based on the average content of the irrigated fields, excluding alfalfa, and the rate of water moving through these profiles suggested that 28 to 34 kg of nitrogen per hectare were lost annually to the water table. This indicated that feedlots contribute very large amounts of nitrate to the soil profile with respect to irrigated land. An important observation is that feedlots are usually located near homesteads and thus have a pronounced effect on rural water supplies.

The amount of nitrate found under cultivated dry land was significant in relation to historic loss of total nitrogen during cultivation. Studies have shown that total nitrogen in dry-land soils decreases about 50% during 30 to 50 years of cultivation. A large part of this decrease cannot be accounted for by crop removal. Lotspeich et al. (1969) pointed out the negligible loss of nitrogen in the Great Plains because of low rainfall. Losses by volatilization and erosion were emphasized but also seemed to be minimal.

Collected data suggest that leaching losses may have been greatly underestimated. There is an accumulation of nitrate in the 2.4- to 3.0-meter depth just below the rooting depth of most dry-land crops. The rainfall in the study area averaged about 38 cm per year.

Stewart et al. (1968) list the chemical data for water samples

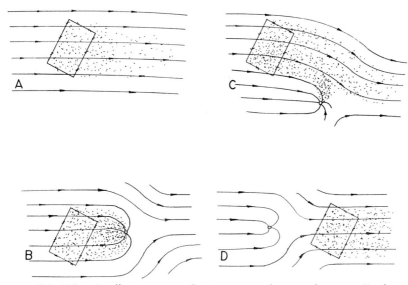

FIG. 7.3. Feedlot sources of nitrogen and groundwater. (Engberg, 1967.)

taken from beneath feedlots and adjacent irrigated fields. The average concentration of ammonium nitrate of the waters beneath 28 irrigated fields was 0.2 mg/l. On the other hand, water from beneath 29 feedlots averaged 4.5 mg/l ammonium nitrogen. It was also observed that samples high in organic carbon contained high amounts of ammonium nitrogen. Nitrite was usually high under feedlots. These results indicate the kinds and amounts of materials moving through soil to groundwater.

The importance of well location with respect to feedlots was demonstrated by Engberg (1967). In a study in Holt County, Nebraska, high nitrate concentrations were observed in domestic wells. In Figure 7.3A, an example is given of undisturbed lateral movement of high nitrate water in the direction of groundwater movement. Figures 7.3B and 7.3C illustrate well pumping that induces movement of high nitrate water into wells. Figure 7.3D illustrates a properly located well that will be free of nitrate. (Also see Fig. 7.4.)

The aforementioned studies make it apparent that livestock-feeding operations are becoming more concentrated and that their effect on groundwater and surface water is indeed noticeable as a source of nitrogen.

RURAL WASTE

Barnyard Wastes

The California State Water Pollution Control Board (1953) reports 1,300 mg/l of ammonia and organic nitrogen in percolate from refuse.

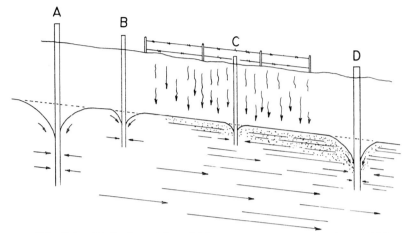

FIG. 7.4. Wells A and B yield low nitrate water, C and D yield high nitrate water. (Engberg, 1967.)

Feeds

Nitrates are likely to be found in feeds including forages, hay, weeds, fodder, silages, or pasture grasses grown on soils that have received heavy applications of manure or nitrogen fertilizers (Hanway et al., 1963). This is especially true when drought, shade, disease, herbicide applications, or other interfering factors affect normal growth and development of the plant. Nitrate concentrations are highest in immature plants. Stems of plants concentrate the majority of nitrate; intermediate levels are found in the leaves, and low levels in the grain.

URBAN WASTE

Domestic Wastewater

Domestic wastewater effluents range in concentrations from 18 to 28 mg/1 of nitrogen (exclusive of molecular nitrogen) without specific treatment for nitrogen removal, according to the Task Group 2610 Report (1967).

Ammonia nitrogen is the predominant form of nitrogen in effluents from primary and high-rate treatment plants.

Although it is not normal to add sewage to a water supply, it is possible that by filtration and proper sewage treatment, waters that once contained sewage could safely be added to a water supply. The concentration of nitrogen in a settled domestic sewage is approximately 80 to 120 mg/1.

The urban runoff which accumulated from three streams in an area containing large reservoirs, roads, and some logging, but no human habitation, is shown in Table 7.7 (Sylvester, 1961). The

TABLE 7.7.   Mean nutrient concentrations from runoff sources in parts per billion.

	Total Phosphorus (P)	Soluble Phosphorus (P)	Nitrates (N)	Total Kjeldahl Nitrogen (N)
Urban street drainage	208	76	527	2,010
Urban street drainage (median) ...	154	22	420	410
Streams from forested areas	69	7	130	74
Subsurface irrigation drains	216	184	2,690	172
Surface irrigation drains	251	162	1,250	205
Green Lake	76	16	84	340

Source: Sylvester (1961).

sources were the Yakima River irrigation return flow drains and the Green Lake in Washington near Seattle. Nitrate nitrogen levels were generally above 200 μg/l. The mean nutrient concentration was about 800 μg/l.

The average per-capita refuse originating from food and other materials imported into the Lake Tahoe watershed is 0.9 kg per day of which 1% is nitrogen (McGauhey et al., 1963).

Nitrogen compounds used for crop fertilization and disposal of sewage and industrial wastes were pinpointed as sources of groundwater nitrate (Navone et al., 1963).

Groundwater Infiltration

Nitrate movement downward in a silt loam is relatively small (Herron et al., 1968) and corroborates the fact that there is a lack of downward movement of nitrogen from the surface.

Fifty wells were examined in a 31-square-kilometer area (Behnke and Haskell, 1968) in the northeastern section of Fresno, California. Most of the wells were unperforated, open-bottomed casings 27 to 43 meters long. Behnke and Haskell identified areas of increased nitrate concentrations on a contour map and drew a nitrate concentration map of the area. The background nitrate concentration was 11 to 15 mg/l. In a zone directly under the Clovis sewage treatment plant, a concentration of 35 mg/l nitrate was found. A second area of 25 mg/l concentration extended in a zone in a southwesterly direction and coincided with the strike of the flow line in the same vicinity as determined by a water-table contour map. A third zone of nitrogen underlies a subdivision containing individual septic tanks. The nitrate concentration again ranged from 35 to 25 mg/l. It was noted that nitrate concentrations decreased from 50 to 25 mg/l in a lateral distance of eight-tenths of a kilometer. This study also found the nitrate concentrations in the top 3 meters of the groundwater body was one-third greater than in the rest of the water column.

Leaching and Erosion

A study conducted in California (Stout and Bureau, 1967) showed that a major part of the nitrate reaching underground aquifers was from urban areas and sewage fields. In addition, it was found that agricultural crops reduce the amount of nitrate in irrigation water that returns to lower soil depths.

In Missouri, where the precipitation normally exceeds evapotranspiration, soils are acid on the surface. Salts that weather from soil minerals are regularly leached and are a normal constituent of drainage water. Hence, elements from the land that can pollute streams are derived more from erosion sediments than from leachates. The main sources of sediment that enter water courses are soil eroded from urban developments, from highway construction areas, and from agricultural land. Losses of essential mineral nutrients during the past half century in the United States have been greater from erosion than from crop removal. On soils that have low exchange capacities, leaching of nitrate can be serious.

Storm Water

Storm-water runoff, because of storm overflows, can supply some nitrogen to rivers. For example, analysis of River Erwell at Ratcliffe showed that ammoniacal nitrogen was in the order of 4.9 mg/l and albuminoid nitrogen in the order of 32.6 mg/l (Klein et al., 1962).

Storm runoff measured over a year's period from an 11-hectare residential, commercial, urban area indicated that phosphorus (as phosphate) and total nitrogen are 9 and 11%, respectively, of the estimated raw sewage content from sources in the area. At Coshocton, Ohio, two storms with 5.61 and 12.93 cm of rainfall per storm produced runoff of 61.7 to 714 kiloliters per hectare. Phosphate in the runoff water ranged from 0.06 to 0.47 kg/ha and total nitrogen ranged from 0.22 to 6.86 kg/ha (U.S. Public Health Service, 1964).

INDUSTRIAL WASTE

Several substances containing nitrogen are commonly found in industrial wastes. For example, ammonia is a waste material from gas and coke manufacturing and other chemical manufacturing processes. Cyanide is evolved during gas manufacture, plating, case hardening, and metal cleaning. Nitrogen compounds also originate from explosive factories and other chemical works.

In November 1966 a severe ammonia infestation reached the Becva River in Czechoslovakia. The pollution was caused by a chemical plant where the equipment for the production of granulated superphosphate was taken out of operation. Simultaneously, the ammonia water storage tanks were cleaned. During cleaning, the inlet to the chemical sewage systems became clogged, and the water overflowed into the normal sewage system. This resulted in severe contamination of the river and led to poisoning of fish along a 20-kilometer length from the site of entrance (Dockal and Varecha, 1967).

A study conducted on Lake Norrviken in central Sweden during the years 1961 to 1962 indicated that wastewater from a yeast factory was responsible for more than 80% of the nitrogen and 70% of the phosphorus found in the lake. Only about 40% of the nitrogen and 50% of the phosphorus input to the lake leaves the lake through its outflow. The rest of the phosphorus accumulated in the sediments, but a large fraction of the nitrogen was presumed to undergo denitrification to free nitrogen. On the basis of the ratio of the content of nitrogen to phosphorus in surface sediment, this fraction was calculated to be about 37% of the total nitrogen input to the lake or 60% of the amount which does not leave the lake through the outflow (Ahlgren, 1967).

PRISTINE SOURCES OF NITROGEN

In areas never touched by man for purposes of building or cultivation, nitrate from natural deposits and normal decomposition of organic matter is present in soil profiles and groundwaters. Nitrate accumulates in salty areas of semiarid and arid regions where surface waters evaporate. Also irrigation without adequate drainage accelerates nitrate accumulation. These natural sources cannot be neglected in any appraisal of a nitrate infiltration problem. Unless such additions of nitrogen to a basin or watershed are balanced by withdrawals or denitrification losses, soluble nitrogen will accumulate in surface and soil profiles.

In many cases, natural sources of nitrogen are sufficient to cause large nitrogen inputs into an area. A good example of this situation was reported by Frink (1967) wherein the nutrient input from a largely forested watershed with no overt source of pollution was found to be adequate to support abundant vegetative growth. In addition, a reservoir was noted in which the upper centimeter of the bottom sediment of a lake contained at least 10 times the estimated annual input of nitrogen and phosphorus to the lake. A nitrogen budget of this lake indicated that in kilograms of nitrogen per lake, the annual input from the watershed was 30,700; the output from the lake was 27,500, resulting in a mean net input of 3,200 kg/yr for the lake.

POND WATER

Ponded water also received nitrate from the sources mentioned above. Ponded water that contains abundant algal or other growth, however, has less nitrate than water which does not contain this growth. Apparently the plant growth uses excess nitrate about as rapidly as the nitrate enters the pond. Ponded water also loses nitrate by denitrification and anaerobic decomposition of organic matter in the ponded water. This nitrate may eventually escape as molecular nitrogen.

Autotrophic organisms, particularly those of green algae, metabolically produce hydroxylamine in highly eutrophicated water (Koprivik and Burian, 1966). This biological origin of hydroxylamine is confirmed by the fact that higher concentrations were observed at night than during the day. The occurrence of hydroxylamine in pond water is influenced by its relation to the oxygen content. The authors find great differences between origin and existence of this chemical in water.

Infiltration from Ponds

Passage of water through the ground by infiltration from ponds has little or no effect on nutrient concentrations in the Tahoe Basin near Lake Tahoe, Nevada (McGauhey et al., 1963), and subsequent flow through the ground affects only partial removal of nutrients. Nitrate appears to be transported by groundwater without significant reduction by earth materials. Percolation of water through the ground does materially reduce the concentrations of other chemical constituents. Wisconsin stabilization ponds indicate annual per-capita contributions of 1.9 kg of inorganic nitrogen. Nine Springs sewage treatment plant, serving a 135,000 population with primary and secondary filtration, had an annual per-capita contribution of 3.9 kg inorganic nitrogen. In contrast, surface runoff in one instance was found to contain 43 kg/ha of inorganic nitrogen on a 20% slope and 20 kg/ha on an 8% slope (Eck et al., 1957). The annual contribution of inorganic nitrogen per hectare of drainage area loading Lake Monona was 4.9 kg, Lake Waubesa 5.5 kg, and Lake Kegonsa 7.2 kg (Sawyer et al., 1945). (See Table 7.8.)

MAN-MADE NITROGEN SOURCES

Deforestation

Nitrate concentration in stream water from an experimentally deforested watershed (Likens et al., 1969) increased from 0.9 mg/l before removal of the vegetation to 53 mg/l two years later. The nitrate mobilization was attributed to increased microbial nitrification and was equivalent to all the other net cationic increases and anionic decreases observed in the drainage water of the Hubbard Brook Experimental Forest in central New Hampshire.

Dredging

Enlargement of the Chesapeake and Delaware Canal and its approaches required that large volumes of bottom material be re-

TABLE 7.8 Distribution of nitrogen in ponds.

	Raw Sewage	Ponds							
		1	2	3	4	5	6	7	8
Org.-N (mg/l) ...	26.3	12.5	14.5	11.2	13.7	16.4	8.9	8.1	7.5
NH$_3$-N (mg/l) ...	32.4	46.4	52.5	48.7	45.0	42.5	40.0	28.1	18.9
NO$_3$-N (mg/l) ...	0.0	0.0	0.0	0.3	0.5	0.2	0.5	0.2	0.8
Algae (no./ml) ...	Nil	7×10^3	7.1×10^6	2.4×10^7	1.4×10^7	1.2×10^5	7.2×10^3	2.9×10^3	8.5×10^3

Source: Parker (1962).

moved from channel areas and relocated. In the Chesapeake approach area, about 7.4×10^6 cubic meters of silt and clay were scheduled to be dredged. As a result of data gathered and projected by Biggs, it was concluded that such action would increase the total phosphate and nitrogen by a factor of 50 or 100 over ambient levels in the immediate vicinity of the proposed disposal plant (Biggs, 1968).

SUMMARY AND CONCLUSIONS

It has been shown that there are multiple sources of nitrogen to water supplies. These include atmospheric, geologic, biogenic, rural runoff, urban runoff, sewage, irrigation, return flow, animals, sinkholes, caves, feedlots, pollen, rural waste, industrial waste, pond waters, deforestation, and land stripping, among others.

Generally, salts of nitrogen applied as fertilizer do not move either vertically or laterally to any significant extent. Movement is a function of soil type, soil saturation, applied water volume, and temperature. A few examples of such movement to groundwater and surface-water supplies and the relative significance of such movement were discussed.

Nitrate in a nonsalt form seems to have higher soil infiltration capacity than salt nitrogen. This is dependent, however, upon the physical conditions of the soil and the hydrology of the region.

Other sources not directly used as nutrients to plants, such as soil erosion, urban and industrial wastes, natural soil nitrogen loss, land renovation, deforestation, and atmospheric fallout, were evaluated with respect to their importance as a source of nitrogen in water. In general, industrial waste, rural runoff (including agricultural land and nonagricultural land runoff), farm animal waste, and domestic waste are the dominant sources in surface waters.

In groundwater supplies, specifically wells, the usual sources of nitrogen are feedlots, privies, septic tanks, or other waste forms. A few examples were given of geologic sources within the aquifer either as nitrate deposits or nitrate minerals.

Dissemination of nitrogen from a plant-nutrient source is dependent upon the geology and hydrology extant at the nitrogen origin. With sufficient data describing these variables it should be possible to characterize the potential for retention or loss of nitrogen from the point of origin and the possibility of entrance into a surface or groundwater supply. Certainly, with the varied sources of nitrogen now available, and the increasing amount of man-made nitrogen materials added to the environment each year, a careful check is necessary on the amounts and sources of nitrogen entering water supplies.

REFERENCES

Ahlgren, I. 1967. Limnological studies of Lake Norrviken, a eutrophicated Swedish lake. *Schweiz. Z. Hydrol.* 29:54–90.
Behnke, J. J., and Haskell, E. E., Jr. 1968. Ground water nitrate

distributions beneath Fresno, California. *J. Am. Water Works Assoc.* 60 (4): 477–80.

Biggs, R. B. 1968. Environmental effects of overboard spoil disposal. *J. Sanit. Eng. Div. Am. Soc. Civil Engrs.* 94 (SA-3): 477–87.

Brown, M. A., and Volk, G. M. 1966. Evaluation of ureaform fertilizer using nitrogen-15 labeled materials in sandy soils. *Soil Sci. Soc. Am. Proc.* 30 (2): 278–81.

Calif. State Dept. of Public Health, Bur. of Sanit. Eng. 1963. *Occurrence of nitrate in ground water supplies in southern California.*

Calif. State Water Pollution Control Board. 1953. *Field investigation of waste water reclamation in relation to ground water pollution.* Calif. State Water Pollution Control Board Publ. 6.

Carter, D. L., Robbins, C. W., and Bondurant, J. A. 1969. The effects of irrigation on water quality and pollution in south central Idaho. In *Western Soc. Soil Sci., 1969 Meetings,* Wash. State Univ., Pullman.

Comly, H. H. 1945. Cyanosis in infants caused by nitrates in well waters. *J. Am. Med. Assoc.* 129 : 112–16.

Dockal, P., and Varecha, A. 1967. Destructive pollution of the Becva River by ammonia. *Vodni Hospodarstvi* 17 (9): 388–91.

Domogalla, B. P., Juday, C., and Peterson, W. H. 1925. The forms of nitrogen found in certain lake waters. *J. Biol. Chem.* 63: 269–85.

Doneen, L. D. 1968. *Effects of soil salinity and nitrates on tile drainage in San Joaquin Valley, California.* Water Sci. and Eng. Paper 4002. Sacramento, Calif. (1966) and San Joaquin Master Drain, Appendix Part C. Fed. Water Pollution Control Admin., Southwest Region.

Dugdale, V. A., and Dugdale, R. C. 1965. Nitrogen metabolism in lakes. III. Tracer studies of the assimilation of inorganic nitrogen sources. *Limnol. Oceanog.* 10 (1): 53–57.

Eck, P., Jackson, M. L., Hayes, O. E., and Bay, C. E. 1957. *Runoff analysis as a measure of erosion losses and potential discharge of minerals and organic matter into lakes and streams.* Summary Rept. Lakes Investigation, Univ. of Wis.

Ehrlich, G. G., and Slack, K. V. 1969. Uptake and assimilation of nitrogen in microecological systems. *Am. Soc. Testing Materials.* Spec. Tech. Publ. 448, pp. 11–23.

Engberg, R. A. 1967. *The nitrate hazard in well water.* Nebr. Water Survey Paper 21. Univ. of Nebr. Conserv. and Survey Div. Lincoln.

Feth, J. H. 1966. Nitrogen compounds in water-A review. *Water Resources Res.* 2 (1): 41–58.

———. 1967. *Chemical characteristics of bulk precipitation in the Mojave Desert Region, California.* U.S. Geol. Survey Prof. Paper 575-C, pp. 222–27.

Frink, C. R. 1967. Nutrient budget: rational analysis of eutrophication in a Connecticut lake. *Environ. Sci. Tech.* 1 (5): 425–28.

Grill, E. V., and Richards, F. A. 1964. Nutrient regeneration from phytoplankton decomposing in sea water. *J. Marine Res.* 22 (1): 51–69.

Hanway, J. J., Herrick, J. B., Willrich, T. L., Bennett, P. C., and McCall, J. T. 1963. The nitrate problem. *Agronomy* 615:1.

———. *The nitrate problem.* Iowa State Univ. of Sci. and Tech. Spec. Rept. 34.

Herron, G. M., Terman, G. L., Drier, A. F., and Olsen, R. A. 1968.

Residual nitrate nitrogen in fertilized deep loess-derived soils. *Agron. J.* 60:477–82.

Hutchinson, G. E. 1954. The biogeochemistry of the terrestrial atmosphere. In *The earth as a planet,* ed. G. P. Kuiper, pp. 371–433. Chicago: Univ. of Chicago Press.

Hutchinson, G. L., and Viets, F. G., Jr. 1969. Nitrogen enrichment of surface water by absorption of ammonia volatilized from cattle feedlots. *Science* 166 (3904): 514–15.

Inglish, H. J. 1967. Nitrates in private water supplies in Morgan County, Missouri. *Milk Food Technol.* 30 (7): 224–25.

Johnston, W. R., Ittihadieh, F., Daum, R. M., and Pillsbury, A. F. 1969. *Proc. Soil Sci. Soc.,* p. 287.

Junge, C. E. 1958. The distribution of ammonia and nitrate in rainwater over the United States. *Trans. Am. Geophys. Union* 39 (2): 21–248.

Keller, W. D., and Smith, George E. 1967. Ground water contamination by dissolved nitrate. *Geol. Soc. Am. Spec. Papers* 90:48–59.

Klein, L., Jones, J. R. E., Hawkes, H. A., and Downing, A. L. 1962. *River pollution. II. Causes and effects.* London: Butterworth.

Koprivik, B., and Burian, V. 1966. Origination and occurrence of hydroxylamine in pond water. *Cesk. Hygiena* 11 (5): 268–75.

Koyama, T., and Tomino, T. 1967. Decomposition process of organic carbon and nitrogen in lake water. *Geochem. J.* 1 (3): 109–24.

Krause, H. H., and Batsch, W. 1968. Movement of fall-applied nitrogen in sandy soil. *Can. J. Soil Sci.* 48:363–65.

Likens, G. E., Bormann, F. H., and Johnson, N. M. 1969. Nitrification: importance to nutrient losses from a cutover forested ecosystem. *Science* 163 (3872): 1205–6.

Loehr, R. C. 1969. Animal wastes, a national problem. *J. Sanit. Eng. Div. Am. Soc. Civil Engrs.,* 95 (SA-2): 189–220.

Lotspeich, F. B., Hauser, V. L., and Lehman, O. R. 1969. Quality of water from playas on the southern High Plains. *Water Resources Res.* 5 (1): 48–57.

McGauhey, P. H., Eliassen, R., Rohlich, G., Ludwig, H. F., and Pearson, E. A. 1963. Comprehensive study on protection of water resources of Lake Tahoe Basin through controlled waste disposal. Prepared for the Board of Directors, Lake Tahoe Area Council, Al Tahoe, Calif.

McGuinness, J. L., Harrold, L. L., and Dreibelbis, F. R. 1960. Some effects of land use and treatment on small single crop watersheds. *J. Soil Water Conserv.* 15 (2): 65–69.

Macrae, I. C., Rosabel, R. A., and Salandan, S. 1968. The fate of nitrate nitrogen in some tropical soils following submergence. *Soil Sci.* 105 (5): 327–34.

Matheson, D. H. 1951. Inorganic nitrogen in precipitation and atmospheric sediments. *Can. J. Technol.* 29:406–12.

Metzler, D. F., and Stoltenberg, H. A. 1950. The public health significance of high nitrate waters as a cause of infant cyanosis and methods of control. *Trans. Kansas Acad. Sci.* 53:194–211.

Meyer, J., and Pampfer, E. 1959. Nitrogen content of rainwater collected in the humid central Congo Basin. *Nature* 184:717.

Miller, R. B. 1961. The chemical composition of rainwater at Taita, New Zealand, 1956–1958. *New Zealand J. Sci.* 4:844.

Mink, J. F. 1962. Excessive irrigation in the soils and ground water of Oahu, Hawaii. *Science* 135 (3504): 672–73.

Moe, P. G., Mannering, J. V., and Johnson, C. B. 1967. The loss of fertilizer nitrogen in surface runoff water. *Soil Sci.* 104 (6): 389–94.

——. 1968. A comparison of nitrogen losses from urea and ammonium nitrate in surface runoff water. *Soil Sci.* 105 (6): 428–33.

Navone, R., Harmon, J. A., and Voyles, C. F. 1963. Nitrogen content of ground water in southern California. *J. Am. Water Works Assoc.* 55 (5): 615–18.

Olsen, R. J., Hensler, R. F., Attoe, O. J., Witzel, S. A. 1969. Effect of fertilizer nitrogen, crop rotation and other factors on amounts and movement of nitrate nitrogen through soil profiles. *Agron. Abstr. Am. Soc. Agron.*, 61st Annual Meeting, p. 104.

Overrein, L. N. 1968. Lysimeter studies on tracer nitrogen in forest soil. I. Nitrogen losses by leaching and volatilization after addition of urea-N^{15}. *Soil Sci.* 106 (4): 280–90.

Owens, M., and Wood, G. 1968. Some aspects of the eutrophication of water. *Water Res.* 2:151–59.

Paloumpis, A. A., and Starrett, W. C. 1960. An ecological study of benthic organisms in the three Illinois river flood plain lakes. *Am. Midland Naturalist* 64 (2): 406–35.

Parker, C. D. 1962. Microbiological aspects of lagoon treatment. *J. Water Pollution Control Federation* 34:149–61.

Peterson, H. B., Bishop, A. A., Law, J. P., Jr. 1969. Problems of pollution of irrigation waters in arid regions. In *AAAS international conference on arid lands in a changing world* (preprint).

Pratt, P. F., Cannell, G. H., Garber, M. J., and Blair, F. L. 1967. Effect of three nitrogen fertilizers on gains, losses, and distribution of various elements in irrigated lysimeters. *Hilgardia* 38 (8): 277.

Preul, H. C., and Schroepfer, G. J. 1968. Travel of nitrogen in soils. *J. Water Pollution Control Federation* 40 (1): 30–48.

Putnam, H. D., and Olsen, T. A. 1959. *A preliminary investigation of nutrients in western Lake Superior, 1958–1959.* School of Public Health, Univ. of Minn.

——. 1960. *An investigation of nutrients in western Lake Superior.* School of Public Health, Univ. of Minn.

Sawyer, C. N., Lackey, J. B., and Lenz, R. T. 1945. *An investigation of the odor nuisances occurring in the Madison lakes, particularly Monona, Waubesa and Kegonsa from July 1942 to 1944.* Report of Governors Committee. Madison, Wis. 2 volumes.

Sinha, H., and Prasad, K. 1967. Performance, transformation and movment of urea in acid soils. *J. Indian Soc. Soil Sci.* 15 (4): 281–87.

Smith, G. E. 1967. Fertilizer nutrients as contaminants in water supplies. In *Agriculture and the quality of our environment.* Publ. 85, pp. 173–86. Am. Assoc. for the Advancement of Sci.

Stewart, B. A., Viets, F. G., Jr., Hutchinson, G. L., Kemper, W. D., Clark, F. E., Fairbourn, M. L., and Strauch, F. 1967. *Distribution of nitrates and other water pollutants under fields and corrals in middle South Platte Valley of Colorado.* USDA, ARS 41–134.

Stewart, B. A., Viets, F. G., Jr., and Hutchinson, G. L. 1968. Agriculture's effect on nitrate pollution of ground water. *J. Soil Water Conserv.* 23 (1): 13–15.

Stout, P. R., and Burau, R. G. 1967. The extent and significance of fertilizer build-up in soils as revealed by vertical distribution of nitrogenous matter between soils and underlying water reservoirs. In *Agriculture and quality of our environment*. Publ. 85, pp. 283–310. Am. Assoc. for the Advancement of Sci.

Sylvester, R. O. 1961. *Nutrient content of drainage water from forested, urban and agricultural areas.* Algae and Metropolitan Wastes. U.S. Public Health Serv. SEC TR W61-3, pp. 80–87.

Sylvester, R. O., and Seabloom, R. W. 1963. Quality and significance of irrigation return flow. *J. Irrigation Drainage Div. Am. Soc. Civil Engrs.* 89 (IR-3). Proceedings Paper 3624, pp. 1–27.

Task Group 2610-P Report. 1966. Nutrient-associated problems in water quality and treatment. *J. Am. Water Works Assoc.* 58 (10): 1337–55.

Task Group 2610-P Report. 1967. Sources of nitrogen and phosphorus in water supplies. *J. Am. Water Works Assoc.* 59:344–66.

Timmons, D. R., Burwell, R. E., and Holt, R. F. 1968. Loss of crop nutrients through runoff. *Minnesota Sci.* 24 (4): 1.

U.S. Geological Survey, Water Resources Division. 1965. Conference on Nitrogen Chemistry, 1965. Menlo Park, Calif., Sept. 21–22.

U.S. Public Health Service. 1964. Basic and Applied Sciences Branch, Division of Water Supply and Pollution Control. Activities Report July 1, 1963–June 30, 1964.

Weidner, R. B., Christianson, A. G., Weibel, S. R., and Robeck, G. G. 1969. Rural runoff as a factor in stream pollution. *J. Water Pollution Control Federation* 41 (3): 377–84.

White, A. W., Burnett, A. P., Jackson, W. A., and Kilmer, V. J. 1967. Nitrogen fertilizer loss in runoff from crop land tested. *Crops Soils* 19 (4): 28.

Whitehead, E. I., and Moxon, A. L. 1952. *Nitrate poisoning.* S. Dak. State College Bull. 424.

CHAPTER EIGHT

CHEMISTRY OF NITROGEN IN SOILS

F. J. STEVENSON and G. H. WAGNER

T HE importance of N from the standpoint of soil fertility has long been recognized, and our knowledge concerning the nature, distribution, and transformations of N compounds in soil is extensive. Early work dealt largely with practical aspects of maintaining a reserve of humus N for plant growth; more recently, interest has been centered on the efficient use of fertilizer N. Increasing attention is now being given to problems associated with the disposal of nitrogenous wastes on farmland and of the fate of applied N as related to water quality.

A schematic diagram depicting the cycle of N in soil is given in Figure 8.1. Ammonium (NH_4^+) added as fertilizer, or formed from decay of plant and animal residues, is temporarily held by the exchange complex of the soil but is eventually oxidized to nitrate (NO_3^-) unless it becomes fixed by humus or clay minerals. Immobilization by microorganisms leads to conversion of NH_4^+ and NO_3^- to the humus form. The NO_3^- is subject to leaching, and it can be converted to gaseous products through a process called denitrification. Losses of N can also occur through chemical reactions involving nitrite (NO_2^-).

The above considerations emphasize that a close relationship exists between inorganic and organic forms of N, and that the subject of soil N deals not only with the nature and distribution of various inorganic and organic compounds but of their interactions with each other and with mineral matter. An understanding of the chemistry of soil N complexes, and of the reactions they undergo, is of considerable importance from the standpoint of evaluating agricultural practices as they relate to the occurrence of NO_3^- and nitrogenous organic substances in natural waters.

The purpose of this chapter is to summarize our knowledge of the kinds and amounts of N compounds in soil. Brief mention will be made of chemical transformations involving NH_4^+ and NO_2^-. The subject of biological transformations will be mentioned only as

F. J. STEVENSON is Professor of Soil Chemistry, Department of Agronomy, University of Illinois. G. H. WAGNER is Associate Professor, Department of Agronomy, University of Missouri.

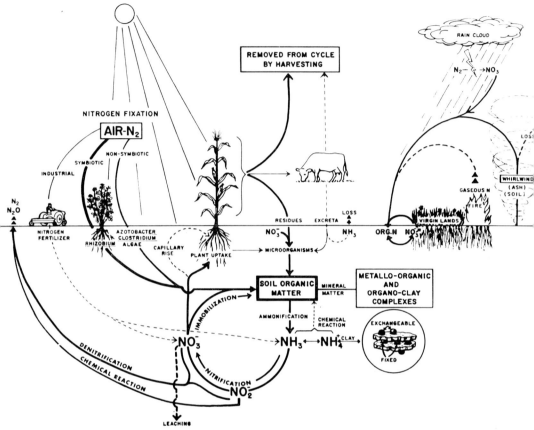

FIG. 8.1.   The N cycle in soil. (From Stevenson, 1965.)

far as it contributes to our understanding of the chemistry of soil N.

INORGANIC FORMS OF N IN SOIL

Examination of Figure 8.1 shows that several mineral forms of N other than NH_4^+ and NO_3^- are possible in soil. They included nitrite (NO_2^-), elemental N (N_2), and nitrous oxide (N_2O). Nitrite and N_2O, along with nitric oxide (NO) and nitrogen dioxide (NO_2), can be found in soil only under very special circumstances (see sections dealing with denitrification and nitrite reactions). Other inorganic N compounds, such as hydroxylamine (NH_2OH) and hyponitrous acid (HON = NOH), may occur as intermediates in biological transformations of N but for the most part they are unstable and have only a transitory existence. Elemental N is a common constituent of soil air; unfortunately, it cannot be used directly by plants.

Although plants are capable of utilizing organic N compounds (for example, amino acids), practically all of the N taken up from the soil exists in inorganic forms (as NH_4^+ and NO_3^-).

Exchangeable NH_4^+ and NO_3^-

Several recent reviews (Bremner, 1965; Harmsen and Kolenbrander, 1965; Stevenson, 1965) have emphasized that only a small fraction of the N in soils, generally less than 0.1%, exists in available mineral compounds (as exchangeable NH_4^+ and NO_3^-). Thus, only a few pounds of N may be available to the plant at any one time, even though 2 or 3 tons may be present in combined forms. The slow conversion of nitrogenous organic substances to available mineral forms by microorganisms has been attributed to their stabilization by ligninlike substances and to the protective action of clay minerals. The formation of stable complexes can be considered beneficial, because the N is protected against decomposition and subsequent leaching as NO_3^-.

Levels of exchangeable NH_4^+ and NO_3^- vary from day to day and from one season to another, and will depend upon such factors as climate (temperature, rainfall), organic matter content, presence or absence of growing plants, C/N ratio of added residues, and time and rate of application of nitrogenous fertilizers. Some important aspects regarding available N in soils are itemized below.

1. The quantity of available N in unfertilized soil at any one time is markedly influenced by climatic patterns (Harmsen and van Schreven, 1955; Harmsen and Kolenbrander, 1965). For example, in soils of the temperate humic climatic zone, the content of inorganic N in the surface layer is lowest in winter due to leaching, rises in spring as mineralization of organic N commences, decreases in summer through consumption by plants, and increases once again in the fall when plant growth ceases and the dead residues start to decay. The level in winter seldom exceeds 10 ppm but may increase 4- to 6-fold or more during the spring (Harmsen and van Schreven, 1955). The winter minimum is usually ascribed to leaching.

2. Biological turnover leads to the interchange of NH_4^+-N and NO_3^--N with the N locked up in organic forms. Accordingly, the amount of mineral N in the soil at any one time represents a balance between the opposing processes of mineralization and immobilization, and will be determined to a large extent by the activity of the soil microflora and the C/N ratio of decomposing residues. A C/N ratio above a critical value of 20 to 25 (equivalent to 1.5 to 2.0% N) results in a net immobilization of N whereas a ratio below this value leads to net mineralization.

3. Growing plants have a depressing effect on the level of mineral N in soils. The decrease when soils are cropped cannot be accounted for entirely by plant uptake, and may be due to one or more of the following: (1) inhibition of nitrification by excretion products of plant roots, (2) immobilization of mineral N by

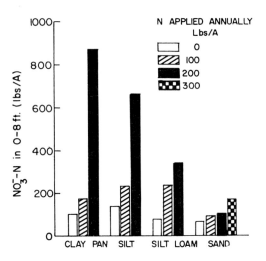

FIG. 8.2. Nitrate-N in the upper 8 feet of 4 soil types after the annual application of N fertilizer for 7 years to continuous corn in Missouri. (Adapted from Smith, 1968.)

rhizosphere microorganisms, and (3) enhanced denitrification in the root zone.

4. The repeated annual application of fertilizer N can lead to a buildup of NO_3^--N in the soil, particularly those with medium and heavy textures. Figure 8.2 shows the increase in NO_3^--N in the upper 8 feet of 4 different soil types following the annual application of N for 7 years to continuous corn in Missouri. Extremely high levels of NO_3^--N (2,000 to 4,000 lb/acre) have been observed in soil under feedlot areas (Stewart et al., 1967; Smith, 1968).

5. Rapid changes in NH_4^+ and NO_3^- levels can occur as a consequence of volatilization. Losses as free NH_3 are particularly serious in calcareous and alkaline soils but volatilization also takes place in neutral and slightly acidic soils when sufficient NH_3 is present to raise the pH in localized zones. The latter situation often arises when nitrogenous wastes and NH_4^+-type fertilizers are applied at high rates. Hutchinson and Viets (1969) concluded that absorption of NH_3 volatilized from cattle feedlots contributes significantly to N enrichment of nearby surface waters.

   Losses of NO_3^- by bacterial denitrification (see next section) and through chemical reactions involving NO_2^- (see section on Nitrite) are also of considerable practical importance. The various channels of N volatilization are discussed in detail elsewhere (Allison, 1965).

6. Nitrate is the form of N that is most mobile and which is of greatest concern from the standpoint of leaching losses and movement into water supplies. The magnitude of NO_3^- leaching is difficult to estimate and will depend upon a number of variables, including (1) quantity of NO_3^-, (2) amount and time of rainfall, (3) infiltration and percolation rates, (4) evapotranspiration, (5) water-holding capacity of the soil, and (6) presence of

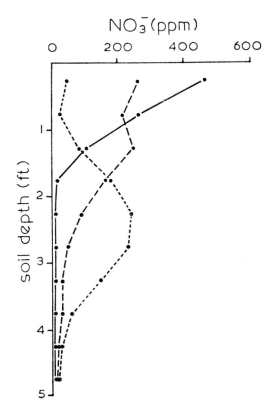

FIG. 8.3. Distribution of NO_3^--N in a clay loam soil after 7.4 (———), 15.4(— —), and 23.7 (- - -) inches of rain. Sodium nitrate had been applied at the rate of 2,000 lb/acre, or 330 lb N/acre. (From Wetselaar, 1962.)

growing plants (Allison, 1965). Leaching is generally greatest during cool seasons when precipitation exceeds evaporation; downward movement in summer is restricted to periods of heavy rainfall. Nitrate (as well as NH_4^+) can also be lost by erosion.

Nitrate moves downward in soil as a wave having the shape of a normal distribution curve; this wave becomes wider and flatter as the NO_3^- is pushed deeper into the subsoil. Nitrate distribution patterns observed by Wetselaar (1962) for three levels of rainfall are shown in Figure 8.3.

Denitrification as a Factor Controlling Nitrate Levels

Under suitable conditions NO_3^- is lost rapidly from soil by bacterial denitrification (see review of Broadbent and Clark, 1965). The ability to reduce NO_3^- to N gases is limited to those organisms which can utilize the oxygen of NO_3^- (and NO_2^-) as a substitute for molecular oxygen in conventional metabolism. The organisms mainly involved are heterotrophic and belong to the genera *Pseudomonas*, *Micrococcus*, *Achromobacter*, and *Bacillus*. Several chemoautotrophs

(Micrococcus denitrificans; Thiobacillus denitrificans) are also capable of converting NO_3^- to N_2 but they are not believed to be important in most soils.

The following pathway represents the probable mechanism of bacterial denitrification.

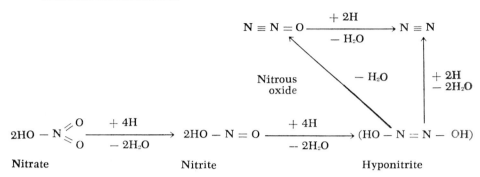

Nitrate   Nitrite   Hyponitrite

Nitrous oxide represents an intermediate in the denitrification process and is normally reduced further to N_2; consequently, the N_2O has only a transitory existence in the soil.

Optimum conditions for denitrification are as follows:

Poor drainage: Moisture status is of importance from the standpoint of its effect on aeration. Denitrification is negligible at moisture levels below two-thirds of the water-holding capacity but is appreciable in flooded soils. The process may occur in anaerobic microenvironments of well-drained soils, such as small pores filled with water, the rhizosphere of plant roots, and the vicinity of decomposing plant and animal residues.

Temperature of 25° C and above: Denitrification proceeds at a progressively slower rate at temperatures below 25° C and practically ceases at 2° C.

Soil reaction near neutral: Denitrifying bacteria are sensitive to high hydrogen ion concentrations. Their activity in acidic soils (< pH 5) is limited.

Good supply of readily decomposable organic matter: The amount of organic matter available to denitrifying microorganisms is generally appreciable in the surface horizon but negligible in the subsoil. Significant amounts of soluble organic matter may be found under feedlots, as well as in the lower horizons of soils amended with large quantities of organic wastes.

Denitrification can be considered a desirable process when it occurs below the rooting zone, because of reduction in the NO_3^- content of groundwater. Dentrifying microorganisms are known to be present at considerable depths in soil, and it is possible that some of the NO_3^- leached into the subsoil may be volatilized before reaching the water table. Meek et al. (1969) concluded that much of the NO_3^- leached into the subsoil in irrigation waters was lost through denitrification. Stewart et al. (1967) found that NO_3^- levels in soil under feedlots decreased sharply with increasing depth and concluded that the decrease was due to denitrification.

Under optimum conditions, NO_3^--N can be volatilized quantitatively in a comparatively short time (24 to 36 hours). This suggests that the denitrification process can be utilized to eliminate excess NO_3^- from soil, thereby reducing the NO_3^- content of percolating water. For example, the disposal of nitrogenous wastes on farmland results in the generation of large quantities of NO_3^-, which must be removed if groundwater contamination is to be avoided. In fine-textured soils, reduction in NO_3^- content could be accomplished by artificially subjecting the soil to successive cycles of submergence and drying. The anaerobic conditions created during waterlogging would result in a significant loss of NO_3^- produced by oxidation of NH_4^+ during the aerobic cycle. A similar procedure may prove effective in reducing the NO_3^- content of soil under feedlots.

Fixation of NH_4^+ by Clay Minerals

The NH_4^+ produced in soil through microbial activity, or added as fertilizer, can be fixed by clay minerals (Nômmik, 1965). Fixation results from a replacement of NH_4^+ for interlayer cations that expand the lattice (Ca^{2+}, Mg^{2+}, Na^+, H^+), but not by those that contract the lattice (K^+, Rb^+, Cs^+). Soils containing large amounts of vermiculitic- or illitic-type minerals have the capacity for fixing 1 to 6 m.e. of NH_4^+ per 100 g, or from about 280 to 1,680 lb per acre plow depth. Practically no fixation will occur when the clay fraction is predominantly kaolinitic.

The availability of NH_4^+ to both nitrifying microorganisms and higher plants can be reduced by fixation. However, various studies have shown that fixation is usually not a serious problem under normal fertilizer practices. Potassium, being a fixable cation, is effective in blocking the release of fixed NH_4^+; thus, the application of large amounts of K^+ simultaneously or immediately following an NH_4^+ addition may diminish the availability of the fixed NH_4^+ to higher plants.

Naturally Occurring Fixed NH_4^+

For many years, soil scientists assumed that the major inorganic forms of N in soils were exchangeable NH_4^+ and NO_3^-. Now it is known that soils contain fixed NH_4^+—that is, NH_4^+ held within the lattice structures of silicate minerals. Present estimates are that 4 to 10% of the N in the surface layer of the soil occurs as fixed NH_4^+. The proportion generally increases with depth, and in some subsoils as much as 50% of the N may exist in this form.

The distribution of fixed NH_4^+ in representative soils of several great soil groups is shown in Figure 8.4. With the exception of the Podzols, the A_1 horizons contained about 60 to 150 ppm of fixed NH_4^+-N, equivalent to about 120 to 300 lb of N per acre plow depth of soil. The rooting zone may contain as much as 1,600 lb of N per

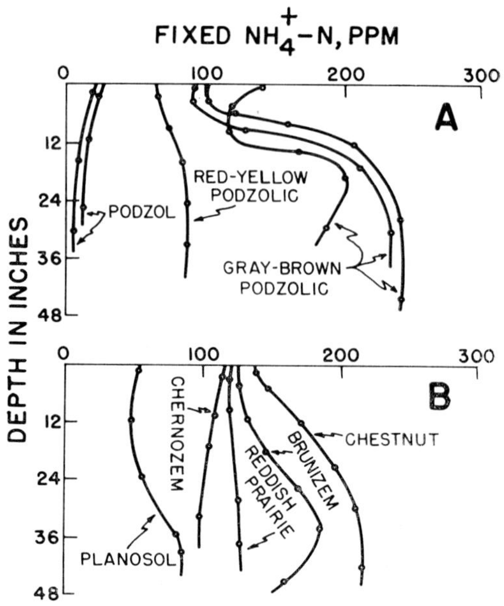

FIG. 8.4. Distribution of fixed NH_4^+-N in soils representative of several "great soil groups." (Adapted from Stevenson and Dhariwal, 1959.)

acre as fixed NH_4^+. The fixed NH_4^+ content is related to clay mineral composition; soils rich in micaceous (illitic) types contain the largest amounts.

The proportion of the soil N as fixed NH_4^+ increases slightly when soils are cropped, indicating that the native fixed NH_4^+ is less available to plants and microorganisms than the humus N. Increases in the content of fixed NH_4^+ have been reported through N fertilization (Harmsen and Kolenbrander, 1965).

Fixation of NH_3 by Organic Matter

It is well known that NH_3 can be "fixed" by reaction with lignins and humic substances (Mortland and Wolcott, 1965; Broadbent and Stevenson, 1966). Fixation is associated with oxidation (uptake of oxygen) and is favored by an alkaline reaction. Thus, the application of alkaline fertilizers such as aqueous- or anhydrous NH_3 to soil may result in considerable fixation. The NH_3 fixed by organic matter is not immediately usable by plants, although it does become available eventually through the mineralization process.

The nature of the reaction of NH_3 with soil humus is not known. It is believed, however, that aromatic compounds containing two or more hydroxyl groups are involved. The initial step involves the consumption of oxygen and the formation of a quinone, which subsequently reacts with NH_3 to form complex polymers. Catechol (I), for example, is readily converted in alkali to o-quinone (II), which can be hydrated to form benzenetriol (III) (see Mortland and Wolcott, 1965). Further oxidation yields o-hydroxyquinone (IV) and p-hydroxy-o-quinone (V).

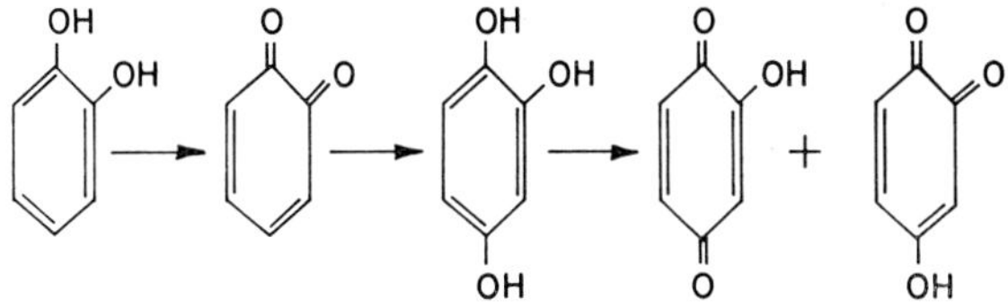

I   II   III   IV   V

The incorporation of NH_3 into p-hydroxy-o-quinone (V) is postulated to produce structures of the types represented by VI and VII.

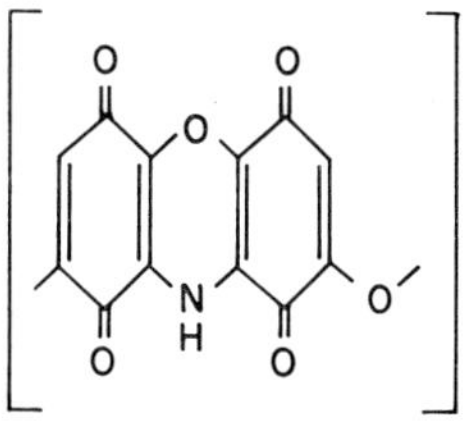

VI 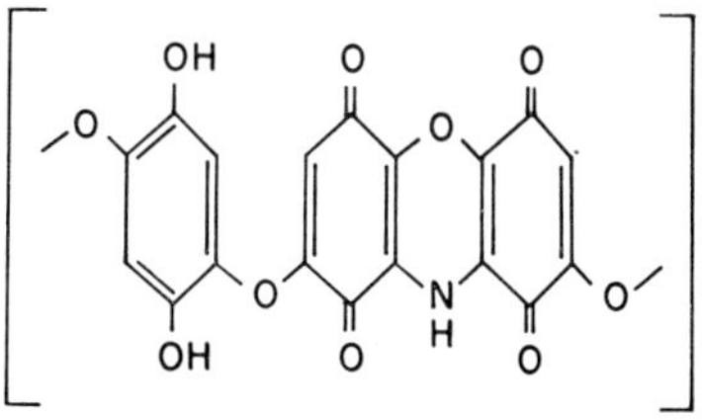   VII

Nitrite

Nitrite is not usually present in detectable amounts in well-drained neutral or slightly acidic soils. Accumulations occur, however, in calcareous soils, and recent work indicates that this ion often persists, albeit temporarily, when NH_4^+- or NH_4^+-type fertilizers are applied to soil. This NO_2^- accumulation has been attributed to inhibition of nitrification at the NO_2^- stage. Presumably, NO_2^- oxidizing organisms (*Nitrobacter*) are more sensitive to NH_3 and an adverse soil reaction than NH_4^+ oxidizers (*Nitrosomonas*). According to Hauck and Stephenson (1965), large fertilizer granules, high application rates, and an alkaline pH in the zone of fertilization are particularly favorable for NO_2^- accumulations.

The possibility that gaseous loss of fertilizer N may accompany temporary NO_2^- accumulations has been mentioned in the reviews of Allison (1965) and Broadbent and Stevenson (1966). Classical reactions involving NO_2^- include (1) double decomposition of NH_4NO_2 ($NH_4NO_2 \rightarrow 2H_2O + N_2$), (2) the Van Slyke reaction ($RNH_2 + HNO_2 \rightarrow ROH + H_2O + N_2$), and (3) decomposition of HNO_2 ($3HNO_2 \rightarrow 2NO + HNO_3 + H_2O$). All three are favored by a low pH (<5.0); thus, losses would be greatest from acid soils. It should be pointed out, however, that acidic conditions are created in fertilizer bands when NH_4^+ is oxidized to NO_2^- and NO_3^-.

The NO formed by decomposition of HNO_2 has a strong tendency to react with oxygen to form NO_2 ($2NO + O_2 \rightarrow 2NO_2$), which in turn readily dissolves in water to form HNO_2 and HNO_3 ($2NO_2 + O_2 + H_2O \rightarrow HNO_2 + HNO_3$). Consequently, the amounts of NO and NO_2 in the soil air are believed to be inconsequential.

Recently it has been suggested that certain soil components

promote the decomposition of NO_2^-. One theory is that organic constituents are involved (Broadbent and Stevenson, 1966; Bremner and Nelson, 1968). Another view is that metallic cations are responsible (Wullstein, 1967).

ORGANIC FORMS OF N

The organic N in soil consists of two main groups of compounds: (1) nitrogenous biochemicals synthesized enzymatically by microorganisms living on plant and animal residues, and (2) products formed by secondary synthesis reactions and which bear no resemblance to any of the substances occurring in plant and animal tissues. The N in the second group probably exists as part of the structures of the so-called humic and fulvic acids. The two groups are not easily separated, because some of the biochemicals (e.g., amino acids) may be covalently bound to the humic matter.

Nitrogenous Biochemicals

AMINO ACIDS

The recent application of chromatographic methods to studies of soil N have resulted in the isolation of an impressive number of amino acids from soil hydrolysates, and these studies have confirmed earlier reports indicating that 20 to 50% of the organic N occurs in the form of amino acids (Bremner, 1965, 1967). In addition to the 20 to 22 amino acids generally found in proteins, a variety of other compounds have been identified, including α-amino-n-butyric acid, γ-aminobutyric acid, β-alanine, α,ε-diaminopimelic acid, and 3,4-dihydroxyphenylalanine. The occurrence of α,ε-diaminopimelic acid is of particular interest because this amino acid appears to be confined to certain bacteria, where it occurs as a structural component of the cell wall. The presence of ornithine, β-alanine, and γ-aminobutyric acid in a variety of natural products is now well established.

Many unidentified ninhydrin-reacting substances have also been detected in soil hydrolysates. Thus far, over 50 compounds have been reported; the identity of the majority has not been established. Some of the amino compounds may be artifacts produced during hydrolysis.

The persistence of certain microbially synthesized amino acids has been reported by Wagner and Mutatkar (1968) in a study of the humification of ^{14}C glucose. The highest specific activities were found in those amino compounds known to be constituents of cell walls of microorganisms (alanine, glycine, glutamic acid, and lysine). Glucosamine, an amino sugar found in bacterial and fungal cell walls, also contained large quantities of ^{14}C. The cell walls of certain dark pigmented (melanic) fungi appear to be especially resistant to decomposition (Hurst and Wagner, 1969).

The reviews of Bremner (1965, 1967) show that conflicting results have been obtained concerning the relative distribution of amino acids in different soil types and between various horizons of the same profile. Data obtained for the Morrow Plots at the University of Illinois indicate that basic amino acids are selectively preserved through long-time cropping; this trend has yet to be confirmed. Variations in amino acid composition may exist between soils from different climatic regions of the earth.

Considerable controversy exists as to whether proteins as such occur in significant amounts in soil organic matter. The well-known ligno-protein theory advanced by Waksman has yet to be confirmed; many investigators believe that the theory in its original form is obsolete. Swaby and Ladd (1962) failed to detect proteins in humic acids, using sensitive chemical tests, and concluded that neither proteins nor ligno-protein complexes accounted for a significant part of the soil N. On the other hand, results obtained using proteolytic enzymes, partial hydrolytic procedures, and infrared spectrophotometry suggests that in some humic acids peptide linkages are present. Some of the amino acid-N in soil may occur as mucopeptides. Free amino acids have but a transitory existence, and the amount of N in this form rarely exceeds more than a few ppm.

The relative importance of clay and humus particles in binding amino acids, peptides, and proteins is unknown. However, for the surface layer of normal agricultural soils, the role played by humic and fulvic acids cannot be overemphasized. In argillaceous subsoils, a significant proportion of the proteinaceous material may be held by clay minerals, perhaps on interlamellar surfaces.

AMINO SUGARS

Several studies have indicated that 4 to 10% of the N in the surface layer of the soil occurs in the form of N-containing carbohydrates, namely, the amino sugars. In some soils, the proportion may increase with depth. Amino sugars are widely distributed in microbial tissues; hence, their presence in soil is to be expected.

Research conducted at the University of Illinois indicates that a wide variety of amino sugars are present in soils, including glucosamine, galactosamine, fucosamine, and muramic acid. The latter is a common constituent of the cell walls of bacteria. Free amino sugars have yet to be found in soils.

OTHER BIOCHEMICALS

A wide array of naturally occurring nitrogenous compounds other than amino acids and amino sugars have been found in soils, but in very low amounts. They include a variety of amines, several chlorophyll derivatives, amino acid amides (asparagine and glutamine), and purine and pyrimidine bases. All of these compounds combined account for no more than 1 to 2% of the soil N (Bremner, 1965, 1967).

Unknown Forms of Organic N

The considerations mentioned in the previous section emphasize that no more than one-half of the soil organic N can be accounted for as amino acids, amino sugars, purine and pyrimidine bases, and other known compounds. Since practically all of the organic N in soil is of microbial origin, and because the N of microbial tissues occurs almost exclusively in the above-mentioned compounds, the conclusion seems justified that during humification, conversion of the microbially synthesized products to more stable humus forms has occurred. The N content of humic and fulvic acids varies widely, values between 0.4 and 5.0% having been reported.

The relative distribution of the forms of N in acid hydrolysates of humic and fulvic acids is illustrated in Figure 8.5. It is noteworthy that as much as one-third of the N in humic acids cannot be solubilized by hydrolysis with 6 N HCl; as much as one-half of that in fulvic acids is liberated as NH_3. The nature of this N is uncertain, but most of it may occur as part of the structures of humic substances.

In considering the properties of humus N, some discussion of the nature of humic and fulvic acids is desirable. These constituents can best be described as a series of acidic, yellow- to black-colored, moderately high-molecular-weight polymers which have characteristics unlike any organic compounds occurring in living organisms. The modern view is that they represent a heterogeneous mixture of molecules which range in molecular weight from as low as 2,000 to perhaps over 300,000. Interrelationships between such properties as color, elemental composition, acidity, degree of polymerization, and molecular weight are outlined schematically in Figure 8.6. No sharp division exists between the various fractions.

FIG. 8.5. Relative distribution of the forms of N in humic and fulvic acids. The broken portion of the bars indicates the range of values reported.

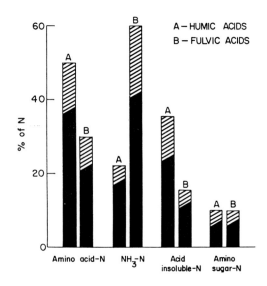

Fulvic acid		Humic acid	
Light yellow	Yellow-brown	Dark brown	Gray-black

– – – – – – – – – – increase in degree of polymerization – – – – – – – – – – – – – – ➤

2,000? – – – – – – increase in molecular weight – – – – – – – – – – – – – ➤ 300,000?

45% – – – – – – – increase in carbon content – – – – – – – – – – – – – – ➤ 62%

48% – – – – – – – decrease in oxygen content – – – – – – – – – – – – – – ➤ 30%

1,400 – – – – – – decrease in exchange acidity – – – – – – – – – – – – – ➤ 500

FIG. 8.6. Chemical properties of humic and fulvic acids. The yellow-colored fulvic pigments are relatively mobile and can act as carriers of N in streams and lakes (see text). (Adapted from a drawing by Scheffer and Ulrich, 1960.)

The yellow-colored pigments shown in Figure 8.6 correspond to the crenic and apocrenic acids of Berzelius, and they are the constituents often found in the colored waters of lakes and streams. Because of their low molecular weights, fulvic acids are highly mobile and can migrate through the soil profile in percolating waters.

The N of soil humic substances may occur in the following forms:

1. As a free amino ($-NH_2$) group
2. As an open chain ($-NH-$, $=N-$) group
3. As part of a heterocyclic ring, such as an $-NH-$ of indole and pyrrole or the $-N=$ of pyridine
4. As a bridge constituent (see structures VI and VII)

Very little is known regarding the manner whereby N is incorporated in humic and fulvic acids, but one or more of the processes illustrated in Figure 8.7 (and discussed below) are probably involved.

FIXATION OF NH₃ BY OXIDIZED LIGNINS

The interaction between NH_3 and oxidized lignins has been suggested as a possible pathway of humus formation. The autoxidation of both humic acids and lignin under alkaline conditions in the presence of aqueous NH_3 yields stable N-containing complexes. Reactions of the type discussed earlier are probably involved. Part of the fixed N cannot be solubilized by subsequent acid hydrolysis.

POLYMERIZATION OF QUINONES WITH AMINO ACIDS

Many scientists now support the theory that humic constituents originate through condensation of quinones with N-containing compounds, such as amino acids. According to this concept, polyphenols, either derived from the biological breakdown of lignin or synthesized

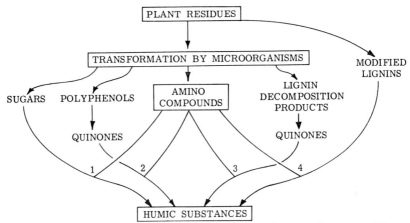

FIG. 8.7. Mechanisms of formation of soil humic substances. Nitrogenous substances (e.g., amino acids) synthesized by microorganisms during the decomposition of plant and animal residues are seen to react with modified lignins (reaction 4), quinones (reactions 2 and 3), and reducing sugars (reaction 1) to form complex polymers containing N as part of their structures.

by microorganisms, are oxidized enzymatically by phenoloxidases to quinones, which then react with amino acids to form humic substances. In the process, cyclic N compounds are formed.

Flaig's (1966) concept of humus formation is as follows:

1. Lignin, freed of its linkage with cellulose during decomposition of plant residues, is subjected to oxidative splitting with the formation of primary structural units (derivatives of phenylpropane).
2. The side chains of the lignin-building units are oxidized, demethylation occurs, and the resulting polyphenols are converted to quinones by polyphenoloxidases.
3. Quinones arising from the lignin (as well as from other sources) react with N-containing compounds to form dark-colored polymers.

The importance of microorganisms as a source of polyphenols for humus synthesis has recently been emphasized. Kononova (1966), for example, has postulated that humic substances can be formed from polyphenols synthesized by cellulose-decomposing myxobacteria in soil. Many fungi are known to produce humic acidlike substances. According to Swaby and Ladd (1962) humic molecules are formed from free radicals (quinones) produced enzymatically within deceased cells while autolytic enzymes are still functioning but before cell walls are ruptured by microbes.

CONDENSATION OF SUGARS AND AMINES

The formation of brown nitrogenous polymers by condensation of carbonyl-containing compounds (reducing sugars) and amino derivatives (amino acids) occurs extensively in stored food products and the reaction has been postulated to occur in soils. A major objection to this theory is the slow rate at which sugar-amine condensation reactions occur. However, drastic changes in the environment (freezing and thawing, wetting and drying), together with the intermixing of reactants with mineral material having catalytic properties, may facilitate condensation.

EFFECT OF CULTIVATION OF THE N DISTRIBUTION IN SOILS

It is well known that the N content of most soils declines when land is cultivated for the first time. Under average farming conditions in the Corn Belt region of the United States, about 25% of the N is lost the first 20 years, about 10% the second 20 years, and about 7% the third 20 years. This loss of N is not spread uniformly over all of the N fractions. Long-time cultivation has been found to result in increases in the proportion of the total N as fixed NH_4^+, amino sugars, and hydrolyzable N. The changes are small, however, and no single component can be considered to be the major source of mineral N for plant growth. Methods of estimating available N by analysis of any given fraction would appear to be unsatisfactory.

Research conducted at the University of Illinois indicates that when soils are cropped those compounds intimately bound to clay minerals are selectively preserved. Figure 8.8 shows that the proportion of the organic N in the Morrow Plots which was solubilized through destruction of clay with HF increased with decreasing N content. Thus, it appears that loosely bound substances are lost first, followed in order by those held by strong cohesive forces. The content of soluble organic N compounds in drainage waters would be expected to be particularly low in soils from intensively cultivated areas.

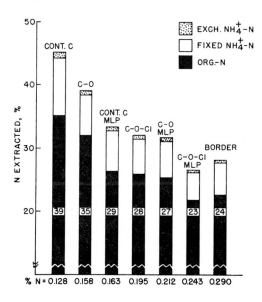

FIG. 8.8. Organic N and NH_4^+ extracted from the Morrow Plot soils by extraction with a 2.5N-HF:0.1N-HCl solution. The values in the solid portion of the bars represent the percent recovery of organic N. C = corn, O = oats, Cl = clover, MLP = manure, lime, and phosphate. (From Stevenson et al., 1967.)

Figure 8.8 further shows that the percentage of the total N as fixed NH_4^+ was highest in those soils where organic matter had been depleted through intensive cultivation (see section on Naturally Occurring Fixed NH_4^+).

SUMMARY

This brief review has served to emphasize the complex nature of soil N. Other than gaseous forms, the inorganic N consists primarily as NH_4^+ and NO_3^-. Part of the NH_4^+ is bound to colloidal surfaces and behaves according to classical reactions of exchange chemistry. Nitrate is free to move with the soil water and is the form of N which is of greatest concern from the standpoint of pollution of water supplies. Many soils contain appreciable amounts of NH_4^+ that cannot be utilized directly by plants and microorganisms; this NH_4^+ is held within the lattice structures of clay minerals.

Less than one-half of the organic N in soils can be accounted for in known compounds (amino acids, amino sugars, purine and pyrimidine bases, etc.). The remainder may occur as part of the structures of humic and fulvic acids. Part of the N added to soils as fertilizers can be converted to organic forms by chemical reactions involving NH_3 and NO_2^-; this combined N is only slowly mineralized and may persist in soil for prolonged periods.

Bacterial denitrification is an important factor regulating NO_3^- levels in natural soil and may serve as a means of reducing the NO_3^- content of groundwater when land is used for the disposal of nitrogenous wastes.

REFERENCES

Allison, F. E. 1965. Evaluation of incoming and outgoing processes that affect soil nitrogen. In *Soil nitrogen*, ed. W. V. Bartholomew and F. E. Clark, pp. 573–606. Madison, Wis.: Am. Soc. Agron.

Bremner, J. M. 1965. Organic nitrogen in soils. In *Soil nitrogen*, ed. W. V. Bartholomew and F. E. Clark, pp. 93–149. Madison, Wis.: Am. Soc. Agron.

———. 1967. Nitrogenous compounds. In *Soil biochemistry*, ed. A. D. McLaren and G. H. Peterson, pp. 19–66. New York: Marcel Dekker.

Bremner, J. M., and Nelson, D. W. 1968. Chemical decomposition of nitrite in soils. *Trans. 9th Intern. Congr. Soil Sci. Australia* 2:495–503.

Broadbent, F. E., and Clark, F. 1965. Dentrification. In *Soil nitrogen*, ed. W. V. Bartholomew and F. E. Clark, pp. 344–59. Madison, Wis.: Am. Soc. Agron.

Broadbent, F. E., and Stevenson, F. J. 1966. Organic matter interactions. In *Agricultural anhydrous ammonia: technology and use*, ed. M. H. McVickar et al., pp. 169–87. Madison, Wis.: Am. Soc. Agron.

Flaig, W. 1966. The chemistry of humic substances. In *The use of isotopes in soil organic matter studies*, pp. 103–27. New York: Pergamon Press.

Harmsen, G. W., and Kolenbrander, G. J. 1965. Soil inorganic nitrogen. In *Soil nitrogen*, ed. W. V. Bartholomew and F. E. Clark, pp. 43–92. Madison, Wis.: Am. Soc. Agron.

Harmsen, G. W., and van Schreven, D. A. 1955. Mineralization of organic nitrogen in soil. *Advan. Agron.* 10:299–398.

Hauck, R. D., and Stephenson, H. F. 1965. Nitrification of nitrogen fertilizers. Effect of nitrogen source, size and pH of the granule, and concentration. *Agr. Food Chem.* 13:486–92.

Hurst, H. M., and Wagner, G. H. 1969. Decomposition of ^{14}C-labeled cell wall and cytoplasmic fractions from hyaline and melanic fungi. *Soil Sci. Soc. Am. Proc.* 33:707–11.

Hutchinson, G. L., and Viets, F. G., Jr. 1969. Nitrogen enrichment of surface water by absorption of ammonia volatilized from cattle feedlots. *Science* 166:514–15.

Kononova, M. M. 1966. *Soil organic matter*, 2nd ed. New York: Pergamon Press.

Meek, D. B., Grass, L. B., and MacKenzie, A. J. 1969. Applied nitrogen loss in relation to oxygen status of soils. *Soil Sci. Soc. Am. Proc.* 33:575–78.

Mortland, M. M., and Wolcott, A. R. 1965. Sorption of inorganic nitrogen compounds by soil minerals. In *Soil nitrogen*, ed. W. V. Bartholomew and F. E. Clark, pp. 150–97. Madison, Wis.: Am. Soc. Agron.

Nômmik, H. 1965. Ammonium fixation and other reactions involving a nonenzymatic immobilization of mineral N in soil. In *Soil nitrogen*, ed. W. V. Bartholomew and F. E. Clark, pp. 198–258. Madison, Wis.: Am. Soc. Agron.

Scheffer, F., and Ulrich, B. 1960. *Humus und Humusdüngung*. Bd. 1. Stuttgart, Germany: Ferdinand Enke.

Smith, G. E. 1968. Contribution of fertilizers to water pollution. In *Water pollution as related to agriculture*, pp. 13–28. Paper presented at joint seminar, Univ. of Mo., Columbia, and Mo. Water Pollution Board, Columbia.

Stevenson, F. J. 1965. Origin and distribution of nitrogen in soil. In *Soil nitrogen*, ed. W. V. Bartholomew and F. E. Clark, pp. 1–42. Madison, Wis.: Am. Soc. Agron.

Stevenson, F. J., and Dhariwal, A. P. S. 1959. Distribution of fixed ammonium in soils. *Soil Sci. Soc. Am. Proc.* 23:121–25.

Stevenson, F. J., Kidder, G., and Tilo, S. N. 1967. Extraction of organic nitrogen and ammonium from soil with hydrofluoric acid. *Soil Sci. Soc. Am. Proc.* 31:71–76.

Stewart, B. A., Viets, F. G., Jr., Hutchinson, G. L., and Kemper, W. D. 1967. Nitrate and other water pollutants under fields and feedlots. *Environmental Sci. Tech.* 1:736–39.

Swaby, R. J., and Ladd, J. N. 1962. Chemical nature, microbial resistance, and origin of soil humus. *Trans. Intern. Congr. Soil Sci. (New Zealand), Com. IV and V*, pp. 197–202.

Wagner, G. H., and Mutatkar, V. F. 1968. Amino components of soil organic matter formed during humification of ^{14}C glucose. *Soil Sci. Soc. Am. Proc.* 32:683–86.

Wetselaar, R. 1962. Nitrate distribution in tropical soils. III. Downward movement and accumulation of nitrate in the subsoil. *Plant Soil* 14: 19–31.

Wullstein, L. H. 1967. Soil nitrogen volatilization. *Agr. Sci. Rev. 2nd Quart.*, pp. 8–13.

CHAPTER NINE

FERTILIZER MANAGEMENT FOR POLLUTION CONTROL

W. P. MARTIN, W. E. FENSTER, and L. D. HANSON

THE rapid increase in fertilizer usage has been due largely to low fertilizer costs and the necessity for higher economic yields. Reliance on legumes and the use of animal manures, both for nitrogen and erosion control, have given way to chemical fertilizers in many areas. This higher fertilizer usage has vastly increased crop residues which, in themselves, tend to protect the soil surface and improve soil structure for moderating erosion. Crop varieties, with high yield potentials, have also played a major role in increased crop production. In order for these new varieties to attain their maximum yield potentials, increased fertilizer rates have been necessary. In addition to farm uses, fertilizers are being used more on parks, playgrounds, golf courses, home lawns, roadbanks, forest recreation areas, and even in forest lands.

The rapid expansion in fertilizer use has raised many questions concerning nutrient pollution of our surface and groundwaters. Since the population of the United States is rapidly increasing, it probably will be essential that our land acres produce food and fiber at capacity levels in the future. This will necessitate the continued rise of high rates of fertilizer. However, management practices must be followed such that the high yields attained are also consistent with a clean and safe environment.

FERTILIZER USE IN THE NORTH-CENTRAL STATES

In the east north-central states of Wisconsin, Michigan, Illinois, Indiana, and Ohio, 8.1 million tons of fertilizers were used in 1968,

W. P. MARTIN is Professor and Head, Department of Soil Science, University of Minnesota. W. E. FENSTER is Assistant Professor and Extension Specialist in Soils, Department of Soil Science, University of Minnesota. L. D. HANSON is Associate Professor and Extension Specialist in Soils, Department of Soil Science, University of Minnesota.

Miscellaneous Publication Paper No. 1360 of the University of Minnesota Agricultural Experiment Station, St. Paul.

See Hargett (1969) for the statistics used in this section.

or an average of about 135 pounds of plant nutrients per acre on some 56 million harvested acres, 32% of which was applied in the fall. This is approximately four times the usage in 1945. Nitrogen has shown the most spectacular increase, 46,000 tons in 1945 to 1.3 million tons in 1968, or almost 30 times as much.

In the west north-central states of North and South Dakota, Minnesota, Iowa, Nebraska, Kansas, and Missouri, 7.8 million tons were used in 1968, or an average of about 65 pounds of nutrients per acre on some 117 million harvested crop acres, and some 34% was used in the fall. This is approximately 17 times the usage in 1945 and again nitrogen has shown the most spectacular gains, increasing from less than 6,000 pounds in 1945 to over 2 million pounds in 1968, over 300 times as much.

The north-central states are among the high-use states, and in the western and central parts the rapid expansion of irrigation enterprises is accelerating the use of fertilizer nutrients to maximize production. Projection estimates suggest further expansion, perhaps even a doubling in fertilizer use in the next 15 years, so that the Midwest will account for some 40% of the total used in the United States (Beaton and Tisdale, 1969).

Although the aforementioned figures are spectacular in terms of increasing usages of plant nutrients in fertilizers, their utilization by crops must be balanced against the pollution aspects of the soil-water system. Many of these factors have been covered in great detail in the preceding chapters, however, it will be necessary to provide modest documentation in order to relate principles of soil and crop management for production to the problem of minimizing potential pollution of water supplies from use of fertilizers (Soileau, 1969). The discussion will be confined to *nitrogen* and *phosphorus*, the two nutrient elements of principal concern in water pollution and eutrophication.

FERTILIZER USE VS CROP HARVEST REMOVALS

It should be pointed out that our cropping programs have, in general, been exploitive of plant nutrients and that we are still removing more nutrients than are being replaced by way of fertilizers, or from other sources. White (1965) evaluated the situation and estimated that major crops in the United States on our 294 million cropped acres were removing about 8.8 million tons of nitrogen (including nitrogen fixed in leguminous plants of approximately 3 million tons) and 2.8 million tons of phosphate. Only in the case of phosphorus are the additions equivalent to the withdrawals, and when it is considered that crop use efficiencies are substantially less than 50% of that applied, we are still "mining" rather than "enriching" our soils with plant nutrients.

Stanford (Wadleigh, 1968) has estimated that in the past 100 years there has been a loss of organic matter in the top 40 inches of the cropped agricultural soils of the United States of some 35 billion tons, or a loss of 1,750 million tons of organic nitrogen. Nitrogen fertilizer application, though appearing to be large and now approaching annual crop removal levels, is small in terms of "historical losses."

In Minnesota, for example, on approximately 18 million acres of cropland, nitrogen withdrawals average close to a million tons annually and phosphorus some 200,000 tons. Less than a quarter of this amount is being added by way of fertilizers, so even taking into account nutrients added through manures and legumes, two to three times as much chemical fertilizer could be justified for crop production at current levels.

It is evident, however, that we may reach application levels where the additions of plant nutrients surpass crop removals and in local situations now, very high application rates of nitrogen particularly are sometimes noted (Beaton and Tisdale, 1969). It is possible to enrich local water supplies, especially where soils are not adequately protected from erosion. It is necessary, therefore, that attention be given now to those management factors that can assure the crop production needed and at the same time minimize the potential for nutrient pollution.

EROSION AND SEDIMENTATION

The conservation movement of the past 30 years has stimulated and supported a major research effort which has documented the seriousness of erosion and sedimentation both from the standpoint of land destruction and water degradation. It has been estimated that some 4 billion tons of sediment are washed into waterways and reservoirs annually; this is equivalent to about 4 million acres of good top soil 6 inches deep (Stallings, 1957; Smith and Wischmeier, 1962; Wadleigh, 1968). Marked abatement of this erosion and sediment delivery can be accomplished by erosion control structures, crop rotations, use of minimum tillage, and utilization of crop residues both by incorporation to improve structure and by mulching to protect soil surfaces.

Smith and Wischmeier (1962) developed a "universal rainfall erosion equation" by integrating data from some 35 field research stations. This equation aids in management decisions designed to keep soil losses in the field below established "tolerance" limits of 3 to 4 tons per acre annually. The equation identifies key determinants in soil loss and sediment delivery and defines them in terms of average annual erosion-producing rainfall, soil erodibility, topography, cropping and cultural practices, and erosion control activities (Ballantyne et al., 1967). In the future these activities will likely take on the increasingly important role of controlling lake-destroying sediments.

A further consideration of interest is the nutrient aspects of the land sediments reaching water. Most researchers have felt that just as fertile soils produce more land plants via higher equilibrium levels of available nutrients, so do fertile sediments provide more nutrients for aquatic plants.

The physical removal of nutrient elements by erosion is nonselective in the sense that the elements may be removed in any chemical form. The process, however, tends to be selective in that the organic matter and finer particles of soil are more vulnerable to erosion than are the coarser soil fractions (Barrows and Kilmer, 1963). Organic matter is among the first constituents to be removed because of its low density and high concentration in surface soils. Hays et al. (1948) reported 951 pounds per acre of organic matter lost annually from moderately eroded Fayette silt loam and 668 pounds from a severely eroded phase. Significant quantities of nitrogen and phosphorus may be removed in the organic phase. Massey and Jackson (1952) calculated regression equations for the enrichment ratios of organic matter and plant nutrients from Almena, Fayette, and Miami soils in Wisconsin, using runoff plot and small watershed data, and concluded that they were removed selectively in the following order: organic matter, organic and ammoniacal nitrogen, and finally "available" phosphorus.

Losses reported for soluble nitrogen salts and unreacted phosphatic fertilizer compounds in runoff waters are exceedingly low and appear to be of little significance (Barrows and Kilmer, 1963; Biggar and Corey, 1968; Wadleigh, 1968). However, existing data are insufficient to evaluate the influence of such factors as source, rate, placement, and time of application of fertilizer relative to the occurrence of runoff. Hauser (1968) recently sampled closed playas on the Texas high plains entrapping runoff waters from heavily fertilized adjacent fields and found them virtually free of nitrates. Samples taken on five different sampling dates contained less than 0.5 ppm of nitrate nitrogen, on an average, and the same values were recorded for playas whose watersheds were 95% native grasses. Rogers (1942) applied triple superphosphate at the rate of 200 pounds per acre to Dunmore silt loam in permanent pasture, followed immediately by a series of 1-inch rains from a rainfall simulator. The first rain removed 9.1% of the applied phosphorus and the second 4.3%. As much as 22% of the phosphorus applied to a dry bare soil was removed when rain was applied immediately after fertilization. Phosphorus solution and immobilization by soil fixation could not occur with sufficient rapidity under these extreme conditions to prevent some loss in the runoff waters.

It is evident that erosion can and does in many instances cause significant losses of soil and organic matter with concomitant removal of nitrogen and phosphorus. Previously mentioned erosion control measures can reduce these losses by 75% and more (Wadleigh, 1968).

PHOSPHORUS IN SOIL AND NATURAL WATER SUPPLIES

Recently there has been increased appreciation of the significance of phosphorus in the process of lake eutrophication (Megard, 1969). The nitrogen-fixing capability of blue-green algae often diminishes the significance of nitrogen as a nutrient and increases that of phosphorus. The phosphorus regimes in soil versus water vary markedly in that only a small portion of the soil phosphorus is in an available form, whereas that in water is almost totally available. The amount of phosphorus in soils is, therefore, much larger than that in our natural waters. Soils may vary from 100 to 4,000 pounds of total phosphorus (1,000 pounds per acre average) in the plow layer, only 5 to 10% of which contributes to the "labile pool" of potentially available phosphorus (Bailey, 1968; Black, 1968). An example of a quantity of phosphorus contained in a Minnesota lake to a depth where light was sufficient for photosynthesis is 2.8 pounds per acre. This amount is sufficient for profuse algae growth (Megard, 1969).

Lysimeter and other types of experiments have demonstrated that phosphorus does not significantly leach downward as a result of water percolation; drainage waters thus contain small concentrations. The highest amount reported was that in California on well-drained soils receiving large amounts of fertilizer and water by way of irrigation, where Johnston et al. (1965) recorded a mean concentration of 0.08 ppm of phosphorus in the irrigation drainage. Water moving into natural waters from underground flow will contain phosphorus at levels consistent with those found generally in uncontaminated waters or from 0.01 to 0.03 ppm (Maderak, 1963). Agricultural land drainage is usually in this same range (MacGregor and Hanson, 1969).

The magnitude of runoff and sediment sources of phosphorus is under extensive investigation at the present time. Past work has tended to emphasize erosion.

Many experiments on soil loss from erosion have been carried on by the Missouri Agricultural Experiment Station, dating from 1917 (Duley and Miller, 1923). In an experiment on Shelby loam, with plots 90 feet long and having a 3.86% slope, loss of phosphorus by erosion was 18 pounds per year with continuous corn and 6.2 pounds with a good rotation of corn, wheat, and clover. Under continuous bluegrass, only 0.1 pound of phosphorus was lost by erosion, demonstrating the effectiveness of plant protection against soil loss (Miller et al., 1932).

Bedell et al. (1946) demonstrated the loss of organic phosphorus through erosion. Where corn was grown under prevailing management practices, over 4.5 tons of solids were removed per acre, carrying approximately 20 pounds of phosphorus. Nearly 60% of the phosphorus lost was in the organic form. Eroded soil from natural runoff-erosion plots on a Barnes loam soil, 7% slope, at Morris, Minnesota, contained 500 to 2,000 ppm total P (Timmons et al., 1968). These were agricultural soils which had been adequately fertilized, and cropping patterns varied from clean-cultivated fallow, through continuous corn to corn-oats-hay in rotation.

Recent studies have indicated that lake sediments are not contributing to lake water pollution by supplying phosphate and indeed will be able to extract phosphate from the waters with which they come in contact. The phosphate potential for lake bottom sediments from several western Minnesota lakes with varying degrees of eutrophication were determined and the "index" factors were found to vary from 8.22 to only 8.59, indicating a high degree of phosphate adsorption capacity (White and Beckett, 1964; Holt et al., 1969; Latterell et al., 1969).

The runoff source of phosphorus appears to be more important than was previously suspected. Of particular interest is Holt's (1969) observation that spring snow melt waters carry much higher amounts of phosphorus than runoff waters during other times of the year as measured on natural-rainfall-runoff plots. This is presumably coming from plant residues that have been frozen over winter, allowing the nutrients to be washed out in the spring. Also, soil contact is prevented by a mat of organic material on the soil surface and the frozen soil itself. Amounts, though small, were five to six times higher in snow melt runoff than in water percolating through the soil. This observation was supported by Hanson and Fenster (1969) in data comparing the phosphorus concentration of tile line waters (soil percolation) and adjacent drainage ditch waters (percolation plus snow melt) in the spring of 1969 for sampling sites on 20 farms in southern Minnesota's corn- and soybean-growing area. Soils at the sampling sites were Webster and Glencoe clay loams. Tile line outlet waters averaged 0.03 ppm phosphorus vs. 0.16 ppm for the adjacent ditches, or five times as much.

It will be difficult to intercept snow melt runoff coming off the large areas of natural grasslands. Diversion of surface runoff waters to seepage areas may in some instances be feasible, but often at considerable expense. Water which has percolated through a mineral soil is essentially stripped of its soluble and particulate phosphate and will not be a significant source of phosphorus in natural water supplies whether or not it comes from fertilized or unfertilized soils. Land leveling, retention terraces, and other erosion control measures can be designed to help on cultivated soils. Spreading of fertilizer and manures on frozen soils on rolling land adjacent to water supplies should be avoided (Corey et al., 1967).

MANAGEMENT OF SOIL NITROGEN

In many ways the questions raised concerning fertilizer management for control of pollution are premature in that water quality benchmarks for lake eutrophication or for public and animal health have not been jointly established or agreed upon. However, regardless of interpretation with respect to these two facets of the problem, it is important that nitrogen movement and losses be reviewed as related to land management activities. Most modern crop production practices will affect the soil nitrogen regime in some degree and it is difficult to generalize about them because of the complex nature of the soil-climate-plant system. Interactions among soil, climate, irrigation, drainage, tillage, fertilizer, and crop are exceedingly complicated and becoming more so with rapidly changing patterns of fertilizer use and tillage methods.

Nitrogen in the Soil

Tillage is a significant factor in the release of nitrogen, since it markedly speeds up oxidation of organic matter with release of, and subsequent nitrification of, ammonia. The high organic matter soils of the north-central states containing 0.2 to 0.4% by weight of nitrogen have a potential for production of nitrate which is substantial, and yields of 200 to 400 pounds per acre annually without supplementary nitrogen were not uncommon during the early years of cultivated agriculture in the region (Black, 1968). To a large extent, nitrogen fertilizers as currently used can be considered a replacement for lower "yields" of tillage-induced soil-organic-matter-released nitrogen. From this perspective, chemical nitrogen fertilizer use is not essentially different from the older agronomic practices of cultivation and the use of legumes and animal manures to shift the nitrogen equilibrium in favor of the crop plant.

Allison (1955, 1965) has extensively reviewed nitrogen balances in soils and concludes that as long as it remains in the organic form it is comparatively safe from loss except through erosion. Normally, however, as noted above, soil organic nitrogen is slowly converted to ammonia by heterotrophic soil microorganisms and then into nitrites and nitrates by the nitrifying bacteria, and in these forms it is subject to the same losses as nitrogen from fertilizer sources. In the absence of a crop or leaching, as much as 5 to 10% of the nitrogen may accumulate as nitrate during a 6-month period in cultivated soils. A crop such as corn removes 2 to 3% of the nitrogen in the plow layer during one growing season. Small grain crops remove half as much as corn. Nitrogen returned to the soil in crop residues may contribute as much as 20% of the total nitrogen assimilated by the crop.

Many investigators, using lysimeters, have reported on leaching losses of nitrogen in the form of nitrates (Bizzel, 1944; Allison, 1955, 1965; Allison et al., 1959; Black, 1968; Webber, 1969b). Allison (1955), for example, summarized the results of 157 lysimeter experiments conducted at several locations in the United States. These included 51 lysimeters kept fallow and 106 that were cropped to nonlegumes. The unaccounted-for nitrogen averaged 15% of that added or which became available in the soil. He noted that this nitrogen loss could not be assigned to denitrification, which under normal soil conditions is quite small. Nitrogen recovered in the crop from added fertilizer nitrogen, or from that which became available in the soil, was usually less than 50%. Significantly, however, Pearson et al. (1961) showed that equivalent nitrogen recoveries for three successive crops ranged from 70 to 77% in the humid southeast if nitrogen was applied at a time when leaching was at a minimum and when crops were present to effect assimilation. Two hundred pounds of nitrogen per acre were applied to corn in the spring with two additional crops being grown during the following 16 months. It was concluded that in general, leaching losses of nitrogen are small if an actively growing crop is present at all times, and if the rate of nitrogen additions clearly approximates the needs of the crop. If much nitrogen is added or released as nitrate in the late fall, the losses are likely to be large unless a cover crop or permanent sod is present.

Russell (1961) documents that nitrates are always lower in cropped land than under fallow, not only because the crop is extracting nitrate for growth but because the crop depresses the rate of nitrification in soil. Nitrogen present in a cropped soil as nitrate and in the crop was less than the nitrate in an adjacent fallow soil. Nitrates accumulated during the spring and summer in the fallow soil, but not in the cropped soil. Fallow soil also appeared to lose substantial amounts of nitrates by early winter, presumably because of leaching into the subsoil.

Smith (1968) in Missouri has also found that nitrates in small amounts may reach groundwater supplies. Soil samples in foot increments were taken to a depth of 10 feet in Putnam silt loam which had been in continuous corn for 20 years and had received 120 pounds of nitrogen as ammonium nitrate per acre annually. Nine pounds per acre per year more nitrogen was found in the surface 10 feet of soil than where no nitrogen was applied. Other nitrate movement studies have been underway for 7 years on soils with widely different characteristics. Rainfall has ranged from 30 to 50 inches per year and corn yields from 60 to more than 150 bushels per acre. Nitrates in small amounts have accumulated progressively in the 8-foot profile samples at all levels of application above 100 pounds per acre except in the sandy soils where leaching has presumably moved nitrates below the depth of sampling.

Higher nitrogen losses have been measured by Johnston (1965) in connection with a study of tile drainage and wastewater management in the San Joaquin Valley of California. He noted that 9 to 70% of the nitrogen applied just prior to the 1962 irrigation season or with the irrigation water was lost either in the drainage effluent or in the tailwater. It was noted that the presence of a continuous water table at or above the tile systems was necessary to obtain the data presented. Nitrogen rates varied from 84 to 260 pounds per acre and crops were cotton and rice.

Gardner (1965) notes that the downward movement of water through the "macropore systems" of medium-textured soils is rather rapid. The larger the total pore volume of this system, the more readily the water will move. The presence of a crop, however, tends to reduce this downward movement because of evapotranspiration. The crop, therefore, greatly minimizes leaching losses of nitrogen both directly, by assimilation, and indirectly, by reducing the amount of leachate.

A suggested way of evaluating probable leaching losses of nitrogen and how to minimize them is to make use of precipitation-evapotranspiration curves as noted by Allison (1965). Using this approach, for an example, the results for central Minnesota show that there is little cr no leaching or movement of water through the soil during the summer months, and during the winter months the soils are frozen. Fall and spring are the months when drainage occurs in the Midwest (Blake et al., 1960). In drier regions of the Great Plains states, the soil is rarely filled to field capacity beyond the root zone, except under irrigation, and hence there will be little leaching of nitrogen. These data emphasize the importance of a crop for minimizing leaching losses and the importance of avoiding the accumulation of nitrates in soils in late fall.

It should perhaps be noted that nitrates reaching the drainage ditch, lake, or reservoir are either quickly used by plants or denitrify in the anaerobic high-energy environment of decomposing plant materials (Allison, 1965). Keeney et al. (1969) were not able to detect nitrates in Wisconsin lake sediments, nor are nitrates commonly found in more than trace amounts in surface waters (Maderak, 1963).

Sources of Nitrate in Water Supplies

Natural sources of nitrogen, as well as those from fertilizers, leguminous crops, and animal waste disposal operations, must be evaluated for perspective in considering ways in which soil management may minimize the nitrate pollution of water supplies. These quantities are difficult to estimate, so considerable watershed monitoring will be needed in the future. Unless additions of nitrogen from all sources which go into a watershed are balanced by withdrawals such as by harvest and removal of crops or denitrification, nitrate-nitrogen will accumulate in surface water or groundwater (Stewart et al., 1968).

Nitrate contamination of water supplies from barnyards or concentrated livestock feeding operations has been well documented and corrective measures are being instituted in many states to moderate the problem via collecting basins, oxidation trenches or lagoons, and land spreading of the animal manures. Since the animal manures are a source of plant nutrients released during decomposition, they are in the same category as fertilizers when applied to cropland in evaluating management procedures which will minimize pollution.

Smith (1965, 1967) researched sources of nitrogen in some 6,000 rural water supplies in Missouri and concluded that animal wastes and septic tank drainage coming from poorly constructed shallow wells were the main sources of water contamination. He suggested that fertilizer nitrogen was not at this time significant overall, though in some instances application rates go beyond efficient crop utilization levels.

In Minnesota, also, nitrate contamination of rural wells has been noted for many years, long before nitrogen fertilizers were used to any extent. Shallow wells in glacial drift and in the Shakopee and Oneota dolomites, with recharge directly from the drift, are higher in dissolved solids and often contaminated with nitrates above Public Health Service standards. This occurs most notably in communities without municipal sewage disposal systems and where large numbers of livestock are concentrated. However, recent summary reports by the Minnesota State Department of Conservation (Maderak, 1965) on the chemical quality of groundwaters show that wells from deep aquifers such as the Jordan and St. Peter sandstones, with recharge from the northern Minnesota lake and forest areas, are very low in nitrates and dissolved solids. In general, change in the quality of water for the major aquifers from 1899 to 1963 has been minor.

Schmidt (1956) studied the problem of anoxemia in very young infants as related to nitrate contamination of rural wells varying in depth from 15 to 50 feet in southern Minnesota's prairie soil area. Soils obviously containing high levels of organic nitrogen from livestock had the highest nitrifying capacities, and water supplies with concentrations of nitrate of 75 to 130 ppm were located near such soils. Normal field soils were associated with subsoil drainage waters of up to 18 ppm and well waters of up to 35 ppm nitrate. The high organic matter soils of southwestern Minnesota present ideal conditions for nitrification and release of nitrogen from the organic nitrogen complex with cultivation so that supplementary nitrogen from animal manures or other sources can result in high nitrate production which may move into shallow wells which are improperly located or constructed. This illustrates that fertilizer rates applied must be evaluated in terms of the "background" level of fixed nitrogen in the soil water.

Stout and Burau (1967) studied nitrate accumulations in the groundwaters of a closed 10-square-mile basin near San Luis Obispo, California. This area, containing 2,700 intensively cropped acres, is urbanized with 13,500 people and the domestic and irrigation waters are supplied exclusively from wells with a rapid recharge. These well waters ranged from 5 to 130 ppm in nitrate. The nitrogen pool was substantial and mostly associated with the native soil organic matter complex supplemented with sewage waste from area homes and to a lesser extent from lawn and farm fertilization. Cropland management recommendations were developed by Stout and Burau to include nitrogen fertilizer rates consistent with the needs of the crop, mostly fruits and vegetables, and to include the amounts of nitrate-nitrogen in the well waters which were used for irrigation. It was recommended that domestic waters be taken from prehistoric deep waters which are unaffected by tillage and hydraulic sewage disposal systems.

One of the more recent and well-documented studies on sources of pollution of underground supplies was made in the middle South Platte River valley in Colorado (Stewart et al., 1968). This valley is intensively farmed and irrigated, has some 600,000 cattle in feedlots, and is surrounded by many cultivated dryland fields. Twenty-foot cores from the soil surface to water table or bedrock from 10 to 65 feet deep were taken from 129 sites of differing land use and analyzed for nitrates in transit. Average total nitrate nitrogen in pounds per acre for land use types was as follows: alfalfa, 79; native grassland, 90; cultivated dryland, 261; irrigated fields not in alfalfa, 506; and cattle corrals, 1,436 pounds. In general, there was extreme variation within classes of land use. Calculations based on core averages and rate of water movement through the profile under irrigation indicated that 25 to 30 pounds of nitrate nitrogen per acre were being lost annually to the water table. Though the losses were small from irrigated fields compared to those from feedlots, they contributed much more total nitrate because acreages were much more extensive.

Management to Minimize Nitrogen Losses

In summary, it is evident that leaching of nitrates below the rooting zone of plants can and does occur in soils, depending upon nitrogen supplies present, and that it may be larger on sandy soils under irrigation than on heavier textured soils during summer when evapotranspiration is greater than precipitation. Under fallow or in late fall and early spring when soils are not frozen, movement of nitrates downward within the soil profile occurs and some may eventually reach underground water supplies. Erosion losses of nitrogen are mostly associated with the selective removal of organic nitrogen compounds in the erosion debris. Thus, to minimize losses and moderate potential pollution, soil management should include erosion control practices, soil nitrogen should be kept to a minimum during the colder months of the year or in the absence of a crop, and fertilizer nitrogen should be added in amounts which allow for, but do not greatly exceed, the amounts needed for efficient crop production. It may be necessary to again emphasize the value of split applications of nitrogen fertilizer for efficiency of utilization via the irrigation waters, with starter and nitrogen side-dressing of corn and summer top-dressing of meadow and turf—all good crop production management recommendations. Late season or fall application of nitrogen should be in the ammoniacal form where soils are subject to leaching. Temperatures should be low enough that nitrification is negligible.

Alexander (1965) noted that the optimum temperature for nitrification falls between 30° and 35° C. There is no fixed minimum temperature above freezing, but rates are low. However, nitrate will continue to be formed throughout the autumn in small amounts and may be lost by leaching in those situations where there is movement of water through the profile. This nitrate may be utilized by soil microorganisms if carbonaceous crop residues are incorporated in the fall.

Chemical inhibitors to delay oxidation of ammonia to nitrates and nitrites have been suggested (Black, 1968). Alexander (1965) listed many inhibitors and summarized the literature on their use. Turner and Goring (1966) examined a number of researchers on the use of 2-chloro-6-(trichloro-methyl) pyridine, one of the more effective inhibitors, and concluded that yield and nitrogen content of several crops could be increased by the use of this inhibitor. In general, the inhibitors appeared to be more effective at temperatures below 21° C and much less effective at temperatures up to 32° C. Studies by Janssen and Wiese (1969) in Nebraska and by Huber et al. (1969) in Idaho support these conclusions. Further investigation is warranted to improve use reliability and for reduction in price.

Under irrigated soil conditions, or farming situations where there is control over the water table, it may be possible to dissipate some nitrate entering tile lines with controlled denitrification. Meek et al. (1969), using simulated tile lines in soil columns, reduced nitrates in the tile effluent to an average value of 0.5 ppm by submerging the tile lines, thus creating an anaerobic environment.

The role of deep-rooted crops, like alfalfa, in a rotation and of cover crops in the fall to remove nitrogen and enhance the organic nitrogen reserve should not be minimized for selected locations. Stewart et al. (1968) showed that little nitrate was present under alfalfa fields and grasslands to depths of 20 feet. Where the water table is within this depth, some nitrate may even be removed from the water table.

Sod crops and crop residues left on soil surfaces during noncropping seasons can also reduce erosion as will minimum tillage. The adoption of minimum tillage practices (Cook, 1962) would appear to be particularly warranted as a management tool for protection of the organic nitrogen pool against rapid oxidation and yield of nitrates. This practice also protects against destruction of soil aggregates, preserves structure, and decreases runoff (Burwell et al., 1968). Infiltration is increased, which provides more water for use by plants and a more extensive plant cover.

As noted in an earlier section, nitrogen is a key element in crop production because of its transitory nature in soils, and it is becoming more economical to add too much fertilizer nitrogen rather than to risk not applying enough. It is evident now that in selected locations, movement of surplus nitrates into water supplies can be serious, not only as a potential pollutant but also as a loss to the efficiency of production. University and commercial soil and plant tissue testing laboratories and procedures are generally available for making fertilizer recommendations, and these are geared for efficiency of production at yield potential levels estimated to be feasible for a given soil and climatic area. Nitrogen recommendations, particularly, are based on the nitrogen requirement of the crop for maximum efficient production (in the case of crops like sugar beets, potatoes, or malting barley where surplus nitrogen reduces quality, it should be the "minimum" requirement for maximum production of a product of acceptable quality, as suggested by Stanford et al., 1965), efficiency of utilization of nitrogen fertilizers used, and the nitrogen-supplying capability of the soil via release of nitrogen from the organic nitrogen pool (Fenster et al., 1969). As noted earlier, when irrigation waters from surface wells containing nitrates are used, cropland management recommendations can be developed to include the amounts of nitrogen which will be supplied with the irrigation waters (Stout and Burau, 1967). Realistic recommendations can help avoid overapplication. The environmental quality factor will have to be brought into the formulation of responsible recommendations.

A number of researchers are attempting to determine what constitutes an acceptable application rate for nitrogen that will both sustain production and minimize pollution.

Webber (1967) in Ontario, Canada, has postulated an application rate for farm manures which would not release on decomposition over 300 pounds per acre of ammonia-nitrogen which could be oxidized to nitrate. This amount could presumably be utilized by corn or by hay-pasture crops and removed with the crop or be dissipated otherwise, such as by denitrification or tied up by microorganisms in the decomposition of crop residue. At this level, it was suggested that there would be little nitrate in surplus which would move into underground water supplies. It was further suggested that for small grains, or sandy soils under irrigation, a lower figure would have to be used. The figure for "safe" application levels of nitrogen for different crop management systems is currently being checked out, using 32-inch diameter, 42-inch deep lysimeters on a Guelph loam.

In Missouri Smith (1968) suggested an application rate no higher than is required for optimum yields, approximately 100 pounds of nitrogen per acre, if nitrates are not to reach groundwater supplies. As noted earlier, nitrate movement studies have been underway for 7 years on soils with widely different characteristics and where corn yields have varied from about 60 to more than 150 bushels per acre. Nitrates accumulated progressively in 8-foot profiles at all levels of application above 100 pounds per acre annually.

Cooke (1969) suggests that use efficiency of nitrogen fertilizers which currently average less than 50% must be increased in the future not only for reduction in crop production costs but to avoid loss of nitrogen by leaching. Promising researches relate to the control of ammonia oxidation and other reactions in soils as noted earlier and perhaps also the decomposition of urea, higher analysis and more readily available compounds of phosphorus reacted with ammonia, pelleting of fertilizers to control solubility rates and with the seed for immediate utilization, and "agronomic control" by plant analysis with subsequent and immediate application of fertilizer if needed by aerial topdressings or perhaps in the irrigation waters. Different soils, climates, and cropping systems would have to be given individual research attention.

CONCLUSIONS

Nitrogen and phosphorus, as nutrient elements, are important to both land and aquatic plants, and normally reach water supplies via land runoff in the erosion debris which is selectively enriched in organic nutrient materials or via the leachate which may contain mobile nitrate ions.

Fertilizer usages in the midcontinent area are rapidly increasing to maximize production and increase efficiency, and further increases are anticipated. Current information suggests that phosphatic fertilizers incorporated in the soil are not contaminating natural waters, but nitrogen fertilizers may be contributory in selected situations. For example, where application rates, together with soil supplies, have exceeded crop needs and/or excessive leaching occurs induced by overirrigation of sandy soils, nitrates can be contributed to underground water supplies.

Fertilizer phosphorus quickly converts to unavailable forms in mineral soils and the evidence indicates that one of the ways of reducing the level of soluble phosphorus in water would be to effect soil contact such as by filtration through the soil medium. Some phosphorus is removed from frozen plant materials with snow melt waters which is difficult to control except perhaps by diversion terraces into seepage areas.

Nitrogen fertilizer application rates should approximate crop needs, which for a given soil type and climatic zone are based on production potential estimates for the crops to be grown. One hundred pounds of nitrogen per acre can apparently be safely applied to cropped soils without major contribution of nitrate to the leachate, and up to 300 pounds per acre in some instances, though much more research is needed in this area.

Management recommendations refined through the years for maximizing production are not incompatible with the objective of reducing nutrient contamination of natural waters. These involve an emphasis on erosion control measures to include vegetative cover which, in addition to a reduction in runoff and erosion, removes fertilizer nutrients with the harvest and effects water transpiration to reduce leaching. Other factors include the use of cover crops where adapted and incorporation of crop residues in the fall for protection of soil surfaces and utilization of plant nutrients, minimum tillage to improve structure and reduce the mineralization of organic nitrogen reserves, and an emphasis on increasing fertilizer use efficiencies by the crop, such as by split applications and the use of ammoniacal forms of nitrogen in the fall.

Further research is needed on nutrient balances and reactions in soils to maintain supplies at levels needed for crop production; to increase the efficiency of use as a percentage of that supplied, currently less than 50%; and to minimize loss of nitrate to water supplies. This would include research on nitrification-inhibiting chemicals so as to retain nitrogen in the ammoniacal form, pelleting, or other to reduce solubility or application with the seed to increase uptake, and plant analysis monitoring of nutrients with needed applications applied quickly, perhaps by air or in the irrigation waters.

Water quality standards as established by the federal and state water pollution control groups should be compatible with the need for maintaining adequate nutrients for efficient crop production consistent with management programs designed to minimize losses to adjacent water supplies.

REFERENCES

Alexander, M. 1965. Nitrification. In *Soil nitrogen,* ed. W. V. Bartholomew and F. E. Clark, pp. 307–43. Madison, Wis.: Am. Soc. Agron.

Allison, F. E. 1955. The enigma of soil nitrogen balance sheets. *Advan. Agron.* 7:213–50.

———. 1965. Evaluation of incoming and outgoing processes that affect soil nitrogen. In *Soil nitrogen,* ed. W. V. Bartholomew and F. E. Clark, pp. 573–606. Madison, Wis.: Am. Soc. Agron.

Allison, F. E., Roller, E. M., and Adams, J. E. 1959. *Soil fertility studies in lysimeters containing lake land sand.* USDA Tech. Bull. 1199.

Bailey, G. W. March 1968. *Role of soils and sediment in water pollution control. I. Reactions of nitrogenous and phosphatic compounds with soils and geologic strata.* Fed. Water Pollution Control Adm., Southeast Water Lab. Bull., U.S. Dept. Interior.

Ballantyne, C. R., Schaller, F. W., and Phillips, J. A. Dec. 1967. *Erosion control factors and universal soil loss equation.* Iowa State Univ. Coop. Ext. Serv. Bull., p. 410.

Barrows, H. L., and Kilmer, V. J. 1963. Plant nutrient losses from soils by water erosion. *Advan. Agron.* 15:303–16.

Beaton, J. D., and Tisdale, S. L. 1969. *Potential plant nutrient consumption in North America.* Sulphur Inst. Tech. Bull. 16.

Bedell, G. D., Kohnke, H., and Hickok, R. B. 1946. The effects of two farming sytems on erosion from cropland. *Soil Sci. Soc. Am. Proc.* 11:522–26.

Biggar, J. W., and Corey, R. B. 1968. Nitrate and phosphate in lakes and streams. Unpublished mimeo., Univ. of Wis., Madison.

Bizzel, J. A. 1944. *Lysimeter experiments. VI. The effects of cropping and fertilization on the losses of nitrogen from the soil.* Cornell Agr. Exp. Sta. Memo. 256, pp. 1–14.

Black, C. A. 1968. *Soil-plant relationships.* 2nd ed. New York: John Wiley.

Blake, G. R., Allred, E. R., Van Bavel, C. H. M., and Whisler, F. D. 1960. *Agricultural drought and moisture excesses in Minnesota.* Minn. Agr. Exp. Sta. Tech. Bull. 235, pp. 1–36.

Burwell, R. E., Sloneker, L. L., and Nelson, W. W. 1968. Tillage influences water intake. *J. Soil Water Conserv.* 23:185–87.

Cook, R. L. 1962. *Soil management for conservation and production.* New York: John Wiley.

Cooke, G. W. 1969. *Fertilizers in 2000 A.D.* Intern. Superphosphate and Compound Manufacturers' Assoc., Bull. 53, pp. 1–13.

Corey, R. B., Hasler, A. D., Lee, G. F., Schraufnagel, F. H., and Wirth, T. L. Jan. 1967. *Excessive water fertilization.* Report to the Water Subcommittee, Natl. Resources Com. of State Agencies, Wis.

Duley, F. L., and Miller, M. F. 1923. *Erosion and surface runoff under different soil conditions.* Mo. Agr. Exp. Sta. Bull. 63.

Fenster, W. E., Overdahl, C. J., and Grava, J. 1969. *Guide to computer programmed soil test recommendations in Minnesota.* Minn. Agr. Ext. Serv. Spec. Rept. 1.

Gardner, W. R. 1965. Movement of nitrogen in soil. In *Soil nitrogen,* ed. W. V. Bartholomew and F. E. Clark, pp. 555–72. Madison, Wis.: Am. Soc. Agron.

Garman, W. H. 1969. Nitrogen facts and fallacies. *Plant Food Rev.* 15:15–20.

Haas, H. J., Grunes, D. L., and Reichman, G. A. 1961. Phosphorus changes in Great Plains soils as influenced by cropping and manure applications. *Soil Sci. Soc. Am. Proc.* 25:214–18.

Hanson, L. D., and Fenster, W. E. Oct. 1969. Phosphorus and lake quality. *Crops Soils.*

Hargett, N. L. 1969. *1968 fertilizer summary data* Natl. Fertilizer Develop. Center, TVA, Muscle Shoals, Ala.

Hauser, V. L. 1968. Nitrates in playas. *Agr. Res. Notes* 17:15.

Hays, O. E., Bay, C. E., and Hull, H. H. 1948. Increased production on a loess-derived soil. *Am. Soc. Agron. J.* 40:1061–69.

Hemwall, J. B. 1957. The fixation of phosphorus by soils. *Advan. Agron.* 9:95–113.

Holt, F. G. 1969. *Runoff and sediment as nutrient sources.* Water Resources Res. Center Bull. 13, pp. 35–38, Univ. of Minn.

Holt, R. F., Timmons, D. R., and Latterell, J. J. 1969. Accumulation of phosphates in water. In press. *J. Food Agr. Chem.*

Huber, D. M., Murray, G. A., and Crane, J. M. 1969. Inhibition of nitrification—a deterrent to nitrate nitrogen loss and potential water pollution. *Soil Sci. Soc. Am. Proc.* In press.

Janssen, K. A., and Wiese, R. A. 1969. The influence of 2-chloro-6-(Trichloromethyl) pyridine with anhydrous ammonia on corn yield, N-uptake, and conversion of ammonium to nitrate. M.S. thesis, Univ. of Nebr., Lincoln.

Johnston, W. R., Ittihadieh, F., Daum, R. M., and Pillsbury, A. F. 1965. Nitrogen and phosphorus in tile drain effluent. *Soil Sci. Soc. Am. Proc.* 29:287–89.

Keeney, D. R., Konrad, J. G., and Chesters, G. 1969. Nitrogen distribution in some Wisconsin lake sediments. *J. Water Pollution Control Federation.* In press.

Kilmer, V. J., Hays, O. E., and Muckenhirn, R. J. 1944. Plant nutrient and water losses from Fayette silt loam as measured by monolith lysimeters. *Am. Soc. Agron. J.* 36:249–63.

Latterell, J. H., Holt, R. F., and Timmons, D. R. 1969. Phosphate availability in lake sediments. Personal communications; manuscript in press.

MacGregor, J. M., Hanson, L. D., and Ellis, J. E. 1969. Unpublished research and personal communication. Univ. of Minn., St. Paul.

Maderak, M. L. 1963. *Quality of waters, Minnesota—a compilation, 1955–62.* Minn. State Dept. Conserv. Bull. 21.

——. 1965. *Chemical quality of ground water in Minneapolis-St. Paul area of Minnesota.* Minn. State Dept. Conserv. Bull. 23.

Martin, W. P. 1969. Controlling nutrients and organic toxicants in runoff. *Water pollution by nutrients—sources, effects and control.* Water Resources Res. Center Bull. 13, pp. 39–48. Univ. of Minn.

Massey, H. F., and Jackson, M. L. 1952. Selective erosion of soil fertility constituents. *Soil Sci. Soc. Am. Proc.* 16:353–56.

Meek, B. D., Grass, L. B., Willardson, L. S., and MacKenzie, A. J. Aug. 18–22, 1969. Nitrate transformation in a column with a controlled water table. Abstr. Western Soc. Soil Sci., Wash. State Univ., Pullman.

Megard, R. O. 1969. Diagnosing pollution in Lake Minnetonka. *Water pollution by nutrients—sources, effects and control.* Water Resources Res. Center Bull. 13, Univ. of Minn.

Miller, M. F., and Krusekoff, H. H. 1932. *The influence of systems of cropping and methods of culture on surface runoff and soil erosion.* Mo. Agri. Exp. Sta. Res. Bull. 177.

Pearson, R. W., Jordan, H. V., Bennett, O. L., Scarsbrook, C. E., Adams, W. E., and White, A. W. 1961. *Residual effects of fall- and spring-applied nitrogen fertilizers on crop yields in the southeastern United States.* USDA Bull. 1254, pp. 1–19.

Rogers, H. T. 1942. Losses of surface-applied phosphate and limestone through runoff from pasture land. *Soil Sci. Soc. Am. Proc.* 7:69–76.

Russell, E. W. 1961. *Soil conditions and plant growth.* 9th ed. New York: John Wiley.

Schmidt, E. L. 1956. *Soil nitrification and nitrates in waters.* Minn. Public Health Dept. Repts. 7:497–503.

Smith, D. D., and Wischmeier, W. H. 1962. Rainfall erosion. *Advan. Agron.* 14:109–48.

Smith, G. E. 1965. *Water forum: nitrate problems in water as related to soils, plants and water.* Mo. Agr. Exp. Sta. Spec. Rept. 55:42–52.

——. 1967. *Fertilizer nutrients as contaminants in water supplies.* Am. Assoc. Adv. Sci. Publ. 85, pp. 173–86.

——. April 9, 1968. In *Water pollution as related to agriculture,* pp. 13–27. Joint seminar, Univ. of Mo. and Mo. Water Pollution Board, Columbia.

Soileau, J. M. 1969. *Effects of fertilizers on water quality—a collection of abstracts and references.* Natl. Fertilizer Dev. Center, TVA, Muscle Shoals, Ala.

Stallings, J. H. 1957. *Soil conservation.* New York: Prentice-Hall.

Stanford, G., Ayres, A. S., and Doi, M. 1965. Mineralizable soil nitrogen in relation to fertilizer need of surgarcane in Hawaii. *Soil Sci.* 99:132–37.

Stewart, B. A., Viets, F. G., and Hutchinson, G. L. 1968. Agriculture's effect on nitrate pollution of groundwater. *J. Soil Water Conserv.* 23:13–15.

Stout, P. R., and Burau, R. G. 1967. *The extent and significance of fertilizer buildup in soils as revealed by vertical distribution of nitrogenous matter between soils and underlying water reservoirs.* Am. Assoc. Adv. Sci. Publ. 85, pp. 283–310.

Taylor, A. W. 1967. Phosphorus and water pollution. *J. Soil Water Conserv.* 22:228–31.

Timmons, D. R., Burwell, R. E., and Holt, R. F. 1968. Loss of crop nutrients through runoff. *Minn. Sci.* 24:16–19.

Turner, G. O., and Goring, C. A. I. 1966. N-serve, a status report. *Down Earth* 22:19–25.

Wadleigh, C. H. 1968. *Agriculture and the quality of our environment.* USDA Misc. Publ. 1065.

———. Feb. 4, 1968. Nitrate in soil, water and food. Commentator response to article, "Pollution hazard may curb fertilizer use," appearing in *Des Moines* (Iowa) *Sunday Register.*

Wagner, G. H., and Smith, G. E. 1960. *Recovery of fertilizer nitrogen from soils.* Mo. Agr. Exp. Sta. Res. Bull. 738.

Webber, L. R. 1967. *The nature of problem: soil pollution.* Ontario Pollution Control Conf., Toronto, Can.

———. 1969a. *Characteristics of soil percolates following application of liquid manure.* 1968 Progress Rept., Dept. of Soil Sci., Univ. of Guelph, Ontario, Can.

———. 1969b. Animal waste utilization using undisturbed soil lysimeters. Unpublished data and personal communication. Univ. of Guelph, Ontario, Can.

Webber, L. R., and Elrick, D. E. 1966. Research needs for controlling soil pollution. *Agr. Sci. Rev.* 4:10–20.

White, W. C. 1965. Plant nutrient toll 1965. *Plant Food Rev.* 11 (4): 17–18.

White, R. E., and Beckett, P. H. T. 1964. Studies on the phosphate potentials of soils. *Plant Soil* 20:1.

CHAPTER TEN

WORKSHOP SESSION

J. T. PESEK, Leader
R. A. OLSON, Reporter

D R. PESEK opened the session by summarizing its objectives as being a forum for questioning the speakers in the formal program, a second channel for bringing into focus the lacking data which should be filled in by future research, and a means for all interested individuals to make statements and discuss any aspect of the role of fertilizers as water pollutants.

A lively session among the 40 to 50 participants resulted for the prescribed period. Procedure followed was to read prepared statements which had been submitted, followed by discussion from the floor.

The initial statement by Dr. L. B. Baldwin of the University of Florida Extension Service concerned Lake Okeechobee and the St. John's River Basin Water Development Projects which constitute closed water systems. Herewith, an attempt is being made to measure water nutrient levels from the eutrophication standpoint which, it is hoped, will provide information of countrywide interest. Most relevant aspects of Dr. Baldwin's statement were as follows:

> Florida has several important agricultural areas adjacent to large lakes and reservoirs which are a part of well-developed and closely regulated water management projects. In the case of Lake Okeechobee (740 sq. miles) and the peat soil farming area (1,100 sq. miles) around its southern perimeter, water is pumped to the lake during wet periods, and taken from the lake for irrigation. The lake itself is contained by levees, and is regulated seasonally for stage control. During periods of below normal rainfall, discharge may not be necessary, and the lake and agricultural area function as a closed system. This situation may contribute substantially to nutrient buildup in the lake.

> A 2-year study of the nutrient condition in Lake Okeechobee was started in January 1969. It is the purpose of the study to determine the level of nutrients in the lake and in all water entering the lake. This, and subsequent studies, may show that eutrophication of the lake, under present or proposed future stages, will be accelerated by

J. T. PESEK is Professor and Head, Department of Agronomy, Iowa State University. R. A. OLSON is Professor, Department of Agronomy, University of Nebraska.

nutrients from agricultural lands. All aspects of this situation involve important segments of Florida's economy.

A similar study is underway in the St. John's River Basin, which is also part of a controlled system. These studies should produce data of interest and use to other areas of the country. Subsequent studies of fertilizer-soil-water management and water system management should also be of importance.

Discussion on this topic centered particularly around source of phosphorus that might be responsible for its buildup in lake and stream waters in an area such as Okeechobee which is surrounded by peat and muck soils. Dr. Black expressed belief from the phosphorus chemistry standpoint that any phosphorus that did accumulate in this situation would not be from mineralization of the peat and muck but rather would come from other sources.

Dr. George Smith noted the occurrence of the substantial phosphate deposits a short distance to the north in Florida and questioned the relevance of phosphate rock origin to current considerations in the St. John's-Okeechobee projects. Environmental conditions were entirely different, however, and presumably there would be no corollary between the two.

The next statement was by Dr. Robert D. Harter of the University of New Hampshire who wrote concerning the perplexing nature of phosphorus in surface water and its role in eutrophication. The relevant portion of his statement was as follows:

> Even in highly eutrophic lakes, the amount of phosphorus in solution is small; much less, in fact, than is needed for plant growth. Yet, luxurious algal blooms are common. Where, then, do they obtain the needed phosporus?

> Studies of the phosphorus cycle in lakes are being conducted, and nutrient budgets of lakes are being worked out. An increasing amount of this type of study is needed. However, the contribution of the lake sediment has frequently been ignored in these deliberations. Lake sediment has been shown to have a large adsorption capacity for phosphorus. Further research is needed on the fate of phosphorus which is unaccounted for in nutrient budgets, and is assumed to be adsorbed by the sediment.

> Soil scientists have for years attempted to identify the phosphorus compounds in soil. Long-term fertility plots have been shown to contain increased amounts of hydroxyapatite, variscite, and other highly insoluble phosphorus compounds. However, there is little information on the length of time needed for formation of the most insoluble crystals and the kinetics of formation. Before the eutrophication process can be completely understood and any measure of control or reversal initiated, we need to know whether the same insoluble phosphorus compounds are formed in lake sediment. If they are not, we need to know why. If they are, we need to work out the kinetics of formation, with an eye to increasing the rate of phosphorus fixation in highly insoluble forms.

Discussion following this statement centered on equilibria established between the solid/liquid phase, the time required for equilibria to be reached, the turnover time involved with algal uptake, the role of carbon dioxide on algal uptake at low concentrations, and water stratification implications on equilibria.

A significant observation in this respect is the lack of algal problems with high sediment levels in the water. This is responsible for the fact that the high stem dams of the Missouri River and elsewhere are now creating taste and odor problems in municipal water supply systems in their vicinities which did not exist before impoundment and sedimentation occurred. Also relevant is water depth, evidenced by the lack of stratification in the shallow eastern part of Lake Okeechobee compared with considerable stratification in the deeper western part of the lake and a much greater eutrophication of the former. Lake depth also influences the problem of bottom rooted plants, complimented by water clarity.

There was agreement that studies are needed to establish the fate of phosphorus in lake sediments, including the kinetics of formation of insoluble phosphorus compounds. Although some work was recognized as being underway in Wisconsin, Oregon, and elsewhere, much more is needed in various sections of the country with a variety of soil sediments, kinds of clay minerals, and environmental conditions, especially temperature. A number of questions were raised without specific answers, to wit: (1) When and where should sampling be done of stream and lake waters for expressing nutrient concentrations—that is, a need exists for *sampling standards.* (2) How do we best measure phosphorus in stream or lake sediments, by water extraction? (3) Do bottom rooted plants serve as a phosphorus pump from these sediments, exuding phosphorus to algae in the upper waters?

The next statement by Dr. J. Lunin of ARS-SWC accepted that phosphorus movement into lakes and streams is simplified by reason of the adsorbed state of the element on sediments. Movement of nitrates, however, is a much more difficult problem. The most pertinent aspects of his statement follow:

A nitrogen balance would be highly desirable to determine. But how do we quantify deep percolation and denitrification losses? We can study nitrogen transformation processes in the laboratory and greenhouse, with lysimeters, and on field plots. Indeed, we are studying only segments of a problem. To truly evaluate the contribution of nitrogen fertilization to the nitrate content of a stream, lake, or groundwater source, we must integrate multiple effects found within the watershed supplying that water resource. It is obvious that we must take into consideration all the hydrologic parameters of that watershed because nitrates move with water.

The question is, How can we evaluate agriculture's contribution to the nitrate content of a given water resource? Let us define the research required to develop and implement a workable water quality model for a watershed that would integrate all climatic, agronomic, animal, etc., effects within that watershed.

Discussion here recognized that nitrate buildup is usually noted whenever streams are running high with runoff. A key question raised was, How often do geologic sources of nitrate influence reported stream values, especially with the high runoff conditions? There was group concurrence that a great deal of deep profile investigation is needed for tracing the course of nitrate from the topsoil to the groundwater. North Dakota, for example, commonly finds a pool of nitrate at the 2-foot depth, more or less. There may well be similar accumulation zones at considerable depths in other regions that are of rather ancient origin.

The statement of Dr. James P. Law, Jr., Research Soil Scientist of the FWPCA, made particular reference to nitrate buildup in irrigated areas.

The switch to high-value crops, increased fertilization rates, and increased irrigation contributes to increased rates of water quality degradation, especially where shallow groundwater exists as the only dependable supply for rural domestic, municipal, and livestock requirements. These facts suggest the need for serious scrutiny of present fertilizer application methods and rates.

The time-worn practice of applying fertilizer for entire crop needs as one or two slug-feedings during the growing season could very well be shown to be both wasteful and impractical. In tile-drained areas it has, in fact, been shown that large percentages of the fertilizer nutrients applied are lost from cropland in the drainage water. Other studies have shown increased crop yields by adding fertilizer requirements in small increments throughout the growing season—for example, irrigating grain crops with sewage effluents containing limited quantities of nutrients (Ref: A. D. Day and co-workers in Arizona). Fertilizer elements in excess of immediate crop needs are subject to loss by leaching below the root zone and eventual occurrence as pollutants in water supplies, both surface and groundwater.

The following are suggested as areas worthy of research, with the objectives of correcting some of the present pollution problems relative to fertilizer application methods and rates:
1. Subsurface irrigation lends itself to automation and much more efficient water use, which can be beneficial in controlling leaching losses of fertilizer elements. The control of surface evaporation in subsurface systems also alleviates the salinity problem associated with irrigation return flow.
2. Spoon-feeding fertilizer elements in small increments throughout the growing season would greatly lessen the possibility of wasteful losses of fertilizer to surface and groundwater supplies. Economic benefits of fertilizer applications would be increased. Soluble fertilizer fed directly in the irrigation water is an example. The closely controlled application of subsurface systems would be a beneficial method.
3. Further studies into application of slow-release fertilizers by conventional methods are suggested. The objectives should be to maximize fertilizer benefits and minimize environmental pollution.
4. Control of excess plant nutrients arising from fertilizer application depends on a better understanding of the movement and ultimate fate of these materials. Studies aimed at clarification of nutrient transport and deposition mechanisms may furnish new leads to better control.

Discussion following Dr. Law's paper was concerned especially with determining what is economic rate of fertilizer application without building excess residual in the soil. It is common opinion that some nominal excess in application rate, as in the order of 50%, is necessary, due to portions of the soil root zone being dry during parts of the season. The pertinent question then is just how much nutrient exists residually in the entire rooting profile at the beginning of the crop season for determining what would be the economic rate of application.

A primary question from this area is, How do we go about measuring fertilizer influence on groundwater? Some of the barometer watersheds as in Oregon and the Treynor watershed in Iowa may be revealing in the near future.

The statement of Dr. Ronald G. Menzel of ARS-USDA was similar to that posed by Dr. Lunin, as follows:

> Nitrate concentrations in groundwater or surface water mean very little by themselves. One must understand the dynamics of each situation. Where is the nitrate coming from? Where is it going? How rapidly? Only by answering these questions can we relate fertilizer practices to water contamination. Therefore, it appears that measurements of groundwater movement, chemical and biological transformations of nitrogen, and gaseous losses of nitrogen are critically needed.
>
> One major problem is interrelating the different measurements involving nitrogen transformations and movement. Those measurements that have to be made in the laboratory must somehow be extrapolated to field conditions. For example, it may be necessary to estimate denitrification losses in the field from laboratory measurements. Can these be made more realistic by increasing sample size, controlling composition of the gaseous and aqueous phases, increasing static pressure, or by other means? At the same time, we need to attempt direct measurements of denitrification in the field. Possibly an indicator reaction, similar to the reduction of acetylene as an indicator of nitrogen fixation, can be found for denitrification. If so, the difficulty of distinguishing denitrified nitrogen from atmospheric nitrogen might be avoided.

Discussion in this case brought out that there has been an increase of about 15% in recent years of water supplies in Iowa with greater than 45 ppm nitrate. An interesting proposal for the immediate locality was one that would take all of the wastewater from the city of Ames, Iowa, which now goes into water courses and use it year around for irrigating some 1,000 acres of land in the immediate vicinity. Thereby, stream pollution would be alleviated at the same time that many of the fertility requirements of a substantial area of land were taken care of.

Further discussion centered around ways of removing nitrate that has accumulated in a soil zone before it reaches the underlying groundwater. One under investigation is the addition of an energy source to an anaerobic zone where nitrate has accumulated to promote denitrification.

A statement by Dr. T. R. Smith of the FWPCA supplied data on nitrate and tile drains in streams of Illinois as follows:

> Water discharged from tile drains in prairie soils in Vermilion County, Illinois, was studied in the spring of 1968.

In the Middle Fork Vermilion River Basin, two tile drains averaged 13.5 and 17.3 mg/l nitrate nitrogen and at the same time the river averaged 9.1 mg/l. At baseflow and with no tile discharge, the river contained 0.24 mg/l nitrate nitrogen. The North Fork Vermilion River Basin yielded similar data.

The data indicate that most of the nitrate was coming from agricultural land and that it was a widespread condition, otherwise, the river would have had a much lower nitrate concentration during spring runoff.

Nitrate losses in these concentrations pose the possibility of polluting reservoirs and groundwater supplies.

It appears that research may be needed on this matter to determine whether nitrates could be used more efficiently, with less being lost in drainage water and at the same time maintain high crop yields.

This problem could occur anywhere in the humid prairie region.

Complementary to this statement was a report from Story County, Iowa, of 5 to 40 ppm nitrate nitrogen in tile drains. It was further contended that nitrate has been increasing steadily in rivers of Illinois in the last 10 to 20 years, much more rapidly during the last 5 years, and especially in the most productive agricultural areas of the state. These increases coincide closely with the pyramidal growth in fertilizer nitrogen consumption during the interval involved.

Acknowledged was the need to study again the amount of nitrogen received in precipitation under modern conditions. Results could be quite different from those obtained early in the century.

From these discussions the following summary statements and questions evolved:

1. Recognizing that phosphorus accumulates in water largely through sediments, how do we go about reducing the phosphorus level maintained in the equilibrium solution?
2. We do not know with certainty the source of nitrogen in waters. A good deal of research is needed for locating the source and means of abatement.
3. What quality of water should the public have reasonable right to expect, keeping in mind the services demanded and the quality levels attainable in relation to economic considerations?
4. It would be most helpful if agronomists, engineers, and hydrologists would work together closely in solving the problems involved.
5. It should be made clear that controls on the use of fertilizers would necessitate some radical changes in our American eating habits, to the very great dissatisfaction of many. Fertilizers have done much toward making this the best fed nation on earth.

PART THREE

PESTICIDES AS WATER POLLUTANTS

CHAPTER ELEVEN

CHEMISTRY AND METABOLISM OF INSECTICIDES

PAUL A. DAHM

As man embarked on global travel during the eighteenth and nineteenth centuries, a number of events occurred that had immense consequences in relation to pest control. The world was searched for new plants to adorn the greenhouses that were part of every gentleman's residence. These plants brought new pests that flourished in their new environments. Similarly, other pests were distributed by shipments of infested food, grain, and other products. In fact, most of today's major pest control problems exist because of man's ignorance and indiscretion. Attempts to control these problems led to the development of chemical pesticides. Reviewing the history of some of these early developments (Ordish, 1968) will prepare us to consider a few examples of modern insecticides.

Until about 1840 most farmers regarded pests as something one had to accept, as the will of God. By the late 1840s M. Grison of Versailles discovered that lime-sulfur was a cure for powdery mildew, *Uncinula necator,* a serious pest of grapes that came from America. Soon after it was discovered that the disease could be arrested by dusting plants with sulfur. This was the first large-scale successful use of chemicals for pest control.

The next significant step occurred when pioneers introduced the potato plant to beetles, *Leptinotarsa decemlineata,* feeding on wild solanaceous plants growing on the eastern slopes of the Rocky Mountains from Canada to Texas. This beetle, soon known as the Colorado potato beetle, displayed a strong preference for its new food, the potato. The beetle began spreading eastward at an average rate of about 85 miles a year, often destroying entire potato crops wherever it appeared. Virtually nothing checked the multiplication and spread of the beetle until about 1865 when an arsenic-containing

PAUL A. DAHM is professor of Entomology, Department of Zoology and Entomology, Iowa State University.

Journal Paper No. J-6509 of the Iowa Agriculture and Home Economics Experiment Station, Ames. Projects No. 1351, 1435, and 1686. Preparation of this paper was supported by Public Health Service Research Grant ES-00205 from the Division of Environmental Health Sciences and North Central Regional Project NC-85.

chemical known as Paris green was used as a spray on potato plants to kill the beetles. Although Paris green was quite toxic and likely to injure plant foliage, it remained the leading stomach poison for insect control until the introduction of lead arsenate in 1892.

A combination of copper sulfate and lime, subsequently called Bordeaux mixture, was discovered by accident in the 1880s to be an effective fungicide for the control of downy mildew, *Plasmopara viticola*.

Chemical control of pests was well launched by these discoveries during the latter part of the nineteenth century. At the Columbian Exposition in Chicago in 1893 there were some 42 patented insecticides offered by several manufacturers.

Until 1940 insecticides consisted mostly of arsenicals, fluosilicates, plant-derived chemicals, various petroleum products, synthetic thiocyanates, and several fumigant chemicals. Discovery of the broad-spectrum insecticidal properties of p,p'-DDT and γ-HCCH (lindane) in the 1940s stimulated a pesticide bonanza. The millenium, however, had not arrived. When populations of both harmful and useful insects were drastically reduced by these modern chemicals, nontarget arthropods occasionally became pests because their predators were no longer plentiful enough to reduce their populations. Insecticide-resistant strains of more than 200 species of arthropod pests also developed, owing to chemical selectivity of the new insecticides. Although benefits from modern pesticides are manifold, their use has been progressively questioned, especially since publication of *Silent Spring* by Rachael Carson (1962). We are now at a stage at which people from several disciplines and with different expertise are looking critically at many facets of pesticide use. Also, a variety of pest-control methods are being examined with the hope of reducing some of the problems caused by chemical agents.

In 1966 over half of all U.S. farmers used weed-, insect-, or disease-control chemicals on their crops. In this same year about 29% of the farmers used insecticides on one or more crops. But only 5% of the crop, pasture, and range acres, or about 12% of the crop acres excluding pasture and rangeland, were treated for insect control (Fox et al., 1968). An estimate of the use of insecticides in the 48 contiguous states in the early 1960s showed that less than 5% of the acreage had insecticides applied; about 0.4% of the total area generally considered favorable to wildlife had insecticides applied; and 85% of the acreage planted by U.S. farmers to crops each year was not treated with insecticides (Hall, 1962). In actual quantities, about 156 million pounds of insecticide products were used on farms in the 48 contiguous states in 1964. This amounts to about 70 pounds for each commercial farmer in the United States. Of the total, about 143 million pounds were used on crops (including crops, pasture, rangeland, and land in summer fallow) and 13 million pounds for other purposes (principally livestock and livestock buildings). Although alternative methods of controlling insect pests are being developed and employed, it has been estimated that conventional insecticides are still needed to control 80 to 90% of insect problems affecting agriculture (Knipling, 1969).

The abundance and mobility of water and its solvent properties have resulted in a variety of relationships between water and insecticides. Fundamentally, water can transport insecticides, and insecticides can pollute water. Many insecticides are applied to plants or soil for protection or beautification. Such applications are made to fields, lawns, orchards, forests, gardens, greenhouses, nurseries, and shrubs. Although soil is the principal recipient of insecticidal chemicals, water is their principal distributor after application. Insecticides may pollute water when they are applied to areas harboring insects and related arthropods and to domestic animals and their wastes. Insecticidal pollution of water may also occur when man accidentally or irresponsibly misuses these chemicals. Back-siphoning of spray materials into wells when filling spray equipment, damage to containers of insecticidal chemicals in transit, improper disposal of insecticides in all forms, excessive applications, and various misapplications are examples of these misuses. Occasionally, industrial wastes containing insecticides may lead to water pollution. And there is continuous cycling of small quantities of insecticides by volatilization from the earth into the atmosphere and precipitation back onto soil and water.

The three major classes of insecticides presently in use are chlorinated hydrocarbons, organophosphates, and carbamates. Of the eight insecticides used most in the United States in 1964, four were chlorinated hydrocarbons (DDT, DDD, aldrin, and toxaphene), three were organophosphates (methyl parathion, parathion, and malathion), and one was a carbamate (carbaryl) (Table 15, Eichers et al., 1968). These will serve as examples around which to discuss the metabolism of insecticides.

DDT AND RELATED CHEMICALS

Both praising and damning declarations have been made about DDT since its introduction as an insecticide in the 1940s. Campaigns against this chemical have recently been waged so vigorously in communication media and in legislative and judicial branches of our government that there is considerable doubt that DDT will survive as an insecticide. Mankind is giving a pragmatic twist to the future use of DDT by applying the Socratean adage, "To know is to suffer." DDT has probably been studied more intensively and extensively than any other synthetic chemical. It is one of the cheapest organic pesticides. Its chemical stability and biological effects have been praised or criticized, depending upon how one reacts to the need for and presence of this chemical in the environment. The principal metabolites of DDT are well known (Fig. 11.1). The best known metabolic route involves dehydrochlorination of DDT to DDE, 1,1-dichloro-2,2-bis(p-chlorophenyl) ethylene, because this reaction is the primary reason for resistance of insects to DDT (Sternburg et al., 1953). Strains of insects resistant to DDT have a large proportion of their population possessing an enzyme that can dehydrochlorinate DDT to less-toxic DDE (Lipke and Kearns, 1960). Susceptible strains

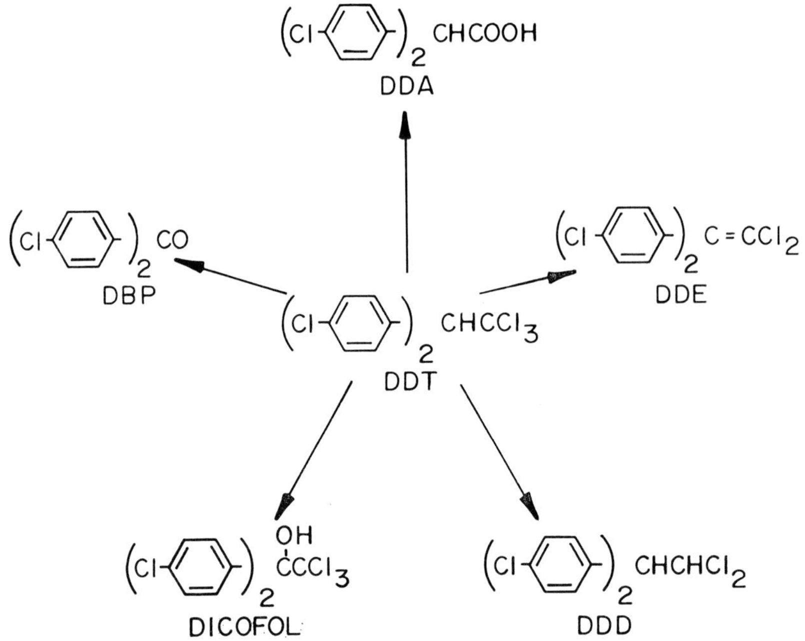

FIG. 11.1.   The principal metabolites of DDT.

of insects have relatively few individuals with this biochemical pro-
ficiency; hence, they succumb to the insecticide. DDE is also the
most common metabolite of DDT found in avian tissues. It has been
suggested that DDE plays a major role in causing thinness of eggshells in certain species of birds (Heath et al., 1969), possibly by
inducing hepatic microsomal metabolism of steroids. One of the
earliest metabolic discoveries about DDT was its conversion to DDA,
bis(p-chlorophenyl) acetic acid, in mammals (White and Sweeney,
1945; Jensen et al., 1957; Durham et al., 1963), including man
(Neal et al., 1946; Durham et al., 1965). DDA is readily excreted in
the urine. Biological reductive dechlorination of DDT to
DDD(=TDE), 1,1-dichloro-2,2-bis(p-chlorophenyl) ethane, has been
proved comparatively recently (Finley and Pillmore, 1963; Barker
and Morrison, 1964; Walker et al., 1965). This reaction occurs most
readily under anaerobic conditions in animal tissues and in microorganisms. It is now quite acceptable to report DDD as a metabolite
of DDT but for many years the possibility of this compound being
formed biologically was scoffed at by some scientists. DDD is a commercial insecticide in its own right. Replacement of hydrogen on the
tertiary carbon of DDT by a hydroxyl group forms a metabolite of low
toxicity to insects and mammals but of high toxicity to mites (Tsukamoto, 1959; Agosin et al., 1961). A commercial miticide called dicofol
(Kelthane®, 4,4′-dichloro-α-[trichloromethyl] benzhydrol) is identical

TABLE 11.1 Toxicity of DDT and metabolites to adult male rats.

Chemical	Acute Oral Toxicity LD_{50}	Relative Toxicity
	(mg/kg)	
DDT (technical)	217	1.0
DDA	740	3.4
DDE	880	4.1
Dicofol (=Kelthane®) ..	1,100	5.1
DDD (=TDE)	>4,000	>18.0

Source: Gaines (1969).

to this metabolite. Another metabolite of DDT is DBP, p,p'-dichloro-benzophenone (Menzel et al., 1961; Abou-Donia and Menzel, 1968); this compound has frequently been reported in metabolism studies with insects. Although several criteria should be used to compare the toxicity of chemicals, the most complete comparison of the toxicity of DDT with its principal metabolites can be made on the basis of acute oral toxicity values (Table 11.1). The toxicity of the chemicals in this table is inversely related to the numerical values.

Many metabolites of DDT other than the five already described have been reported (Abou-Donia and Menzel, 1968). A recent discovery about DDT metabolism is the in vivo isomerizations that lead to the formation of p,p'-DDT from feeding o,p'-DDT to rats (Klein et al., 1964) and the formation of o,p'-DDT and o,p'-DDD from feeding p,p'-DDT and p,p'-DDD to young chickens (Abou-Donia and Menzel, 1968). The approximately 20% of o,p'-DDT in technical DDT is converted to p,p'-DDT and then to p,p'-DDE in living avian tissue; in the anaerobic conditions after death, o,p'-DDT is metabolized to o,p'-DDD (French and Jefferies, 1969). The absence of o,p'-DDT and metabolites in field specimens is ascribed to the rapid rate of breakdown and a masking of the o,p'-DDD residue during analysis by the relatively large amounts of p,p'-DDE. These examples illustrate the complexity of metabolism studies and the pitfalls of interpreting analytical data.

The exact biochemical cause of the toxicity of DDT and related chemicals to certain organisms has never been proved. Several theories on how DDT acts have been promulgated. An extensive study of feeding DDT in the diet of rats suggested that the effects of DDT depend not only on DDT but also on some unidentified secondary factor (Ortega et al., 1956). An example of this hypothesis is the suggestion that DDE is the major factor in toxicity of DDT and that the amount of DDE produced from DDT determines the level of toxicity of DDT in different species (Bailey et al., 1969). An earlier study, however, suggested that residues of DDE were not critical in birds that died from DDT (Stickel et al., 1966). These examples are cited to illustrate the confusion about the toxicity of DDT, its metabolites, and related compounds. The estrogenic activity of o,p'-DDT (Bitman et al., 1968) and the conversion of analogues of DDT to estrogenic metabolites (Welch et al., 1969) are interesting new developments that may link DDT metabolism studies with the claim that this insecticide is the indirect cause of a reduction of eggshell thickness associated with failing reproduction and population decline of certain predatory birds (Stickel, 1968; Porter and Wiemeyer, 1969). In the past, surveys have not usually distinguished between the presence of p,p'- and o,p'-DDT. A change in analytical procedures could clarify how widespread the latter isomer really is.

Although the use of DDT as an insecticide is declining, the environment will continue to be monitored for this chemical and its metabolites. A review of the voluminous data on DDT, its analogues, and its metabolites in the environment is beyond the scope of this presentation. I predict, however, that interpreting these data in terms of biological effect or no-effect will provide a continuing debate for many years. Methoxychlor, 2,2-bis(p-methoxyphenyl)-1,1,1-trichloroethane, is an insecticidal analogue of DDT that has much lower mammalian toxicity than DDT. For example, the acute oral LD_{50} of methoxychlor to rats seems to be somewhere between 5 to 7 g/kg (Smith et al., 1946; Hodge et al., 1950). This insecticide shows little tendency to be stored in the body fat and other lipids. If there is a general ban on the use of DDT, methoxychlor may serve as a replacement for DDT in a few pest control situations, but the organophosphate and carbamate insecticides currently available will probably fill most of the gaps left by withdrawing DDT from pest control use.

ALDRIN AND DIELDRIN

Aldrin is one of a group of chlorinated hydrocarbon insecticides that also includes dieldrin, endrin, and heptachlor. Interrelationships of structure and activity are known for about 500 of these so-called cyclodiene compounds (Soloway, 1965). The following comments draw upon recent reviews of the metabolism of these insecticides (Brooks, 1966, 1968, 1969; Korte, 1968). The 1969 review by Brooks is especially comprehensive in its treatment of the subject. Biological epoxidation of aldrin (Fig. 11.2), isodrin, and heptachlor produces dieldrin, endrin, and heptachlor epoxide, respectively. The epoxidation of these insecticides is interesting because the metabolites, dieldrin, endrin, and heptachlor epoxide, are about as toxic as, and more persistent than, their parent compounds (Gaines, 1960, 1969).

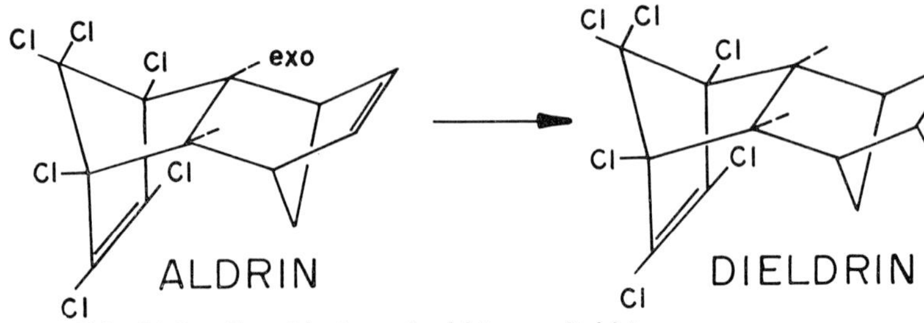

FIG. 11.2. Epoxidation of aldrin to dieldrin.

Many efforts have been directed toward finding metabolic products of dieldrin, endrin, and heptachlor epoxide (and other members of this group of insecticides). Until recently these epoxides were considered stable in metabolizing systems. It was sometimes thought that the insecticides were stored in fat, as the epoxides in those instances in which epoxidation could occur, and ultimately excreted intact in the feces. It is now known that these compounds are amenable to further metabolism, including hydroxylation, hydrolytic (or oxidative) elimination of chlorine atoms (when present) other than those of the intact hexachloronorbornene nucleus, and hydrolysis of epoxide rings. In vivo studies with rats have shown that aldrin is converted to polar metabolites from either dieldrin formed from aldrin or dieldrin administered separately (Datta et al., 1965; Korte, 1968). Metabolites of dieldrin have been found also in urine from man (Cueto and Hayes, 1962) and rabbits (Korte, 1968). A more recent study revealed two metabolites from rats fed a diet containing 100 ppm of dieldrin (Richardson et al., 1968). The mixed-function oxidases that metabolize so many foreign substances are also involved in cyclodiene metabolism in insects and mammals in vitro. The nature of the metabolites so far isolated, the parallel between microsomal enzyme induction and increased metabolism in vivo observed for some mammals, and the action of synergists in insects provide a link between the in-vivo and in-vitro processes.

The toxicology and no-effect levels of aldrin and dieldrin have been extensively reviewed by a panel selected by the the Secretary of Health, Education, and Welfare from nominations by the National Academy of Sciences (Hodge et al., 1967). The following statements are from the summary of this review. The acute oral toxicity for either aldrin or dieldrin ranged from 20 to 70 mg/kg among 12 species of animals; the estimated lethal dose for man is approximately 5 g. The mortality among several species of animals, after either repeated short-term or chronic doses, ranged from 0.5 to 300 ppm. No body weight changes occurred among several species of animals at 2 ppm or less in the diet. Pathological conditions were observable at levels in the diet ranging from 0.5 to 10 ppm among several species of animals. And, typical diets in England and in the United States are estimated to contain 1 to 2 ppb of dieldrin; dieldrin concentrations in human fat probably average about 0.2 ppm.

Insecticides of the cyclodiene group have had low residue tolerances imposed upon them from the beginnings of their use. Further residue tolerance restrictions have been placed on these chemicals in recent years. Environmental persistence and unfavorable biological effects of some of the cyclodiene insecticides and development of resistance to these insecticides by some species of insects and other arthropods suggest that the use of these insecticides will decline.

TOXAPHENE

An anomalous situation exists with respect to our knowledge of toxaphene, an insecticide used more extensively in the United States in 1964 than any other insecticide (Eichers et al., 1968). The extensive use of toxaphene, since it became available for commercial use about 1947 (Parker and Beacher, 1947), has not been accompanied with published information about its composition and metabolism. Toxaphene is a chlorinated camphene having an approximate empirical formula of $C_{10}H_{10}Cl_8$; it contains 67 to 69% chlorine. Toxaphene is a general convulsant that acts on the central nervous system. In this respect it is similar to DDT and the cyclodiene insecticides. In contrast to them, however, little is known about the metabolism of toxaphene. It is probably slowly detoxified in the liver. This assumption is based on its close chemical relationship to camphor, which is detoxified in the liver, and the isolation of ethereal sulfate and glucuronic acid conjugates of toxaphene in the urine (Conley, 1952).

Although toxaphene is a highly chlorinated organic compound, and hence readily detected by electron-capture gas chromatography (GLC), there is a paucity of residue and metabolism data that distinguish between components of the technical product. Residues of toxaphene cannot be determined quantitatively in environmental samples by GLC because toxaphene is a mixture of compounds that gives a continuum of curves with a wide spread of retention times. This results in mutual interference from many common pesticides. This difficulty is illustrated in Figure 11.3 by GLC curves of toxaphene, DDT, and a combination of the two insecticides (Benevue and Beckman, 1966). These GLC curves are especially pertinent because one of the major markets for toxaphene has been a 2:1 combination of toxaphene and DDT as an insecticide for use on cotton.

The difficulties of estimating the components of toxaphene are illustrated in studies of the persistence of toxaphene in lakes in which it has been used as a substitute for rotenone to reduce rough fish populations (Johnson et al., 1966; Terriere et al., 1966). Various formulations of toxaphene showed slightly different gas chromatograms, the components of toxaphene seemed to be degraded at different rates, and the components had different toxicities for fish (Johnson et al., 1966). It is clear that until the chemistry and metabolism of toxaphene are better known, the fate of this insecticide in natural waters will be poorly understood.

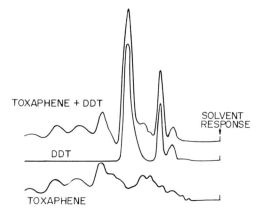

FIG. 11.3. GLC curves of toxaphene, DDT, and a combination of the two insecticides. (Benevue and Beckman, 1966.)

TOXAPHENE + DDT

SOLVENT RESPONSE

DDT

TOXAPHENE

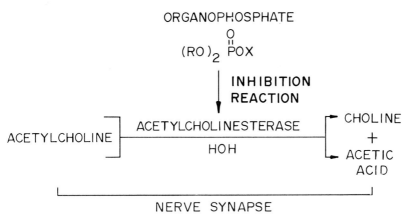

NERVE SYNAPSE

FIG. 11.4. The principal toxic action of organophosphate insecticides.

PARATHION AND MALATHION

Parathion, methyl parathion, and malathion are members of a large class of organophosphate insecticides. "Organophosphate" is often employed as a generic term to cover all the toxic organic compounds containing phosphorus. Organophosphates are more specifically designated as phosphates, phosphonates, phosphorothionates, phosphorothiolates, phosphorodithioates, phosphoramidates, etc., depending upon the atoms attached to the phosphorus; for examples, see O'Brien (1960). There is an extensive literature on these compounds, including books concerned exclusively with organophosphates (O'Brien, 1960; Heath, 1961).

The most important reaction of organophosphates is with acetylcholinesterase, an enzyme involved in the transmission of nerve impulses (Fig. 11.4). Acetylcholine, a chemical mediator of nerve impulses at synapses, is normally hydrolyzed very quickly by acetylcholinesterase. Any disruption of this reaction causes acetylcholine to accumulate. Acetylcholine is itself a moderately toxic chemical. It acts as a poison and causes well-known symptoms of poisoning. Organophosphates with a P$=$O structure irreversibly react with cholinesterases, preventing these enzymes from accomplishing their hydrolytic function.

Parathion was introduced about 1944 in Germany. As recently as 1964, methyl parathion (the dimethyl analogue of parathion) and parathion were the most widely used organophosphates in the United States (Eichers et al., 1968). Although methyl parathion and parathion are chemically very similar, each seems needed to control different species of pest insects; therefore, both exist on the commercial market. Both are quite toxic chemicals; for example, their acute oral LD_{50} values with male rats are 14 and 13 mg/kg for methyl parathion and parathion, respectively (Gaines, 1969). Because their properties and metabolism are so nearly alike, further attention will be given only to parathion.

The toxicity of parathion develops from a desulfuration reaction

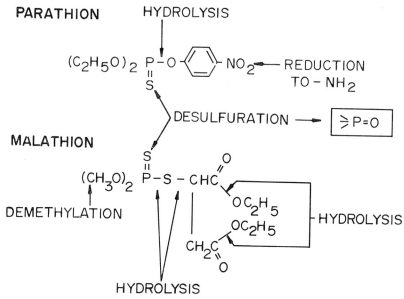

FIG. 11.5. Some points of metabolic attack on parathion and malathion.

that changes P=S to P=O (Fig. 11.5). This converts parathion to paraoxon, a compound with strong cholinesterase-inhibiting properties. This important intoxication reaction occurs with all organophosphates having a P=S structure and is especially catalyzed by liver microsomal enzymes. These enzymes require reduced nicotinamide adenine dinucleotide and oxygen with in vitro reactions. Two primary degradation reactions of parathion and paraoxon are shown in Figure 11.5. One of these is a hydrolytic reaction that yields diethylthiophosphoric acid and p-nitrophenol. This reaction is catalyzed by liver microsomal oxidases similar, if not identical, to those that effect conversion of parathion to paraoxon (Nakatsugawa et al., 1969). The p-nitrophenol from parathion degradation appears in urine and provides a sensitive indicator of exposure to parathion before any significant decline in cholinesterase activity can be detected (Davies et al., 1966). The second degradation reaction illustrated for parathion in Figure 11.5 involves reduction of the p-nitro group of parathion and paraoxon to form aminoparathion and aminoparaoxon, respectively. This reaction occurs under a variety of conditions (O'Brien, 1960; Lykken and Casida, 1969; Mick and Dahm, 1970).

The metabolism of parathion has been investigated with several species of animals, plants, and microorganisms (O'Brien, 1960; El-Refai and Hopkins, 1966). Other reported metabolites of parathion and paraoxon include desethyl parathion, desethyl paraoxon, diethyl phosphoric acid, ethyl phosphoric acid, and phosphoric acid. All metabolites of parathion, except paraoxon, are less toxic than the parent insecticide.

Malathion was accepted for commercial use as an insecticide in

1952. Since then, it has been used to control many species of insects and other arthropods. It is a major insecticide used throughout the world, owing partly to its low toxicity to mammals. For example, its acute oral LD_{50} in adult male rats is 1,375 mg/kg (Gaines, 1969). The major intoxication route for malathion is desulfuration to malaoxon (Fig. 11.5) and inhibition of acetylcholinesterase by the malaoxon produced (O'Brien, 1960). It is the detoxication reactions that set malathion apart and are responsible for its remarkably low toxicity to mammals. The most important reactions involve the hydrolysis by carboxylesterase of one of the two available carboxylic ethyl esters of malathion and malaoxon as shown in Figure 11.5 (Dauterman and Main, 1966). Malathion monoacid, the major metabolite of malathion, has been identified as O,O-dimethyl-S-(1-carboxy-2-carbethoxy) ethyl phosphorodithioate (Chen et al., 1969). Other detoxication reactions shown in Figure 11.5 produce hydrolytic products, such as malathion diacid, malaoxon mono- and diacids, O,O-dimethyl phosphorodithioate, O,O-dimethyl phosphorothioate, dimethyl phosphate, monomethyl phosphate, and phosphoric acid (O'Brien, 1967).

Malathion gained further prominence when Frawley et al. (1957) showed that simultaneous administrations of malathion and EPN, O-ethyl O-p-nitrophenyl phenylphosphonothioate, to dogs and rats caused strong synergistic effects in the form of cholinesterase inhibition. Several later studies showed that EPN inhibits the carboxylesterase that hydrolyzes malathion and malaoxon. A number of other combinations of organophosphates also have been synergistic (O'Brien, 1967). Fears that ingestion of mixtures of low levels of organophosphates, and possibly other chemicals, as residues on foods might produce overt symptoms of cholinesterase depression have so far proved false.

Malathion is comparatively more toxic to insects than to mammals, seemingly because of less effective hydrolytic detoxication by carboxylesterases in insects. EPN fails to synergize the toxicity of malathion to insects, and certain strains of insects resistant to malathion have a high carboxylesterase level (O'Brien, 1967).

The metabolism of organophosphate insecticides has received special attention in recent reviews by Fukuto and Metcalf (1969) and Lykken and Casida (1969). From these and other sources it can be concluded that organophosphate insecticides include chemicals that range from high toxicity (e.g., parathion) to low toxicity (e.g., malathion). These insecticide molecules usually possess several places that are vulnerable to metabolic attack, and the metabolic products are more water soluble than the parent insecticides. Organophosphates are physically and chemically less stable than organochlorine insecticides (e.g., DDT and dieldrin) and therefore present less of a hazard for environmental contamination than organochlorines.

CARBARYL

Carbaryl (=Sevin®) is the most widely used insecticide belonging to a group of esters of N-methyl and N-dimethyl carbamic acid. The carbamate insecticides show somewhat erratic patterns of selec-

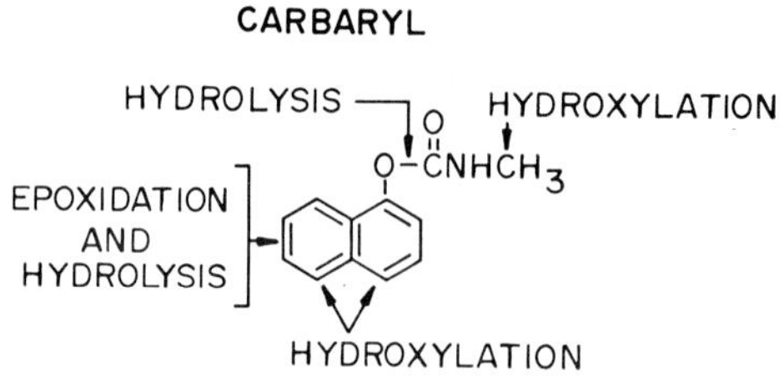

CARBARYL

FIG. 11.6. Some points of metabolic attack on carbaryl.

tive toxicity to insects. These insecticides are fairly potent inhibitors of cholinesterases, and the symptoms resulting from this action are typically cholinergic. The inhibitory action of carbamates, however, is reversible, in contrast to the action of organophosphates.

Carbaryl quite readily undergoes several metabolic reactions (Fig. 11.6), including hydroxylation attack on the N-methyl group and two locations on the napthol ring and epoxidation followed by epoxide cleavage and hydrolysis on the nonphenolic ring. Each of these initial oxidation products subsequently conjugates and is excreted as a sulfate or glucuronide in mammals, but may persist as a glycoside in plants. Hydrolysis of the carbamyl ester linkage releases 1-napthol, which is rapidly metabolized. Additional information about the metabolism of carbaryl and other carbamate insecticides is included in reviews by Fukuto and Metcalf (1969) and Lykken and Casida (1969). Carbamates are currently viewed as competitors of organophosphates for pest-control purposes.

SUMMARY

Insecticides occur in the environment because of purposive applications for pest control and because of accidents and carelessness. The major problems with insecticides arise from the contamination of the environment and food and the development of resistant arthropod-pest populations. The persistence of insecticides in the atmosphere, water, soil, plants, animals, and microorganisms is being investigated. Alterations of insecticides occur under both metabolic and nonmetabolic conditions.

Knowledge of the metabolism of insecticides is prerequisite to their development and use for insect control. Identification and toxicological assessment of metabolic products should precede establishment of residue and other safety factors. More basically, metabolism studies of insecticides reveal intoxication and detoxication processes and how these relate to physiological effects and problems of resistance. Some of the ways that organic insecticides are metabolized in living organisms are hydrolysis, hydroxylation, dehalogenation, dehydrohalogenation, desulfuration (=oxidation), O-dealkylation, N-dealkylation, reduction, and conjugation. Metabolic attack occurs at one or more sites on an insecticide molecule. Plants and animals often metabolize insecticides by similar pathways. With some insecticides, primary metabolic attack may form compounds whose toxicity approximately equals or is greater than the parent insecticide (e.g., aldrin→dieldrin; parathion→paraoxon). Further metabolism produces compounds of much lower toxicity. Other insecticides are detoxified directly (e.g., DDT→DDE, although DDE may have subtle physiological effects on nontarget organisms). The metabolism of an insecticide from administration to target sites and in and out of storage tissues generally produces compounds of greater water solubility to facilitate excretion of metabolites. Because the persistence of some of our present organochlorine insecticides (e.g., DDT, DDD, cyclodienes) creates environmental problems, future insecticide developments will probably give special attention to effective chemicals that degrade to compounds with negligible environmental effects.

Although this review is primarily concerned with metabolism, numerous nonmetabolic factors exert effects on the structure and persistence of insecticides. Some of these nonmetabolic factors include light, water, heat, acidity and alkalinity, atmospheric constituents, metal ions, and soils. An indication of the nonmetabolic complexities of the decomposition of insecticides is given in a review by Crosby (1969). Furthermore, the solubilities of insecticides in soil and water are especially important in relation to their movement and persistence in the environment. An exhaustive search of the literature by Gunther et al. (1968), however, revealed only limited useful data on water solubility.

REFERENCES

Abou-Donia, M. B., and Menzel, D. B. 1968. The metabolism in vivo of 1,1,1-trichloro-2,2-bis(*p*-chlorophenyl) ethane (DDT), 1,1-dichloro-2,2-bis(*p*-chlorophenyl) ethane (DDD) and 1,1-dichloro-2,2-bis(*p*-chlorophenyl) ethylene (DDE) in the chick by embryonic injection and dietary ingestion. *Biochem. Pharmacol.* 17:2143–61.

Agosin, M., Michaeli, D., Miskus, R., Nagasawa, S., and Hoskins, W. M. 1961. A new DDT-metabolizing enzyme in the German cockroach. *J. Econ. Entomol.* 54:340–42.

Bailey, S., Bunyan, P. J., Rennison, B. D., and Taylor, A. 1969. The metabolism of 1,1-di(*p*-chlorophenyl)-2,2-dichloroethylene and 1,1-di(*p*-chlorophenyl)-2-chloroethylene in the pigeon. *Toxicol. Appl. Pharmacol.* 14:23–32.

Barker, P. S., and Morrison, F. O. 1964. Breakdown of DDT in mouse tissue. *Can. J. Zool.* 42:324–25.

Benevue, A., and Beckman, H. 1966. The examination of toxaphene by gas chromatography. *Bull. Exptl. Contamination Toxicol.* 1:1–5.

Bitman, J., Cecil, H. C., Harris, S. J., and Fries, G. F. 1968. Estrogenic activity of *o,p'*-DDT in the mammalian uterus and avian oviduct. *Science* 162:371–72.

Brooks, G. T. 1966. Progress in metabolic studies of the cyclodiene insecticides and its relevance to structure-activity correlations. *World Rev. Pest Control* 5:62–84.

———. 1968. Perspectives of cyclodiene metabolism. *Symposium on the Science and Technology of Residual Insecticides in Food*

Production with Special Reference to Aldrin and Dieldrin. Sponsored by Shell Chemical Co.

——. 1969. The metabolism of diene-organochlorine (cyclodiene) insecticides. *Residue Rev.* 27:81–138.

Carson, R. L. 1962. *Silent spring.* Boston: Houghton Mifflin.

Chen, P. R., Tucker, W. P., and Dauterman, W. C. 1969. Structure of biologically produced malathion monoacid. *J. Agr. Food Chem.* 17:86–90.

Conley, B. E. 1952. Pharmacologic properties of toxaphene, a chlorinated hydrocarbon insecticide. *J. Am. Med. Assoc.* 149:1135–37.

Crosby, D. G. 1969. The nonmetabolic decomposition of pesticides. *Ann. N.Y. Acad. Sci.* 160:82–96.

Cueto, C., Jr., and Hayes, W. J., Jr. 1962. The detection of dieldrin metabolites in human urine. *J. Agr. Food Chem.* 10:366–69.

Datta, P. R., Laug, E. P., Watts, J. O., Klein, A. K., and Nelson, M. J. 1965. Metabolites in urine of rats on diets containing aldrin or dieldrin. *Nature* 208:289–90.

Dauterman, W. C., and Main, A. R. 1966. Relationship between acute toxicity and in vitro inhibition and hydrolysis of a series of carbalkoxy homologs of malathion. *Toxicol. Appl. Pharmacol.* 9:408–18.

Davies, J. E., Davis, J. H., Frazier, D. E., Mann, J. B., and Welke, J. O. 1966. Urinary *p*-nitrophenol concentrations in acute and chronic parathion exposures. *Advan. Chem. Ser.* 60:67–78.

Durham, W. F., Ortega, P., and Hayes, W. J., Jr. 1963. The effect of various dietary levels of DDT on liver function, cell morphology, and DDT storage in the rhesus monkey. *Arch. Intern. Pharmacodyn.* 141 (1–2): 111–29.

Durham, W. F., Armstrong, J. F., and Quimby, G. E. 1965. DDA excretion levels. *Arch. Environ. Health* 11:76–79.

Eichers, T., Andrilenas, P., Jenkins, R., and Fox, A. 1968. *Quantities of pesticides used by farmers in 1964.* USDA, Agr. Econ. Rept. 131.

El-Refai, A., and Hopkins, T. L. 1966. Parathion absorption, translocation, and conversion to paraoxon in bean plants. *J. Agr. Food Chem.* 14:588–92.

Finley, R. B., Jr., and Pillmore, R. E. 1963. Conversion of DDT to DDD in animal tissue. *BioScience* 13:41–42.

Fox, A., Eichers, T., Andrilenas, P., Jenkins, R., and Blake, H. 1968. *Extent of farm pesticide use on crops in 1966.* USDA, Agr. Econ. Rept. 147.

Frawley, J. P., Fuyat, H. N., Hagan, E. C., Blake, J. R., and Fitzhugh, O. G. 1957. Marked potentiation in mammalian toxicity from simultaneous administration of two anticholinesterase compounds. *J. Pharmacol. Exptl. Therap.* 121:96–106.

French, M. C., and Jefferies, D. J. 1969. Degradation and disappearance of ortho, para isomer of of technical DDT in living and dead avian tissues. *Science* 165:914–16.

Fukuto, T. R., and Metcalf, R. L. 1969. Metabolism of insecticides in plants and animals. *Ann. N.Y. Acad. Sci.* 160:97–111.

Gaines, T. B. 1960. The acute toxicity of pesticides to rats. *Toxicol. Appl. Pharmacol.* 2:88–99.

——. 1969. Acute toxicity of pesticides. *Toxicol. Appl. Pharmacol.* 14:515–34.

Gunther, F. A., Westlake, W. E., and Jaglan, P. S. 1968. Reported solubilities of 738 pesticide chemicals in water. *Residue Rev.* 20:1–148.

Hall, D. G. 1962. Use of insecticides in the United States. *Bull. Entomol. Soc. Am.* 8:90–92.

Heath, D. F. 1961. *Organophosphorus poisons.* New York: Macmillan (Pergamon).

Heath, R. G., Spann, J. W., and Kreitzer, J. F. 1969. Marked DDE impairment of mallard reproduction in controlled studies. *Nature* 224:47–48.

Hodge, H. C., Maynard, E. A., Thomas, J. F., Blanchet, H. J., Jr., Wilt, W. G., Jr., and Mason K. E. 1950. Short-term oral toxicity tests of methoxychlor (2,2 di-(*p*-methoxy phenyl)-1,1,1-trichlorethane) in rats and dogs. *J. Pharmacol. Exptl. Therap.* 99:140–48.

Hodge, H. C., Boyce, A. M., Deichmann, W. B., and Kraybill, H. F. 1967. Toxicology and no-effect levels of aldrin and dieldrin. *Toxicol. Appl. Pharmacol.* 10:613–75.

Jensen, J. A., Cueto, C., Dale, W. E., Rothe, C. F., Pearce, G. W., and Mattson, A. M. 1957. DDT metabolites in feces and bile of rats. *J. Agr. Food Chem.* 5:919–25.

Johnson, W. D., Lee, G. F., and Spyridakis, D. 1966. Persistence of toxaphene in treated lakes. *Intern. J. Air Water Pollution* 10:555–60.

Klein, A. K., Laug, E. P., Datta, P. R., Watts, J. O., and Chen, J. T. 1964. Metabolites: reductive dechlorination of DDT and DDD and isomeric transformation of *o,p'*-DDT to *p,p'*-DDT in vivo. *J. Assoc. Official Agr. Chemists* 47:1129–45.

Knipling, E. F. 1969. Alternative methods of controlling insect pests. *Food Drug Admin. Papers* 3 (1): 16–24.

Korte, F. 1968. Metabolism of aldrin, dieldrin, and endrin. *Symposium on the Science and Technology of Residual Insecticides in Food Production with Special Reference to Aldrin and Dieldrin.* Sponsored by Shell Chemical Co.

Lipke, H., and Kearns, C. W. 1960. DDT-dehydrochlorinase. *Advan. Pest Control Res.* 3:253–87.

Lykken, L., and Casida, J. E. 1969. Metabolism of organic insecticide chemicals. *Can. Med. Assoc. J.* 100:145–54.

Menzel, D. B., Smith, S. M., Miskus, R., and Hoskins, W. M. 1961. The metabolism of C^{14}-labeled DDT in the larvae, pupae, and adults of *Drosophila melanogaster. J. Econ. Entomol.* 54:9–12.

Mick, D. L., and Dahm, P. A. 1970. Metabolism of parathion by two species of *Rhizobium. J. Econ. Entomol.* In press.

Nakatsugawa, T., Tolman, N. M., and Dahm, P. A. 1969. Degradation of parathion in the rat. *Biochem. Pharmacol.* 18:1103–14.

Neal, P. A., Sweeney, T. R., Spicer, S. S., and von Oettingen, W. F. 1946. The excretion of DDT (2,2-bis-(*p*-chlorophenyl)-1,1,1-trichloroethane) in man, together with clinical observations. *Public Health Rept.* 61:403–9.

O'Brien, R. D. 1960. *Toxic phosphorus esters.* New York: Academic Press.

———. 1967. *Insecticides. Action and metabolism.* New York: Academic Press.

Ordish, G. 1968. 150 years of crop pest control. *World Rev. Pest Control* 7:204–13.

Ortega, P., Hayes, W. J., Jr., Durham, W. F., and Mattson, A. 1956. *DDT in the diet of the rat.* Public Health Monograph 43.

Parker, W. L., and Beacher, J. H. 1947. *Toxaphene, a chlorinated hydrocarbon with insecticidal properties.* Univ. of Del. Bull. 264, Tech. 36. Newark, Del.

Porter, R. D., and Wiemeyer, S. N. 1969. Dieldrin and DDT: Effects on sparrow hawk eggshells and reproduction. *Science* 165:199–200.

Richardson, A., Baldwin, M., and Robinson, J. 1968. Identification of metabolites of dieldrin (HEOD) in the faeces and urine of rats. *J. Sci. Food Agr.* 19:524–29.

Smith, M. I., Bauer, H., Stohlman, E. F., and Lillie, R. D. 1946. The pharmacologic action of certain analogues and derivatives of DDT. *J. Pharmacol. Exptl. Therap.* 88:359–65.

Soloway, S. B. 1965. Correlation between biological activity and molecular structure of the cyclodiene insecticides. *Advan. Pest Control Res.* 6:85–126.

Sternburg, J., Vinson, E. B., and Kearns, C. W. 1953. Enzymatic dehydrochlorination of DDT by resistant flies. *J. Econ. Entomol.* 46:513–15.

Stickel, L. F. 1968. *Organochlorine pesticides in the environment.* Bur. of Sport Fisheries and Wildlife, Spec. Scientific Rept., Wildlife No. 119, Wash., D.C.

Stickel, L. F., Stickel, W. H., and Christensen, R. 1966. Residues of DDT in brains and bodies of birds that died on dosage and in survivors. *Science* 151:1549–51.

Terriere, L. C., Kugemagi, U., Gerlach, A. R., and Borovicka, R. L. 1966. The persistence of toxaphene in lake water and its uptake by aquatic plants and animals. *J. Agr. Food Chem.* 14:66–69.

Tsukamoto, M. 1959. Metabolic fate of DDT in *Drosophila melanogaster.* I. Identification of a non-DDE metabolite. *Botyu-Kagaku* 24:141–51.

Walker, K. C., George, D. A., and Maitlen, J. C. 1965. *Residues of DDT in fatty tissues of big game animals in the states of Idaho and Washington in 1962.* USDA, ARS 33-105.

Welch, R. M., Levin, W., and Conney, A. H. 1969. Estrogenic action of DDT and its analogs. *Toxicol. Appl. Pharmacol.* 14:358–67.

White, W. C., and Sweeney, T. R. 1945. The metabolism of 2,2-bis-(p-chlorophenyl)1,1,1-trichloroethane (DDT). I. A metabolite from rabbit urine, di(p-chlorophenyl) acetic acid; its isolation, identification, and synthesis. *Public. Health Rept.* 60:66–71.

CHAPTER TWELVE

THE PESTICIDE BURDEN IN WATER AND ITS SIGNIFICANCE

H. PAGE NICHOLSON

CONTAMINATION of the environment by pesticides has been a subject of mounting concern for over 20 years. Within the past year (1969) we have seen this concern, largely focused on DDT, reach a pitch where an aroused public is demanding action. This is indicated by the frequency and nature of coverage in the nation's press, the appointment of committees at the highest levels of government to consider the problem, and the number of restrictive bills prepared for presentation to various state legislatures and to the Congress. Arizona, in January 1969, banned the use of DDT for agricultural and commercial purposes for a 1-year trial period. Michigan has restricted its employment to control of mice and bats and for emergency public health purposes on approval of application. Steps have been taken in a number of other states to reduce or better control the use of DDT.

We in this country are not alone in our anxiety. Sweden has placed DDT under a 2-year ban. The Soviet Union is considering such a ban. Hungary has banned all organochlorine insecticides, and Britain is reportedly phasing them out.[1] All of this comes at a time when world food production is at an all-time high and vector-borne diseases of man and animals are more nearly arrested than ever before—a condition that must in part be credited to the effectiveness of DDT and other pesticides.

DEFINITION OF THE PROBLEM

Pesticide Production and Usage

It is necessary to consider the amount and nature of pesticide manufacture and usage to gain perspective about the potential for

H. PAGE NICHOLSON is Chief, Agricultural and Industrial Water Pollution Control Research Program, Southeast Water Lab., FWPCA, USDI, Athens, Georgia.

1. *Chattanooga* (Tennessee) *Times,* June 11, 1969.

pesticide involvement in water pollution. Although the United States production of pesticides exceeded one billion pounds in 1967, not all was used domestically; about 40% was exported and an additional 12 million pounds, primarily herbicides, were imported (Mahan et al., 1968). It is not known how many of the 750 basic pesticidal chemicals listed by Gunther et al. (1968) were included in these production figures. Some idea can be obtained, however, from knowledge that less than half this number were registered for use and covered by legal tolerances or exemptions in the United States in 1966 (Westlake and Gunther, 1966). Only 14 insecticides, 8 fungicides, and 5 herbicides accounted for nearly 54% of the tonnage manufactured in the United States in 1967 (Mahan et al., 1968).

From these data it may be concluded, at least with respect to the quantities of pesticides used within the United States, that the potential for widespread water pollution is currently limited to a relatively few compounds. These figures, however, do not preclude the possibility of local pollution problems associated with the manufacture or processing of any pesticide, nor from accidental spills or careless use.

Environmental Contamination and Significance

The acute effects of gross pesticide pollution are well known and depend upon the toxicity of the compound in question and its concentration in the environment. Widespread and chronic environmental pollution problems involve only those pesticides and degradation products that are not only toxic but also possess the characteristic of extended persistence sufficient to allow their escape from control after application, coupled with the ability to be taken up and concentrated in living organisms. The latter has been called "biological magnification." The pesticides most frequently involved are the organochlorine insecticides DDT, TDE, endrin, heptachlor, aldrin, dieldrin, chlordane, toxaphene, Strobane, and BHC or its gamma isomer, lindane (Nichloson, 1969). More recently, the organic mercury compounds have been implicated (Smart, 1968; Novick, 1969).

Among these compounds, DDT has been the most objectionable. The universal occurrence of traces of DDT is now common knowledge. It is used throughout much of the world and its secondary dispersion is aided by wind, water, and the movement of animals in which residues have accumulated.

We are faced with mounting evidence that traces of DDT are not as innocuous as many have believed. Transovarially conveyed DDT was shown to be responsible for significant losses of lake trout fry in a New York fish hatchery (Burdick et al., 1964), and investigations are being made to determine if losses of coho salmon fry in Michigan hatcheries are similarly caused.

A drastic decline in populations of fish-eating raptorial birds, such as the bald eagle and osprey, has long been associated circumstantially with the advent and use of DDT. Only recently has supporting evidence been produced to suggest that DDT and its metabolite, DDE, can cause an imbalance in calcium metabolism resulting in eggshell thinness and loss of eggs in the nest through breakage (Hickey and Anderson, 1968). The hypothesis that sublethal amounts of persistent chlorinated hydrocarbon pesticides are involved is further strengthened by experimental studies with dieldrin and DDT, using captive sparrow hawks (Porter and Wiemeyer, 1969).

Finally, we have experienced recently (March 1969) the seizure by the Food and Drug Administration of 28,000 pounds of coho salmon, caught commercially from Michigan streams, because the fish contained up to 19 ppm of DDT, an amount deemed to be excessively high (Congressional Record, 1969). This seizure was a severe blow to commercial fishing and recreational interests of the states adjacent to Lake Michigan as this new fishery was proving to be an economic bonanza (Henkin, 1969).

It should be pointed out that in each of these instances of insecticide-related loss, the insecticide must first have entered water.

Concentrations in Water

A synoptic survey for chlorinated hydrocarbon insecticides in waters of 56 of the nation's major drainage basins and 3 of the Great Lakes was made by the U.S. Public Health Service on whole-water samples collected during the period September 18–29, 1964 (Weaver et al., 1965). The samples from 96 sites in 41 states were analyzed by thin layer chromatography and microcoulometric titration gas chromatography. The wide distribution of dieldrin, endrin, and DDT, with its metabolite DDE, is significant (Table 12.1). Concentration values in water all were less than one ppb.

TABLE 12.1. Chlorinated hydrocarbon insecticides and related compounds in major rivers of the United States.

Compound	Geographic Distribution (No. states with positive or presumptively positive samples)	No. Rivers and Lakes Positive	Sampling Stations Positive	
			Positive and Quantified	
			No.	Range ppb*
Dieldrin	36	39	56	0.002–>0.118
Endrin	28	23	30	0.003–>0.094
DDT	28	22	23	0.007–0.087
DDE	28	17	18	0.002–0.018
TDE	1	1	1	0.083
Aldrin	10	1	1	0.085
Heptachlor	16	0	0	. . .
Heptachlor epoxide	0	0	0	. . .
BHC	2	0	0	Trace

Source: Adapted from data by Weaver et al. (1965).
Note: Except Alaska and Hawaii.

* Minimum detectable concentrations of dieldrin, endrin, DDT, DDE, aldrin, and heptachlor ranged from 0.002 to 0.010 ppb. Comparable values for TDE, heptachlor epoxide, and BHC were 0.075, 0.075, and 0.025 ppb, respectively.

TABLE 12.2. Pesticides in ten selected western streams, 1965–66.

Compound	No. Samples Positive of 114 from 11 Stations	Range of Concentration
		(ppb)
Lindane	46	0.005–0.020
Dieldrin	29	0.005–0.015
Heptachlor epoxide	20	0.005–0.090
DDE	18	0.005–0.020
DDT	14	0.025–0.110
Heptachlor	14	0.005–0.015
TDE	13	0.005–0.015
Endrin	7	0.010–0.040
Aldrin	4	0.005–0.015
2,4-D	0	...
2,4,5-T	0	...
Silvex	0	...
Total	75 positive for one or more pesticides	0.005–0.110

Source: Adapted from data by Brown and Nishioka (1967).

Similarly, the U.S. Geological Survey, in October 1965, began the collection and analysis of water samples with associated suspended sediment from selected streams west of the Mississippi River (Brown and Nishioka, 1967; Manigold and Schulze, 1969). The samples, taken monthly, were examined by electron capture gas chromatography for the common chlorinated hydrocarbon insecticides and the herbicides 2,4-D, silvex, and 2,4,5-T. Results of the first year's work on 10 rivers are summarized in Table 12.2, and those for the subsequent 2 years from 19 rivers are given in Table 12.3.

All 12 pesticides or derivatives were recovered at one time or another. Sixty-six percent of 114 water samples taken during the first year were positive for 1 or more pesticides. Forty-nine percent of 333

TABLE 12.3. Pesticides in nineteen selected western streams, 1966–68.

Compound	No. Samples Positive of 333 from 20 Stations	Range of Concentration
		(ppb)
DDT	82	0.01–0.12
DDE	49	0.01–0.06
2,4-D	41	0.01–0.35
TDE	35	0.01–0.04
2,4,5-T	28	0.01–0.07
Heptachlor	27	0.01–0.04
Dieldrin	24	0.01–0.07
Silvex	14	0.01–0.21
Lindane	13	0.01–0.02
Aldrin	11	0.01–0.04
Endrin	4	0.01–0.07
Heptachlor epoxide	2	0.02–0.04
Total	164 positive for one or more pesticides	0.01–0.35

Source: Adapted from data by Manigold and Schulze (1969).

samples were positive in the subsequent 2-year period. Concentration values all were less than 1 ppb.

Lindane, dieldrin, and heptachlor epoxide were recovered most frequently during the period October 1965 through September 1966. During the following 2 years DDT, DDE, and the herbicide 2,4-D were most commonly found. No explanation was offered for this difference in frequency of recovery.

The concentration of chlorinated hydrocarbon insecticides in water alone, however, does not necessarily correctly reflect the availability of these compounds to living components of the hydrosphere. Studies in the major agricultural river basins of California have indicated that an average pesticide concentration of 0.10 ppb to 0.20 ppb in water may mean that bottom sediments contain 20 ppb to 500 ppb of the compounds (Bailey and Hannum, 1967).

A pond near Denver was treated with 0.02 ppm of DDT, and the insecticide was quantified in water, mud, vegetation, fish, and crayfish for 16 months (Bridges et al., 1963). As the DDT residues in the water decreased to none detectable at 4 weeks, residues in the mud increased to 8.3 ppm at 24 hours and disappeared in 12 months; vegetation residues were 30.7 ppm within 30 minutes and declined to 0.6 ppm at 12 months; rainbow trout, black bullhead, and crayfish still contained DDT and the metabolites TDE and DDE at 16 months.

Quite clearly DDT is remarkably hydrophobic and does not remain in water in very large quantities. It does tend to concentrate and persist in other compartments of the hydrosphere. Such data give reason to pause and reconsider whenever the urge strikes to set permissible limits for this and similar compounds in water alone where the objective is to maintain a suitable overall environment for aquatic life.

SOURCES OF WATER CONTAMINATION

Pesticides may enter water in a variety of ways. These include runoff from the land, industrial waste discharges, carelessness and accidents, and by direct application to control unwanted plant and animal pests (Nicholson, 1969). Other sources may be airborne residues, products of home use and garbage disposals (sewers), dumped products containing residues higher than tolerances, dead animals and animal excreta, and decaying plant tissues (Westlake and Gunther, 1966). The significance of these additional sources remains to be more fully documented, but their validity as sources is not questioned. Contamination may be more or less continuous, generally at very low levels (less than 1 ppb), or in brief episodes that may reach concentrations sufficient to kill fish and other aquatic life.

Runoff

Runoff from the land is probably the most widespread single source of low level surface water contamination by pesticides and has been demonstrated repeatedly (Nicholson et al., 1962; Hindin et al., 1964; Nicholson et al., 1964; Lauer et al., 1966; Nicholson et al., 1966; Bailey and Hannum, 1967). Runoff may be more or less continuous throughout the year at levels generally less than 1 ppb or may occur sporadically (Nicholson, 1969). Transport from land to water may occur while the pesticide is adsorbed on eroded particulate matter, while in solution in runoff water, or by both means. It has been shown that sodium humate, a common soil constituent, solubilizes DDT in water (Wershaw, 1969). This phenomenon would be expected to facilitate the transport of DDT.

Factors that control the runoff of pesticides are the nature of the pesticide and the extent to which it is used, edaphic considerations, climatic factors, topography, and land usage and management practices. Pesticides having short half-lives do not possess the runoff potential of persistent types. High-humus-type soils will yield less insecticide than will sandy soils (Lichtenstein, 1958). Heavy rainfall immediately following application of chlorinated hydrocarbon-type insecticides is a classic cause of runoff that sometimes causes fish kills (Young and Nicholson, 1951).

Industrial Waste

Perhaps the second most significant source of pesticides in water is industry. The types of industries involved include producers of basic pesticides, pesticide formulators, cooperage firms that reclaim used pesticide drums, textile plants that moth-proof woolen yarns and fabrics with dieldrin, and paper manufacturing industries that use phenylmercury acetate (PMA) as a fungicide.

Releases from industrial sources may be continuous in manufacturing or process effluents, or occasional in high concentration slug discharges following in-plant mishaps or breakdowns. In the latter case, biological catastrophies may result in receiving streams.

As an example of a plant breakdown, an instance that occurred in Alabama may be cited (Alabama Water Improvement Commission, 1961). A plant which manufactures parathion and methyl parathion normally treats its wastes very effectively by neutralization with strong alkali followed by double activated sludge treatment through its own plant and that of a nearby city. During a breakdown in 1961 neither treatment plant could handle the load of toxic materials and 60% of the combined industrial effluent containing parathion and city sewage was discharged untreated to a creek until corrective action could be taken. Fish, turtles, and snakes died along 28 miles of the stream whose average discharge at the time was 211 million gallons a day at a velocity of ¾ mile per hour. The creek entered the Coosa River which then had an average discharge about 28 times greater than that of the creek. Even with that dilution, traces of parathion residues were recovered 90 miles down the Coosa and some lesser fish kills occurred in it. Unfortunately, water samples were not taken for analysis until the third day after fish were first observed dying. At that time a maximum 0.21 ppm of parathion was found at a point on the creek 22 miles from the city. On that same day, 667 ppm of parathion was reported in thickened sludge at the city sewage treatment plant.

A second example involved a manufacturer of DDT who provided minimal waste treatment. The DDT content of water in a ditch receiving these wastes was 0.1 ppm to 7.8 ppm. Bottom samples analyzed from 0.6% to 2% DDT along the half-mile length of this ditch after it had been carrying away wastes from this industr.al plant for 1½ years.[2]

Barthel et al. (1969), in their study of pesticide residues in the sediments of the lower Mississippi River and its tributaries, found 5 pesticide-formulating companies that dumped waste materials in city sewers, in channels and sloughs near their plants, and on city and privately owned dumps where they could be washed away by rainfall. Residues found included dieldrin, aldrin, endrin, isodrin, chlordane, lindane, and DDT analogs and metabolities. Many of the residues in river bottom sediments were in concentrations less than 0.05 ppm, but some ranged in the thousands of ppm in the vicinity of industrial plants.

Accidents and Carelessness

Although strenuous efforts have been made within agricultural and related industries to minimize accidents and carelessness with pesticides, some instances of water pollution from these causes still are reported. An instance of carelessness having potentially serious human health implications occurred in Florida in 1964 (Florida State Board of Health, 1964).

A rancher instructed his hired hand to dispose of approximately 50 four-pound bags of over-age 15% parathion dust. This was done without the rancher's knowledge, by dumping them from a highway bridge into the Peace River 1 mile upstream from the municipal water intake of Arcadia, a town of about 6,000 people. The act was discovered when boys fishing near the bridge hooked a bag and reported it.

The town fortunately had an auxiliary well and immediately reverted to it. The citizens were instructed not to use the water, and flushing of the mains was begun. Subsequent analysis of water samples showed that parathion concentration in the distribution system was generally less than 1 ppb. However, a series of samples taken from a tap at the local bus station ranged from 10 ppb to 380 ppb.

Investigation revealed that the bags of parathion had been dumped in the river about 10 days before their discovery. They were polyethylene lined and resisted rapid disintegration. All but 8 to 12 bags were eventually recovered. Those unrecovered bags that disintegrated apparently did so over a period of several weeks. This may have been the reason that residue levels sufficiently high to be a threat to human health or the fish in the river did not occur. Parathion residue occurred in the river water for about 2 weeks after dis-

2. Charles Kaplan, FWPCA, Southeast Region, Atlanta, Georgia, personal communication.

covery at concentrations generally less than 1 ppb.

Accidents also have caused real or potential water pollution problems. In March 1965, during the night, 2,500 to 3,000 pounds of 5% chlordane wettable powder spilled from a truck passing through Orlando, Florida. After recovering what could be salvaged, about 1,300 to 1,700 pounds was hosed into the street's storm drainage system from which it passed into a dry creek bed not far from one of the city's lakes. When the potential for damage to the lake was realized, the contaminated water and soil were removed for safe disposal elsewhere.

Other Sources

The chemical control of aquatic weeds, rough fish, and aquatic insect pests often results in some pesticide residue in water. These activities are generally managed by professionals so that undesirable consequences are minimized. Toxaphene, however, that was first used for control of rough fish in lakes in the early 1950s has sometimes caused trouble. Although toxaphene-treated lakes may generally be restocked within 6 months to a year later, occasionally a lake may remain toxic to restocked fish for 5 years (Kallman et al., 1962; Terriere et al., 1966). Such was the case at Miller Lake in Oregon that was treated in 1958 at an estimated rate of 40 ppb. The initial residues declined sharply to less than 2 ppb and remained near the level for approximately 5 years (Terriere et al., 1966).

Airborne dust containing pesticides may also contribute to pesticide levels in water either by direct deposition or by deposition on land with subsequent runoff. Dust deposited on Cincinnati, Ohio, in January 1965, originating from the southern high plains of Texas and adjacent states, was shown to contain 0.6 ppm DDT, 0.5 ppm chlordane, 0.2 ppm DDE, 0.2 ppm Ronnel, 0.04 ppm heptachlor epoxide, 0.04 ppm 2,4,5-T, and 0.003 ppm dieldrin (Cohen and Pinkerton, 1966).

Local drift of dusts and sprays from areas of pesticide application is well known and can also be a source of water contamination.

Urban storm water has also been suggested as a carrier of pesticides (Weibel et al., 1966). The significance of urban sites and activities as sources of water pollution by pesticides is now being investigated at Michigan State University.

CONTROL OF PESTICIDE POLLUTION

Can anything practical be done to control water pollution by pesticides? The answer is most definitely yes.

Point sources can be controlled most easily. These are industrial sources where waste effluents enter watercourses through single or adjacent outfalls. A variety of effective waste treatment systems are now employed. Research and demonstration grant funds are available through the Federal Water Pollution Control Administration for studies leading to the development of improved waste treatment measures. Research on chemical degradation of pesticides is expected to result in knowledge that can be engineered into effective new treatment technology.

Since the more persistent chlorinated hydrocarbon insecticides are recognized as being more troublesome than less refractory pesticides, their usage can be minimized or reserved for those purposes where substitutes will not do.

Advanced concepts of pest control are being developed that range from male sterilization techniques to use of micro quantities of pesticides that are effective, yet not as wasteful of toxicants as are present techniques. The acceptance of levels of pest control somewhat less than eradication also is being emphasized. The latter involves reduction of pest population levels only to that point where economic loss will not result.

Scientists at the Southeast Water Laboratory are working to develop a means to predict runoff pollution and to prevent it from occurring (Nicholson, 1969). The Universal Soil Loss Equation, developed by soil conservationists to guide conservation farm planning throughout the United States, is being considered as the basis for a new formula for predicting pesticide loss from the soil. Knowing what to anticipate, control would be accomplished by using recommended chemicals and practices.

REFERENCES

Alabama Water Improvement Commission. 1961. A report on fish kills occurring on Choccolocco Creek and the Coosa River during May 1961.

Bailey, T. E., and Hannum, J. R. 1967. Distribution of pesticides in California. *J. Sanit. Eng. Div. Am. Soc. Civil Engrs.* 93 (SA5): 27–43.

Barthel, W. F., Hawthorne, J. C., Ford, J. H., Bolton, G. C., McDowell, L. L., Grissinger, E. H., and Parsons, D. A. 1969. Pesticides in water. *Pesticide Monitoring J.* 3:8–66.

Bridges, W. R., Kallman, B. J., and Andrews, A. K. 1963. Persistence of DDT and its metabolites in a farm pond. *Trans. Am. Fisheries Soc.* 92:421–27.

Brown, E., and Nishioka, Y. A. 1967. Pesticides in selected western streams—a contribution to the national program. *Pesticide Monitoring J.* 1:38–46.

Burdick, G. E., Harris, E. J., Dean, H. J., Walker, J. M., Skea, J., and Colby, D. 1964. The accumulation of DDT in lake trout and the effect on reproduction. *Trans. Am. Fisheries Soc.* 93: 127–36.

Cohen, J. M., and Pinkerton, C. 1966. Widespread translocation of pesticides by air transport and rain-out. In *Organic pesticides in the environment, Advan. Chem. Ser. 60.* Wash., D.C.: Am. Chem. Soc.

Congressional Record—Senate (S9417) Aug. 8, 1969.

Florida State Board of Health. 1964. Report of Peace River parathion incident Dec. 23, 1964. Jacksonville: Bur. of Sanit. Eng.

Gunther, F. A., Westlake, W. E., and Jaglan, P. S. 1968. Reported solubilities of 738 pesticide chemicals in water. In *Residue Reviews,* ed. F. A. Gunther, pp. 1–148. New York: Springer-Verlag.

Henkin, H. 1969. Problems in PPM. *Environment* 11:25, 32–33,37.

Hickey, J. J., and Anderson, D. W. 1968. Chlorinated hydrocarbons and eggshell changes in raptorial and fish-eating birds. *Science* 162:271–73.

Hindin, E., May, D. S., and Dustan, G. H. 1964. Collection and analysis of synthetic organic pesticides from surface and ground water. In *Residue Reviews,* ed. F. A. Gunther, pp. 130–56. New York: Springer-Verlag.

Kallman, B. J., Cope, O. B., and Navarre, R. J. 1962. Distribution and detoxification of toxaphene in Clayton Lake, New Mexico. *Trans. Am. Fisheries Soc.* 91:14–22.

Lauer, G. J., Nicholson, H. P., Cox, W. S., and Teasley, J. I. 1966. Pesticide contamination of surface waters by sugar cane farming in Louisiana. *Trans. Am. Fisheries Soc.* 95:310–16.

Lichtenstein, E. P. 1958. Movement of insecticides in soils under leaching conditions. *J. Econ. Entomol.* 51:380–83.

Mahan, J. N., Fowler, D. L., and Shepard, H. H. 1968. *The Pesticide Review 1968.* Wash., D.C.: USDA, Agr. Stabilization and Conserv. Serv.

Manigold, D. B., and Schulze, J. A. 1969. Pesticides in selected western streams—a progress report. *Pesticide Monitoring J.* 3:124–35.

Nicholson, H. P. 1967. Pesticide pollution control. *Science* 158:871–76.

———. 1969. Occurrence and significance of pesticide residues in water. *J. Wash. Acad. Sci.* 59:77–85.

Nicholson, H. P., Webb, H. J., Lauer, G. J., O'Brien, R. E., Grzenda, A. R., and Shanklin, D. W. 1962. Insecticide contamination in a farm pond. I. Origin and duration. *Trans. Am. Fisheries Soc.* 91:213–17.

Nicholson, H. P., Grzenda, A. R., Lauer, G. J., Cox, W. S., and Teasley, J. I. 1964. Water pollution by insecticides in an agricultural river basin. I. Occurrence of insecticides in river and treated municipal water. *Limnol. Oceanog.* 9:310–17.

Nicholson, H. P., Grzenda, A. R., and Teasley, J. I. 1966. Water pollution by insecticides: a six and one-half year study of a watershed. *Proc. Symp. Agr. Waste Waters,* Rept. 10, pp. 132–41. Davis: Univ. of Calif.

Novick, S. 1969. A new pollution problem. *Environment* 11:3–9.

Porter, R. D., and Wiemeyer, S. N. 1969. Dieldrin and DDT: effects on sparrow hawk eggshells and reproduction. *Science* 165:199–200.

Smart, N. A. 1968. Use and residues of mercury compounds in agriculture. In *Residue Reviews,* ed. F. A. Gunther, pp. 1–36. New York: Springer-Verlag.

Terriere, L. C., Kiigemagi, U., Gerlach, A. R., and Borovicka, R. L. 1966. The persistence of toxaphene in lake water and its uptake by aquatic plants and animals. *J. Agr. Food Chem.* 14:66–69.

Weaver, L., Gunnerson, C. G., Breidenbach, A. W., and Lichtenberg, J. J. 1965. Chlorinated hydrocarbon pesticides in major U.S. river basins. *Public Health Rept.* 80:481–93.

Weibel, S. R., Weidner, R. B., Christianson, A. G., and Anderson, R. J. 1966. Characterization, treatment, and disposal of urban stormwater. *Third Intern. Conf. Water Pollution Res.*, Munich, Germany. Section I, Paper 15, pp. 1–15. Wash., D.C.: Water Pollution Control Federation.

Wershaw, R. L., Burcar, P. J., and Goldberg, M. C. 1969. Interaction of pesticides with organic material. *Environ. Sci. Technol.* 3:271–73.

Westlake, W. E., and Gunther, F. A. 1966. Occurrence and mode of introduction of pesticides in the environment. In *Organic pesticides in the environment, Advan. Chem. Ser. 60,* pp. 110–21. Wash., D.C.: Am. Chem. Soc.

Young, L. A., and Nicholson, H. P. 1951. Stream pollution resulting from the use of organic insecticides. *Progressive Fish-Culturist* 13:193–98.

CHAPTER THIRTEEN

HERBICIDE RESIDUES IN AGRICULTURAL WATER FROM CONTROL OF AQUATIC AND BANK WEEDS

F. L. TIMMONS, P. A. FRANK, and R. J. DEMINT

Herbicides are essential and widely used tools in our modern agriculture. In 1964 approximately 120 million acres of cultivated fields, pastures, grazing lands, and forested areas were treated with 200 million pounds of herbicides for weed control (U.S. Department of Agriculture Census, 1964). In 1967 the total sales of herbicides had increased to 348 million pounds. A small but relatively significant proportion of those herbicides were used to control weeds in irrigation and drainage canals, on ditchbanks, in farm ponds, and in irrigation reservoirs.

Thus far, monitoring studies have shown few significant herbicide residues in our streams, ponds, and lakes resulting from runoff from treated fields, rangelands, and forests. There is some concern about the effects on water quality of herbicides appied directly into or over the water or on adjacent banks from which drift, overlap spray, or runoff may get into surface water supplies.

This chapter reports the extent of herbicide use for control of aquatic and bank weeds, the levels of residues found in water after such applications, the rate of dissipation of such residues, and whether and to what extent herbicides in irrigation water are found in irrigated crops used for food or feed. Only limited information is presented on herbicide residues in water from other sources.

EXTENT OF HERBICIDE USE FOR CONTROL OF AQUATIC AND BANK WEEDS

No statistics are available on the total amount of herbicides used annually in the United States for control of aquatic and bank weeds. However, several examples of the extent of aquatic areas where weeds are serious problems and the amount of herbicides used in

F. L. Timmons is Research Agronomist, Crops Research Division, ARS, USDA, Laramie, Wyo. P. A. Frank is Plant Physiologist, Crops Research Division, ARS, USDA, Denver. R. J. Demint is Research Chemist, Crops Research Division, ARS, USDA, Denver.

certain areas provide reliable indications of the total amounts used in and adjacent to water.

About 150 species of aquatic and semiaquatic marginal plants create weed problems in one or more aquatic situations in the United States (Timmons, 1967). According to the latest available statistics (U.S. Department of Agriculture Census, 1959, 1964), there are more than 2 million ponds and reservoirs, 189,000 miles of drainage ditches, and 173,000 miles of irrigation canals. Most of the ponds and drainage ditches are in the north-central and southern states. Three-fourths of the irrigation canals and most of the reservoirs which supply irrigation water are in the western states. The numerous reservoirs in the southern and north-central states are used primarily for recreation and municipal purposes. All of these aquatic areas are infested or susceptible to infestation by aquatic and bank weeds.

In 1957 a careful survey was conducted by the Agricultural Research Service and the Bureau of Reclamation (Timmons, 1960) to determine the extent of weed infestation, annual losses caused by weeds, and the cost of weed control on irrigation systems of the 17 western states. The survey revealed that 63% of the 144,000 miles of canals were infested with aquatic weeds. More than 75% of the 530,000 acres of ditchbanks were infested with 1 or more of 4 kinds of bank weeds. In that year, 54% of the weed-infested canals and 80% of the weed-infested ditchbanks were treated for weed control, mostly with herbicides.

A questionnaire survey made in 1961 (Timmons, 1963) among agencies and aquatic weed specialists revealed that aquatic and marginal weeds were serious problems in most ponds and drainage ditches in the north-central, southern, and western states. The extensive annual losses from lack of drainage and water utilization caused by those weeds were reported in *Agriculture Handbook 291, Losses in Agriculture, 1965.*

An extensive weed control program has been continued since 1957 on western irrigation systems. The herbicides used most extensively in the control programs are xylene; (2,4-dichlorophenoxy) acetic acid (2,4-D); (2,4,5-trichlorophenoxy) acetic acid (2,4,5-T); copper sulfate; 2,2-dichloropropionic acid (dalapon); and 3-amino-s-triazole (amitrole). Aromatic weed oils are used extensively in the southwestern states. The amounts of herbicides ordered by irrigation districts in Oregon, Washington, and Idaho for use on irrigation systems during 1969 were xylene, 800,000 gal; acrolein, 22,000 gal; copper sulfate, 216,000 lb; 2,4-D, 187,000 lb; 2,4,5-T, 9,200 lb; dalapon, 3,500 lb; and amitrole + ammonium thiocyanate (amitrole-T), 5,000 lb.[1] This is for only 3 of the 17 western states. Most of the other western states do not use herbicides as extensively as do the 3 northwestern states.

General information indicates that weed problems in drainage ditches of eastern states are as critical and probably more so than those in western irrigation systems. However, the use of herbicides does not seem to have been as extensive for control of weeds in those drainage ditches except possibly in Florida and Louisiana. Mechanical methods have not proved to be adequate substitutes for herbicides in drainage ditches and ponds in those states.

Irrigation and drainage of agricultural land are important factors in the conservation and use of water resources in the southeastern states. The aquatic weed problems in lakes, streams, and water-control canals in that region are much more extensive and serious than in the north-central states. A survey was conducted in 1963 in 8 Gulf and South Atlantic Coast states (U.S. Department of the Army, 1965). The survey showed total infestations of 162,000 acres of water hyacinth (*Eichhornia crassipes* [Mart.] Solms), 99,000 acres of alligator weed (*Alternanthera philoxeroides* [Mart.] Griseb.), and 207,000 acres of submersed weeds. The survey did not include farm ponds and tidal marsh areas, most of which are heavily infested by aquatic and marginal weeds in those states.

Herbicides, chiefly 2,4-D, have been used extensively since about 1950 for the control of water hyacinth and certain other floating and emersed weeds in Florida and Louisiana. During the extensive unrestricted use of 2,4-D prior to 1967, no serious problems of injury to fish, livestock, or man from use of treated water were apparent. During the 4 years 1959–62, approximately 188,000 acres of water hyacinth and alligator weed were sprayed with 2,4-D in the U.S. Army Corps of Engineers Expanded Aquatic Plant Control Program. That did not account for the herbicide usage by other agencies and private individuals during those years.

Aquatic herbicides such as 2,4-D; 6,7-dihydrodipyrido[1,2-*a*:2′, 1′-*c*]pyrazinediium salts (diquat); 7-oxabicyclo[2.2.1]heptane-2,3-dicarboxylic acid (endothall); dalapon; and 2-(2,4,5-trichlorophenoxy) propionic acid (silvex) are used to a considerable extent in the southeast, especially in Florida. The highly successful aquatic and marginal weed program of the Central and Southern Flood Control District is an excellent example of what can be accomplished by extensive and careful use of all available registered herbicides for control of aquatic and marginal weeds.

At present 6 herbicides are registered by the Pesticides Regulation Division of the Agricultural Research Service for control of algae, 4 for control of floating weeds, 6 for control of emersed weeds, and 12 for control of submersed weeds. In addition, 17 herbicides are registered for control of ditchbank weeds. That is a total of 35 different herbicides registered for the control of aquatic or bank weeds.

HERBICIDE RESIDUES IN WATER

The principal means by which herbicides enter water are (1) from surface-runoff water during irrigation or rainfall; (2) by application of herbicides to soil or water for control of submersed weeds in canals, ponds, or lakes; (3) by herbicide treatment of floating and emersed weeds, and (4) from treatment of banks of streams and canals for control of bank and marginal weeds.

---

1. W. D. Boyle, Bureau of Reclamation, Boise, Idaho, 1969, personal communication.

Residues in Surface Runoff

During a 3-year program of monitoring agricultural pesticide residues, herbicides were found only rarely, and usually in concentrations less than 10 ppb (U.S. Department of Agriculture, 1969). Monitoring studies in an area of irrigated agriculture showed that before use, irrigation water contained very small quantities (<1 ppb) of pesticides of any kind. Of a number of herbicides used in the area monitored, no detectable residues of these were found in waste irrigation water.

In other monitoring studies (Marston et al., 1968) small quantities of amitrole were detected in runoff water for 5 days following aerial spraying of a 100-acre watershed for control of salmonberry. A maximum concentration of 155 ppb amitrole was found 30 minutes after spraying began, but was reduced to 26 ppb after 2 hours. On the other hand, amitrole was found in runoff water for only 35 hours from a similar but larger watershed treatment (Norris et al., 1967). When 2.1 acres of a 46.5-acre rangeland watershed were treated with 9.3 lb per acre of 4-amino-3,5,6-trichloropicolinic acid (picloram), the runoff water from this watershed contained picloram in concentrations of 0.37 to 0.046 ppm for 11 months (Davis et al., 1968). No picloram was found after this period. Concentrations of 1.5 to 2.0 ppm of 2,4-D were detected in runoff water for a period of 7 days following treatment of 150 acres of forest with 40 lb per acre of the nonyl ester of 2,4-D (Aldhous, 1967). In a subsequent sampling of the runoff water 28 days after treatment, the residue of 2,4-D was below the detectable level of 0.005 ppm.

Experimental data showing the extent of herbicidal residues in runoff water are limited. Where residues were shown to occur, in most cases the total volume of water affected was not large.

Residues in Water from Control of Submersed Weeds

Recommendations for control of submersed weeds usually specify herbicide-usage levels in terms of ppm of the herbicide in water. Therefore, the initial residue level most often represents the recommended or predetermined concentration of herbicide found to be effective for control of the weed species present. A number of herbicides and recommended application rates for control of submersed weeds are given in Table 13.1.

Submersed weed control in waterways such as irrigation canals is accomplished primarily by the use of acrolein, aromatic solvents, and copper sulfate. Diquat, endothall, and the ester of 2,4-D are used less frequently. Copper sulfate is commonly used for control of algae; however, low concentrations applied over extended periods have been reported recently to provide good control of vascular weeds (Bartley, 1969). Where very little water movement occurs in waterways, good weed control is obtained with diquat and the amine salts of endothall.

When maximum possible herbicide residues were found in water from the applications recommended in Table 13.1, all of the applied

TABLE 13.1. Herbicides and application rates recommended for control of submersed aquatic weeds.

Herbicide	Form	Application Rates*
Acrolein	Liquid	0.1–0.6 ppm[†]
		4–7 ppm[‡]
Aromatic solvents	Emulsified	600–740 ppm[§]
Copper sulfate	Pentahydrate	0.1–2.0 ppm
Dichlobenil	Granular	10–15 lb/a
		0.9–1.4 ppm[‖]
Diquat	Cation	0.25–1.5 ppm
Endothall	Disodium salt	0.5–4 ppm
	Amine salt	0.05–2.5 ppm
Fenac	Granular	15–20 lb/a
		1.4–1.8 ppm[‖]
Silvex	Potassium salt	1.5–2 ppm
2,4-D ester	Granular	20–40 lb/a
		1.8–3.6 ppm[‖]

* From USDA (1969) *Suggested Guide for Weed Control.* Agr. Handbook 332. Application rates are in terms of acid equivalent or active ingredient.

† For extended application time in flowing water.

‡ For treatment of weeds in quiescent water.

§ Emulsifier added at concentrations of 1.5 to 2.0%.

‖ Ppm concentration arbitrarily expressed in terms of 4 ft of water.

herbicide recovered in water usually dissipated rapidly. Volatile herbicides such as acrolein and aromatic solvents (mostly xylene) are lost from water at relatively rapid rates. Diquat concentrations are rapidly reduced by weed growth, organic matter, and sediment (Coats et al., 1966). Granular formulations may prevent occurrence of high concentrations of certain herbicides in water by confining portions of the herbicides at the hydrosoil surface. Granular formulations of 2,6-dichlorobenzonitrile (dichlobenil) and the ester of 2,4-D are notable in this respect. Following treatment of 2 ponds with 0.58 and 0.40 ppm of granular dichlobenil, only 0.32 and 0.23 ppm, respectively, were recovered (Frank and Comes, 1967). Likewise, in a pond treated with 1.33 ppm of granular butoxyethanol ester of 2,4-D, the maximum residue level of 2,4-D observed was 0.067 ppm. At the same time, relatively high concentrations of both herbicides were found in the upper 1 inch of hydrosoil. On the other hand (2,3,6-trichlorophenyl) acetic acid (fenac) was rapidly lost from granules and nearly all of the herbicide applied was found in water above the granules which remained at the bottom of the pond or lake. During 1966 the Tennessee Valley Authority used large-scale applications of granular butoxyethanol ester of 2,4-D at rates of 40 to 100 lb per acre for control of Eurasian watermilfoil (*Myriophyllum spicatum* L.). The highest concentration of 2,4-D recorded at any of the water-treatment plants where water was monitored was 2 ppb (Smith and Isom, 1967).

Residues in Water from Control of Floating Weeds

Herbicide residues resulting from treatment for control of floating weeds are dependent not only on the application rate and water depth but also on the type of floating weeds and the amount of exposed water surface. Very few residue data on these applications are available.

In one series of experiments, pools 10 feet in diameter containing growths of alligator weed were sprayed with propylene glycol butyl ether (PGBE) ester of silvex at 8 lb per acre (Cochrane et al., 1967). Highest possible concentrations of silvex residues would have ranged from 2.70 to 3.04 ppm if all of the herbicide applied was found in the water. However, the greatest recovery of silvex in water at any time was approximately 1.6 ppm. In this study no estimates of uncovered water surface were made. In similar studies involving applications of the dimethyl amine salt of 2,4-D and the PGBE esters of 2,4-D and silvex applied at 4 lb per acre on water hyacinth or alligator weed, almost all of the maximum residue levels were between 1 ppm and 650 ppb (Averitt, 1967). In both of the above studies, the highest concentrations of herbicides did not appear in the water until approximately 1 to 2 weeks after the treatments. The authors concluded that the herbicides were absorbed by the plants and later released into the water through roots and other submersed plant tissues.

Residues from Ditchbank Weed Control

Spreading weed infestations have caused irrigation system managers and maintenance workers to become more conscious of weed control on banks of waterways. Where periodic treatment with 2,4-D was once considered adequate for ditchbank maintenance, extensive and varied weed control programs involving other herbicides or mixtures are now common. Among the most serious ditchbank weeds are several species such as sedges—for example, *Carex aquatilis* Wahl and reed canary grass *(Phalaris arundinacea* L.)— which grow at the water margin. The proximity of weeds to water almost invariably results in some herbicide entering the water during herbicide application. Principal factors affecting the amount of herbicide found in the water are treatment rate, water volume, nature of the weed growth, and spray overlap at the water's edge.

A number of ditchbanks were sprayed with various herbicides and the water sampled and analyzed to determine the quantities of residues present (Frank and Demint, 1967, 1968). Herbicides, treatment rates, and water volumes, along with the highest concentrations of herbicides found in the water of a number of irrigation waterways, are shown in Table 13.2. With one exception, all treatments were made on 1 bank, with a vehicle-mounted boom traveling in an upstream direction. Both banks of the Boulder Feeder Canal were treated prior to the entry of water. The 98 ppb of amitrole

TABLE 13.2. **Highest concentrations of residues found in irrigation water following ditchbank treatment with several herbicides.**

Herbicide and Irrigation Waterway	Treatment Rate	Volume of Water Flow	Highest Concentration of Residue
	(lb/a)	(cfs)	(ppb)
Amitrole			
Boulder Feeder Canal* ..	6	50	98
Farmer's ditch	4	4	24
Manard lateral	4	40	31
Yolo lateral	3	23	43
Dalapon			
Five-mile lateral	20.0	15	399
Lateral no. 4	6.7	290	23
Manard lateral	9.6	37	39
Yolo lateral	10.5	26	162
TCA			
Lateral no. 4	3.8	290	12
Manard lateral	5.4	37	20
Yolo lateral	5.9	26	69
2,4-D†			
Lateral no. 4	1.9	290	5
Manard lateral	2.7	37	13
Yolo lateral	3.0	26	36

Source: Unpublished data from P. A. Frank and R. J. Demint, *Annual Report of Weed Investigations.* USDA, ARS, Denver, Colo.

* Both banks treated for distance of 0.7 mile.

† N-oleyl 1,3-propylenediamine salt.

represent the herbicide picked up by the initial water filling the canal and were of very short duration. Minimum and average residue values for all treatments were considerably less than the maximum levels shown in the table. It will be shown later that residues in the concentrations listed in Table 13.2 would be most unlikely to injure crops or produce significant residues in crop plants.

DISSIPATION OF HERBICIDE RESIDUES FROM WATER

Dissipation is an extremely important factor in the use of herbicides for control of aquatic and bank weeds. Most of the herbicides registered for use in aquatic situations have water-use restrictions which require at least partial dissipation of the herbicide before normal water use is resumed. The pathways leading to dissipation are almost as varied as the chemicals themselves. Volatilization is the most important factor in the dissipation of aromatic solvents and acrolein. Sorption processes predominate in the disappearance from water of herbicides such as diquat, paraquat, and possibly endothall. Biological and chemical degradation account for much of the loss of 2,4-D, silvex, dichlobenil, and other herb cides.

The dissipation of herbicides in water has been studied most extensively in small ponds, pools, and reservoirs. Data from some of

TABLE 13.3. Residue dissipation in ponded water following application of herbicides.

Herbicide	Application Rate	Concentration Detected			
		Highest		Final	
	(ppm)	*(ppm)*	*(days)*	*(ppm)*	*(days)*
	Liquid applications				
Amitrole*	1.0	1.34	1.0	0.08	201
Fenac*	4.0	5.2	1.0	2.4	202
Diquat*	2.5	3.27	2.0	N.D.	30
Paraquat*	2.1	1.05	1.0	N.D.	38
2,4-D methylamine salt†	1.5	0.139	1.0	0.004	41
Silvex, PGBE ester‡§	2.9	1.6	7.0	0.02	182
Diquat‖	0.62	0.49	1.0	0.001	8
Paraquat‖	1.14	0.55	1.0	0.001	12
Endothall‖	1.0	0.18	2.0	0.001	36
Copper¶	0.50	0.42	0.1	0.19	3
Endothall**	1.2	0.79	4.0	0.54	12
	Granular applications				
Dichlobenil‖	0.58	0.32	36	0.004	160
Dichlobenil‖	0.40	0.23	8	0.001	160
Fenac‖	1.56	1.61	18	0.38	160
Fenac‖	1.0	0.71	8	0.07	160
2,4-D butoxyethanol ester‖ ...	1.33	0.067	18	0.001	36

* Grzenda, Nicholson, and Cox (1966).

† Averitt (1967).

‡ Cochrane et al. (1967).

§ Average of three treatments.

‖ Frank and Comes (1967).

¶ Toth and Riemer (1968).

** Yeo (1969).

the more typical studies were compiled and are shown in Table 13.3. Some of the most effective aquatic herbicides, such as dichlobenil, fenac, and silvex, were found to be among the more persistent compounds. The excellent and often complete control of weeds by these herbicides may be attributed in part to their persistence. Diquat, paraquat, 2,4-D, and endothall disappeared from ponded water at rapid to moderate rates. While rapid dissipation from water is desirable from the standpoint of residues, it may also result in the total ineffectiveness of diquat and paraquat in waters containing suspended sediment or organic matter (Coats et al., 1966). In some cases dissipation of the herbicides from water was found to be accompanied by accumulation of high concentrations of the herbicides in the hydrosoil (Frank and Comes, 1967).

Dissipation of herbicide residues in the flowing water of canals, ditches, and streams has been studied less extensively than in ponds and very few data are published. Most of the studies reported here were carried out recently by personnel of the Agricultural Research Service and cooperators.

While aromatic solvents have been used many years for control of submerged weeds in irrigation canals, it was not until 1967 that the dissipation of this herbicide was studied in some detail (Frank and Demint, 1967). Two canals carrying 11 and 13 cubic feet per second (cfs) of water were treated with 575 and 550 ppm emulsified xylene, respectively. Loss of xylene, largely by way of volatilization, was rapid. After traveling 9 miles, the concentration of xylene in the canal treated at the rate of 550 ppm was reduced to 17 ppm. The concentration of xylene in the second canal was reduced to 6 ppm after a downstream flow of 8 miles.

Acrolein is another highly volatile herbicide and is used for control of submersed weeds in large irrigation canals. The loss rate of acrolein from concentrations of 0.6 and 0.7 ppm was determined for a canal carrying 132 to 135 cfs of water (Battelle-Northwest Laboratories, 1966, 1968). In 2 tests, the loss of acrolein was shown to be temperature dependent. In water of 64° F the original concentration of 0.7 ppm of acrolein was reduced by 98% while the water traveled a distance of 19 miles. At the lower and less typical temperature of 48° F, the loss was only 62% at a distance 27 miles downstream from the point of application. The dissipation data of both aromatic solvent and the acrolein showed a linear relationship between the log of the herbicide concentration and distance of water flow downstream.

Copper sulfate is frequently used to control algae in irrigation canals. The commonly used slug treatment of 1 lb of copper sulfate pentahydrate per cfs of water flow, when applied to a 411-cfs canal in Washington, gave concentrations of 1.6, 0.36, 0.23, and 0.04 ppm at 0.5, 6, 12, and 23 miles downstream, respectively (Nelson et al., 1969). A 3-year study was made to determine the efficacy of daily application of copper sulfate for control of submersed weeds in irrigation canals (Bartley, 1969). Five pounds of copper sulfate were applied per hour to a flow of 26 cfs of water. An average maximum concentration of 0.21 ppm copper ion was found 0.25 mile below the treatment site. The copper ion concentration was reduced 86% to 0.03 ppm 9 miles downstream.

In one study a single bank of each of 2 irrigation laterals was sprayed with amitrole in an upstream direction for a distance of 0.5 mile. Treatment rates were 3 and 4 lb per acre. Overlap of the spray pattern at the water's edge was estimated to vary from 12 to 24 inches. Water samples taken at varying distances downstream from the area treated with 4 lb per acre of amitrole showed a reduction in residue levels from 31 to 24 ppb over a 4.5-mile distance of water flow. Reduction of amitrole residue from the bank treated at the rate of 3 lb per acre was 43 to 26 ppb over a distance of water flow of 3 miles.

Frequently it is necessary to treat canal banks for weed control prior to filling with water for the growing season. One such canal was treated with a 4-foot swath on both banks for a distance of 0.7 mile. On turning 50 cfs of water into the canal, an initial concentration of 98 ppb of amitrole occurred in the water front. This residue level was reduced to 46 ppb at 1.3 miles downstream and after

TABLE 13.4. Dissipation of herbicides in irrigation water.

Miles Downstream	Dalapon	TCA	2,4-D
	(ppb)	(ppb)	(ppb)
		Manard lateral	
0.5	66	31	25
4.25	40	20	14
		Yolo lateral	
0.5	289	...	55
3.0	182	...	36

flowing 9 miles, the residue level in the water amounted to only 23 ppb.

Two irrigation laterals (Yolo and Manard) were treated with a commonly used mixture of herbicides. A study was made of the resulting residue levels in the water and the extent of dissipation of these levels as the water traveled downstream. Water volume and the treatment rates of dalapon, trichloroacetic acid (TCA), and 2,4-D used are shown in Table 13.2. Residue levels in the irrigation water 0.5 mile below the treatment sites and at the ends of the laterals are shown in Table 13.4. The input of herbicide during bank treatments such as these was quite variable. At any instant it may vary as much as ± 100% of the average or calculated input. Also, as the water traveled downstream, water containing the maximum residue level became a smaller fraction of the total volume of residue-bearing water. For this reason values based on the average residue levels may reflect more accurately the dissipation of herbicides in flowing water.

In other studies, dalapon, amitrole-T, and the isooctyl ester of 2,4-D were applied directly to irrigation water at constant rates, and reduction in residue levels was determined as the water flowed downstream. A canal which carried 16 cfs of water was sprayed for 75 minutes to provide a mile of water containing 400 ppb of 2,4-D. The dissipation of residues of 2,4-D was nonlinear. The 400 ppb were reduced to maximum residue levels of 383, 285, 210, 206, and 190 ppb at distances of 0.1, 1, 3, 5, and 8 miles downstream, respectively. These data show an initial rapid loss during the first 3 miles of water flow, followed by a slow but constant decrease up to 9 miles.

Another canal, which carried 19 cfs of water, was sprayed with a solution of the sodium salt of dalapon for 51 minutes to provide a mile of water containing 100 ppb of dalapon. A plot of maximum concentration in ppb against mileage gave a straight line with a slope of 5.6. Another canal which carried 49 cfs of water was similarly treated for 18 minutes with amitrole-T to provide a half-mile length of water containing 50 ppb of amitrole (Demint et al., 1969). A similar plot, for the 5.25 miles sampled, gave a straight line with a slope of 6. Using these rates of dissipation, downstream mileage at which total dissipation might occur was calculated as 18 miles for dalapon and slightly under 9 miles for amitrole. The conformance to linearity was an indication that only 1 factor was involved for these 2 water-soluble herbicides. Dissipation was achieved through elongation of the herbicide cloud. The magnitude of the dilution was so great as to obscure possible losses from sorption or degradation. Caution should be exercised in attempting to use these dissipation rates to predict the complete disappearance of these herbicides to other canals. Among the complicating factors are time required for complete dispersion, canal capacity changes attendant with flow rate changes, the retarding effect of bank treatments compared with idealized applications to the center of the canal, and length of bank treatments.

HERBICIDES IN IRRIGATED CROPS

Nearly all of the herbicides used for weed control in irrigation canals or on canal banks have been tested on most of the important field crops at 1 to 4 of our Agricultural Research Service research stations in the western states (Arle, 1950; Bruns, 1954; Bruns et al., 1955, 1958, 1964; Arle and McRae, 1959). The treated water was applied by flood or furrow irrigation methods in 1 to 3 acre-inches of water.

In general, xylene-type aromatic solvents, acrolein, amitrole, and dalapon were found to cause no injurious effects on crop growth or yields at concentrations or rates used for weed control. Even 2,4-D at rates up to 1 lb, and usually 2 lb, per acre did not affect growth or yields of such sensitive crops as cotton, grapes, and sugar beets.

The results of this research have verified the extensive experience and observation in connection with the widespread use of irrigation water on crops from canals treated with aromatic solvents, acrolein, or copper sulfate and on which bank weeds were treated with 2,4-D, dalapon, amitrole, 2,4,5-T, or silvex. No known substantiated instances of damage to crops by any of the extensive uses during 5 to 20 years have been reported. This extensive use and experience have been documented in annual weed and pest control reports of the 7 Bureau of Reclamation regional offices.

In 1966 equipment was developed at Prosser, Washington, for field application to crops by sprinkler irrigation of water containing herbicides. This provided an opportunity to compare the effects of herbicides in water on irrigated crops when applied by overhead sprinkler and furrow methods. It also provided an opportunity to compare the amounts of herbicide residues assimilated by the crops when treated water was applied by each of the 2 methods.

In 1967, 2,4-D and silvex were applied to crops at rates of 0.1, 0.5, and 2.5 lb per acre by furrow irrigation. These rates provided concentrations of 0.22, 1.11, and 5.55 ppm, respectively, in 2 acre-inches of water. Only at the highest rate of silvex did significant yield reductions occur in beet tops and bean seed. Small but statistically nonsignificant reductions were measured in beet tops and roots for the 2 highest rates of 2,4-D. There was no reduction in yield of corn fodder or grain by either herbicide at any of the 3 rates.

Both 2,4-D and silvex were applied at rates of 0.01, 0.1, and 1.0 lb per acre by sprinkler irrigation. These rates provided concentrations of 0.022, 0.22, and 2.22 ppm in 2 acre-inches of irrigation water. Surprisingly, both 2,4-D and silvex produced significant increases in the yields of sugar beet tops and roots at all 3 rates. Neither 2,4-D nor silvex affected the yield of corn. The 2 highest rates of silvex reduced the yield of soybean seed, but the lowest rate of silvex and none of the rates of 2,4-D reduced the yield of soybeans. The rates for sprinkler irrigation were lower than those used for furrow irrigation.

In samples taken 7 days after furrow irrigation, the highest rate of 2,4-D resulted in a residue of 0.11 ppm in beet roots, fresh weight (Bruns and Comes, 1968). No residues were found in other crop tissues. Samples of crop tissues taken at maturity showed no residues of either herbicide after irrigations containing 0.22 or 1.11 ppm.

Low concentrations of 2,4-D were found in most crop tissues in samples taken 2 days after sprinkler irrigation at all rates. However, the highest concentrations from the 2 lower rates ranged up to 3.94 ppm dry weight basis in beet roots. These concentrations were lower than the tolerance of 5 ppm already established for 2,4-D in some food and feed crops. Also, sugar beet roots would never be used for feed or sugar production at that stage of growth. It is possible that sweet corn roasting ears or soybeans as hay might be harvested at that immature stage of growth. At maturity, when all of these crops are usually harvested, none of the crops contained any 2,4-D from the 2 lower rates and only beet roots contained 0.06 ppm from the highest rate, 1 lb per acre (2.22 ppm). This is 40 to 50 times the highest concentration of 2,4-D found in water thus far, following applications for control of aquatic or bank weeds.

No silvex residues were found in any crop tissue receiving the lowest rate of 0.1 lb per acre (0.22 ppm). By normal harvest time at crop maturity, most of the silvex residues had disappeared, even in crops irrigated with the highest concentration.

Silvex residues in crop tissues following sprinkler irrigation were found in all crop tissues from the 2 highest rates in samples taken 2 days after harvest. Also, soybean and corn foliage and beet roots contained measurable residues from the lowest rate. However, by normal harvest date at crop maturity, no residues were present in any crop tissues from the 2 lower concentrations of 0.022 and 0.22 of silvex in irrigation water.

Additional data on residues of 6 different herbicides in 6 different irrigated crops are being obtained in our contract research with Stanford Research Institute. In this contract the crops were grown in 2-gallon greenhouse crocks. Each crop was irrigated at early growth and late growth stages with 2 concentrations of each herbicide. The treated water was applied in 1 acre-inch by both flood or soil and overhead sprinkler irrigation methods. Results are now available on 5 of the herbicides in all 6 crops (Stanford Research Institute, 1968, 1969).

No 2,4-D was found in onions or soybeans from the highest

rates of 0.22 and 1.11 ppm and the residues were negligible in carrots, milo, or potatoes. Even in leaf lettuce the residues were less than one-tenth the tolerance established for 2,4-D on some food crops.

No silvex was found in milo, carrots, or lettuce from the highest concentrations of 0.22 and 1.11 ppm, and residues were very low in potatoes, soybeans, and onions.

No amitrole residues were found in any of the tissues of greenhouse-grown and treated crops or in field-grown beans, corn, and wheat at Bozeman, Montana, which were furrow irrigated with water containing 4 lb per acre of amitrole. In another experiment at Prosser, Washington, no amitrole residues were found in crops furrow irrigated with water containing up to 2.5 lb per acre of amitrole (Bruns and Comes, 1966).

The dalapon residues were determined in greenhouse-grown crops treated and analyzed by Stanford Research Institute. The highest rate used was 0.5 lb per acre (2.22 ppm) except on potatoes, carrots, and onions. For the latter 3 crops, the rates were increased 5-fold. Despite the heavy rates of treatment on carrots and onions, the dalapon residues were very low. The highest concentrations of dalapon were in soybeans, 1.18 to 2.79 ppm. These concentrations were less than one-tenth the tolerance of 30 ppm of dalapon established by the U.S. Food and Drug Administration for asparagus.

No diquat was found in any of the 6 crops which were irrigated by soil-flooding or overhead sprinkling at 0.09 or 0.45 ppm. Because of the rapid dissipation of diquat in water, irrigation water would seldom, if ever, contain a residue of 0.45 ppm following a normal application for weed control.

The same equipment that was used at Prosser, Washington, for comparing effects and residues from furrow and sprinkler irrigation of 2,4-D and silvex in 1967 was used for comparing furrow and sprinkler irrigation of acrolein in 1966, and again in 1968 (Bruns and Comes, 1966, 1968). The concentrations used were 0.1, 15, and 60 ppm in 1966 and 0.1, 0.6, and 15 ppm in 1968. Only the highest concentration, 60 ppm by furrow irrigation, caused injury to soybean and sugar beet foliage. The injury from sprinkler irrigation was greater than that from furrow irrigation but no injury occurred from concentrations used for weed contol. None of the furrow irrigation treatments reduced corn yields. Analyses of water samples showed that only 5 to 10% of the acrolein was lost from the water during furrow irrigations. However, 60 to 90% of the acrolein was lost from the water during sprinkler irrigation before the water fell on the crop plants. That probably explains why no damage to crops was ever reported by farmers who applied acrolein-treated water directly from canals by sprinkler irrigation. Battelle Laboratories found no acrolein in any of the crop samples.

SUMMARY

The effectiveness of herbicides and the economics involved in agricultural production have caused their extensive use for weed control in and adjacent to aquatic areas, especially on irrigation systems. As additional data concerning residues and toxicity are developed, and as adequate tolerances are established for residues, greater use of herbicides in and around agricultural waters may be expected.

Maximum residues of herbicides used for weed control in farm ponds and reservoirs are low, ranging from a fraction of 1 ppm to several ppm. In most cases these levels are of short duration. With the exception of aromatic solvents and copper sulfate, most herbicides occur in irrigation water at concentrations under 100 ppb. Only under the most adverse conditions in small irrigation laterals are significantly greater residues found. The transport of herbicide residues in irrigation water prevents extensive exposure of any given irrigated area. However, the flowing water may at times carry residues to areas where their presence may be objectionable. While reduction in residue levels varies with the canal and herbicide, many residues are dissipated after a water flow of 10 to 15 miles. In most cases, the dissipation can be attributed to dilution in water or absorption by bottom mud.

The concentrations of herbicides found in irrigation water are unlikely to cause injury in crops. Crop tolerance studies showed that crops can tolerate greater quantities of herbicides than would be found in the water after applications for weed control. Where residues were found in crops following irrigation with water containing herbicides, the levels were generally much lower than tolerances already established for the same or similar crops.

REFERENCES

Aldhous, J. R. 1967. 2,4-D residues in water following aerial spraying in a Scottish forest. *Weed Res.* 7:239–41.

Arle, H. F. 1950. The effect of aromatic solvents and other aquatic herbicides on crop plants and animals. *Proc. Western Weed Control Conf.* 12:58–60.

Arle, H. F., and McRae, G. N. 1959. Cotton tolerance to applications of acrolein in irrigation water. *Western Weed Control Conf. Res. Progr. Rept.*, p. 72.

Averitt, W. K. 1967. Report on the persistence of 2,4-dichlorophenoxyacetic acid and its derivatives in surface waters when used to control aquatic vegetation. Univ. of Southwestern Louisiana, Lafayette. Unpublished.

Bartley, T. R. 1969. Copper residue on irrigation canal. Paper 98 presented at meeting of Weed Sci. Soc. Am., Feb. 11–13, Las Vegas, Nev.

Battelle-Northwest Laboratories. 1966, 1967, 1968. Progress reports on herbicide residues in irrigated crops. Unpublished.

Bruns, V. F. 1954. The response of certain crops to 2,4-dichlorophenoxyacetic acid in irrigation water. I. Red Mexican beans. *Weeds* 3:359–76.

Bruns, V. F., and Clore, W. J. 1958. The response of certain crops to 2,4-dichlorophenoxyacetic acid in irrigation water. II. Concord grapes. *Weeds* 6:187–93.

Bruns, V. F., and Comes, R. D. 1966, 1967, 1968. Annual report of weed investigations in aquatic and noncrop areas. USDA, ARS,

Crops Res. Div. Unpublished.

Bruns, V. F., Hodgson, J. M., Arle, H. F., and Timmons, F. L. 1955. *The use of aromatic solvents for control of submersed aquatic weeds in irrigation channels.* USDA Circular 971.

Bruns, V. F., Yeo, R.R., and Arle, H. F. 1964. *Tolerance of certain crops to several aquatic herbicides in irrigation water.* USDA Tech. Bull. 1299.

Coats, G. E., Funderburk, H. H., Lawrence, J. M., and Davis, D. E. 1966. Factors affecting persistence and inactivation of diquat and paraquat. *Weed Res.* 6:58–66.

Cochrane, D. R., Pope, J. D., Jr., Nicholson, H. P., and Bailey, G. W. 1967. The persistence of silvex in water and hydrosoil. *Water Resources Res.* 3:517–23.

Davis, E. A., Ingebo, P. A., and Pase, C. P. 1968. Effect of a watershed treatment with picloram on water quality. *Forest Serv. Res. Note RM-100.* Fort Collins, Colo.: USDA.

Demint, R. J., Frank, P. A., and Comes, R. D. 1969. Amitrole residues and dissipation rate in irrigation water. Submitted for publication.

Frank, P. A., and Comes, R. D. 1967. Herbicidal residues in pond water and hydrosoil. *Weeds* 15:210–13.

Frank, P. A., and Demint, R. J. 1967, 1968. Annual report of weed investigations. USDA, ARS. Unpublished.

Grzenda, A. R., Nicholson, H. P., and Cox, W. S. 1966. Persistence of four herbicides in pond water. *J. Am. Waterworks Assoc.* 58:326–32.

Marston, R. B., Schults, D. W., Shiroyama, T., and Snyder, L. V. 1968. Amitrole concentrations in creek waters downstream from an aerially sprayed watershed sub-basin. *Pesticides Monitoring J.* 2:123–28.

Nelson, J. L., Bruns, V. F., Coutant, C. C., and Carlile, B. L. 1969. Behavior and reactions of copper sulfate in an irrigation canal. *Pesticides Monitoring J.* In press.

Norris, L. A., Newton, M., and Zavitkovski, J. 1967. Stream contamination with amitrole from forest spray operations. *Western Weed Control Conf. Res. Progr. Rept.* pp. 33–35.

Smith, G. E., and Isom, B. G. 1967. Investigations of effects of large-scale applications of 2,4-D on aquatic fauna and water quality. *Pesticides Monitoring J.* 1:16–21.

Stanford Research Institute. 1968, 1969. Progress reports on herbicide residues in irrigated crops. Unpublished.

Timmons, F. L. 1960. *Weed control in western irrigation and drainage systems.* USDA, ARS 34–14.

———. 1963. Herbicides in aquatic weed control. *Proc. 16th Southern Weed Conf.,* pp. 5–14.

———. 1967. The waterweed nuisance. In *U.S. Dept. of Agriculture yearbook of agriculture,* pp. 158–61.

Toth, S. J., and Riemer, D. N. 1968. Algae control in inland water. *Weeds Trees Turf* 7:14–18.

U.S. Dept. of Agriculture. 1959, 1964. *Agriculture census.*

U.S. Dept. of Agriculture. 1969. *Monitoring agricultural pesticide residues 1965–1967.* ARS Rept. 81-32.

U.S. Dept. of the Army. 1965. *Expanded project for aquatic plant control.* House Document 251, 89th Congress, 1st Session.

Yeo, R. R. 1969. Dissipation of endothall in water and effects on aquatic weeds and fish. *Weed Science.* In press.

CHAPTER FOURTEEN

PESTICIDES AND PEST MANAGEMENT FOR MAXIMUM PRODUCTION AND MINIMUM POLLUTION

DON C. PETERS

T HE late Paul Errington, an ecologist in our department, once said that the human mind craves constants but in biology deals with variables. The words maximum and minimum both connote such relative value judgments. Furthermore, pesticide usage has been accompanied by certain ironies—controlling disease-carrying insects has contributed to our population crisis, and while crop protection has been a major factor in increased production, this has often been followed by reduced prices. In an era when science and technology are playing a major role in shaping our society, it is altogether too easy for the individual scientist to lose his objectivity and assume that his particular insights entitle him to become a demagogue. The subject of pesticides has certainly lead to such polarity (Carson, 1962; Rudd, 1964; Egler, 1964a, 1964b; Whitten, 1966; McLean, 1967). The challenge today is for an enumeration of alternatives in environmental management and an admission that with any strategy there will be a certain amount of compromise. Pesticide usage continues to be confronted with the need for compromise. We may be near the end of the golden age of agricultural pesticide technology since there seems to be a geometric increase in regulations regarding the chemical inputs for pest control. Wellman (1969) estimated that the cost of developing a typical pesticide is now $4.1 million, up from $2.5 million in 1964.

In an effort to facilitate your understanding of this area, I would like to outline the pest management strategies available, relate them to specific production commitments, and then consider the ramifications to the role of agriculture in clean water. Consideration needs to be given to both the quantity and quality aspects of this subject so that we can propose a rational compromise between pests and pollution.

In entomology we often refer to pest population reductions which occur without the influence of man as being natural controls. (The

DON C. PETERS is Professor, Department of Zoology and Entomology, Iowa State University.

term control has been overworked to include the agent, the action, and the results.) Natural control can be subdivided into climatic, edaphic, and biotic aspects. The reason for mentioning natural control is that we hope we can understand it and capitalize upon it as we try to improve direct or applied pest control.

Modern agriculture is still largely dependent on proper climatic conditions. The same sunlight, moisture, and nutrients are utilized by weeds as well as planted crops. Crop adaptation is a matter of growing the crop in an area where it has at least some competitive advantages and applying additional controls as needed. Since each organism has specific moisture, light, and temperature requisites, it follows that pest species are not uniformly distributed and man can capitalize on this knowledge. However, some diseases and insects may be carried great distances by winds. The most dramatic illustration of wind distribution would probably be the cereal rusts which have been referred to as continental pathogens because they spread from the subtropical regions to the north to cover the entire cereal acreages in North America.

In nature, diversity appears to be a solution to catastrophic outbreaks and destructive changes. Dasmann (1968) said that complexity appears to be accompanied by stability and man seeks to simplify the complex so that he can manage it. If a great variety of plants are growing in an area, the chance of spread for a host-specific disease is greatly reduced. For this reason the chances for insect and disease outbreaks are much greater in cultivated monocultures than in natural areas. Under the conditions in northern forests, age may act as diversity. As man has tried to manage forests and prevent fires, he has occasionally allowed large areas with trees of the same age to grow up. These may be attacked by insects or pathogens which normally attack only a specific age category. When such attacks occur the losses are more severe than would be true of a forest with diverse age groups or species of trees.

I feel that a better understanding of the balance of nature is needed for a meaningful communication of the science of pest control. "Key factor analysis" is a recent concept used by insect ecologists such as Clark et al. (1967) in trying to characterize the major factors contributing to population levels of insect groups. An extension of this approach may be the reason why in each crop we have a few major persistent pests, several species which become pests during sporadic outbreak periods, and an additional group of potential pests associated with a larger number of species which cause no damage but occur in the area as scavengers or parasites and predators. The interactions between these groups are frequently drawn in a web configuration, but this may communicate a concept of peaceful cooperation whereas intense competition for resources is more in line with the "key factor" approach. Work summarized in the National Academy of Science (NAS) publication on insects (1969) indicates that food may be a key factor in regulating a pest, but that parasites and predators, disease, weather, and migration have been found to be key factors with as great a frequency. As an illustration, the Colorado potato beetle in Canada was found to be limited by food. However,

I doubt that any potato farmer would consider it reasonable to allow this vegetative feeder to completely devour the above-ground parts of the plant before some direct means of control was sought.

It is my impression that similar relationships between crops and pests exist in the realm of plant pathogens and to a different degree in weed competition. I feel that the work of Kooper (1927) and Holm (1969) relating to the competition between plants by growth inhibition of one species by another encourages speculation that if we knew what inhibits some seed growth in the presence of other plants a more effective weed control could be achieved. Species competition should be managed for our good.

One other point I would like to emphasize before discussing applied controls is that when man put his hand to the plow and began to modify plant diversity, he began a high-risk enterprise. There are still no absolute measures of what is progress as far as manipulating the disturbed cultivated environment. Many of us have gone along with Swift's adage of the man "who can make two ears of corn or blades of grass to grow where but one grew before," but I feel that most thinking biologists today have conceded that man is not capable of continuing to feed himself and his progeny unless he devises effective means of regulating his population. The question of the quality of our environment is another thing that merits more attention.

APPLIED CONTROLS

Applied controls are those biological, cultural, legal, or chemical practices which man utilizes in an effort to reduce losses caused by pests. Each of these has its disadvantages and advantages and the cost/benefit ratio needs to be continually investigated in a dynamic agriculture and civilization. Paul Sears, in a recent visit to Iowa State, warned that another danger in this scientific age was doing things simply because they became technically feasible. For example an insect-free cornfield may not be the most desirable condition. Let us first consider biological control which may be either natural or applied. Biological control probably has its main desirable aspects in that it usually produces no side effects and frequently is a one-time operation. Once it is set in motion there need not be an annual cost for crop production. Biological control works best where some damage can be incurred to the crop without serious economic loss and where the soil is not disturbed. This means that we should look for the most frequent successes in forest lands and in orchards, and the least successes for biological control in the intensive cultivation practices of truck farming.

The three main aspects involved in the utilization of parasites and predators are introduction, conservation, and augmentation. While the introduction of an insect species for control of another insect or weed is a complicated matter (NAS, 1968b), there have been sufficient successes in this area, particularly in those instances where the pest was not native, that continued work is certainly justified. It has been estimated that if the program is effective, 80% of the introductions are effective within three generations. By the conservation of parasites and predators, I have reference to such situations as strip mowing of alfalfa so that the shelter for predators is not completely eliminated at any one time during the production period. The augmentation of field populations by laboratory-reared parasites and predators has met with varying success. It seems to show more promise where the target insect infests a localized area and where the parasites and predators are limited to the immediate area. I know of no successful program of augmentation in the Upper Mississippi Valley.

Insect pathologists have been working on diseases of insects for over a hundred years, and a recent report (NAS, 1969) indicated that there were 1,165 microorganisms which attacked insects. In this region disease agents have been used against the European corn borer and Japanese beetles. However, there is a possibility of the insects developing resistance to these diseases. A recent paper by Hoage and Peters (1969) demonstrated the ability of honeybees to develop larval resistance to American foulbrood disease. Similar disease resistance probably occurs in nature as part of the overall web of competition and survival of the fittest.

I have chosen only to mention and not discuss some other concepts in biological control such as the areas of competitive displacement, antimetabolites, feeding deterrents, or genetic regulation of pests since these are still largely in the investigative stage and lack working field programs to confirm their potential.

Host-plant resistance is frequently considered as a part of the biological control approach and certainly it is a modification of the host organism in an effort to reduce losses from pest infestations. It is doubtful if we would be able to continue cultivation of any of the cereal crops without disease-resistant cultivars. And yet in the case of the cereal rusts, we are probably witnessing evolution working at an extremely rapid and efficient rate but not toward our varietal improvement goals. Van der Plank (1968) is optimistic and states that crop breeders should continue their work on developing disease-resistant lines.

By contrast to the great number of disease races that have cropped up in relation to varietal resistance, the story on insect-resistant crops is not nearly so complex. Three exceptions are the corn leaf aphid and pea aphid races or "biotypes" reported by Cartier and Painter (1956) and Cartier et al. (1965) and the Hessian fly where there are currently at least four races (Gallun et al., 1961). Host-plant resistance is probably the most ideal means of controlling the major disease and insect pests of the major crops. Development of resistant varieties does entail a considerable expenditure of time and the cooperative effort of a team of investigators and therefore will probably be limited to only the major pests of the various cultivated crops. The potential for breeding insect- and disease-resistant animals is certainly not great. I have no idea of how one would go about breeding a corn plant for resistance to foxtail competition. All of the biological control approaches require a lot of specific research before they can be utilized.

Cultural pest control is among the oldest of man's practices in trying to come to grips with his pests. Sanitation as illustrated by crop residue destruction and animal waste removal is an important means in reducing the breeding potential of a number of pests. Tillage practices can have an impact on any of the three pest groups that we have been considering. By way of illustration, it is hard to say whether the Iowa farmer should plow his cornstalks under to control European corn borers, weeds, or the yellow leaf blight disease. Reduced tillage may encourage some pest species, but increased tillage will also destroy many of the organisms that would tend to afford a competitive balance between the organisms in the field.

The economics of current production practices in the Corn Belt leave little leeway for pest management in timing the planting operation or the intensity of fertilization. Since both of these need to be maximized from an agronomic standpoint, workers in pest management are confronted with the need to devise some means of compensating for agronomic practices which may be at odds with optimum pest control. Early harvesting can certainly help to avert some of the potential losses that might otherwise be attributed to stalk-attacking insects or diseases.

Physical or mechanical controls are seldom of importance in the large acreages of cultivated crops common in modern agriculture, but such things as the flaming of alfalfa fields may reduce the alfalfa weevil threat and give some reduction in the chickweed problem as well.

Another illustration of mechanical means is the light trap. As far as reducing crop pests, light traps have been of limited value, with the most favorable data coming from the tobacco-growing area in North Carolina (Lawson et al., 1966). There is also a report of reduction in *Heliothis* spp. as cotton pests in Texas, following the use of artificial light (Nemec, 1969).

Insect sterilization has received a lot of popular publicity in the past 10 years because of the success of the screwworm program in southeastern United States (Bushland et al., 1958) and more recently in the Texas area. However, there are several drawbacks to this approach. It is extremely expensive in comparison to other programs with which entomologists have been associated. Sterilization would not appear to be practical where a pest overwinters in an extensive area or where numbers are not severely reduced in the spring. Chemosterilants have been and are being investigated but in the past decade they have not proved to be commercially acceptable in even a single field program in the United States.

The potential use of attractants and repellents still must be considered nebulous, although there have been some excellent results where attractants and insecticides were combined on island situations in eradication programs (Beroza, 1966). Personally, I have serious reservations about man's ability to totally eradicate any insect pest species from the continents. Eradication of weeds and diseases is even less likly (NAS, 1968a).

Chemical control of pests is an old practice. It probably began when the Arabians discovered the benefits of sulfur for louse control for their horses or with the early observations of the herbicidal effects of salt water. It has only been during the last 40 years that man has begun to synthesize chemicals rather than to depend upon those which he could obtain by mining or refining. The intensity to which he has used these synthesized products has had a considerable influence in the gains in production potential on a number of crops as illustrated in a paper by Decker (1964). I have tried to update these production figures in Table 14.1. Insecticide use on oats, hay, and soybeans has been low. For oats and hay the returns have been low but the per acre net return from soybeans has been almost as good as corn. The relative increases in per acre yields for corn, cotton, and potatoes since the advent of DDT and other organic insecticides has been much greater than for oats, hay, or soybeans. I certainly do not believe that the yield increases are entirely caused by insect control, but the insecticides must obviously be aiding a total production program. There may also have been a profit differential that justified the decision to use the chemicals at the time the first synthetic pesticides were applied. The economics of production would appear to continue to dictate similar pesticide use patterns.

The hope held out for growth-regulating hormones as "third generation insecticides" by Williams (1967) may be only a hope, and certainly many of us will need to change our attitude about taxes if these hormonal mimics are to be used. I doubt whether industry will be willing to expend the resources necessary to develop these specific means of control. I would expect the financial returns to be considerably less favorable than with the conventional multi-use pesticides available today. Persing (1965) wrote that if DDT were specific for houseflies, its profits would not have equaled research and development costs. I have heard a lot of talk to the contrary, but specific pesticides have not been forthcoming in the past decade. A good demonstration of the problem is a product by the name of Manazon which is excellent for aphid control but apparently the company owning this product does not feel that it would be a profitable product to develop at this time. By contrast, the top ten pesticides in 1967 sales were all broad-spectrum materials (Mahan et al., 1968).

There are certainly many pitfalls that can arise from over-dependence on use of chemicals in crop production. Smith (1967, 1969a, 1969b) has done an excellent job of describing some such problems in cotton production and he also tells of the potential integrated control has as a means of maximizing the effectiveness of chemical applications. As Mills (1968) indicated, we need to continue to sharpen our entomological knowledge of space and time in insecticide applications. Knipling (1966) has calculated that 1 lb of the most effective boll weevil insecticide would be enough to kill all the boll weevils in the United States if applied topically in the spring when weevil levels are lowest.

These are the pest control alternatives available. The next question is, How and to what extent are these being used in various production programs?

TABLE 14.1. Average yields for selected crops in 48 states.

Crop	Percent Acres Treated in 1966	Yield per Acre for Years Indicated						
		1901–40	1941–45	1946–50	1951–55	1956–60	1961–65	1966–68
Oats	1	29.4	32.2	33.9	34.6	39.7	45.1	49.2 bu.
Ratio*			1.10	1.15	1.18	1.35	1.54	1.68
Hay	3	1.81	1.36	1.35	1.46	1.66	1.76	1.94 tons
Ratio			0.75	0.75	0.81	0.92	0.97	1.07
Soybeans	4	...	18.5	20.4	20.0	23.2	24.2	25.5 bu.
Ratio				1.11	1.08	1.26	1.31	1.38
Corn	33	26.0	33.1	37.0	40.2	51.2	65.9	76.5 bu.
Ratio			1.27	1.42	1.54	1.97	2.53	2.94
Cotton	54	186.0	262.0	273.0	326.0	434.0	492.0	479.0 lb.
Ratio			1.41	1.47	1.76	2.34	2.65	2.58
Potatoes	89	63.0	85.0	132.0	153.0	183.0	196.0	211.0 cwt.
Ratio			1.35	2.09	2.43	2.90	3.12	3.35

* Ratio of production in each period to production from 1901 to 1940, except in soybeans where ratio base used was 1941–45.

PEST MANAGEMENT IN THE SEVERAL AREAS OF PRODUCTION

There are a number of functional considerations or variants involved in considering the pest problems as related to the food, shelter, and clothing areas of production. There is also a need to keep in mind the "aesthetic needs" of man. How many "Madison Avenue"-gendered needs can we afford on our crowded planet?

In the area of food production, the cereal crops and potatoes are the major carbohydrate sources. In the United States, the percentage of cereal crops receiving insecticide treatment in 1964 was around 3% for small grains, but about 33% for corn, of which a large percentage was for soil insect control. According to Fox et al. (1968) chemicals for disease control were used on less than 0.5% of the acres on all of these crops, while herbicides were used on 57% of the corn acres and about 30% of the acres planted to the other grain crops.

The amount of money spent on livestock pest control, according to Gale et al. (1968), was less than 5% of the total farm use, and the estimated pounds of insecticide were an even smaller ratio. In spite of this relatively small volume, the point source principle used in identifying and detecting pollution may present problems for pesticide usage on livestock and poultry. However, the major problem is from misuse or contamination, since there is little likelihood of water contamination from the materials used in fly control today.

Production of fruits and vegetables is the most intensive high-value crop production program, but as pointed out previously there is a considerably greater potential for biological strategies to effectively control orchard pests as compared to truck farming operations. In 1966 Fox et al. (1968) found that 28% of the vegetable acres in the 48 contiguous states were treated with a herbicide, whereas the percentage of apple acres treated was 16%, and that for other deciduous fruits was only 13%. Similar figures on insecticides indicate that use on vegetables was 56%, on apples 92%, and on other deciduous fruits 72%. Apparently, the consumer insistence on perfect fruit has encouraged a lot of spraying. While Irish potatoes would normally be considered a carbohydrate source, the percentage of crop acres on which insecticides were used was 89% over the contiguous states, but reached 100% in the southeastern and southern plains states. The demand for fruits and vegetables free of insect damage has certainly been met with an intensive use of pesticides. With current harvesting and processing it is doubtful if this usage can be changed.

Turning to clothing, I have already indicated that a very small percentage of the total amount of pesticides is used on livestock and as one would expect the amount of pesticides used in wool production would be minimal. By contrast the proportion of herbicide and insecticide usage in cotton production would be far greater than that for other field crops with the exception of tobacco and potatoes. According to Gale et al. (1968), in 1964 the United States average per acre pesticide expenditure was $11.27 for cotton compared to only $1.87 per acre of corn. This illustrates the deceptive potential of figures since there were 66 million acres of corn as compared to 14 million acres of cotton. Therefore the total expenditure for cotton was only 20% greater than for corn pesticides. In another sense pesticide use on cotton is much more intensive and does not allow for as great a dilution as it enters the environment.

The current trend is toward more synthetic fibers. There are some indications that these too may possibly have some harmful side effects. Determining the long-term influences of these products on experimental animals should be pursued with the same rigor as has the toxicology of chemical control agents.

Man's need for shelter is influenced by diseases and insects only to the extent that he utilizes wood in providing these shelters. The critical times for timber seem to be during the establishment of the young trees, as the standing crop nears harvest, during the processing period, and after the structure has been completed, when termite and decay problems may arise. Economics of lumber production are such that it has not been feasible to treat large acreages repeatedly. Consequently current estimates are that less than 5% of our forest lands have ever been sprayed with any insecticides. The hazard is that when forest areas are sprayed it is usually done in large contiguous blocks treated as part of a federally coordinated program. Such massive programs usually involve large aircraft in terrain where it is not expedient to avoid spraying of streams and other areas where fish and wildlife are concentrated. Therefore, while the direct problems of chemical treatment to the wood are nil, the ramifications to the fish and wildlife populations may be considerable, since the only logical places for significant wildlife populations are in the forests and ranges of the United States.

I would like to consider the aesthetic ramifications associated with agricultural production. One concern is with the farm fence row. To many people the uniform growth of grasses which can be achieved by annual 2,4-D spraying is desirable. Others like a diversity in plants and do not find this uniform grass population appealing. It is certainly true that this is a more costly practice than allowing the plants to grow as they wish. It is difficult to extrapolate Scott's (1938) data to modern times with increased miles traveled on our primary and secondary roads, but it is time we determine if wildlife would increase if ditches and roadsides were left to grow up in a natural vegetation as game cover.

Most of us became too embroiled in the Dutch elm disease control program to consider it with much objectivity. While this has basically been an urban rather than a rural problem, I believe that there are lessons to be learned from the successes and failures of various strategies and tactics tried in controlling this pest. The Iowa Cooperative Extension Service (1961) outlined a 4-step program of (1) evaluation and education, (2) sanitation, (3) maintenance, and (4) spraying. Steps 1 through 3 were seldom executed effectively, but the extension entomologists were certainly blamed for any robins that died after DDT spraying. All phases of agriculture must get involved in public information and communication.

Home gardens, lawns, and flowers are not usually considered an agricultural problem and yet in the area of pesticide pollution they should not be overlooked. I submit that there is as great a probability that the suburbanite will dump the leftover spray into the sewer as there is that the agriculturalist will dispose of his leftover pesticides in such a manner as to directly contaminate water sources. When one considers the population ratio between rural and suburban peoples in the United States today, the magnitude of this problem becomes obvious.

ROLE OF AGRICULTURAL PESTICIDE IN CLEAN WATER

What then are the ramifications of pest management to agricultural waters? If we assume that changes will be brought about by the due process of legislation and education I think we can make some fairly good assumptions and suggestions as to what can be done to educate ourselves about the proper use of pesticides in farm production programs. Figures 14.1 and 14.2 on land uses and relative intensity of pesticide use on crops in the United States should put the problem in perspective. First let us consider small grain production. With the present net return from these crops, it is doubtful whether additional chemicals will be used in an effort to achieve more efficient production. These crops are grown on relatively large acreages and there is little likelihood that yield can be increased without the addition of irrigation. Cultural practices and host plant resistance should continue to be mainstays of pest control on small grains.

After visiting with agronomists, agricultural engineers, and others interested in corn production, I believe that future corn production will see increased emphasis on narrow row spacing with a moderating trend in the immediate future to 30-inch row spacing. Even the shift to 30-inch row spacing means essentially a 30% increase in insecticide usage to achieve the same amount of rootworm protection as compared to 40-inch row spacing. To partially offset this we have been working (Peters, 1965; Munson et al., 1970) to try to combine one chemical treatment for both corn rootworms and European corn borer control. Some of the current insecticides under investigation might control corn leaf aphids also, and thereby get three birds with one stone. The emphasis on minimum tillage will need to be watched and possibly modified in the future in line with efficient

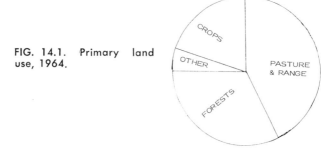

FIG. 14.1. Primary land use, 1964.

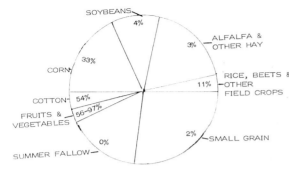

FIG. 14.2. Insecticide use on U.S. crops, 1964. Insecticides were applied on 2% of the small grain acreage. Small grains were grown on more acres than any other crop.

use of herbicides and insecticides. Disease problems may become greater if crop residue is left on the soil surface. The ideal system for corn would be to maintain the intertillage system so that the space between the row need not be treated with pesticide.

We have been searching for a replacement for aldrin and hepta-chlor, the two major chlorinated hydrocarbons still used in corn insect control. To date we have not found a product that will control white grubs, wireworms, or cutworms at economically feasible rates. The carryover problem of herbicides is one reason given for planting corn after corn. This means that the use of persistent herbicides has intensified the need for corn rootworm control measures since corn rootworms do economic damage mainly in fields of corn following corn. If this situation can be alleviated we would hope that the acres treated for corn rootworms can be stabilized or even reduced. However, it is possible that with a major change in crop sequence patterns other insect pest problems may increase in importance; Cole (1966) has pointed out that all communities harbor opportunistic species. The disease problem seems to be increasing under higher plant populations. Some promising disease control chemicals are being evaluated but the potential economics of such pesticide usage has not been worked out.

At the risk of sounding provincial, I would like to emphasize that soybeans should be grown in the northern part of the United States rather than as a replacement for cotton. In the South chemicals will have to be used to control corn earworms, stink bugs, and other insect pests of soybeans, whereas these insects have not occurred in damaging numbers in soybean culture in the Upper Mississippi Valley. I feel that this is a place where timely legislative action could reduce the overall pesticide burden in the United States.

Cotton culture is an enigma for it is profitable under the present allotment system to use relatively large quantities of pesticides to maximize yield on a per acre basis. If allotment were on a basis of pounds of lint cotton per farm unit it might be possible to reduce pesticides. Another consideration might be the emphasis of production on those areas where cotton pests are less of a problem. Additional irony in this situation is that while Smith (1969b) and his associates in California have done an excellent job of describing integrated control to the scientific community, the amount of pesticide money spent per acre of cotton production in California was higher in 1966 than any other area of the country. It is hoped that the California entomologists can devise as efficient a means of communicating to the growers in the state as they have to the scientific community.

There is still a demand for tobacco products. This high intensity crop will probably continue to utilize large amounts of pesticides in localized areas. If hopes are realized, continued work on mechanical or biological controls can reduce the insecticide usage for this crop. While the total tonnage of pesticide used may be small, the likelihood of local stream or pond contamination is still very real. Potatoes and sugar beets also present a problem since the net return to the grower is very small unless a high yield per acre can be achieved. Therefore, we again have the potential of a point source contamination situation. Since these crops are grown by relatively few farmers it should be possible to amplify the educational effort toward the reduction of unnecessary treatments or low return treatment.

The juxtaposition of metropolitan areas and intensive truck farming will continue to be the cause of friction in pesticide usage. The high value commodities would seem to justify the use of pesticides in order to insure a favorable return to the grower; however, the chance of water contamination is a continuing problem when such usage is adjacent to streams, ponds, and lakes with high recreational demand.

Every effort should be made to encourage fruit growers to investigate the feasibility of enhanced biological control in their orchards. An important corollary for such a program to be completely successful is that we will also need to educate the consumer to accept less than perfect produce.

There is currently a boom in large feedlot operations in the southwestern states of Texas, Oklahoma, Kansas, and Colorado. This has been brought about, in part, by increased irrigation of sorghum and corn as a grain source for livestock feed. These lots tend to be large and the livestock are confined. If we continue to emphasize that "the solution to pollution is dilution" then this is a step in the wrong direction. It is true that these are areas where the moisture problems in feedlots are reduced, but if pesticides are needed to control flies and other insect problems under the crowded livestock condition, it is only conjectural as to what would be the concentration of insecticide in the small amount of runoff that might occur from these areas.

If we really feel that the chlorinated hydrocarbons are a detriment to our society, we should encourage an immediate ban on all small-package registrations of these products. This is an area in which misuse is most likely to occur since the homeowner-gardener is not confronted with the cost/return ratio to the extent that people in crop production are.

I feel that I must take a stand in opposition to many of the large federal insecticide pest control programs. These have been subject to considerable criticism, for even though they achieve a major cost reduction per treated unit, the tendency, as pointed out by Cope and Springer (1958), is that by achieving these efficiencies in distribution there is a comparative loss in target precision and effectiveness. I believe the Plant Pest Control Division would do well to continue its emphasis on the distribution of biological control agents or attractants. The substitution of Mirex bait in the fire-ant program was certainly a progressive step in the right direction.

In summary, I would say that the various agencies in pest control have been and continue to be concerned about the use of pesticides in relation to the total environment. We are working and will continue to work to the limit of personnel and funds available. The need for increased funds in the future is great since the newer strategies are of a nature that will require public support for their application. Recently a national joint task force on pollution proposed less than a 1% increase in effort for the pesticide area for the next decade! If the public demand for sophistication in pest control is to be achieved, more imaginative research support will have to be found. Man is the dominant species on earth today and the question is not if he will modify the environment, but the question is how can he modify the environment in such a way as to achieve a stability which will allow his long-term existence.

Starr's (1969) article on social benefits versus technological risk merits careful consideration. In order to maximize pest management for maximum production, crop protectionists should expect a reasonable risk ratio along with other agricultural, industrial, and urban sources of water pollution. The alternative loss of 10 to 30% of our basic agricultural production to pests and diseases needs to be held before the consuming public.

REFERENCES

Beroza, Morton. 1966. *The future role of natural and synthetic attractants for pest control in pest control by chemical, biological, genetic, and physical means.* USDA, ARS.

Bushland, R. C., Knipling, E. F., and Lindquist, A. W. 1958. Eradication of the screw-worm fly by releasing gamma-ray sterilized males among the natural population. *Proc. Intern. Conf. Peaceful Use Atomic Energy Geneva* 12:216–20.

Carson, Rachel. 1962. *Silent spring.* Boston: Houghton Mifflin.

Cartier, J. J., and Painter, R. H. 1956. Differential reactions of two biotypes of the corn leaf aphid to resistant and susceptible varieties, hybrids and selections of sorghums. *J. Econ. Entomol.* 49:498–508.

Cartier, J. J., Isaak, A., Painter, R. H., and Sorensen, E. L. 1965. Biotypes of pea aphid *Acythosiphon pisum* (Harris) in relation to alfalfa clones. *Can. Entomol.* 97:754–60.

Clark, L. R., Geier, P. W., Hughes, R. D., and Morris, R. F. 1967. *The ecology of insect populations in theory and practice.* London: Methuen.

Cole, Lamont C. 1966. The complexity of pest control in the environment. In *Scientifiic aspects of pest control,* pp. 13–25. Nat. Acad. Sci., Nat. Res. Council Publ. 1402, Wash., D.C.

Cooperative Extension Service. 1961. *Diseases and insects attacking Iowa elms.* Iowa State Univ. Pamphlet 250 (Rev.)

Cope, O. B., and Springer, P. F. 1958. Mass control of insects: the effects on fish and wildlife. *Entomol. Soc. Am. Bull.* 4:52–56.

Dasmann, R. F. 1968. *Environmental conservation.* 2nd ed. New York: John Wiley.

Decker, George C. 1964. The past is prologue. *Entomol. Soc. Am. Bull.* 10:8–15.

Egler, F. E. 1964a. Pesticides in our ecosystem. *Am. Scientist* 52 (1): 110–36.

———. 1964b. Pesticides in our ecosystem: communication. II. *BioScience* 14 (11): 29–36.

Fox, Austin, Eichers, T., Andrilenas, P., Jenkins, R., and Blake, H. 1968. *Extent of farm pesticide use on crops in 1966.* USDA, Agr. Econ. Rept. 147.

Gale, J. F., Andrilenas, P., and Fox, A. 1968. *Farmers' pesticide expenditures for crops, livestock, and other selected uses in 1964.* USDA, Agr. Econ. Rept. 147.

Gallun, R. L., Deay, H. O., and Cartwright, W. B. 1961. *Four races of Hessian fly selected and developed from an Indiana population.* Purdue Univ. Res. Bull. 732.

Hoage, T. R., and Peters, D. C. 1969. Selection for American foulbrood resistance in larval honey bees. *J. Econ. Entomol.* 62: 896–900.

Holm, LeRoy. 1969. Chemical interactions between plants on agricultural lands. *Down Earth* 25:16–22.

Knipling, E. F. 1966. New horizons and the outlook for pest control. In *Scientific aspects of pest control,* pp. 455–70. Nat. Acad. Sci., Nat. Res. Council Publ. 1402. Wash., D.C.

———. 1968. The role of chemicals in the general insect control picture. *Entomol. Soc. Am. Bull.* 14:102–7.

Kooper, W. J. C. 1927. Sociological and ecological studies on weed vegetation of Pasurian. *Rec. Trav. Bot. Neerl.* 24:1–255.

Lawson, F. R., Gentry, C. R., and Stanley, J. M. 1966. Experiments on the control of insect populations with light traps in pest control by chemical, biological, genetic, and physical means. USDA, ARS.

McLean, L. A. 1967. Pesticides and the environment. *BioScience* 17:613–17.

Mahan, J. N., Fowler, D. L., and Shepard, H. H. 1968. *The pesticide review 1968.* USDA, Agr. Stabilization and Conserv. Serv.

Mills, H. B. 1968. Summary and conclusions in *Symp. on the Science and Technology of Residual Insecticides in Food Production with Special Reference to Aldrin and Dieldrin.* Shell Oil Co.

Munson, R. E., Brindley, T. A., Peters, D. C., and Lovely, W. G. 1970. Control of both the European corn borer and corn rootworms with one application of insecticide. Submitted to *J. Econ. Entomol.*

National Academy of Sciences. 1968a. *Plant-disease development and control.* Principles of plant and animal pest control. Vol. 1.

———. 1968b. *Weed control.* Principles of plant and animal pest control. Vol. 2.

———. 1969. *Insect-pest management and control.* Principles of plant and animal pest control. Vol. 3.

Nemec, S. J. 1969. Use of artificial lighting to reduce *Heliothis* spp. populations in cotton fields. *J. Econ. Entomol.* 62:1138–40.

Persing, C. O. 1965. Problems in the development of tailor-made

insecticides, specific insecticides. *Entomol. Soc. Am. Bull.*
11:72–74.

Peters, D. C. 1965. Chemical control of resistant corn rootworms in Iowa. *Entomol. Soc. Am. Bull.* 20:58–61.

Rudd, R. 1964. *Pesticides and the living landscape.* Madison: Univ. of Wis. Press.

Scott, T. G. 1938. Wildlife mortality on Iowa highways. *Am. Midland Naturalist* 20:527–39.

Smith, R. F. 1967. Principles of measurements of crop losses caused by insects. FAO Symp. on Crop Losses, Rome, 2–6 Oct. 1967, pp. 205–24.

———. 1969a. The importance of economic injury levels in the development of integrated pest control programs. *Qualitas Plant. Mater. Vegetabiles* 17:81–92.

———. 1969b. Patterns of crop protection in cotton ecosystems. Mimeo of talk given at Cotton Symp. on Insect and Mite Control Problems and Res. in Calif., 12–13 March 1969, Hotel Claremont, Berkeley, Calif.

Starr, Chauncey. 1969. Social benefits versus technological risk. *Science* 165:1232–38.

Tukey, John W., chairman. 1965. *Restoring the quality of our environment.* Report of the Environmental Pollution Panel of President's Science Advisory Committee.

U.S. Dept. of Agriculture. 1966a. *Field crops by states, 1959–64.* Statistical Bull. 384.

———. 1966b. A century of agriculture in charts and tables. *Agriculture Handbook 318.*

Van der Plank, J. E. 1968. *Disease resistance in plants.* New York and London: Academic Press.

Wellman, Richard H. 1969. Ag chemicals industry faces big changes. *Chem. Eng. News,* pp. 22–23.

Whitten, J. L. 1966. *That we may live.* Princeton, N. J.: D. Van Nostrand.

Williams, Carroll M. 1967. Third-generation pesticides. *Scientific Am.* 217:13–17.

CHAPTER FIFTEEN

WORKSHOP SESSION

DON C. PETERS, Leader
H. B. PETTY, Reporter

THE general public at present suffers from lack of factual and realistic information pertaining to (1) the real role and importance of pesticides in food production, (2) the present restrictive regulations which govern labeling, sale, and use of pesticides, (3) the accident-safety record of pesticide use, and (4) the food-monitoring work of the HEW, FDA, which so carefully protects our food supply from any contamination that could be considered deleterious. The general public is unaware of extensive use-education programs and they have the opportunity to read only the overpublicized alarm stories, many of which are not realistic. There is a need, therefore, for the Cooperative Extension Services to expand their programs to include more than just agriculture.

PESTICIDES AND CLEAN WATER

Those interested in clean water and pesticides must realize that as long as chemical tests in parts per trillion can be made, trace amounts of the pesticides or their metabolites will at some stage be found in water. Thus, permissible levels in water must be established if we are to continue use of any pesticides. Such levels might be established only for drinking water, or they might include marine waters, irrigation waters, or waters for swimming, boating, and fishing. It would be possible to consider overall environmental permissible levels or international permissible levels. It would be impossible to set levels defined by (1) the lowest level of testing accuracy and (2) the level at which it could be guaranteed that there was not, nor ever would be, any deleterious effects of any kind.

Aquatic herbicides, to be effective, are applied to water or immediately adjacent to water. There are at present very few tolerances established for these aquatic herbicides in water. Some older ones such as arsenic do have established levels. Tolerances have been established for food crops for the "newer" herbicides but not

DON C. PETERS is Professor, Department of Zoology and Entomology, Iowa State University. H. B. PETTY is Professor and Extension Entomologist, University of Illinois.

for water. It is imperative that permissible levels be established soon.

Chlorinated hydrocarbon insecticides present a different problem. Some people believe that permissible levels in water can be set, others do not. Although the hydrocarbons are occasionally applied directly to water, their appearance in water usually results from a nonwater use. This can be runoff from actual use, but it can also be manufacturing waste. These insecticides are not water soluble and escape from it at every opportunity; thus they accumulate on the aquatic plants and bottom sediment where so many of our aquatic organisms live. The organisms concentrate these chemicals in their bodies, sometimes to thousands of times the amount in the water.

All chlorinated hydrocarbons accumulate in living organisms in varying degrees. Of the many, only a few present problems. Dieldrin probably persists in the environment longer than others, although DDT approaches it in persistence. Dieldrin content in fish is in relation to water content, not food content. When fish are fed excessive amounts of dieldrin there is a quick uptake, but the body content returns to the water-dieldrin equilibrium within a month. This is the opposite to DDT. Although DDT and its metabolites stay in the environment, DDT is apparently responsible for the upset in the calcium metabolism in some birds. Endrin, with the highest acute toxicity, does not persist as long as the other two and organisms cleanse themselves of endrin readily. Endrin is, at the moment, suspected of systemic absorption.

Although it is difficult to set permissible levels for chlorinated hydrocarbons for all situations, levels have been set for drinking water. As a result of a committee of about 50 experts pooling their knowledge. in May 1968 the Water Pollution Control Administration published "Water Quality Criteria."

It is possible to set permissible levels for the organophosphates since the amount which will produce cholinesterase inhibition can be defined with some accuracy. As much as 10% inhibition may be permissible. Furthermore, the residues of organic phosphates in water are short-lived and runoff from agricultural use, if found at all, is present for a very short time. Manufacturing wastes may be more important than use runoff. However, one point to be considered is the speed of reversibility of phosphate effect (comparatively low) and carbamate effect (comparatively high) on cholinesterase levels.

Manufacture of these products provides another avenue for contamination. There are examples where waste from pesticide manufacturing plants seriously contaminated miles of streams. A permissible level for these products in factory effluent must also be set.

PESTICIDES AND THEIR METABOLITES

Knowledge of the metabolism of barbiturates 15 years ago has been greatly enlarged upon and even changed. The same thing is happening with pesticides. DDT is not a single compound but a mixture of many materials. Recently in vivo isomerizations have been authentically reported in feeding experiments in which o,p'-DDT was fed and p,p'-DDT was formed in the animal. Similarly, p,p'-DDT was fed and o,p'-DDT was formed in the animal. It has also been published in *Science* that o,p'-DDT has pronounced estrogenic effects.

Reference has been made to the absence or the quick disappearance of organophosphates. Do we know the metabolites of phorate, Dyfonate, carbofuran, etc.? How about amino parathion and its effects? In short, we need to know more about the biological effects of pesticide metabolites than we do at present. A small amount of a toxic chemical can be tolerated by most organisms. A person can ingest a very low level of parathion and be unable to detect a reaction, except through very rapid sampling, as parathion is detoxified rather quickly. But with an increase in this level of intake, one soon starts detecting it or some of its metabolites. A little more and symptoms of intoxication are evident.

Is it possible to determine the no-effect level for pesticides and their metabolites for the most important sensitive species of animals? It might be man, the peregrine falcon, or others, but we could establish a base line. We will have to settle on the most toxic form of a given chemical as well as the most sensitive species. In the case of DDT is it the p,p'-isomer, the o,p'-isomer, DDE, or possibly DDD? What is the important sensitive species for which we can determine an environmental level for any given pesticide? Is this level consistent with its use in agriculture and public health? Is this kind of approach a practical one? What is best for our human society? These were some of the unanswered questions concerning pesticides and the quality of our environment.

ROLE OF PESTICIDES

Pesticides protect plants and animals from pest losses to the benefit of mankind. This should be done so as not to harm man now or in the future. However, no scientist ever could or would positively guarantee that no harm could ever occur from the use of a certain chemical. To answer every question that could be posed would require 30 years of search for answers, and such detail, if not scientifically impossible, is financially impossible.

Without pesticides, food production would be reduced some 40 to 50%, and the quality would be greatly reduced. Bread as we know it would still be present but would contain insect fragments and some rodent excrement. Today food processors are on the horns of a dilemma—foods are inspected for both insect fragments and pesticide, and an entire day's pack can be confiscated if contamination (by either) is found in any one can or case of processed food.

In the past, tolerances were established for chemicals on food crops. The safety factor was considered to be 100 to 1. That concept is no longer valid. We are now searching for minor or hidden effects. We have searched for flaws in DDT for some 25 years and can still find a few weaknesses. The Russians are interested in carbamates and are diligently searching for hazards. We constantly search for metabolites, side effects, etc. In the meantime, we have constant pleas for help to control pests in order to enhance food supplies.

PESTICIDES AND THE GENERAL ENVIRONMENT

Little can be learned about pesticide contamination until the materials are used in our environment. Mock environments can be assembled, but based only on our past experience with DDT and other chlorinated hydrocarbons. Had it not been for widespread use of these materials it is doubtful that we would have been able to foresee and prevent any of our present-day problems. We can theorize, but until we use a chemical and find it in streams, for example, we do not know the actual environmental problems involved.

As greater chemical detection finesse is attained we change our views about residues. The one philosophy that might be acceptable is the one used by the USDA in clearing labels—if you can use an insecticide in such a way as to avoid having a residue, then there should be no permissible level.

Coho salmon survival from eggs from Lake Michigan was lower than from eggs from Lake Superior. It seems that more information is needed on this entire situation.

GENERAL COMMENTS

We too often view insecticides as though a single one will be with us for a lifetime. Actually, DDT lasted about 10 to 15 years, others a shorter time. The commercial life of an insecticide is a matter of years, not decades, so the time to find the answer to the questions is limited. Resistance of insects to an insecticide can develop rapidly and a product can be on the market and gone before problems even arise. Insecticides of the future will have a short commercial life, not a long one.

We have alarmed people who now want to do something about pollution, including pesticides, and we are in no position to answer all the questions and supply the guidance needed. We need much more research which will cost taxpayers large sums of money if they want answers first.

It was the hope of the group that public pressure was not dictating programs and answers. Science must be cold-blooded and give answers based on fact, not emotion. However, science does dictate its needs and we do respond to this.

Overcaution so far as our environment is concerned should be the goal for pest control specialists, and we should not use pesticides unless their use can be completely justified. On this basis, DDT and other insecticides should not be banned from use but should be usable at least on a permit basis. With proper discretion in use, it is possible that no permit, ban, or other restrictive measures would be necessary.

PART FOUR

ANIMAL WASTES AS WATER POLLUTANTS

CHAPTER SIXTEEN

LIVESTOCK OPERATIONS
AND FIELD-SPREAD MANURE
AS SOURCES OF POLLUTANTS

J. R. MINER and T. L. WILLRICH

D ISCHARGE of livestock and poultry manure into the environment is a practice as old as the animal. Historically, animal manure was randomly deposited on the land surface where the nutrients were utilized by growing vegetation and the organic matter was incorporated into the soil humus. Current livestock manure production, in excess of 1.5 billion tons per year (Wadleigh, 1968), results from a combination of the historical range or pasture production and some degree of confinement in which traditional on-site soil incorporation may not be applicable as a manure disposal system. As much as 50% of the current manure production is from confinement production (Law and Bernard, 1969).

POLLUTION CHARACTERISTICS OF ANIMAL WASTES

The major water pollutants arising from animal manures are oxygen-demanding matter (principally organic matter), plant nutrients, and infectious agents. Color and odor are potential polluting constituents of secondary importance. Organic matter from livestock wastes, like that from other sources, serves as a substrate for aerobic bacteria when it enters a receiving stream. Associated with bacterial metabolism is the utilization of dissolved oxygen. When the rate of oxygen utilization exceeds the reaeration rate of the stream, oxygen depletion occurs. Whenever sufficient organic matter enters, oxygen concentrations will be reduced below the level necessary for fish survival, and in more severe cases, complete oxygen depletion will occur and cause the development of anaerobic conditions.

J. R. MINER is Assistant Professor, Department of Agricultural Engineering, Iowa State University. T. L. WILLRICH is Professor, Department of Agricultural Engineering and Extension Agricultural Engineer, Iowa State University.

Journal Paper No. J-6378 of the Iowa Agriculture and Home Economics Experiment Station, Ames. Project No. 1730. Prepared for presentation to A Conference Concerning the Role of Agriculture in Clean Water, Ames, Iowa, November 18–20, 1969.

TABLE 16.1. Pollutional characteristics of untreated animal wastes, summary of values.

Animal	Animal Weight	Solids	BOD	Nitrogen	Phosphorus
		(lb/day)	(lb/day)	(lb/day)	(lb/day P$_2$O$_5$)
Beef cow ...	1,000	10.0	1.0	0.3	0.1
Dairy cow ..	1,000	10.0	1.2	0.4	0.1
Swine	100	0.9	0.25	0.06	0.02
Poultry	5	0.06	0.015	0.003	0.003

Organic matter in wastewater has historically been measured as biochemical oxygen demand (BOD). This measurement evaluates the concentration of oxidizable organic material that can be utilized by aerobic bacteria in terms of how much oxygen they will require to metabolize this material during a specified time, generally 5 days, and at a specific temperature, generally 20° C. Having determined the BOD and knowing the quantity of waste produced, it is possible to determine a daily BOD production for various animal species. The BOD of animal wastes has been evaluated by numerous researchers (Jeffrey et al., 1964; Taiganides et al., 1964; Dornbush and Anderson, 1965; Hart and Turner, 1965; Witzel et al., 1966; Dale and Day, 1967; Jones et al., 1968). From these data, representative BOD quantities from various animals can be determined. These values are summarized in Table 16.1.

Chemical oxygen demand (COD) is another measure of organic and other oxygen-demanding water based on chemical rather than biological oxidation. The COD exceeds the BOD of a waste due to the inability of aerobic bacteria to completely oxidize the more resistant constituents under the conditions of the BOD test. Table 16.2 compares the BOD and and COD of various wastes by using untreated municipal sewage as a reference.

In addition to oxygen depletion and resulting changes in aquatic life, decomposing organic matter contributes to color, taste, and odor problems in public water systems utilizing surface sources. Such problems are often difficult to solve, yet are of great significance. Reduced inorganic substances, such as ammoniacal nitrogen, exert an oxygen demand in addition to organic matter. Ammoniacal nitrogen exert an oxygen demand in addition to organic matter. Ammoniacal nitrogen concentrations ranging from 1 to 139 mg/l were found in feedlot runoff (Miner et al., 1966) and from 197 to 332 mg/l in swine manure lagoon effluent (Koelliker, 1969).

TABLE 16.2. BOD and COD concentrations in various wastes.

Source	BOD	COD
	(mg/l)	(mg/l)
Untreated domestic sewage	100–300	400–600
Dairy cattle manure (Dale and Day, 1967)	25,600	
Swine manure (Scheltinga, 1966)	27,000–33,000	70,000
Chicken droppings (Niles, 1967)	24,000	172,000

Nitrogen and phosphorus are the plant nutrients of primary concern. These elements are present in sufficient quantities to increase nutrient concentrations in surface water bodies and thus stimulate the growth of aquatic plants. In addition, nitrate toxicity due to increased nitrogen concentration in groundwater is important in many rural areas.

Livestock wastes are sources of infectious agents that may infect other animals and, in some instances, man. Among the potential water-borne diseases transmissible from animals are anthrax, brucellosis, coccidiosis, encephalitis, erysipelas, foot rot, histoplasmosis, hog cholera, infectious bronchitis, mastitis, Newcastle disease, ornithosis, gastroenteritis, and salmonellosis (Wadleigh, 1968). Although water-borne diseases are relatively rare in our country, increasing emphasis on water-based recreation creates new opportunities for this mode of infection. Leptospirosis has been spread from cattle to swimmers by the water-borne route (Diesch and McCulloch, 1966). Samples of cattle feedlot runoff, as small as one ml, showed the presence of *Salmonella* organisms even though there were no symptoms of infection observed in the cattle (Miner et al., 1967). By using the fecal-coliform—fecal-streptococcus ratio (Kenner et al., 1960) it is possible to distinguish between livestock and human wastes. When stored in a lagoon or applied to the soil, pollutional bacteria—coliform and enterococcal—die off rapidly (McCoy, 1967). Thus, little public health hazard would appear due to lagooned livestock wastes. It was further noted that for bovine wastes the predominant enterococci were *Streptococcus durans* and *S. faecium* rather than *S. faecalis* found in the human intestine. This suggests a different interpretation of enterococcal counts for animal than for human waste sources.

Since livestock wastes are not usually collected, transported, treated, and discharged into a receiving stream, as municipal sewage almost always is, a quantified prediction of water-quality deterioration caused by animal wastes cannot be made as it can for municipal sewage. Calculation of a population equivalent for the wastes from various animals assumes that the total wastes from these animals are discharged into streams and released at a uniform rate either with or without treatment. Neither assumption is valid except in a most unusual situation.

However, the potential for livestock wastes to pollute water is influenced by the ways in which it is collected, stored, and treated as well as the final method of disposal. Seven major potential pollution sources exist in connection with livestock wastes.

SURFACE WATER POLLUTION POTENTIAL

Runoff from Range and Pasture Operations

Where animals graze a vegetated land area (range or pasture), little interest has been shown by water pollution control agencies. Manure is uniformly distributed in a light application, liquids are absorbed by the soil, and the vegetative cover utilizes the added nutrients and inhibits erosion. Low-intensity rainfalls are usually absorbed by the soil and high-intensity rainfalls in excess of soil infiltration rates provide sufficient dilution water to minimize the concentration of potential pollutants in the runoff.

In range and pasture systems, one can visualize extensive waste treatment taking place as any runoff-carried pollutants pass over the soil surface. Vegetative cover provides effective screening as well as settling areas for particulate matter. Mixing and aeration stimulate biological treatment of soluble organic matter. Thus, with respect to water pollution potential, range or pasture livestock production is of less concern than confinement production. However, when one considers the use of a farm pond as a domestic water source, utilization of the watershed as a pasture is discouraged because of the high-quality water requirements and the relatively long die-off periods exhibited by pathogenic organisms in such a system (Andre et al., 1967).

Runoff from Cropland following Manure Application

When manure is spread on frozen or snow-covered fields, or when heavy rainfall occurs immediately following manure application, considerable runoff and a resulting organic matter and nutrient loss is possible. Data from Wisconsin indicate that spring application of manure caused no increase in loss of nitrogen in runoff. Manure application on snow-covered ground that was followed by a rain increased nitrogen losses from a normal 3 to 4 pounds per acre annually to over 23 pounds (Hensler et al., 1969). Additional runoff losses are possible where manure is stockpiled prior to spreading in such a way that runoff has direct access to a surface stream.

Runoff from Feedlots and Similar Unroofed Enclosures

Animals produced in feedlots, pens, and other uncovered enclosures in such a concentration as to remove the vegetative cover present pollution hazards unlike the pasture systems. During and immediately after rain and spring thaws, water flows over manure-covered feeding areas and carries both particulate and soluble manure components with it. This pollution source has received considerable public interest due to the occurrence of dramatic fish kills and other gross pollution incidents. The action of animal hooves on a feeding surface creates an area void of vegetation and one through which infiltration rates are greatly reduced. However, considerable surface storage capacity is available on feeding areas in the hoof depressions.

CATTLE FEEDLOT RUNOFF QUALITY

Data exist on the quality of runoff from cattle feedlots (Smith and Miner, 1964; Miner et al., 1966; Loehr, 1968). They indicate cattle feedlot runoff to be of highly variable quality, depending upon such factors as rainfall intensity, temperature and feedlot surface moisture content, and manure accumulation. Organic content as COD in cattle feedlot runoff ranged from 3 to 11 times the COD in untreated domestic sewage (Miner et al., 1966). Although runoff from feeding areas confining animals other than cattle may be expected to be high in organic matter, no data are currently available concerning these sources. In addition to the high-strength character istics of feedlot runoff, the slug effect upon a receiving stream is particularly damaging. When feedlot runoff is uncontrolled, particularly from a lot located adjacent to receiving streams, the large volume of relatively high-strength wastewater enters the stream quickly and consequently allows little time for dilution by runoff from clean areas. Thus, one technique proposed for the reduction of feedlot runoff damage is the construction of flow control structures that spread the discharge of runoff over a longer time period. Of particular concern to pollution agencies have been large feedlots (capacity over 1,000 head), lots located near or adjacent to streams, or lakes and lots whose runoff enters groundwater supplies through abandoned wells, springs, sinkholes, or other openings.

In assessing the significance of cattle feedlot runoff compared with other waste sources within a drainage basin, one must look at both the quantity and quality of runoff. Assuming an earthen lot with a 2% slope, about 11 inches of annual runoff might be expected from 30 inches of annual rainfall, with runoff occurring during 30 days of the year. At an average of 1,000 mg/l of BOD, the runoff from a feedlot on each of these 30 days would be equivalent to the untreated sewage from a community of 500 people per acre of feedlot surface. Although such an average is of little help in actual situations, it indicates that runoff from cattle feedlots is a significant source of organic wastes, but it is not of the same magnitude as one gets if he bases his predictions on standard population equivalents for various livestock.

CONTROL OF CATTLE FEEDLOT RUNOFF

In response to fish kills attributable to feedlot drainage (Loehr, 1968) and for other reasons, such as stream enrichment, various pollution control measures have been devised. The first step in most programs is to divert any water falling outside the feedlot so that it will not flow across the feedlot and thereby minimize the quantity of polluted runoff. The second step is generally the construction of a runoff collection and impoundment system that will prevent the immediate and uncontrolled entry of runoff into a stream. Facilities to settle manure solids are frequently incorporated into either the runoff collection system by the design of channels for low flow velocities or by the construction of separate settling basins. Settling facilities are designed for flow velocities of 1 foot per second or less and for dewatering so collected solids will dry more rapidly and thus more easily. Where solids are to be removed from a settling basin with a dragline, a maximum basin width of 50 feet is desirable.

Runoff impoundment basins generally provide sufficient capacity to hold 3 to 6 inches of runoff from the contributing area. The final design capacity is a function of the climatological features of the area and the proposed method for disposing of collected runoff. In some parts of the country where seasonal and annual evaporation losses sufficiently exceed rainfall quantities, it is possible to design runoff impoundment basins so that most or all collected water will be lost by evaporation and seepage. This approach is not applicable in humid regions, however.

Where evaporation and seepage losses are not sufficient for runoff disposal, collected wastewater may be spread on land or treated prior to release into a stream or surface water body. Problems associated with wastewater treatment are (1) the necessity of frequent operator attention, (2) the difficulty in producing a high-quality effluent, and (3) the costs involved in such treatment.

Discharge from Waste Storage or Treatment Units

Roofed livestock confinement units offer advantages to the producer in ease of mechanizing feed and water distribution and manure collection as well as offering the possibility of environmental control. Such units range from unheated structures with natural ventilation to totally enclosed buildings with mechanical ventilation as well as heating and cooling equipment.

To perform satisfactorily, an enclosed livestock building must incorporate a compatible manure management system. A manure management system may logically incorporate (1) a means to separate the manure from the animal and to collect it in some logical place, (2) a method to transport it, (3) a storage device, (4) one or more treatment units, and (5) a final disposal or utilization scheme. These functions must be mutually compatible as well as being compatible with the remainder of the production unit. They must not only control the escape of potential water pollutants but also minimize the potential for odor, insect, and rodent nuisances, and operate with a minimum of labor, capital investment, and operating costs.

Totally roofed animal units eliminate the open-lot runoff problem but they offer the greatest potential for water pollution of all the livestock production schemes. They also offer the greatest potential for essentially pollution-free operation. System design and management determine the degree of pollution that will develop, if any. As an example, a 1,000-head beef unit would be equivalent to a community of 6,000 people, based on BOD, if the raw wastes were dumped into a stream every day, or a community of up to 600,000 if the accumulated wastes were dumped every 100 days. However, with proper waste collection, transport, and application to cropland, the manure from this operation need not contribute to water pollution.

Liquid manure systems are most common in roofed confinement units. Liquid manure may be applied to the soil with or without treatment as just discussed. Treatment for release into high-quality surface waters has not been recommended due to the inability of currently available systems to produce an acceptable effluent at a reasonable cost.

GROUNDWATER POLLUTION POTENTIAL

Percolate from Feedlots and Similar Unroofed Enclosures

Whenever water passes through a layer of manure and percolates into the underlying soil, it will carry certain components of the manure with it. Because of soil puddling and compaction by animal hooves, however, the infiltration rate in an animal feeding area will usually be low. Thus, only a very small quantity of water would be expected to enter the groundwater supply as long as the lot is in continuous use to confine animals. Where soil and groundwater samples have been collected near old feedlots, elevated nitrate-nitrogen concentrations have been detected (Smith, 1967). Data collected from beneath feedlots and irrigated fields of the South Platte Valley in Colorado also indicated elevated nitrogen concentrations in groundwater near feedlots (Stewart et al., 1968). They also noted high organic carbon concentrations in groundwater samples as much as 35 feet beneath feedlots. High organic carbon concentrations caused much of the nitrogen to be present as ammonium nitrogen. Thus, localized pollution of the water-table aquifer with nitrogen near and under animal feeding areas does take place. However, due to the limited acreage being used for feedlots, widespread groundwater pollution due to infiltration from animal feeding areas is not likely.

Percolate from Disposal Areas

Most animal manure is spread on cropland. This includes not only manure and other wastes scrapped from open feedlots but also that hauled, both solid and liquid wastes, from confinement buildings and barns as well. This manure is field spread not only because of its fertilizer value but also as a convenient and least-cost disposal technique in most situations. Current manure-spreading techniques include not only conventional solid manure spreaders but also liquid-hauling tanks and irrigation equipment. Two potential modes of pollution exist for manure applied to cropland: (1) runoff due to rainfall or snowmelt carrying it to surface streams or impoundments and (2) percolation into the groundwater.

Where collected feedlot runoff or liquid manure is spread on cropland, forest land, or pasture, the greater portion of pollutants will be removed from the wastewater before it becomes a portion of the groundwater recharge. Soil has the ability to remove all suspended solids and much of the dissolved material. BOD and COD removal should present no problem as long as the infiltration capacity of the soil is maintained. Soil also has the ability to absorb large quantities of phosphorus. Nitrogen, however, can escape to the groundwater and thus sufficiently increase the nitrate concentration in a localized area so that the groundwater would be of inferior quality for some uses.

Recent work with application of anaerobic animal wastes to grassland indicates that with proper management extensive biological denitrification is possible (Koelliker and Miner, 1969). In one trial, using anaerobic lagoon effluent, 2,300 pounds of nitrogen per acre were applied in 30 inches of lagoon effluent. Losses to groundwater (250 lb/A) and in runoff (170 lb/A) were 420 pounds per acre. A net nitrogen loss within the soil profile of 400 pounds per acre was measured. Thus, a loss of 2,020 pounds of nitrogen per acre due to denitrification took place during the 3-month trial period.

Percolate from Field-spread Manure

Groundwater pollution due to field-spread manure has generally been of little significance, due to the associated organic matter which tends to release nitrogen over an extended time period and due to the conventional rates of manure application. This mechanism allows the nutrients greater opportunity to be used by crops or be incorporated into the soil. The soil is also effective in removing potentially infectious bacteria; 14 inches of silt loam soil removed the initial concentrations of 1×10^5/ml of *Escherichia coli* and of 1×10^6 to 1×10^7/ml of enterococci (McCoy, 1969).

SUMMARY

1. Potential water pollutants from animal manures are oxygen-demanding matter, plant nutrients, infectious agents, and color- and odor-contributing substances.
2. Total solids in animal manures are about 300 times more concentrated than in municipal sewage. The BOD of undiluted animal manures is about 100 times greater than the BOD of municipal sewage.
3. Ammoniacal nitrogen concentrations in diluted and decomposed animal wastes, such as lot runoff and lagoon effluent, are sufficient to exert a major oxygen demand or produce a toxic level to fish in a receiving stream.
4. The incidence of water-borne diseases transmitted from animal to man is low even though a dozen or more diseases can be transmitted by this route. Fecal enterococcal counts must be interpreted differently for animal-manure-polluted water than for human-waste-polluted water since nonpathogenic enterococci apparently predominate in some animal wastes. Most infectious agents die off rapidly when animal wastes are treated or applied to the soil.
5. Data concerning pollutants removed by runoff from livestock range and pasture operations are sparse. Logic indicates that this potential source is relatively insignificant when compared to other sources.

6. Runoff from manured cropland will transport greater quantities of pollutants if the manure has been spread on frozen or snow-covered fields.

7. Highly concentrated open feeding areas offer the potential for runoff-caused pollution problems, due to the low infiltration rates and high manure density. Runoff control is one key to pollution prevention. Manure cleaned from lots and collected runoff requires some means of disposal. Land application is the current disposal means of preference.

8. Roofed confinement livestock buildings make possible a high degree of control over manure disposal. A proper means for control of this material requires systems for manure collection, transport, storage, treatment, and/or disposal or utilization. Hydraulic manure transport systems offer improvements in labor requirements but unless some means of water reuse is planned, excessive waste disposal expense is encountered. Improper manure disposal from such a unit causes the greatest pollution threat of the systems mentioned.

9. The application of livestock manure to the soil is both a logical and historically verified practice. Technological, social, and economic factors have in recent years made this practice less acceptable. Applied in proper quantities with alert management, and with improved methods of application, manure disposal by return to the soil should be encouraged. This disposal may necessitate treatment and conditioning prior to disposal to minimize odors or water pollution.

REFERENCES

Andre, D. A., Weiser, H. H., and Maloney, G. W. 1967. Survival of bacterial pathogens in farm pond water. *J. Am. Water Works Assoc.* 59 (4): 503.

Dale, A. C., and Day, D. L. 1967. Some aerobic decomposition properties of dairy-cattle manure. *Trans. Am. Soc. Agr. Engrs.* 10 (4): 546–48.

Diesch, S. L., and McCulloch, W. F. 1966. Isolation of pathogenic leptospires from waters used for recreation. *Public Health Rept.* 81 (4): 299–304.

Dornbush, J. N., and Anderson, J. R. 1965. Lagooning of livestock wastes in South Dakota. *Proc. 1964 Ind. Waste Conf.* Lafayette, Ind.: Purdue Univ. Eng. Ext. Ser. 117, pp. 317–25.

Hart, S. A., and Turner, M. E. 1965. Lagoons for livestock manure. *J. Water Pollution Control Federation* 37 (11): 1578–96.

Hensler, R. F., Olsen, R. J., Witzel, S. A., Attol, O. J., Paulson, W. H., and Johannes, R. F. 1969. Effect of method of manure handling on crop yields, nutrient recovery and runoff losses. Presented at meeting of Am. Soc. Agr. Engrs., 22–25 June 1969, W. Lafayette, Ind.

Jeffrey, E. A., Blackman, W. C., and Ricketts, R. L. 1964. *Aerobic and anaerobic digestion characteristics of livestock wastes.* Univ. of Mo. Eng. Ser. Bull. 57.

Jones, D. D., Jones, B. A., and Day, D. L. 1968. Aerobic digestion of cattle wastes. *Ill. Res.* 10 (2): 16–18.

Kenner, B. A., Clark, H. F., and Kablet, P. W. 1960. Fecal streptococci: quantification of streptococci in feces. *Am. J. Public Health* 50 (10): 1553–59.

Koelliker, J. K. 1969. Soil percolation as a renovation means for livestock lagoon effluent. Unpublished Master's thesis, Iowa State Univ., Ames.

Koelliker, J. K., and Miner, J. R. 1969. Use of soil to treat anaerobic lagoon effluent renovation as a function of depth and application rate. Paper 69-460 presented at meeting of Am. Soc. Agr. Engrs., 22–25 June 1969, W. Lafayette, Ind.

Law, J. B., and Bernard, H. 1969. The impact of agricultural pollutants on subsequent users. Paper 69-235 presented at meeting of Am. Soc. Agr. Engrs., 22–25 June 1969, W. Lafayette, Ind.

Loehr, R. C. 1968. *Pollution implications of animal wastes—a forward oriented review.* U.S. Dept. of Interior, Fed. Water Pollution Control Admin., Robert S. Kerr Water Res. Center, Ada, Okla.

McCoy, E. 1967. Lagooning of liquid manure (bovine): bacteriological aspects. *Trans. Am. Soc. Agr. Engrs.* 10 (6): 748–87.

———. 1969. Removal of pollution bacteria from animal wastes by soil percolation. Paper 69-430 presented at meeting of Am. Soc. Agr. Engrs., 22–25 June 1969, W. Lafayette, Ind.

Miner, J. R., Lipper, R. I., Fina, L. R., and Funk, J. W. 1966. Cattle feedlot runoff: its nature and variation. *J. Water Pollution Control Federation* 48 (10): 1582–91.

Miner, J. R., Fina, L. R., and Piatt, C. 1967. *Salmonella infantis* in cattle feedlot runoff. *J. Appl. Microbiol.* 15 (3): 627–28.

Niles, C. F. 1967. Egglaying house wastes. *Proc. 22nd Ind. Waste Conf.* Lafayette, Ind.: Purdue Univ. Eng. Ext. Serv. 129, p. 334.

Scheltinga, H. M. J. 1966. Aerobic purification of farm waste. *J. Proc. Inst. Sewage Purification*, pp. 585–88.

Smith, G. E. 1967. Fertilizer nutrients as contaminants in water supplies. In *Agriculture and the quality of our environment*, ed. N. C. Brady, pp. 173–86. Norwood, Mass.: Plimpton Press.

Smith, S. M., and Miner, J. R. 1964. Stream pollution from feedlot runoff. *Trans. 14th Ann. Conf. Sanit. Eng.*, pp. 18–25. Univ. of Kans., Lawrence.

Stewart, B. A., Viets, F. G., and Hutchinson, G. L. 1968. Agriculture's effect on nitrate pollution. *J. Soil Water Conserv.* 23 (13): 13–15.

Taiganides, E. P., Hazen, T. E., Baumann, E. R., and Johnson, H. P. 1964. Properties and pumping characteristics of hog waste. *Trans. Am. Soc. Agr. Engrs.* 7 (2): 123–29.

Wadleigh, C. H. 1968. Wastes in relation to agriculture and forestry. USDA Misc. Publ. 1065.

Witzel, S. A., McCoy, E., Polkowski, L. B., Attoe, O. J., and Nichols, M. S. 1966. Physical, chemical and bacteriological properties of bovine animals. In *Management of farm animal wastes*. St. Joseph, Mich.: Am. Soc. Agr. Engrs. SP-Oe66, pp. 10–14.

CHAPTER SEVENTEEN

MANURE DECOMPOSITION AND FATE OF BREAKDOWN PRODUCTS IN SOIL

T. M. McCALLA, L. R. FREDERICK, AND G. L. PALMER

H UGE quantities of animal waste are accumulating in small areas because of the increasing confinement of animals in large numbers for meat, milk, and egg production (Wadleigh, 1968). The production of enormous amounts of urine and fecal material has caused unparalleled disposal problems and a threat to water quality (Commoner, 1968). The best way to dispose of animal waste is to put it on the land for decomposition and mineralization. But what is the highest concentration of animal waste can be applied to the land without upsetting favorable microbial decomposition patterns, producing a toxic effect on the crop, or polluting the runoff and groundwater?

There are some waste treatments that can be applied to animal manure to remove its high oxygen demand and inorganic nutrients, but these treatments are not yet economically feasible.

Much can be done in the management of the animal waste on site (for example, on beef cattle feedlots) to create a favorable environment for decomposition so that a considerable amount of the manure can be decomposed to CO_2 and N_2, which will dissipate into the atmosphere (Dale and Day, 1967; McCalla and Viets, 1970). Phosphates are readily adsorbed by the soil and thus may be removed effectively from solution. Therefore, correct management can reduce eutrophication[1] in streams and lakes.

T. M. McCALLA is Microbiologist, USDA, Lincoln, Nebraska. L. R. FREDERICK is Professor, Department of Agronomy, Iowa State University. G. L. PALMER is Instructor, Department of Agronomy, Iowa State University.

Contribution from the Northern Plains Branch, Soil and Water Conservation Research Division, ARS, USDA, in cooperation with the Nebraska Agricultural Experiment Station, and from the Agronomy Department, Iowa State University, Ames. Published as Paper No. 2742, Journal Series, Nebraska Agricultural Experiment Station; and Paper No. J6431, Iowa Agricultural Experiment Station, Project 1378.

1. Eutrophication is an excessive enrichment of water with nutrients, such as nitrates and phosphates, which will promote a luxuriant growth of algae (algal bloom).

TABLE 17.1. Chemical composition of various fresh manures, litter free.

Chemical Constituents	Sheep Manure*	Horse Manure†	Cow Manure*
	(percent of dry material)		
Ether-soluble substances	2.83	1.89	2.77
Cold water-soluble organic matter .	19.19	3.19	5.02
Hot water-soluble organic matter ..	5.73	2.39	5.32
Hemicelluloses	18.46	23.52	18.57
Cellulose	18.72	27.46	25.43
Lignin	20.68	14.23	20.21
Total nitrogen	4.08	1.09	2.38
Ash	17.21	9.11	12.95

Source: Waksman (1938).
* Solid and liquid excreta.
† Solid excreta only.

MANURE COMPOSITION

Fresh manure contains from 30 to 85% water. The rest of the constituents in manure are inorganic and organic solids, liquids, and gases. The composition of manures is shown in Tables 17.1, 17.2, 17.3, and 17.4.

Manure contains all the inorganic nutrients needed by plants. These nutrients are worth slightly more than $1 per ton (Table 17.4). When putting large quantities of manure on land, materials such as ammonia may accumulate in concentrations toxic for the growth of plants (McCalla and Haskins, 1964; Megie et al., 1967). Using average figures for production of manure per animal unit and agricultural statistics for the number of animals present in the various states, an estimate of the N, P, and K in manure produced by livestock in the north-central region of the United States was made. For the western north-central states, the manure contained per year 2,100,000 tons N, 300,000 tons P, and 1,300,000 tons K. Similar figures were obtained for the eastern north-central states. These figures are approximately comparable to the nutrients applied as fertilizer in 1968, except that about 50% more phosphorus was applied as fertilizer.

Roughly, 90% of the dry matter in manure is organic waste material from animal digestion of feeds. Animal rations consist largely of carbohydrates (sugars, starches, celluloses, and hemicelluloses), some proteins, fats, small amounts of lignin, and numerous inorganic nutrients, such as nitrogen, phosphorus, potassium, and a number of micronutrients (Hemingway, 1961; Gilbertson et al., 1970). In a high-concentrate ration, about 70 to 80% of the organic nutrients are utilized by the animal. The substances used by the animal are mostly carbohydrates, some proteins, small amounts of minerals, and other substances. The animal waste is more concentrated than the feed in lignin and minerals upon deposition in feedlot or confinement structure and is less concentrated in carbohydrates. But the manure retains about 60 to 75% digestible materials. Some fats are present, and also humiclike substances resistant to

TABLE 17.2. Characteristics of animal manures.

Animal	Moisture	Characteristics								Volatile Solids	Fat
		N	P	K	S	Ca	Fe	Mg			
	%					(lb/ton manure)					
Dairy cattle	79	11.2	2.0	10.0	1.0	5.6	0.08	2.2	322	7
Fattening cattle	80	14.0	4.0	9.0	1.7	2.4	0.08	2.0	395	7
Hogs	75	10.0	2.8	7.6	2.7	11.4	0.56	1.6	399	9
Horses	60	13.8	2.0	12.0	1.4	15.7	0.27	2.8	386	6
Sheep	65	28.0	4.2	20.0	1.8	11.7	0.32	3.7	567	14

Source: Loehr (1968).

TABLE 17.3. Trace element content of manures (as ppm, dry-matter basis).

Element	Minimum	Maximum	Average
Boron	4.5	52.0	20.2
Manganese	75.0	549.0	201.1
Cobalt	0.25	4.70	1.04
Copper	7.6	40.8	15.6
Zinc	43.0	247.0	96.2
Molybdenum	0.84	15.83	2.37
Molybdenum*	0.84	4.18	2.06

Source: Atkinson et al. (1954).

Note: Data from 44 samples of farmyard manure, representing fresh cow, horse, swine, sheep, poultry, and mixed manures, and composted cow and mixed manures.

* With one exceptionally high value omitted.

TABLE 17.4. Chemical analysis of slurry manure (a mixture of feces and urine) from confined beef cattle feeding in Nebraska.

Constituent	Wet Weight Basis	Each Ton Contains	20 T/A Supplies
N	0.29%	5.8 lb.	116 lb.
P_2O_5	0.18%	3.6 lb.	72 lb.
K_2O	0.31%	6.2 lb.	124 lb.
Moisture	85.0 %		
Volatile solids	11.6 %		
Total solids	15.33%		
Ash	3.73%		
NH_4	0.05%		
NO_3N	0 %		
COD	121,000 mg. O_2/liter		
pH	7.3		
Conductivity	4.5 mmhos/cm²		

Note: Acknowledgment is made of the assistance of J. R. Ellis, USDA-ARS-SWC, in making these determinations.

TABLE 17.5. Particle size analysis of fresh manure (oven-dry weight basis).

Particle Size	Percent of Total
4.00 mm or greater	2.45
4.00 mm but >2,000μ	25.09
<2,000μ but >500μ	36.69
<500μ but >210μ	4.75
<210μ but >2μ	1.01
<2μ	30.02

Source: Unpublished data, T. M. McCalla and J. S. Boyce (1969).

decomposition (Jansson, 1960a, 1960b; Alexander, 1961). Antibiotics may also occur in the animal waste (Morrison et al., 1969).

The mechanical size of the particles in manure is shown in Table 17.5. The solids consist of undigested fragments of grain, bran, fibrous materials, and about 30% colloidal materials.

The microbial population of animal waste is composed mainly of bacteria, fungi, actinomycetes, and protozoa. Cells of microbes and cells from the lining of the intestinal tract of the animal in feces amount to about 40% of the feces (Crampton and Harris, 1969). Among the bacteria, the enterococci and coliforms are very numerous, with coliform counts as high as 18 billion excreted per animal per day (Table 17.6).

Fresh manure, a manure-soil-urine mixture from next to the concrete feeding apron, and dry manure from the middle of the feedlot were collected in eastern Nebraska. A manure suspension, 5% by weight (oven-dry basis), was made by shaking manure and distilled water for 1 hour. After standing for 0, 1, and 24 hours, both solubility of substances and suspension of the manure, and the number of microorganisms in the supernatant, were determined (Table 17.7). Highest solubility and suspension of combustible material were found in fresh manure, and greatest solubility and suspension of noncombustible material were found in samples collected next to the feedlot bunkers. Appreciable numbers of microbial pollution indicators were present, and they remained in suspension even after 24 hours of settling. The amount of phosphorus and nitrate in suspension and solution remained high after settling. Concentration of total P of material in suspension and solution was approximately 68 to 113 ppm and for NO_3-N was 8.5 to 23 ppm. The pH decreased sharply when the fresh manure suspension was allowed to stand for 24 hours. Thirty percent of the manure was in particle sizes less than 2μ. Salter and Schollenberger (1939) found up to 50% of manure was humus. *Shigella* and *Salmonella* were not found in the manure samples. The orders of magnitude of the microbial counts in the manure suspension were: total count, 10^8; anaerobes, 10^5 to 10^6; *Escherichia coli*, 10^5; enterococci, 10^4 to 10^6; and total fungi, 10^3 to 10^5 per ml of manure suspension.

MANURE DECOMPOSITION IN FEEDLOTS, CONFINEMENT AREAS, AND IN THE SOIL

Decomposition in Storage

Animal waste may remain where deposited in feedlots and confinement buildings for considerable time before disposal, and much decomposition may occur. For example, manure from beef cattle with a high-roughage diet was incubated in a growth chamber simulating spring and summer climatic conditions at Lincoln, Nebraska. Urine was added twice weekly to the incubated manure samples to equal two stocking rates: 50 and 250 ft^2 per animal. After 3 weeks of decomposition, 90% of the nitrogen added initially in the manure

TABLE 17.6. Estimated daily per capita discharge of coliforms in animal feces.

Item	Human	Cow	Hog	Sheep	Ducks	Turkeys	Chickens
Moisture content (%)	77.0	83.3	66.7	74.4	61.0	62.0	71.6
Average weight of 24-hr fecal discharge (wet weight in grams)	150.0	23,600.0	2,700.0	1,130.0	336.0	448.0	182.0
Coliforms per gram (millions)	13.0	0.23	3.3	16.0	33.0	0.29	1.3
Total coliforms discharged per day (millions)	1,950.0	5,428.0	8,910.0	18,080.0	11,088.0	130.0	237.0

Source: Geldreich et al. (1962).

TABLE 17.7. Numbers of microorganisms and chemical tests on 5% suspension of manure in distilled water. Numbers per ml or mg/ml or ppm of manure suspension.

Kind of Manure Sample	H₂O	pH	Bacteria per ml	Fungi per ml	Anaerobes per ml	E. coli per ml	Enterococci per ml	Nonvol. res. wt. In suspension	Vol.* res. wt. In suspension	Total Phosphorus	NO₃-N
	%		($\times 10^6$)	($\times 10^4$)	($\times 10^5$)	($\times 10^5$)	($\times 10^4$)	(mg/ml)		(ppm for solution)	
D_0	95	7.8	490.0	0.3	1.7	7.0	7.0	4	18	60	13.8
D_1		7.2	303.0	0.3	0.3	13.0	17.0	6	25	113	13.7
D_{24}		7.6	120.0	5.7	0.1	0.29	8.8	6	19	88	14.5
M_0	95	8.2	245.0	3.0	21.3	7.0	293.0	19	24	60	23.7
M_1		8.6	257.0	13.0	27.3	3.0	183.0	12	18	88	23.9
M_{24}		7.8	73.0	10.0	0.99	2.9	487.0	7	13	60	23.5
F_0	95	6.8	303.0	63.0	†	†	53.0	6	6	100	8.5
F_1		5.6	187.0	10.0	3.0	13.0	71.0	4	4	100	10.6
F_{24}		4.94	8.5	24.0	†	0.4	80.0	4	3	88	10.7

Source: Unpublished data, T. M. McCalla and J. R. Ellis, (1968).

* = combustible at 550° C.

† = numbers below or above dilutions made.

D = dry manure
M = mixture of soil, manure, and urine near feed bunker
F = fresh manure
0 = 0 times of standing after shaking
1 = 1 hour of standing after shaking
24 = 24 hours of standing after shaking

247

or subsequently in the urine was lost into the atmosphere with the stocking rate of 50 ft² per animal. In the decomposing manure, NH_3 concentrations were high, pH ranged from about 8 to 9, nitrates accumulated only to a slight extent, COD values remained high, and salt concentration increased. About 50% of volatile solids were lost in 4 months (McCalla et al., 1969b). In Connecticut, 3 bushels of fresh manure from dropping pits lost 55% of the organic matter and 77% of the N when stored for 20 weeks in a laying house (Perkins et al., 1964). With the loss of carbon and nitrogen, mineral content increased, readily available organic materials decreased, and resistant materials such as lignin accumulated (Burnett and Dondero, 1969). Manure oxygen demand is characterized as BOD[2] and COD[3] values (McCalla et al., 1969b).

The BOD:COD ratio generally is about 8.5:10 for beef cattle manure (Lipper, 1969). Morrison et al. (1969) showed that excreted chlortetracycline in beef cattle feedlot waste, arising from antibiotic supplementation of the ration, had a half-life of 1 week at 37° C and greater than 20 days at 28° C and 4° C. By altering decomposition patterns, antibiotics or other chemicals may affect release of nuisance odors.

The microorganisms found in manure during decomposition are bacteria, fungi, actinomycetes, and protozoa (Witzel et al., 1966; McCoy, 1967, 1969). Many of the *E. coli*, enterococci, and other intestinal and disease microorganisms are short-lived in the soil (King, 1957; Burroughs, 1967; Klein and Casida, 1967). In a manure decomposition study at Nebraska, the *E. coli* and enterococci disappeared rapidly, and none remained after the second and third months. Fungi numbers were very low initially, but increased during the incubation period. Bacilli decreased; total bacteria increased (McCalla et al., 1969b).

Decomposition in Soil

The addition of large amounts of manure will stimulate the growth of saprophytic bacteria, fungi, and actinomycetes in the soil. Aerobic, mesophilic bacteria metabolizing cellulose are much more numerous in manured fields. Protozoan and actinomycete numbers and CO_2 production are increased by manure additions (Alexander, 1961).

Manure from a high-concentrate ration contains about 10 to 15% lignin. Most of the other energy material decomposes rather rapidly in the soil. Polysaccharides, including cellulose and starch, and most protein materials decompose rapidly, although some of the proteinaceous material, probably associated with lignin or keratin, is fairly resistant to decomposition (Polheim, 1965). Consider-

---

2. Biological oxygen demand is the oxygen consumed by microbes in the process of oxidizing the organic materials during a 5-day incubation period. This is basically an indication of the readily oxidizable material present.
3. Chemical oxygen demand is a chemical evaluation of the total oxidizable material using sulfuric acid and potassium dichromate, the measure being the quantity of oxygen used in this process.

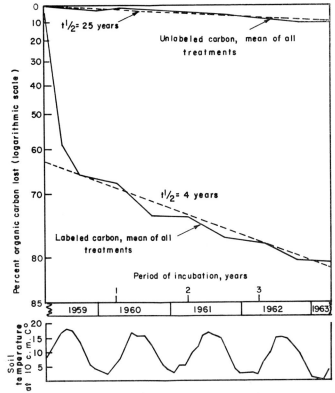

FIG. 17.1. Losses of unlabeled (soil) and labeled (ryegrass) carbon from soils incubated in the field with labeled ryegrass. (Jenkinson, 1965.)

able carbon and nitrogen are found in microbial cells formed during decomposition. Of labeled C added as 0.6% ryegrass to Broadbalk field soils, Jenkinson (1966) found that 30 to 33% remained in the soil after 1 year, of which about one-third was in microbial cells. After 4 years, 19% of the labeled C still remained, and only about 19% of that was in microbial cells. The carbon turnover rate appeared to vary with stage of decomposition: the original residues decomposed rapidly with a half-life estimated to be 14 to 30 days. After the first year, the biomass has a half-life of 1 year, and the residual C has a half-life of about 4 years, while the soil humus has a half-life of about 25 years (Figure 17.1). About 50 to 60% of the nitrogen in manure applied to soil will be mineralized the first year.

Factors Affecting Decomposition

Under aerobic conditions, carbonaceous materials are rapidly oxidized to CO_2; microbial cells are synthesized; and nitrates, sulfates, and inorganic phosphate tend to accumulate. Manure added in large quantities to the soil has a tremendous O_2 demand. Well-

TABLE 17.8. Generalized presentation of breakdown products of manure decomposed under aerobic and anaerobic conditions.

Type of Material	Aerobic				Anaerobic			
	Carbon compounds	Nitrogen compounds	Phosphorus compounds	Sulfur compounds	Carbon compounds	Nitrogen compounds	Phosphorus compounds	Sulfur compounds
Breakdown products	CO_2	NO_3^-	$H_2PO_4^-$	$SO_4^=$	CO_2, CH_4	N_2, NH_3	$H_2PO_4^-$	$S^=$
	Microbial cells				Organic acids	Pyridines		Mercaptans
					Alcohols	Indoles		H_2S
					Cells	Skatoles		
						Amines		

drained soil is aerobic, but the soil environment may become anaerobic, particularly if conditions are favorable for decomposition and there is an excess of water.

Under anaerobic conditions, which will occur in a very wet soil (as in overirrigation), denitrification can occur. A considerable amount of the nitrogen may be lost into the atmosphere, because 1 unit of N can be lost for each 3.1 units of carbohydrate metabolized to CO_2.

Many anaerobic decomposition products, such as organic acids (acetic, butyric, propionic, isobutyric) and other compounds, may be unfavorable for plant growth. The iron may be reduced to a ferrous condition. Foul-smelling compounds, such as indole, skatole, mercaptans, hydrogen sulfide, and amines, are byproducts of protein decomposition (Table 17.8).

Temperature is another important factor. When the soil is cold, decomposition is slow. Rothwell (1955) found that breakdown rates at 45°, 60°, 70°, and 80° F were about 30, 60, 70, and 80%, respectively, of the rate at 95° F.

The maximum amount of manure that the soil will accommodate in decomposition has not been determined. Indeed, if the land were covered with several inches of manure, considerable decomposition would occur in the manure pack where thermophilic bacteria may be active in the decomposition. Temperature in manure packs will reach 160° F even in winter.

FATE OF BREAKDOWN PRODUCTS IN SOIL

Application of animal waste to the surface or incorporation in the soil is followed by further decomposition. Manure should be immediately plowed under to minimize N loss (Table 17.9). About three-fourths or more of the organic materials will be decomposed in the first year. The mineralization of the animal waste will result in nitrogen, phosphorus, potassium, and micronutrients becoming available to plants, but there is no evidence that manure is superior to inorganic fertilizer (Tables 17.10 and 17.11). Further evidence is needed to evaluate any contribution due to organic matter present

TABLE1 17.9. **Effect of plowing manure under at different times after application on crop yield.**

	Relative Value in Increasing Crop Yields	
	Oats (15 experiments)	Potatoes (1 experiment)
Manure plowed under immediately	100	100
Manure plowed under 6 hours after spreading	79	86
Manure plowed under 24 hours after spreading	73	70
Manure plowed under 4 days after spreading ..	57	44

Source: Salter and Schollenberger (1939).

TABLE 17.10. Long-time yields with manure and fertilizer are comparable.

Place	Crop	Years	Manure	Fertilizer	None
			(bu/a)	(bu/a)	(bu/a)
Rothamstead, England	Wheat	>150	32	34	12.6
Ohio	Corn	> 75	58	56	32.0
Missouri	Wheat	> 50	19	20	10.0

or microorganisms carried and growth-promoting or growth-inhibiting effects possible. Embleton and Jones (1956) showed that yield of oranges was the same when 2 pounds of nitrogen were applied per tree as manure or as commercial fertilizer annually when the soil was tilled, but was lower with manure applications when the soil was not tilled. Manure was also an efficient source of phosphate and potash for the trees.

Excessive mineralization of animal waste in the soil may result in leaching of nitrate into the groundwater and runoff with N and P. Huge quantities of animal waste applied to the land may result in accumulation of some organic and inorganic constituents in concentrations that may become toxic to plants, particularly under anaerobic decomposition conditions (Megie et al., 1967). For example, corn seeds planted into manure will not germinate (Figure 17.2).

Gaseous products, such as CO_2, NH_3, NO_2, N_2O, and N_2, become a part of the soil air and may return to the atmosphere. Small amounts of organic acids and other odor-forming compounds are gaseous. When released in the soil, some (e.g., NH_3, NO_2, H_2S) may be sorbed, and others (e.g., organic acids) may be metabolized, lowering the volatilization.

The readily decomposable organic constituents will be rapidly utilized by microorganisms. Of the materials remaining, humuslike substances become a part of the humus complex of the soil (Dorr, 1965). The ultimate accumulation of organic constituents in the soil, however, will be only a small fraction of the total organic material applied to the land. Salter and Schollenberger (1939) indicated that the beneficial physical effects on the soil of adding manure are probably overestimated.

There is a considerable backlog of information on the applica-

TABLE 17.11. Corn yield of three varieties with manure and fertilizer on sandy clay loam.

Treatment ($N + P_2O_5 + K_2O$)	Variety		
	AES704	C103XB14	WF9XB14
(lb/a)		(bu/a)	
(1) 1240 + 730 + 1030	147	159	143
(2) 1270 + 750 + 600 + 66 T manure ..	143	168	144
(3) 800 + 515 + 600 + 66 T manure ..	141	154	144

Source: Unpublished data, D. G. Woolley and L. R. Frederick (1960).
Note: Nos. 1 and 3 have comparable amounts of N, P, K.

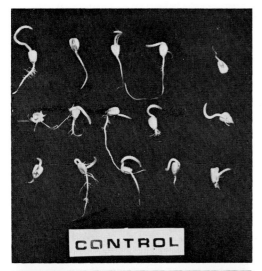

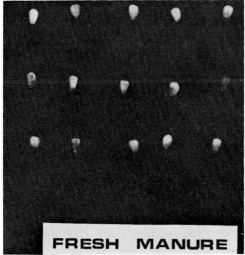

FIG. 17.2. The influence of manure on the germination of corn after 5-day incubation at 25° C. The control was planted in soil and the other seeds were planted in fresh manure.

tion of animal waste in small to moderate amounts to the land and its effect on crops and on the physical, chemical, and biological properties of the soil (Hastings, 1938; Salter and Schollenberger, 1939). But there are many unanswered questions in regard to the application of large amounts of animal waste to the land, such as the effect on crop growth and on the pollution of surface and groundwaters.

REFERENCES

Alexander, Martin. 1961. *Soil microbiology*. New York: John Wiley.
Atkinson, H. J., Giles, G. R., and Desjardins, J. G. 1954. Trace element content of farmyard manure. *Can. J. Agr. Sci.* 34:76–80.

Burnett, W. E., and Dondero, N. C. 1969. The microbiology and chemistry of poultry waste decomposition and associated odor generation. (Mimeo.) Presented Cornell Animal Waste Management Conf., Syracuse, N.Y., 13–15 Jan. 1969.

Burroughs, A. L. 1967. Viral respiratory infection in commercial feedlot cattle. *Am. J. Vet. Res.* 28:365–71.

Commoner, Barry. 1968. Threats to the integrity of the nitrogen cycle: nitrogen compounds in soil, water, atmosphere, and precipitation. (Mimeo.) Presented Ann. Meeting Am. Assoc. Advan. Sci., Dallas, Tex., 26 Dec. 1968.

Crampton, E. W., and Harris, L. E. 1969. *Applied animal nutrition.* 2nd ed. San Francisco: W. H. Freeman.

Dale, A. C., and Day, D. L. 1967. Some aerobic decomposition properties of dairy cattle manure. *Trans. Am. Soc. Agr. Engrs.* 10:546–48.

Dorr, R. 1965. The characterization of the organic substance in manures. II. Groups of organic manures and residues, and a proposed scheme of a simple analysis based on the oxidizable carbon. *Landwirtsch. Forsch.* 18:238–46. (#10096, Biol. Abstr., 1968)

Embleton, T. W., and Jones, W. W. 1956. Manure as a source of nitrogen. *Calif. Agr.* 10:14–15.

Geldreich, E. E., Bordner, R. H., Huff, C. B., Clark, H. F., and Kabler, P. W. 1962. Type distribution of coliform bacteria in the feces of warm-blooded animals. *J. Water Pollution Control Federation* 34:295–301.

Gilbertson, C. B., McCalla, T. M., Ellis, J. R., Cross, O. E., and Woods, W. R. 1970. Beef feedlot wastes: characteristics of runoff, solid wastes and nitrate movement on dirt feedlots as affected by animal density and feedlot slope. *J. Water Pollution Control Federation.* (Submitted.)

Hastings, Stephen H. 1938. Influence of farm manure on yields and sucrose of sugar beets. *USDA Tech. Bull.* 614.

Hemingway, R. G. 1961. The mineral composition of farmyard manure. *Empire J. Exptl. Agr.* 29:14–18.

Jansson, S. L. 1960a. On the properties of organic manures. I. Actual humus properties. *Uppsala Lantbrukhogskolans Ann.* 26:51–75.

———. 1960b. On the properties of organic manures. III. Potential humus properties. *Uppsala Lantbrukhogskolans Ann.* 26:135–72.

Jenkinson, D. S. 1965. Studies on the decomposition of plant material in soil. I. Losses of carbon from ^{14}C-labelled ryegrass incubated with soil in the field. *J. Soil Sci.* 16:104–15.

———. 1966. Studies on the decomposition of plant material in soil. II. Partial sterilization of soil and the soil biomass. *J. Soil Sci.* 17:280–302.

King, N. B. 1957. The survival of *Brucella abortus* in manure. *J. Am. Vet. Med. Assoc.* 131:349–52.

Klein, D. A., and Casida, L. E., Jr. 1967. *E. coli* die-out from normal soil as related to nutrient availability and the indigenous microflora. *Can. J. Microbiol.* 13:1461–70.

Lipper, R. I. 1969. Design for feedlot waste management—history and characteristics. Presented at seminar, Design for Feedlot Waste Management, Topeka, Kans., 23 Jan. 1969.

Loehr, Raymond C. 1968. *Pollution implications of animal wastes—*

a forward-oriented review. U.S. Dept. Interior, Fed. Water Pollution Control Admin., Robert S. Kerr Water Res. Center, Ada, Okla.

McCalla, T. M., and Haskins, F. A. 1964. Phytotoxic substances from soil microorganisms and crop residues. *Bacteriol. Rev.* 28:181–207.

McCalla, T. M., and Viets, F. G., Jr. 1970. *Chemical and microbial studies of wastes from beef cattle feedlots.* Nebr. Exp. Sta. Publ. (In press.)

McCalla, T. M., Ellis, J. R., Gilbertson, C. B., and Woods, W. R. 1969a. Chemical studies of runoff from rain and snowmelt from beef cattle feedlots. *Agron. Abstr.*, pp. 84–85.

McCalla, T. M., Ellis, J. R., and Woods, W. R. 1969b. Changes in the chemical and biological properties of beef cattle manure during decomposition. *Bacteriol. Proc.*, pp. 4–5.

McCoy, Elizabeth. 1967. Lagooning of liquid manure (bovine): bacteriological aspects. *Trans. Am. Soc. Agr. Engrs.* 10:784–85.

———. 1969. Removal of pollution bacteria from animal waste by soil percolation. (Mimeo.) Paper #69–430, presented at the Ann. Meeting of the Am. Soc. Agr. Engrs., Lafayette, Ind., 22–25 June 1969.

Megie, Christian A., Pearson, R. W., and Hiltbold, A. E. 1967. Toxicity of decomposing crop residues to cotton germination and seedling growth. *Agron. J.* 59:197–99.

Morrison, S. M., Grant, D. W., Nevins, M. P., and Elmund, K. 1969. Role of excreted antibiotic in modifying decomposition of feedlot waste. (Mimeo.) Paper presented at the Cornell Animal Waste Management Conf., Syracuse, N.Y., 13–15 Jan. 1969.

Perkins, H. F., Parker, M. B., and Walker, M. L. 1964. *Chicken manure—its production, composition, and use as a fertilizer.* Ga. Agr. Exp. Sta. Bull. N.S. 123.

Polheim, P. 1965. Characterization of the organic matter in manures. I. Classification of organic manures on the basis of solubility of organic substances and of nitrogen in organic bond. *Landwirtsch. Forsch.* 18:228–37. (#10099, Biol. Abstr., 1968)

Rothwell, D. F. 1955. The influence of temperature and nitrogen on the decomposition of plant materials mixed with soil. Ph.D. thesis. Purdue Univ. Library.

Salter, Robert M., and Schollenberger, C. J. 1939. *Farm manure.* Ohio Agr. Exp. Sta. Bull. 605.

Stewart, B. A., Viets, F. G., Jr., Hutchinson, G. L., Kemper, W. D., Clark, F. E., Fairbourn, M. L., and Strauch, F. 1967. Distribution of nitrates and other water pollutants under fields and corrals in the middle South Platte valley of Colorado. USDA, ARS 41–134.

Taiganides, E. P., and Hazen, T. E. 1966. Properties of farm animal excreta. *Trans. Am. Soc. Agr. Engrs.* 9:374–76.

Wadleigh, Cecil H. 1968. Wastes in relation to agriculture and forestry. USDA Misc. Publ. 1065.

Waksman, Selman A. 1938. *Humus.* 2nd ed. Baltimore: Williams and Wilkins.

Witzel, S. A., McCoy, E., Polkowski, L. B., Attoe, O. J., and Nichols, M. S. 1966. Physical, chemical and bacteriological properties of farm wastes (bovine animals). In *Proc. Symp. Management of Farm Animal Wastes*, pp. 10–14.

CHAPTER EIGHTEEN

MANURE TRANSFORMATIONS
AND FATE OF DECOMPOSITION
PRODUCTS IN WATER

ROSS E. McKINNEY

W̌HEN animal manure is mixed with water, the biochemical reactions are both rapid and predictable. The keys to the chemical transformations in aqueous suspension of manures lie in the chemical composition of the manures, the microbes present, the environmental conditions, and the time of exposure. It is important to understand each of these major variables and their interactions. Too cften engineers and scientists examine only a portion of the problem and fail to recognize the fundamental concepts that underlie all manure transformations in water.

CHEMICAL CHARACTERISTICS OF MANURES

The chemical characteristics of manure are primarily dependent upon the chemical characteristics of the feed processed through the animals. Only a small fraction of the feed eaten by any animal is processed into animal tissue. The feed is transformd internally into materials which can be either absorbed or passed through the animal. Waste products of metabolism are largely collected in the urine and are passed out of the animal along with the solid manure.

Not very much research has been carried out correlating the chemical characteristics of feed and the chemical characteristics of manure, yet a major part of the problem in evaluating the chemical characteristics of manure lies in knowledge of the chemical variations in feeds. With hogs, approximately 30% of the feed consumed is converted to animal tissue and 70% is excreted in the form of urine and manure (Irgens and Day, 1965). With cattle, the conversion rate is lower, approximately 10%. With a feed consumption of 5.0 lb/day for a 100-lb hog, the manure should contain 3.5 pounds of the feed along with the excess water, which will be approximately 1 gallon. This would indicate that hog wastes should contain 300,000

Ross E. McKINNEY is Professor, Department of Civil Engineering, University of Kansas.

mg/l total solids. Generally, additional wasted water results in lower values of solids than indicated. It is important that complete material balances be made to determine the fate of all materials fed to the animal. It may well be that attention to the complete animal system could result in more efficient feeds and lower manure productions.

Interest in animal manure pollution problems has stimulated interest in chemical analysis of manures with respect to water pollution parameters. A recent study on hog manure (Schmid and Lipper, 1969) indicated that the volume of urine and manure should be approximately 0.9 gal/day/100 lb live weight for hogs in confinement fed a sorghum-grain-soybean meal ration. The COD of the manure was 0.52 lb/day/100 lb live weight, while the BOD_u was 0.20 lb/day/100 lb live weight. A review of published data (McKinney and Bella, 1968) indicated an ultimate BOD of 0.50 lb/day/100 lb live weight. There is no doubt that variation in feed composition is a significant factor in the variation in manure characteristics.

Beef cattle manure collected at the University of Wisconsin (Witzel et al., 1966) yielded 1.0 lb BOD_5/day/1,000 lb live weight and 3.3 lb COD/day/1,000 lb live weight. Since cattle tend to be fed more varied rations than hogs, the chemical characteristics of the manure will also be more varied.

MICROORGANISMS

Manure contains a tremendous population of microorganisms. Unfortunately there have been few studies to delineate the various types of microorganisms in manure. Beef cattle being rumen organisms have a more complex microbial flora than hogs. One of the few studies (McCoy, 1967) on beef cattle manure indicated a wide variety of bacteria related to the feed consumed by the cattle. As expected there were proteolytic microorganisms, lactic acid producers, as well as cellulose and pectin fermenters. The presence of methane-producing bacteria has been well established in cattle manure. Special microbial techniques are required to enumerate the rumen bacteria due to the anaerobic environment in the rumen and the varied metabolic characteristics of these microorganisms.

It suffices to say that the microbial population in animal manure is more than adequate to bring about the chemical transformations which will occur when the manure is mixed with water.

ENVIRONMENTAL CONDITIONS

Anaerobic Environment

When manure is mixed with water, microbial activity is very rapid. The oxygen is removed so quickly that it has no significant effect on the anaerobic bacteria which were growing in the manure prior to its discharge from the animal. The complex organics are hydrolyzed further to yield organic acids from proteins and cellulose.

The ammonia released from the protein helps prevent the pH from dropping too rapidly. But as the cellulose is decomposed, the pH can drop sharply, causing the environment to retard further bacterial action. As the pH drops below 5.5, microbial activity slows and only the acid-forming bacteria continue metabolism. Eventually the acid buildup will cause all microbial activity to cease. The acidified manure will remain stable until the acids are either removed or neutralized. If the acidified manure is agitated, numerous odorous compounds will be discharged from the liquid phase.

If the pH of the manure does not drop below 6.0, the methane bacteria will metabolize the organic acids, producing a satisfactory environment for further metabolism. The ammonia released from protein metabolism reacts with carbon dioxide to form ammonium bicarbonate, which acts as a buffer to hold the pH at a favorable level. Under these conditions the acid-forming bacteria continue to metabolize the complex organics, forming organic acids which are immediately neutralized by the ammonium bicarbonates. The neutralized acids are metabolized by the methane bacteria to reform the ammonium bicarbonate buffer. The nonbiodegradable organics remain untouched.

The extent of degradation of organic matter by the acid-producing bacteria and the methane bacteria depends largely upon the time of contact and the extent of mixing. These two environmental factors are very important in determining the extent of metabolism. There is no simple formula for determining the time of contact for metabolism to be carried to completion. It suffices to say that the more microbes present, the higher the temperature, and the better the mixing, the shorter will be the time for metabolism. There are basic limits to this concept. The amount of organic food present will limit the maximum microbial population which can be maintained. Temperatures above 37° C will become toxic to the mesophilic bacteria and will require the development of thermophilic bacteria if metabolism is to continue. Generally it is not possible to obtain too much mixing but it should be recognized that little additional benefit can be derived from mixing above the optimum level.

One of the most critical environmental factors affecting anaerobic metabolism has been shown to be toxicity related to soluble cations (McCarty and McKinney, 1961). It was demonstrated that ammonium ions were toxic to the methane bacteria in anaerobic digestion systems. Since animal urine contains considerable amounts of urea which is readily hydrolyzed to form ammonium ions, ammonium ion toxicity should be an important factor in the complete anaerobic metabolism of concentrated manures. This fact has been confirmed recently (Schmid and Lipper, 1969) in studies on controlled anaerobic digestion of hog manure.

It should be recognized that the acid-forming bacteria merely hydrolyze the biodegradable components of the organic manures. There is no change in the COD or the BOD of the wastes. If the manure contains large quantities of inert, nonbiodegradable materials, there will be little apparent change. BOD and COD reductions occur when the methane bacteria convert the soluble organics to methane, an insoluble gas that is discharged to the atmosphere above the liquid. If the methane were not lost from the liquid phase, there would be no decrease in COD or BOD of the system, only transformation of the biodegradable organics from one form to another form.

If the water diluting the manure contains nitrates or sulfates, the bacteria will reduce the nitrates to nitrogen gas while oxidizing the organic matter or will reduce the sulfates to sulfides. Nitrogen gas does not create a BOD or COD and would result in stabilization of the organic matter. On the other hand, the hydrogen sulfide would exert an oxygen demand unless it was lost to the atmosphere. It should be recognized from an energy standpoint that microbes will reduce nitrates completely before reducing sulfates (McKinney and Conway, 1957). Both nitrates and sulfates will be reduced before methane will be formed. This relationship is very important in understanding anaerobic transformations.

Aerobic Environments

In an aerobic environment free dissolved oxygen is present for the microbial reactions. Initially the organic matter is oxidized to carbon dioxide, water, and ammonia. The oxidation reaction results in energy transfer from the manure to the microbial cells. The microbes use this energy to synthesize new microbial protoplasm. Aerobic metabolism results in approximately one-third of the organic matter metabolized being oxidized and two-thirds of the organic matter being converted to cellular protoplasm.

With true aerobic conditions the bacteria growth stimulates the growth of protozoa. Like the bacteria, the protozoa oxidize a definite amount of organic matter while converting a portion of the organic matter to new protozoan cells. The protozoa use bacteria as their source of food, thereby reducing the total amount of bacteria in the liquid.

As long as dissolved oxygen remains in the liquid the bacteria will metabolize all of the biodegradable organics contained in the manure. The metabolism of the protein components produces ammonium bicarbonate which holds the pH at the proper level, between 6.5 and 8.5, for good bacterial growth. If sufficient time is allowed, nitrifying bacteria will grow and oxidize the ammonium ions to nitrites and then to nitrates. Since this reaction results in the conversion of a base to an acid, there will be a definite pH drop. The degree of pH drop depends primarily upon the amount of buffer present that is not related to ammonium ions. If oxygen should become limiting after nitrification has occurred, denitrification will result. The bacteria metabolizing the organic manure will use nitrates almost as readily as oxygen and will reduce the nitrogen gas. Denitrification is as odorless as aerobic metabolism since metabolism is complete.

One of the major problems in aerobic metabolism of animal manure is supplying sufficient oxygen to maintain the aqueous system aerobic. This can be done only with dilute aqueous suspensions of manure. Failure to maintain aqueous manure systems aerobic has caused numerous problems in trying to arrive at satisfactory aerobic treatment systems. Dilution can be carried out by the addition of fresh water or by the use of treated effluent.

The aqueous suspension of manure after aerobic metabolism will contain the bacteria produced from the metabolic reactions as well as the inorganic salts in the urine and in the manure and the nonbiodegradable organics, both suspended and dissolved. The bacteria will undergo endogenous metabolism with time until only an inert residual of dead cells will remain. The inert residual of dead cellular solids will contain about one-fifth of the volatile solids in the original microbial mass produced and all of the inorganic solids in the original microbial mass. Thus it is that neither aerobic nor anaerobic metabolism will result in complete degradation of manure in aqueous systems. Yet, microbial transformations can convert unstable manure which is difficult to handle into a fluid material which is easy to handle and contains all of the elements in the original manure. This permits easier spreading of treated manures onto fields without the creation of obnoxious odors and nuisance conditions.

AQUEOUS TREATMENT SYSTEMS

There is no doubt that mixing animal manures with water will result in serious environmental pollution problems as a result of uncontrolled microbial reactions which will be predominantly anaerobic. For this reason it is necessary to develop systems which employ controlled microbial reactions in order to transform the manure into a form where it can be returned into the environment without creating a serious pollution problem. A number of aqueous treatment systems have been developed and studied to date.

Oxidation Ponds

The simplest form of liquid treatment for animal manures is the oxidation pond. In all respects, oxidation ponds have not proved successful for animal wastes. Oxidation ponds have tended to produce obnoxious odors and poor quality effluents (Clark, 1965; Hart and Turner, 1965).

Fundamentally, there is no reason why oxidation ponds could not be used to treat animal manures satisfactorily. The problem lies in use of inadequate dilution of the concentrated manures. Generally, animal manure lagoons are designed to operate on minimum water volumes in order to eliminate any effluent. The net result is that concentrated manure is discharged at a single point in the oxidation pond. The heavy manure solids tend to settle out around the inlet, creating an anaerobic environment at a single point. The building up of solids results in an acid environment due to anaerobic metabolism and failure to distribute the acids into the liquid so that methane fermentation can occur. Anaerobic metabolism also results in carbon dioxide formation. The carbon dioxide is released as a gas as acids build up and depress the pH. The carbon dioxide gas causes solids to rise to the surface and permits odorous compounds to be released into the environment.

The important concept to recognize in the use of oxidation ponds is dispersion of the organic matter throughout the pond liquid. It must be recognized that simple oxidation ponds cannot be used for animal manures. There is no way for the manure to be dispersed in a simple pond system. It is possible to use a large pump to dilute the manure prior to its addition to the oxidation pond. The treated effluent could be used to flush the manure from the animal house. Unfortunately, the quantity of liquid which would have to be recycled is quite large, around 200 gallons per day per hog or 1,000 gallons per day per steer.

It is essential that there is adequate volume in the oxidation pond for good metabolism. A 4-foot deep oxidation pond can handle around 40 lb BOD_5/acre/day. This would require 1 acre of oxidation pond for 200 hogs or 40 steers. For either confined hog growing or cattle feedlots, the use of oxidation ponds requires far too much land area. A 50-sow farrowing house would require 0.3 acres of oxidation ponds to treat the wastes, provided there was good mixing. Larger installations create even greater problems due to mixing.

Aerated Lagoons

Mechanical aerators have been added to oxidation ponds in an effort to produce better mixing and to add additional oxygen. In an effort to reduce power costs to a minimum, the mechanical aerators are generally undersized for the pond volume. Best results are obtained when mixing relationships are balanced against oxygen transfer characteristics. Some research (McKinney and Benjes, 1965) indicated that a mechanical surface aerator was capable of transferring 1.5 pounds of oxygen per HP-hr with a residual DO of 1.0 mg/l and that $\frac{1}{4}$ HP was required to reproduce good mixing in 1,000 cu ft of pond volume. This meant that a 5-HP surface aerator could transfer 7.5 pounds of oxygen per hour and mix 20,000 cu ft of wastes. The 5-HP surface aerator could treat the wastes from 225 hogs or 45 head of cattle. The very long detention time, over 50 days, would result in a high degree of stabilization of the BOD but would still produce a large mass of solids for disposal.

Oxidation Ditch

One of the most effective forms of the aerated lagoon concept has been the use of the oxidation ditch under a slotted floor. Mechanical rotor aerators circulate the wastes under the slotted floor and aerate the mixture. The aerobic environment results in stabilization of the manure in an odor-free environment. Although the concept of the oxidation ditch was originally tried in Europe, the first successful field scale unit for treating animal wastes in the United States was put into operation at the Paul Smart hog farm near Lawrence, Kansas, in January 1966. The results obtained from the study of several units (McKinney and Bella, 1968) indicated that mechanical rotor aerators were capable of treating the wastes from up to 275 hogs with a 5-HP unit. This would mean that the same unit could treat the wastes from 55 head of cattle.

Foaming has been a serious problem in starting oxidation ditches as well as in improperly loaded units. A number of investigators (Sheltinga, 1966; Moore et al., 1969) have reported foaming problems. Aside from start-up, foaming occurs only when the unit is overloaded. Maintenance of proper aerobic conditions with adequate mixing eliminates foaming due to the manure. Excessive use of detergents or disinfectants could result in foaming but this would occur only under abnormal conditions. Foaming should never be a problem in a well-operated treatment unit.

The oxidation ditch system is capable of metabolizing all of the biodegradable components of the manure but normally will contain a large quantity of living microbial cells which would exert a high oxygen demand, around 1,000 mg/BOD_5. These microbial cells can be further treated by oxidation ponds or mixing with soil. Further aeration alone will also result in their stabilization.

Anaerobic Lagoons

Recently it has been shown that properly designed anaerobic lagoons can be used for pretreatment of manure. Field units for hogs (Curtis, 1966; Willrich, 1966) indicated 100 cu ft of anaerobic lagoon per 100-lb hog. By and large the anaerobic lagoons were merely large sludge-holding ponds. Periodically solids were removed and placed on the land. An anaerobic lagoon for dairy cattle (Loehr and Ruf, 1968) operated at 9 lb BOD_5/day/1,000 cu ft. Cattle-waste anaerobic lagoons have been operated at higher organic loadings than hog-waste lagoons as a result of the nature of the wastes. Cattle wastes generally have a higher population of methane bacteria and a better buffering capacity. This generally permits cattle-waste lagoons to operate more efficiently. The problem with efficient operation of anaerobic lagoons lies in adequate mixing. Gas production by the methane bacteria alone will not produce the desired degree of mixing as heavy organic loads and untreated solids will accumulate in the anaerobic lagoon. It should be recognized that anaerobic treatment of cattle manure will result in only 20% total solids reduction. While the lagoon system will remove 80 to 85% of the solids, the accumulated solids must be removed eventually.

Concentration of solids to 10% would require approximately one-half cu ft per day per head of cattle for sludge storage alone. It is important that sludge storage be provided for a period of 6 months to a year to reduce the time intervals for sludge removal. In effect, sludge storage capacity should equal the active anaerobic lagoon capacity for beef cattle.

EVALUATION OF AQUEOUS TREATMENT SYSTEMS

With regard to aqueous treatment systems for animal manure, it is apparent that aqueous treatment systems are not desirable for animal wastes except in special situations. The concentrated animal wastes are not normally mixed with water and can be handled best as solid wastes. This is especially true of cattle manure.

The advent of confined animal growing has posed some changes in the philosophy of handling manure as a solid waste. Chicken houses have been designed to collect manure as a solid on moving belts and to transport it from the source to a point of concentration. On the other hand, confined hog houses have too much fluid manure for handling as solids. The oxidation ditch has proved a satisfactory system for both collection and treatment of hog manure; it is designed to replace conventional collection and disposal methods. It should be recognized that the treated hog manure must be returned to the soil the same as untreated manure. The soil is the ultimate acceptor of all animal wastes. It is vital that this concept be acknowledged and accepted as one of the basic factors in manure disposal.

Studies are currently underway to demonstrate the use of the oxidation ditch for handling cattle manure from animals grown in confinement like hogs. There is no reason why it should not work.

Regardless of the treatment system used, the biological treatment will reduce only a small fraction of the total solids of the manure. The residual solids and the soluble salts pose a major disposal problem that must be considered as part of the total manure disposal problem. Fortunately, biological treatment of the manure destroys the obnoxious qualities and results in a material which can be handled relatively easily without the creation of sanitary problems.

REFERENCES

Clark, C. E. 1965. Hog waste disposal by lagooning. *J. Sanit. Eng. Div. Am. Soc. Civil Engrs.* 91 (SA6): 27–41

Curtis, D. R. 1966. Design criteria for anaerobic lagoons for swine manure disposal. In *Management of farm animal wastes.* Am. Soc. Agr. Engrs. Publ. SP-0366, pp. 75–80.

Hart, S. A., and Turner, M. E. 1965. Lagoons for livestock manure. *J. Water Pollution Control Federation* 37:1578–96.

Irgens, R. L., and Day, D. L. 1965. Laboratory studies of aerobic stabilization of swine wastes. *Farm structures eng. rept.* Univ. of Ill. Agr. Exp. Sta.

Loehr, R. C., and Ruf, J. A. 1968. Anaerobic lagoon treatment of milking-parlor wastes. *J. Water Pollution Control Federation* 40:83–94.

McCarty, P. L., and McKinney, R. E. 1961. Salt toxicity in anaerobic digestion. *J. Water Pollution Control Federation* 33:399–415.

McCoy, E. 1967. Lagooning of liquid manure (bovine): bacteriological aspects. *Trans. Am. Soc. Agr. Engrs.* 10:784–85.

McKinney, R. E., and Bella, R. 1968. *Water quality changes in con-*

fined *hog waste treatment.* Kans. Water Resources Res. Inst. Rept. Univ. of Kans.

McKinney, R. E., and Benjes, H. H., Jr. 1965. Evaluation of two aerated lagoons. *J. Sanit. Eng. Div. Am. Soc. Civil Engrs.* 91 (SA6): 43–55.

McKinney, R. E., and Conway, R. A. 1957. Chemical oxygen in biological waste treatment. *Sewage Ind. Wastes* 29:1097–1106.

Moore, J. A., Larson, R. E., and Allred, E. R. 1969. Study of the use of oxidation ditch to stabilize beef animal manure in cold climates. In *Animal waste management,* pp. 172–77. Cornell Univ.

Scheltinga, H. M. 1966. Biological treatment of animal wastes. In *Management of farm animal wastes.* Am. Soc. Agr. Engrs. Publ. SP-0366, pp. 140–43.

Schmid, L. A., and Lipper, R. I. 1969. Swine waste characterization and anaerobic digestion. In *Animal waste management,* pp. 50–57. Cornell Univ.

Willrich, T. L. 1966. Primary treatment of swine wastes by lagooning. In *Management of farm animal wastes.* Am. Soc. Agr. Engrs. Publ. SP-0366, pp. 70–74.

Witzel, S. A., McCoy, E., Polkowski, L. B., Attoe, O. J., and Nichols, M. S. 1966. Physical, chemical and bacteriological properties of farm wastes (bovine animals). In *Management of farm animal wastes.* Am. Soc. Agr. Engrs. Publ. SP-0366, pp. 10–14.

CHAPTER NINETEEN

DISEASE TRANSMISSION
OF WATER-BORNE ORGANISMS
OF ANIMAL ORIGIN

STANLEY L. DIESCH

CENTURIES prior to the era of bacteriology, man realized that water was somehow involved in the transmission of disease.

Before consideration of current problems of disease transmission related to water, the historical implication of water and disease will be briefly reviewed. The early miasmatic theory of disease taught that all disease was due to emanations from water, earth, and influence of the stars, moon, winds, and seasons. More than 2,500 years ago during the pre-Christian era, the role of water was further described by Hippocrates, the "father of medicine," in his treatise, "Airs, Waters and Places" (Chadwick and Mann, 1950). He related causes of disease to different waters, the wind, and to the slope of the land. These findings were further advanced during the early Christian period and the Middle Ages. During this time epidemics of certain diseases such as typhoid and cholera were associated with floods and the rise and fall in the level of groundwater. The theory of poisonous miasmata and vapors (arising from decaying filth) held until the end of the nineteenth century. Some early observations were inadequate and unsound, but others represented correct observations of fact.

During the nineteenth century, researchers, including Henle, Snow, Budd, and Pasteur, developed the germ theory of disease. In 1876 Robert Koch proved the germ theory by his classical work on anthrax. Historical aspects of bacteriology are well described in a book by Bulloch (1938). The golden era of bacteriology has existed and developed for nearly 100 years. Major emphasis has been on the importance of the microbiologic agent in causation of communicable diseases.

Recognition that predisposing or contributing factors of disease must be identified, and multiple causes of disease ex'st, has broadened man's efforts to consider the total perspective of disease—the interrelationship of the agent, host, and environment complex.

STANLEY L. DIESCH is Associate Professor, Department of Veterinary Microbiology and Public Health, University of Minnesota.

CONCEPTS OF DISEASE TRANSMISSION

Knowledge of epidemiology as related to disease transmission is essential. Epidemiology is the study of disease as related to the host, agent, and total environment—or the ecology of disease.

Of the many infectious diseases affecting animals, more than 150 are classified as zoonoses, or those infections or infectious diseases transmitted under natural conditions between vertebrate animals and man (WHO, 1967b). Zoonoses associated with food-producing animals are usually considered occupational. An increasing number of zoonotic diseases associated with recreational activities are being reported.

The infectious disease process contains six necessary factors. These factors are considered as links in a chain and all are essential in disease development. The six essential factors are as follows:

1. Causative or etiological agent

    Infection represents entry and development or multiplication of an infectious agent in the body of man or animal. The parasitic agent usually lives at the expense or detriment of the host. Fortunately, many organisms are not pathogenic for man and animals. Certain organisms have specificity and will infect only a selected species. For example, hog cholera virus will not infect man or other animals.

2. Reservoir of the infectious agent

    Reservoirs are man, animals, plants, soil, or inanimate organic matter. Here an infectious agent lives and multiplies. With few exceptions, pathogens are not capable of prolonged growth or multiplication outside the living body. Significance of the animal reservoir depends upon man's direct or indirect association. Man has much greater direct exposure to domestic animals than wild animals. Animals and man are potentially and indirectly associated with animal pathogens through waters. Man remains the most significant reservoir of infection for his species, and animals for their kind.

3. Escape of organisms from the reservoir

    Escape and subsequent discharge of the organism into the environment may occur through natural body openings (respiratory, intestinal, urinary), by way of open lesions, and by mechanical means (blood-sucking arthropods). A variation exists in time duration of escape of pathogens. This is dependent on the course of disease in the host animal. In general the duration of communicability of an infectious agent varies inversely with the degree of communicability.

4. Transmission of the infection from the reservoir to the new host

    Transmission occurs by direct and indirect methods. Direct contact occurs when organisms pass immediately to the new host by physical contact. Indirect contact occurs when there is a transfer of infectious agents between the reservoir and the new host without direct association. These organisms must be capable of surviving outside the body and a vehicle or vector must transfer the organisms. The classification of indirect methods of transmission are vectors (arthropods or other invertebrates) and vehicles (all nonliving objects or substances that are contaminated and transfer the infectious organisms). Vehicles include water, milk, other foods, air, and fomites.

5. Entry of organisms into new hosts

Before entry, the organisms must pass defensive barriers of the host. With exceptions, the mode of entry into man or animal corresponds with the mode of exit.

6. Susceptible host

Man and animals possess defense mechanisms or resistance, which protect against invasion of the pathogenic microorganisms. Immunity implies the development of absolute protection in a susceptible host against disease by artificial or natural means.

Development of a disease in man or animal depends on completion of several concurrent events and includes the strength of the six essential links of the chain.

The following important factors concern the susceptible host. *Age* usually increases resistance, for the longer man or animal lives, the greater is the opportunity for contact with specific microorganisms and for development of immunity. *Incidence of disease in a community* is significant, for greater occurrence of disease increases opportunities for exposure. *Opportunities for spread* include biological, social, and physical factors. Environmental factors such as water supply, sanitation, housing, and crowding are involved.

The occurrence of disease in populations has been inadequately reported. Cases (with clinical signs or symptoms) may be reported but many infected carrier (subclinical or inapparent) animals may exist in a population. Because the carriers are often not recognized, they are more capable of transmitting disease to populations. The case-carrier concept may be viewed as a floating iceberg, with a small fraction of the ice observed (cases) and the remainder under water inapparent (carriers). This phenomenon varies with each disease entity.

If a disease outbreak is manifest in a population, the outbreak exists until there is a death, disablement, recovery, and/or development of resistance against the specific disease. Infected animals may shed millions of organisms into the environment, and these organisms may find a susceptible host. Errington (1963) has stated, "Nature's way is any way that works."

To prevent, control, and eradicate animal disease, treatment with antibiotics and chemotherapeutics, and prevention by use of vaccines and bacterins, have been developed. Quarantine, test, and slaughter programs of identified infected animals have been used.

THE CHANGING ENVIRONMENT OF ANIMALS AND MAN

A few decades ago a predominantly rural America existed with wide dissemination of livestock populations. The raising of livestock and rural living remain predominant in many areas of the world. Today, fewer farms have greater concentrations of livestock. In the United States in 1937, 24.3% of 128,649,000 people lived on farms containing 94,694,000 animal units. In 1967, 5.4% of 198,608,000 people lived on farms containing 120,439,000 animal units. In three decades there has been a 21.3% increase in animal units, with a 65% decrease in human farm population and a 35% increase in total population (USDA, 1968b).

An increasing number of animals are raised in confinement. In the United States on January 1, 1969, there were 23,040,000 cattle on feed in lots. Of these, 10,823,000 were found on 2,080 lots, each with 1,000 or more head of cattle (USDA, 1969). It is not uncommon to find feedlots of 10,000 cattle or broiler farms of 100,000. This concentration can greatly enhance disease-prevention programs, but may by increased contact cause greater problems in disease transmission.

The environment of the agricultural worker allows greater exposure to infectious and parasitic diseases than is encountered in urban surroundings (WHO, 1962).

As man migrated from the farms to the cities, controlled sewage disposal and chlorination of water supplies have reduced the incidence of illnesses such as typhoid fever, paratyphoid, dysenteries, and cholera. Perhaps man, as a result of control of specific waterborne diseases, has developed a placid attitude concerning water-associated disease.

Living in the city, man has increasingly been seeking his outdoor recreational activities in rural areas. Most people seeking outdoor recreation wish to be near water. Swimming will be the most common form of outdoor recreation by the year 2000 (U.S. Outdoor Recreation Res. Rev. Comm., 1962). Being exposed to the environment of domestic and wild animals and surface waters will increase man's exposure to waterborne infections.

Water is absolutely essential to maintain the bodies of both man and animal. In the United States much of man's water supply for household use is from deep wells or chlorinated, treated supplies. Man continues to be exposed to surface water through occupational and increasing recreational activities. Confined animals receive much of their water from deep wells, but those on ranges in pasture largely consume water from ponds, streams, rivers, and lakes. Economics of agriculture demands the fullest utilization of land. Often land adjacent to surface water can be used only for pasturing of livestock. Millions of food-producing and wild animals are found here. If infected, pathogens escape into surface waters via respiratory discharges, drainage of wounds, feces or urine, or dead animals. Transmission of organisms from reservoir to water also occurs by soil runoff, flooding, wind, and other ways. Due to the dilution, pathogens discharged into water may be of relatively low densities. The general concept that running water undergoes purification is counteracted by the fact that infected animals may shed millions of pathogens for days, weeks, or months.

TRANSMISSION OF DISEASE

In consideration of agriculture's role in maintaining clean water, concern is for the *cause* and *effect* or the *effect* and *cause* relationship of waters contaminated with pathogenic organisms. When total ecology of disease is studied, complexity is greatly increased and by definition decreased by the numerous interrelated factors involved. To document water's role as a vehicle in disease transmission, information gathered from a literature review will be used. Specific disease entities are grouped by classification based on etiology of the causative organism.

In view of the scope of this subject it will be impossible to discuss all diseases individually. No reference will be made to prevention, control, and treatment. This information is available in literature cited. Specific examples in each category are briefly described, with emphasis on resistance and transmission of the agent.

INFECTIOUS DISEASES OF ANIMALS AND MAN

Bacterial Diseases

Species of vegetative bacteria vary greatly in their ability to survive away from the host. Spore forms are very resistant to physical and chemical agents whose action can greatly affect the growth rate and death (Merchant and Packer, 1967).

In 1854 water first assumed an important role in the transmission of disease when John Snow was able to demonstrate the relationship between human cholera and water from the Broadstreet pump in London. Since the development of the bacteriologic era, numerous documentations of water transmission of disease have been made.

SALMONELLOSIS

In the United States the major zoonotic disease is salmonellosis. Approximately 20,000 human cases are reported each year, but estimates are that between 1 to 2 million cases occur (Steele, 1968). The disease is widespread in food-producing animals, poultry, and other animals (Edwards and Galton, 1967). These are the major reservoirs for man. In acute cases in calves, 10,000,000 organisms per gram of feces have been reported.[1]

Salmonella survive in water and the environment for extended periods of time (Kraus and Weber, 1958; Andre et al., 1967; Gibson, 1967). The bacteria could survive several weeks to 3 months in drinking water and natural surface water (Kraus and Weber, 1958). Hibbs and Foltz in 1964 isolated *Salmonella* from two calves, creek water, and a human being. Schaal (1963) reported enzootic salmonel-

---

1. K. L. Loken, 1967, personal communication.

losis in cattle as a result of drinking contaminated brook water. In May 1965 a serious epidemic of waterborne *Salmonella typhimurium* occurred, with three human deaths (NCDC, 1965). Of the human cases reported each year, more than half are sporadic. The remainder are associated with epidemics that can usually be traced to contaminated foods of animal origin or to water (McCroan et al., 1963; Steele, 1968).

More than 1,300 serotypes of *Salmonella* have been identified. These bacteria are ubiquitous and shed in the feces of infected animals. Surface waters serve as potential vehicles for transmission of *Salmonella* to other animals or man.

In 1966 a large waterborne outbreak of human cases occurred at Riverside, California, from a *Salmonella*-contaminated water supply. Although the source of contamination was not identified, it was speculated the water may have been contaminated by seepage from distant cattle feedlots (Decker and Steele, 1966). Due to the widespread occurrence of reservoirs and environmental contamination, salmonellosis continues to be a major disease entity.

LEPTOSPIROSIS

Leptospirosis, caused by a spirochete, has been classified as a waterborne zoonosis. In the United States and many areas of the world, leptospirosis is found in domestic animals and wildlife. In domestic animals the bacteria are found primarily in cattle and swine and may be shed in the urine for several months. Counts of 100 million leptospires per ml of urine have been reported (Gillespie and Ryno, 1963).

Leptospires may live in water for several weeks (Chang et al., 1948; Gillespie and Ryno, 1963; Ryu and Liu, 1966). However, the changing environment may complicate survival (Diesch et al., 1969). Fresh water in all forms in nature is a major factor in the circulation of leptospires in enzootic foci. The conventional idea that stagnant waters and slow-moving streams are potentially infectious is not necessarily valid. The infectiousness of rapid-flow water in the jungle and increased infectiousness with flooding has been shown (WHO, 1967a). Leptospires have been isolated from fast-moving streams (Gillespie and Ryno, 1963).

Human outbreaks have occurred when people have come in contact with contaminated water through swimming or occupational exposure. In the United States since 1941 approximately 1,000 human cases have been reported. Swimming has accounted for 10 outbreaks that involved 233 human cases.[2] In 1964 *Leptospira pomona* was isolated from the swimming site in a creek where human cases occurred in 1959 and 1964 following swimming. Cattle and other animals frequented this stream (Diesch and McCulloch, 1966). Sixty-one human cases occurred in Washington following swimming in water contaminated by infected cattle (NCDC, 1965a).

Between 1951 and 1960 the estimated annual loss to the dairy and milk industry was more than $12 million per year (USDA, 1965). In 1969 the Leptospirosis Committee of the United States Animal

2. W. F. McCulloch, 1969, personal communication.

Health Association stated that leptospirosis is not amenable to eradication. It is likely that water will continue to serve as a vehicle of transmission of leptospirosis to animals and man and remain one of the major sporadic diseases associated with water transmission.

ANTHRAX

In addition to being one of the oldest known diseases affecting man and animals, anthrax was the first zoonotic disease associated with an etiologic agent.

Anthrax spores are one of the most resistant of pathogenic bacteria. Spores stored in soil contained in a rubber-stoppered bottle remained viable for 60 years (Wilson and Russell, 1964). Field observations indicate similar duration of viability in alkaline, undrained soils in warm climates (Blood and Henderson, 1968). There have been instances of animals becoming infected on anthrax areas 25 years after the original cases of disease (Merchant and Packer, 1961).

A major mode of dissemination of spores is by surface waters flooding contaminated ground, causing transfer of spores to widespread areas. Many water courses in anthrax districts in the United States are contaminated (Stein, 1942; Jones, 1963).

Reported human cases of anthrax have declined steadily during the past 50 years (Brackman, 1964). Most of the human cases reported in the United States in recent years have been associated with imported goat hair and coarse wool. Estimates indicate that a decade ago the worldwide yearly incidence was 20,000 to 100,000 cases (Glassman, 1958).

Animals are most commonly infected by ingestion of contaminated food and water. Potential infection will exist for many years, especially in the contaminated anthrax districts where surface water plays a major role in transmission.

TULAREMIA

Tularemia is a widespread, highly contagious disease that has been isolated from more than 100 kinds of wild and domestic animals (Steele, 1968). In U.S. agricultural animals, the disease is reported most commonly in sheep. The bacteria do not form spores. Researchers reported water and mud contamination and the occurrence of tularemia in beaver and muskrat as widespread phenomena in northwestern United States. The tularemia organism has been found in all streams tested with any frequency in the Bitter Root Valley (Hamilton area) of Montana (Parker et al., 1951).

The organisms are believed to be able to multiply in the mud, leaf mold, and materials that make up the beds and shores of the streams. The aerobic organism is recoverable from running waters only, and never found in still or stagnant streams. During a 7-year period in one stream, *Francisella tularensis* has been recovered from approximately 30% of the specimens tested.[3]

---

3. Cora R. Owen, 1969, personal communication.

Tularemia can be transmitted by many different routes (Shaughnessy, 1963). There is evidence that the bacteria will penetrate the intact skin (Quan et al., 1956).

Four clinical and four probable human cases were associated with contaminated water (Jellison et al., 1950). Two of the cases were associated with contaminated water supply (spring water); the bacteria of tularemia were isolated from water collected from the faucet. In another report (Jellison et al., 1942) contamination of four streams was found. One stream remained contaminated for 33 days after any beavers were known to be present. Since contamination of water may persist for months and perhaps for years, drinking of water from streams in endemic regions should be avoided. During a tularemia epidemic that occurred in Vermont, 47 human cases were linked to contact with muskrats; the tularemia organism was isolated from the mud and water of a trapping site (Young et al., 1969). This was North America's largest outbreak of tularemia in man linked to aquatic mammals. Since the disease is established in wildlife populations it does not presently appear amenable to control.

BRUCELLOSIS

Brucellosis is a contagious disease of cattle, swine, and goats and a major occupational disease of man.

The bacteria are shed in the excretions and secretions, especially uterine, of infected animals. In pastures and barnyards, brucellae have survived 65 to 182 days or more in dead fetuses and fetal membranes, and 2 months in manure (Bosworth, 1934). In tap water the organism remains viable 10 to 120 days at 25° C and in bovine urine up to 4 days (Van Der Hoeden, 1964). Brucellae survived in grass for 100 days in winter and 30 days in summer. It survived freezing temperature over 824 days in cattle urine, lake water, tap water, raw milk, bovine feces, and soil (Ogarkov, 1962). In the United States, 1975 is the target date for the eradication of brucellosis. According to Harris (1950), water, except when grossly contaminated with brucella organisms, seems to be an unlikely source of human infection.

ERYSIPELAS

Erysipelas is of major importance and widely distributed, causing swine erysipelas and affecting turkeys. The bacteria occasionally cause erysipeloid in man.

The organism is resistant to drying and remains viable a month or more in the dark and 10 to 12 days in sunlight (Morse, 1963). It exists in soil as a saprophyte and retains virulence. Persistence in soil is variable and determined by temperature, pH, and other factors. It is reported viable 4 to 5 days in drinking water and 12 to 14 days in sewage (Reed, 1965). Soil, food, and water are readily contaminated by infected animals through large numbers being discharged in the urine. From soil experimentally inoculated, the organisms were recovered to a maximum of 21 days. Persistence was longer during winter and spring (Rowsell, 1958). Surface waters may transmit the disease from one farm to another (Karlson, 1967a). Since the bacteria can pass through the stomach without loss of viability, carrier animals may continuously contaminate the soil (Rowsell, 1958).

TUBERCULOSIS

Although in the United States bovine tuberculosis is no longer of major importance, the disease is still of major importance in some areas of the world.

The bacteria are resistant to chemical and physical agents (Middlebrook, 1965). In some instances virulent bovine tubercle bacilli can survive 6 months exposure in soil, in soil-dung mixture, and in dung (Maddock, 1933). It is reported (Christiansen, 1943; Blood and Henderson, 1968) that stagnant drinking water may cause infection up to 18 days after being used by a tuberculous animal. Viable organisms were isolated from the soil 6 or 8 weeks after feces were dropped, but the duration varies widely—being longer in wet weather. According to Karlson (1967b), the bacillus is transmitted through feed and sometimes water.

In the United States in recent years only a rare human case was caused by the bovine strain (Feldman, 1963).

TETANUS

The disease is widespread and usually associated with the entry of the bacteria into a wound. The organism, a sporeformer, is widely distributed in nature and is abundant in animal or human feces, especially of horses and other herbivorous animals (Sterne and Van Heyningen, 1965; Merchant and Packer, 1967). The spore form resists boiling for more than 1 hour. The spores are capable of persisting in the soil for a number of years (Blood and Henderson, 1968). With the rapid increase of the horse population in the United States, the subsequent contamination of the soil will likely increase. Surface water may play a major role in the dissemination of the tetanus spores.

COLIBACILLOSIS

Colibacillosis has worldwide distribution and it is, under certain conditions, associated with enteric infections in man and animals. It is found universally in the intestinal tracts of man and animals. The organism is usually destroyed at 60° C for 30 minutes. Heat-resistant strains may survive (Merchant and Packer, 1967) and individual cells survive freezing in ice for 6 months. The organism is transmitted by water, feces, and flies contaminated with fecal material. Some strains are hazards to both man and animal and may cause illness of the newborn (Morgan, 1965). The number of *E. coli* organisms found in water indicate the extent of fecal contamination. Attempts to document association between cases in agricultural animals and man appear to be inconclusive.

Rickettsial Diseases

Agents of rickettsial diseases other than Q fever depend on arthropod vectors for transmission of disease and on human or animal hosts for their mechanisms (Fox, 1964).

Q FEVER

Q fever is found in man and animals on every continent of the world. It has a widespread host range (Babudieri, 1959). In the United States it has agricultural significance in sheep, goats, and cattle. The organism, an intracellular parasite, has greater resistance to physical and chemical agents than other pathogenic *Rickettsia* and has more resistance than most nonsporogenic bacteria. The agent is viable in skim milk for 42 months and tap water for 36 months (Ignatovich, 1959). Welsh et al. (1959) isolated the organism from standing water (surface pools) on infected sheep ranches in California over a 6-week period during the lambing season, and from the soil up to 148 days. Stoenner (1964) reported that the role of microenvironments on mobile fomites was significant in extending the hazards of the disease to diverse occupational groups not normally considered at risk. He estimated that in the United States at least 25% of the dairy herds and a higher percentage of sheep and goat herds are infected. Q fever usually appears as inapparent infection in domestic livestock.

The exact mode of transmission is unknown but dust-laden air, containing animal waste, and ticks are considered important. One organism has been suggested as an infectious dose for man (Tigertt et al., 1961). The role of water in transmission has not been determined.

Viral Diseases

There are an estimated 500 known animal viruses (Green, 1965). Counterparts of major groups of viruses known to infect man are also found in domestic animals. According to Abinanti (1964), no thorough investigation has been made to determine which virus may be present in milk and other animal by-products or under what conditions they are destroyed.

In an extensive review of enteroviruses of animals it was concluded that the enterovirus problem of animals parallels that reported in man and that a multitude of organisms may be isolated from feces of different animal species (Kalter, 1964). In recognition that human health is closely related to health of animals, viruses are considered the least-explored infectious agents (Sinha et al., 1960).

In general, viruses do not survive for long periods of time outside the animal host (Gratzek, 1967). Viruses possess about the same degree of resistance to heat, drying, and chemical agents as many of the vegetative forms of bacteria. Most are unaffected by concentrations of antibiotics that will destroy bacteria.

According to Prier and Riley (1965), some information on survival of viruses in water is available, but most of the data have been obtained from distilled-water studies under controlled temperatures. They stated that compared to bacterial and protozoal agents, viruses in natural waters, except under unusual circumstances, are presumed to survive only for a short period of time. However, Brown and McLean (1967) stated that enteroviruses are more resistant to halogens than bacteria and unless residual free chlorine is sufficiently high, water, although free of viable bacteria, may contain active virus.

Joyce and Weiser (1965) reported that a study of farm ponds over a 6-month period revealed no enteroviruses or specific bacteriophages. They experimentally inoculated pond water with enteroviruses which survived for long periods of time (present up to 91 days) at simulated temperature extremes and over pH ranges of extremes found in natural pond waters. The virus survived longer in slightly and heavily polluted waters than in moderately polluted waters. Chemicals found in farm ponds did not appear to inhibit viral survival. Based on experimental findings, the conclusion was that farm pond water poses a definite site for storage of enteroviruses.

Less is known regarding the role of water in transmission of viruses than bacteria. Many of the viral diseases are transmitted by arthropods. Approximately 200 viruses have been classified as arboviruses (Merchant and Packer, 1967). The nonarthropod-borne viral diseases are fewer in number but many are associated in the United States with animal industries.

Many classes of viruses are excreted in the feces of animals. Included are picornaviruses (enteroviruses), reoviruses (respiratory-enteric viruses), herpesviruses, adenoviruses, and myxoviruses (Gratzek, 1967).

According to Prier and Riley (1965), natural water is of minor significance when compared with other factors that affect viral transmission of disease between individuals and herds.

Geldreich (1965), in describing the origin of microbiologic pollution in streams, stated that water contaminated by fecal pollution may also contain viruses excreted by warm-blooded animals.

Although man is primarily involved in viral hepatitis transmission, this agent, with high resistance and capable of being transmitted via surface waters, can serve as a study model. Mosley (1963) reports a total of 31 human epidemics presumed to have been transmitted by water. The hepatitis virus is not destroyed by chlorination or pasteurization (Anderson et al., 1962). According to Mosley (1963) only the viral agent of infectious hepatitis has been clearly associated with waterborne transmission in man's drinking water. Water may also have a role in transmission of poliovirus, Coxsackie, ECHO, and adenovirus (Clarke and Chang, 1959; Brown and Mc-Lean, 1967; Chang, 1968).

The role of water in transmission of viral diseases has not been adequately documented or perhaps considered. The following viral diseases of domestic animals are examples to show the variation in viral resistance.

NEWCASTLE

This virus causes an acute systemic infection of fowls, may infect man, and is highly resistant to detrimental factors of the environment. In chicken down and dust the virus remains active for many weeks at ordinary temperatures (Bernkoph, 1964).

HOG CHOLERA

Hog cholera is an acute, highly contagious disease of swine, caused by a relatively stable virus. One report stated that the virus at 37° C survived for 7 but not for 15 days (Bruner and Gillespie, 1966). Survival time may be longer and varies with environmental conditions. Transmission is believed to be primarily by contact with infected swine, or indirectly by secretions and excretions. The target date for eradication of hog cholera in the United States is 1975.

FOOT-AND-MOUTH DISEASE

Foot-and-mouth disease is an extremely acute contagious disease of all cloven-footed animals that rarely infects man. The virus is resistant to external influence including common disinfectants. It may persist for more than 1 year in infected premises. The virus is rather susceptible to heat and pH change and insensitive to cold. Many methods of transmission occur, with the common method believed to be ingestion of contaminated feedstuff (Blood and Henderson, 1968).

OTHER DISEASE AGENTS (VIRAL-LIKE)

The role of water in the transmission of many agents of disease is unknown. Of recent interest are three disease entities causing similar chronic neurologic disorders: scrapie in sheep, mink encephalapathy, and Kuru in man. The etiologic agents are extremely resistant and have long incubation periods (McDaniel, 1969). The agent of scrapie in sheep resists exposure to 75° C for 1 hour, is ether resistant, and brain tissue in 10 to 12% formalin is still viable after 4 to 28 months (Merchant and Packer, 1967). The role of water transmission is unknown.

Fungal Diseases

DEEP SYSTEMIC MYCOSES

The agents of systemic mycotic diseases of importance are actinomycosis, nocardiosis, aspergillosis, phycomycosis, candidiasis, histoplasmosis, North American blastomycosis, coccidioidomycosis, cryptococcosis, and sporotrichosis. With the exception of candidiasis the others are found free living in nature and are not considered to be zoonotic. These diseases are known as occupational fungi. The fungi are cultured with ease from soil containing chicken manure, starling roost, and pigeon feces (Harrell, 1964). Animals and man are susceptible to these fungi found in the environment. The spores are airborne-transmitted. Infected animals are not considered reservoirs for the transmission of disease to man (Menges, 1963; Maddy, 1967).

HISTOPLASMOSIS

Histoplasma infection of man and animals is widespread in midwestern United States. It is reported sporadic in animals (Blood and Henderson, 1968). Evidence is lacking on the role of water in transmission of fungal disease. Gordon et al. (1952) first reported the isolation of the spore of *H. capsulatum* from river water.

Experimentally the fungus will remain viable as long as 621 days in water (Metzler et al., 1956). The fungus will grow in ordinary river water. Ordinary water purification processes uniformly removed spores from the water. It was found that the spores are more resistant to chlorine than polio virus or enteric bacteria. According to Furcolow (1965), present evidence of transmission by the water supply is not considered important. Since spores can easily be washed into streams, spore content in water storage should be considered in endemic areas.

SUPERFICIAL MYCOSES—RINGWORM

Certain ringworms are transmitted from animal to man (Bridges, 1963). The ringworms are considered as major zoonoses. Direct transmission is the method of common spread. The fungal spores remain viable for years in a dry environment (Blood and Henderson, 1968). The role of water in the transmission of the spores has not been determined.

Parasitic Diseases

The diseases associated with helminths and other parasites is an old science. Helminths were considered important until the discovery of the microscope. Then the era of bacteriology rapidly developed and pushed the macroscopic forms of parasites into the background. Approximately 60 years ago, with the development of tropical medicine, worms again become prominent as causative agents of disease (Cameron, 1962).

Protozoan and helminth diseases are widespread in animals associated with agriculture. Helminths include the trematodes or flukes, cestodes or tapeworms, and nematodes or roundworms.

Trematodes or flukes are rare in North America except for "swimmers itch" in northern lakes. In the United States cestode diseases are not public health problems of magnitude. The nematodes cause many diseases in man and animals, including fish (Steele, 1968).

In general, larvae and eggs of parasites are relatively resistant to the external environment. It has been reported (Blood and Henderson, 1968) that during comparatively dry seasons and short pasture, dung pats can act as reservoirs for larvae for up to 5 months in the summer and 7 to 8 months in the winter. Under warm and wet conditions, helminth parasites survive in large numbers for as long as 6 to 8 weeks, appear relatively resistant to cold, and may survive through the winter.

Ascarids and the larvae of hookworm may be contracted from water or soil (Faust et al., 1968). The life cycle of the fluke evolves in a mollusk, usually a snail. The fluke of "swimmers itch" develops in a snail. From a single egg, thousands of cercariae emerge in water and attack any warm-blooded animal, including man. Tapeworm eggs pass through in feces and all require an intermediate host to complete the cycle.

BALANTIDIASIS

Balantidiasis is a protozoan disease of cosmopolitan distribution, usually observed in warm climates. It is a parasite of the intestine and most commonly found in swine, monkeys, and man (Faust, 1963; Van Der Hoeden, 1964). Human infection results from ingesting contaminated food and water. According to Hoare (1962), over 90% of the people are infected in some countries.

TOXOPLASMOSIS

Toxoplasmosis is an intracellular protozoan infecting animals and man. The disease has a wide host range. The mode of transmission is not known (Jacobs, 1964). According to Jacobs (1956), despite the sea of toxoplasma infection around us the mode of transmission is still in doubt.

ASCARIASIS

Up to 200,000 eggs per day are produced by one female ascarid (Faust et al., 1968). The eggs are very resistant to cold and survive most readily in moist surroundings. Survival up to 5 years has been recorded (Blood and Henderson, 1968).

STRONGYLOIDES

Strongyloides is a dermatitis developed in trappers, hunters, and oil workers from swampy areas of southern Louisiana. Infectious larvae of the strongyloides species infecting swamp-inhabiting mammals were associated with the disease (Burks and Jung, 1960).

TAENIASIS

Beef infected with cysticercosis, the beef tapeworm, causes taeniasis in man. The tapeworm is spread to cattle by human defecation in feed pens and cattle pasture or through distribution of human sewage and septic tank effluent to pastures. Researchers in Great Britain concluded that tapeworm eggs can survive most urban and rural human sewage treatment processes and then pass on in final effluent or air-dried sludge. This material, if used on pastures or if it finds its ways to streams, can infect livestock (Silverman and Griffiths, 1955). In fiscal 1968 in the United States, 12,723 beef carcasses were reported infected on slaughter (USDA, 1968a). Prevalence in man is unknown.

SUMMARY AND CONCLUSIONS

There is a growing public concern for the environment and the need for a reevaluation of water's role as a vehicle in transmission of animal diseases associated with agriculture. Documented cases of infectious diseases of animal origin in man and animals have been associated with water transmission. Following a literature review, it is apparent that adequate consideration of water transmission has not been made. In many case reports reviewed, no epidemiologic studies were made to determine the source of infection. In this chapter an effort is made to indicate the potential epidemiologic significance based on the variability of the resistant characteristics of various kinds of pathogenic organisms and their potential for water transmission.

Much of the past documentation of water transmission has been associated with bacterial agents. The role of animal viruses and other agents is practically unknown, and with available methods, the significance in disease transmission via water cannot be measured. Pathogenic organisms of animals are found in surface waters, but for a multiple of factors, disease only occasionally occurs in man or animals. Factors involved may be the dilution of water, with a low density of organisms found; the chain of events necessary to produce the infectious disease process does not develop; or man and animals are not exposed. If the disease does develop, it is not always diagnosed or reported.

Although in recent years chronic diseases of man have been of major consideration, the potential of zoonotic diseases through occupational and recreational exposure may be increasingly significant in the future. Water is only one of the methods of disease transmission, but water is essential for life—all animals and man have exposure to water.

In the United States the predicted concentration of populations of food-producing animals may better facilitate the control and eradication of animal disease by preventive medicine practices rather than treatment. Developing problems, such as animal waste disposal and the subsequent environmental effect, increase with livestock concentration. Future population growth and new developments will change occupational and recreational methods, and these factors will upset the ecologic systems in nature that exist today. One cannot predict what will happen in the future due to these ecologic changes.

Ecologic studies of disease in the environment of nature are filled with the variabilities of the agent-host-environment complex and are difficult to define. This research needs new approaches.

The future effect of changing agricultural practices, growth and concentration of animal and human populations, and man's increasing exposure to water will effect a challenge to all scientific disciplines to assess the interrelated disease associations.

REFERENCES

Abinanti, F. R. 1964. Respiratory viruses of animals. In *Occupational diseases acquired from animals*, ed. H. J. Magnuson, pp. 53–71. Ann Arbor: Univ. of Mich. School of Public Health.

Anderson, G. W., Arnstein, M. G., and Lester, M. R. 1962. *Communicable disease control.* 4th ed. New York: Macmillan.

Andre, D. A., Weiser, H. H., and Malaney, G. W. 1967. Survival of bacterial enteric pathogens in farm pond water. *J. Am. Water Works Assoc.* 59:503–8.

Babudieri, B. 1959. Q fever a zoonosis. In *Advances in veterinary science*, ed. C. A. Brandly and E. L. Jungherr, pp. 81–182. New York and London: Academic Press.

Bernkopf, H. 1964. Newcastle disease. In *Zoonoses*, ed. J. Van Der Hoeden, pp. 396–400. Amsterdam, London, New York: Elsevier.

Blood, D. C., and Henderson, J. A. 1968. *Veterinary medicine.* 3rd ed. Baltimore: Williams and Wilkins.

Bosworth, T. J. 1934. Persistence of *Brucella* on the aborted foetus and its membranes. *Univ. of Cambridge, Inst. of An. Pathol., Rept. of the Director* 4:65–71.

Brackman, P. S. 1964. Anthrax. In *Occupational diseases acquired from animals*, ed. H. J. Magnuson, pp. 216–27. Ann Arbor: Univ. of Mich. School of Public Health.

Bridges, D. H. 1963. Fungous diseases. In *Diseases transmitted from animals to man*, ed. T. G. Hull, 5th ed., pp. 453–507. Springfield, Ill.: Charles C Thomas.

Brown, J. R., and McLean, D. M. 1967. Water-borne diseases, an historical review. *Medical Services J. Can.*, pp. 1011–26.

Bruner, D. W., and Gillespie, J. H., eds. 1966. *Hagan's infectious diseases of domestic animals.* 5th ed. Ithaca: Cornell Univ. Press.

Bulloch, W. 1938. *The history of bacteriology.* London, New York, Toronto: Oxford Univ. Press.

Burks, J. W., and Jung, R. C. 1960. A new type of water dermatitis in Louisiana. *Southern Med. J.* 53:716–19.

Cameron, T. W. M. 1962. Helminths of animals transmissible to man. In *Progress of medical science, pathology and bacteriology,* ed. R. W. Reed and G. C. McMillan. *Am. J. of Med. Sci.* 130/354, 157/381.

Chadwick, J., and Mann, W. N., collaborators. 1950. *The medical work of Hippocrates. A new translation from the original Greek made especially for English readers.* Oxford: Blackwell Scientific Publ.

Chang, S. L. 1968. Waterborne viral infections and their prevention. *Bull. World Health Organ.* 38:401–14.

Chang, S. L., Buckingham, M., and Taylor, M. P. 1948. Studies on *L. icterohaemorrhagiae.* IV. Survival in water and sewage. Destruction in water by halogen compounds, synthetic detergents and heat. *J. Infect. Diseases* 82:256–66.

Christiansen, M. J. 1943. Graemarks infektion og kvaegtuberkulose. *Maadskrift Dyrlaeger* 54:241–305.

Clarke, N. A., and Chang, S. L. 1959. Enteric viruses in water. *J. Am. Water Works Assoc.* 51:1299–1317.

Decker, W. M., and Steele, J. H. 1966. Health aspects and vector control associated with animal wastes. *Proc. Nat. Symp. Animal Waste Management,* pp. 18–20. Mich. State Univ., East Lansing.

Diesch, S. L., and McCulloch, W. F. 1966. Isolation of pathogenic leptospires from waters used for recreation. *Public Health Rept.* 81:299–304.

Diesch, S. L., McCulloch, W. F., Braun, J. L., and Crawford, R. P., Jr. 1969. Environmental studies on the survival of leptospirosis in a farm creek following a human leptospirosis outbreak in Iowa. Proc. Ann. Conf. *Bull. Wildlife Disease Assoc.* 5:166–73.

Edwards, P. R., and Galton, M. M. 1967. Salmonellosis. *Advan. Vet. Sci.* 1:63.

Errington, P. L. 1963. The phenomenon of predation. *Am. Scientist* 51:180–92.

Faust, E. C. 1963. Infections produced by animal parasites. In *Diseases transmitted from animals to man,* ed. T. G. Hull, 5th ed., pp. 433–52. Springfield, Ill.: Charles C. Thomas.

Faust, E. C., Beaver, P. C., and Jung, R. C. 1968. *Animal agents and vectors of human disease,* 3rd ed. Philadelphia: Lea and Febiger.

Feldman, W. H. 1963. Tuberculosis. In *Diseases transmitted from animals to man,* ed. T. G. Hull, 5th ed. Springfield, Ill.: Charles C Thomas.

Fox, J. P. 1964. Rickettsial diseases other than Q fever as occupational hazards. In *Occupational diseases acquired from animals,* ed. H. J. Magnuson, pp. 98–109. Ann Arbor: Univ. of Mich. School of Public Health.

Furcolow, M. L. 1965. Environmental aspects of histoplasmosis. *Arch. Environ. Health* 10:14–10.

Geldreich, E. E. 1965. Origins of microbial pollutions in streams. In *Transmission of viruses by the water route,* ed. G. Berg, pp.

355–61. New York, London, Sidney: Interscience Publishers.
Gibson, E. A. 1967. Disposal of farm effluent. *Agriculture* 74 (4): 183–88.
Gillespie, R. W. H., and Ryno, J. 1963. Epidemiology of leptospirosis. *Am. J. Public Health* 53:950–55.
Glassman, H. N. 1958. World incidence of anthrax in man. *Public Health Rept.* 73:22–24.
Gordon, M. A., Ajello, L., Georg, L. K., and Zeidberg, L. D. 1952. *Micro sporum gypseum* and *Histoplasma capsulatum* spores in soil and water. *Science* 116:208.
Gratzek, J. B. 1967. General aspects of viral diseases. In *Veterinary bacteriology and virology*, ed. I. A. Merchant and R. A. Packer, 5th ed., pp. 582–88. Ames: Iowa State Univ. Press.
Green, M. 1965. Major groups of animal viruses. In *Viral and rickettsial infections of man*, ed. F. L. Horsfall and I. Tamm, 4th ed., pp. 11–18. Philadelphia, Toronto: J. B. Lippincott.
Harrell, E. R. 1964. The known and the unknown of the occupational mycoses. In *Occupational diseases acquired from animals*, ed. H. J. Magnuson, pp. 176–78. Ann Arbor: Univ. of Mich. School of Public Health.
Harris, H. J. 1950. *Brucellosis* (undulant fever). 2nd ed. New York: Paul B. Hoeber.
Hibbs, C. M., and Foltz, V. D. 1964. Bovine salmonellosis associated with contaminated creek water and human infection. *Vet. Med.* 59:1153–55.
Hoare, C. A. 1962. Reservoir hosts and natural foci of human protozoal infections. *Acta Trop.* 19:281–317.
Ignatovich, V. F. 1959. The course of inactivation of *Rickettsia burneti* in fluid media. *J. Microbiol. Epidemiol. Immunol.* 30:134–41.
Jacobs, L. 1956. Propagation, morphology, and biology of toxoplasmosis. *Ann. N.Y. Acad. Sci.* 64:154–79.
———. 1964. Actual and potential importance of protozoal and helminth zoonoses as occupational hazards. In *Occupational diseases acquired from animals*, ed. H. J. Magnuson, pp. 344–49. Ann Arbor: Univ. of Mich. School of Public Health.
Jellison, W. L., Kohls, G. M., Butler, W. J., and Weaver, J. A. 1942. Epizootic tularemia in the beaver, *Castor canadensis*, and the contamination of stream water with *Pasteurella tularensis*. *Am. J. Hyg.* 36:168–82.
Jellison, W. L., Epler, D. C., Kuhns, E., and Kohls, G. L. 1950. Tularemia in man from a domestic rural water supply. *Public Health Rept.*, pp. 1219–26.
Jones, T. L. 1963. *Diseases of cattle*. 2nd ed. Santa Barbara, Calif.: Am. Vet. Publ.
Joyce, G., and Weiser, H. H. 1965. Survival of enteroviruses and bacteriophage in farm pond waters. *J. Am. Water Works Assoc.* pp. 491–501.
Kalter, S. S. 1964. Enteroviruses in animals other than man. In *Occupational diseases acquired from animals*, ed. H. J. Magnuson, pp. 126–59. Ann Arbor: Univ. of Mich. School of Public Health.
Karlson, A. G. 1967a. The genus *Erysipelothrix*. In *Veterinary bacteriology and virology*, ed. I. A. Merchant and R. A. Packer, 7th ed., pp. 466–74. Ames: Iowa State Univ. Press.

———. 1967b. The genus *Mycobacterium*. In *Veterinary bacteriology and virology*, ed. I. A. Merchant and R. A. Packer, 7th ed., pp. 441–65. Ames: Iowa State Univ. Press.

Kraus, P., and Weber, G. 1958. Untersuchungen über die Haltborheit von Krankheitserregern intrink-und oberflächerwasser. *Zentr. Bakteriol. Parasitenk. Abt. I. Orig.* 171:509–23.

McCroan, J. E., McKinley, T. W., Brin, A., and Ramsey, C. H. 1963. Five salmonellosis outbreaks related to poultry products. *Public Health Rept.* 78:1073–80.

McDaniel, H. A. 1969. Comparative chronic neurological disorders. In *Midwest interprofessional seminar on diseases common to animals and man.* (Abstr.) Ames: Iowa State Univ.

Maddock, E. C. G. 1933. Studies on the survival time of the bovine tubercle bacillus in soil, soil and dung, in dung and on grass, with experiments on the preliminary treatment of infected organic matter and the cultivation of the organisms. *J. Hyg.* 33:103–17.

Maddy, K. T. 1967. Epidemiology and ecology of deep mycoses of man and animals. *Arch. Dermatol.* 96:409–17.

Menges, R. W. 1963. A review and recent findings on histoplasmosis in animals. *Vet. Med.* 58:331–38.

Merchant, I. A., and Packer, R. A. 1961. *Veterinary bacteriology and virology.* 6th ed. Ames: Iowa State Univ. Press.

———. 1967. *Veterinary bacteriology and virology.* 7th ed. Ames: Iowa State Univ. Press.

Metzler, D. F., Ritter, C., and Culp, R. L. 1956. Combined effect of water purification processes on removal of *Histoplasma capsulatum* from water. *Am. J. Public Health* 46:1571–75.

Middlebrook, G. 1965. The mycobacteria. In *Bacterial and mycotic infections of man,* ed. R. J. Dubos and J. G. Hirsch, 4th ed., pp. 490–521. Philadelphia, Montreal: J. B. Lippincott.

Morgan, H. R. 1965. The enteric bacteria. In *Bacterial and mycotic infections of man,* ed. R. J. Dubos and J. G. Hirsch, 4th ed., pp. 610–48. Philadelphia, Montreal: J. B. Lippincott.

Morse, E. V. 1963. Swine erysipelas. In *Diseases transmitted from animals to man,* ed. T. G. Hull, 5th ed., pp. 186–209. Springfield, Ill.: Charles C Thomas.

Mosley, J. W. 1963. Epidemiologic aspects of viral agents in relation to water-borne disease. *Public Health Rept.* 78:328–30.

National Communicable Disease Center. 1965a. *Leptospirosis.* Zoonosis Surveillance Rept. 7.

———. 1965b. *Morbidity and mortality weekly rept.,* vol. 14, no. 22, June 5.

Ogarkov, V. I. 1962. Infectiousness of various objects and materials contaminated with *Brucella. J. Microbiol.* (Moscow) 4:88.

Parker, R. P., Steinhaus, E. A., Kohls, G. M., and Jellison, W. L. 1951. *Contamination of natural waters and mud with* Pasteurella tularensis *and tularemia in beavers and muskrats in the northwestern United States.* U.S. Nat. Inst. of Health Bull. 193. Public Health Serv. 1–61.

Prier, J. E., and Riley, R. 1965. Significance of water in natural virus transmission. In *Transmission of viruses by the water route,* ed. G. Berg, pp. 287–300. New York, London, Sidney: Interscience Publishers.

Quan, S. F., McManus, A. G., and von Fintel, H. 1956. Infectivity of tularemia applied to intact skin and ingested in drinking water. *Science* 123:942–43.

Reed, R. W. 1965 *Listeria* and *Erysipelothrix*. In *Bacterial and mycotic infections of man*, ed. R. J. Dubos and J. G. Hirsch, 4th ed., pp. 757–62. Philadelphia, Montreal: J. B. Lippincott.

Rowsell, H. C. 1958. The effect of stomach contents and the soil on the viability of *Erysipelothrix rhusiopathiae*. *J. Am. Vet. Med. Assoc.* 132:357–61.

Ryu, E., and Liu, C-K. 1966. The viability of leptospires in the summer paddy water. *Japan. J. Microbiol.* 10:51–57.

Schaal, E. 1963. Enzootic salmonellosis in a herd of cattle caused by infected brook water. *Deut. Tieraerztl. Wochschr.* 70:267–68.

Shaughnessy, H. J. 1963. Tularemia. In *Diseases transmitted from animals to man*, ed. T. G. Hull, 5th ed., pp. 588–604. Springfield, Ill.: Charles C Thomas.

Silverman, P. H., and Griffiths, R. B. 1955. A review of methods of sewage disposal in Great Britain with special reference to the epizootiology of *Cysticercus bovis*. *Ann. Trop. Med. Parasitol.* 49:436–50.

Sinha, S. K., Fleming, L. W., and Scholes, S. 1960. Current considerations in public health of the role of animals in relation to human viral diseases. *J. Am. Vet. Med. Assoc.* 136:481–85.

Steele, J. H. 1968. Occupational health in agriculture. *Arch. Environ. Health* 17:267–85.

Stein, C. D. 1942. Anthrax. In *Keeping livestock healthy*. USDA Yearbook of Agriculture, pp. 250–62.

Sterne, M., and Van Heyningen, W. E. 1965. The clostridia. In *Bacterial and mycotic infections of man*, ed. R. J. Dubos and J. G. Hirsch, 4th ed., pp. 454–72. Philadelphia, Montreal: J. B. Lippincott.

Stoenner, H. G. 1964. Occupational hazards of Q fever. In *Occupational diseases acquired from animals*, ed. H. J. Magnuson, pp. 36–52. Ann Arbor: Univ. of Mich. School of Public Health.

Tigertt, W. D., Benenson, A. S., and Gochenour, W. S. 1961. Airborne Q fever. *Bacteriol. Rev.* 25:285–93.

U.S. Dept. of Agriculture. 1965. *Losses in agriculture*. ARS Agricultural Handbook 291.

––––. 1968a. *Livestock Slaughter Inspection Division Rept.*

––––. 1968b. *Statistical report.*

––––. 1969. Cattle on feed. *Statistical Report*, 1 Jan.

U.S. Outdoor Recreation Resources Review Commission. 1962. *Outdoor recreation for America, a report to the President and to the Congress.* Wash., D.C.

Van Der Hoeden, J. 1964. Brucellosis. In *Zoonoses*, ed. J. Van Der Hoeden, pp. 95–132. Amsterdam, London, New York: Elsevier.

Welsh, H. H., Lennette, E. H., Abinanti, F. R., Winn, J. F., and Kaplan, W. 1959. Q fever studies. XXI. The recovery of *Coxiella burnetii* from soil and surface waters of premises harboring infected sheep. *Am. J. Hyg.* 70:14–20.

Wilson, J. B., and Russell, K. E. 1964. Isolation of *Bacillus anthracis* from soil stored for 60 years. *J. Bacteriol.* 87:237.

World Health Organization. 1962. *Occupational health problems in agriculture.* Fourth report of the joint ILO/WHO committee on occupational health. Tech. Rept. Ser. 246.

———. 1967a. *Current problems in leptospirosis research.* Report of a WHO expert group. Tech. Rept. Ser. 380.

———. 1967b. *Joint FAO/WHO expert committee on zoonoses.* Third Rept. Tech. Rept .Ser. 378.

Young, L. S., Bicknell, D. S., Archer, B. G., Clinton, J. M., Leavens, L. J., Feeley, J. C., and Brachman, P. S. 1969. Tularemia epidemic: Vermont, 1968. Forty-seven cases linked to contact with muskrats. *New Engl. J. Med.* 280:1253–60.

CHAPTER TWENTY

ANIMAL WASTE MANAGEMENT TO MINIMIZE POLLUTION

J. A. MOORE

THE practice of managing animal waste to control pollution began when animals were confined. Today livestock operations tend to be more confined and continue to increase in size. This requires a higher degree of waste management. Social attitudes are changing the definition of pollution and the degree of acceptability, thus requiring more waste management. Taste and color, odors, dust, organic and inorganic matter, plant nutrients, insects, and pathogenic bacteria are all pollutional factors which can result from the mismanagement of animal waste.

Management is defined by Webster as "the act or art of planning, organizing, coordinating, directing, controlling, and supervising any project or activity with the responsibility for results." Looking particularly at animal waste management this act may be broken down into four separate functions: collection, storage, treatment, and utilization or disposal. Not all systems contain all of the above processes and for any one system the order may be changed. This chapter will look at these four steps as they affect water pollution.

While all the steps will be discussed separately there is a very definite relationship among the functions. In most livestock operations, the ultimate utilization or disposal practice will strongly dictate the nature of the other processes employed in the waste management system.

Manure varies in composition and characteristics because of differences in specie, breed, age of the animal, and the ration. Number of animals, geographic locations, climatic conditions, proximity to populated areas, and land availability should be considered in selecting a workable and satisfactory management system.

COLLECTION

The collection process can be divided into two types: wet or dry. The dry system can be defined as that which does not add any dilu-

J. A. MOORE is Instructor, Department of Agricultural Engineering, University of Minnesota.

tion or conveying water to the waste. Dry systems minimize the volume of waste material that must be further processed, while wet systems utilize the efficiency obtained with liquid-carried transportation. The low cost of water and the efficiency of pumping systems can make liquid collection very attractive if utilization or disposal of this additional volume of wastewater is available.

In dry systems the manure is usually deposited on the floor, pen, or under the cage and collected and removed to the next process at some given frequency. In the open feedlot operation, the manure may be stored in a lot for several months before being collected and removed. Many dairy operations use mechanical equipment to remove waste from the building on a daily basis. Gutter cleaners, shuttle stroke and endless belt conveyors, powered carts, and small and large tractors are examples of some of the mechanical equipment which has been developed to reduce the labor required for collection.

Flushing gutters have been used successfully in poultry, swine, and dairy operations which use liquid collection systems. If disposal is no great problem, clean water can be used for flushing; in other operations some treatment can be employed to permit the recycling of flushing water. In operations using flushing systems the installation of impervious channels or conduits is essential. If any of this wastewater is allowed to escape, either by design or otherwise, undesirable conditions result.

Manure solids which are allowed to settle out on the bottom or sides of waterways will continually be rewet and stink, attract flies and rodents, and be very unsightly.

Since water is being used as a carrier for the manure, it is important that this liquid does not seep into the soil or through cracks in the conveying system. If the above occurs, the solid will be left high and dry and can create the nuisance conditions mentioned above. A loss of water will result in a buildup of solids on the surface and "polluted" water moving into the soil and eventually the groundwater.

Some operations use sloping bottom ponds to collect and hold the waste slurry for bimonthly flushing. If water is allowed to seep out, the collection process has failed and the above-mentioned conditions result.

The development of slatted floor structures has expanded the use of storage tanks under the housing area to collect and store manure. The use of fully slatted floors can eliminate the need for labor, either hand or mechanical, in the collection process.

In almost all construction the under-the-floor storage tank is designed to function as part of the structural members of the building foundation. These components are almost always concrete and serve as a water-tight storage unit, thus eliminating any water pollution.

STORAGE

Storage may be the first process in the waste management system. Many beef feedlots and poultry operations allow manure to build up and employ only annual or semiannual clean-out schedules.

In some poultry operations shallow liquid pits are constructed under the cages and manure is collected and stored in these for a bimonthly flushing. This storage process in liquids for a short period of time minimizes odor production and eliminates flies. When these shallow pits become full, the slurry may be flushed to a larger tank for some additional storage or immediate removal and disposal. These units are usually concrete lined, which prevents any deep percolation losses.

Storage of the manure collected in tanks under slat floors may extend over long periods of time and accomplish several purposes. Storage tanks eliminate the need for labor in the collection process. Feces deposited in the slats by the animals are worked through so the livestock operator need exert no energy in getting this waste into the tank. These tanks can contain the waste until the land, or some other treatment or disposal system, is in condition to accept the manure. The effectiveness of adding this organic matter and plant nutrients to the soil is reduced in the winter when heavy snowfall and freezing temperatures are encountered.

If animal waste is collected and spread in the winter, the waste may actually be stored above the land in a frozen condition until spring. Because of the cold weather experienced in northern climates, very little processing in the way of anaerobic or aerobic microbial activity takes place during the winter. Depending upon the amount of precipitation, slope of the ground, and overland flow from higher elevations, this site may continue to serve as storage until the animal waste is completely stabilized, leached, or mechanically incorporated into the soil.

Storage of animal manures is also required after processing in some cases. In operations in which effort and energy are expended to reduce the moisture content, storage can be employed to maintain the product in its postprocess condition. Processes such as drying, composting, and dehydration reduce the moisture content which generally results in lower nuisance levels. This material can then be further processed into feed or fertilizer or applied on the land as the demand and time allow. Storage requires that external moisture sources, such as rainfall and snow, be kept from the processed manure. If this objective is met, then any water pollution threat is eliminated.

TREATMENT

Many may consider processing as a step or method involved in preparing a marketable product, and treatment as any step or method involved in stabilizing or reducing waste products. Here, treatment and processing will be used to mean any method involved in an attempt to make the product marketable or reduce or stabilize the material.

Dry Systems

By far the most effective way to minimize the water pollution is to remove moisture from the manure and then provide safeguards to eliminate or minimize its subsequent contact with water. The major treatment systems which remove moisture from the waste are drying, dehydration (which differ only in the amount of moisture removed), incineration, and composting.

Natural drying is extensively used as a treatment process in the arid regions of the Southwest. This method is employed because of the low humidity and high temperature which are encountered in this area. The very conditions which allow this system to be used also reduce water pollution potential. Dust can be a major nuisance in these areas.

When wet periods in winter or high intensity summer thundershowers occur, dikes or catchments can be used to collect and contain the runoff until evaporation can remove the water. By removing the solids from catchments or sedimentation chambers and frequently scraping the pens, runoff water quality can be improved. In many areas in the Southwest continuously running surface waters are not common, and generally the water table is very deep. These two factors greatly reduce the water pollution hazard.

In systems employing dehydration or incineration, water contact and subsequent pollution are avoided. Most operations process the waste directly from the defecation site. Since dehydration is relatively expensive, the resulting product is usually stored or further processed without the opportunity to contact and pollute water.

In the incineration process the remaining ashes possess little threat to water pollution when compared to the original product. Incineration can be accomplished without polluting the air, but this is an expensive operation and is not widely used as a disposal system for animal manures.

Composting is a process of promoting aerobic degradation of organic wastes in a relatively dry condition. This can be accomplished in a pile or windrow, much the same as you might make leaf or vegetable waste compost in your backyard, only on a larger scale. This process is usually mechanized and can take place in a large revolving drum which may be heated and ventilated. When this method is employed on a large scale it is not a great contributor to water pollution.

Wet Systems

Water pollution hazards are increased in liquid waste management systems. The relatively inexpensive price of water allows operators to use liquid systems for the advantage obtained in the transportation of this material. Liquid systems have many things in common with municipal sewage treatment plants and all of the engineering and biological principles apply.

For economic reasons the livestock operator is unable to handle and treat animal waste in the same manner as domestic sewage. Actually sewage is about 99% clean water and 1% waste. To dilute animal waste to the same consistency and employ similar treatment systems would be economically prohibitive. It has been reported that homeowners pay about 0.9 cents per pound for municipal refuse collection, treatment, and disposal, while a similar operation would cost the dairyman $200 per cow, per year (Hart, 1964a).

Since many treatment operations were developed by Civil Sanitary Engineers, we will use their terms to describe three of the basic treatment processes which do apply to animal manure.

PRIMARY TREATMENT

The first treatment process is called primary treatment. In this process floating, suspended, and settleable solids of untreated waste are reduced by sedimentation and screening.

Screening. Screening of animal waste as a treatment process has not been used in any commercial livestock operations. Researchers have evaluated it and reported that dairy cattle waste strained through a No. 4 (4.76-mm opening) sieve removes 50% of the solids by weight and 36% of the BOD_5 in a 2% solids slurry (Dale and Day, 1967). A similar study found that only 12% of the total solids of the dairy waste and none of the solids of chicken waste were held above a No. 8 sieve (2.38-mm opening) (Sobel, 1966). While they do not agree, both of these studies indicate that screening can serve to take out some of the undigested corn kernels, hay stems, and silage which are common to most feeds. These materials are relatively inert and not amenable to biologic treatment.

Sedimentation. Sedimentation has been and can be a very effective treatment method of animal waste. Gravity is the principal force causing matter to settle in water. While the principles of this phenomenon are well defined and understood, no formula, theoretical or empirical, has been devised that is applicable to practical sedimentation-basin design because of the widely varying conditions occurring during operation. Some of the conditions which affect the efficiency of the operation are size of particles (the greater the size, the more rapid is the rate of settling), specific gravity of the particles, concentration of the suspended matter, period of retention, and the velocity of flow through the basin.

Sedimentation can serve as a treatment scheme before a secondary system or be designed to function at the same time. Beef cattle feedlots serve as a good example to employ either or both of these systems. Natural precipitation that falls on or is allowed to run through open feedlots becomes polluted and may have a suspended solids concentration as high as 10,300 mg/l (Miner et al., 1966).

Several studies (Miner et al., 1966; Loehr, 1969; Norton and Hansen, 1969) have reported the relationships and effects of the intensity, duration, slope, etc., on the quality and quantity of runoff water from cattle feedlots.

Laboratory studies have been conducted on animal manure to determine the settleable matter. The test is defined in standard methods, but basically measures the solid material that will settle from a 1-liter sample in 60 minutes.

The suspended and dissolved solids were found to be a function of dilution, ration, and detention time, with dairy manure settling from 20% to 95% in 1 hour as the dilution ratio changed from 2:1 to 10:1 (Sobel, 1966). Similar settling curves have been plotted for chicken manure with dilution ration and settling time as the variables. When looking at this method as a treatment system it is helpful to realize that it is the organic nonsettleable suspended solids and the organic dissolved solids which leave the settling chamber and exert the BOD in the effluent. In beef cattle waste this amounts to 39% of the manure added to the system (Ward and Jex, 1969).

SECONDARY TREATMENT

There are two different biological processes which constitute secondary treatment systems: aerobic and anaerobic systems. However, it is customary to recognize three major subtypes of energy-yielding metabolism: fermentation, aerobic respiration, and anaerobic respiration (Stanier et al., 1965). These three processes are distinguished from one another by differences of the ultimate electron acceptor.

Anaerobic Systems. Anaerobic respiration can be defined as those biological oxidations which use an inorganic compound other than oxygen as the final electron acceptor. Nitrates, sulfates, and carbonates are commonly used as the electron acceptor by anaerobic bacteria.

One of the main advantages this type of system has to offer in the treatment of animal waste is the high degree of stabilization that is possible. Unlike the aerobic oxidation, the anaerobic conversion to methane gas yields little energy to the microorganisms. This low energy conversion does not support the growth of a large number of new cells and the resulting end products are primarily carbon dioxide and methane gas.

Since cell growth is slow there is a low production of waste biological sludge. Nutrient requirements are low for this type of system and since oxygen is not required, the power requirements for operation are reduced. In many municipal operations methane gas is collected and can be used as a heat source for the waste digestor, heating buildings, or generating electricity.

It has been shown that as much as 90% of the degradable organics of a waste can be stabilized in anaerobic treatment while only about 50% is stabilized in an aerobic system (McCarty, 1964a). While the system has advantages, the disadvantages begin to weigh very heavily when treating wastes with BOD concentration of less than about 10,000 mg/l.

The major disadvantage of the anaerobic system is the high temperature required for optimum operation; temperatures about 90° F are preferred. While heating the digestors is a common practice for municipality and some industrial wastes, agriculture has yet to make widespread use of this technique. Most livestock operators are not interested in developing the stalls required to run a good anaerobic digestor. This usually involves a knowledge of mixing ratios, pH control, etc.

Using other than oxygen as the electron acceptor results in the production of some foul odors. With the present public awareness and demand for high environmental quality, the anaerobic systems are definitely handicapped because of the odor production characteristics. Because of the low energy realized in the process, the treatment is not rapid and requires a longer period of time for start-up and adjustment to temperature and loading changes.

However, the use of unmanaged anaerobic lagoons to treat animal waste is widespread in this country. In this sense an anaerobic lagoon can be defined as a tank, pit, or reservoir over 5 feet deep which receives animal waste in some dilute concentration. The 5-foot minimum depth eliminates the transfer and mixing of oxygen from the surface by thermal current or wind action.

Many authors (Hart, 1963; McCarty, 1964b; Hart and Turner, 1965; Curtis, 1966; Willrich, 1966; Loehr, 1967, 1968; Gramms et al., 1969; Schmid and Lipper, 1969) have studied anaerobic lagoons in the laboratory and field for all the major farm animals. The loading rates reported for each animal ranged from near zero to 4,000 chickens, 250 hogs, or 45 cattle per 1,000 cubic feet of liquid; the loading rates most often suggested were about one-half of these maximum values.

There is no standard measurement by which all of the above investigators can compare results. Each is likely to have his own list of objectives and criteria to measure the success of his project and then to project loading rates. Sludge buildup rate is one operational parameter which affects the frequency of cleanout. This is a rather costly operation and in some locations the use of additional land for a larger or second lagoon will eliminate this cost.

Lagoons can be operated on a batch or continuous basis. Generally the effluent from an anaerobic lagoon cannot be discharged to a surface waterway. Sprinkling onto pasture or a waste disposal plot may provide a final disposal site for excess liquid. Recycle of flushing or wash water is one method of reducing effluent from the waste disposal system.

Some locations will allow the construction of a lagoon site with a designed seepage rate, while other sites may be required to construct an impervious lagoon.

Temperature is perhaps the variable which has the greatest influence on the performance of an anaerobic lagoon. Amount of mixing, pH, salinity, detention time, and type of ration fed to the animals will also affect the operation of the system.

Aerobic Systems. Respiration (aerobic metabolism) is that class of biological oxidations which utilizes molecular oxygen as the final electron acceptor.

Oxygen is transferred naturally in turbulent flowing streams and rivers and in shallow ponds and lagoons. Algae can also be a major contribution of oxygen to a pond. However, the relationship is not always favorable as algae produce oxygen in the sunlight and consume it at night. If these natural processes are not sufficient, then mechanical means can be employed to provide additional oxygen.

With adequate oxygen and the waste as a food source, aerobic bacteria grow rapidly and degrade soluble organics very effectively. In this growth some of the waste is converted to cells, which constitutes a biological floc. In final settling this sludge material is removed and some of it becomes a solid water product which creates the need for another disposal system.

Oxidation Ponds. Sufficient oxygen levels can be maintained in ponds or lagoons limited to about 4 feet deep if the loading rate is not too great. Generally aerobic lagoons are designed to treat 20 to 40 pounds of BOD/acre/day, depending upon location. Using the 40-pound rate this is equivalent to 2,600 chickens, 100 hogs, or 30 cattle/acre/day. These figures were generated by reviewing several of the articles in the field (Babbit and Baumann, 1958; Porges and Taft, 1964; Clark, 1965; Jeffrey et al., 1965; Loehr, 1968) and summarizing the reported results.

Wind action, temperature, depth, and amount of sunlight will all influence the treatment. If the loading is light or the detention time is long the effluent may be of sufficient quality to allow discharge to a surface waterway. Several lagoons in series are sometimes employed to provide treatment that will allow discharge.

Depth to water table, soil type, crop, rainfall, slope of the land, and water quality will influence final disposal at this effluent. In areas where evaporation is greater than rainfall, a final liquid disposal system may not be necessary.

In many treatment systems supplemental air has to be provided, and this can be done with rotors or aerators which strike the surface of the water and increase oxygen transfer or by employing compressors and bubbling air up through the liquid. While the above equipment is expensive, the freedom from noxious odors may be worth the price. Waste digestion and odor control are factors which must be considered in a livestock production operation today.

Aerated Lagoons. Some manufacturers of floating aerators have guaranteed that their equipment will supply about 3 pounds of oxygen per horsepower hour at standard conditions (Dale et al., 1969). An operator can determine the total oxygen demand of his waste load and select the necessary equipment. In design it is best to supply twice the oxygen demand to ensure sufficient dissolved oxygen in the entire system.

Oxidation Ditches. While floating aerators (vertical shaft units) splash, mix, and reaerate the liquid in a lagoon, rotors (horizontal shaft units) are used to accomplish the same functions in an oxidation ditch. These units are generally constructed under a slatted floor building. As such they are almost always water tight and prevent any seepage losses.

Most rotors can transfer 1 to 1.5 pounds of oxygen/hr/foot of rotor length. This system holds much promise to contain and treat the waste in an odor-free environment; several investigators (Irgens and Day, 1966; Dale and Day, 1967; McKinney and Bella, 1967; Jones et al., 1969; Ludington et al., 1969; Moore et al., 1969) have studied the loading rates and operation characteristics of this system.

There are over 100 oxidation ditches in use in this country. Most of these units are in hog operations, with only limited application to beef wastes. The above researchers suggest that 10 ft³/hog and 60 ft³/beef animals are loading rates that can be applied to oxidation ditches.

These systems can be operated on a batch basis or with a continuous overflow, which requires an additional treatment system. As indicated above temperature and loading rate will influence the pollutional reduction and rate of solids buildup.

Trickling Filter. The trickling filter is an aerobic system that is widespread in the treatment of domestic wastes. While it has been demonstrated in a laboratory study that this method can be applied to dairy waste, the system has economic and management requirements which have limited its agricultural application (Bridgham and Clayton, 1966).

Combination Systems. Investigators (Agnew and Loehr, 1966; Webster and Clayton, 1966; Loehr, 1969) have explored the advantages of combining an anaerobic and aerobic process to form a complete treatment system. It would appear that some combination of the two can utilize the advantages of both and provide a good system. Field trials to date do not allow the projection of sizes and loading rates required for commercial units.

TERTIARY TREATMENT

Secondary treatment systems may have removed up to 90% of the original organic matter. In the event additional treatment is required, this is called tertiary or third-degree treatment. Since most of the solids have been removed and much of the oxygen-demand materials have been oxidized, this additional treatment may be aimed at nutrient removal.

Nutrients, primarily nitrogen and phosphorus, can be responsible for the growth of algae and other unwanted plants. Tertiary treatment is presently being implemented in a few domestic waste treatment plants.

Like most cities of several years ago, the animal industry is today thinking about primary and secondary treatment and has not yet been encouraged to employ tertiary treatment systems. Nutrients are generated in large quantities in livestock operations, and these do represent a very real pollution potential. While application of nutrient removal systems for animal wastes is some distance in the future, proper management of this material can maximize the benefit of utilization and minimize the pollution from disposal.

UTILIZATION AND DISPOSAL

Almost all of the utilization and disposal of animal manures will be through land application. Some attempts have been made to recover portions of the waste product for the drug industry, but these have generally met with limited success and less application. Incineration does a good job of disposing of manure and almost eliminating all water pollution potential, but cost has kept this from widespread use.

It is not within the scope of this chapter to review or report any or all of the volumes of work that have been published by agronomists, soil scientists, engineers, and others on the effect of animal manure on soil and crop responses. Many report that animal manure cannot compete with manufactured fertilizers and this is very true, but manure will continue to be produced and we must look to least-cost disposal systems which still maintain our environment quality if we wish to continue producing livestock.

Work done at Rutgers University shows that engineering systems can be developed to apply liquid manure to the soil (Reed, 1966). This plow-furrow-cover system employs equipment which opens a plow furrow, applies up to 225 tons of liquid manure per acre and then covers up this material, which maximizes soil contact and stabilization and minimizes environmental pollution (Reed, 1969).

Chopper pumps are now available that can move any material that will flow to the pump (Hart et al., 1966). Large rubber nozzles on sprinkler heads will allow irrigation systems to convey and spread liquid manure. The old manure spreader has seen several new developments in recent years to increase its capabilities.

Plow-furrow-cover, like all other forms of land application, needs careful review by scientists from all disciplines to determine the pollution effect, immediate and long-range, on the surrounding soil, water, and air.

Techniques are available to collect, store, and treat animal manure. The one large remaining task and challenge is to determine the limits of our environment to accept, utilize, or dispose of animal wastes. It is wonderful to live in a country that has the capabilities to send men to the moon and back. It is, however, somewhat disturbing to realize that some of our people are standing knee deep in brown gold to do it. Time and effort will solve the problem; let us exert the effort and shorten the time.

REFERENCES

Agnew, R. W., and Loehr, R. C. 1966. Cattle-manure treatment techniques. In *Management of farm animal wastes*, SP-0366, pp. 81–84. St. Joseph, Mich.: Am. Soc. Agr. Engrs.

Babbit, H. E., and Baumann, E. R. 1958. *Sewerage and sewage treatment*. 8th ed. New York: John Wiley.

Bridgham, D. O., and Clayton, J. T. 1966. Trickling filters as a dairy-manure stabilization component. In *Management of farm animal wastes*, SP-0366, pp. 66–68. St. Joseph, Mich.: Am. Soc. Agr. Engrs.

Clark, C. E. 1965. Hog waste disposal by lagooning. *J. Sanit. Engrs. Div. Am. Soc. Civil Engrs.* 91 (SA6): 27–46.

Curtis, D. R. 1966. Design criteria for anaerobic lagoons for swine manure disposal. In *Management of farm animal wastes*. SP-0366, pp. 75–80. St. Joseph, Mich.: Am. Soc. Agr. Engrs.

Dale, A. C., and Day, D. L. 1967. Some aerobic decomposition properties of dairy cattle manure. *Trans. Am. Soc. Agr. Engrs.* 10 (4): 546–51.

Dale, A. C., Ogilvie, J. R., Chang, A. C., Douglass, M. P., and Lindley, J. A. 1969. Disposal of dairy cattle wastes by aerated lagoons and irrigation. In *Animal waste management*, pp. 150–59. Ithaca: Cornell Univ.

Gramms, L. C., Polkowski, L. B., and Witzel, S. A. 1969. Anaerobic digestion of farm animal wastes (dairy bull, swine, and poultry). Paper 69-462 presented at annual meeting of Am. Soc. Agr. Engrs., 22–25 June, Purdue Univ., Lafayette, Ind.

Hart, S. A. 1963. Digestion tests of livestock wastes. *J. Water Pollution Control Federation* 35 (6): 748–57.

———. 1964a. Manure management. *Calif. Agr.*, pp. 5–7. (Dec.)

———. 1964b. Thin spreading of slurried manures. *Trans. Am. Soc. Agr. Engrs.* 7 (1): 22–28.

Hart, S. A., and Turner, M. E. 1965. Lagoons for livestock manure. *J. Water Pollution Control Federation* 37 (11): 1578–96.

Hart, S. A., Moore, J. A., and Hale, W. F. 1966. Pumping manure slurries. In *Management of farm animal wastes*, SP-0366, pp. 34–38. St. Joseph, Mich.: Am. Soc. Agr. Engrs.

Irgens, R. L., and Day, D. L. 1966. Aerobic treatment of swine waste. In *Management of farm animal wastes*, SP-0366, pp. 58–60. St. Joseph, Mich.: Am. Soc. Agr. Engrs.

Jeffrey, E. A., Blackman, W. C., Ricketts, R. 1965. Treatment of livestock waste—a laboratory study. *Trans. Am. Soc. Agr. Engrs.* 8 (1): 113–17.

Jones, D. D., Day, D. L., and Converse, J. C. 1969. Field tests of oxidation ditches in confinement swine buildings. In *Animal waste management*, pp. 160–71. Ithaca: Cornell Univ.

Loehr, R. C. 1967. Effluent quality from anaerobic lagoons treating feedlot waste. *J. Water Pollution Control Federation* 39:384–91.

———. 1968. *Pollution implications of animal wastes—a forward oriented review*. U.S. Dept. of Interior, Fed. Water Pollution Control Admin., Robert S. Kerr Water Res. Center, Ada, Okla.

———. 1969. Treatment of wastes from beef cattle feedlots—field results. In *Animal waste management*, pp. 225–41. Ithaca: Cornell Univ.

Ludington, D. C., Bloodgood, D. E., and Dale, A. C. 1969. Storage of poultry manure with minimum odor. *Trans. Am. Soc. Agr. Engrs.* (In press.)

McCarty, P. L. 1964a. Anaerobic waste treatment fundamentals. I. Chemistry and microbiology. *Public Works,* pp. 107–12. (Sept.)

———. 1964b. Anaerobic waste treatment fundamentals. IV. Process design. *Public Works,* pp. 95–99. (Dec.)

McKinney, R. E., and Bella, R. 1967. Water quality changed in confined waste treatment. Project Completion Report, Kans. Water Resources Res. Inst., Manhattan.

Miner, J. R., Fina, L. R., Funk, J. W., Lipper, R. I., and Larson, G. H. 1966. Stormwater runoff from cattle feedlots. In *Management of farm animal wastes,* SP-0366, pp. 23–27. St. Joseph, Mich.: Am. Soc. Agr. Engrs.

Moore, J. A., Larson, R. E., and Allred, E. R. 1969. Study of the use of the oxidation ditch to stabilize beef animal manure in cold climates. In *Animal waste management,* pp. 172–77. Ithaca: Cornell Univ.

Norton, T. E., and Hansen, R. W. 1969. Cattle feedlot water quality hydrology. In *Animal waste management,* pp. 203–16. Ithaca: Cornell Univ.

Porges, R., and Taft, R. A. 1964. Principles and practices of aerobic treatment in poultry waste disposal. Paper presented at the Natl. Poultry Ind. Waste Management Symp., 20 May, Lincoln, Nebr.

Reed, C. H. 1966. Disposal of poultry manure by plow-furrow-cover method. In *Management of farm animal wastes,* SP-0366, pp. 52–53. St. Joseph, Mich.: Am. Soc. Agr. Engrs.

———. 1969. Specifications for equipment for liquid manure disposal by the plow-furrow-cover method. In *Animal waste management,* pp. 114–19. Ithaca: Cornell Univ.

Schmid, L. A., and Lipper, R. I. 1969. Swine wastes, characterization and anaerobic digestion. In *Animal waste management,* pp. 50–57. Ithaca: Cornell Univ.

Sobel, A. T. 1966. Physical properties of animal manures associated with handling. In *Management of farm animal wastes,* SP-0366, pp. 27–32. St. Joseph, Mich.: Am. Soc. Agr. Engrs.

Stanier, R. Y., Doudoroff, M., and Adelberg, E. A. 1965. *The microbial world.* 2nd ed. Englewood Cliffs, N. J.: Prentice-Hall.

Ward, J. C., and Jex, E. M. 1969. Characteristics of aqueous solutions of cattle manure. In *Animal waste management,* pp. 310–26. Ithaca: Cornell Univ.

Webster, N. W., and Clayton, J. T. 1966. Operating characteristics of two aerobic-anaerobic dairy manure treatment systems. In *Management of farm animal wastes,* SP-0366, pp. 61–65. St. Joseph, Mich.: Am. Soc. Agr. Engrs.

Willrich, T. L. 1966. Primary treatment of swine wastes by lagooning. In *Management of farm animal wastes,* SP-0366, pp. 70–74. St. Joseph, Mich.: Am. Soc. Agr. Engrs.

CHAPTER TWENTY-ONE

WORKSHOP SESSION

T. E. HAZEN, Leader
R. I. LIPPER, Reporter

In the moderator's opening remarks, he mentioned two possible areas of discussion that seemed to be suggested from information presented in the papers of the Wednesday afternoon session. One area concerned use of the soil as the ultimate *receptor* of either treated or untreated animal wastes. The other was whether the state of the art is such that more emphasis on broad-based systems analysis is appropriate.

After much discussion, it was apparent that no one wished to challenge the general concept of returning livestock wastes to the land. However, there was ample evidence of anxiety over the many information gaps that affect intelligent application of the concept. Much discussion was directed toward the various aspects of nitrate as a pollutant.

Tolerances of man and domestic animals to nitrates in water supplies are not well defined. Needs were expressed for much more specific information. With respect to water for human consumption, the expressed need for more definite information on tolerance limits was countered by the assertion that public water supplies must meet the needs of those with the lowest tolerance. J. E. Box pointed out that bio-contamination is always associated with blue babies. T. L. Willrich gave the history of the development of the present 10 mg/l (N) standard by Comely and cited one controlled study under way involving children of various ages in care homes. It appears to be accepted that the criterion now in use for babies and pregnant women is very conservative for normal adults. Suggestions that the pressures of a growing population and increased use of fertilizer may in time indicate the need for special drinking water were in sharp contrast with other views—namely, that increases in ground-water nitrates cannot be tolerated regardless of source and that algal blooms must be precluded in surface waters even if those waters are not to be used for drinking. A defense was offered for algae on the basis that they potentially have the ability to remove

T. E. HAZEN is Professor, Department of Agricultural Engineering, Iowa State University. R. I. LIPPER is Professor, Department of Agricultural Engineering, Kansas State University.

nitrates and phosphates, and under some circumstances have other redeeming characteristics. The assertion that increasingly stringent water quality standards will be required for the 1980s and beyond seemed to imply that little is to be gained now by looking for maximum tolerances in man as influenced by the many variables involved.

A case was made for the usefulness of more information regarding the influence of nitrates on livestock.

Monitoring of nitrates in groundwater is being done in numerous localities. High nitrates in well waters often are associated with feedlots or rural home waste disposal. High nitrates have been found in wells at depths of 80 to 90 feet. W. H. Walker said that the Illinois State Water Survey is obtaining background levels of N in wells at depths to 100 feet and that NO_3 levels as high as 1,200 ppm have been found in Illinois water supplies. Many are in the range of 200 to 300 ppm. N. J. Thul said that the Kansas Department of Health is sampling wells around large feedlots. Large seasonal variations (up to 100 ppm) in nitrate levels of effluent from field tile drains under cultivated land were reported by Willrich. The need for a broad and extensive interdisciplinary approach to reconcile potentially conflicting demands for clean water and a highly productive agriculture was indicated.

Other questions concerning the returning of livestock wastes to land were numerous and varied. There are several current research projects in which very heavy applications of wastes are being incorporated into soil. The fate of nitrogen is a common concern, but the behavior of numerous other possible water, soil, and plant contaminants is also being investigated. Interest in management schemes to maximize nitrogen losses from the soil is evident. Discussions regarding the salt content of wastes and its effect on soil structure and water intake rate reflect the complexity of the research needed. Effects on germination and on plant growth and composition are being given some attention and appear to require more extensive examination. Research relating to these questions was cited in the Northeast Region by P. E. Schleusener; in Nebraska, Texas, and Colorado by T. M. McCalla; in Kansas by W. L. Powers; in Iowa by J. Koelliker; in Georgia by J. E. Box; and in Mississippi by J. B. Allen. The need for better delineation of objectives to be achieved and criteria for successful systems was recognized. The emphasis again was on working from a broad interdisciplinary base, development of better regional planning counsels, and avoidance of parochial concerns through team efforts. Acknowledgment of the rural-urban interface is demonstrated by projects concerned with disposal of urban wastes on cropland as well as those directed at minimizing the assault of animal waste management practices on the sensibilities of urban dwellers.

In the other major area covered by the discussion, it was admitted that livestock waste management cannot now be planned with adequate consideration being given to all other important interacting factors. Continued emphasis toward development of system components was defended on the grounds that better components are required as building blocks for systems. On the other hand, studies of system concepts can indicate where further component development is likely to be most productive and it was asserted that rudimentary systems analysis would be in order now.

A question was raised concerning importance of the deficiencies in characterization of wastes with respect to the rations and species of origin. There was no disagreement with the answer that there is an obvious relationship, but it is not known how positive the correlation may be. The choices are to become more precise or to accept the heterogeneity and widen the margin for error.

Other items that were discussed briefly are as follows: lagoon criteria, performance, and pollution hazards; pollution tracers and indicators; potential for beef confinement feeding systems; and allowable cost allocations for agricultural pollution control.

PART FIVE

AGRICULTURAL POLLUTION IMPLICATIONS

CHAPTER TWENTY-TWO

MOVEMENT OF AGRICULTURAL POLLUTANTS WITH GROUNDWATER

HARRY E. LE GRAND

AN unbiased view of pollution of groundwater from agriculture-related products would emphasize the fact that numerous rural wells and springs are polluted. It would also emphasize the fact that only a very small proportion of rural groundwater is polluted. These facts are merely a starting point for a general assessment of the degree to which groundwater may be polluted by agriculture-related products.

An ideal assessment would include an evaluation of cases of polluted groundwater in relation to unpolluted groundwater to determine specific causes of pollution. From such an assessment it is hoped would come simple and concrete guidelines or standards to prevent pollution.

The following considerations indicate that the development of simple standards for prevention of pollution of groundwater from agriculture-related products is difficult.

1. Substances that can become pollutants are numerous and diversified. (Common potential pollutants include animal fecal wastes, fertilizers, pesticides and associated chemicals, and inorganic salts.)
2. The environment below ground surface in which agriculture-related pollutants may occur is complex and generally not easily determined. (A dry, sandy, clay deposit in a desert might be acceptable for pollutants whereas a rocky ground with a near-surface water table could be unacceptable.)
3. The distribution of these potential pollutants ranges greatly from place to place and time to time. (Wastes from small cow pastures contrast sharply with wastes from large feedlots, and a single pesticide application on a crop contrasts with repeated application on some orchards.)
4. The toxicity and attenuation properties of pollutants range greatly. (Some pesticides in small quantities are known to be harmful to some wildlife. The attenuation, or weakening tendencies, of

HARRY E. LeGRAND is Research Hydrologist, U.S. Geological Survey, USDI, Raleigh, N.C.

Publication authorized by the Director, U.S. Geological Survey.

each possible pollutant is dependent on complex factors of its environment and on its own inherent characteristics.)

Much fruitful research has been done on the behavior of agriculture-related products in soils, but the movement of these products as pollutants downward into the groundwater system has received less attention. The approach taken here is to discuss briefly some of the geologic conditions and hydrologic factors that affect the movement of pollutants in the ground environment.

DISTRIBUTION OF POLLUTANTS RELATING TO AGRICULTURE

Increasing attention is being focused on the broad spectrum of pollution, and the effect of agriculture on environmental quality is continually being assessed. A symposium presented at the meeting of the American Association for the Advancement of Science in 1966 (AAAS, 1967) included a group of papers that discussed the effect of agriculture on the quality of our environment. An excellent summary report by Wadleigh (1968) discussed wastes in relation to agriculture and forestry. A group of symposium papers discussing the effects of pesticides on soil and water was published by the Soil Science Society of America (1966). At the request of the President of the United States several government agencies contributed to a report (A Report to the President, 1969) on the control of agriculture-related pollution. This latter report listed the following eight pollutants of special concern: sediment, animal wastes, wastes from industrial processing of raw agricultural products, plant nutrients, forest and crop residues, inorganic salts and minerals, pesticides in the environment, and air pollution. All of these except sediment, forest and crop residues, and air pollution are especially pertinent to the quality of groundwater.

Some brief facts indicating the magnitude of agriculture-related pollutants at the land surface are stated below.

Animal Wastes

The volume of wastes from livestock and poultry production is estimated at 1.7 billion tons annually. About one-half of this amount is produced by animals in concentrated production systems. The degree of concentration and the size of individual production units are increasing rapidly (A Report to the President, 1969, p. 2). "The daily wastes from poultry, cattle, and swine alone are equivalent to 10 times the wastes of the human population of the United States" (Taiganides, 1967, p. 388).

Plant Nutrients

"In 1967, 39 million tons of chemical fertilizers were applied in the United States and further large increases in use are projected.

The principal nutrients supplied were nitrogen, phosphorus, and potassium" (*A Report to the President, 1969*, p. 4).

Inorganic Salts and Minerals

"Though the presence of dissolved salts and minerals in waters is universal, their presence in detrimental concentrations is generally associated with part of the irrigated cropland in arid regions of the country and not with the relatively humid East. Salinity from natural sources stems mainly from the saline characteristics of soils and from the geologic formations from which the soils are formed. The salts have not been leached out because of the scarcity of precipitation. In agricultural operations in the arid part of the nation, water is supplied to crops in the necessary quantities to sustain growth. Concentration of the salts occurs in the soil as a result of water loss through evaporation and transpiration" (*A Report to the President, 1969*, p. 61). The part of the irrigated water reaching the water table tends to be higher in dissolved salts than it was originally; there may be as much as a ton of salt per acre-foot of water, as is the case of water from parts of the Colorado River (Thomas, 1956, p. 551). Thus, the accumulation of salts in the soil, which may result in a downward leaching of the salts into the zone of saturation, tends to deteriorate the quality of groundwater in some irrigated arid lands.

Pesticides

"Today, in the United States 8,000 manufacturing firms mix about 500 chemical compounds into more than 60,000 formulations registered for use as pesticides. In 1964, the U.S. chemical industry produced 783 million pounds of pesticides. . . ." (*Fish, Wildlife, and Pesticides*, 1966, p. 2). Traces of one or more chlorinated hydrocarbons have been reported in every major river system of the United States.

BEHAVIOR OF POTENTIAL POLLUTANTS IN THE GROUND

If there were no appreciable attenuation, a potential pollutant could conceivably pass in sequence through the following parts of the environment: (1) land surface, (2) zone of aeration (the zone between the land surface and the water table), (3) the zone of saturation (the groundwater reservoir) to a stream, (4) stream course, and (5) the sea. Almost never does a pollutant persist throughout the sequence of travel, and generally it is dissipated in the zone of aeration.

The great variety of potential agricultural pollutants differ in their behavior in the ground. The pollutants start to move with water from precipitation or from solutions containing toxic elements. Pollutants in waste solutions are already mobile, but solid wastes must undergo leaching before pollutants from them become entrained in subsurface water. The entrainment may be retarded, short-lived, or complicated by tendencies of pollutants to lose effectiveness by (1) decay or some other inherent power to decrease potency, (2) sorption on earth materials, and (3) dilution through dispersion and diffusion. Assessing the degree to which pollutants will become attenuated and predicting the limits of individual polluted zones are central objectives.

Decay

In the sense used here decay refers to any of the mechanisms by which materials foreign to the ground may be destroyed, inactivated, or dissipated as to toxicity. Some pollutants degrade and lose their potency with passing time; others degrade in contact with oxgyen, particularly on the land surface, in surface water, or in the zone of aeration above the water table. Animal wastes degrade in an oxygen-rich environment that favors biological decomposition. Some pesticides are broken down by microorganisms in the soil, but others (Alexander, 1967, p. 335) resist biodegradation.

Sorption

Although moving in the same direction as water, some pollutants move slowly or scarcely at all as they are physically retained by, or react chemically with, earth materials. The extent to which pollutants are retained depends on the character of the pollutant and on that of the earth materials through which they move. Clays tend to retain, by ion exchange or some other sorptive mechanism, many pollutants better than do sands. Dense rocks in which permeability, and thus the sorbing surface, is restricted to fractures and solution openings have poor sorption characteristics, and in these rocks the water and the entrained pollutants may move at about the same rate.

Dilution

Almost all agriculture-related pollutants mix to a considerable degree in water. Dispersion and dilution are commonly favorable considerations, at least at a certain stage or position of pollutant movement. However, dispersion is not desirable where dilution is insufficient to lower the concentrations of certain pollutants to limits acceptable for organisms that use the water. For example, where concentrated toxic pollutants leak to the ground, consideration may be given to recovering and containing them before they disperse into the ground.

A method of evaluating collectively all aspects of attenuation has not been developed. Precise values for sorption and dilution in the environment are difficult to determine. Generally we do not separate our reliance on sorption, on dilution, or on "delay and decay" in the ground before the pollutant reaches points of water use. Yet, a crude evaluation of each method of attenuation in each case of possible pollution might be helpful.

HYDROGEOLOGIC FRAMEWORK

A potential pollutant at the ground surface may be considered to be in a geologic environment of solid earth materials that include a complex arrangement of soils and rocks. It is also in a hydrologic environment that may give it mobility as some water from precipitation moves into the zone of aeration and down into the zone of saturation. Thus, the hydrogeologic setting represents an environment in which two opposing tendencies are at work—the tendency for a pollutant to move with subsurface water and the opposing tendency for it to be almost immobile or weakened by a combination of dilution, sorption on earth materials, or some "die-away" mechanism. The great range in geologic and hydrologic conditions prevents good rule-of-thumb techniques for determining the safe distribution of agriculture-related products at the land surface.

The soil zone is the "action zone" where fertilizers, manure, and pesticides may start to become pollutants of groundwater. It is the action zone for biodegradation and other attenuation methods. The chemical and biological character, texture, permeability, and thickness of the soil zone are important features.

Beneath surface soils in some places are unconsolidated sedimentary materials of clay, silt, and sand. In other places hard, dense rocks underlie soils. Rocks at considerable depth may not be significant because they lie below the paths of most ground-surface pollutants.

Permeability is an important characteristic because it controls the rate of movement of water and pollutants that might be with it. The permeability of some clays may be many hundreds of times less than that of some sands. Zones of greater permeability tend to parallel, or coincide with, rock formational boundaries even if the rocks are appreciably inclined. Differences of permeability in the horizontal field, although common, are in many cases more gradual than in the vertical field. The point to be made is that water and included waste will tend to take preferred paths, flowing readily through permeable zones and shunning or flowing with difficulty through relatively impermeable materials.

The water table is an important consideration of groundwater pollution, especially in view of the ease of attenuation of most pollutants where the water table is deep and where the overlying zone of aeration is composed of sands, silts, and clays. The frequency of precipitation in humid regions is sufficient to keep the water table relatively close to the ground surface in areas of moderate permeabilities, and the consequent mounding of water beneath interstream areas causes a continuous subsurface flow of water to nearby perennial streams. Thus one can get a general idea of the gross direction of movement of groundwater in humid regions; in arid regions, however, the areas of natural groundwater discharge are more widely scattered, and the general movement of water may be less discernible. In arid regions some reaches of most streams lose water —that is, water from the streams may seep into the ground as opposed to the gaining type of stream in humid regions.

In many cases of pollution, the movement of water in the ground has been altered by man's activities, such as pumping of wells or adding liquids to the ground. Pumping of a well causes a cone of depression on the water table, resulting in a flow of water toward the well from the surrounding area. Opposite hydrologic conditions result when liquids are added to the ground in one place, as a mound on the water table is developed and groundwater moves outward from the spot. Knowledge or inferences about earlier conditions may guide decisions about remedial action on some pollution problems.

POLLUTION PATTERNS IN HYDROGEOLOGIC SETTINGS

Fertilizers and pesticides are spread usually over the land surface in their conventional use, and occasional applications for both, rather than continual applications, are the rule. Both the lack of concentration and the lack of continual application tend to weaken the ability of these possible pollutants to move downward with infiltrating water through the soil zone or through the entire zone of aeration to the water table.

Of the fertilizer nutrients, phosphate and nitrate are the ions of chief concern as to possible pollution of water resources. Phosphorus tends to be sorbed by soils so well that it is rarely a serious threat. Nitrate is a common constituent in groundwater, generally in proportions of no more than a few milligrams per liter. In fact, the average sample of groundwater in the humid southeastern part of the United States has less than one milligram per liter of nitrate. Yet, in local areas and in certain groundwater systems the nitrate content averages several milligrams per liter. It may originate from natural sources, livestock feeding operations, sewage disposal systems, legume residues, manures, or excessive use of chemical fertilizers. It is difficult to single out the source of nitrate in groundwater, but Smith (1967, p. 184) points out that leachates from highly fertile, unfertilized agricultural lands may have a higher content of plant nutrients than the percolates from nearby fertilized, well-managed cropland low in natural fertility. Nitrate and chloride are good precursors of pollution, and an increase in these ions with time may aid planning in avoiding serious pollution. With the exception of isolated cases, there is little evidence to support statements that fertilizer nutrients are polluting water supplies (Smith, 1967, p. 185). A special study of a fertilized terrain in southwestern Wisconsin (Minshall et al., 1969, p. 713) confirms this view; it was found after 2 years of data collecting that water of streams during their low-flow period (representing outflow of groundwater) in this region appeared to be a relatively unimportant carrier of plant nutrients. With excessive and improper use, however, in the future nitrates could become a problem when excess nitrogen is added to some soils.

Analyses of groundwater for pesticide content are relatively rare; most of the analyses are related to local research programs not yet completed or are from isolated samples of water from wells near places where concentrated pesticides may have spilled to the ground. The absence of a systematic sampling and monitoring program of groundwater is probably based on the assumption that the soil zone and zone of aeration are effective in attenuating pesticides above the water table. The work of Sheets (1967), Alexander (1967), and other workers indicates the tendency for the bulk of pesticides to be degraded, volatilized, or fixed on soils. That microbial decomposition of pesticides is less rapid in subsoil than in surface soil appears to be a valid assumption that should be investigated (Sheets, 1967, p. 322). Even in the subsoil, sorption is still effective, as indicated by research on DDT (Scalf et al., 1968).

Some groundwater samples from Arkansas and Mississippi in the Mississippi River Delta were analyzed for pesticide residues as a result of a research project undertaken by the USDA (ARS 81-13). This study reports analyses made in 1964 and indicates that most of the well water sampled contained no detectable pesticide residue. However, detectable residues were identified in a few samples, generally in quantities of only a fraction of a microgram per liter. At the time the report was completed, the presence of the residues in the well water was not explainable. It should be noted that none of the wells contained pesticide residues throughout the year. This study of pesticides in the Mississippi River Delta serves to show the difficulty of evaluating the possibility of contaminating groundwater. Iverson (1967, p. 161) reports that analyses "of hundreds of samples of water have produced evidence that neither deep nor shallow wells are being contaminated by insecticides if the well is constructed in such a manner as to provide water fit for human consumption." Evidence from different sources suggests the general freedom of groundwater from pesticides, but a monitoring program to determine the distribution of pesticides in groundwater seems justified.

There are certain conditions that could readily lead to local pollution of groundwater by pesticides and related chemicals. Where such materials are dumped on the ground in concentrated form, especially near shallow wells or in areas where the soil is thin or highly permeable, pollution of groundwater could be serious. Soils are thin in many areas underlain by limestone, where rolling sinkhole topography results in quick drainage of surface water into caverns. In some limestone terranes the groundwater moves rapidly to streams, and pollutants have little chance to be attenuated (Deutsch, 1963, p. 33). Attenuation of pollutants is much better where the pollutants are in contact with the ground only occasionally, as with agricultural pesticide use.

Although there is a tendency for animal organic wastes to become more localized each year, both animal and human wastes in rural areas are much more dispersed than those in urban areas. Thus, unlike procedures in urban areas where organic wastes are generally contained, diluted with water, transported, and treated, the waste-handling procedures in rural areas result in wide distribution to the ground; the percentage of water added to wastes in rural areas is generally much less than that in urban areas. It is difficult to assess the potential of rural organic wastes to pollute water. Overland run-off can leach wastes and result in stream pollution. There is vertical leaching into the ground environment of animal and human wastes. Gillham and Webber (1968) reported a significant increase in the nitrogen content in the groundwater as it passed beneath a barnyard. Two counter tendencies prevail. The tendency for pollution from leached wastes to move downward and to become entrained with the subsurface water is mostly offset by the tendency of the waste materials to be attenuated by degraduation in the soil, by sorption, and by dilution. Hence, pollution of groundwater is less common than might be expected in view of the widespread occurrence of surface contaminants. Yet, serious problems do exist. The potential for polluting groundwater is great where concentrated wastes, as at feedlots, are exposed to thin soils on cavernous limestone formations or to thin or sandy soils on fractured rocks.

Where pollutants escape attenuation by sorption and decay in the zone of aeration, attenuation in the underlying zone of saturation may be chiefly by dilution in groundwater. As might be expected in the groundwater reservoir, the polluted zone is normally more

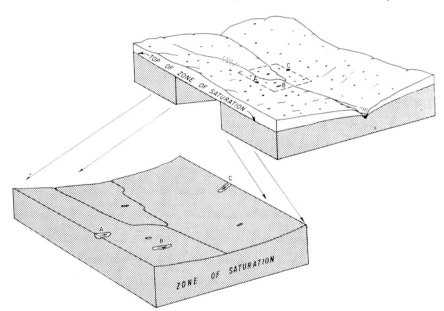

FIG. 22.1. Generalized block-diagram, showing isolated polluted zones at the land surface (dots in block on right) and the relative extent to which pollution is carried downward to the zone of saturation in block on left. Sites **A, B,** and **C** represent pollution concentrations, such as feedlots, great enough to pass through the zone of aeration and along the top of the zone of saturation for some distance toward the surface stream.

pronounced at the water table than at greater depths, and the polluted zone tends to be elongated in the direction of groundwater movement. Patterns of polluted zones on the water table have been described schematically by LeGrand (1965) and are shown in Figure 22.1. Although zones of pollution from agriculture-related products have rarely been described, their patterns on the water table are similar to patterns formed by industrial pollutants. A large but commonly shaped polluted zone (Fig. 22.2) resulted from waste-disposal practices at a chemical factory in Colorado (Walker, 1961); the map shows the movement of chlorates and 2,4-D-type compounds, as well as the anticipated area of influence from waste basins. Very rarely would a contaminated groundwater zone in agricultural areas be as large as that shown in Figure 22.2, but the "down-gradient" shape is typical.

CONCLUSIONS

The volume of groundwater polluted by plant nutrients, animal wastes, and pesticides appears to be small. Admittedly, there are

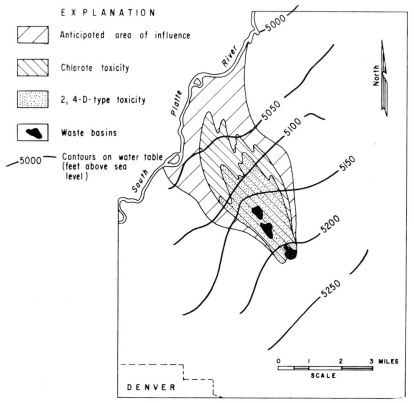

FIG. 22.2. Patterns of polluted groundwater formed from seepage of chemicals from waste basins. (Modified after Walker, 1961, p. 492.)

numerous cases of farm wells being polluted, and numerous small polluted zones of water occur in the upper part of the zone of saturation. Sufficient safeguards are available to minimize ground-water pollution to the extent that good agricultural practices should not be deterred.

The zone of aeration above the water table, which normally contains in its upper part the soil zone, attenuates almost all of the foreign bodies that are potential pollutants of the underlying ground-water. Chemical fertilizers, animal wastes, and pesticides vary great-ly in their tendency to degrade in ground environments. They all degrade better under a set of hydrogeologic conditions. The follow-ing environmental factors tend to reduce the chances of pollution of water from wells and springs:

1. A deep water table, which (a) allows for sorption of pollutants on earth materials, (b) slows subsurface movement of pollutants, and (c) facilitates oxidation or other beneficial "die-away" effects.
2. Sufficient clay in the path that pollutants will move so that re-tention or sorption of pollutants is favorable. (However, excessive clay may result in poor surface permeability, thereby allowing much water and pollutants to move overland to surface streams.)
3. A gradient of the water table beneath a waste site away from nearby wells.
4. A great distance between wells and wastes so that advantages of the above factors can accumulate.

Dispersion has been a major factor in minimizing the pollution of groundwater in agricultural regions of the United States. In their conventional uses both fertilizers and pesticides have been widely but thinly applied. Both human and animal wastes have caused only minor pollution problems until recent years, but the increasing concentrations of animal wastes in large feedlots is a matter of growing concern. Disposal of containers of pesticides and other toxic chemicals in rural areas by design or accident will pose ques-tions of the possibility of groundwater pollution.

Soils maps and results of hydrogeologic studies should furnish a good background for evaluating the potential of certain agriculture-related products to pollute groundwater. Yet no magic or simple quantitative system for predicting accurately the fate of the variety of pollutants in the ground environment is likely to be developed soon. Although extremely unfavorable ground conditions are easy to determine, most earth materials have the capacity to attenuate pollutants to some degree. The exercise of good judgment in manag-ing agriculture-related products that can become pollutants of groundwater is essential.

REFERENCES

Alexander, Martin. 1967. The breakdown of pesticides in soils. In *Agriculture and the quality of our environment,* ed. N. C. Brady, pp. 331–42. Norwood, Mass.: Plimpton Press.

American Association of Advancement of Science. 1967. *Agriculture and the quality of our environment,* ed. N. C. Brady, Norwood, Mass.: Plimpton Press.

Deutsch, Morris. 1963. *Ground-water contamination and legal controls in Michigan.* U.S. Geol. Survey Water-Supply Paper 1691.

Gillham, R. W., and Webber, L. R. 1968. Groundwater contamination. *Water Pollution Control* 106 (5).

Iverson, L. G. K. 1967. Monitoring of pesticide content in water in selected areas of the United States. In *Agriculture and the quality of our environment,* ed. N. C. Brady, pp. 157–62. Norwood, Mass.: Plimpton Press.

LeGrand, H. E. 1965. Patterns of contaminated zones of water in the ground. *Water Resources Res.* 1 (1): 83–95.

Minshall, N. M., Starr, Nichols, and Wetzel, S. A. 1969. Plant nutrients in base flow of streams in southwestern Wisconsin. *Water Resources Res.* 5 (3): 706–13.

Scalf, M. R., Hauser, V. L., McMillion, L. G., Dunlap, W. J., and Keeley, J. W. 1968. *Fate of DDT and nitrate in ground water.* Robert S. Kerr Water Res. Center, Ada, Okla., and Southwestern Great Plains Res. Center, Bushland, Tex., Spec. Publ.

Sheets, T. J. 1967. Pesticide buildup in soils. In *Agriculture and the quality of our environment,* ed. N. C. Brady, pp. 311–30. Norwood, Mass.: Plimpton Press.

Smith, G. E. 1967. Fertilizer nutrients in water supplies. In *Agriculture and the quality of our environment,* ed. N. C. Brady, pp. 173–86. Norwood, Mass.: Plimpton Press.

Soil Science Society of America. 1966. *Pesticides and their effects on soils and water.* ASA Spec. Publ. 8.

Taiganides, E. P. 1967. The animal waste disposal problem. In *Agriculture and the quality of our environment,* ed. N. C. Brady, pp. 385–94. Norwood, Mass.: Plimpton Press.

Thomas, Harold E. 1956. Changes in quantities and qualities of ground and surface waters. In *Man's role in changing the face of the earth,* ed. William L. Thomas, pp. 542–63. Chicago: Univ. Chicago Press.

U.S. Dept. of Agriculture. 1966. *Monitoring agricultural pesticide residues.* ARS-81-13.

U.S. Dept. of Agriculture. 1969. *Control of agriculture-related pollution.* A report to the President. Submitted by the Sec. of Agr. and the Dir. of the Office of Sci. and Technol.

U.S. Dept. of Interior. 1966. *Fish, wildlife and pesticides.* U.S. Fish and Wildlife Serv. Unnumbered pamphlet.

Wadleigh, C. H. 1968. *Wastes in relation to agriculture and forestry.* USDA Misc. Publ. 1065.

Walker, T. R. 1961. Ground-water contamination in the Rocky Mountain arsenal area, Denver, Colorado. *Bull. Geol. Soc. Am.* 72:489–94.

CHAPTER TWENTY-THREE

EFFECTS OF AGRICULTURAL
POLLUTION ON EUTROPHICATION

D. E. ARMSTRONG and G. A. ROHLICH

EUTROPHICATION refers to the process of enrichment of water with nutrients (Stewart and Rohlich, 1967). An obvious effect of eutrophication is an increase in the biomass which can be supported in a body of water. Although the increase in yield of a crop after fertilization is desirable in terrestrial situations, the effects of eutrophication of waters are often undesirable. Generally the aesthetic value of a lake is lowered through excessive growth of aquatic weeds and algae and production of floating algal scums which are a nuisance to those who use the water for recreational purposes. Other effects include undesirable odors and tastes, and impairment of water treatment operations—for example, through clogging of filters by algae.

It should be recognized that lake eutrophication is a natural process of lake maturation. Precipitation and natural drainage contribute nutrients which support and enhance the growth of phytoplankton and littoral vegetation. However, the acceleration of eutrophication as a result of man's activities in altering the landscape through agricultural development, urbanization, and waste discharge is of major concern.

While lake eutrophication involves enrichment with nutrients, the stage or rate of lake eutrophication is not controlled solely by the quantities of nutrients present or entering the receiving body of water. The interrelationships of climatic, physical, chemical, and biological factors which affect lake metabolism are highly complex. As illustrated by Rawson (Fig. 23.1), the morphology of the basin, geological characteristics of the area, temperature, nutrient input, and many other factors influence the metabolism of a lake. Because of the complex interrelationships involved, establishing reliable measurements of lake eutrophication rate and stage has been a major problem (Fruh et al., 1966).

Interest in control of eutrophication has focused on limiting

D. E. ARMSTRONG is Assistant Professor of Water Chemistry, University of Wisconsin. G. A. ROHLICH is Director, Water Resources Center, and Professor of Sanitary Engineering, University of Wisconsin.

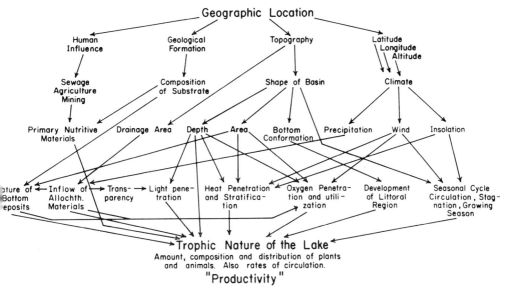

FIG. 23.1. Chart suggesting the interrelations of factors affecting the metabolism of a lake. (Rawson, 1939.)

the amounts of nutrients entering the water. The success of this approach depends on whether the available nutrient supply can be reduced to the extent that growth of aquatic plants is limited. Nutrients which have received the most attention are nitrogen and phosphorus because, following carbon, they are required in the greatest amounts for the production of green plants.

Importantly, the amounts of nitrogen and phosphorus available to aquatic plants in lakes depend not only on the amounts entering the body of water but also on the chemical, biochemical, and physical processes occurring within the lake as shown in Figure 23.2 (Armstrong et al., 1969). The available nitrogen and phosphorus pool (mainly the dissolved inorganic nitrogen and phosphorus compartment) is regulated by a number of interrelated processes. For example, uptake or release of available nutrients by the bottom sediments may occur, depending on sediment properties and environmental conditions. Microorganisms may compete with plants for available nutrients. It should be emphasized that both quantities in compartments and rates of interchange among compartments are important. For example, rapid exchange of nutrients between the sediments and water might supply sufficient quantities for plant growth even at low concentrations of nutrients in the lake water.

FACTORS CONTROLLING NITROGEN AND PHOSPHORUS TRANSPORT IN AGRICULTURAL DRAINAGE

The forms and chemistry of nitrogen and chemistry of nitrogen and phosphorus in soils have been discussed previously and will be

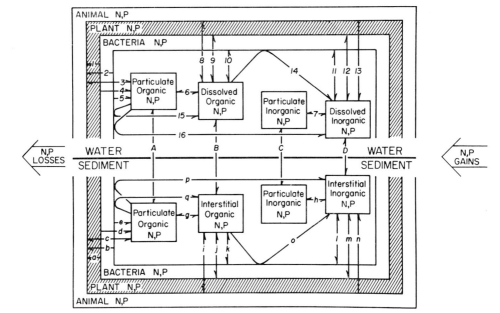

FIG. 23.2. Major components of the nitrogen and phosphorus cycles in lakes. (Armstrong et al., 1969.)

reviewed only briefly here (see review by Biggar and Corey, 1969).

Most of the nitrogen in soils (perhaps more than 95% of the total soil nitrogen) is organic. Much of the organic nitrogen (about 50%) is present in amino form. The main inorganic forms are nitrate and ammonium; nitrite is usually present only in small amounts, though a small portion of the total soil nitrogen, nitrate, and ammonium is of primary importance because it is in the form of nitrogen utilized by plants. Quantities of ammonium and nitrate depend mainly on the processes of organic nitrogen mineralization and inorganic nitrogen immobilization, and soil organic nitrogen or organic matter contents provide a good indication of the nitrogen fertility of the soil.

Phosphorus in soils exists in inorganic and organic forms. The inorganic phosphorus content varies from about 25 to 97% of the total and is in the range of 50 to 75% for many soils. Total phosphorus ranges from 100 to 2,000 ppm and is often about 1,000 ppm. Dissolved inorganic phosphorus is the form directly available to plants but organic phosphorus is available through conversion to inorganic phosphorus. The amount of dissolved inorganic phosphorus in the soil solution is low, usually about 0.01 to 0.1 ppm, due to adsorption of phosphorus by the iron, aluminum, and calcium components of the soil.

Water reaching the soil surface is disposed of by (1) surface runoff, (2) groundwater runoff (interflow), (3) deep percolation,

(4) storage, and (5) evaporation and transpiration (Biggar and Corey, 1969). Of these, the first three—namely, surface runoff, groundwater seepage, and percolation to perched water tables or deeper aquifers—contribute to eutrophication by transporting nutrients to streams and lakes. Surface runoff may directly enter streams and subsequently lakes. Some of the water that enters the soil drains downslope and may reappear at a lower elevation as surface water or seepage. Water percolating to the groundwater may transport nutrients to rivers and lakes which receive a major portion of their water from groundwater flow. According to Biggar and Corey (1969), irrigation, which involves a recycling of water derived from runoff, seepage, and percolation, often increases the amounts of nutrients transported to lakes and streams by these waters.

The amounts of nutrients transported in agricultural drainage are determined in part by the chemical forms of the nutrients and the processes controlling their retention in the soil. Runoff water carries nutrients in both dissolved and particulate forms, while water percolating through the soil generally carries only dissolved forms. Because inorganic phosphorus is retained more strongly than inorganic nitrogen by soil particles, the forms of nitrogen and phosphorus transported differ appreciably for runoff and percolate waters. Ammonium and particularly nitrate are quite soluble and tend to move downward in the soil with percolating water, thereby lowering the amounts at the soil surface. Since runoff waters tend to transport forms located near the soil surface, ammonium and nitrate are carried in runoff waters in dissolved or paticulate form to a lesser extent than are the more insoluble nutrients. Due to the low anion exchange capacity of soils and the high solubility of nitrate, the downward movement of nitrate with percolating waters is quite rapid. Thus, the extent to which nitrate is leached depends to a large extent on the quantity of water percolating through the soil and the degree to which nitrate levels are in excess of plant and microbial needs. Although ammonium is soluble, the downward movement of ammonium is retarded by retention at cation exchange sites. Furthermore, conversion of ammonium to nitrate in soils through nitrification is generally quite rapid.

Inorganic phosphorus tends to be strongly retained by soil particles, and phosphorus received by the soil as commercial fertilizer, plant residue, and manure tends to remain at the soil surface, thereby enhancing the possibility of transport by runoff in particulate and soluble forms. Biggar and Corey (1969) have suggested that due to the low mobility of phosphorus in soils, application of phosphorus to the soil surface will tend to saturate the phosphorus adsorption sites and cause the concentration of phosphorus in solution near the soil surface to be relatively high. Some of the phosphorus in solution would tend to move downward but would be rapidly adsorbed at the undersaturated adsorption sites beneath the surface. However, at the surface, phosphorus in solution would be maintained at a relatively high concentration and the phosphorus concentration in runoff waters in contact with these surfaces might be relatively high. Whether the dissolved phosphorus would remain in solution

would depend on the phosphorus adsorption capacity of the suspended soil particles and stream sediments in contact with the
runoff water.

Both organic nitrogen and organic phosphorus as well as inorganic phosphorus are of low mobility in soil and are likely transported to a large extent in particulate form in runoff waters. However, because the amount of organic nitrogen in soil is high as
compared to inorganic nitrogen, quantities of soluble organic nitrogen transported may be significant relative to amounts of inorganic
nitrogen. Particulate forms are generally of less interest than dissolved forms regarding their effects on the receiving water due to
the lower plant availability of these forms and the possibility that
the particulate material will settle to the bottom of streams or lakes.
However, it should be recognized that the new environment, for
example an anaerobic lake bottom, may markedly increase the
mobility of nutrients contained in these particles. On the other
hand, eroded soil particles transported to streams or lakes may decrease the available nutrient supply in the water. For example,
phosphorus-deficient soil particles entering a lake may remove phosphorus from solution by adsorption and transport the adsorbed
phosphorus to the lake bottom.

In summary, it is generally expected that inorganic nitrogen is
transported mainly as nitrate by percolating waters, although the
amounts of ammonium and nitrate carried in runoff waters may be
highly significant in terms of the receiving water. Similarly, the
largest amount of phosphorus is likely transported in particulate
form in runoff waters, but the amount of dissolved phosphorus in
runoff water may be of equal or greater importance even though
lower in quantity. Obviously these statements are highly generalized
and will not apply in many situations. An important example is the
situation in which the soil is frozen. In this case, soluble and particulate forms of both nitrogen and phosphorus would be carried in
surface runoff.

Because concern over the quality and the nutrient content of
agricultural drainage has developed only recently, relatively few

TABLE 23.1. Nitrogen and phosphorus content of waters in surface and subsurface drains and in shallow wells.

Constituent	Surface Drain	Subsurface Drain	Shallow Well
		mg/l	
		Irrigation Season	
NO$_3$-N	0.8	2.5	2.3
Dissolved P	0.19	0.22	0.12
Total P	0.27	0.28	0.16
		Nonirrigation Season	
NO$_3$-N	1.9	2.5	0.16
Dissolved P	0.20	0.23	0.08
Total P	0.26	0.26	0.10

Source: Sylvester and Seabloom (1962) as reported by Biggar and Corey
(1969).

TABLE 23.2. Constituents in runoff waters from a 1.45-acre winter wheat field near Coshocton, Ohio.

Constituent	In Runoff		In Rainfall
	Range	Average	
		(mg/l)	
Suspended solids	5–2074	313.0	11.7
Total N	2.2–12.7	9.0	1.17
Inorganic N	0.2–8.2	5.0	0.86
Total hydrolyzable P	0.08–1.07	0.6	0.03

Source: Weibel et al. (1966) as reported by Biggar and Corey (1969).

investigations have involved quantitative evaluation of the factors controlling the amounts of nitrogen and phosphorus reaching streams and lakes from agricultural sources. However, some data are available which are useful in considering the amounts of nutrients transported in this manner.

Sylvester and Seabloom (1962) studied the amounts of nutrients carried to surface drains, subsurface drains, and shallow wells for irrigated and nonirrigated situations in the Yakima Basin (Table 23.1). Surface drains should reflect surface runoff, subsurface drains the nutrients leached to shallow depths, and shallow wells the nutrients carried in percolating water to the groundwater. As expected, the amount of phosphorus carried to the groundwater was small, although amounts appearing in shallow drains were comparable to the amounts in subsurface drains. The quantities of nitrate appearing in subsurface drains and shallow wells reflected the mobility of nitrate in percolating waters. Recycling of the water through irrigation tended to increase the amounts of nutrients in the groundwater.

Weibel et al. (1966) measured the nutrient concentrations in runoff waters from a small wheat field in Ohio (Table 23.2). It is of interest to note the relatively high concentrations reported for runoff, the range in amounts of suspended solids, and the relatively large amounts of materials in the rainfall.

Further indication of the importance of runoff is obtained from the results of Duley and Miller (1923) shown in Table 23.3. Annual

TABLE 23.3. Annual nitrogen and phosphorus content of runoff and eroded material from a shelby loam soil of 3.6% slope.

Cropping System	Pounds per Acre		
	Total N	NO₃⁻-N	Total P
Not cultivated	99.0	1.38	48.0
Spaded 8″ deep	74.0	0.56	33.0
Bluegrass sod	0.6	0.07	0.1
Wheat	30.0	0.32	11.0
Rotation—corn,			
wheat, clover	6.0	0.02	2.0
Corn annually	40.0	0.02	8.0

Source: Duley and Miller (1923) as reported by Biggar and Corey (1969).

TABLE 23.4. Estimated amounts of nitrogen and phosphorus in agricultural drainage.

Drainage Area	Pounds per Acre of Land per Year			
	Inorganic N	Organic N	Inorganic P	Organic P
Lake Monona	4.4	1.6	0.06	...
Lake Waubesa	4.9	1.8	0.10	0.29
Lake Kegonsa	6.4	1.8	0.10	0.31

Source: Sawyer (1947).

amounts transported ranged from 0.6 to 99 lb/acre of total nitrogen, 0.02 to 1.38 lb/acre of NO_3-N, and 0.1 to 48 lb/acre of total phosphorus. Of particular interest is the marked effect of the cropping system and the low amount of NO_3-N transported relative to total nitrogen.

From another point of view, Sawyer (1947) estimated the amounts of nitrogen and phosphorus carried from the watershed to three Wisconsin lakes based on analysis of one tributary to each lake (Table 23.4). The estimated pounds of nutrients lost per acre of land per year were from 4.4 to 6.9 for inorganic nitrogen, 1.6 to 1.8 for organic nitrogen, 0.06 to 0.10 for inorganic phosphorus, and 0.29 to 0.31 for organic phosphorus. Estimates of nutrient losses for harvested areas of the United States (Table 23.5) reported by Lipman and Conybeare (1936) were 4 to 6 times greater for nitrogen and 4 to 40 times greater for phosphorus than the values estimated by Sawyer (Table 23.4). Leaching estimates were based on lysimeter and river analysis, while erosion estimates involved amounts of eroded material lost at various locations and the nutrient content of the soil in the corresponding region.

CONTRIBUTION OF AGRICULTURAL DRAINAGE TO THE NITROGEN AND PHOSPHORUS STATUS OF WATERS

Although eutrophication of surface waters through transport of nutrients from surrounding lands is a natural process, primary concern is focused on whether the activities of man are increasing the amounts of nutrients transported in agricultural drainage as well as from other sources and whether practices can be implemented which will lessen the nutrient influx and thereby preserve the quality of our waters.

The relative contribution of agriculture to the nutrient budget of a lake depends on types of activities occurring in the drainage basin of the lake. For example, lakes located in rural areas may be influenced primarily by agricultural drainage, while the effect of extensive urban development in the drainage basin may be to lower the relative importance of agricultural drainage. Furthermore, the types of agricultural practices and activities also influence the quality of agicultural drainage, and consequently the relative role of agriculture in eutrophication. For example, animal feeding and soil

TABLE 23.5. Loss of plant nutrients from harvested crop areas in the U.S.A., 1930.

	Pounds per Acre per Year		
	N	P	K
Intertilled crops			
Leaching	17.1	. . .	39.1
Erosion	48.1	21.0	280.7
Annual crops not intertilled			
Leaching	32.5	. . .	37.6
Erosion	11.1	4.9	65.0
Biennial and perennial crops			
Leaching	23.0	. . .	. . .
Erosion	24.2	10.6	141.1

Source: Lipman and Conybeare (1936) as reported by Biggar and Corey (1969).

management practices can have a marked effect on the quality of agricultural drainage.

An indication of the effect that certain agricultural activities and management practices can have on the quality of agricultural drainage is shown in the following examples.

Animal wastes are one of the largest sources of agricultural wastes (Loehr, 1969), and concern has been focused on the impact of these wastes on water quality, particularly the amount of nitrogen transported in runoff and percolate waters from animal feedlots which represent a concentrated source of these wastes. The survey of well waters in Missouri conducted by Smith (1964) seemed to show a relation between animal population and the nitrate content of the groundwater.

Stewart et al. (1967) compared the nitrogen and phosphorus contents of the surface groundwater beneath feedlots to that beneath nearby irrigated fields (Table 23.6). Their results show that concen-

TABLE 23.6. Concentrations of constituents in surface of groundwater beneath four feedlots and adjacent irrigated fields.

	Depth to Water Table	MG/L in Water of			
		NO_3^--N	NH_4^+-N	Total dissolved P	Organic C
	(meters)				
Feedlot	10	8.6	5.1	0.25	130
Irrigated field ..	10	0.1	0.0	0.06	18
Feedlot	5	18.0	5.7	0.36	130
Irrigated field ..	3	31.0	0.1	0.04	12
Feedlot	4	21.0	5.8	0.22	90
Irrigated field ..	3	8.5	0.0	0.01	9
Feedlot	11	1.1	38.0	1.3	170
Irrigated field ..	11	18.0	0.4	0.05	26

Source: Stewart et al. (1967).

trations of nitrate, ammonium, phosphorus, and organic carbon were generally higher beneath the feedlots. However, because of the greater area occupied by irrigated lands, it was suggested that for this area irrigated lands were contributing more nitrate to the groundwater than were the feedlots.

Although attention is usually focused on runoff and percolates, the recent results of Hutchinson and Viets (1969) indicate that volatilization of ammonia from feedlots can cause transport of significant quantities of nitrogen to nearby surface waters (Table 23.7). Depending on feedlot size and distance from the feedlot, about 4 to 35 kilograms of NH_3-N/hectare (one-half of the values obtained by adsorption of ammonia in acid traps) were transported to nearby surface waters. These amounts were much larger than the quantity of NH_4-N contained in precipitation (the precipitation values shown in Table 23.7 are for a 3-month period).

The results of Weidner et al. (1969) recorded in Table 23.8 indicate the effect that soil management and crop rotations can have on the amounts of nutrients carried in runoff waters. Improved management reduced nitrogen in runoff by about 63% and phosphorus by 70%. These values were estimated from correlations between the quality parameters and total solids in the runoff, and it is seen that the main effect of improved management was to reduce the total solids transported in the runoff. Improved management primarily involved contour tillage, liming of the soil, and increased fertilization.

The data obtained by Johnson et al. (1965) suggest the importance of fertilizer and cropping practices on the quality of agri-

TABLE 23.7. Absorption of ammonia volatilized from cattle feedlots.

| | Ammonia-N (kilograms per hectare) | | |
| | Absorption* | | |
Site Description	Weekly	Annual	Precipitation
Control—no feedlots or irrigated fields nearby	0.15	3.9	0.22
Small feedlots within 0.8 to 4 km	0.34	9.1	0.29
0.2 km east of 800-unit feedlot and 0.6 km west of about 800-unit feedlot	0.57	15.0	0.32
0.5 km southwest of 9,000-unit feedlot (shore of Clark Lake)	0.62	17.0	0.29
2 km northwest of 90,000-unit feedlot (shore of Seeley Lake)	1.3	34.0	0.53
2 km east of 90,000-unit feedlot	1.3	34.0	0.40
0.4 km west of 90,000-unit feedlot	2.8	73.0	0.61

Source: Hutchinson and Viets (1969).

* Absorption in 0.01 N H_2SO_4; absorption by lake water estimated to be one-half of these.

TABLE 23.8. Estimated annual amounts of constituents in runoff from rural land as affected by management practice (prevailing or improved) and cover crop.

| | Pounds per Acre of Constituent in Runoff for Cover Crop of | | | | | |
| | Corn | | Wheat | | Meadow | |
Constituent	Pre-vailing	Im-proved	Pre-vailing	Im-proved	Pre-vailing	Im-proved
Total solids	33,200.0	3,660.0	1,730.0	480.0	Trace	Trace
BOD	120.0	28.0	16.0	4.0	...	...
COD	1,300.0	480.0	170.0	64.0	...	...
Hydrolyzable P ...	9.2	2.8	1.2	0.36	...	...
Total N	237.0	88.0	31.0	11.0	...	...

Source: Weidner et al. (1969).

cultural drainage (Table 23.9). The experiments were performed on soils described as deep, permeable, silty clays, with tile drains located at depths of 5.5 to 7 feet. More nitrogen was contained in both tile drain effluents and surface runoff from fertilized than from nonfertilized systems. However, phosphorus losses were low compared to the phosphorus content of the irrigation water, suggesting a net removal of phosphorus from the irrigation water by the soil. Similarly, in the nonfertilized system, less nitrogen was lost than applied in the irrigation water.

To evaluate the importance to eutrophication of agricultural drainage relative to other nutrient sources, all nutrient sources for the particular water must be considered. Estimates have been made of the nutrient sources for Lake Mendota, Wisconsin, the surface waters of Wisconsin, and the water supplies of the United States. Review of these estimates is useful in evaluating the contribution of agricultural drainage to the nitrogen and phosphorus status of natural waters.

TABLE 23.9. Nitrogen and phosphorus balance for tile-drained soils under different cropping and fertilizer treatments.

| | | Pounds Applied | | Pounds Lost | | |
System	Nutrient	Fertilizer	Irrigation	Drainage effluent	Surface runoff	Applied Nutrient Lost
						(%)
6	N	22,216	1,263	14,836	1,539	70
	P	4,025	373	25	109	3
7	N	14,112	347	843	414	9
	P	2,328	54	3	11	1
14	N	0	1,317	282	132	31
	P	0	165	6	16	13
16	N	3,864	1,357	1,528	191	33
	P	0	156	22	4	17

Source: Johnson et al. (1965).

Lake Mendota, Wisconsin

Lake Mendota, Wisconsin, provides an example of a lake influenced to a major degree by rural and urban areas. Because of the importance of the lake to the region and concern over its eutrophic nature, an attempt was made to estimate the amounts of nitrogen and phosphorus entering the lake from various sources (Lee et al., 1966; Schraufnagel et al., 1967).

Lake Mendota is approximately 9,730 acres in surface area, with a maximum depth of 24 meters. Madison, with a population of about 175,000, is the largest city in the watershed.

The Lake Mendota watershed covers about 142,000 acres and is described by Schraufnagel et al. (1967) as an area occupied by permeable, calcareous, loamy glacial deposits, with a significant covering of loess. Most soil development is in the loess cover, with some development occurring in the glacial till immediately below the loess. Many of the soils were developed under prairie vegetation and are characterized by an A horizon 8 to 16 inches thick and relatively high in organic matter. Slopes in most of the watershed are gentle. Numerous small, undrained depressions occur in the uplands, and several large, wet lands containing organic soils are located in the watershed. Numerous dairy farms occupy the area; the estimated dairy cow population is 100 cows per square mile.

RURAL RUNOFF

The contribution of rural runoff to the nitrogen and phosphorus budgets of Lake Mendota was estimated by considering the land use in the watershed and the amounts of nutrients lost from each type of land (Lee et al., 1966; Schraufnagel et al., 1967). The distribution of land in the watershed according to use is shown in Table 23.10. A large portion (102,500 acres or 73%) of the watershed is devoted to cropland, with smaller areas in woodland (7%), pasture (8%), wetland (5%), and urban centers (7%).

Estimates of the amounts of nitrogen and phosphorus contributed to Lake Mendota from the various types of rural lands are shown in Table 23.11. The largest contribution was estimated to

TABLE 23.10.   Estimated land use in the Lake Mendota watershed.

Land Use	Acres	Percent of Watershed
Cropland	103,500	73
Corn and row crops	51,000	36
Oats	18,500	13
Hay and pasture	34,000	24
Woodland	10,000	7
Pasture and other	11,400	8
Major wetland	7,100	5
Urban	10,000	7
Total	142,000	100

Source: Water Subcommittee (1967).

TABLE 23.11. Estimates of the annual amounts of nitrogen and phosphorus contained in runoff waters in the Lake Mendota watershed.

| | Pounds per Acre | | Pounds per Watershed | |
Land Use	Nitrogen	Phosphorus	Nitrogen	Phosphorus
Cropland and pasture ...	0.06	0.04	6,900	5,400
Woodland	0.03	0.003	300	30
Wetland	...	...	...	...
Manured land	3.0	1.0	45,000	15,000
Total			52,200	20,430

Source: Water Subcommittee (1967).

be from manured land, accounting for about 87% of the nitrogen and 73% of the phosphorus. Cropland contributed about 27% of the phosphorus and 13% of the nitrogen. Although insufficient data were available to estimate the contribution of wetlands, it was believed that the amounts of nitrogen and phosphorus received, particularly from drained marshes, would be significant.

The contributions from manured lands were calculated by assuming that one-half of the manure from dairy cattle was applied to frozen soil and that 3 pounds of nitrogen and 1 pound of phosphorus were lost for each 10 tons per acre application of manure. These estimates were based on observation of Midgley and Dunklee (1945) for a frozen soil of 8% slope. Amounts from cropland and pasture were estimated from concentrations in runoff from a Miami silt-loam soil with 10% slope (Eck et al., 1957) and assuming 2 inches of runoff per year. Only water-soluble forms of nitrogen and phosphorus were considered. Values for wooded areas were obtained from the nitrogen and phosphorus contents of streams flowing through these areas (Sylvester, 1960) and were considered very rough estimates as they did not distinguish between amounts contributed by surface runoff and base flow.

OTHER SOURCES

The relative importance of rural runoff, percolate waters, and other sources is shown from the estimates of the total nutrient budget of Lake Mendota recorded in Table 23.12 (Lee et al., 1966). Rural runoff was the largest phosphorus contributor (42%), while groundwater accounted for the major portion of nitrogen (52%). However, the quantity of nitrogen contributed by rural runoff (52,-000 lb/yr) was larger than the corresponding quantity of phosphorus (20,000 lb/yr). For nitrogen, precipitation on the lake surface was the second largest contributor (20%), followed by rural runoff (11%) and municipal and industrial wastewaters (10%). For phosphorus, municipal and industrial wastewaters were the second largest source (36%), followed by urban runoff (17%).

The large amount of soluble nitrogen contributed by groundwater shows the importance of nitrate transport from soils to groundwater by water percolating through the soil. Estimates for the contribution of groundwater included both that entering the lake directly (about 30 cfs) and that reaching the lake through contributing to the flow of surface tributaries (about 35 cfs). Concentrations of NO_3-N of 2.5 mg/l for groundwater entering through surface tributaries and 1 mg/l for direct-entering groundwater were assumed. A lower NO_3-N concentration for groundwater entering below the surface was used because it was assumed that denitrification was of greater importance in these waters than in surface tributaries.

It is of interest to compare the estimates in Table 23.12 with values obtained by measuring flow and nutrient concentrations in the tributaries entering Lake Mendota (Rohlich, 1963). Tributary measurements, which do not include groundwater entering the lake beneath the surface, indicated that 259,700 pounds of inorganic nitrogen and 343,400 pounds of total nitrogen entered the lake during the year October 1948 to October 1949. This compares with a total estimated nitrogen budget of 478,300 pounds per year in Table 23.12. The total phosphorus contribution from tributaries indicated from direct measurements was 53,389 pounds per year compared with an estimate of 47,000 pounds per year in Table 23.12.

Briefly, estimates of contributions from other sources shown in Table 23.12 were obtained as follows: Quantities of nitrogen and phosphorus in municipal and industrial wastewaters were estimated from the individual sources, including municipal-treated domestic wastes from small villages in the watershed, private domestic waste disposal systems, milk and cheese processing and canning companies, and a car wash. Treated domestic wastes from the city of Madison are not discharged into Lake Mendota. Urban runoff values were estimated from data obtained for Cincinnati, Ohio (Weibel et al., 1964), with allowances made for the higher degree of industrialization of Cincinnati than of Madison. For precipitation, a value of 10 pounds of nitrogen per acre per year was used (Shah, 1961); the value of 1,300 pounds of phosphorus per year for Lake Mendota

TABLE 23.12. Estimated sources of nutrients for Lake Mendota, Wisconsin.

Nutrient Source	Pounds per Year		Percent of Total	
	Nitrogen	Phosphorus	Nitrogen	Phosphorus
Municipal and industrial waste water	47,000*	17,000*	10	36
Urban runoff	30,300†	8,100†	6	17
Rural runoff	52,000†	20,000†	11	42
Precipitation on lake surface	97,000	1,300	20	3
Groundwater	250,000	600	52	2
Nitrogen fixation	2,000	...	< 1	...
Marsh drainage	.... Not estimated			
Total	478,300	47,000		

Source: Nutrient Sources Subcommittee (1966).

* Total of nutrient forms.

† Soluble nutrient forms.

is an average value derived from several sources. The quantity of nitrogen-fixation was based on a rate of 0.02% of nitrogen fixed per day as reported by Goering (1963) and the assumption that nitrogen-fixation occurs 3 months per year and in the top 3 meters of the lake. Although marsh drainage was not estimated, its contribution may be significant.

Nutrient Sources for Waters in Wisconsin

Using an approach similar to that described for the Lake Mendota watershed, the amounts of nitrogen and phosphorus reaching surface waters of the state of Wisconsin from various sources were estimated by Schraufnagel et al. (1967).

The importance of rural sources relative to other sources differed somewhat from the values for Lake Mendota (Table 23.13). Rural sources were estimated to contribute 54% of the nitrogen. Of this, the largest portion (42%) came from the groundwater. Rural sources accounted for 30% of the phosphorus, 21.5% arising from manured land runoff. However, municipal treatment facilities were the largest phosphorus contributor (55.7%), while groundwater contributed the largest portion of nitrogen, as was the case for Lake Mendota.

Nutrient Sources for Water Supplies of the United States

In 1967 a Task Group of the American Water Works Association prepared a report on the sources of nitrogen and phosphorus in

TABLE 23.13. Estimated amounts of nitrogen and phosphorus reaching Wisconsin surface waters.

Source	Thousands of Pounds per Year		Percent of Total	
	Nitrogen	Phosphorus	Nitrogen	Phosphorus
Municipal treatment facilities	20,000	7,000	24.5	55.7
Private sewage systems	4,800	280	5.9	2.2
Industrial wastes	1,500	100	1.8	0.8
Rural sources				
Manured lands ...	8,110	2,700	9.9	21.5
Other cropland ...	576	384	0.7	3.1
Forest land	435	44	0.5	0.3
Pasture, woodlot, and other	540	360	0.7	2.9
Groundwater	34,300	285	42.0	2.3
Urban runoff	4,450	1,250	5.5	10.0
Precipitation on water areas	6,950	155	8.5	1.2
Total	81,661	12,558	100.0	100.0

Source: Water Subcommittee (1967).

TABLE 23.14. Estimated amounts of nutrients contributed from various sources for water supplies of the U.S.

	Millions of Pounds per Year		Percent of Total*	
Nutrient Source	Nitrogen	Phosphorus	Nitrogen	Phosphorus
Domestic waste	1,100–1,600	200–500	10	22.0
Industrial waste ...	>1,000	...	7	...
Rural runoff				
Agricultural land	1,500–15,000	120–1,200	60	42.0
Nonagricultural				
land	400–1,900	150–750	8	29.0
Farm animal waste .	>1,000	...	7	...
Urban runoff	110–1,100	11–170	4	6.0
Rainfall	30–590	3–9	2	0.4

Source: AWWA Task Group 2610-P (1967).
* Percentages are based on mean value of ranges given.

water supplies in the United States (McCarty et al., 1967). Their estimates are shown in Table 23.14. These estimates are for all water supplies, including groundwater. Thus the contribution by rural runoff includes drainage to the groundwater as well as surface runoff. It should be noted that the percentages shown in Table 23.14 were calculated from the means of the ranges of values reported by the Task Group and they may differ appreciably from the actual average contribution for each source. Consequently the percentages are useful only for very rough approximations. Futhermore, in the manner calculated, the percentages total 100, even though farm animal waste and industrial waste contributions of phosphorus were not estimated.

The values in this table suggest that agricultural land is an important contributor of nitrogen and phosphorus to water. About 60% of the nitrogen and 42% of the phosphorus were estimated to come from agricultural land. To arrive at these figures it was assumed that the 308 million acres of cultivated land in the United States contributed 5 to 50 pounds of nitrogen per acre per year or a total of 1,500 to 15,000 million pounds of nitrogen per year. As estimated, phosphorus contribution of 0.4 to 4 pounds per acre per year gave the total estimated amount of 120 to 1,200 million pounds per year.

It should be emphasized that the nutrient budget estimations that have been discussed were based on data obtained on a small scale in most cases, and extrapolation of these localized evaluations to an entire watershed or larger area gives estimations of a rather low reliability. More precise estimations based on more extensive evaluation of representative watersheds would certainly be useful in planning management programs to control the influx of nitrogen and phosphorus into water supplies. Nutrient sources are numerous and generalizations as to which source is the most important cannot be made. However, these estimations indicate that the contribution of agriculture is significant. The challenge is that this contribution should be reduced by improved and more efficient agricultural management practices.

REFERENCES

Armstrong, D. E., Spyridakis, D. E., and Lee, G. F. 1969. Cycling of nitrogen and phosphorus in natural waters with particular reference to the Great Lakes. Presented at the ACS Symp. on the Chemistry of the Great Lakes, Minneapolis, Minn.

Biggar, J. W., and Corey, R. B. 1969. Agricultural drainage and eutrophication. In *Eutrophication: causes, consequences, correctives.* Proc. Intern. Eutrophication Symp., Madison, Wis. Wash., D.C.: Natl. Acad. Sci.

Duley, F. L., and Miller, M. F. 1923. *Erosion and surface runoff under different soil conditions.* Mo. Agr. Exp. Sta. Res. Bull. 63.

Eck, P., Jackson, M. L., and Bay, C. E. 1957. Annual report AES Project 791 (Phase 5).

Fruh, E. C., Stewart, K. M., Lee, G. F., and Rohlich, G. A. 1966. Measurements of eutrophication and trends. *J. Water Pollution Control Federation* 38:1237–58.

Goering, J. J. 1963. Studies of nitrogen-fixation in natural fresh waters. Ph.D. thesis, Zoology Dept., Univ. of Wis.

Hutchinson, G. L., and Viets, F. G., Jr. 1969. Nitrogen enrichment of surface water by adsorption of ammonia volatilized from cattle feedlots. *Science* 166:514–15.

Johnson, W. R., Illihadich, F., Daum, R. M., and Pillsbury, A. F. 1965. Nitrogen and phosphorus in tile drain effluent. *Soil Sci. Soc. Am. Proc.* 29:287–89.

Lee, G. F., chairman, Nutrient Sources Subcommittee. 1967. Report on the nutrient sources of Lake Mendota. Water Chemistry Program, Univ. of Wis., Madison. (Mimeo.)

Lipman, J. G., and Conybeare, A. B. 1936. *Preliminary note on the inventory and balance sheet of plant nutrients in the United States.* N. J. Agr. Exp. Sta. Bull. 607.

Loehr, R. C. 1969. Animal wastes—a national problem. *J. Sanit. Eng. Div. Am. Soc. Civil Engrs.* 95:189–221.

McCarty, P. L., chairman Task Group 2610-P. 1967. Sources of nitrogen and phosphorus in water supplies. *J. Am. Water Works Assoc.* 59:344–66.

Midgley, A. R., and Dunklee, D. E. 1945. *Fertility runoff losses from manure spread during the winter.* Univ. of Vt. and State Agr. College Agr. Exp. Sta. Bull. 523.

Rawson, D. C. 1939. Some physical and chemical factors in the metabolism of lakes. *AAAS Bull.* 10:9–26.

Rohlich, G. A. 1963. Origin and quantities of plant nutrients in Lake Mendota. In *Limnology in North America,* ed. D. C. Frey. Madison: Univ. of Wis. Press.

Sawyer, C. N. 1947. Fertilization of lakes by agricultural and urban drainage. *J. New Engl. Water Works Assoc.* 61:109–27.

Schraufnagel, F. H., chairman, Working Group on Control Techniques and Research on Water Fertilization. 1967. Excessive water fertilization. Report to Water Subcommittee, Nat. Resources Committee of State Agencies, Wis. (Mimeo.)

Shah, K. S. 1961. Sulphus and nitrogen brought down in precipitation in Wisconsin. Master's thesis, Soils Dept. Univ. of Wis., Madison.

Smith, G. E. 1964. Nitrate problems in plants and water supplies in Missouri. 92nd Ann. Meeting, Am. Public Health Assoc., New York City.

Stewart, B. A., Viets, F. G., Jr., Hutchinson, G. L., and Kemper,

W. D. 1967. Nitrate and other water pollutants under fields and feedlots. *Environ. Sci. Technol.* 1:736–39.

Stewart, K. M., and Rohlich, G. A. 1967. *Eutrophication—a review.* Publ. 34, State Water Quality Control Bd., Calif.

Sylvester, R. O. 1960. *Limnological aspects of recreational lakes.* Public Health Serv. Publ. 1167.

Sylvester, R. O., and Seabloom, R. W. 1962. *A study on the character and significance of irrigation return flows in the Yakima River Basin.* A report from the Univ. of Wash.

Weibel, S. R., Anderson, R. J., and Woodward, R. L. 1964. Urban land runoff as a factor in stream pollution. *J. Water Pollution Control Federation* 36:914–24.

Weibel, S. R., Weidner, R. B., Cohen, J. M., and Christianson, A. G. 1966. Pesticides and other contaminants in rainfall and runoff. *J. Am. Water Works Assoc.* 58:1075–84.

Weidner, R. B., Christianson, A. G., Weibel, S. R., and Robeck, G. G. 1969. Rural runoff as a factor in stream pollution. *J. Water Pollution Control Federation* 41:377–84.

CHAPTER TWENTY-FOUR

EFFECTS OF AGRICULTURAL POLLUTANTS ON RECREATIONAL USES OF SURFACE WATERS

ROBERT S. CAMPBELL and JAMES R. WHITLEY

RECREATIONAL use of surface waters involves the employment of leisure time for enjoyment of fishing, boating, swimming, and the esthetic values of water. Pollution is the addition of material to water which produces results undesirable to man, including death of organisms, impairment of metabolic life processes, or the production of nuisance odors and algal scums.

Man's full recreational enjoyment of water demands the presence and diversity of animals and plants. The ecology of these living organisms, and the impact of agricultural pollutants on them, is best understood with reference to the aquatic community.

THE AQUATIC COMMUNITY

The aquatic community is the interdependent group of plants and animals living in a lake, pond, or stream. Interdependence is most easily seen in food-procuring activities, where each organism functions as a food *producer* or as a *consumer*. This complex community is dependent on photosynthesis in the same way that all agricultural production is ultimately dependent on food synthesis by green plants. The process of photosynthesis converts sunlight energy to chemical energy which is incorporated into carbohydrates, fats, and proteins. Thus, algae and rooted green plants are the *producers* in the aquatic community and comprise the principal source of food for the dependent group of *consumer* animals. In streams and rivers rooted plants and algae are less abundant than in lakes. Plant materials produced on the land and washed into streams and lakes are an additional food source for *consumers*.

Figure 24.1 shows that ingestion of green plants by animals initiates the transfer of sunlight energy to one or more levels of

ROBERT S. CAMPBELL is Professor of Zoology, University of Missouri. JAMES R. WHITLEY is Supervisor, Water Quality Investigations, Missouri Department of Conservation.

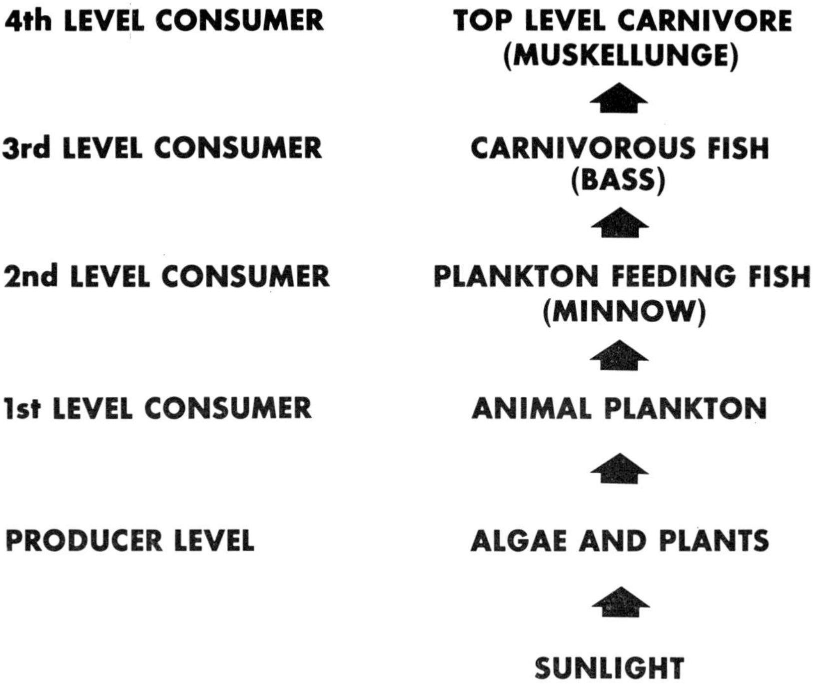

4th LEVEL CONSUMER   **TOP LEVEL CARNIVORE**
                               (MUSKELLUNGE)

3rd LEVEL CONSUMER   **CARNIVOROUS FISH**
                               (BASS)

2nd LEVEL CONSUMER   **PLANKTON FEEDING FISH**
                               (MINNOW)

1st LEVEL CONSUMER   **ANIMAL PLANKTON**

PRODUCER LEVEL   **ALGAE AND PLANTS**

SUNLIGHT

FIG. 24.1. A simplified food chain involving one **producer** link and four **consumer** links. **Arrows** indicate direction of flow of energy.

consumers, and demonstrates the dependence of each *consumer* level on lower levels of *consumers* and ultimately on *producers*. At death organisms are mineralized by *decomposer* bacteria and nutrients are released to be incorporated by *producers*. Any factor which adversely affects the environment of this complex community may affect directly all levels *(producer, consumer, decomposer)* in the community. If only one level is directly affected, all other levels will be affected indirectly because of their interdependence. Thus, environmental pollution, however slight, may have far-reaching effects on the entire aquatic community. For example, any agricultural practice which increases soil erosion and turbidity of water will interfere directly with the photosynthetic process and indirectly with the poundage of fish produced in that body of water.

We are concerned in this chapter with the aquatic communities of streams and lakes. Agricultural pollutants that have a profound impact on the aquatic community include (1) pesticides, (2) irrigation return water, (3) eroded soil, and (4) agricultural fertilizers and animal wastes.

PESTICIDES

Trace levels of pesticides in water may be concentrated in the tissues of aquatic organisms. If these organisms are in turn eaten, pesticides are further concentrated in the consuming animals. Thus, in one food chain, pesticides may become progressively concentrated in animal tissues at successive levels, so in the third and fourth consumer levels the concentration may exceed the concentration in the water by several thousandfold. This phenomenon of biological magnification occurs with the chlorinated hydrocarbon insecticides because they are selectively absorbed into the oils, fats, and waxes in the living organisms in the aquatic environment. Most surface waters in the United States now contain DDT and its related compounds (American Chemical Society, 1969). An example of this type of pesticide magnification is the death of fish-eating birds resulting from the use of DDD to control gnats in Clear Lake, California (Hunt and Bischoff, 1960; Rudd, 1964).

DDD was applied in 1949, 1954, and 1957, with near-complete control of the gnat. Prior to 1949, more than 1,000 pairs of western grebes nested at the lake but apparently did not breed subsequent to treatment. Grebes did continue to visit the lake annually. There was a die-off in 1954, 1955, and 1957, attributed to high levels of DDD in the tissues. Inspection of the aquatic food chain showed that DDD levels in tissues were progressively greater at successive consumer levels (Table 24.1).

A problem closely related to biological magnification of chlorinated hydrocarbons is the development of resistance to pesticides by organisms. The development of resistance is a well-known obstacle in the control of insect pests with insecticides. Vinson et al. (1963) reported resistance in fish to chlorinated hydrocarbons. The ability of nontarget organisms to become resistant would seem to be beneficial. However, resistance can be distastrous to fish popula-

TABLE 24.1. Biological magnification, Clear Lake aquatic food chain. Concentrations are maximal. Values for vertebrates are for visceral fat.

Food Chain Level	Organism	Concentration of DDD	Concentration of DDD in Excess of That in Water
		(ppm)	
Third-level consumer	Predaceous birds (grebes)	1,600.0	80,000 ×
	Carnivorous fish (largemouth bass)	1,700.0	85,000 ×
Second-level consumer	Plankton-feeding small fish	10.0	500 ×
First-level consumer Producer level	Animal plankton Plankton algae	5.3	265 ×
Water	.....	0.02	...

Source: Modified from Rudd (1964).

tions. Ferguson (1967) reports that some fish populations from heavily treated areas can tolerate up to 1,500 times the dose of some insecticides that is lethal to nonresident fishes. Ferguson states, "Resistant fishes are able to tolerate massive body burdens of these compounds in their tissues, and these residues constitute the source of concern regarding the ecological significance of resistance." He concludes, "Our findings indicate that although selection of a resistant fishery may permit exposed populations to survive, it may ultimately produce a biological product dangerous to consumers of all sorts, including man himself."

A critical review of the literature on the effects of pesticides on fishes (Johnson, 1968) emphasizes the following points: (1) Spraying of streams has, in some instances, destroyed most of the aquatic insects. (2) Pesticides do alter the composition of aquatic communities. This can involve reduction in game fish, elimination of predators with subsequent increase in prey species, and reduction in members of the zooplankton and bottom-dwelling invertebrates. (3) The degree of toxicity may be dependent on the position of the plant or animal in the food chain—the fourth-level carnivore may be affected more than the first-level consumer, due to biological concentration of pesticides. (4) Most studies with fish have concerned acute toxicity where the effect is measurable by death. When fish survived, the implication was that the pesticide was not toxic at the level tested; the possibility of damage through long-term exposure at sublethal concentrations was not answered. (5) Acute toxicity is mainly injurious to the nervous system of fish. (6) There are reports of damage in fish to the liver, gonads, blood, gills, and interference with normal physiological processes.

A typical example of fish loss from exposure to DDT, applied in concentrations of 0.5 to 1 pound per acre, is cited from Cope and Springer (1958): "Large numbers of dead trout, whitefish, and suckers, including many young-of-the-year, were noted three months after the spraying along a 100-mile stretch of the river. Great reductions in numbers of aquatic invertebrates again took place. This loss of food appears to have been the chief cause of the fish die-off."

Burdick et al. (1964) compared fry survival from eggs gathered from 12 lakes receiving varying amounts of DDT from the watershed. The authors concluded that fry mortality was induced when concentrations of DDT in the egg exceeded approximately 3 ppm. During the study period when the watershed of Lake George, New York, was treated with amounts of DDT ranging from 0.30 to 0.57 pounds per acre, concentration of the pesticide ranged from 4 to 15 ppm in egg tissue and 112 to 515 ppm in egg oil.

In recent months coho salmon from Lake Michigan were removed from the market by the Food and Drug Administration because they contained excessive residues of DDT. Some countries and the states of Arizona and Michigan have banned the use of DDT, and others are considering similar action.

The major concern of conservationists regarding chlorinated hydrocarbon pesticides is the problem of persistence. The severe ecological effects resulting from pesticide levels which are hardly measurable in the aquatic environment suggest that there is no safe level of application of these persistent chemicals which is consistent with economic agricultural use. These long-lasting compounds spread worldwide throughout the environment and concentrate in dangerous amounts through the food chain. There are alternatives to the use of persistent pesticides in agriculture—namely, organic phosphates and carbamates, and more intensive employment of biological controls.

IRRIGATION RETURN WATER

Irrigation was the greatest single use of water in the United States in 1960, accounting for 135 out of a total use of 322 billion gallons per day (U.S. Bureau of the Census, 1962). Water quality changes resulting from irrigation include temperature increase and total salinity increase. The more serious effects from temperature elevation are reduction in the dissolved oxygen supply and increased toxicity of polluting substances. An effect on fish of salinity increase, caused by irrigation return water, was described for the San Joaquin River, California, by Radtke and Turner (1967). Concentrations of dissolved substances in excess of 350 ppm blocked the upstream spawning migration of striped bass. However, at lesser concentrations of 100 to 350 ppm, upstream migration occurred as indicated by a 4- to 12-fold increase in gill-net catch.

ERODED SOIL

Photosynthesis in water is restricted to that upper euphotic zone which receives 1% or more of incident sunlight. For example, the euphotic zone in Lake Erie, 1939–40, varied in thickness from 32 feet when turbidity was 5 ppm to 3 feet when turbidity was 115 ppm (Chandler, 1942). This reduction of light penetration by suspended soil reduces total photosynthesis and hence total production within the aquatic community. Chandler and Weeks (1945) proposed that increased turbidity in 1942 in Lake Erie appeared to have resulted in a 19% reduction of spring phytoplankton from the 1941 level. Butler (1964) wrote that primary productivity in central Oklahoma farm ponds varied inversely with turbidity. Summer photosynthetic rate in one clear pond was three times that of a turbid pond.

The effects of turbidity on fish and other consumer organisms are varied, but the overall result is one of reduction in total production. According to Trautman (1957), "Studies made since 1925 have proved that since then, if not before, soil suspended in water has been the universal pollutant in Ohio, and the one which has most drastically affected the fish fauna. Clayey soils, suspended in water, prohibited the proper penetration of light, thereby preventing development of the aquatic vegetation, of the food of fishes, of fish eggs and of fry."

These views are supported by Cordone and Kelley (1961): "There is abundant evidence that sediment is detrimental to aquatic life in salmon and trout streams. The adult fishes themselves can apparently stand normal high concentrations without harm, but deposition of sediments on the bottom will reduce the survival of eggs and alevins, reduce aquatic insect fauna, and destroy needed shelter. There can scarcely be any doubt that prolonged turbidity of any great degree is also harmful."

Whether the physical contact of suspended solids is directly detrimental to adult fishes is not resolved. Laboratory studies on 16 species of freshwater fishes suggested that "the direct effect of montmorillonite clay turbidity is not a lethal condition in the life of juvenile to adult fishes at turbidities found in nature" (Wallen, 1951). Wallen reported that most individuals survived for a week or longer exposures to 100,000 ppm suspended clay, a value at least 10× greater than expected turbidities in natural waters. On the other hand, Herbert and Merkens (1961) concluded that continual abrasion by suspended solids in concentrations of 90 to 810 ppm in experimental tanks may have induced gill thickening which was observed in some trout but not in others. They suggest that such gill alteration may make fish more susceptible to other stresses in the environment and thus reduce survival chances.

Effects of turbidity on bass and sunfish, measured over 2 growing seasons in 12 ponds in Illinois where turbidity was approximately 25 ppm in the clearer ponds and in excess of 100 ppm in the most turbid, are described by Buck (1956): (1) The average total weight of fish in the clear ponds was 5.5 times greater than in muddy ponds at the end of the second growing season; (2) growth rate in length of first-year bass was three times greater in the clear ponds than in muddy ponds; (3) the weight increase in bass at the end of the second growing season was 5.5 times greater in the clear ponds; (4) bass reproduction was suppressed in the more turbid ponds. He found similar results in studies on 14 hatchery ponds and 2 large reservoirs. Swingle (1949) also reported the failure of largemouth bass to spawn in ponds receiving a large inflow of highly turbid water.

Angler success for most game species is improved in clearer water. "The clear reservoir attracted more anglers, yielded greater returns per unit of fishing effort, as well as more desirable species, and was immeasurably more appealing in the aesthetic sense" (Buck, 1956). Catch success for game fish is directly related to water clarity. In Little Dixie Lake, Missouri, in 1969, extended summer rains restricted water visibility to a depth of 8 to 16 inches, June through July. In August, water visibility increased to a depth of 37 inches. The catch of bass immediately increased 5-fold (J. L. Choate, personal communication). Similarly, more bass and bluegill were taken by anglers in Fork Lake, Illinois, during periods of increased water transparency (Bennett et al., 1940). Angler use of the Meramec River watershed (Missouri) dropped one-third when the water flow was above normal and muddy, resulting in an estimated annual economic loss of $60,775 to the residents (Brown, 1945).

AGRICULTURAL FERTILIZERS AND ANIMAL WASTES

The slow process of aging of lakes and ponds is accompanied by a gradual increase in nutrients with concomitant increased production of animal and plant life. Associated with this is a reduction in dissolved oxygen in deeper water because of accumulated organic matter, and a loss in water transparency due to blooms of algae and animal plankton. The term applied to aging is eutrophication and is defined as the intentional or unintentional enrichment of water (Hasler, 1947). Serious aspects of eutrophication include impairment of esthetic qualities by unsightly nuisance algae and dense growth of rooted plants and a hastening of lake extinction, since the accumulated organic matter and eroded soils ultimately fill the lake basin. Agricultural pollutants which hasten eutrophication include inorganic fertilizers and animal wastes.

It is currently thought that nitrogen and phosphorus are the elements most responsible for lake eutrophication (Mackenthun, 1968). Large quantities of nitrogen and phosphorus are contributed to surface waters by agricultural drainage (Sawyer, 1947; Task Group Report, 1967; Mackenthun, 1968). It is shown (Table 24.2) that concentrations in agricultural drainage and irrigation return water are several times greater than in uncontaminated lakes and streams, and as great or greater than in eutrophic lakes.

Concentrations of total phosphorus less than 0.01 ppm usually limit biological activity, whereas nuisance algal blooms may be expected when total phosphorus exceeds 0.05 to 0.1 ppm. The relationship of nitrogen and phosphorus enrichment to eutrophication is discussed by Armstrong and Rohlich (see Chapter 23).

It has been suggested that there is a relationship between weight of the fish population and water fertility (Moyle, 1956; Table 24.2). The relationship of the standing crop of fish in pounds per acre to total phosphorus in ppm was 40 to 0.02, 90 to 0.034, 150 to 0.058, and 370 to 0.126. However, increase in standing crop is accompanied by a change in species composition. For example, in Minnesota lakes (Moyle, 1956), as the standing crop of fish increased from 40 to 370 pounds per acre, the structure of the fish population changed from one involving lake trout in the 40 pounds per acre lakes to one including yellow perch, walleye, northern pike, bass, and bluegill in lakes of intermediate poundage; and finally, in the 370 pound per acre lakes, to one where two-thirds of the standing crop were undesirable fish such as carp.

Marked biological changes associated with eutrophication include loss of esthetic values associated with loss of water clarity and development of algal blooms, and major changes in fish fauna and fish food organisms. Such changes have been described for Lake Erie (Beeton, 1965) and for lakes Zurichsee, Switzerland, and Mendota, Wisconsin (Hasler, 1947). More general aspects of biological problems in recreational lakes are described by Mackenthun et al. (1964). An annotated bibliography on nitrogen and phosphorus in water was compiled by Mackenthun (1965).

TABLE 24.2. Concentrations of nitrogen and phosphorus in milligrams per liter (ppm) in different aquatic communities, and the relationship of nitrogen and phosphorus levels to biological activity.

Item	Soluble Phosphorus (as P)	Total Phosphorus (as P)	Inorganic Nitrate Nitrogen (as N)	Total Nitrogen (as N)	Ref.
Uncontaminated surface water ...	...	0.01–0.03	...	...	Mackenthun (1968)
Streams, forested area, little habitation or land use ...	0.007	0.069	0.130	0.204	Sylvester (1961)
Eutrophic Green Lake, Seattle ...	0.016	0.076	0.084	0.340	Sylvester (1961)
Sewage ...	1–13	3.5–9.0	7–40	18–50	Bartsch (1961) Task Group Report (1967)
Seepage water from agricultural soils, Illinois ...	0.2–0.7	...	...	...	Engelbrecht and Morgan (1961)
Surface irrigation return flow ...	0.162	0.251	1.250	1.455	Sylvester (1961)
Cattle feedlot wastes ...	16.3	...	0.1–11	...	Miner et al. (1966)
Limiting factor to biological activity ...	...	<0.01	...	...	Sawyer et al. (1945)
Nuisance algal blooms expected when values exceed ...	0.01	0.05–0.10	0.3	...	Sawyer (1947) Mackenthun (1968)
Fish production: 40 lb/a ...	...	0.020	...	...	Moyle (1956)
370 lb/a ...	...	0.126	...	...	Moyle (1956)

Note: The values of N and P in relationship to animal and plant production should be considered only as indicative of general relations since there is much variation among lakes and many factors affect production.

TABLE 24.3. Wastes of hogs and cattle in Missouri expressed as human population equivalents.

Population	Number in Missouri, 1969*	Individual Pounds BOD per Day	Approximate Population Equivalent
Man	4,320,000	0.17	4,320,000
Hogs and pigs	4,257,000	0.41	10,260,000
Cattle and calves	4,748,000	1.20	33,520,000

Source: Modified from Ray (1965).

* USDA Statistical Reporting Service.

Animal wastes which enter surface waters have such a high oxygen demand that they rapidly exhaust the dissolved oxygen. Ray (1965) expressed animal waste in terms of "human population equivalents" by dividing the oxygen requirements (pounds BOD per day) of animal waste by 0.17, the value for human wastes. The population equivalents calculated for hogs and cattle on farms in Missouri, 1969, are shown in Table 24.3. Clearly the organic load of animal wastes represents a potential oxygen demand on receiving waters in excess of that imposed by human waste. The concentration of animals in feedlots with uncontrolled drainage results in exaggerated surface water degradation at the locations of those drainages. Dissolved oxygen concentration should be above 5 ppm for a diversified warm-water fauna (Federal Water Pollution Control Administration, 1968). Lower concentrations adversely affect the respiratory rate and general metabolism; prolonged concentrations as low as 2 ppm are often fatal to fish.

Cross and Brasch (1969) described a change in land use pattern in the Neosho River watershed, Kansas, from seasonal grazing to year-round maintenance of cattle, with many concentrated in feedlots. Associated with this change was a loss of 5 species of fishes and a decline in abundance of at least 20 species. Numerous fish kills were attributed to pollution from cattle feedlots whose wastes drained into streams.

Smith and Miner (1964) considered animal feedlot runoff a significant source of water pollution in Kansas. They described runoff water quality as follows: (1) very high organic content, (2) concentrations of ammonia frequently in excess of 10 ppm, and (3) heavy bacterial populations. The existence of pollution was usually indicated by fish kills which they attributed to ammonia and low dissolved oxygen.

PUBLIC LAWS

With the recent adoption of water quality standards by the states, minimal limits for the addition of agricultural pollutants to state waters were set by state law and are backed by federal enforcement.

The Federal Water Pollution Control Act of 1948 (Public Law

660) formed the basis for federal-state cooperation and for enforcement of federal regulations on interstate waters through the attorney general. With the adoption of the Federal Water Quality Act of 1965 (Public Law 234) Congress authorized the states and the federal government to establish water quality standards for interstate waters. After holding public hearings the states adopted standards and submitted them for review by the secretary of the interior. As of May 1969, there was whole or partial acceptance of water quality standards by all 50 states.

The development of standards considers the uses to be made of the water in question, the assignment of specific water quality criteria to protect the water use, and plans for implementation and enforcement. Water quality criteria differ from state to state and for different waters within a state.

A standard reference for water quality criteria which will protect recreational and other uses of surface water is the Report of the National Technical Advisory Committee to the Secretary of the Interior (Federal Water Pollution Control Administration, 1968). Criteria adopted by the state of Missouri are cited as examples of their application to agricultural pollutants:

> All tributary streams and all municipal, industrial, agricultural, and mining effluents shall not create conditions in the stream which will adversely affect the present water uses or the future water uses as they become current.
>
> *Pesticides.* Substances toxic to man, fish, and wildlife or detrimental to agricultural, mining, industrial, recreational, navigational, or other legitimate uses shall be limited to nontoxic or nondetrimental concentrations in the streams.
>
> *Irrigation Return Water.* Effluents shall not elevate or depress the average cross-sectional temperature of the stream more than 5°F. The stream temperature shall not exceed 90°F due to effluents.
>
> *Eroded Soil.* There shall be no turbidity of other than natural origin that will cause substantial visible contrast with the natural appearance of the stream or with its legitimate uses. There shall be no noticeable man-made deposits of solids either organic or inorganic in nature on the stream bed.
>
> *Animal Wastes.* Dissolved oxygen in the stream shall not be less than 5 ppm at any time due to effluents or surface runoff.
>
> The intent of enforcement of water quality standards (and the specific water quality criteria) is the orderly development and improvement of the nation's water resources, guaranteeing their long-time preservation for industrial, municipal, and agricultural uses, for recreation, and for esthetic enjoyment.

CONCLUDING STATEMENT

Unquestionably many agricultural pollutants affect recreation through alteration of water quality and degradation of fish and aquatic life. The more serious polluting agents we judge to be eroded soil, nutrients, and pesticides. We sense there is an awareness and appreciation of the problem among those concerned with agriculture.

While the problems relating to agricultural pollution are complex, and the solutions will not easily be attained, it seems reasonable that in many instances alternative procedures can be developed. Pollution control measures are available (e.g., pesticides) which will allow continuation of agricultural production and enhance and protect water quality and recreation. While these procedures may be costly to apply, the expenditure should be judged in light of its contribution toward the preservation of man's environment. Especially in the instance of pesticide use, protection of water quality may be requisite to protection of the health of man from unknown long-term effects of pesticides. Reduction and control of agricultural pollutants are essential to develop and maintain a high-quality environment. Quality of life and quality of environment are synonymous.

REFERENCES

American Chemical Society. 1969. *Cleaning our environment: the chemical basis for action*. Am. Chem. Soc., Wash., D.C.

Bartsch, A. F. 1961. Induced eutrophication—a growing water resource problem. In *Algae and metropolitan wastes*, pp. 6–9. U.S. Dept. of Health, Education and Welfare.

Beeton, A. M. 1965. Eutrophication of the St. Lawrence Great Lakes. *Limnol. Oceanog.* 10:240–54.

Bennett, C. W., Thompson, D. H., and Parr, S. A. 1940. A second year of fisheries investigations at Fork Lake, 1939. Lake Management Rept. 4. *Ill. Nat. Hist. Surv., Biol. Notes* 14:1–24.

Brown, C. B. 1945. Floods and fishing. *Land* 4:78–79.

Buck, D. H. 1956. Effects of turbidity on fish and fishing. *Trans. 21st North Am. Wildlife Conf.*, pp. 249–60.

Burdick, G. E., Harris, E. J., Dean, H. J., Walker, T. M., Skea, J., and Colby, D. 1964. The accumulation of DDT in lake trout and the effect on reproduction. *Trans. Am. Fisheries Soc.* 93:127–36.

Butler, J. L. 1964. Interaction of effects by environmental factors on primary productivity in ponds and microecosystems. Ph.D. thesis, Okla. State Univ. Graduate School.

Chandler, D. C. 1942. Limnological studies of western Lake Erie. II. Light penetration and its relation to turbidity. *Ecology* 23:41–52.

Chandler, D. C., and Weeks, O. B. 1945. Limnological studies of western Lake Erie. V. Relation of limnological and meteorological conditions to the production of phytoplankton in 1942. *Ecol. Monographs* 15:435–57.

Cope, O. B., and Springer, P. F. 1958. Mass control of insects: the effects on fish and wildlife. *Bull. Entomol. Soc. Am.* 4:52–56.

Cordone, A. J., and Kelley, D. W. 1961. The influences of inorganic sediment on the aquatic life of streams. *Calif. Fish Game* 47:189–228.

Cross, F. B., and Braasch, M. 1969. Qualitative changes in the fish-fauna of the upper Neosho River system, 1952–1967. *Trans. Kans. Acad. Sci.* 71:350–60.

Engelbrecht, R. S., and Morgan, J. J. 1961. Land drainage as a source of phosphorus in Illinois surface waters. In *Algae and metropolitan wastes,* pp. 74–79. U.S. Dept. of Health, Education and Welfare.

Federal Water Pollution Control Administration. 1968. *Water quality criteria.* Report of the Nat. Tech. Advisory Committee to the Sec. of the Interior.

Ferguson, D. E. 1967. The ecological consequences of pesticide resistance in fishes. *Trans. 32nd North Am. Wildlife Nat. Resources Conf.,* pp. 103–7.

Ferguson, D. E., Culley, D. D., Cotton, W. D., and Dodds, R. P. 1964. Resistance to chlorinated hydrocarbon insecticides in three species of freshwater fish. *BioScience* 14:43–44.

Hasler, A. D. 1947. Eutrophication of lakes by domestic sewage. *Ecology* 28:383–95.

Herbert, D. W. M., and Merkens, J. C. 1961. The effect of suspended mineral solids on the survival of trout. *Intern. J. Air Water Pollution* 5:46–55.

Hunt, E. G., and Bischoff, A. I. 1960. Inimical effects on wildlife of periodic DDD applications to Clear Lake. *Calif. Fish Game* 46:91–106.

Jamison, V. C., Smith, D. D., and Thornton, J. F. 1968. *Soil and water research on a clay pan soil.* USDA, ARS Tech. Bull. 1379.

Johnson, D. W. 1968. Pesticides and fishes—a review of selected literature. *Trans. Am. Fisheries Soc.* 97:398–424.

McKee, J. E., and Wolf, H. W. 1963. *Water quality criteria.* 2nd ed. Calif. State Water Quality Control Bd. Publ. 3-A.

Mackenthun, K. M. 1965. *Nitrogen and phosphorus in water.* An annotated selected bibliography of their biological effects. Public Health Serv. Publ. 1305.

———. 1968. The phosphorus problem. *J. Am. Water Works Assoc.* 60:1047–54.

Mackenthun, K. M., Ingram, W. M., and Porges, R. 1964. *Limnological aspects of recreational lakes.* Public Health Serv. Publ. 1167.

Miner, J. R., Lipper, R. I., Fina, L. R., and Funk, J. W. 1966. Cattle feedlot runoff—its nature and variation. *J. Water Pollution Control Federation* 38:1582–91.

Moyle, J. B. 1956. Relationships between the chemistry of Minnesota surface waters and wildlife management. *J. Wildlife Management* 20:303–20.

Piest, R. F., and Spomer, R. G. 1968. Sheet and gully erosion in the Missouri Valley loessal region. *Trans. Am. Soc. Agr. Engrs.* 11:850–53.

Radtke, L. D., and Turner, J. L. 1967. High concentration of total dissolved solids block spawning migration of striped bass, *Roccus saxatilis,* in the San Joaquin River, California. *Trans. Am. Fisheries Soc.* 96:405–7.

Ray, A. D. 1965. Pollution from industrial wastes and sewage. In *Water Forum,* pp. 31–36. Spec. Rept. 55, College of Agr., Univ. of Mo., Columbia.

Rudd, R. L. 1964. *Pesticides and the living landscape.* Madison: Univ. of Wis. Press.

Sawyer, C. N. 1947. Fertilization of lakes by agricultural and urban drainage. *J. New Engl. Water Works Assoc.* 61:109–27.

Sawyer, C. N., Lackey, J. B., and Lenz, R. T. 1945. *An investigation of the odor nuisances occurring in the Madison lakes, particu-*

larly Monona, Waubesca and Kegonsa from July 1942 to July 1944. Rept. of the Governor's Committee, Madison, Wis.

Smith, S. M., and Miner, J. R. 1964. Stream pollution from feedlot runoff. *Trans. 14th Ann. Conf. Sanit. Eng.* Univ. of Kans. Publ., Bull. of Eng. and Architecture 52:18–25.

Swingle, H. S. 1949. Some recent developments in pond management. *Trans. 14th North Am. Wildlife Conf.*, pp. 295–310.

Sylvester, R. O. 1961. Nutrient content of drainage water from forested, urban and agricultural areas. In *Algae and metropolitan wastes*, pp. 80–87. U.S. Dept. of Health, Education and Welfare.

Task Group Report. 1967. Sources of nitrogen and phosphorus in water supplies. *J. Am. Water Works Assoc.* 59:344–66.

Trautman, M. B. 1957. *The fishes of Ohio*. Columbus: Ohio State Univ. Press.

U.S. Bureau of the Census. 1962. *Statistical abstract of the United States*.

Vinson, S. B., Boyd, C. E., and Ferguson, D. E. 1963. Resistance to DDT in the mosquito fish, *Gambusia affinis. Science* 139: 217–18.

Wallen, I. E. 1951. The direct effect of turbidity on fishes. *Bull. Okla. Agr. Mech. College* 48:1–27.

The White House. 1965. *Restoring the quality of our environment*. Rept. of the Environ. Pollution Panel, President's Sci. Advis. Committee.

CHAPTER TWENTY-FIVE

EFFECTS OF SURFACE RUNOFF ON THE FEASIBILITY OF MUNICIPAL ADVANCED WASTE TREATMENT

E. ROBERT BAUMANN and SHELDON KELMAN

THE state of Iowa has been a national leader in water pollution control for nearly half a century. Its first stream control law, passed in 1923, gave the State Department of Health regulatory and enforcement authority. At the time the 1923 law was passed, almost 200 municipal sewage treatment plants were already in operation (Iowa Water Pollution Control Commission, 1969). These plants were in the smaller towns and served 350,000 persons, or 30% of the population connected to municipal sewers.

The pollution control law has been revised twice, the latest revision being enacted in 1965. This legislation created the Iowa Water Pollution Control Commission as the policy-making body in Iowa's water pollution activities. Present stream water quality regulations, in effect, necessitate secondary treatment (85 to 90% removal of BOD) on all interior streams.[1] Plant construction has steadily progressed so that as of January 1, 1969, there were 510 municipal water pollution control plants in operation or under construction, and the population served by treatment had increased to 99.3% of the sewered population. Municipalities not presently treating their wastes are smaller communities which now have plants in the planning or construction stage. One hundred percent of the medium size and larger communities had sewage treatment facilities at the beginning of 1969. This record of water pollution control ranks Iowa with the most progressive states in the nation.

Of the industries, Iowa's meat-packing plants represent the largest potential source of industrial water pollution. Every meat-packing plant in the state has a treatment plant in operation or under construction (Iowa Water Pollution Control Commission, 1969), and this represents some 3.5 million population equivalent being treated.

E. ROBERT BAUMANN is Professor, Department of Civil Engineering, Iowa State University. SHELDON KELMAN is Assistant Professor, Department of Civil Engineering, Iowa State University.

1. In October 1969, the FWPCA adopted national regulations requiring Iowa to provide secondary treatment also for all wastes discharging to both the Mississippi and Missouri rivers.

With the exception of packing plants on border streams, all packing-plant wastes receive at least secondary treatment.

Although this municipal and industrial waste treatment record is impressive, much work remains before the quality of the water in our streams is adequately protected. Some cities have grown to the point where their treatment facilities are undersized and/or obsolete. Most secondary treatment facilities do not provide sufficient treatment efficiency in the wintertime (only 65 to 75% removal of BOD) due to the effects of cold weather on the efficiency of biological treatment on trickling filters. Recently, some authorities have been calling for still higher levels of wastewater treatment to alleviate water pollution problems. Iowa's interior streams are characterized in much of the state by extremely low minimum flows and relatively high summer temperatures. At Ames, for example, the design flow in the Skunk River (7-day low flow with a frequency of occurrence of once in 10 years) is only 0.1 cfs while the Ames waste discharge currently approximates 5.0 to 6.0 cfs. Even when low flow augmentation is available from the proposed Ames reservoir, the design stream flow will be increased to only 30 to 40 cfs. Under these conditions—typical of those for many of Iowa's cities and industries—maintenance of current water quality standards in Iowa streams will require better waste treatment. The treatment needs indicated include:

1. increased carbonaceous BOD removal
2. increased oxidation of the ammonia in the treated waste to nitrate
3. increased phosphate removal

The increased removal of carbonaceous BOD is required to maintain the oxygen level in the stream to protect fish life. The oxidation of ammonia to nitrate is required to reduce the ammonia levels in the stream below levels toxic to fish. Unfortunately, the increased oxidation of ammonia to nitrate, together with the availability of phosphates in the stream, results in significant algal growths. Such algal growths can have a detrimental effect on water quality because:

1. they increase the carbonaceous BOD in the stream and may result in significantly lowered DO levels at night
2. they increase the turbidity and suspended solids load in the stream and can impart tastes and odor to the water

Before increased treatment requirements (advanced waste or tertiary treatments) are imposed on cities and industries, it would appear desirable to consider first whether such wastes are the more significant contributors of carbonaceous BOD, nitrates, and phosphates to Iowa streams. Agriculture which contributes carbonaceous BOD from animal wastes, plant residues, etc., and phosphates and nitrates from the above sources and from fertilizer applications may contribute such significant quantities of similar pollutants on an uncontrolled area basis as to negate any desirable effect of increased municipal and/or industrial waste treatment.

This chapter is designed to explore the relative effects of both municipal-industrial and agricultural wastes as they affect treatment requirements which may be imposed on municipal use of the stream for receiving treated wastes.

MUNICIPAL-INDUSTRIAL WASTE TREATMENT

Each treatment process achieves certain end results. For many years all Iowa municipal and industrial wastes have received primary treatment. Primary treatment is commonly a settling process which removes floating and settleable material, including a portion of the suspended solids and its associated organic carbon. The organic carbon is measured by the amount of oxygen bacteria required to oxidize it in a fixed time period under aerobic conditions. Thus the organic carbon removal is typically described as a reduction in biochemical oxygen demand or reduction in BOD_5 (measured in 5 days at 20° C). Primary treatment will remove over 95% of the floating and settleable solids, from 60 to 70% of suspended solids, and from 30 to 40% of BOD_5. Since much of the organic carbon is present in solution or in colloidal suspension, most (60 to 70%) is not removable by sedimentation.

All Iowa municipal-industrial wastes will ultimately require secondary treatment prior to discharge to Iowa's surface waters. Secondary treatment normally employs a biological process utilizing bacteria and other simple forms of life to convert much of the remaining suspended and soluble organic carbon to biological cell protoplasm and energy. These process units are then followed by sedimentation tanks to remove the cells produced. Typical domestic effluents after secondary treatment contain only 10 to 20% of their original suspended solids and BOD and involve pollutant removal efficiencies of 80 to 90% under ideal conditions.

Primary and secondary treatments (complete treatment) remove only part of the wastes in wastewater. The organic material present is partially oxidized and partially converted into settleable cell protoplasm. This reaction can be represented empirically as[2]

$$COHNSP + O_2 \xrightarrow{\text{bacteria}} \text{protoplasm} + CO_2 + H_2O + NO_2^- + NO_3^- + NH_3^+ + SO_4^{--} + PO_4^{---} + \text{organic } P$$

Thus, it can be seen that although secondary treatment removes 80 to 90% of the organic carbon and reduces the oxygen demand on the stream which receives the treated wastes, these wastes will contain significant amounts of NO_2, NO_3, and NH_3 as well as phosphorous compounds, substances that are also applied to land in the form of common fertilizers. These compounds have become increasingly important since in recent years the widespread use of phosphate builders in detergents has more than doubled the concentration of phosphorus

---

2. Note: C = carbon; O = oxygen; H = hydrogen; N = nitrogen; S = sulfur; P = phosphorus.

in municipal wastewaters. In addition, significant concentrations of nonbiologically degradable organics will remain in the wastewater.

Nitrogen and phosphorus in municipal and industrial wastewaters add to the concentrations of these fertilizer elements in surface waters. Such nutrient enrichment of water is termed eutrophication and is of concern since it stimulates algal growth. This process can be represented as

$$PO_4^{---} + NO_3^- + CO_2 + \text{sunlight} \xrightarrow{\text{Algae}} \text{COHNSP (Algae protoplasm)}$$

Algae thus defeat the purpose of secondary treatment by creating more organic carbon (which we have just removed by primary and secondary treatment) in surface waters.

In the past 10 years attention has been focused on the problems created by such eutrophication. Many studies have been made of the various methods intended to solve this problem by achieving a higher degree of wastewater treatment. These methods employ an additional treatment step, usually termed tertiary treatment. Tertiary treatment is designed to achieve either a better degree of suspended solids and BOD removal and/or the removal of nonbiologically degradable organic and inorganic compounds, especially nitrogen and phosphorous compounds. Tertiary treatment, now economically and technically feasible, can result in BOD and phosphate removals of above 98% and the effluent quality would be as good or better than that of the receiving stream.

Among the processes which can be used singly or in combination to achieve these results are

1. lime or alum precipitation of phosphates
2. air stripping of ammonia at high pH levels
3. activated carbon adsorption of dissolved organics
4. pulsed adsorption beds (PAB) for increased biological removal of dissolved organics
5. sand or diatomaceous earth filtration for removal of residual biological cells and suspended organics
6. ion exchange for removal of specific cations and anions

All of these processes are expensive relative to present treatment methods. To put such a program into effect on a statewide basis for all municipal and industrial wastewater will cost many millions of dollars. Adding typical tertiary processes, such as lime precipitation for phosphorus removal and air stripping of ammonia, could triple the cost of wastewater treatment for a typical Iowa city.

EFFECTS OF NUTRIENTS IN SURFACE WATERS

To understand why there is a concern over the addition of nitrates and phosphates to surface water, it is first necessary to consider its effect on water uses. The presence of pyrophosphates and/or triphosphates has been shown to interfere with the efficiency of potable water treatment processes, including the coagulation-flocculation-sedimentation process and the lime-softening process. These problems become noticeable (Task Group Report, 1966) at combined triphosphate and pyrophosphate levels of 0.3 mg/l, measured as P. Shrobe (1967) found that approximately half the phosphates discharged in treated wastewater are orthophosphates and this ratio continues several miles downstream from the treatment plant. Most of the remaining phosphate will be in the condensed forms discussed above. Since typical Iowa rivers have been found to contain peak orthophosphate levels approaching 3 mg/l (Dept. of Civil Engineering, Engineering Research Institute, 1969), it can be assumed that similar levels of condensed phosphates will also be present below sewage discharges, creating potable water treatment difficulties.

Two of the principal nitrogen compounds, nitrates and ammonia, also cause problems. The United States Public Health Service drinking water standards limit the concentration of nitrates in potable water to 45 mg/l as nitrate. This limit is based on the fact that higher levels cause methemoglobinemia in infants. In general, nitrate levels in surface waters are well below this limit; however, there are times when Iowa rivers contain more than 45 mg/l nitrates (Engineering Research Institute, 1969). Ammonia causes problems by increasing significantly the chlorine demand of water if an uncombined or "free" chlorine residual is required. Ammonia is also detrimental to stream water quality since it is toxic to fish. The Iowa water quality standards for fishing streams limit the allowable ammonia concentration to 2 mg/l.

The major water quality problem created by nitrogen and phosphorus, however, is concerned with their stimulation of algae growth. Algae create problems in potable water treatment by clogging filters and causing undesirable tastes and odors. These problems were estimated in 1967 to affect as much as 56% of total municipal surface water supplies in the United States (Task Group Report, 1966).

Algae interfere with recreational use of rivers and lakes by coloring the water green and forming unsightly floating mats. Fish may be affected when large numbers of algae are present by lowering significantly the DO during the night. This algae oxygen demand can deplete the dissolved oxygen sufficiently to lead to fish kills. Fish may also find it hard to feed if the algae color the water and obscure their vision.

The conservationist pressures to solve the problems created by eutrophication are becoming greater every year. However, before we move toward requiring tertiary treatment of municipal and industrial wastes to control nutrient discharges in agricultural regions, we need to determine whether even 100% tertiary treatment of these wastewaters will correct the problems of eutrophication or even contribute to the correction. To accomplish this, we need to determine the relative nutrient contributions from various sources.

SOURCES OF NUTRIENTS

Several potential sources of nitrogen and phosphorus which can enter the surface waters of Iowa are readily recognized. For years, industrial and municipal wastes have been pointed out as the major contributors of N and P. In recent years, attention has been focused on the potential contribution from surface runoff. Corey et al. (1967) have listed the following available nitrogen sources for plant growth: soil organic matter, animal manure, legume fixation, commercial fertilizer, and fertilizer naturally present in precipitation. The same sources, of course, are potential contributors of nitrogen to runoff.

The average daily N and P contribution of each person connected to a sewer is well established. Given sewered population data, the quantities of nitrogen and phosphorus discharged in domestic wastewater can readily be computed (an example will be discussed later in this chapter). Other sources of these nutrients may equal or even exceed the quantities in domestic wastewater. Industrial wastes, especially those from packinghouses, contain large quantities of nitrogen and phosphorus, since meat is a protein containing high concentrations of both N and P.

Animal wastes form an increasing source of such nutrients. Both wild and domestic animals are significant sources of fertilizer elements. When storm runoff occurs, large quantities of animal wastes are washed into streams. In Iowa, for example, we have a domestic population of 2.75 million. This state is noted, however, for its production of pork and beef. Approximately 6,100,000 swine and 3,300,000 beef animals are on feed at any one time. Nearly 46,000 cattle feedlots are recorded in Iowa. The daily waste from these animals is equivalent to the daily waste from a human population of 65 to 90 million people. Naturally, not all this waste finds its way into our streams. But when it rains—as it does in Iowa 20 to 30 times per year with intensities of 1 inch/hour or more—several days' accumulation of these wastes may find their way into our surface waters. Feedlot regulations are now designed to control runoff from feedlots that feed over 100 head of cattle. Such animal wastes, together with dairy and poultry wastes, can be significant contributors of carbonaceous and nitrogenous BOD, ammonia, and nitrogen to our surface waters.

Another increasing source of the nutrients which enhance eutrophication is that derived from row crop agriculture. Nitrogen fertilizer use in the United States has increased from 2.15 million tons in 1957 to 6.56 million tons in 1968 (Sulphur Institute, 1969). The 1957 figure represents 76% of total United States consumption of nitrogen at that time (Sauchelli, 1961). During approximately the same time period, phosphorus use in fertilizers has risen from 0.99 million tons in 1958 (Van Wazer, 1961) to 2.02 million tons P in 1968 (Sulphur Institute, 1969). The 1958 figure represents 70% of that year's total United States consumption of phosphorus. Other large uses of phosphorus include use in detergents (13.3%) and in animal feeds (8.4%). Reportedly, commercial fertilizers are the source of only 10 to 20% of the gross nitrogen available for agriculture (Corey et al., 1967; Willrich, 1969).

The United States as a whole is in a nutrient mining phase; i.e., more nutrients are removed in the harvested crops than are replaced by all nutrient inputs, including commercial fertilizers. This is usually true for most Iowa crops. Corn can be an exception, however. High rates of nitrogen application in excess of 150 to 200 pounds per acre may cause a nitrogen accumulation situation rather than a mining situation depending on the amount of corn grain and stalks that are harvested. If only the grain is harvested, about 1 to 1.2 pounds of nitrogen are required per bushel of corn. If the whole plant is harvested for silage, about 2 pounds of nitrogen are removed for each bushel of corn produced.

TVA statistics (National Fertilizer Development Center, 1968) indicate that the average 1968 Iowa application rate of nitrogen on corn was 120 pounds N per acre. The USDA Statistical Reporting Service stated the average Iowa corn yield for 1968 was 93 bushels per acre.

WATER QUALITY IN DES MOINES RIVER—BOONE TO DES MOINES

For the past 2 years, the Sanitary Engineering Section of the Engineering Research Institute at Iowa State University has been making surface water quality studies between Boone and Des Moines as a part of a "Preimpoundment Survey of Water Quality in the Des Moines River above Saylorville Reservoir." This study is supported by the Rock Island District, Corps of Engineers. Among the parameters measured weekly are stream flow, BOD, COD, suspended solids, turbidity, the various forms of nitrogen, phosphates, and the algal count.

Total algal counts have been extremely high as shown by the algal count data for 1968. For example, in the first 6 months of 1968, the phytoplankton count averaged 96,000 cells/ml, ranging from 17,000 to 281,000 cells/ml. These values appear to be 5 to 10 times the typical values reported for similar rivers in a National Water Quality Network Report published 8 years ago (U.S. Dept. of Health, Education and Welfare, 1962.

Because of these high algal counts which have increased significantly in recent years, a mass balance on the nutrients entering the Des Moines River from the watershed above Boone was attempted. It was hoped that such a balance would reveal the probable sources of these nutrients and their magnitudes. The area, land use, and population of the basin were used to estimate possible levels of pollutants from domestic, industrial, and agricultural sources. The drainage area of the Des Moines River at Boone is 5,490 mi^2 of which 18% is in Minnesota and the remainder in Iowa (Iowa Natural Resources Council, 1953). The total area of the basin above Boone is equal to 9.78% of the area of the state of Iowa. Based on data from Iowa Water Resources Council Bulletin No. 1 (1953) and the 1960 census, a sewered population of 103,741 contributes treated wastewater directly to the river above Boone. In addition, consideration must be made of the nonsewered rural population, most of which use septic tanks. At the present time, roughly half the Iowa population of 2,783,000 can be classified as being rural (Iowa Natural Resources Council, 1953). Part of the wastes from this population eventually reaches a stream by surface runoff or by illegal connections to drain tiles, or enters the groundwater and reaches a stream during low flow periods. Since the rural population is rather evenly distributed throughout the state, the ratio of the basin's rural population to the state's rural population should be roughly equal to the ratio of the two areas. The estimated rural population calculated on this basis is 135,600. Some of the nutrients in the rural wastes are removed by plant uptake or lost by denitrification, soil adsorption, etc., and we can assume that only 50% reaches a stream. The effective total population contributing wastewater to the Des Moines River is thus 171,500. An average value for nitrogen in wastewater is about 10 pounds per capita per year (Task Group Report, 1967). At this rate we could expect roughly 4,700 pounds nitrogen per day or 860 tons of nitrogen per year from domestic wastewater. Similarly an average value for phosphorus in wastewater is 3 pounds per capita per year, which would result in a discharge of 1,410 pounds phosphorus per day or 256 tons per year in domestic wastewater in the basin. These estimates assume typical low removal efficiencies of these constituents in wastewater treatment. In the case of nitrogen, the form may merely be changed, i.e., to ammonia or to nitrate. In the case of phosphorus, it may be converted from organic phosphates to ortho-phosphate.

Major sources of industrial wastes in the basin are an anhydrous ammonia plant and several packing plants. Information from the records of the Iowa State Department of Health indicates that approximately 2,300,000 pounds of live weight of beef and hogs are killed each weekday at the packing plants in the basin above Boone. These plants will have losses of about 1 pound N and 0.1 pound P per 1,000 pounds live weight killed, based on a U.S. Department of Health, Education and Welfare publication (1954) and based on sampling experience of the authors. These losses would thus total about 2,300 pounds N and 230 pounds P each weekday or 300 tons N and 30 tons P yearly. The fertilizer plant contributes comparatively little N and no P to the Des Moines River. Most of these nutrients will be discharged in treated wastewater to the Des Moines River.

The possible losses of nutrients from growing corn, the dominant crop in the 5,490 mi^2 basin, can be estimated based on crop patterns. The harvested area of corn in 1968 in Iowa is believed to be about 10,200,000 acres (USDA Economic Research Service and Statistical Reporting Service, 1964), and if the watershed is assumed to have a proportionate acreage in corn the watershed corn acreage would be 1,000,000 acres. Timmons et al. (1968) have shown that with 3 inches of runoff 20.3 pounds per acre of nitrogen was lost annually from continuous corn plots. If this value is accepted *for discussion purposes*, then corn acreage in the basin could have contributed approximately 10,000 tons of nitrogen annually to the Des Moines River above Boone.

Timmons et al. (1968) also found that phosphorus losses with 3 inches of runoff from continuous corn plots were 0.2 pounds per acre. If this value is accepted, then the 1,000,000 acres of cornfields in the watershed could lose 100 tons of phosphorus annually to the river. Since corn is the predominant row crop in Iowa and receives 95% of the applied commercial fertilizer (USDA, ERS and Stat. Rep. Serv., 1964), no estimate was made of the nutrient contributions from other crops or noncultivated land.

A rough estimate can be made of nutrient contribution to the Des Moines River from animal wastes. Loehr (1969) has presented data indicating hogs produce wastes with 0.05 pound N and 0.03 pound P_2O_5 per 100 pounds animal weight per day. Beef cattle produce wastes with 0.40 pound N and 0.12 pound P_2O_5 per 1,000 pounds animal weight per day. Since we have 6,100,000 swine and 3,300,000 beef cattle on feed in Iowa at any one time, it is possible to calculate their pollution potential. In making this estimate it was assumed that the distribution of animals was uniform throughout the state, the average animal was half-grown, and 25% of the animal waste nutrients (a guess) were lost in runoff. Based on these assumptions, the quantities of nutrients lost from feedlots in the basin each year could well approximate 3,600 tons N annd 500 tons P. Additional quantities of nutrients are lost from poultry and dairying operations but are not included in this estimate.

The N and P estimated from these sources are tabulated in Table 25.1. These estimates can now be compared to the gross amounts determined from actual stream data collected between 1967 and 1969. Analyses for the various forms of nitrogen and orthophosphate were made weekly from samples collected from the flowing river water. No analyses were made of bottom sediments, but during high flow periods the water was highly turbid and contained large quantities of sediment. The analyses were performed according to the procedures outlined in "Standard Methods" (American Public Health Association, 1965). Since the test for orthophosphate is performed in an acid medium, part of the phosphate adsorbed on sediment is desorbed and detected by this method.

The concentration of N and P in the Des Moines River at Boone, based on these weekly analyses, is shown in Figure 25.1, together with river flows. Similarly, Figure 25.2 shows the pounds per day of N and P in the river at Boone.

During the first year of the study (1967–1968) rainfall was below

TABLE 25.1. Estimated sources of nitrogen and phosphorus in the Des Moines River basin above Boone, 1968.

	Ton N/Yr	Ton P/Yr	Lb N/Day	Lb P/Day
Domestic wastewater	860	256	4,700	1,410
Packinghouse wastes .	300	30	1,650	165
Animal wastes	3,600	500	20,000	2,700
Agricultural losses ..	10,000	100	55,000	550
Total	14,760	886	81,350	4,825

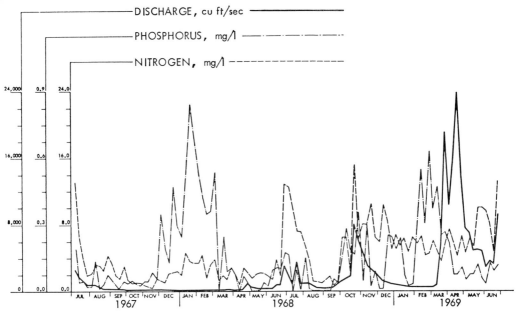

FIG. 25.1. Concentration of nutrients and flow in the Des Moines River at Boone, Iowa.

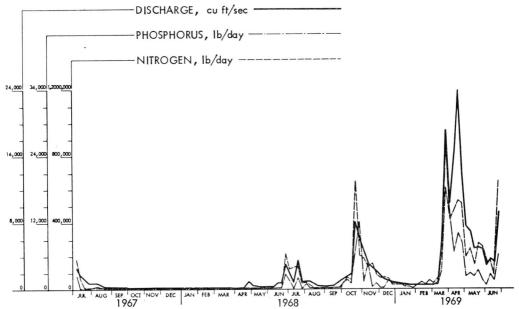

FIG. 25.2. Pounds of nutrients per day and flow in the Des Moines River at Boone, Iowa.

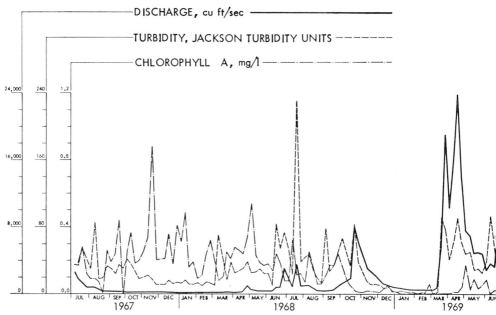

FIG. 25.3.   Chlorophyll A, turbidity, and flow in the Des Moines River at Boone, Iowa.

average, totaling 26.8 inches at Boone and only 18.4 inches at the Des Moines airport. As a result, runoff and river flows during this period were exceptionally low. Nitrogen levels were lower than the estimated wastewater contributions for most of this year. Under these conditions of flow and low turbidity, high concentrations of chlorophyll A, a measure of algal activity, were found, as shown in Figure 25.3. Figure 25.4 is a plot of the nitrogen and chlorophyll data during winter to summer at this low flow period. The dashed lines at 6,350 pounds nitrogen per day represent the amount of nitrogen expected in the river water from domestic and industrial wastewater.

Several researchers (Willrich, 1969) have reported drain tile concentrations of 15 to 25 mg/l of nitrate N and 0.1 mg/l of P. On this basis, we might conclude that groundwater entering the river during the low flow periods might approximate these same levels of N and P. However, we have no real data to indicate the groundwater contributions of N and P from this source, and have attributed all of the N and P in the river during low flow periods to municipal and industrial wastes. The uptake of nitrogen by algae and attached plants can account for the fact that the quantities of nitrogen observed were lower than the estimated wastewater contributions for extended periods.

The second year of the study (1968–1969) was a wet period during which rainfall totaled 37.8 inches at Boone. During the second year, when runoff and the river flows were relatively low, the nitrogen content of the river water was approximately at the level estimated to

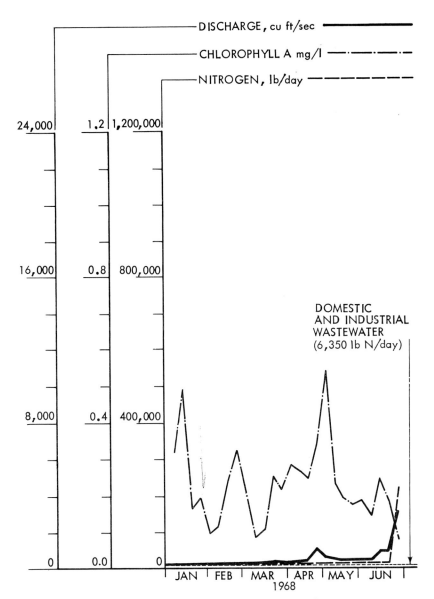

FIG. 25.4. Nitrogen, chlorophyll A, and flow in the Des Moines River during a dry period.

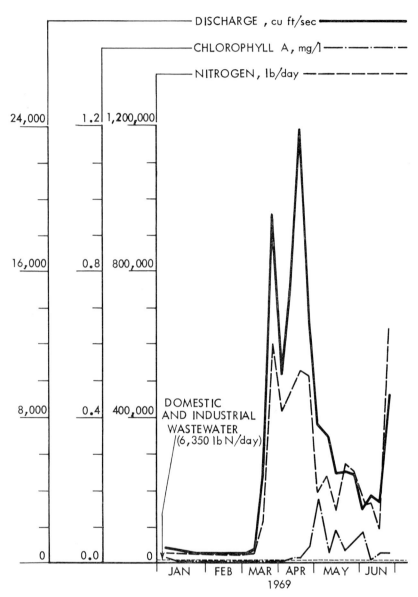

FIG. 25.5. Nitrogen, chlorophyll A, and flow in the Des Moines River during a wet period.

result from the continuous domestic and industrial wastewater contribution. At times of high runoff and river flow, the nitrogen content was correspondingly high. Figure 25.5 shows the relationship between nitrogen content, flow, and chlorophyll A during winter to summer of the wet year. It is apparent that during low flow periods mestic and industrial wastewater is the principal source of nitrogen. During high runoff periods, large quantities of nitrogen are entering the stream over extended periods of time; but due to high turbidity, algal growth is low.

By assuming that the product of the weekly analysis for nitrogen and flow represented the average weekly nitrogen load, it was possible to compute the weekly and annual nitrogen load to the river. The values for the weeks of incomplete data were estimated. The annual nitrogen totals for the first and second years were 2,207 and 24,230 tons, respectively. During the first year, the first 2 weeks and the last week were exceptionally wet. When these 3 weeks were eliminated, the river nitrogen content during the remaining 49 continuous weeks was 647 tons. The nitrogen total during these 49 dry weeks was 60% of the estimated wastewater nitrogen. The nitrogen total for the second wet year was 164% of the estimated combined wastewater, animal waste, and agricultural loss contributions. Apparently during a wet year the additional nitrogen derived from runoff is equal to about 31% of all the nitrogen contained in the fertilizer and animal wastes generated that year in the basin. Annual gross nitrogen inputs originate from many sources, including mineralization of organic matter, animal waste, commercial fertilizers, and that received from the atmosphere by legume fixation, soil absorption, precipitation, and dust sedimentation. The exact quantities derived from each source have not been and cannot be determined from the data in this study.

BOD loads in the river also increased dramatically during periods of peak runoff. During the dry first year the average BOD load was 28,100 pounds per day, the equivalent of untreated wastes from a population of 165,000. During the second wet year the average BOD load in the stream was 127,000 pounds per day, the equivalent of untreated wastes from a population of 750,000. The peak BOD during the second year, experienced on March 26, was 916,000 pounds per day. The carbonaceous BOD (subtracting the oxidation of nitrogenous compounds) was equivalent to untreated wastes from a population of 4,200,000. These values demonstrate the effect of runoff on stream quality in a watershed where the total population is 238,000.

Figures 25.1 and 25.2 also show the concentration and pounds per day of phosphorus in the river at Boone. Only orthophosphate in the flowing water was measured and no analysis was made of organic phosphate, phosphorus in bottom deposits, etc. Figure 25.6 shows winter and summer data during this low flow period. The dashed line at 1,575 pounds P per day represents the amount of phosphorus expected from domestic and industrial wastewater sources. During this first year of the study, the dry conditions resulted in little runoff. Much of the phosphorus in the wastewater either precipitated

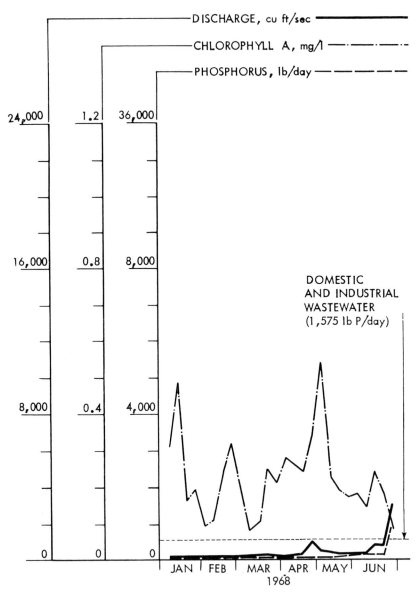

FIG. 25.6.   Phosphorus, chlorophyll A, and flow in the Des Moines
River during a dry period.

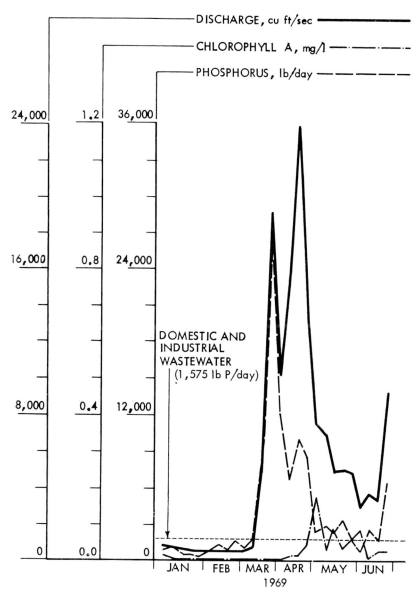

FIG. 25.7. Phosphorus, chlorophyll A, and flow in the Des Moines River during a wet period.

359

out or was utilized by algae (which were present in unusually high concentrations), resulting in low levels in the stream.

Figure 25.7 illustrates the river phosphorus content during the winter and spring of the year (1968–1969). During this wet period when runoff and river flows were high, phosphorus levels rose to as high as 19 times the level expected from wastewater alone. At low river flows the phosphorus levels were again well below the domestic and industrial wastewater level. Apparently the phosphorus is associated with channel scour and bottom sediments. It is interesting to note that the phosphorus levels both increased and decreased faster than the river flows, indicating that the phosphorus was bound to sediment particles.

As with the nitrogen data, it was assumed that the product of the weekly analysis for phosphorus and flow represented the average weekly phosphorus load in the river. The values for the weeks of incomplete data were estimated. The annual phosphorus totals for the first and second years were 50 tons and 1,653 tons, respectively. The total for the first dry year is 18% of the estimated domestic phosphorus alone. The total for the second wet year is nearly 6 times the estimated wastewater phosphorus alone and 186% of the estimated combined contributions from wastewater, animal wastes, and agricultural losses. The additional phosphorus in the stream derived from runoff during a wet year is equal to about 6% of all the phosphorus contained in the applied fertilizer and animal wastes generated in the basin.

Based on the assumptions made in this analysis, it would appear that treating domestic and industrial wastewater to remove the nutrients will benefit the receiving stream only during dry weather flows, given present inputs from all other sources. During wet weather most of the nutrients in the water will originate from sources other than domestic and industrial wastewaters.

CONCLUSIONS

The protection of the quality of water in Iowa streams requires that attention be directed at the various contributors of the significant pollutants. Attention is currently being directed at municipal and industrial waste discharges, since these enter streams through a point source and are easily controlled. All such wastes must be given secondary treatment prior to discharge to Iowa's streams. As more stringent treatment requirements are demanded in the future, there is some question as to whether nutrient removals from municipal and industrial wastes will be sufficient to protect the stream.

This study indicated that during periods of dry weather when light and turbidity conditions are favorable for phytoplankton growth, the principal source of the N and P required to support such growth is derived from municipal and industrial wastewater discharges. Removal of N and P from such wastewater discharges will help reduce phytoplankton growth.

In periods of high stream flow, when turbidity levels are high enough to be unfavorable to phytoplankton growth, runoff from urban and rural lands and channel erosion are probably the principal contributors of N and P to the stream. Removal of N and P from municipal and industrial wastes during these periods will not reduce nutrient levels significantly. However, these are not the periods when eutrophication is a problem in flowing streams. In those situations where the stream flow is impounded, the runoff sources predominate and the clarified water in the reservoir will support large phytoplankton blooms. Under the latter conditions, tertiary treatment of municipal and industrial wastes will be of less benefit until runoff contributions of N and P are also controlled.

REFERENCES

American Public Health Association. 1965. *Standard Methods for the Examination of Water and Wastewater.* 12th ed. New York.

Corey, R. B., Hasler, A. D., Lee, G. F., Schraufnagel, F. H., Wirth, T. L. Jan. 1967. Excessive water fertilization. Rept. to Water Subcommittee, Nat. Resources Committee of State Agencies, Madison, Wis.

Dept. of Civil Engineering. Oct. 1966–Sept. 1967. Annual rept. Coralville project. Univ. of Iowa, Iowa City.

Engineering Research Institute. Fiscal year 1968–69. Preimpoundment water quality study, Saylorville reservoir, Des Moines River, Iowa. Sanit. Eng. Sec., Iowa State Univ., Ames.

Iowa Natural Resources Council. 1953. *An inventory of water resources and water problems, Des Moines River Basin.* Bull. 1.

Iowa Water Pollution Control Commission. Apr. 1969. *Statement in support of the Iowa water quality standards and plan for implementation and enforcement, Mississippi River Basin.*

Loehr, Raymond C. 1969. Animal wastes—a national problem. *J. Sanit. Eng. Div. Am. Soc. Civil Engrs.* 95 (SA2): 189.

National Fertilizer Development Center. 1968. Fertilizer summary data 1968. TVA, Muscle Shoals, Ala.

Sauchelli, V., ed. 1960. *Chemistry and technology of fertilizers.* Am. Chem. Soc. Monograph Ser. 148. New York: Reinhold.

Shobe, William R. 1967. A study of diatom communities in a hardwater stream. Unpublished Ph.D. thesis, Iowa State Univ., Ames.

Sulphur Institute. 1969. *Potential plant nutrient consumption in North America.* Tech. Bull. 16, Wash., D.C.

Task Group 2610-P Report. 1966. Nutrient-associated problems in water quality and treatment. *J. Am. Water Works Assoc.* 58 (10): 1337.

———. 1967. Sources of nitrogen and phosphorus in water supplies. *J. Am. Water Works Assoc.* 59 (3): 344.

Timmons, D. R., Burwell, R. E., and Holt, R. F. 1968. *Minnesota science.* Univ. of Minn. Agr. Exp. Sta. 24 (4).

USDA Economic Research Service and Statistical Reporting Service. 1964. *Fertilizer use in the United States.* 1964 estimates, Statistical Bull. 408.

U.S. Dept. of Health, Education and Welfare. 1954. *An industrial waste guide to the meat industry.* Publ. 386.

———. 1962. *Plankton population dynamics.* Natl. Water Quality Network Suppl. 2, Public Health Serv. Publ. 663.

Van Wazer, V. R. 1961. *Phosphorus and its compounds. II. Technology, biological functions, and applications.* New York: Interscience Publishers.

Willrich, Ted L. 1969. Personal communication. Agr. Eng. Ext., Iowa State Univ., Ames.

PART SIX

AGRICULTURE'S INVOLVEMENT IN POLLUTED AND CLEAN WATER

CHAPTER TWENTY-SIX

LEGAL ASPECTS

N. WILLIAM HINES

IN view of the preceding extensive technical discussions, it is unnecessary to emphasize the "iceberg" character of agriculture's contribution to the pollution load carried by our waters. The highly publicized forms of agricultural pollution, such as the wastes from concentrated feedlot operations, are analogous to the tip of an iceberg—they signal the presence of a much larger mass of pollution that exists just below the surface of visibility. The law's present concern with agricultural pollution reflects and reinforces this distinction between overt instances of pollution from identifiable point sources and subtle, broad-gauge pollution from materials carried to waterways through surface runoff and underground drainage from agricultural lands. Thus far, the law recognizes and enforces some duties in respect to agricultural pollution from point sources and has created regulatory schemes to control this type of pollution. Little legal attention, however, has been devoted to the larger problem of nonpoint pollution from land runoff containing animal and vegetable wastes, agricultural chemicals, and silt. Because this book brings together experts from so many disciplines, I will assume that my specific responsibility as a representative of the legal community is twofold: (1) to describe what the law now requires and permits in the area of water pollution from agricultural sources, and (2) to suggest how the law might constrain or promote the implementation of pollution policy changes affecting agricultural production.

PRIVATE LAW DUTIES OWED LOWER RIPARIAN OWNERS

Under the common law doctrine of riparian rights, which was uniformly adopted in the eastern United States, rights and duties relating to water use were incident to the ownership of land on the banks of a watercourse. Each riparian owner was said to have a right to use the water that flowed by for any beneficial purpose so long as his use did not unreasonably interfere with the use of the common watercourse by another riparian owner. Stated in water quality terms, the right of each riparian owner was said to be that of having

N. WILLIAM HINES is Professor of Law, University of Iowa.

the water flow by his land "unimpaired in quality." This was interpreted to mean that he had a right to receive the water in a quality state reasonably suitable for the use he wished to make of it. If some upstream riparian user was diminishing the water quality below this level, his pollution was actionable and the injured riparian could sue for damages or could seek to enjoin the polluting activity. The technical form of action under which such suits were brought is called nuisance; therefore, you frequently see this private-law approach referred to as the "nuisance theory."

The essence of private nuisance is an interference with a property owner's use and enjoyment of his land, and under the riparian theory water rights are an incident to the ownership of riparian land. A nuisance may be either private or public, depending upon whether it harms only a few persons or affects the interests of the general public. For example, stream pollution that damages only isolated downstream users is a private nuisance, but if the pollution causes a fish kill, it is a public nuisance. If the nuisance is public, it subjects the polluter to criminal punishment, and actions to abate it may be brought by public officials (see Prosser, *Law of Torts*, 605–23 [1964]).

In many states the nuisance concept has been legislatively endorsed and the procedures for remedying the situation specified by statute. For example, Iowa Code provides:

> 657.1 *Nuisance—what constitutes—action to abate.*
> Whatever is injurious or offensive to the senses, or an obstruction to the free use of property, so as essentially to interfere with the comfortable enjoyment of life or property, is a nuisance, and a civil action by ordinary proceedings may be brought to enjoin and abate the same and to recover damages sustained on account thereof.
>
> 657.2 The following are nuisances:
> (4) The corrupting or rendering unwholesome or impure the water of any river, stream, or pond, or unlawfully diverting the same from its natural course or state, to the injury or prejudice of others.

Relatively few reported cases can be found in which agricultural pollution has been attacked as either a private or public nuisance. In fact, no higher court case can be found where a nuisance suit was brought to remedy an injury caused by water-borne agricultural chemicals or silt. A look at a recent private nuisance action arising in Kansas as the result of pollution caused by feedlot wastes should serve to illustrate the application of the nuisance law.

Some of you may be familiar with the litigation which reached the Kansas Supreme Court in 1968 under the title *Atkinson v. Herington Cattle Company* (200 Kan. 298, 436 P.2d 816). To my knowledge it is the only feedlot pollution case to be decided by a state supreme court in the modern era. Under the facts alleged, farmer Cecil Atkinson's water supply for his Grade A dairy operation was Level Creek and a well 400 feet distant from the creek. The Herington feedlots, on which were fed as many as 7,500 cattle, drained into Level Creek $1\frac{1}{4}$ miles upstream from Atkinson's farm, causing the

water, as it passed through Atkinson's property, to have a foul manure odor and a dark yellow-brown color. The water in Atkinson's
well had many of the same properties and was grossly unfit for human or animal consumption. Atkinson sued Herington and Swift
and Company jointly, claiming the latter party was a joint venturer
in the feedlot enterprise, the cattle being supplied by Swift and fed
by Herington on a contract basis. Evidence was submitted by a host
of expert witnesses, including bacteriologists, chemists, geologists,
and sanitary engineers. Veterinarians testified that Atkinson's cows
had died from nitrate poisoning. The trial court awarded Atkinson
$29,060 actual damages and $7,500 punitive damages against both
defendants jointly. Punitive damages are awarded in cases where the
defendant is deserving of punishment for his willful and malicious
invasion of another person's rights. The purpose of such an award
is to make an example of the defendant and thereby deter others
from the commission of like wrongs.

On appeal, the Supreme Court sustained the actual damage
award, but denied the punitive damages. The court said that although there was conflict over the details of how the water became
polluted and the precise physical effects of the pollution, ample evidence existed to support the lower court's finding that Herington
had unreasonably polluted Level Creek and that Atkinson's damages
resulted from that pollution. The court's statement of its ruling was
as follows: "Runoff becomes a harmful substance when it combines
bacteria and chemicals in such an amount as to produce excessive
pollution resulting in injury." On the punitive damage issue, the
court found the evidence inadequate to support the awarding of
such exemplary damages because the evidence showed that Herington took immediate, although as it developed ineffective, steps to try
to remedy the situation upon receiving the first complaint from Atkinson.

Because in this case the injured party recovered substantial
damages from the agricultural polluter, it should not be inferred that
such is always the result. Nuisance cases are generally hard to win
for a variety of factors, including the difficulties of proving the source
and effect of the alleged pollution, the possibility that a complaint is
not made quickly enough to protect the right asserted, and the willingness of the courts to engage in a balancing process which pits the
social utility of the polluter's economic activity against the personal
loss of the complainant. Additionally, courts of law are not particularly well suited to the determination of the typical pollution suit.
The perceived inefficiency in placing direct reliance on the judicial
system to control pollution is the reason we presently assign the
major responsibility in this area to public pollution control agencies.

REGULATION OF AGRICULTURAL POLLUTION
BY PUBLIC AGENCIES

Public regulation of pollution generally is carried on by control
agencies established by local, state, interstate, and federal governmental units. Traditionally, pollution control by state level agencies

has been the mainstay of water quality regulation. Nearly every state has a pollution control law administered by a separate agency of a special division within a larger agency (see Hines, *Nor Any Drop to Drink: Public Regulation of Water Quality Part I: State Pollution Control Programs*, 52 Iowa L. Rev. 186 [1966]). The concentration of control activity at the state level continues to hold true today; however, Congress's enactment of the Water Quality Act of 1965 interjected the federal government very directly into the business of pollution control on most of the nation's waterways. The 1965 Act required the establishment of federal water quality standards for all of the interstate waters in the country. As defined by federal authorities, nearly all larger streams, rivers, and lakes are interstate waters. The 1965 Act authorized the individual states to develop standards for the waters within their jurisdiction, but required that these standards be acceptable to the federal government.

If you read the newspapers, you know that the establishment of federal standards has led to a number of serious disputes between state pollution control agencies and the federal officials responsible for approving the standards adopted by the states. Although a number of the states in the Missouri and Mississippi basin have encountered problems in obtaining approval of their standards, Iowa has been the chief antagonist of the FWPCA's requirements for accepting state standards. This dispute came to a head when Secretary of Interior Hickel announced on October 29, 1969, that he was imposing federal standards on Iowa, the first action of its kind under the 1965 Act.

This is probably not a good occasion to air in detail the dispute between the Iowa Pollution Control Commission and the FWPCA; however, it is worthy of note that the major issue is the requirement of secondary treatment for all sewage discharged into Iowa's 27 interstate streams. Other standards imposed relate to water temperature, phenols, and continuous disinfection of all municipal waste. Only the standard limiting phenol levels to one part per billion would appear remotely related to agricultural pollution. That standard speaks in terms of phenols "from other than natural sources," so arguably phenols produced by decomposition of vegetative agricultural wastes may not be covered by the standard because, except in a rare case, it would be impossible to distinguish these from phenols produced by decomposition of natural vegetation. On a more general level, it is worthy of note that the federal Guidelines for Establishing Water Quality Standards make no specific mention of regulation to control agricultural pollution, nor has the FWPCA's application of these standards demonstrated any immediate concern for problems of agricultural pollution, except in a research capacity.

It thus seems a safe conclusion that the current furor around the country over the establishment of water quality standards has very little to do with agricultural pollution. Municipal and industrial pollution are the immediate targets of the federal-state effort to peel back the flood of pollutants. Only when these obvious point sources of pollution are brought under control is attention likely to shift to cleaning up agriculture's insidious wastes. Given the present rate of success in controlling municipal and industrial wastes, it will probably be some time before the spotlight shifts to agricultural pollution. Two notable exceptions exist to the current disinterest in agricultural pollution. Pollution control agencies have taken a direct interest in the regulation of feedlot wastes and chemical pesticides used in agriculture and have attracted widespread attention. Both of these areas deserve special comment. The pollutional effects of chemical fertilizers and soil erosion have received much less attention. No regulatory interest has been addressed to the enormous volume of animal and crop wastes periodically washed into streams by surface runoff from agricultural lands. Some experts suggest that shock loads of these organic materials that reach watercourses as the result of heavy rains or rapid thaws pose the most serious agricultural pollution problems (see Morris, Pollution Problems in Iowa, Paper presented to the Iowa Academy of Sciences, April 18, 1969).

Regulation of Feedlot Wastes

At the outset it should be noted that pollution resulting from concentrated feedlot operations is a type of agricultural pollution that is fundamentally different from the great bulk of agriculture's contribution to the pollution load of our waters. Feedlot pollution emanates from a readily identifiable source—it is point pollution— and it is susceptible to the same types of treatment procedures as are applied to municipal wastes and organic industrial wastes. The similarity of feedlot pollution to municipal and industrial wastes, plus its severe pollutional effects (a feedlot of 20,000 cattle is said to produce a waste with a population equivalence of a city of over 300,000 people), no doubt explains the prevalence of efforts to regulate feedlot wastes in the midwestern states where this type of agricultural practice is popular.

Several states have enacted legislation regulating the waste discharge practices of feedlots. The Kansas statute, for example, provides that any feedlot operator feeding more than 300 cattle, 100 hogs, or 500 sheep must register with the health department and provide pollution control facilities if needed to prevent pollution runoff from the premises (Kan. Stat. Ann. 47–1505). Arizona requires feedlot operations with more than 500 cattle to obtain a license and to provide reasonable methods to dispose of excrement and control drainage (Ariz. Rev. Stat. Ann.§§ 24–391–397). In most other states, the pollution control agencies are working to promulgate regulations relating to feedlot wastes under their general power to make rules and regulations necessary to perform their regulatory function. Considerable discussion has centered on what a good regulation should provide (see Matthews, *A Recommended Procedure for Developing a Model Feedlot Regulation*, proceedings of Animal Waste Management Conference, Cornell Univ., Ithaca, N.Y., 1969).

Iowa's recently promulgated regulation covering cattle feedlots is worthy of note. In 1968 hearings conducted around the state on proposed feedlot regulations provoked considerable interest in agricultural circles. The 1969 session of the Iowa legislature amended the pollution control law to require registration of all livestock and poultry operations where a potential for water pollution exists. Under the amendment the Commission cannot require waste disposal facilities unless it is determined that the registrants are in fact polluting water or may reasonably be believed to threaten pollution. The thrust of the regulations recently issued under this amendment is to specify the feedlot situations in which a pollution potential exists, and therefore in which registration is required. The regulations require registration of cattle feedlots which confine more than 1,000 cattle or which contribute effluent to a watercourse draining more than 3,200 acres above the lot, which watercourse is less distant than 2 feet per head of cattle, or from which the runoff flows into an underground conduit or drainage well. If the control agency determines that the registered feedlot is, or reasonably may be, a source of pollution, then the feedlot is required to obtain a permit for disposal of wastewater. Permits are granted on a showing of adequate water pollution control facilities constructed in accordance with plans and specifications approved by the agency. The regulation specifies terraces or retention ponds sufficient to contain a surface runoff of 3 inches as the minimum pollution control facility permissible.

Iowa's regulations seem to meet most of the objectives suggested by Matthew in his recommended model feedlot regulations. One facet of the regulations that is not clear relates to the enforcement of the registration and permit requirements. What penalty is incurred by failure to register a feedlot required to be registered or failing to obtain a permit under circumstances where the regulations would require a permit? If the feedlot is actually creating a situation of pollution, the Commission can issue an abatement order without relying on any violation of the regulations. If only a potential for pollution exists, it is not certain what steps, if any, the Commission can take to compel compliance with the registration and permit requirements. Presumably the permit required by the regulations is a permit of the type covered by Iowa Code 455B.25, which makes the construction of disposal systems or use of a new waste outlet without permit an unlawful act. The feedlot operator who does nothing about his wastes would seemingly not be guilty of an unlawful act under this section. Iowa Code 455B.24 concerning contempt citations for failure to obey orders of the Commission has been interpreted as referring to abatement orders based on proof of pollution. Orders are not ordinarily issued on a showing of pollution potential. The injunction power granted the agency under Iowa Code 455B.23 applies to situations in which a person is placing wastes in a location where they will probably cause pollution. Under this provision the Commission could apparently enjoin the waste disposal activity of a feedlot operator if it appeared likely to cause pollution. This brief excursion through the enforcement section of the Iowa law proves nothing more than the need to make sure regulatory schemes fit the enforcement pattern of the statute under which they operate. If registration is the key to controlling feedlot pollution, it appears desirable to put some teeth in the registration requirement by indicating the penalty for failure to comply.

Pesticide Regulation

Pesticides have been in the headlines for much of the last year; not so much as water pollutants as total environment pollutants. The so-called hard pesticides, DDT and the other chlorinated hydrocarbons, have received the lion's share of attention, with 2-4,D and related herbicides taking a secondary position. The toxic effect of the existing chemical biocides on man is still hotly debated; less disputed are the obvious incursions that have been made on the food chains and eco-systems of lower animals.

Because they enter the environment at a multitude of contact points, the most effective method for controlling pesticide pollution seems to be to regulate their initial use. Almost every state has some form of pesticide registration law that requires the filing of an ingredient statement, the label, and directions for use (see Iowa Code § 206.4). Many states have additional provisions regulating the use of pesticides by commercial applicators (see Iowa Code § 206.5). These latter statutes were primarily aimed at assuring technical competency on the part of persons who applied chemicals for hire; they do not reach the individual applying chemicals to his own property.

In sharp contrast to this traditional approach of minimum regulation are the actions taken by several states recently in prohibiting the use or banning the sale of certain pesticides thought to be dangerous. Arizona declared a 1-year moratorium on the use of DDT and DDD in January 1969. In April, the Michigan Agricultural Commission decided to ban the sale in the state of all products containing DDT. In August, Wisconsin created a Pesticide Review Board for the purpose of governing the use of pesticides. Actions outlawing or phasing out DDT were taken by one house of the legislature in California, Wisconsin, and Illinois (*New York Times*, Apr. 30, 1969, p. 43; July 19, 1969, p. 30; Nov. 4, 1969, p. 6). This bustling of state regulatory activity presaged the announcement by HEW Secretary Finch on November 13, 1969, that the federal government had decided to halt DDT use in this country within the next 2 years.

To appreciate the nature and extent of the federal power in this area it is necessary to understand the federal regulation of pesticides used in agricultural production. The Food and Drug Administration within HEW is authorized by Congress to safeguard the safety and quality of food products and drugs distributed in interstate commerce. If you remember your high school civics, you may recall that the federal government has no general police power, but must regulate through the specific enumerated powers granted by the Constitution. Thus purely intrastate marketing of agricultural products is not subject to the FDA requirements. Since the Pesticide Chemicals in or on Raw Agricultural Commodities Act of 1954, pesticide residues have been one of the elements of food quality the FDA has been responsible for regulating. The FDA, therefore, sets the levels of tolerance of pesticide residue that will be permitted on foodstuffs marketed in interstate commerce.

Responsibility for the regulation of agricultural chemicals marketed in interstate commerce rests with the USDA under the Federal Insecticide, Fungicide and Rodenticide Act (7 U.S.C. § 135). This act makes it a criminal offense to sell any "economic poison" which has not been fully and accurately registered with the USDA. The secretary of agriculture determines what chemicals are economic poisons, and chemical biocides are uniformly so classified. Any party seeking to register a chemical to be used on food crops must indicate the crops on which the chemical is to be used, the quantity to be used for each crop, and describe the exact procedure of use. Additionally, test data must be provided to show the safety of specific residues of the chemical in or on foodstuffs. If no residue should be left under correct application procedures, the product is registered as a "no-residue" chemical. If a residue subsequently shows up, the registrant has violated the act.

This is what happened in the great cranberry snafu of 1958. The herbicide amenotraezole was registered on a no-residue basis, then when a residue appeared because of improper use, FDA panicked the buying public by announcing the confiscation of 300,000 pounds of cranberries. Testing ultimately showed that relatively few of the cranberries were contaminated and cranberry growers were reimbursed $8.5 million for their losses. A similar problem arose in 1963 concerning endrin residue on brussels sprouts. Endrin had been registered on a no-residue basis at a time when the testing devices could detect residues of no smaller amounts than 0.1 ppm. Improved testing techniques enabled inspectors to find a 0.03-ppm residue and the products were pulled from the market.

If the chemical will leave a residue, the product will not be registered until a residue tolerance level has been set by FDA. The tolerance level is set on the basis of information submitted to FDA by the applicant, showing the expected amounts of residue, the effect of such a residue on test animals, the pattern of normal use of the foodstuff, and a workable method of analysis for enforcing the tolerance level. If USDA is satisfied with the tolerance level set by FDA, the chemical is then authorized.

Thus working in concert, as they apparently plan to do, HEW and USDA can, through reduction of the permissible tolerance levels of DDT, eliminate its use in conjunction with agricultural products. Critics of the federal government's past activities in pesticide control have asserted that one of the major weaknesses has been the lack of coordination between FDA and HEW (see Note, *Agricultural Pesticides: The Need For Improved Control Legislation*, 52 Minn. L. Rev. 1242 [1968]). Perhaps the joint plan to phase out DDT signals a new era in effective cooperation between these two agencies.

Lawyers active in environmental defense litigation claim that the most difficult problem in pesticide regulation is uncovering the scientific facts about the relative toxicity of the different chemicals. They suggest that this difficulty could be substantially cured if the regulatory agencies held public hearings where experts could be produced and cross-examined on the questions concerning the danger of chemicals to various forms of life. The lawyers argue that the adversary process used in our courts is peculiarly suitable for testing the reliability of the evidence presented by proponents and opponents of controversial chemicals. The one experiment with this method before a special hearing board in Wisconsin suggests that there is merit in the argument for adversary proceedings before agencies charged with protecting environmental quality. Until recently, such a requirement would have been meaningless because only the chemical industry would have been represented. Today, however, a number of citizen groups are ready and able to present the case for the public interest in a safe and wholesome environment (see Foster, Counsel for the Concerned Conference on Law and the Environment, Sept. 11–12, 1969, Warrenton, Va.).

Looking to the future, the agricultural producer should expect much closer state and federal regulation of both the chemicals available to him and his procedures in applying them. Special pesticide-regulating agencies are likely to be created by many states. From a purely legal standpoint, given the range of uncertainty concerning the long-range effects of pesticides on the environment, almost any type of restrictive state regulation is likely to be sustained as a valid exercise of the state's police power. However, chemical biocides play such a major role in modern commercial agriculture that it is inconceivable that many of the other important chemicals will be dealt with as harshly as DDT. Much more likely is regulation designed to encourage selective use of chemicals and substitution of softer chemicals or biologic techniques for the more toxic pesticides. Because pesticides entering water directly from agricultural land are believed chiefly to travel adsorbed to sediment particles washed away by soil erosion, more careful attention to land-use practices is likely to be required by law.

Chemical Fertilizers

It is frequently asserted that the increasing levels of nitrates and phosphates in midwestern waters are caused by residues from chemical fertilizers carried to watercourses by runoff and percolation of precipitation falling on agricultural cropland. Some experts dispute this explanation, claiming that agricultural fertilizers make only a very minor contribution to the current high levels of nitrates and phosphates compared to the amounts contributed by natural sources and by organic effluents discharged by municipalities and industries (see Smith, Fertilizer Nutrients in Water Supplies, in *Agriculture and the Quality of Environment*, 1967). One point upon which considerable agreement exists is that to the extent chemical nutrients reach watercourses, they are principally transported there aboard soil particles lost through erosion. Thus if chemical fertilizers are proved to be a source of nitrate pollution, methods for controlling silt pollution, discussed below, should have a double-barreled effect in reducing the amount of chemicals washed into watercourses.

At present the use of chemical fertilizers is subject to no regulation at either the local or national level. The legal disinterest in chemical fertilizers is typified by the Iowa Pesticide Statute which expressly provides that in products where pesticides and fertilizers are mixed, the fertilizer is to be treated as an inert ingredient (Iowa Code

§ 206.4). Looking to the future, if it is proved that substantial quantities of phosphates and nitrates from chemical fertilizers are washing into streams, it should be anticipated that fertilizer use itself will be regulated. Limits could be placed on the volume and strength of chemical fertilizers that can be applied at one time or during one season, and controls may be adopted governing the timing and methods of fertilizer application. Such regulations would not be different in kind from the controls now being exercised over pesticide use in some parts of the country. There seems little doubt that whether such controls were necessary to prevent nitrate poisoning or to reduce the nutrient load carried by our waters, and thereby reduce pollution caused by nuisance aquatic growths, it would be a valid exercise of the state's police power (see Williamson v. Lee Optical, 348 U.S. 483 [1955]; Brackett v. City of Des Moines, 246 Iowa 249, 67 N.W.2d 542 [1954]).

Silt

Recent studies on water quality in the Mississippi River show that sediment from the over 16 million acres of Iowa agricultural land which drains into the river will reduce the recreational value of the river more rapidly than either municipal or industrial pollution. Soil erosion is acknowledged to be the single largest pollutant of nearly all mid-continent streams draining land intensively used for agricultural production. Also, as noted earlier, soil erosion is thought to be the principal vehicle for transporting agricultural pesticides and chemicals from the site of their application to our waterways. Only recently, however, has soil erosion been thought of in terms of a water pollution problem (see Browning, Agricultural Pollution, Sources and Control, in *Water Pollution Control and Abatement* [1967]), and it is still true that the major concern is the loss to the land of valuable soil and not the diminution in the value of waters resulting from the silt and chemical loads imposed upon them.

Since the 1930s a substantial government effort has been committed to reducing soil erosion from agricultural land; however, little or none of this effort qualifies as regulation in the usual sense of the term (see Wyoming, Proposed Soil Conservation Act, 13 Rocky Mtn. L. Rev. 115 [1941]). Essentially, what has been accomplished has been carried out through spending programs by the state and federal governments, the federal purse providing most of the money. The basic unit for the prevention of soil erosion is the soil conservation district (see Hardin, *The Politics of Agriculture*, 70–84 [1952]).

Generally the approach of the soil conservation districts has been one of offering instruction and incentives for voluntary improvement in soil management techniques. Financial assistance is conditioned upon acceptance and performance of an approved soil conservation program. Doubts have been expressed concerning the actual enforcement of these agreements against farmers who are remiss in performing the required conservation practices. The "tread softly" approach of the soil conservation district is exemplified by the frequent unwillingness to enforce an erosion control agreement against a subsequent buyer of the land.

Gains through voluntary programs are impressive, but it seems doubtful whether soil erosion can be brought under control without compulsion. Through the modern concept of zoning, the law provides a viable and well-established method for accomplishing the desired land-use results. Regulating the use of agricultural lands to assure responsible soil management will be very difficult for many members of the agricultural community to accept, but it is doubtful whether any less drastic approach can achieve the requisite conservation objectives. In most states soil conservation districts are authorized to adopt land-use control regulations (Iowa districts are not granted this power) if a majority of the landowners in the district vote in favor of such a plan. Even where it exists, the power to regulate agricultural practices through zoning has rarely been exercised. Although 32 states authorize such land-use control, only a handful of districts in 3 states have ever adopted such measures (see Parks, *Soil Conservation Districts in Action*, 1952).

If the soil conservation district or conservancy district is not able or willing to employ land-use controls, some other agency may be expected to fill the gap. It is not unlikely that if pollution control commissions ever turn their attention to agricultural pollution, they may find the imposition of land-use regulation the only feasible way to control pollution from soil erosion. Such regulation would restrict types of plantings, prohibit certain cultivation techniques on various soil types and slopes, and prescribe or ban a variety of soil management practices. If the land-use control technique is used, there seems little doubt that it would be a constitutionally valid form of regulation. (For a discussion of the application of due process standards to resource regulation see Hines, *A Decade of Experience Under the Iowa Water Permit System*, Ag. Law Center Mono #9, 1966, 74–82).

An idea currently receiving considerable attention in water management circles is the proposal to create watershed authorities empowered to manage comprehensively the water resources and water-related land resources of a hydrologically defined area. (For a discussion of this agency see Hines, *Controlling Industrial Water Pollution*, 9 Bos. Coll. Ind. & Comm. L. Rev. 605–11 [1968]). If such agencies ever become a reality, they would seem to be the ideal unit to enact and enforce land-use regulations designed to prevent soil erosion and protect water quality. In fact, it is difficult to see how such an agency could comprehensively regulate water quality in an agricultural area without land-use control powers. Conferring land-use regulation powers on a management agency, whose jurisdiction corresponds to the physical contours of the watershed, avoids the type of administrative problems created by the fact that soil conservation districts are generally oriented to political boundaries rather than drainage patterns. Some states have already adopted legislation authorizing creation of watershed districts for the purpose of managing and conserving water and water-related land resources. (Nebraska and Minnesota have such statutes, Timmons & Bromm, *Nebraska*

Water Resource Districts, Nebr. Ag. Econ. Report No. 49; 9 Minn. State. Ann. § 112.34–85 [1964]).

It may well be that rural watersheds containing primarily agricultural water users will be the most practical place to test the watershed management model. Concentrations of people and industry create factors that may militate against organizing the management agency on a purely hydrologic basis.

CONCLUSION

The force of the law has not been brought to bear on agriculture as it has on other major sources of water pollution. Agricultural pollution has thus far been ignored because it is less visible and more difficult to correct than are wastes from municipalities and industry. Currently, only those types of agricultural pollution that are obvious and subject to direct control receive legal attention. As water quality regulation in this country matures and point sources of pollution are brought under control, agriculture's more subtle contributions to the undesirable properties of our wastes will attract regulatory concern. In the background, the private law will continue to provide a remedy for the individual who can prove a direct harm caused by pollution and can conclusively identify the polluter.

Public regulation of agricultural pollution will take two primary forms: (1) direct restrictions on the use of chemical inputs to agricultural production, and (2) regulation of land-use patterns and practices. Examples of the first type of regulation are prohibitions or limitations on the use of certain chemical biocides, fertilizers, and other additives. Assuming a reasonable case can be made for the need for such regulations, no legal constraints exist to their enactment and enforcement.

In the second category, land-use regulations seem very likely to be necessary to effect a meaningful reduction in the soil erosion currently darkening streams, constricting waterways, filling reservoirs with siltation, and transporting chemicals from field to watercourse. The ideal construct might involve the employment of land-use controls by a comprehensive watershed management authority. If this does not come to pass, exercise of such powers by other local districts such as soil conservation districts, conservancy districts, or drainage districts would be feasible, as would granting similar powers to the local pollution control agency.

CHAPTER TWENTY-SEVEN

ECONOMIC ASPECTS

JOHN F. TIMMONS

O$_F$ all the industries in the United States, agriculture possesses the greatest potential for affecting the quality of the nation's water resources. In fact agriculture's potential for lowering water quality appears greater than that for all other industries in the United States combined. This potential arises from the fact that agricultural activities are scattered over most of the nation's surface, with access to practically all the nation's waters. This potential is augmented by modern technologies involving chemicals, concentrated feedlots, tillage practices, irrigation systems, and drainage networks. This potential exists even though less than 5% of the nation's people are engaged in agriculture, which produces about 5% of the gross national product.

DEFINITION OF TERMS

In this chapter the term agriculture is limited to food and fiber production on the nation's farms, ranches, feedlots, gardens, and plantations. All firms that process agricultural products or manufacture agricultural inputs are excluded from this definition.

Water quality refers to all properties of water which affect its use. The term pollution is not used in this chapter because it not only differs in meaning among people but also has become emotion laden, thereby interfering with the communication of objective ideas. Instead, quality levels of particular water supplies viewed in terms of particular quality levels demanded for specific purposes are used.

The term management means that water quality can be altered and affected by purposeful and positive actions of private and public entities and by combinations of the two. Management applied to water quality is regarded as motivated by minimizing disutilities and maximizing utilities in the use of water in the interest of increasing net satisfactions available to people.

JOHN F. TIMMONS is Professor of Economics, Iowa State University.

Journal Paper No. J-6469 of the Iowa Agricultural and Home Economics Experiment Station, Iowa State University, Project No. 1445.

ROLE OF ECONOMICS

Water quality management decisions (including quality standards, demand-supply interrelationships, implementing water quality
changes, and cost allocations incurred by such implementations) involve the use of the science of economics. Economics is primarily
concerned with decision-making processes in allocating scarce resources among multiple and frequently competing ends in a manner
that offers maximum net benefits for the decision maker and his
clientele. Since waters of particular qualities are scarce and their use
demands are competitive, water management comes within the pur-
view of economic analysis. However, the usefulness of economic analysis in planning, programming, and implementing water quality
needs and adjustments is limited by the physical and technological
data available to the economist.

Economic analysis will yield results no better than the physical
and technological coefficients with which the economist works. And
the results may be even less useful unless the economist adapts his
theories, models, and tools of analysis to the unique and complex
problems of water quality. This means that the economist must work
closely with agronomists, engineers, biologists, hydrologists, geologists, limnologists, and other scientists in our multidisciplinary
search for ways and means of making qualities of waters serve mankind's needs. Our work here at Iowa State with Professors Johnson,
Baumann, Willrich, Dougal, and other engineers, as well as our work
with Professors Shrader, Moldenhauer, and other agronomists, is
illustrative of the nature of water research which is both productive
and satisfying.

OBJECTIVES

The general purpose of this chapter is to present some of the
more relevant economic concepts that with the work of other sciences
will help to assess and explain agriculture's role in water quality
management in terms of the associated problems and their remedies.

This general purpose may be restated in terms of three specific
questions:
1. What levels of water quality are desired?
2. How may these desired levels of water quality be provided at the
   least cost to all users, including agriculture and the public?
3. How may costs and benefits of managed changes in water
   quality be assigned among users, including agriculture and the
   public?

QUALITY HETEROGENEITIES OF WATER SUPPLIES
AND WATER DEMANDS

Historically, the quantity theory of water buttressed by the several doctrines of water rights has tended to impute homogeneous
properties to all water or at least to specific hydrologic units. How-

ever, it has become increasingly obvious that water is extremely heterogeneous in terms of (1) its properties, (2) its permitted uses, and (3) its demanded uses. Modern technologies with their fallouts and wastes affecting water quality, multiple demands for water each with specific quality requirements, and increasing population densities emphasize quality to the extent that the quality theory of water equals and frequently exceeds the importance of the traditional quantity theory.

From an economic viewpoint it is helpful and realistic to think of water in terms of many water factors (productive) and numerous water commodities (consumptive). Water may be regarded as differentiated in terms of kinds and grades by its quality as linked with spatial and temporal occurrences (Ackerman and Lof, 1959).

Let us examine this concept further by delving into (1) quality-differentiated water supplies and (2) quality-differentiated demands, each associated with spatial and temporal availabilities.

Water Supplies Quality Differentiated

The common chemical formula for water, H_2O, has tended to impute a homogeneity to water which actually does not exist. To H_2O must be added other chemicals, compounds, organisms, temperature, color, and all other characteristics relevant to its use. Thus, water as found in its several sources is not a simple compound but may become very complex. This complexity varies among existing supplies and conditions of use. These variations are introduced by natural as well as by man-made actions. These variations are compounded by variations in spatial and temporal occurrences of water even within and among segments of the same water source.

The quality of a particular water supply for purposes of management becomes relevant only in terms of uses to which it is put. Thus, a particular supply—a lake, an aquifer, or stream segment— can be appraised in terms of use criteria. Therefore, we must look into the properties demanded by particular uses as the criteria for analyzing a particular supply.

Water Demands Quality Differentiated

Different uses of water require different properties of water and vary in their toleration of particular properties (Timmons and Dougal, 1968). For example, living cells may require the presence of certain minerals in water, whereas battery cells may not tolerate the same minerals. Even organisms vary in their mineral requirements and toleration of minerals. Quality of water must necessarily be viewed in terms of a particular use if quality is to be manageable. Different qualities are required (or tolerated) for animal consumption, navigation, power, irrigation, food processing, air conditioning, recreation, and manufacturing. Even within each of these major categories, demands are specialized. Beer, aluminum, paper, and synthetic fiber production each possesses important quality differentiations.

Water quality suited for one use may be absolutely unsuited for another use. Thus, it appears there is little, if any, relevancy for a universal water quality standard. Instead, quality standards must be developed in relation to specific uses to be made of particular water supplies at particular points or periods of time in the process of satisfying specific human wants. Such differentiations will likely extend to segments of the same water course, be it a stream, lake, or aquifer. In other words, the quality mix of a particular water supply must be analyzed in terms of uses to which it is put (Timmons, 1967).

Gearing Supply Qualities to Demand Qualities

Strategic to analyzing agriculture's role in water quality management is the identification of uses made or to be made of water affected by agricultural uses. Also strategic is the determination of water qualities required or tolerated by these uses. Only in this manner may agriculture's contributions to water quality changes be determined and evaluated in a relevant manner.

In recent years many projections of aggregate water demands have been made. Projections for future water demands are basic and necessary in providing essential elements of a normative and predictive framework for planning and carrying out water policy. But, in the future, these projections should not be considered as aggregates. On the contrary, they must be disaggregated into segmented differentiations derived from relevant estimators (Ackerman and Lof, 1959). Included as estimators by uses are qualities by amounts of water demanded. Also included are the spatial and temporal occurrences of quality-linked supplies available for serving quality-linked amounts to the estimated demands. Finally, the estimator of costs is involved in terms of least cost alternatives for gearing (bringing or keeping) supply qualities to demand qualities.

In regard to demand estimators, one further point should be considered. This involves a more refined differentiation into direct and derived components. Such a differentiation becomes important in systems analysis involving regional accounts as well as in those allocations which must be made through ordinal rather than cardinal-oriented criteria. Thus, not only must we undertake to solve the complex problem of determining the technical coefficients for water used as an input but also the even more difficult one of specifying the demand for water as a "final product," with all of the difficulties inherent in nonquantifiable parameters which must be ordered by ordinal criteria.

COSTS AND BENEFITS ASSOCIATED WITH WATER QUALITY MANAGEMENT INCLUDING LEAST COST METHODS TO MEET DEMAND QUALITIES

Continuing our reasoning that demand-oriented qualities set the criteria for defining objectives (or standards) to be achieved or maintained in water supplies, we turn attention to the means for implementing these objectives (standards). Products and services in these uses provide the basis for approximating benefits and costs or utilities and disutilities which cannot be quantified in the market.

Directions for Water Quality Management

Using demand-oriented qualities of water as criteria, three management directions are opened up for consideration. Direction I is that the supply-oriented qualities can be lowered without adverse effects on other uses than on the use lowering the quality. Under this Direction, water is regarded as a legitimate dilution agent for the wastes and fallouts of agricultural or other uses. Under this Direction, wastes from agricultural feedlots and fields with their chemicals would use water as a dilution agent since this use would not interfere with other uses. In other words, the benefit from agricultural waste disposal would accrue to agricultural activities with no costs to other uses. Therefore, net benefits would be maximized in the process. Direction II involves the prevention of reduction in water quality levels. Under this alternative, agricultural benefits would have to be less than benefits accruing to other uses, costs considered. Of course, one important component of costs to agriculture would be foregoing uses of certain technologies lowering water levels. Pesticides and fertilizers might be examples. If such technologies were foregone, the yields and production of food and fiber would probably decline, which would adversely affect the public as consumers through scarcities and higher prices of food and fiber. Direction III involves the raising of water quality uses where warranted by higher productivity uses. Under this Direction agriculture would be expected to curtail certain technologies which were being used in order to upgrade water quality for other uses which are deemed more productive in the use of higher water quality. As was the case under Direction II above, costs to agriculture and to the consuming public would have to be taken into account.

Differences between Directions II and III are essentially those of prevention in II and reduction in III of certain uses associated with agriculture. Under II the use of certain practices would be prevented from taking place. Under III the use of certain practices would be terminated. The major difference is in terms of implementation of water quality changes where practices have already been capitalized into the agricultural business (under III) and where practices have not yet been capitalized into the agricultural business (under II).

QUALITY USE INTERRELATIONSHIPS

With these differences in mind, let us consider three major types of interrelationships among water uses. These relationships are (A) complementary, (B) neutral, and (C) competitive.

Under Relationship A (complementary) one use contributes to the benefits or utilities of another use without experiencing costs or disutilities. An example would be use of a pesticide by one farmer wherein the pesticide drift to the neighbor's crops would result in additional benefits to the neighbor. Another example would be an irrigator whose herbicides returned to the canal and benefited downstream uses of the water through preventing the clogging of the canal with vegetative growth.

Under Relationship B (neutral) one use has no effect, neither beneficial nor detrimental, on other uses. Other uses can tolerate or are unaffected by quality changes left in the wake of previous uses.

Under Relationship C (competitive) one use exerts a detrimental effect on other uses of water through lowering water quality required by other uses. This Relationship is the one presenting the major problems in water quality management. Here is where decisions must be made in water management. Alternatives A and B do not require management decisions among uses since effects of wastes of fallouts from one use are either complementary or neutral with other uses. This would include Direction I discussed earlier, with Directions II and III falling into Alternative C.

Under Alternative C, water quality downward changes beneficial for one use will adversely affect other uses. Conversely, water quality upward changes will adversely affect uses effecting the change but with beneficial effects on other uses. The major problem encompasses (1) the identification of all kinds of costs and benefits (utility and disutility) associated with each use before and after the change effected in water quality and (2) the assignment of weights in ordinal or cardinal terms to *each* identified kind of cost and benefit (utility and disutility).

Use and Technological Benefits and Costs

In the process of maximizing net benefits (net utilities) among competing uses, benefits and costs of competing uses must be identified and estimated. At this point it is helpful to distinguish between use benefits and costs and technological benefits and costs.

USE BENEFITS AND COSTS

Use benefits and costs are associated with products and services produced or left unproduced by a use due to water quality changes. This assumes that *any* change in cost due to water quality change would be responsible for changes of production. Because of economies of scale or the fixed-variable cost mix, the effect is more likely to be reflected in level of production and prices at which products and services are made available. This in turn is responsive to price elasticity, substitution, and production lags of products and services.

TECHNOLOGICAL BENEFITS AND COSTS

Technological benefits and costs refer to specific techniques within a particular use of water. Assume that three techniques of disposing or controlling cattle feedlot runoff are available. These are (1) open field disposal, (2) playa lake disposal, and (3) natural evaporative system (Owens and Griffin, 1968). Further assume that each technique is equally effective in producing the level of water quality demanded by the highest use of water affected by the feedlot. Also, assume that the cost effects on gains of cattle are affected only by the relative costs of the techniques employed. According to a Texas study, the investment cost per head of cattle for a 25,000-head feedlot would be $1.04, $0.83, and $1.49, respectively, for the three techniques. Costs per head would annualize at $0.18, $0.13, and $0.14, respectively. Thus, Technique 2 would represent the least-cost method.

In another example, three alternative techniques are available for disposal of liquid wastes from confined hogs. These are (1) hauling and field spreading, (2) total lagooning of wastes, and (3) spreading and hauling except for the period July 15 to October 15, when the wastes would be lagooned as reported in an Illinois study (Kesler and Hinton, 1966). Assume that the conditions imposed on the above cattle feedlot techniques were imposed in the hog-lot study. For 500 hogs, the per 1,000 gallon annual cost of disposing of liquid manure was $3.82, $1.78, and $4.37, respectively, for the above three techniques which on a per hog basis is $0.69, $0.32, and $0.79, respectively. On the basis of a 2,500-hog operation the results are $1.69, $1.54, and $2.02, respectively, for the above techniques and $0.30, $0.28, and $0.36, respectively, on a per hog basis. Thus, Technique 2 appears superior for both levels of operation, although the spread of advantage lessens with size of operation (or scale).

The conditions assumed in the above two examples can be relaxed, and revised results obtained with additional information and more complex analysis.

ASSIGNMENT OF BENEFITS AND COSTS ACCRUING FROM WATER QUALITY CHANGES TO WATER USES

If agriculture's behavior in water quality management were as simple as illustrated in the above examples under the assumptions applied, agriculture's role in water quality management would be easily interpreted and easily implemented. Unfortunately this is not the case. In this section, attention is devoted to three particular problems which complicate the understanding and the implementation of agriculture's role in water quality management. Although there are other problems, the three selected for emphasis here are (1) externalities, (2) measurement, and (3) intervention.

The Problem of Externalities

The user of water may be in a position to keep the benefits from use while shifting costs to other users by lowering water quality. If he had to bear the shifted costs, he would be motivated to use the water in a manner consistent with quality demanded by other uses.

On the other hand, a user of water may be in such a position that if he makes an outlay to maintain or improve water quality, he cannot capture the benefits from his outlay which shift to other users. If he could capture such benefits, he would be motivated to make outlays which would maintain or improve the quality of the water after it leaves his use. Such terms as "side effects," "spillover effects," or "second party" effects have been applied to such shifts of costs and benefits.

To the economist these conditions are termed externalities. The rationale for this term is that the consequences of the actions are external to the firm responsible for the actions. Externalities are classified as economies and diseconomies. Beneficial effects are called external economies and harmful effects are called external diseconomies. Both have in common the phenomenon that the incidences of the effects are shifted beyond the user that causes them. The reason for this shift may be either of spatial or temporal origin or both.

External economies (beneficial effects) become important in water quality management if the economies affect the user's decisions. If the user would use the water in the same way regardless of whether or not he could capture the consequential economies, there is no incentive effect on his decision. This was the case with the irrigator using herbicides and the farmer using pesticides, mentioned earlier in this chapter. However, if as is more frequently the case, the water user would not be able to capture external economies in the form of improved water quality resulting from his outlays for improving or maintaining water quality levels, external economies become very important in water quality management.

Although the problem of external economies is important, external diseconomies appear far more important in agriculture's role in water quality management. For example, wastes from chemical fertilizers and pesticides and livestock wastes reaching into streams, lakes, or aquifers may foreclose other uses entirely or make other uses more expensive to undertake. Or they may endanger life and health of human beings. Dr. Kneese concludes that "a society that allows waste dischargers to neglect the offsite costs of waste disposal will not only devote too few resources to the treatment of waste but will also produce too much waste in view of the damage it causes" (Kneese, 1964). Externalities are powerful concepts developed by economists as a body of theory within welfare economics, with tools of analysis having application to water quality. Starting with the work of Pareto, published in 1909, and the work of A. C. Pigou, published in 1920, many economists have devoted attention to development of theory and tools which may now be transferred to water quality analysis. In fact, Pigou's work was motivated in part by the apparent effect of smoke from English factories upon the health of English people and the cleanliness of their air environment.

The Problem of Measurement

Along with externalities, the problem of measurement is crucial in water quality management. Traditionally, water has not been allocated through the market sytem as have most other factors, products, and services. Certainly, water quality is not reflected in market values to an appreciable extent. Judging from the changing size of national, state, municipal, and other governmental budgets, an increasing share of the nation's resources is allocated through voting rather than through pricing processes. This creates problems in resource management but these problems are not unfamiliar to the resource economist and are not outside the science of economics.

Professor Gaffney has expressed relevant views on this problem as follows: "Economics, contrary to common usage, begins with the postulate that man is the measure of all things. Direct damage to human health and happiness is more directly 'economic' therefore, than damage to property, which is simply an intermediate means to health and happiness . . . money is but one of many means to ends, as well as a useful measure of value. . . . 'Economic damage' therefore includes damage to human functions and pleasures. The economist tries to weigh these direct effects of people in the same balance with other costs and benefits. . . ." (Gaffney, 1965).

There exist four major alternatives for dealing with the measurement problems in water quality measurement: (1) expand and create market mechanisms for differential water pricing by qualities or grades; (2) develop institutional pricing through synthesized market prices and costs as weights assignable to water grades or qualities; (3) legal action through legislation and/or executive order with a public welfare basis; and (4) combinations of the three.

Expand and Create Market Mechanisms for Differential Water Pricing by Qualities or Grades

One alternative for dealing with measurement problems of water quality would be to create market mechanisms wherein water is priced by grades as a factor or as a product. Then water could be metered and sold by private, government, or quasi-public entities. Qualities of water could be conserved as a condition of sale or repurchase and minimum quality levels could be warranted to buyers and sellers.

Institutional Pricing

Another alternative is to assign prices to water by quality both in terms of quality used and quality returned. There are two major approaches to assigning relative weights to water qualities: value productivities and opportunity costs.

VALUE PRODUCTIVITY

Through this approach various water qualities or grades of water would be assigned values through a synthetic market of shadow prices indicative of imputed values through input-output analysis. Or, alternatively, water could be assigned weights by grades of quality on the bases of relative contributions by uses to state, regional, or national products of incomes through sector accounting processes.

OPPORTUNITY COSTS

Another approach which is complementary to the value productivity and income-generated ideas briefed above is based upon opportunity costing analysis wherein the cost is suggested in the form of shadow prices estimated from relinquished or diminished options.

Four components of opportunity costing analysis are considered here: (1) relinquished use options, (2) diminished use options, (3) relinquished supply-source options, and (4) relinquished supply treatment options. The first two components are very similar to the case cited by Professor Gaffney wherein each wild duck in Ventura County, California, used $560 worth of water valued in terms of lima bean production sacrificed by water used in the duck club (Gaffney, 1962).

Under (1) relinquished use options, the price of a particular use may be imputed from the cost of the use option(s) relinquished in the achievement of the particular use. For example, the denial or forced cessation of use of water from a stream by an industrial plant results in an annual loss of $100,000 worth of product as the plant goes out of business in order to protect the annual production of 25,000 trout. In this example, the production of trout becomes the use allocated. Even though the price of trout may be difficult to determine in the market, the price may be estimated from the cost of the relinquished use forced out in the allocation process. In this instance, the trout would have an imputed price of $4 each.

Continuing with the same example, let us illustrate (2) diminished use options by assuming that the 25,000 trout could be produced annually with a reduction in product by the industrial plant of $50,000 annually. In this case, the use diminished amounting to $50,000 would impute a price to the trout of $2 each.

Illustrating (3) relinquished supply source options, let us assume that the industrial plant could either obtain its water from another source or could release its effluent in another manner. Let us further assume that this alternative source of water or effluent disposal would cost the plant $50,000 more than the cost of the use of the trout stream. In this case, the relinquishment of the use of the stream by the plant in order for the 25,000 trout to be produced would yield an imputed price to the trout of $2 each.

Illustrating (4) relinquished supply treatment options, let us assume further that the industrial plant could treat its effluent in a manner that would not affect adversely trout production in the stream for a cost of $25,000 but the plant would remain in business with a net product value of $75,000 rather than $100,000. In this instance the price imputed to the trout would be $1 each.

Through these illustrations it would appear there are numerous criteria and tools whereby the allocation of water qualities may be evaluated. Also, it is obvious that present legal systems of water allocation do not discern *between* use quality values and *within* use quality levels of application. Consequently water becomes a free resource to the extent of its availability as determined by existing water rights with no incentive to economize by grades and qualities.

Legal Allocation and Restraint

Under this alternative water would be allocated by qualities for specified uses and with specified return qualities. Also, wastes and fallouts associated with livestock and crop productions would be controlled by legislation or executive action. This would be carried out under public health and welfare criteria just as cyclamates were banned, DDT is in the process of being banned, and tobacco would be banned if tobacco interests were less influential and subordinated to the public interest.

Combinations

Most likely problems of measurement will involve each of the three preceding approaches in some sort of combination. The precise application (and combination) remains to be decided upon.

The Problem of Intervention

Through the Water Quality Act of 1965 and the Clean Waters Restoration Act of 1966, the federal government has intervened in the identification, measurement, and implementation of water quality levels. Most states have water quality control legislation such as the Iowa Water Pollution Control Act of 1965.

Public intervention has come rapidly as revealed in state and federal legislation. But there remains much to be accomplished in moving from legislation to effective implementation of what the legislation purports to do.

Under the Iowa Act "it is hereby declared to be the public policy of this state to conserve the waters of the state and to protect, maintain, and improve the quality thereof for public water supplies for the propagation of wildlife, fish, and aquatic life, and for domestic, agricultural, industrial, recreational, and other legitimate (beneficial) uses; to provide that no waste be discharged into any waters of the state without first being given the degree of treatment necessary to protect the legitimate (beneficial) uses of such waters; to provide for the prevention, abatement, and control of new, increasing, potential, or existing pollution (Acts, 1965).

Shortly after enactment of the Iowa legislation, I wrote as follows: "In the implementation, administration, and future amending of the Iowa Law, the concept 'degree of treatment' will necessarily have to be determined. . . . In the process, difficult decisions will be called for when uses compete with each other for waters of particular qualities. It remains doubtful that existing knowledge is sufficient to make such decisions if they are to result in maximizing the aggregate and variable components of satisfactions which are demanded by our society from water" (Timmons, 1967).

Subsequent conflicts between the federal and state water pollution control commissions concerning quality standards as well as intrastate conflicts among interest groups emphasize the problems encountered and the nature and magnitude of the remaining action in public interventions.

TOWARD RESOLUTION OF WATER QUALITY MANAGEMENT PROBLEMS ORIGINATING WITHIN AGRICULTURE

The first step toward meeting water quality management relating to water use within agriculture is being taken through becoming aware of the importance of water quality problems. This book is part of this step. The need for information and facts is urgent and apparent as the basis for understanding water quality problems and management solutions. There is a real danger that action will move faster than our factual basis for action and public understanding of the facts will accommodate. Thus, there is an urgency for research and education to provide foundations on which action may be formulated and implemented. Public pressure for the action will likely continue to press for solutions to water quality problems.

Because of the urgency for relevant information useful to policy and action formulation, research efforts must be planned, undertaken, and completed with both care and dispatch.

The guidelines for research and education are becoming increasingly clear. Some of them are suggested in this chapter. The need to recognize the quality heterogeneities of water from demand and supply orientations is evident. The importance of demand orientations and requirements is paramount in specifying quality standards which vary among uses, spatially and temporally. Supply qualities must be geared to qualities demanded by uses. Least-cost methods are necessary in meeting demand qualities. In assigning benefits and costs to water uses, the problems of externalities, measurement, and intervention are crucial.

Economics with its legacy of methods, theory, and its corps of resource economists is a necessary part of the multidisciplinary approach in planning and in carrying out relevant research necessary for education, legislation, and administration of water quality management.

REFERENCES

Ackerman, E., and Lof, G. 1959. *Technology in water development.* Baltimore: Johns Hopkins Press.

Acts, 1965. Sixty-first General Assembly, Regular Session, State of Iowa, p. 436.

Gaffney, Mason. 1962. Comparison of market pricing and other means of allocating water resources. In *Water law and policy in the southeast.* Inst. of Law and Government, Univ. of Ga.

———. 1965. *Applying economic controls.* Bull. Atomic Scientist, p. 20.

Kesler, R. P., and Hinton, R. A. 1966. *An economic evaluation of liquid manure disposal from confinement finishing hogs.* Bull. 722. Urbana: Univ. of Ill.

Kneese, Allen V. 1964. *The economics of regional water quality management,* p. 43. Baltimore: Johns Hopkins Press.

Owens, T. R., and Griffin, W. L. 1968. *Economics of water pollution control for cattle feedlot operations.* Spec. Rept. 9. Tex. Tech. College, Lubbock.

Timmons, John F. 1967. Economics of water quality. In *Water pollution control and abatement,* ed. Ted L. Willrich and N. W. Hines, p. 36. Ames: Iowa State Univ. Press.

Timmons, John F., and Dougal, M. D. 1968. *Economics of water quality management. Proc. Intern. Conf. Water Peace,* vol. 6. Wash., D.C.: USGPO.

CHAPTER TWENTY-EIGHT

ALLIANCE FOR ACTION

JOHN M. RADEMACHER

T HIS is the age of the environmental specialist. "Ecology," a word heard only in scientific circles 5 years ago, is rapidly becoming the "in" word of the militant generation.

The role of agriculture in clean water is vital to the Midwest and to the nation. In the preceding chapters are discussions by experts of the problems which affect us all. It is hoped that our conference reinforced our alliance for action. In this pollution problem we must respond with the attitude of action and do a job of cleaning up our rivers and streams.

We Americans are forever proclaiming that the only certainties in man's existence are death and taxes. Massive evidence is accruing in our "effluent" society that would add a third certainty—the problem of waste and what to do about it. The disposal of animal and human wastes is one of the foremost problems facing mankind, and the problem proliferates while we deliberate and debate.

On the east coast of the United States a megalopolis stretches from Boston southward to Washington. The 30 to 50 million people crowded into this narrow corridor represent the most concentrated mass of humanity in North America. The human wastes from this teeming hive exude massive pollution loads, with the vividly described degrading effects upon the Potomac, Delaware, Hudson, and Charles rivers already legend (Fry, 1966).

Yet by comparison these cities are "small-town" in terms of gross organic pollution when you consider the loads dumped into the Missouri River. Organic loads equivalent to 80 to 100 million population equivalents have been measured in the river at Omaha and at Kansas City. Dissolved oxygen levels below Kansas City all the way to St. Louis are at times below 4 mg/l and on occasion have dropped to 1.0 mg/l or less (Lightfoot, 1968). This occurs not at low flow but during a rising stage when rain washes the landscape—the countryside as well as the cities—and floods into the mighty Missouri.

The answer as to the source of such loads does not rest in human

JOHN M. RADEMACHER is Regional Director, Missouri Basin Region, FWPCA, Kansas City, Missouri.

population figures because the Missouri basin has less than 8 million people. But in terms of animal population we are really loaded—20 million cattle, 16 million hogs, and 7 million sheep. Put in terms of population equivalents, we have close to 370 million as the potential organic load at any one time. This then, in large part, is where the organic source in the Missouri River is derived, and with the practice of confined feeding of the animals on the increase (U.S. Dept. Interior, 1968), the percent of that potential getting to the stream will not diminish.

No longer is pollution the vested onus of cities and industries— the farmer has also reaped a piece of the action. The spectrum of pollution problems has broadened and agriculture with its silt loads, organic loads, salt loads, nutrient loads, pesticides, etc., is definitely within the overall area of concern.

When 22 out of 36 reported fish kills in one state were identified as being caused by direct agricultural farming and feeding wastes, that concern is real (State of Kansas, 1967).

When an agricultural pesticide has become a ubiquitous partner in the makeup of all flora and fauna from pole to pole and ocean to ocean, the concern is not only real but takes on the menacing proportions of the dreaded radioactive pollutants.[1]

As a result a new dimension has been added to the role of agriculture—a clean water responsibility. This is not to say agriculture did not recognize the need for clean water in the past; it has always claimed clean water as a right.[2] But the agricultural industry now has to look at its own operations and recognize it can cause pollution and that it must prevent or minimize the potential of that pollution.

In developing an alliance for action to control agricultural pollution let us recognize that each problem area must be approached generally in similar fashion—that is, waste source identification, estimate of effect, and control. However, the specific solutions to silt pollution, salt pollution, pesticide pollution, and animal wastes do not mutually satisfy each other, and this chapter could not do justice in attempting to explore the many and differing requirements for all. Where silt is basically a conservation and management program for all of agriculture, the salt problem is almost exclusively relegated to irrigation agriculture and the basic economic detriments to downstream users as the result of concentration and leaching. Pesticides relate directly to policy decisions at the highest levels to formulate and use particular products and toward research to find more effective yet less toxic compounds as far as the environment is concerned. Only with animal wastes do we have a pollutant which lends itself to more classical solutions and involves the farmer and feeder directly on a day-to-day basis (Shuyler, 1969). For this reason let us look at the animal waste problems and see how the various interests and pieces fit together.

---

1. Conclusion based upon reports from many sources on DDT levels throughout the world.
2. Historical premise—SCS, FFA, 4H, Grange all pushed for clean water in past.

THE TECHNICAL BASE

The acquiring of the technical information is the first needed step—the full development of the technical base. This does not mean that control actions should or will wait for the full development of the technical base. Rather, it means that control efforts must be intensified now, using the known information. Concurrently, the technical base will be strengthened.

The technical base incorporates, among other items, a thorough knowledge of the waste sources, the water uses, and the water quality and quantity. Responsibility for use of these items of information rests with the federal and state water pollution control agencies, although the resources of other federal and state agencies and the industry normally provide significant inputs to this data bank system, and this goes beyond the normal meaning of cooperation—it means participation on the part of all parties.

THE INVENTORY

The development of an inventory noting animal production, concentration, and location is an essential element of the technical base for the animal waste problem. There is no one best method of quantifying and qualifying the problem. While each state is unique, there are many elements of information common to all states. A combination of inventory systems is being used in the various states and there is no reason to alter this. However, a system of state program accountability and actual inventory evaluation through selected random checks is needed. For instance, aerial photographs could be used in selected basins in those states where control efforts have not begun or where adequate progress is not being made. It also appears that mandatory registration is not only highly desirable from the standpoint of prevention but would basically fill the waste source inventory needs.

Population equivalent values are continually based on the total animal waste production with little regard for the fact that only part of the waste actually enters surface water and groundwater. By using inventory data, together with sampling and other surveillance techniques, the relative amount of pollution from animal wastes can be determined.

RESEARCH—DEMONSTRATION—DEVELOPMENT

Although Harold Bernard from our research program in Washington will go into specific details, I do want to touch on this important area.

There are many gaps in our knowledge concerning the most efficient and effective means of controlling pollution. This will require that specific research and development needs be delineated in accordance with the expected trends of the feedlot industry. Not only must this research answer the most pressing present problems but also must simultaneously provide the foundation of long-range plans for developing sufficient technology to control feedlot pollution 5, 10, or 25 years from now. It has been estimated that by the early 1970s, approximately 2,500 large commercial feedlots in the United States will supply 70% of the nation's finished cattle (U.S. Dept. Agriculture, 1967). These lots will in all probability require treatment beyond or in excess of that currently being used.

Feedlot pollution runoff could be greatly reduced with a minimum expenditure by using known information. A comprehensive demonstration project encompassing optimum management techniques to determine and illustrate the amount that pollution can be reduced should be of high priority. Since past studies have usually dealt with existing conditions, it is important to quantify and qualify the feedlot runoff under optimum management practices. The information obtained should give impetus to the implementation of sound management practices throughout the nation. Furthermore, the information obtained will also serve as base-line data for further research to develop treatment processes for the large lots.

REGULATIONS

Regulations are, in effect, the blueprints for the animal waste control program. They act as a guide to planning, construction, and enforcement. Regulations are needed to ensure the feedlot operator that the measures he is taking will guarantee a reasonable tenure of operation. It is necessary that the operator know the controls being installed are adequate and that frequent changes will not be sought by the official agency. Uniformity which concurrently allows for flexibility must be built into the regulations.

The existing legislation pertaining to feedlot pollution control should be thoroughly evaluated. Many of the basic concepts contained in the regulations are sound; however, more attention should be directed to management practices which would prevent the wastes from entering surface water or groundwater.

Our laws must give due consideration to the location of feedlots. Feedlots have generally been located without regard to the soil inventory and associated topographical characteristics. It may be not only desirable but also necessary to employ zoning regulations to prevent the encroachment of the animal population into urban areas and prevent the encroachment of the human population into the feedlot areas.

Regulations should also provide for a continuing, comprehensive animal inventory, state by state, drainage basin by drainage basin, which would provide definitive data on the character and composition of agricultural effluents, points of discharge, and other pertinent information.

Mandatory registration, including an animal population and concentration inventory, should be an integral part of feedlot regulations. Most of the states that have enacted legislation do require some form of registration; however, regulations enacted by some of the states do not require registration until pollution results. This puts the burden of finding feedlot pollution on the state water pollution control commission. Furthermore, this is undesirable as the regulation makes no provision for such preventive measures as properly locating new feedlots.

Model regulations and basic criteria need to be drafted and developed. These should be refined and applied by each state to fit its particular need. Here again, a cooperative effort on the part of federal and state agencies, university specialists, and representatives from the feeder groups could serve the cause of clean water by working together to develop these regulations and criteria.

MANAGEMENT SYSTEMS

A sound animal waste management program encompasses prevention, reduction, treatment, and disposal of animal wastes. The inauguration of this program cannot wait while all the data are collected and assembled. To wait for all the answers before taking action would squander time—time that we do not have. To wait may mean the degradation of many waters beyond the point of recovery, with accompanying health hazards of undefined proportions. Echoing Aristotle: "The ultimate end . . . is not knowledge, but action. To be half right on time may be more important than to obtain the whole truth too late."

A much broader view of waste management will be dictated by socioeconomic changes. While the return of the wastes to the land may not be competitive with commercial fertilizers on an immediate crop production basis, it may be highly profitable in terms of public welfare over both the short and long range to use these wastes to reclaim marginal lands. We are losing approximately a million acres of agricultural land each year as a result of urban growth, highway construction, and other natural and man-made incursions into the reserve of productive land (Moore, 1968). It is difficult to equate the true worth to society for the reclamation of lands. Certainly it extends much beyond the yearly crop production.

To date, the kaleidoscope of alternatives to reduce animal waste pollution has been honored more fully in principle than in practice. The simplest and most economical method of controlling pollution resulting from feedlot runoff is to minimize the quantity of runoff by preventing outside surface water from entering the lot. The majority of feedlot operators have not used techniques which minimize the quantity and strength of runoff waste.

CONTROL-TREATMENT DEVICES

Once all the management factors have been used to minimize the quantity and strength of the runoff waste, treatment may be necessary. The most logical place to treat or reduce the wastes is at the source.

Treatment and disposal of animal wastes center largely on processes currently used for domestic and industrial waste treatment. While investigations have shown that animal wastes are amenable to most of these processes, the treatment results have usually been unsuccessful because of a lack of understanding of the characteristics of the wastes, the magnitude of the problem, and economic constraints currently imposed by society.[3]

The percent removal concept of municipal sewage treatment is not applicable to the control of feedlot pollution. Cattle feedlot runoff is a highly concentrated organic waste (Dague, 1969). The strength may equal that of normal domestic sewage or may be 10, 100, 1,000 or more times greater. Feedlot runoff may still contain *after treatment* as high pollutional parameters as domestic sewage *before treatment* if percent removal is the only criterion used for treatment. Therefore, a "residual" concept of waste treatment is proposed. That is, acceptable treatment is that which reduces the pollution to a prescribed level or residual which would assure adequate treatment.

No one treatment process or treatment system will be the solution for all animal production units. A variety of management and treatment systems will have to be developed.

LOOKING TO THE FUTURE

Surveys reported by Colorado, California, and USDA during the early growth of the commercial feedlot indicated that optimum feedlot capacity ranged between 10,000 and 20,000 head. Today 30,000-head capacities are routine with 40,000- to 70,000-head lots becoming more prominent in the Panhandle area of Texas (Owens and Griffin, 1968). Thus it becomes apparent that growth is still a part of this industry.

There does not appear to be an optimum size feedlot. In all probability large-scale animal production facilities will increase and the problems will grow unless action is taken now.

Finally, we must consider the effects of animal waste control on the economy. We have made cost estimates of nationwide water pollution control (U.S. Dept. Interior, 1968–69). Still, net profit is a key guideline to feedlot operations. This is proper and must be recognized. However, it must also be recognized that when public agencies develop progressive programs to alleviate environmental contamination, the taxpayer usually pays the bill. An enlightened public has shown in all fields of environmental contamination, including water pollution control, that it is willing to pay, in dollars, the added costs of maintaining a high quality environment rather than risk its destruction.[4]

---

3. Personal assessment of situation.
4. Based on observation and federal and state legislative action over the past 14 years.

Agriculture must accept waste treatment as a legitimate production cost so that the natural resources of this country may be handed to posterity undamaged and undestroyed. Agriculture must recognize that the ultimate cost of pollution abatement will be carried by the public.

If it is the public who must bear the cost, then agriculture must have the courage to include waste treatment as a part of its production costs.

REFERENCES

Dague, Richard R. 1969. Animal wastes—a major pollution problem. Second Compendium of Animal Waste Management, June 1969.

Fry, Keith. 1966. Land runoff—a factor in Potomac basin pollution, 1966. Interstate Commission on the Potomac River Basin, Wash., D.C.

Lightfoot, E. 1968. Waste utilization and conservation. Presented at Joint Seminar, Univ. of Mo. and Mo. Pollution Board, Columbia, 9 April 1968.

Moore, Joe G., Jr. 1968. Remarks before the Western Reg. Conf. of Trout Unlimited, Denver, Colo., 27 Sept. 1968.

Owens, T. R., and Griffin, Wade L. 1968. Economics of water pollution control for cattle feedlot operations. Dept. Agr. Econ., Texas Tech. College, Lubbock.

Shuyler, Lynn R. 1969. Using feedlot waste—design for feedlot waste management. Second Compendium of Animal Waste Management, June 1969.

State of Kansas. 1967. Plan of implementation for water quality control and pollution abatement, June 1967.

U.S. Dept. of Agriculture. 1967. *Agriculture statistics—1967.* Wash., D.C.: USGPO.

U.S. Dept. of Interior. 1968. *Pollution implications of animal wastes —a forward oriented review.* FWPCA, Robert S. Kerr Water Research Center, Ada, Okla., July 1968.

U.S. Dept. of Interior. 1968–1969. *Cost of clean water.* FWPCA Publ.

CHAPTER TWENTY-NINE

ACCOMPLISHMENTS AND GOALS

HAROLD BERNARD

T HOUGH the Federal Water Pollution Control Administration has conducted research on some facets of agricultural pollution for many years, for all practical purposes impetus was not given to the program until the Federal Water Pollution Control Act of 1966, as amended, became law. The Act extended the research and development capabilities of the FWPCA. Whereas the agency had conducted research through universities and nonprofit organizations, the new law permitted us to participate financially with the particular industries producing the pollution problem to help them solve their problem. One section of the law requires the FWPCA to demonstrate new and novel techniques and systems for abating pollution from industrial sources. It enables us to join with a user and participate in a program up to 70% of the total cost of a project, but not exceeding $1 million.

In the short time the FWPCA has been given this authority, industrial research and demonstration projects totaling more than $100 million in grants have been initiated, with FWPCA contributing approximately $40 million. Of this impressive sum, agricultural pollution accounts for approximately $2 million.

In addition to this type of activity, the agency has a large program with universities, municipalities, and nonprofit institutions to conduct more fundamental studies. Approximately $2 million has also been expended under this authority in the area of agricultural pollution in fiscal years 1969 and 1970. Before expanding on these accomplishments, the goals of the FWPCA should first be explained. All leading authorities agree that due to our population and our productivity, the quality of our environment has suffered tremendously. Unless the situation is reversed, we will have created a "Mission Impossible" and in "ten seconds we will self-destruct."

The goal for the FWPCA is to develop and demonstrate an array of management, prevention, treatment, and control techniques which meet the water quality standards established by the 50 states. This objective applies to the agricultural industry as well as the steel

HAROLD BERNARD is Chief, Agricultural and Marine Pollution Control Branch, Division of Applied Science and Technology, Office of Research and Development, FWPCA.

industry, paper and pulp manufacturers, food processors, mining, oil refinery, etc.

What is a water quality standard? In the Clean Water Act of 1965, Congress required that each state establish criteria for each interstate stream which will guarantee its utility as a water resource for the purposes assigned to the particular stretch of stream. The following water quality standards were established by the state of Nebraska:

CLASS "A" WATER USE—DOMESTIC WATER SUPPLY

1. COLIFORM ORGANISMS—Coliform group and fecal coliform organisms shall not exceed a geometric mean 10,000 total or 2,000 fecal coliform bacteria per 100 ml, based on at least 5 samples per 30-day period. No more than 20% of samples shall exceed 20,000 total or 4,000 fecal coliform bacteria.

2. TASTE & ODOR-PRODUCING SUBSTANCES—Concentration of substances shall be less than that amount which would degrade the water quality for the designated use. Phenols concentration shall not exceed 0.001 mg/l.

3. SUSPENDED COLLOIDAL, OR SETTLEABLE SOLIDS— None from wastewater sources which will permit objectionable deposition or be deleterious for the designated uses. In no case shall turbidity caused by wastewater impart more than a 10% increase in turbidity to the receiving water.

4. TOXIC AND DELETERIOUS SUBSTANCES—None alone or in combination with other substances or wastes in concentration of such nature so as to render the receiving water unsafe or unsuitable for the designated use. Raw water shall be of such quality that after treatment by coagulation, filtration, and sedimentation, the water will meet Public Health Drinking Water Standards. Radiological limits shall be in accordance with the Radiological Health Regulations, State of Nebraska, 1st edition 1966, and as amended in its latest edition.

5. TEMPERATURE—The temperature of the receiving water shall not be increased by a total of more than 5° F from May through October and not more than a total of 10° F from November through April. Maximum rate of change limited to 2° F per hour.

6. DISSOLVED OXYGEN—Greater than 4 mg/l for a monthly mean. Greater than 3 mg/l in any individual sample.

7. HYDROGEN ION—Hydrogen ion concentrations expressed as pH shall be maintained between 6.5 & 9.0 with a maximum total change of 1.0 pH unit from the value in the receiving stream.

8. TOTAL DISSOLVED SOLIDS—A point source discharge shall not increase the total dissolved solids concentration of a receiving water by more than 10% and in no case shall the total dissolved solids of a stream exceed 600 mg/l.

9. RESIDUE OIL & FLOATING SUBSTANCES—No residue attributable to wastewater or visible film of oil or globules of grease shall be present.

10. AESTHETIC CONSIDERATIONS—No evidence of matter that creates nuisance conditions or is offensive to the senses of sight, touch, smell, or taste, including color.

CLASS "B" WATER USE—FULL BODY CONTACT SPORTS

1. COLIFORM ORGANISMS—Shall not exceed a geometric mean of 200 fecal coliform per 100 ml based on at least 5 samples per 30-day period & shall not exceed 400/100 ml in more than 10% of the samples.
2. TASTE & ODOR-PRODUCING SUBSTANCES—None in amounts which would be sufficient to interfere with designated use.
3. SUSPENDED COLLOIDAL, OR SETTLEABLE SOLIDS— Same as Class "A."
4. TOXIC AND DELETERIOUS SUBSTANCES—Same as Class "A."
5. TEMPERATURE—Same as Class "A."
6. DISSOLVED OXYGEN—Same as Class "A."
7. HYDROGEN ION—Hydrogen ion concentrations expressed as pH shall be maintained between 6.5 & 9.0.
8. TOTAL DISSOLVED SOLIDS—Same as Class "C."
9. RESIDUE OIL & FLOATING SUBSTANCES—Same as Class "A."
10. AESTHETIC CONSIDERATIONS—Same as Class "A."

CLASS "C" WATER USES—AGRICULTURAL, PARTIAL BODY CONTACT SPORTS, INDUSTRIAL, FISH & WILDLIFE GROWTH & PROPAGATION

1. COLIFORM ORGANISMS—Same as Class "A."
2. TASTE & ODOR-PRODUCING SUBSTANCES—Same as Class "A." Shall not contain concentrations of substances which will render any undesirable taste to fish flesh, or in any other way make such fish flesh inedible.
3. SUSPENDED COLLOIDAL, OR SETTLEABLE SOLIDS— Same as Class "A."
4. TOXIC AND DELETERIOUS SUBSTANCES—Same as Class "A." Plus ammonia nitrogen concentrations shall not exceed 1.4 mg/l in trout streams nor exceed 3.5 mg/l in warm-water streams where the pH in these streams does not exceed a pH value of 8.3. If the pH of a stream exceeds 8.3, the undissociated ammonium hydroxide as nitrogen shall not exceed 0.1 mg/l in trout streams nor exceed 0.25 mg/l in warm-water streams.
5. TEMPERATURE—*Trout Streams*—Allowable change 5° F, maximum limit 65° F. *Warm Water Streams*—Allowable change 5° F May thru Oct., 10° F Nov. thru April; maximum limit 90° F; maximum rate of change limited to 2° per hour. For Missouri River, from Gavins Point Dam to Sioux City, Iowa, maximum temperature 85° F, allowable change 4° F.
6. DISSOLVED OXYGEN—Oxygen-consuming waste shall not lower the dissolved oxygen in the receiving stream lower than 5 mg/l in a warm-water stream and 6 mg/l in a trout stream.

7. HYDROGEN ION—Same as Class "A."
8. TOTAL DISSOLVED SOLIDS—A point source discharge shall not increase the total dissolved solids concentration of a receiving water by more than 20%, this value shall not exceed 100 mg/l, and in no case shall the total dissolved solids of a stream exceed 1,500 mg/l. For irrigation use the SAR value and conductivity shall not be greater than a C3-S2 class irrigation water as shown in Figure 25 of Agricultural Handbook 60.
9. RESIDUE OIL & FLOATING SUBSTANCES—Same as Class "A."
10. AESTHETIC CONSIDERATIONS—Same as Class "A."

INTERMITTENT STREAMS
1. COLIFORM ORGANISMS—Not to exceed 20,000 per 100 ml as a monthly average value; nor to exceed this value in more than 20% of the samples tested in any one month.
2. TASTE & ODOR-PRODUCING SUBSTANCES—Not applicable.
3. SUSPENDED COLLOIDAL, OR SETTLEABLE SOLIDS— Suspended solids shall not exceed 30 mg/l.
4. TOXIC AND DELETERIOUS SUBSTANCES—Radiological limits same as Class "A"—shall not be toxic to livestock or terrestrial wildlife.
5. TEMPERATURE—[none given].
6. DISSOLVED OXYGEN—BOD shall not exceed 30 mg/l.
7. HYDROGEN ION—Same as Class "B."
8. TOTAL DISSOLVED SOLIDS—[none given].
9. RESIDUE OIL & FLOATING SUBSTANCES—Same as Class "A."
10. AESTHETIC CONSIDERATIONS—Same as Class "A."

Source: State of Nebraska Water Pollution Control Council.

Notes: Wastewater shall not degrade the receiving waters below the stated criteria. These criteria are applicable at flows greater than the lowest flow for seven (7) consecutive days which can be expected to occur at a frequency of once every ten years.

The method of water-sample collection, sample preservation, analysis, and measurement to determine water quality and the accuracy of the results shall be in accordance with the latest edition of *Standard Methods for the Examination of Water and Wastewater,* or by appropriate regulations or procedures approved by the Nebraska Water Pollution Control Council or the Federal Water Pollution Control Administration.

In making tests or analytical determinations of surface waters to determine conformity or nonconformity with the above criteria, samples shall be collected in such a manner and at such locations, times, and frequencies as approved by the Council. Every effort should be made to make the samples representative of the receiving waters after reasonable opportunity for dilution and mixture with the wastewater.

For temperatures: Flows considered are for ice-free conditions.

Table 29.1 is an example of a schedule for implementing pollution abatement from municipalities in a stretch of river. This schedule is an intimate part of every state's standards. Similar schedules are being developed for industrial sources.

It has been estimated that municipalities and states (FWPCA, 1968) will expend some $10 billion in the next 5 to 10 years to collect and treat wastes to the level necessary for effluents to meet the particular standard set for the receiving body of water. Industry will provide treatment facilities that will require similar expenditures. However, this consignment of a significant but small fraction of resources in this short time period is only a temporary expedient. This is illustrated quite succinctly in Figure 29.1.

Up to 1930, when primary treatment was the main treatment concept, BOD released to the streams increased with population growth. The short-lived dip in BOD during the 1930s was due principally to public works projects. The increase in the 1940s was caused by the diversion of all funds to the war effort. The decrease in the rate of rise during the 1950s is a result of an increase in construction of secondary treatment plants, and the downward trend in the 1960s is a reflection of a recognition on the part of the public for all effluents to receive at least an equivalent to secondary treatment. The parts of the curve shown after 1967 are projected on the basis that all municipal wastes will receive secondary treatment by 1972. The continued downward trend of the curve is illustrative of the fact that a greater amount of BOD is removed from effluents by treatment than is contributed by municipalities. Significant gains are postulated. Our stream quality will be enhanced to the levels we enjoyed in 1915. However, this euphoria is short lived, the null point is reached in 1980.

At that time the waste load resulting from our projected increase in population exceeds the removal capacity of the projected treatment plants. The amount of wastes discharged to streams increases until by the year 2000 we have violated our water resources to the same extent in which we are now mired.

To preclude this projected return to our present morass, the nation must develop new techniques and systems to increase the quantity of pollutants removed from municipal waste streams.

Recall that this curve illustrates the effect of only municipal wastes and readily degradable organic constituents (BOD) on our streams. Add to this industrial sources and wastes that exhibit a chemical oxygen demand plus wastes from agricultural activities and you project the potential magnitude of the pollution problem that faces the nation.

There is no attempt here to focus the agency's efforts on pollution from agricultural activities. There is only a desire to place the pollution problem from this source of the nation's economy into a proper perspective and to expend a proportional amount of our energies to minimize pollution from this source within a similar context as that enjoyed by the remainder of the nation's economy.

A recent federal task force composed of seven cognizant Federal agencies studied the problem of pollution from agricultural activities

TABLE 29.1 Municipal sources of pollution to interstate streams of Nebraska.

Stream	Community	County	1960 Population	Type of Treatment	BOD PE to system	BOD PE to stream	Date of Compliance
North Fork Republican River	Haigler	Dundy	268	No Sewer			
South Fork Republican River	None						
Republican River	Benkelman	Dundy	1,400	Secondary (Lagoon)	1,400		
	Stratton	Hitchcock	492	Secondary	450	100	
	Trenton	Hitchcock	914	Primary	850	500	Jan. 1, 1972
	Culbertson	Hitchcock	803	Secondary (Lagoon)	700		
	McCook	Red Willow	8,301	Secondary	15,000	4,000	
	Indianola	Red Willow	754	Primary	720	300	Jan. 1, 1972
	Bartley	Red Willow	309	No Sewer	None		
	Cambridge	Furnas	1,090	Secondary	850	260	
	Holbrook	Furnas	354	Secondary	350	110	
	Arapahoe	Furnas	1,084	Primary	1,000	600	Jan. 1, 1972
	Edison	Furnas	249	No Sewer	None		
	Oxford	Furnas	1,090	Secondary	1,200		
	Orleans	Harlan	608	Secondary (Lagoon)	600		
	Alma	Harlan	1,342	Secondary & Chlorination	4,370	1,000	Jan. 1, 1972
	Republican City	Harlan	139	Secondary	180	45	
	Naponee	Franklin	206	No Sewer	None		
	Bloomington	Franklin	176	No Sewer	None		
	Franklin	Franklin	1,194	Secondary (Lagoon)	1,100		
	Riverton	Franklin	303	No Sewer	None		
	Red Cloud	Webster	1,525	Primary	900		Jan. 1, 1972
	Guide Rock	Webster	441	Primary	280		Jan. 1, 1972
	Superior	Nuckolls	2,935	Secondary	640		
	Hardy	Nuckolls	285	Secondary (Lagoon)	45		
Arikaree River	None						

TABLE 29.1 (continued)

Stream	Community	County	1960 Population	Type of Treatment	BOD PE to system	BOD PE to stream	Date of Compliance
Frenchman River	Imperial	Chase	1,423	Secondary (Lagoon)	1,300		
	Wauneta	Chase	794	Secondary (Lagoon)	700		
	Hamlet	Hayes	113	No Sewer			
	Palisade	Hayes	544	Secondary	500		
	Culbertson	Hitchcock	803	Secondary (Lagoon)	700	160	Jan. 1, 1972
Beaver Creek	Danbury	Red Willow	185	No Sewer			
	Lebanon	Red Willow	143	No Sewer			
	Wilsonville	Furnas	289	No Sewer			
	Hendley	Furnas	79	No Sewer			
	Beaver City	Furnas	818	Secondary (Lagoon)	800		
	Stamford	Harlan	220	No Sewer			
Sappa Creek	None						
Prairie Dog Creek	None						
Little Blue River	Campbell	Franklin	424	Primary	410		
	Bladen	Webster	322	Secondary (Lagoon)	320	280	Jan. 1, 1972
	Ayr	Adams	111	Secondary (Lagoon)	111		
	Deweese	Clay	100	No Sewer			
	Oak	Nuckolls	125	No Sewer			
	Hebron	Thayer	1,920	Primary	1,900	1,200	Jan. 1, 1972

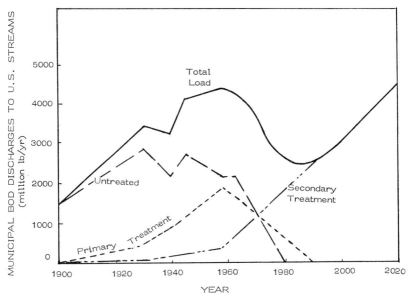

FIG. 29.1. Estimate of BOD discharges to U.S. streams from municipal outfalls, 1900–2020.

and recommended programs for its prevention, control, and treatment. Their recommendations for various areas of concern follow (Office of Science and Technology, 1969):

> The prevention and control of sediment may be accomplished largely by the control of its source, i.e. minimizing soil erosion and curbing sediment delivery from agricultural, range, and forest lands.
>
> To accomplish the control of plant nutrients, emphasis should be on research and action programs on behavior and fate of applied nitrogen, phosphorus, and other nutrients; minimizing runoff and percolation of nutrients by using them more effectively; controlling, treating, or removing excess plant nutrient from surface or sub-surface drainage to maintain the desired quality of receiving waters; effects of nutrients on algae and noxious water plants; use of harvested algae and other water plants.
>
> A research and action program for controlling animal wastes involves minimizing pollution by improved use of existing technology as well as by developing new and improved animal management methods and facility design; waste treatment and disposal methods; and methods for converting wastes to useful products. It also involves minimizing pollution through assisting in the establishment and enforcement of standards and providing criteria for land use planning.
>
> Pollution from irrigation return flows can be reduced by programs designed for decreasing salt concentration of the irrigation supply source; improving irrigation and drainage practices to minimize the effects of salts and minerals on soils and return-water quality; treating or disposing of salts and minerals in return flows;

improving plant tolerance and utilization of salts and minerals.

Intensive cooperative studies are required to more fully evaluate the impact of pesticides on the environment such as: evaluating the nature, extent and impact of pesticides in the ecosystem; reducing the amount of hazardous pesticides in the environment; treating, controlling, or removing pesticides from soil, air, and receiving waters; disposing of pesticide wastes, including used pesticide containers, in a manner least detrimental to the environment, and assisting state regulatory agencies in the establishment of uniform effective pesticide regulatory programs.

In light of these recommendations and our own forecasts on the total pollution problem confronting the nation, the FWPCA embarked on a program to simultaneously develop techniques and systems for controlling and treating pollution from agricultural activities, using existing technology, and to obtain the necessary information and technology that will, in the future, maximize pollution abatement and minimize costs.

As we are by all standards a young organization in this battle to save our environment, and as projects usually run 3 to 4 years, there are not many significant results that can be reported. Let me instead indicate our expenditures for the 2-year period (fiscal years 1969 and 1970), future funding prospects, and the need for additional knowledge and demonstrations of control and treatment methods.

In fiscal years 1969 and 1970 we expended over $4 million in research and demonstrations involving pollution abatement from pesticides, nutrient runoff, irrigation return flows, and concentrated animal feeding operations. Costs have been about equally distributed. It is expected that this level of funding will be somewhat increased in future years. In addition to this direct involvement we are also able to extrapolate from research, development, and demonstration projects in other areas of the total agency program. Notable examples of this are the use of the aeration ditch for pig feeding waste which was initially developed for municipal pollution treatment, activated sludge for animal feeding runoff, and the movement of nitrates in the vadose zone and in aquifers. It is estimated that at least a similar dollar volume of associated research and development is being conducted in the other segments of our program (Fig. 29.2) that can be utilized. Though this is an impressive start, there still is a long road to travel. We need to develop and demonstrate viable and effective means for controlling and treating pollution from all facets of the agricultural economy to match the similar efforts expended for municipal and industrial pollution abatement. I would encourage you to actively use the numerous avenues available in the FWPCA to enable us to help you develop the necessary technology to help your industry.

In summary, products from the agricultural industry are a necessary and vital part of the nation's overall economy. Agricultural activities also are a source of pollution. The public is demanding that our past practices that have violated our environment be stopped

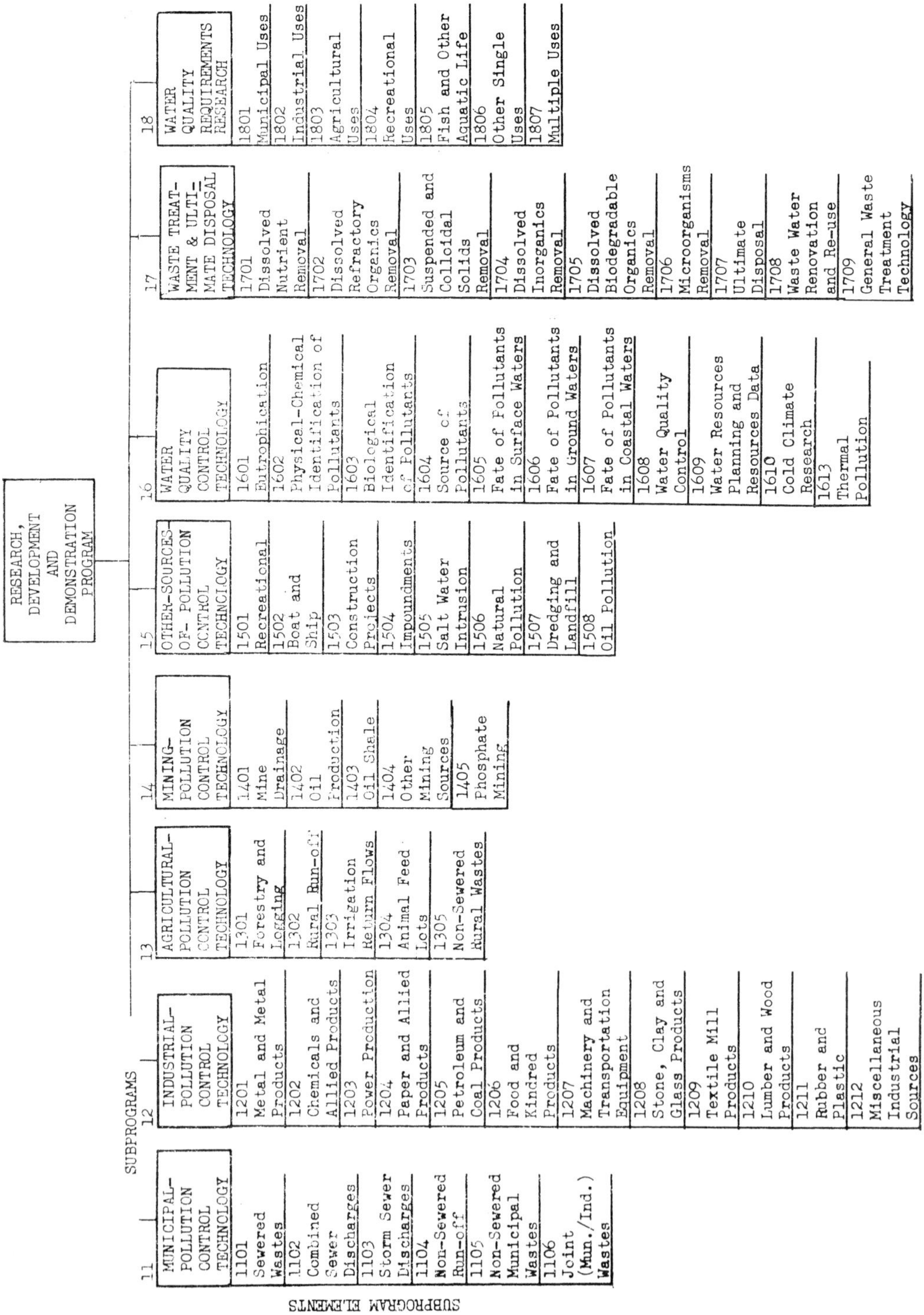

RESEARCH, DEVELOPMENT AND DEMONSTRATION PROGRAM

SUBPROGRAMS

11 MUNICIPAL-POLLUTION CONTROL TECHNOLOGY	12 INDUSTRIAL-POLLUTION CONTROL TECHNOLOGY	13 AGRICULTURAL-POLLUTION CONTROL TECHNOLOGY	14 MINING-POLLUTION CONTROL TECHNOLOGY	15 OTHER-SOURCES-OF-POLLUTION CONTROL TECHNOLOGY	16 WATER QUALITY CONTROL TECHNOLOGY	17 WASTE TREATMENT & ULTIMATE DISPOSAL TECHNOLOGY	18 WATER QUALITY REQUIREMENTS RESEARCH
1101 Sewered Wastes	1201 Metal and Metal Products	1301 Forestry and Logging	1401 Mine Drainage	1501 Recreational	1601 Eutrophication	1701 Dissolved Nutrient Removal	1801 Municipal Uses
1102 Combined Sewer Discharges	1202 Chemicals and Allied Products	1302 Rural Run-off	1402 Oil Production	1502 Boat and Ship	1602 Physical-Chemical Identification of Pollutants	1702 Dissolved Refractory Organics Removal	1802 Industrial Uses
1103 Storm Sewer Discharges	1203 Power Production	1303 Irrigation Return Flows	1403 Oil Shale	1503 Construction Projects	1603 Biological Identification of Pollutants	1703 Suspended and Colloidal Solids Removal	1803 Agricultural Uses
1104 Non-Sewered Run-off	1204 Paper and Allied Products	1304 Animal Feed Lots	1404 Other Mining Sources	1504 Impoundments	1604 Source of Pollutants	1704 Dissolved Inorganics Removal	1804 Recreational Uses
1105 Non-Sewered Municipal Wastes	1205 Petroleum and Coal Products	1305 Non-Sewered Rural Wastes	1405 Phosphate Mining	1505 Salt Water Intrusion	1605 Fate of Pollutants in Surface Waters	1705 Dissolved Biodegradable Organics Removal	1805 Fish and Other Aquatic Life
1106 Joint (Mun./Ind.) Wastes	1206 Food and Kindred Products			1506 Natural Pollution	1606 Fate of Pollutants in Ground Waters	1706 Microorganisms Removal	1806 Other Single Uses
	1207 Machinery and Transportation Equipment			1507 Dredging and Landfill	1607 Fate of Pollutants in Coastal Waters	1707 Ultimate Disposal	1807 Multiple Uses
	1208 Stone, Clay and Glass Products			1508 Oil Pollution	1608 Water Quality Control	1708 Waste Water Renovation and Re-use	
	1209 Textile Mill Products				1609 Water Resources Planning and Resources Data	1709 General Waste Treatment Technology	
	1210 Lumber and Wood Products				1610 Cold Climate Research		
	1211 Rubber and Plastic				1613 Thermal Pollution		
	1212 Miscellaneous Industrial Sources						

SUBPROGRAM ELEMENTS

FIG. 29.2. Research, development, and demonstration program structure. (Office of R&D, FWPCA, Oct. 17, 1968.)

and has indicated a willingness to pay for a clean environment. It is in the best interests of the agricultural industry to help develop and demonstrate its own cures. We would be pleased to help in any of the many ways we can.

REFERENCES

Federal Water Pollution Control Administration. 1968. *Cost of clean water*, vol. 2.

Office of Science and Technology. 1969. *Control of agriculture—related pollution*, a report to the President.

INDEX

Accelerated erosion, 35
Acrolein, 202, 206
Aerated lagoons for treatment of manure, 261
Aerobic environments, effects of on manure, 259–60
Agricultural pollution. *See also* Animal waste problem, factors in controlling
complexity of problem, 391
control of, 391
federal recommendations concerning, 401, 404–5
FWPCA program concerning, 405
Agricultural practices to reduce pollution, 69–70
Agricultural sources of nitrogen in water, 99–120
Agricultural wastes, regulation of chemical fertilizers, 373–74
feedlot wastes, 369–70
pesticides, 371–73
silt, 374–75
Aldrin
biological epoxidation of, 172
metabolism of, 172–73
Algae growth, 348
Amine-sugar condensation, 138–39
Amino acids, 134–35
polymerization of quinones with, 137–38
Amino sugars, 135
Amitrole, 202, 206
Ammonium nitrogen, 102
Anaerobic environment, effect of on manure, 257–59
Anaerobic lagoons for pretreatment of manure, 262
Animal waste management, 241, 286–95. *See also* Animal waste problem, factors in controlling
Animal waste problem
effect of automation on, xxi–xxii
factors in controlling
control-treatment devices, 394–95
economic considerations, 395

growth trend in feedlot industry, 395
inventory, 392
management programs, 394
regulation, 393–94
research, demonstration, development, 392–93
technical base, 392
and growth of food industry, xix–xx
Animal wastes. *See also* Livestock wastes
biochemical oxygen demand (BOD) of, 232
chemical oxygen demand (COD) of, 232
infectious agents in, 233
nitrogen and phosphorus in, 233
pollution characteristics of, 231
Applied pest control, advantages and disadvantages of
biological control, 211–12, 220, 221
chemical control, 213–14
cultural control, 213
insect sterilization, 213
mechanical controls, 213
physical control, 213
Aquatic community
composition of, 63
factors affecting
agricultural fertilizers and animal wastes, 337–39
environmental pollution, 332
eroded soil, 335
irrigation return water, 335
pesticides, 332–35
functions within, 332–33
modus vivendi of, 63
Atkinson v. Herington Cattle Company, 366–67
Atmospheric precipitation, as a source of nitrogen, 96–97

Bacterial diseases, role of water in transmission of, 269–74
anthrax, 271
brucellosis, 272